ENGLISH VERSE 1701—1750

VOLUME 2

ENGLISH VERSE
1701-1750

A CATALOGUE OF SEPARATELY PRINTED POEMS
WITH NOTES ON CONTEMPORARY
COLLECTED EDITIONS

VOLUME 2: INDEXES

D. F. FOXON

Whoever thinks a faultless piece to see,
Thinks what ne'er was, nor is, nor e'er shall be.
Pope, *Essay on criticism*

CAMBRIDGE UNIVERSITY PRESS

Published by the Syndics of the Cambridge University Press
Bentley House, 200 Euston Road, London NW1 2DB
American Branch: 32 East 57th Street, New York, N.Y.10022

© Cambridge University Press 1975

Library of Congress Catalogue Card Number: 70-152637

ISBN: 0 521 08144 0 (set of two volumes)

First published 1975

Printed in Great Britain
at the University Printing House, Cambridge
(Euan Phillips, University Printer)

CONTENTS

INDEX OF FIRST LINES   *page* 1

CHRONOLOGICAL INDEX   61

INDEX OF IMPRINTS   151

INDEX OF BIBLIOGRAPHICAL NOTABILIA   203

INDEX OF DESCRIPTIVE EPITHETS   213

SUBJECT INDEX   217

INDEX OF FIRST LINES

A

A bailiff and a boat-man   H108
A bard, to Phœbus and the world unknown   M376
A bard, unvers'd in politicks, unhir'd   M326
A bard, whom no contending party sways   M305
A beauteous gamester at court end of town   P293
A brawny lump, that scarce knows good from ill   C122
A Britain, who on mountains liv'd   M552
A by-blow struck from Nature's center   L104
A captain once to Britain sail'd   S382
A cavalier, as story says   C342
A certain barber, fraught with much ill nature   A233
A certain fox had stole a neighboors goose   P447
A certain knight of Maltan standard   L20
A certain lady of renown   A114
A certain man, (no matter who   T479
A certain oak of royal growth   M385
A certain pair, who late were ty'd   B407
A chymist that had long essay'd   D336
A circle of ladies, more bright than their pewter   P1141
A cloud of folk met all at once   C451
A convention of late was concluded at Pardo   P711
A cook, who once, had for his guest   A112
A council below,/Summon'd not long ago   C439
A country knight of German race   H257
A country vicar growing lazy   C459
A courtier once, a man of fame   A118
A creature I, of flesh and blood   S666
A cub of France th' imperial eagle tears   K31
A damsel I'm told/Of delicate mold   N197
A dean and prebendary   H108
A dismal song is sung of late   R238
A disregard, where care is most requir'd   W532
A doctor, all inspired with love   C450
A dolphin of note with a whale did agree   T12
A dome of honour, Richmond's neighbouring pride   S344
A drolling sort of fellow made   P425, 426
A fair one sought the silent poplar shade   L30
A famous assembly was summon'd of late   L80
A florist, ever seeking something new   P103
A foe to flatt'ry needs no patron seek   L48
A fox of quality that long   P437
A fox was out upon the pilfering lay   P458
A gentle swain yfed in Kentish mead   P1172
A gentlewoman once of high renown   W400
A German prince of noble race   T521
A ghost I am, of awful worth   G134
A glorious prince he was! whose godlike breast   H85
A gnome sure presided o'er thy heavy lays   N309
A goblin of the merry kind   C372
A godlike man encount'ring hellish foes   C76
A good old blackbird, whose retreat   S679
A good repute, a virtuous name   C102
A goodly teacher of the holy train   C161
A gracious prince as ever people bless'd   L44

A grim old lion sicken'd in his cave   R216
A health to Great Britain, and long may she flourish   D499
A hero scarce could rise of old   E494
A Jew that's well noted for money golore   F26
A journal of my life you urge   G276
A junto lately, or committee   E598
A juncto of knaves met at Paris together   H7
A king in youthfull charms array'd   H401
A kite in a snare was unluckily taken   N236
A knight long absent from the town   T158
A knot of fellows out upon the pad   P455
A lady liv'd in former days   E2
A lady once (so stories say)   W384
A lady, wise as well as fair   S799
A late petition of the clergy   L236
A lawrel'd bard, with wrongs and years oppress'd   T68
A lawland robber in distress   S788
A lyon by his valiant deeds preferr'd   F9
A lyon sunk by time's decay   T374
A lyon whose disputed blood   P507
A lonesome, rude, and indigested heap   B588
A lord, and no lord, once did dwell   L261
A lovely grove, dress'd in perpetual green   P264
A man by his birth and education   C316
A man with expence of wonderful toil   T13
A master of late/Ah! hear the sad fate   H355
A metaphor, in place of proper words   S763
A mighty great fleet the like was ne'er seen   N224
A milk-white hind, immortal and unchang'd   D456
A milk-white rogue, immortal and unhang'd   R173
A miller once of note and might   D269
A modern art, throughout the globe renown'd   A356
A month ago, that rogue, Old-Nick   D247
A mother eagle, weak and blind   E1
A mother, who vast pleasure finds   B77
A mourning muse, with wrongs and years declin'd   T50
A much indebted muse, O York! intrudes   Y43
A muse in arms inspire my willing pen   P608
A nations sense, in humble lines contain'd   G262
A neighbouring priest near Hackney lives   C457
A nightingale whose warbling tongue   I11
A nobler theme my feeble muse invites   P594
A patriot soul by nature is design'd   S369
A peacock nobly born, and bred   S417
A pelican, belov'd by Jove   B179
A person that's devoted to his ease   T517
A picture drawn so full of grace, there's none   R227
A picture I must paint, but yet   P272
A play, with scarce a song— 'tis gross offence   N139
A port in North-Britain lies south of the Clide   C2
A potent family once we were   C321
A presbyter is such a mon'strous thing   D216·5
A pretty, smock-fac'd, prattling boy   T473
A priestly-war I sing, and bloodless field   A200
A princely eagle, that had long been crown'd   F6

A prude, at morn and ev'ning pray'r G58
A purgatory is a jest P614
A quarter-brother barber surgeon H324
A rev'rend parson of the gown S672
A rev'rend starling, learn'd and bold C469
A river insolent with pride Y1
A robin red-breast that had long A335
A Roman bird to Scotland flew R143
A rough unpolish'd formless lump I lay N33
A sad and melancholy tale T46
A salmon of a lord like size T18
A scall'd sorry thing, assuming human shape D413
A seditious old cowardly prater L298
A set of gamesters all together met S724
A set of phrases learnt by rote S857
A sight like this, who can unmov'd survey? B79
A sister of old Levi's tribe M370
A sly and crafty fox B—b tail'd F220
A spacious hive well stock'd with bees M70
A sportive image of the martial race J57
A stately lioness with prudent skill A111
A stately swan, all white and fair S791
A story I'll tell you, a story so merry S470
A tight and trim vessel T19
A time there was e're itch of pow'r began A80
A time there was in ages that have been F3
A tory, a whig and a moderate man C449
A treaty's on foot, look about English boys N189
A trial was lately in Westminster-hall N130
A trifling song ye shall hear T480
A trivial theme no more demands the lay G135
A truth there was in times of old B228
A valiant and virtuous dame K32
A venerable lawrel stood L72
A village swain secure from wants U7
A virgin's pretty toy to guard K95
A voice arose from sorrow's dusky cave B469
A vôtre nez, mon frere, on rit partout de vous D278
A waggish jest, if cleanly told T320
A warning take young women all P1099
A wealthy farmer in the west C43
A well dispos'd and virtuous heart O29
A Welchman, that long,/With a scythe and a prong W284
A whelp of Cerbrus is come here T439
A while to satire we have seen a truce--- S83
A wicked will, alas! who can persuade? W532
A widow kept a favourite cat F13
A widow'd friend invites a widow'd muse O156
A wolf and bear did often meet D273
A woman grown lousey for want of due care S386
A worthy old dame,/Mother Trade was her name N132
A writer held in great renown W537
A young conceited fop, a cit R201
A young man I have been, & now old at last G170
A youth there was possess'd of every charm S380
A zealous brother of the canting crew P153
Ab ab bue, by my shoul I was quite almost mad P757
Abimalech a champion bold and stout E166
About the time that one shall be R305
Above the tallest most exalted view S456
Accept a muse that strives her voice to raise V49
Accept, bright fair! with native smiles, my zeal D567

Accept, dear sire, this humble tribute paid W345
Accept, mighty monarch, our duty at last T341
Accept, my lord, the tribute which I bring O82
Accept, oh Granville! this my rural lay R266
Accept once more, my Celia, e'er we part R251
Accept that tribute which I justly owe A16
Accept, Vanella, what Alexis owes L279
Accept, ye fair, the tribute of a muse! H304
Accept your Britain's smiles once more N266
According to custom,/Which verse-mongers use C274
Achilles' fatal wrath, whence discord rose T281
Ad sacrum incumbas toto quod pectore verum V95
Ad thermas graditur victrix regina calentes P184
Adam the first on apple made his meal C537
Adieu a while forsaken flood G282
Adieu fair ocean, on thee long I liv'd C33
Adieu, my Caelia, oh adieu! R29
Adieu, ye toyish reeds, that once cou'd please P730
Admire not sir, that I so long unseen G205
Adonis dies! the lovely boy expires P102
Advent'rous muse! too daring in thy theme A315
Ae time our poet met wi' Fackney D258
Ae wonny day, last ouk, I'll ne'er forget S721
Ægon, who lov'd the green retreat L222
Æquorei Mavortis opus sulcantia pontum E21
Æsop, a keen satyrick name F243
Æsop, grown weary of the trade P422
Aevo nata, labat quo vis probitatis, & aequi H226
Affairs of state (your garter'd friend suppose A77
Afraid to set so great a name as thine W464
After great Nassaw taught this nation war W525
After invoking of the muse C306
After King Saul had (by the sin he wrought E299
After some short retirements from the bench W100
After the Duke declar'd, with joynt applause K103
After the rebel Lucifer was driv'n S43
After venting all my spight S841
Again Great–Britain's sons auspicious meet W374
Again, Macrinus, comes the genial day B433
Again, my muse! for lofty flights prepare O167
Again, my muse – nor fear the steepy flight S437
Again, my muse, the lyre to Parker string E509
Again? new tumults in my breast? P896
Again the circling year its course has run N43
Again the year returns the day R74
Ah! cease, dear sir, cease to lament his fate W521
Ah! Clio, had thy distant lays T552
Ah! cruel and untimely death E138
Ah cruel death! it's time to give it o'er E227
Ah! cruel death, why dost thou us deprive? E53
Ah! fatal stroak, that from us has remov'd E269
Ah helpless wretch, what shall I do? P758
Ah! how all elements conspire with death E139
Ah how so populous of late E459
Ah is the matchless man the charmer dead? P164
Ah lord! the wound that I had got P748
Ah me! full sorely is my heart forlorn S395
Ah! news tormenting! is my father dead? M541
Ah! now the joy of Greenock's banks is gone E236
Ah! nymph your brow and heavy looks declare G251
Ah! rev'rend friend, since thou art gone, I'll try A132
Ah! Scotland, ah! why are thy muses dumbe? E117
Ah! 'tis too much, relentless fate! H84, R110

INDEX OF FIRST LINES

Ah, why this boding start? this sudden pain   C85

Αἰάζω τον ἄρειον ὀλωλότα ὤλετο Καδκαρς   H408

Aid me, O Venus! beauty's pow'rful queen   H39

Aid sacred nymphs of the Pierian spring   B217

Alak, alas and a-walla-day   K84

Alack and a day/Poor Monsieur they say   G180

Alass, alass! I can't forbear to speak   G324

Alas! and well-a-day! our hopes are lost   K94

Alas, how beast-like the drunkard wallowing lies   E294

Alas! how fragil and uncertain   B63

Alas! no longer now appear   T89

Alas! our kirk has got a scoup   C37

Alas, the very man, whose life we sought   F307

Alas, the warlike hero seems to grieve   T22

Alas! 'tis so; no virtue can withstand   B579

Alass! too oft have I invok'd my muse   H170

Alas what dismal news of late affrights   E57

Alas what sudden news flies o'er the town   P290

Alas! ye bards the elegy's you've made   P647

Alace! Zion! go weep and mourn   K29

Albion, æquoreis circumdata fluctibus ora   D74

Albion disclose thy drowsy eyes, and see   M278

Albion rejoice! thy sons a voice divine have heard   W245

Albion, the glory of her sister isles   C421

Albion, thou art the world's epitome   I68

Alcander wise by long experience grown   A158

Alcides once on Mauritanian ground   E502

Alcipe, il est un dieu. Son pouvoir fit le monde   H385

Alite perfausto regnas, O maxima, tu qua   M418

Alite perfausto, regnat, tu cœlitus orta   M417

All bounteous sire, author of good, whose name   B561

All British men that's loyalists   H393

All Britons, attend,/And an ear to me lend   W42

All Britains rejoyce at this turn of the state   M26

All Britains rejoice/With a general voice   E577, V111

All-conquering death, and even fortune too   O212

All creating father, all sustaining   S397

All creatures date their birth since ancient time   W5

All curious poets keep a muse   Y177

All evils, friend, whatever, great and small   M184

All folks who pretend to religion and grace   S897

All good Christian people   C368

All hail! All hail! Thou happy land   S213

All hail! Great sir! Behold an infant muse   S189

All hail! mysterious; hail! religious rites!   L69

All hail! O awful, sage divinity   J44

All hail! thou most auspicious day   S207

All hail! to Britain's monarch; view nature's act!   C363

All hail to old England so wise and so great   N115

All hail ye soft mysterious pow'rs, which charm   S461

All hearts be swell'd with grief, with tears all eyes   E136

All here below's inconstant, empty, vain   H234

All human race wou'd fain be wits   S888

All humane things are subject to decay   D459, P434

All in amaze at what is past, I stood   R161

All in her bloom the graceful fair   R73

All-in the city West-minster   C150

All in the dark and dolesome hour   B340

All in the late great winter snow   L260

All is not gold, (the proverb says)   N296·5

All kingdoms have their mason-free   F244

All labouring to reform, must miss their aim   C477

All loyal Scots within our land   O243

All men have follies, which they blindly trace   P736

All men of renown give ear   U1

All men to compass happiness essay   H38

All men who're not of sense bereav'd   M226

All must allow, that in the painter's art   L108

All officers would fain appear   R187

All people draw near;/Cit, rustick, and peer   S790

All people now both far and near   L49, S607

All people that hears my complaint for my sake   S605

All people the which in   R243

All pious, loyal souls, who love the truth   E280

All priests are not the same, be understood!   S109

All sing our monarch's praise, nor must his son   P569

All tender-hearted protestants   P685

All the inventions that ever was known   N172

All things created Moses writes   C162

All to the Swan beside the Change   G225

All write at London; – shall the rage abate   Y117

All ye poets of the age   C49, S71

All ye searchers of the fair   P38

All ye that good toping prefer to your rest   N74

All you brave noble men, give ear   P681

All you that are to mirth inclin'd   C171

All you that are willing your cares to beguile   E311

All you that fain would jolly be   M11

All you that have stock, and are mad for a peace   F258

All you that to true English blood do belong   W409

All you that wou'd refine your blood   S405

All you who wou'd feign live a life that is long   A260

Allan is dead!——Ye listing mountains hear!   P108

Alma figlia di Giove inclita madre   M93

Alme Charon, (nam tandem omnes, qui nascimur & qui   B332

Almighty death, by whose decessive blow   E116

Almighty power at length in love doth call   E242

Almighty tyrant death whose pow'rfull sting   F292

Almost four thousand years had past   G115

Aloud I heard the voice of fame   P636

Altho', my dear friends, my eggs are all addle   P182

Altho my lug's nail'd, to the Tron   S629

Altho' (my trusty friend) the muses   D397

Altho not common for our sex   H391

Although the news be spread of late   B46

Am I thus favour'd! Is my dwelling sav'd!   A121

Amazing stroak! A princess great this day   D415

Ambition fires the meanest breast   B64

Ambition is a plant, that's always found   F108

Amelia, beauteous princess, deign to view   C108

Amelia! deign upon thy muse to shine   H116

Amidst a city much decay'd   W170

Amidst th' applause which art and learning brings   J91

Amidst the crowds, that joyn in verse & prose   D298

Amidst the factions, that the world enrage   W301

Amidst the great concerns, which fill thy mind   M563

Amidst the loud applause, which fills the ears   T418

Amidst the noisy town's tumultuous scenes   L74

Amidst the off'rings of the tuneful throng   C430

Amidst the tears that dutifully flow   E43

Amidst the waves and raging billows tost   G266

Amidst those troops, who've put their stables [!] on   S545

Amidst thy triumphs on the deep   N268

Aminadab, a well-enlighten'd Friend   B298
Among the many warm addresses   M333
Among the numerous fools, by fate design'd   M51
Among the various notions of mankind   C168
Among the various presentations   R156
Amongst the numerous crouds, that daily press   P123
Amongst the pure ones all, which conscience doth
    profess   Q6
Amongst the unwholsome Belgick bogs   D532
An antient bard, Simonides his name   C410
An antient metropolis, famous of late   R323
An apothecary cloathed in black   E556
An arch and sturdy bellman of the town   B611
An ass well drubb'd with sturdy oak   R244
An eagle, that long time had been   S690
An honest country-man had got   M73
An honest heathen (no fanatick hears!)   P265
An honest man, once had a mare   M218
An honest old dame,/Mother Trade was her name   E259
An honest shepherd on the wolds   F10
An impious doubt did oft my mind invade   G153
An oaken broken elbow chair   S419
An old baboon, who long had been   A110
An old man, and his graceless young   F44
An opinion, single, is of no weight   S203
An orator dismal of Nottinghamshire   S844
An orator was found in Nottinghamshire   N329
An out landish gard'ner as we do hear tell   H35
An outly of the globe fair Albion reigns   S241
An quia matrona es, generoso stemmate nata   I29
Ancient philosophers declare   S782
And art thou a convert grown!   K72
And art thou then, dear lovely creature   P34
And has all nature, then, espous'd my part?   Y52
An has ald death come in his rage   E206
And has ald death e'n come at last   G253
And has auld death that bloody knave   E52
And has old death that bloody knave   E271
And have the fates, my Strephon, then decreed   C91
And having, with a careless lift   C547
And is he gone to his eternal rest!   W313
And is it so? Is then great Rattray gone?   L144
And is poor Tiger laid at last so low!   E254
And is this all? No, curious maid   P141
And must our deaths be silenc'd too! I guess   E153
And must this house your want of favour mourn   N173
And must we calmly hear his nonsense still   B307
And must we die? Ah wretched fate!   L58
And now awhile let sterner science rest   T103
And shall great Halifax resign to fate   S365
And shall I then for ever silent stand   B559
And shall the patriot who maintain'd your cause   T362
And shall we now turn back   W322
And such are those whose wiley waxen mind   B219
And thus you leave us noble captain   E82
And wilt thou leave young Jemmy in the lurch?   B514·5
Andraea vixti Jacobo semper amicus   P360
Andrews is dead, over's his dying moan   G325
Angelick host! in form and essence bright   H81
Angels and saints, salute the blissful morn   P150
Angligenis lugenda dies! Cur solis ab ortu   I30
Ann, fou as cap or stoup cou'd make her   T100
Anna Caledoniae quae nunc felicior orae   P338

Anna, lady of the ocean   T507
Anna mihi genuit te Margaris Haia, nulli   P295
Anna regali serie creata   H276
Anna Stuartorum decus et spes altera regum   P294
Anna tuæ mater patriæ, primaria mundi   P1101
Anna was once the wise, the great, the good   P97
Anne the new treasure of our Albion   P689
Another scene my pen attempts to show   G210
Antoeus was a mighty lord   A268
Apollo and the muses lend your aid   P287
Apollo and the poets meeting   P1064
Apollo, angry that his sons so long   O208
Apollo, kindly looking down   J27
Apollo now or never shew your art   A345
Apollo, patron of the muse's song   C276
Apollo perplext with poetical duns   T475
Apollo, (the god both of musick and wit)   S223
Apollo was you in a lethargie   N244
Apollo's deity of verse   M116
Appear O James! aproach thy native shore   L43
Appellé sur les pas d'une illustre princesse   L219
Aquarius ebb'd, and Pisces caught i' th' wile   H80
Arbiter Europae, mandato Brittonis Annae   P340
Are all my lawrels come to this?   T485
Are all the Dutch at length come in   D556
Are there such bards, who, fond on courts to wait   C184
Are these the Britons, whom ye stil'd the bold   F74
Are these the marks, then, of our promis'd shame!
    H220
Are these then, France, the arts which you imploy   S64
Are we then lost to sense as well as shame   P456
Are you a brother mason?   F61
Argyle and Mar are gone to war   D260
Arise, behold the royal fleet, whose name   F250
Arise, dead muse, in strains seraphick rise   K103
Arise, my Lycas: in yon' woody wilds   W245·5
Arise, my muse; expand thy soaring wing   A173
Arise, my muse, from low pursuits arise   E484
Arise my muse, thy sable weeds throw by   A156
Arise my soul, and put on strength   H422
Arise my soul with hov'ring wing   D341
Arise O Israel, know the Lord   P61
Arise ye long deceas'd astrologers   M297
Arma virumque cano redivivi stemmatis Angli   H74
Arms, and the hero, who from ruin'd Troy   B374
Arms, and the hero who from Trojan shores   S771
Arms, and the knighted col'nel, muse, relate   D252
Arms and the man I sing, the first who bore   P410
Arms and the man I sing, the first who rose   J96
Arms, and the man I sing, who first from Troy   T444
Arms and the man I sing, who gain'd renown   F308
Arms and the man I sing, who greatly bore   F120
Arms and the man of upper room   G312
Arms and the man renown'd, who last from — [France]
    M81
Arms and the priest I sing, whose martial soul   O282
Arms not the warriors, but the lovers care   L280
Around th' infernal plain she rov'd   J67
Art thou, dear Israel! still the butt of fate?   T574
Artifices cano mellis apes, quas arva secutus   V14
As a fond mother anxious for her son   T379
As a long sword and scarlet cloaths   C401
As a thorn-bush, or oaken-bough   S887

INDEX OF FIRST LINES

As a wild rake that courts a virgin fair   O224
As a young lawyer many years will drudge   E351
As Adam once, with more than royal state   T70
As angels, in their first unsettled state   M141
As A----s was trotting away from the chapter   K48
As at the moon each dog will bark, when bright   P628
As blue-ey'd Kate, sweet-blooming buxom maid   W168
As by some wond'rous sympathy appears   P543
As Cæsar at the end of each campaign   S488
As choicest oar in deepest caves is hid   P735
As Creech swang away in a sanctify'd twine   H199
As Cupid was dispos'd to view   V26
As dandering on the shoar of Leith   W407
As diff'ring parties once did all agree   C358
As drowning men a straw will catch at   M191
As Dryden justly term'd poetick sound   C463
As errant knights by cross indentures   D519
As Hudibrs [!] observes, inspite   P32
As I did travel in the north   C216
As I from hunting came one night   O247
As I have heard, in times of yore   B161
As I in Rosian plains my flocks did feed   P106
As I last night in bed lay snoring   F127
As I on Stephens Green was taking air   D254
As I pass'd o'er Parnassus shady hills   P189
As I thro' the city one morning was walking   O134
As I told you before/You would never give o'er   T125
As I was a walking thro' fair London city   O133
As I was walking up and down   Q1
As in a blowing jasmyn bower   W296
As in some northern region wrapt in night   M150
As in the gay circle Lord Fanny recited   T474
As in those frozen climes, where tedious night   I60
As Indians when a valu'd hero dies   P286
As Jove will not attend on less   S842
As joyful sailors when the tempest's o'er   P660
As late I mus'd upon the fates   D515
As late I walk'd beside that silver spring   D338
As late the thoughtful muse, in pensive mood   B367
As lately through London I rambl'd along   C210
As long as C—le can write, and G—n rage   B303
As lowring lights forebode unwelcome news   F293
As many persons now can tell   N128
As Mar his round one morning took   T283
As men sit under nobles chair   H299
As mercenary canting quacks   B290
As Mort—r lay pensive and with pains   A274
As musing I rang'd in the meads all alone   C47
As nations oft by cunning knaves   W136
As, near Porto-Bello lying   G186
As Neptune with his watery train   K54
As Nero laughing saw fierce fires consume   N36
As of his faction's downfal P---r sings   A365·5
As on a bench near Isis'-banks I sat   B189
As on a bough the blackbird sat   S686
As on a bough the blackbird sate   S700
As on my bed, restless I museing lay   H87
As on the sea-beat shore Britannia sat   T177
As once I lay with thoughts of love possess'd   C69
As once through a village a carrier drove   F20
As once two knights, tho' lords by being m—rs   D239
As one belated on some perilous road   B535
As over Gladsmuir's blood stain'd field   H17

As paupers who on charity are fed   P1022
As poets in the days of yore   S736
As poets say, one Orpheus went   K62
As postcripts after sermons are   M520
As R***** one morning, in cogit'ive mood   S550
As rash hot youths, impatient of delay   P611
As Rochfoucault his maxims drew   S920
As Rome of old, by tyranny oppress'd   T25
As roses in their early bloom   N261
As round their dying parent's bed   F21
As scriblers poor, who write to eat   S717
As Sheba's queen with adoration came   E353
As ship-wrack'd passengers when got to shore   N165
As sly old Lovat to the Tow'r was led   S178
As snarling Momus sung descenting bees   A244
As some brave knight who once with spear and shield   R287
As some faint new-born plant which scarce sustains   F242
As some fond parent, tho' with reason blest   A170
As some raw youth in country bred   S913
As soon as death by sin was usher'd in   E66
As soon as the wind it came kindly about   N95
As Stephen, in his happy state   B407
As story goes, some sage wisakers   B484
As Strephon in a wither'd cyprus shade   P731
As sudden claps of thunder strikes the ear   E180
As Temple notes, not meaning evil   C507
As tender lambs with wolves agree   B15
As tender wives their husbands absence mourn   W9
As that imperial bird employ'd by Jove   F214
As the great dead, by lawful tenure, claim   S331
As the great Founder, when he built his vast   O14
As there are fatal times when Nature's sighs   P167
As those, who hope hereafter heav'n to share   P736
As thro' that lordliest of the creatures, man   S290
As thro' the world's wide wilderness I past   H268
As to the birth of worlds in boundless spaces   S208
As 'tother day I chanc'd to walk   T539
As various arts do shine in various men   C118
As wandring streams by secret force return   S740
As water of all elements   O171
As when a boy is passing thorough   M356
As, when a fire with dreadful blaze   W189
As when a furious tempest from on high   M158
As when a mighty monarch, with renown   W236
As when a missive to poor Ovid came   C343
As when a pregnant cloud dissolv'd to showers   C277
As when a traveller, a long day past   Y54
As when bright Sol extends his glitt'ring stage   J97
As when by some chance-thought, or force of wit   M142
As, when in antient times to mighty Jove   F152
As when learn'd sages optic arts display   E510
As when of old the prince of Roman rakes   E17
As when of old the proud Egyptian land   H173
As when some earthquake in a distant land   J16
As, when some great and gracious monarch dies   D455
As when some tyrant dies that long has made   P446
As when the business of the day is done   P563
As when the deluge first began to fall   S910
As when the dreadful sessions time draws near   P1121

As when the heav'ns are clear, the rising sun   H88
As when the queen of gods and wife of Jove   F276
As wit some mighty product to essay   F173
As with cherubic hosts and choirs divine   H366
As yet unconscious of the latent snare   V13
As youthful Strephon, t'other day   M279
Ascribe to god most solemn praise   H441
Ask Fa-ro-li, please your grace, to sing   M258
Aspasia's to an angel half refin'd   V102
Aspiring muse, commence a noble flight   H68
Aspiring Phoebus, who alone can warm   P119
Assemble loyal Britains, meet with joy   S649
Assist me, a rustick, O muse, to indite   A153
Assist me heav'n, direct me in my choice   B3
Assist me, heavn'ly muse, in lofty verse   V91
Assist me muse, in mournful notes to sing   H174
Assist me, muse, who did inspire   L175
Assist me now ye sacred nine   T112
Assist me sacred muse, the man I sing   T509
Assist me, ye muses, F—ce to sing   K30
Assist Melpomene, thou doleful muse   E75
Assist, my muse, brave Vernon's acts rehearse   M120
Assist, my muse, with brisk satyrick rage   I45
Assist my sacred muse, my pen inspire   N26
Assist, O muse! a youthful bard inspir'd   P1033
Assist, O muse! the bard who racks   B604
Assist, Urania, the advent'rous song   E19
Assist, with aid united, all ye nine   P545
Assist with mournful strains, assist my muse   E237
Assist ye muses (all in number) nine   M186
Assist you tuneful genius of our isle   U10
Astræa, I implore thee, tell me why   K85
Astræa's kind, who taught me how to choose   M413
At a late Derby assizes came forth   P719
At a sessions of late   N145
At a time when the church was much out of repair   V78
At dead of night when midnight hags prepare   C393
At dead of night when peaceful spirits sleep   J112
At Ewelm-town in Oxford-shire   H256
At first our muse in Syracusian strains   B550
At Hackney, or at Chelsea bred   M373
At James's house, is a damnable rout   N53
At Lambeth dwells as fame reports   F146
At last dispelling his lov'd country's fears   T466
At last the long expected day is come   T329
At length auspicious blasts are heard to blow   C257
At length, Britannia, rescu'd from thy fears   S739
At length day breaks, and shades of night give way   A226
At length escap'd from ev'ry human eye   L337
At length for those a satyr's found   L28
At length from love's vile slav'ry I am free   G230
At length, great queen, that glorious work is done   D46·5
At length in pity to a nation's pray'r   M58
At length, O Dorset, not to raise   W302
At length old time brings forth th' important hour   F278
At length propitious heav'n begins to smile   C344
At length the great decisive year is come   A202
At length the hostile din of war is o'er   B505
At length the phrenzy of the realm is o'er   W310
At length, the quære is decided   C286

At length the work is done, a work so great   S520
At length then death has set thee free from care   N135
At length 'tis done - - - Hamilla's from you thrown   D322
At length with vengeance bursts my raging vein   A207
At L—m—th dwells as fame reports   F146
At Madrid, where the kings of Spain   W126
At mid-night hours, when nature seems to nod   A275
At once to raise our rev'rence and delight   L292
At Reswick Monsieur gave us peace   W388
At St. James's of late,/On a great bed of state   B154
At six this morn, disturb'd from pleasing rest   S59
At study still! still mad! come, take the air   B337
At th' oratory near Tower-hill   T21
At the time of the year when the citizens wives   H398
At this unwelcome news lament you nine   E270, H172
At Twickenham, chronicles remark   P782
At your request, sir! which to me's command   P1056
Athyoe alas! who can thy grief express   O256
Attempt, O muse, the pious task, and shed   S745
Attend and prepare for a cargo from Dover   M174, 183
Attend, Calliope; to whom belongs   L188
Attend, illustrious wights, whose favourite joy   S166
Attend malicious S—t si vous plait   E396
Attend, my friends, attend, and ye shall hear   B181
Attend my good friends, and I'll give you a song   N63
Attend, my honest brethren   W480
Attend, my son; while a fond father's care   S147
Attend my V—n, while the daring muse   F45
Attend, O Cambel! nor refuse   O68
Attend, while I relate the fall   E102
Attend, ye brave Britons   W501
Attend, ye Britons, and give ear   Q2
Attend, ye busy mortals, much employ'd   M438
Attend, ye fair, whilst, anxious for your praise   A317
Attend ye good people, give ear to my ditty   M161
Attend, ye guardian angels of the state   N45
Attend, ye princes, and ye kings, give ear   P95
Attend ye youths, with minds retentive   M92
Attend you fools, your character is such   T2
Attend, you loyal Britons, to my lays   R175
Attentive all in solemn silence wait   T134
Attonitus tandem respirat Phœbus, & inquit   D555
Audite, O gentes; linguis animisque favete   D346
Auld Reeky mourn in sable hue   R46
Aurea dicta sacri præconis, & inclyta, nati   T470
Aurora fair, who doth the skye adorn   N27
Aurora, goddess of the purple morn   S507
Aurora quits her ouzy bed   O63
Aurora, saffron rob'd, in glory flames   A348
Aurora, the bright usher of the morn   E328
Auspitious bard! whose late successful lays   R208
Auspicious day! to which we owe   W26
Auspicious muse! to me thy aid dispense   O216
Auspiciously thou, greatest, reignes; who by   M418
Auspiciously thou heav'n-born reigns; who by   M417
Auspicor regi pangere carmen   S608
Author of faith, eternal Word   W318
Authors report, there's to be found   S720
Awake, awake, my lyre   O228
Awake! awake! my silent, sleeping lyre   P720
Awake, awake, whose harmonious souls   C87
Awake, celestial harmony!   H380
Awake, desponding fair one!   F206

Awake my Chloris, hast and dress   A155
Awake, my friend! and strike the sounding lyre!   G143
Awake my Laelius! leave all meaner things   P822
Awake, my muse! awake! expand thy wing!   S106
Awake my muse from thy lethargick dream   S466
Awake my muse, go to   T384
Awake, my muse, in strains melodious show   J18
Awake, my muse; to the Impartial sing   P696
Awake, my muse, whate'er thy name may be   M172
Awake, my song; and leave below   O48
Awake my soul! From Jove begin the song   S32
Awake, my soul, thou drowsy power, awake   S26
Awake, my soul! with joy thy god adore   B575
Awake old Neptune from thy watry bed   A358
Awake, rejoyce, O my soul   T124
Awake! rouse up, shake off your lethargy   W238
Awake, Thalia, and defend   R50
Awake, Thalia! sweep thy string   S653
Awake, thou busie dreamer, and arise   B511
Awake with joyous songs the day   C199
Awake! ye drowsie mortals rise!   C258
Awake, ye lazy powers of peace, awake   O90
Awake, ye nine, and, with superiour art   L111
Awake, ye nine harmonious maids, who dream   B474
Awak'd at last, thanks to thy gracious call   C424
Away, ambition, give me rest   W487
Away with ev'ry trifling theme   P1109
Away with tears, the cypress, and the yew   P602
Awful hero, Marlborough, rise   W294
Awhile forget the scenes of woe   B225
A while to satire we have seen a truce---   S83
Ay me! what aking thoughts possess my mind   C527

B

Bacchus be damn'd, and all his drunken brood   W172
Banish'd by fates decree from lightsome earth   R151
Barbaries patria quando expulit Hellade musas   M195
Barbarus exclusit tumulo me Nassus avito   P376
Base and ungrateful to my proffer'd love   F175
Basely ungenerous mankind deal   J102
Battles no more 'twixt us and France I sing   T492
Be dumb, be dumb, ye inharmonious sounds   T249
Be dumb ye beggars of the rhiming trade   D107
Be hush'd ye gentle winds, nor breath aloud   B581
Be husht ye silent winds and gently breath   F82
Be it remembred now that formerly   B485
Be kind my muse, assist my lays   T481
Be none employ'd to guard the weal   V110
Be present, ev'ry guardian pow'r   B589
Be present to my aid, ye heav'nly quire!   P601
Be wise as Ad—n, as Br—ne be brave   C454
Be wise as Somerset, as Somer's brave   B528
Be't mine the honour, once again to hear   R57
Beam on me, god of wit, seraphick fire   V48
Bear me, auspicious, O ye rural pow'rs   S750
Bearing record in heaven there are three   S186
Beat on, proud billows, Boreas blow   P442
Beaufort, great heir of that distinguished blood   B424·5
Beauty, the fondling mother's earliest pray'r   C55·5
Beauty's a gaudy sign, no more   J34

Beauty's of health the offspring fair   E290
Beauty's soft goddess on a day   M393
Bedoun the bents of Banquo brae   R103
Beer and the men (a mighty theme!) I sing   B160
Before bright Phœbus, with his pompous train   P78
Before her glass, in rapture high   C434
Before I in the widdy swang   M2
Before sin tainted the pure universe   E161
Before the queen o' th' French was grown mis-spir'd   E356
Before the thistle with the roses twin'd   P687
Begin, celestial source of light   F110
Begin, let ransom'd man rejoice   C263
Begin my muse, and strike the adventrous string   T415
Begin, my muse, and strike the lyre!   W35
Begin, my muse! and this strange truth unfold   M556
Begin my muse, begin your mournful strains   E198
Begin my muse, inspire your poets lays   P114
Begin my muse: the dire adventure tell   E517
Begin my muse, the wondrous tale reherse   P463
Begin my muse, with bold unborrow'd praise   T102
Begin, O grateful muse, a second strain   S173
Begin ye sweet melodious heav'nly choir   E170
Begot on board some fly-boat, ship or hoy   S50
Behind an unfrequented glade   P1090
Behold a poor ghost from below   T1
Behold a satyr, on a pinch   A264
Behold a wicked harden'd wretch   S604
Behold Apollo's youngest son   C482
Behold! at length the joyful days return   P578
Behold, Britannia waves her flag on high   P219
Behold he comes to make thy people groan   P98
Behold the church, which some men say has stood   H193
Behold the god of wealth, in whose just reign   M24
Behold the lamb of god, who came   P747
Behold the man! that with gigantick might   O54
Behold the man whom the Judæan race   C261
Behold the ruddy morn springs from afar   P621
Being now on my tour/For higher or lower   L61
Beings, that lifeless meerly being have   L107
Beings, who meerly being have   L105
Bely'd and slander'd by a fiend   H267
Believe me madam, since the fig leaf's on   F42
Believe me, nymph, whilst you contend   T553
Believe me, sir, however strange, 'tis true   F72
Believe us, dread sir,/We come whip and spur   A50
Bellair, a lad, wha spent a hantle time   M304
Bellair, a youth of the poetick train   M304
Bely'd and slander'd by a fiend   H267
Beneath an hawthorn's bush, secreted shade   D362
Beneath the shade of a cool cypress grove   C90
Beneath the shadow of a beaver-hat   G63
Beneath the shelter of these woody hills   D194
Beneath the south-side of a craigy bield   R76
Bennet, the muses ornament, and friend   K18
Bessy Bell and Mary Gray   R36
Best of your sex that ever wore a crown!   B233
Between Ormun and Malburor   N192
Between the hours of twelve and one   P596
Betwixt the banks of pleasant Euphrates   S944
Beyond a park's extensive limits, stands   M476
Beyond the vast circumf'rence of the skies   T416

INDEX OF FIRST LINES

Bibliotheca bonis multisque repleta libellis K42
Black wayward power, who o'er the discontent S658
Blasphemous wretch! How canst thou think or say E23
Bleinheim e're while at ev'ry turn appear'd W3
Bless me! An audience here! I'm all surprize! P1130
Bless my dear Rupert for his ardent pray'r M509
Bless us! how silent is the noisy gown? L243
Bless'd be the man! forever bless'd his name! B554
Bless'd British isle, by heavens propitious hand F216
Bless'd prince! in whom the graces seem combin'd T55
Bless'd was Utopia, when her soveraign's care W68
Blest are the men, in virtuous paths that tread H300
Blest heav'nly mind, which from thy native skys T443
Blest in thy rank, and in each winning grace L226
Blest soul! Thou [who] were wont to be B322
Bloom of beauty, early flow'r P221
Bloom of wit, and choicest flow'r L21
Blow ye zephyrs gentle gales Y22
Blush not, my muse, (unworthy tho' the theme) W522
Boast not of Bollingbroke's retreat N235
Boasts, and the man I sing, whose fame of late B95
Boccace, the scourge of lech'rous monk F230
Boccace, the scourge of wicked monk F228
Bold is the muse to leave her humble cell F106
Bold swearer stop, no farther progress make T266
Bold whiggs and phanaticks, now strive to pull down D354
Books and the man I sing, the first who brings P764
Born in an age, when virtue's vigour fails H225
Born near Avona's winding stream S577
Both antient and modern authors do say J12
Both by the world and thee contemptuous made M497
Bow, wow, oh, curse my collar N326
Boys, that wou'd scholars be, your minds dispose D569
Brave Admiral Matthews has been on the main A61
Brave Admiral Townsend is now on the main N119
Brave Bacchus by all is adored L114
Brave Britton's hear my story V31
Brave Briton's let your voices ring N211
Brave general, whose conduct in the field C361
Brave loyal Britons all rejoice E332
Brave Marlbro' who preserves our Capitol S360
Brave subjects of England rejoice and be glad E329
Bright arts, abus'd, like gems, receive their flaws S89
Bright N---y the lovely, the charming, the fair N118
Bright Sol, thy purest beams display V89
Bright sons of Bacchus and Apollo M351
Bright was the morn, the hemisphere C542
Brisk widows, in their sable N164
Britain arise, in all your glory smile D31
Britains blessing, faiths defender P150
Britannia, famous isle, that all admir'd D53
Britannia! highly favour'd from above N49
Britannia long since was the muses retreat C409
Britannia, queen of isles, whose glorious name S86
Britannia's bards, who rival Greece and Rome P619
Britannia's children! now bewail the day E45
Britannia's guardian, liberty N84
Britannia's heroes, who still dauntless stood S734
Britannia's king in arms in arts renown'd B557
Brittons all your voices raise N194
Briton's awake! and bravely make a stand S483
Britons, behold! what medly virtues meet? T252

Britons behold! your petty tyrant here N230
Britons! for shame, give all these follies o'er C42
Britons, my muse once more inclines to sing B481
Britons, once more in annual joy we meet W32
Briton's rejoice, for Vernon is decreed C315
Britons rejoice! your Io-paeans sing! P618
Britons! these lines I lately took B210
Broke from its charge, my genius flies H452
Brothers in servitude attend the song D388
Bruin and Reynard who had made T316
Bubbies of every form my plume portrays J95
Buckhurst, Such deeds as warranty deraign R159
Budgell! thy Tindall's death demands thy muse E397
But he foresees with prophetick unction P1018
But long had wasting cares the queen opprest S404
But now the queen, long seized with fest'ring pains T136
But there had been mair blood and skaith R37
But what are these to great Atossa's mind? P984
But why shou'd marriage render man undone? B5
By all the gods, I'll fret my guts T156
By Avon's stream (the muses calm retreat) T72
By deathless Phœbus! 'tis not to be born N335
By Ebro's streams the British general sate A25
By him they own'd their sov'reign when they fell P28
By his hall chimney, where in rusty grate J66
By kings and princes, god at first design'd M41
By learned antiquarians we are told S738
By novels from the Irish strand T247
By Ovid, 'mongst many more wonders were told W425
By sleep deserted, when for rest reclin'd E415
By the side of a murmuring stream R286
By thee enjoin'd th' obsequious muse obeys P282
By thee, eternal god of truth, I reign T46
By various means we lose the vital breath P612
By zealous Edward built, for length of years A14

C

Cæsarei cladem thalami, viduumque cubile R194
Call it not love, for love to heaven is fled L147
Call'd, by a heroine, from our isle L219
Calvin lament, thy conquer'd champions mourn R163
Cambray, whilst of seraphick love you set C81
Cambray, whilst of seraphick love you write C82
Can any be with envy so possest P641
Can any knowledge wisemen please H180
Can Christendom's great champion sink away E164
Can I, unmov'd, like a Marpesian rock H179
Can man forbear to check such jilts as you P1051
Can there within these walls pretend to dwell C511
Canace murther'd; – Ha! What is't I hear B347
Candida nympha Chloë, cujus perstringor ocellis E305
Candler has found, (and, doubtless, he alone) O91
Canticum quod rex Solomon canoræ K20
Carmarthen, Oxford, Leeds, great names, and great C509
Carminum præses citharæque Clio O17
Carole Gothorum ductor fortissime, solus P347
Carole Gothorum longe fortissime ductor P346
Carole, si similis fratris, similisve parentis P348

8

INDEX OF FIRST LINES

Carolus Hispaniæ rex Indorumque secundus O249

Casta animi Pallas; puræ rationis amatrix F165

Cato! Well met./Hail vertuous, hopeful youths! C72

Cease bright Sol, your resplendant rays obscure D17

Cease, Britain, from intestine jarrs H273

Cease, cease, proud Jac--- to make a noise O4

Cease, Drusus, cease; make thy strong transports less B291

Cease heathen muse in thy Sicilian hill A357

Cease! thy direful vengeance cease! K71

Celestial dove; by whose enlivening warmth C551, 553

Cœlestial maid, now touch thy golden lyre B98

Celestial muse, that on the blissful plain R274

Cælestial pow'rs, that rule all earthly things S136

Celia long had triumph'd o'er O246

Cælia return'd from visiting R242

Cælia this night has promis'd I J46

Cælia, you rule with such despotick sway W303

Ceres, with each autumnal scene, was fled R268

Change Alley's so thin that a man may now walk S611

Chaste, pious, prudent, C—— the second F248

Chear up and sing ye loyal hearts N203

Chear up Calliope, good news rehearse R149

Cheer up your hearts you brave loyal Brittons N157

Cher & brillant espoir d'un peuple malheureux A1

Children like these, made Niobe compare T588

Children of God, that's by the spirit led G322

'Chloe' see 'Cloe'

Christ is the husband, saints the bride E451

Christ's line and birth St. Matthew first relates W325

Ch-ster, my patron and my aid T357

Churchill is dead! and in that word is lost A187

Chwi-soneddigion mawrion mwyn E287

Cibber (the wonder of a brazen age) U23

Clara, a prude in early bloom P1153

Clarissa ended--- and the dæmons round R219

Clavers and his Highlandmen K39

Cleansing th' Augean stable help'd to raise P552

Clio, behold this charming day W488

Clio, behold this dreadful day W491

Cloe, a country vicar's daughter W578

Cloe, a nymph, divinely fair B108

Cloe, I can, with half an eye F200

Cloe in love's affairs grown nice D356

Clogg'd with a mournful gloom, arose the day T261

Close by the entrance of the woodland plain D72

Close by where Camus moves his languid streams T569

Clystere nuper duriusculam paulo alvum C255

Cochrania dead! we did almost adore G301

Cognovere pias nondum pia secula fraudes C476

Colin, by promise, being oblig'd to pay P753

Collected in myself I'll rule alone D360

Come all good people, give an ear W264

Come all loyal Britains come lssen [!] to me N207

Come all the managers, come forth and moan S556

Come all ye anti-Perkinites O202

Come all ye brave boys, and high-churchmen, draw near T538

Come, all ye freeholders E31

Come all ye gallant knights and 'squires H331

Come, all ye jolly fellows W29

Come, all ye muses, and display N294

Come all ye people far and near E535

Come all ye protestants give ear to my song G176

Come all ye Sussex fox hunters Y19

Come all ye that love laughing, and like not Sir Blue S471

Come all you brave hearts of gold M360

Come all you jolly sailors bold E340

Come all you jolly seamen R225

Come all you jolly weavers N171

Come all you loyal Welchmen H455

Come all you mournful Britains, you who know S524

Come all you poor distressed souls W557

Come all you sportsmen far and near H406

Come all you valiant sailors, of courage, stout and bold S10

Come and give good attention; for my song it is true E575

Come attend British boys,/I'll make you rejoice N81

Come, blessed Jesus, quickly come S361

Come, blooming Venus, beauteous goddess, come A319

Come brave souldiers hast away T315

Come bright Urania, nay come all the nine E248

Come bring the liquor hither B29

Come Britton's now, with joy be fill'd S588

Come Britons rejoice, indulge holy mirth H451

Come buy my new ballad C240

Come citizens all (that your country love) N69

Come citizens, and mourne with me a part? E141

Come, Clio, sing (if such your will is) F153

Come, come, great monarch, come away R172

Come, fair Dorinda, and, while beauty glows P1011

Come, fair muse, of Grub-street D255

Come fairest of our isle, ye graces come H67·5

Come Faustus, in this cool and shady wood B208

Come forth, ye swains, forsake your herds and flocks S513

Come free Brittons lets all rejoice C431

Come from your garrets Grubstreet bards P572

Come gentle ghost that's lanch'd & gone R177

Come, gentle spring, ætherial mildness, come T227

Come give me the cards, let me try this new game Q3

Come, good Father Bacchus, astride on your butt P406

Come hearken now unto my song H323

Come, heavn'ly pensive contemplation, come D61

Come help me now ye muses, to deplore E96

Come hither bold Britons, and I will disclose C479

Come hither, my country 'squire C51

Come hither my queen, and if we must agree W442

Come hither ye dreamers of dreams D185

Come hither ye maidens of country and town B269

Come hither you that would our land enthrall A105

Come hither you who the fair sex reproach F294

Come, honest country-man, what news dost bring? B513

Come jolly Brittons and play your game at whist N199

Come lend an ear good people B200

Come let us joyful anthems raise S140

Come let us mourn for well we may M548

Come let us prepare B220

Come listen a while, and a tale I will tell R231

Come listen a while and I will unfold C381

Come listen awhile, and I'll tell you strange tales H255

Come listen good people and I will relate D462, T321

Come listen, my friends, to a story so new R232

Come listen now to the nations glory   V96
Come listen ye tories and Jacobites now   W344
Come, lord, at this solemnitie   P749
Come loyal Britains all rejoyce, with joyful acclamations   E331
Come loyal churchmen   H428
Come master taylor let us try   M185
Come, Meg, let's fa to wark upo' this green   R59
Come muses all/Lament the fall   E288
Come, my couragious Jack, my metl'd Scot   M200
Come my joy and hearts delight   M22
Come on, my brave boys   N62
Come on thou muse who only dwells   M211
Come out my lads, make haste, come out and play   S415
Come sing, my muse, that ancient Briton   T47
Come sing my muse the noble prince's fame   P33
Come sweet fair maid and grant me love   D340
Come thou my mournful muse to his great name   E186
Come, Wattie, while our hirsels feed thegither   B276
Come weeping friendship! to these mournful plains   A159
Come, where's this wonder? This surprising piece!   T74
Come ye kind angels, and declare the love   C1·5
Come, ye lovers of peace, who are said to have sold   G257
Come ye ministers all so courtly   T584
Come ye old English huntsmen that love noble sport   O118
Come, ye Sachev'lites, lament and mourn   M538
Come, ye souls, who are returning   A169
Come, ye sparks of St. James's who grandeur admire   L91
Come you jovial British fellows   C491
Come you taylors from your houses   P639
Complaints like ours, in Ramah's vale were heard   E171
Complaints like ours thro' Tyber's vales did fly   S142
Compos'd to sleep on Saturn's ominous night   I26
Condemn not, madam, as I write in haste   E376
Condemn'd by fate to wayward curse   C405
Confound all the medals of James the third's face   L308
Conqueritur siquis mores mala tempora culpans   K26
Conquest and triumph the glories proclaim   W21
Constantia, now a saint, was heavenly fair   J57
Consultissime juris, atque rite   P310
Content transcends a crown, 'tis wisdom's mark   S387
Continuat nostras coeli clementia palmas   P1101
Convinc'd by reason, I her laws obey   A218
Corinna, pride of Drury-Lane   S809
Cot-splut-hur-nails! Shall hur sit dumb and mute   S393
Cou'd a surveyor! think this a mystery?   B288
Could all we little folks that wait   P36
Could but success attend my wish   W2
Could I, great Meldrum! thy great worth proclaim   E188
Could mortals taste of heavenly bliss and joy   D477
Could my Hibernian muse but soar on high   H128
Could piety or virtue ought avail   D405
Could the great Lewis from death's shades advance   P616
Could virtue, learning, and religion, all   T260
Could woman's pen attain to Dryden's wit   G10·5
Courage, my friends, 'tis now an equal lay   M387

C—r (the wonder of a brazen age)   U23
Creator! genial source of day!   W295
Credidimus terras Hydram liquisse Britannas   P352
Cretians and Grecians deemed were, to be   M421
Crost in a meaner theam, I mind to prove   C222
Crown'd by the general voice, at last you shew   E402
Crown'd with the sickle, and the wheaten sheaf   T233
Crown'd with the wreath of universal praise   M317
Cruel disease! must now thy spite be shewn   P1031
Cum primum immensi deus unus, trina potestas   S275
Cum suus exanimem populus ploraret Elisam   S489
Cum, varios mundi solis radiantis adinstar   D304
Cumberland, couronné des mains de la victoire   P146
Cur solus, Melibæe, sedes, mœstusq sub umbra   A223
Cur tibi natalem felix Heriote quotannis   P353
Cura quæ vatum, titulis, sacrorum   H143
Curse on the times! for satire reigns o'er all   P702
Curse on thy bribes! shall female love be stain'd   P676
Custom, which every where bears mighty sway   C377
Cutt the name of the man who his mistress deny'd   R144

D

Dædaleas naturæ artes, quas prodiga rebus   B232
Dame Briton of the grange, once fam'd   F1
Damned brazen face, how could you hope   S73
Damon and Thirsis from a mossy rock   A334
Damon, this morn, methought the god of day   D20
Damon, unhappy Damon! sure   D21
Dannistone jubes me digno dicere versu   P354
Dannistone meæ quid turbas otia vitæ   P365
Dans le sein de Thétis, déposant sa lumiere   O172
Dans le temps ancien où l'ignorance florissoit   R213
Dans les soudains transports que m'inspire ta gloire   H386
D'Anvers! no more in weekly libels deal   F92
Daphnis stood pensive in the shade   G44
Dapper spark tho' dwarf in size   P209
Dare you dispute/You sawcy brute   S797
Dark chaos reign'd e're green the earth o'respread   P462
Dark in a closet all alone   W233
Dark in my closet all alone   W235
Dark to futurity, in doubt, and fear   T456
Darling of men, and patron o' the wars   H153
Dat propiæ similem translata metaphora vocem   S763
Daughter of Doris, whose earth-hidden stream   H350
Daughter of Jove! Calliope divine   B365
Daughter of memory, immortal muse   C376
Daughter of Pæon, queen of every joy   A296
Daughters of Jove, and source of sacred song   L171
Daughters of Jove, immortal nine, inspire   B205
David was king, after god's heart anointed   C126
Davidis fautor Jonathan fuisti   P324
D----d brazen face, how could you hope   S73
Dead? and I live to hear it and not dye   E104, 173
Dead to the world's each scene of pomp or care   M234
Dean, Drapier, Tatler, Gulliver   D516
Dear angel divine,/Who brighter doth shine   M201
Dear brethren do ye hear how fine   J7
Dear brother or sire, for I'm sure we're a kin   Y11

INDEX OF FIRST LINES

Dear brother weavers, late of no renown   B603
Dear Captain may I call you so   S463
Dear children, whom the Lord to me hath giv'n   F75
Dear Chloe, while thus beyond measure   C157
Dear Col'nel! Cobham's and your country's friend!   P955
Dear Davy, my dear, how comes it to pass   A18
Dear Dean, if e're again you write   S876
Dear Dick, howe'er it comes into his head   P1078
Dear Dick! since thus conveniently we meet   T434
Dear Doctor – Being you're so kind   S407
Dear doctor, here comes a young virgin untainted   H394
Dear doctor, I send/To you as a friend   L258
Dear Doctor! – While the road to health you shew   E398
Dear father, sure I hope you think   O127
Dear friend, have you heard the fantastical chimes   J103
Dear friend,/'Tis talk'd which I scarce can think true   F185
Dear friend, whose elegiack vein   E418
Dear friends and Christians, what shall I say   A13
Dear friends and countrymen give ear   S603
Dear Goody! you have seen, no doubt   B299
Dear Humpus will you still abuse   O229
Dear J—n, I congratulate   L122
Dear John, what ails ye now? ly still   R56
Dear little Friends, not tainted yet with ill   P1176
Dear Lodge, you know my love for rhime   J43
Dear madam. Before you depart from this nation   E383
Dear Martin Folkes, dear scholar, brother, friend   B614
Dear miss, I thank you for your kind surrender   H395
Dear Nanny, all the world are running   H155
Dear Peter, whose friendship I value much more   B620
Dear Pope, the muses' favourite, and friend!   L269
Dear R******, if I know thy soul aright   H15
Dear reverend sir,/In your epistle   E419
Dear royal youth I'll nere repent   L301
Dear sir,/I'm really sorry that our friend   B612
Dear sir since in cruxes and puns, you and I deal   S899
Dear sister, of the rhyming tribe   F162
Dear sisters come see you how fine   D333
Dear Smed I read thy brilliant lines   S858
Dear to bright honour, to thy country dear   C357
Dear to thy country and thy king   P1044
Deer Tom, pray lay aside your hoe   O127
Dear William, did'st thou never go   S151
Dear William, didst thou never pop   P1086
Dear wise-headed friends, of the Jacobite clan   D69
Death as a champion bold, a gyant fierce   E51
Death, as a king, does all the world engage   T37
Death, dost thou difficult us now to know   E456
Death, that the fort of life had long assail'd   F302
Death who regards not wealth or blood   E65
Death, ye're a slimm and packy lown   G294
Deborah did a divine song compose   F52
Deceptos pastor secum meditatus amores   B329
Defensive folds our midnight flocks inclose   A333
Deign, vocal sisters, ever-tuneful maids   B84
Delia, who once of courts and empires sung   H154
Deliciae generis nostri, mihi rebus in arctis   P355
Deliciæ Veneris Cnidus, hos Cytherea recessus   C215
Dell'uom la prima trasgressione e il frutto   R255

Delphinis quanto balaena Britannica fertur   P357
Deluded man, by flatt'ring hopes betray'd   L291
Deluded mortals, whom the great   S877
Deluding world, which hath so long amus'd   W224
Depress'd, desponding Britain's genius lay   D70
Descend angelick choir again, adorn   C518
Descend my muse, among the tuneful throng   O8
Descend Polymnia! and sing   O35
Descend Urania, haste descend   O57
Descend ye angels, heavenly choir   H319
Descend ye nine, assist me while I sing   G226
Descend ye nine! descend and sing   P904
Descende cœlo, spiritu quæ melleo   S490
Descended from a race renown'd for arms   L95
Descending, whether right or wrong   W466
Descens de la voute étherée   O22
Describe, my muse; in epic numbers tell   H133
Desert, oft hid in shades, when monarchs trace   E509
Desolate Albion, mourn thy cruel fate   P690
Despair, when sprung from great and just disgrace   F23
Despise, my soul, the pompous state   P58
Despising all the idle cant   S177
Desponding artist talk no more   W31
Destructive wars some may delight to sing   G9
Detesting flatt'ry, and to art unbred   P542
Detesting flatt'ry's venal strain   O56
Dexteram læti canimus Jovemque   P364
Dian knew well to chace the tim'rous hare   B6
Dic mihi, chare puer, patri dilecte supremo   N299
Dic mihi mitis Hymen, cui sunt connubia curæ   T166
Dic mihi qui medicae mortalibus auctor es artis   P334
Dicite heroem sociumve, musæ   P400
Dicite jam, Britones, quo Mæcenate poeta   C13
Dicite jam, Britones, quo successore beata   C16
Dick serv'd a widow of no mean esteem   B49
Dick, thour't resolv'd, as I am told   S854
Did once the morning stars admire   P740
Dilate your breasts, brave souls, and scorn to weep   P562
Dim, as the borrow'd beams of moon and stars   D461
Dimply damsel, sweetly smiling   P217
Diogenes sober and wise, is said to have liv'd in a tub   A220
Diogenes surly and proud   W183
Direct thine eye to yonder plains   C417
Discite quam rapidæ vanescunt ludicra vitæ   I24
Disdain not, P—, my verse to hear   P10
Disdain not, Snow, my humble verse to hear   G64
Dismiss'd from life, and from life's anxious cares   E263
Distant a little from the Gallick shore   F25
Distinguish'd praises mark that gracious day   A374
Distinguish'd worth demands the poet's lays   B335
Distrest Ecclesia from the pulpit groans   A19
Diva potens, cœli proles pulcherrima, cujus   K77
Dive, dic vatem medicumve Phœbo   P399
Divine Thalia! charmer of my breast   F275
Divinest Clio, strike the trembling strings   H242
Divinity and justice hand in hand   O174
Do not, most fragrant earl, disclaim   R291
Do thou, fair liberty, descend   S134
Do thou, great goddess, whose superiour sway   L274
Do thou, whom thy great death on earth renowns   O200
Do ye appear in any page   B22

11

Doctor, I thank you, for your inkling R116
Doctor, pray give a repetition D356
Dr. Sammy may I call you so M281
Dr. Smed altho' I'm press'd with cares F53
Doctor, you're right, love only works the cure D217
Does any weary soul thro' sin despair G208
Does Maurus move? Who would not laugh to see C130
Does thy great master, Walpole! for a while M536
Don Carolus, my namesake's son D399
Tonald Bayn her nane dear shoy H206
Donatus, you as opportunely ask T548
Doron, methinks this lovely, gloomy shade E44
Dorset, the grace of courts, the muse's pride P931·5
D'où partent ces coups de tonnerre M139
Down at the foot of Vesulus the cold O95
Down by a chrystal river clear B96
Down by a chrystal river side B97
Draw near, ye sober citizens N307
Drayton, sweet antient bard, his Albion sung K89
Dread not, my muse, the task pursue W471
Dread queen and princess, hail! we thus are met C400
Drunkard, stand, if thou canst, and see within this glass E293
Du bon Charles premier, des bons rois le modele L4
Du heros de la Germanie V116
Dub, dub, dubbadub, says the drum in the morning W49
Dublin, that breeds the poet, breeds the dun P695
Duke Hamilton was as fine a lord D496
Duke William came, and, in a bang N76
Dull is the muse that aids the servile pen E176
Dum fagus (namq; aestus erat) me protegit umbra K74
Dum fastu me, chara Chloe, fas praeter & aequum C157
Dum lustro, celebris quas Dorovernia jactat R111
Dum moriens laetor redeuntis numere vitae P368
Dum novus annus adest: tibimetque secunde Georgi T118
Dum numerat doctam renitens ecclesia prolem L144
Dum patriae servire studes patriaeq; parenti P374
Dum prius cunctis mihi chare, Juli J107
Dum prudens utor rediturae munere vitae P367
Dum rosa purpureo suffunditur ora rubore R304
Dum sic Wilhelmum laudibus evehit B231
Dum studeo fungi fallentis munere vitae P366
Dum tibi laudatur Maij vigesima nona P361
Dum tua bellator, princeps, vexilla secutus S544
Dum tua Teutonici proclamant facta dynastae E603
During the reign of the royal Robert F191
Durst thou attempt to sing of Blenheim's plain T508
D'ye hear the news! Sir Roger he's retir'd E178

E

Each matron, consecreated in the trade E113
Each reverend whore and celebrated thief N287
Each woman is a brief of womankind O252
Early one Sunday, when Aurora's dawn W125
Early queen of light arise S411
Earth, keeps the relicts of a choice dear wife B216
Earth shakes again, and Britain cries V64
Earth trembled, the sun blush'd a crimson red S4·5

Eboracae peragro fines; lustroque viator D232
Ecquid adest spectrum, fallacis lampade lunae E34
'E'er' see 'Ere'
Egregios fuci tractus, calamique labores A204
Eh! bien mon frere, eh! bien, nôtre troupe sacrée D283
Eheu! sereni mollia tempora T172
Eia alacres hilaresque virum cantemus, amœnos K22
Emathian plains with slaughter cover'd o'er R292
Employ'd in learned dissertation C338
Empress of Islse [!], who rules the rolling Forth E210
En! ego musarum blando perculsus amore D527
En Jovis alta ales, quam a terra Marlburus armis I22
Encore; now let's have th' other touch of the song A295
Enfans d'Albion qui tenez le sang A278
Engine strong,/Thick and long! T586
England again, by civil discord torn T562
England lament at Benbows fate severe S162
England of late has fell among the thieves T430
England, thy sun have shined many years R307
Enough, enough; all this we knew before S531
Enough has satire vicious times bewail'd C23
Enough, my muse, 'tis time to lay aside D408
Enough, my soul, let's quit this cool retreat E289
Enough of Grongar, and the shady dales D566
Enthron'd in center of the planets bright S718
Equipt for journey, mounted on a steed T483
E'er bright Aurora streak'd with rose the east S773
Ere (cursed instance!) as the poets feign B323
E'er Europe's peace is broken quite M320·5
E'er Lucifer dispers'd the shades of night P535
E'er that the flood, with unresisted sway P1043
E'er the most high and undistinguish'd light B572
E'er time first mov'd, or e'er the youthful sun B443
Er'e we to play this match prepare R308
E'er yet the earth or heaven, or various frame N248
Erected at last,/To discover each blast N239
E–/rected/To him elected P1180
Ergo age, pars nostri melior, vis vivida, vitae D348
Ergo jaces perdocte senex? Virtutibus annos I25
Esse tibi notum Christum ter Petre negasti P395
Est currens mundus demens, ego credo, rotundus B394
Et me Latine, non solitum, loqui D302
Eternal god, creator of all things! O191
Eternal love, of sweetest poetry B130
Eternal Phœbus! whose propitious ray T335
Æternal spirit of that bless'd abode C475
Ethereal daughter of the lusty spring T171
Aethereal ray that didst inspire D83
Eugene and Boufflers, now contending are G268
Eve, the mother of all living F103
Even as the dew within a rose S195
Ever did the muse the female sex befriend L14
Ex schismatico fit Hortensius H327
Examination's ever-dreaded toils P173
Excuse me, madam, if amidst your tears G45
Exert, my muse, in more transcendent strain K103
Exhilarent alacres Britonum jam gaudia vultus! P185
Expositas late Cami prope flumina merces H237
Extoll my muse, our studious founder, Leigh O3
Extremes on either side are wrong D352·5

INDEX OF FIRST LINES

F

Fabricius to my numbers lend thy ear   G102
Faction and schism that ope' the dreadful way   E602
Fain wou'd my verse, Tyrconnel, boast thy name   S119
Fair Albion's brightest, but abating joys   S560
Fair Albion's sons your tuneful notes advance   T267
Fair as the morning, as the morning early   T77
Fair Cytherea, and her lovely train   C416
Fair daughter once of Windsor's woods!   T293
Fair innocence, the muses loveliest theme   B80
Fair lady your petition with care I did read   O259
Fair liberty, bright goddess, heavenly-born   C522
Fair nymph, ascend to beauty's throne   W255
Fair nymph, who hast with such applause so long   L120
Fair ones! to you who hearts command   P1167
Fair patroness of long departed worth   C410
Fair royal mourner! hear the pious muse   S375
Fair science blasted in its num'rous growth   G136
Faith is the gift of god, and 'tis the scope   T505
Faith, sir, it's strange, and somewhat sad   A256
Fall'n! by the dismal stroak of harshest fate   I29
False Britons who favour the measures of France   P145
Fama cum patrem varii sacelli   H142
Fame, by your leave! ⟨   ⟩ worth   R187·5
Fame, for a while, 'till British arms appear   D218
Fame! let thy trumpet sound   B224
Fame, the charming'st girl on earth   W474
Fame thy loudest blast prepare   S587
Fancy, bright and winged maid   H19
Fancy, creative power, at whose command   M50
Fancy the great Hippocrates's art   P381
Far from her hallow'd grot, where mildly bright   M123
Far from the town remov'd, that faithless den   S667
Far in a lonely vale where poplars spread   S24
Far in a wild, unknown to public view   P72
Far in the watry waste, where his broad wave   M44
Far north from London may be seen   W127
Farewel c—t and farewel pleasure   S36
Farewel, farewel, to rump and good old cause   A161
Farewel great George, not only great but good   P673
Farewell, great man; th' ungrateful land forgive   V77
Farewell, old bully of these impious times   W112
Farewel that liberty our fathers gave   H22
Farewell the great, the good!----this all may cry   T506
Farewel thou last and greatest of thy race   M90
Farewel to Lochaber, and farewell my Jean   R65
Farewel ye gilded follies pleasing troubles   W565
Fast by the banks of Cam was Colin bred   P1065
Fast by the surge my limbs are spread   Y82
Fat Buphalus, his o'er-fed paunch to ease   C255
Fate gave the word, the cruel arrow sped   B502
Father of all! in every age   P982
Father of lights! to thee, from whom   H443
Fatigued with granting mortal pray'rs   U16
Fav'rite of gods and men! spirit refin'd!   A62
Fear god, and his commandments keep   C218
Felicem censes, vetus, o! et fide sodalis   E9
Felix Dupplinio, nuruque felix   P307
Famale [!] Ovington, how poor, and thin   W11
Fergusia once a sovereign free   M162
Fert animus, quo non aliud præstantius ullum   J75
Fetch! fetch the paper! in my rage I said   W546

Few of themselves, of nature all complain   F202
Fie fie Dick,/To take chick   P523
Fill the glasses all round   P1151
Fill up the glass, if ever, now's the time   N13
Finish'd the stage, the croud collected round   E385
Fir'd by the laudable example   H151
Fir'd with just resentment I will write   V97
First is my note, and Blenheim is my name   N295
First, let thy piece, address the mighty man   A74
First – let us not, by reason's rules, intend   M494
First noble master of this honour'd dome!   M307
First to the gods thy humble homage pay   R288
First worship god th' eternal three and one   P62
Fitly to hail this happy day   N341
Five hours, (and who can do it less in?)   S869
Fixt in the spacious main there lays an isle   S77
Flentis hamadryadis luctum, quercumq; dolentem   D231
Flevimus, o utinam possent, Gulielme, dolores   A221
Flocks are sporting, doves are courting   C53
Florinda, whose enchanting face   T28
Flush'd with a double draught of double strong   P154
Fly forked satyr, turn your ill tun'd lays   A361
Fly swift wing'd godess messenger of death   E243
Folks are mad with the cries   C462
Folks talk of supplies   B459
Fond man! Why charm'd? Why wheedled so?   C229
Fond of applause, let other poets raise   U31
Fond to record to future times   S198
For aiding pow'rs this task to undertake   S245
For an apple of gold   C275
For faults and follies London's doom shall fix   N325
For fear our play and prologue both should fail   F277
For fear your ladyship mistake   H290
For heaven's sake, what d' you mean to do?   S196
For her departed lord, does Britain show   B144
For in the word of god, by his command   M227
For Jacob he this law ordain'd   T258
For me how vain to urge my vent'rous flight   H419
For quiet, friend, the sailor prays   M168
For quiet, Y—ke, the sailor crys   J65
For rest, my lord, the sailor prays   S484
For shame give or'e/And write no more   A88
For speaking gospel-truth, it shakes my reason   E295
For th' off'rings paid at some dead worthy's urn   S235
For true religion with a zeal inspir'd   R139
For tyrants dead no statues we erect   T577
For what have these gentry these four years been fighting?   E487
For which of all our gross enormous crimes   F192
For whom is it we weep, and whence arise   S336
Forbear, fond man, to think that thou canst live   V16
Forbear thou great destroyer of mens fame   R154
Forbear, unskillful mortal   C396
Forbear ye bold rapacious worms, forbear   S719
Forbear, ye criticks, to chastise my muse   P992
Foremost and first, a broken scraper   G248, I52
Forgive dear faithless youth my errors past   F199
Forgive me, sacred bard, if I aspire   N256
Forgive me, worthy sir, if I   E389
Forgive my crime, forgive it, gentle shade   W308
Forgive, my lord, that mine, an artless muse   A371
Forgive, my lord, the fond officious muse   L98

13

INDEX OF FIRST LINES

Forgive th' audacious man, ye injur'd fair   P520
Forgive the daring rashness of the muse   D488
Forgive the muse, that boldly dares to roll   C273
Forgive the muse, that, with a heart sincere   D443
Forgive, ye nereids, if I sing no more   D292
Forsook by fortune, unemploy'd by power   C28
Forte sub Auroram (quamprimum Phœbus Eoo   D219
Forth from the silent mansions of the dead   S631
Fortune, that blind, unconstant devil   G275
Four belov'd river gods, move Jove by prayer   V21
Four kings, each god's viceregent   H108
Four lovely lasses, gay and bright   C546
Four monarchs of worth   R321
Four mushroom merchants, insolent and proud   P165
Four sisters once a pretty handsome brood   P445
Frae north'ren mountains clad with snaw   R79
Fre seventeen hondred twenty yere   D486
France, Spain, Rome, and devil (as always) of late   N212
Fratre tuo viso derisit Apollo Gradivum   P385
Fraught with rebellions, feuds, and murthers fell   S150
Free from all the fears   L303
Freedom, goddess frank and fair   S582
Freemen far and near, I pray you come here   B25
French tyranny to such a height is grown   E296
Fresh from his task, the rising bard aspires   B494
Fret not, dear Tom, that thou ha'st lost the race   P480
Friend, finding some weary of more rugged prose   W232
Friend! if I'm late, excuse the failing   F247
Friend Ralph (for that I think's thy name   H263
Friend to the gloomy shade of night!   H20·5
Friends and companions, servants of the fair   S19
Friends, Britons, and countrymen, hark ye draw near   S141
Friends! Britons! Countrymen! I pray from whence   S166
From a beggarly off-spring, from dunghil and dirt   N314
From a dozen of p———s made all at a start   N150
From a poet that's proud of his wit and his parts   N153
From all the mischiefs I shall mention here   H250
From anch'rites lonely caves, from hermites cells   W82
From Blossoms Inn when Bob came down   C80
From Bogie side to Bogie gight   M107
From Cæsar, now, each poet hopes reward   S355
From Cam's fam'd banks, and Granta's green retreats   E488
From Carrick, where the noble Ormond met   S642
From darkest shades, behold I rise   A70
From dirty kennels and a jakes   P47
From distant climes, and long fatigues return'd   A368
From dreams, where thought in fancy's maze runs mad   Y36
From dreary realms where cold and famine reign   S621
From dusky mansions, where misguided souls   G249
From earth's low prospects and deceitful aims   B359
From fate's dank cell to empire call'd   T84
From France from Spain from Rome I come   I38
From gentle skies, and ever blooming plains   B187
From gentler notes of peace and love   J108
From gloomy horrors, big with black despair   F204
From glorious toyls of war   D549

From Granta's stream the loyal muse is come   L99
From Hades, with the rich-man's wish, I'm sent   A363
From happy climes where vertue never dyes   M208
From Harry's daughter, and the Princess Bess   N173
From heaven first my ancient lineage came   O269
From India's burning clime I'm brought   R204
From Isis banks three kindred bards unknown   A191
From joyous songs, and from the vocal groves   O211
From lighter strains, to sing the tragic theme   M570
From loftier subjects the heroick muse   S190
From lofty garret comes your thund'ring verse   D78
From lofty themes, from thoughts that soar'd on high   Y74
From London to Exon/By special direction   M289
From London to Scotland   R115
From lonely vaults can blooming landskips rise   F225
From low and abject themes the grov'ling muse   P226
From low and abject themes the soaring muse   V122
From me, dear Charles, inspir'd with ale   T546
From me Edina, to the brave and fair   R44
From 'mongst the noisey crew, where devils resort   H134
From peaceful bowers, and from silent shades   D497
From pillory, describ'd with wondrous art   T104
From publick noise and factious strife   P1088
From religion dress'd up like a miss for the game   L193
From rosy fingers, morning shook the dew   A5
From royal tombs, we change the awful scene   P581
From Sala's banks our constitutions came   H109
From scenes of blood, and war's destructive deeds   M147
From school and mamma a coxcomb I came   F265
From Sc—th depositions, and gre—ing of men   L302
From shades as deep, and gloomy as the bow'rs   D6
From soft Elysium's fair retreats   D357
From solitude, which ne'er must know an end   J40
From southern climes, where unremitting day   T220
From sultry regions, in the road to hell   W66
From sunless worlds, where Phœbus seldom smiles   D11
From the blest mansions of eternal joy   W22
From the charm'd port escap'd at last   E605
From the cold grave, where kings and prophets sleep   F260
From the creation let the day begin   J15
From the dark caverns of the earth I come   A276
From the dark realms of lowest hell I come   E370
From the dark Stygian lake I come   F248
From the fair banks of Thame this verse I send   W292
From the fine Roman whore, or the Geneva slut   N151
From the lawless dominion of mitre and crown   L167
From the mount of Parnassus November the fift   E610
From the remotest banks of northern Tay   F101
From the sad place where sorrow ever reigns   M434
From this auspicious day three kingdoms date   F113
From this small text the furious priests take pains   S450
From those bright mansions of eternal day   C166
From those dire realms of everlasting gloom   E372
From thy own Westminster's Castalian spring   S285
From time's vast length, eternal and unknown   H93
From town retir'd, where vice and folly reign   C419
From verdant meads, where Isis gentle waves   G171

14

From villainy dress'd in the doublet of zeal   F241, L194

From vulgar eyes, on plains exalted high   B527·8

From warmer lands, ally'd to latest fame   K88·5

From week to week, while venal pens essay   C77

From what bewitch'd unhappy ignorance   D400

From whence, dear child, does all that's good descend?   G162·5

From whence, dear child, does all that's good proceed?   G160

From woods and lawns, serene and hush'd retreats   E366

From your lyre-enchanted tow'rs   S491

Frontello once the blithest of the swains   L323

Full five and fifty winters o'er thy head   D410

Full forty long years has old England complain'd   H252

Full fraught with years and knowledge doth resort   E232

Full thirty years and more we've seen   N93

Full twenty times hath Phœbus' car gone round   H48

Full twenty years exper'ence have I had   T590

G

Gard'ner, thy blood for vengeance cry'd   P268

Gaudia mirifice perfundunt pectora honesta   I6

Geneva's a subject long since out of date   D243

Genius of harmony arise!   W6

Genius of Penshurst old!   C474

Genius of these aspiring times   M227

Genius of verse! with ardour fill my breast   E468

Gentle lyre, begin the strain   H99

Gentle poet, brother swain   T344

Germanicus, for love, and empire, born   H231

Gibbie, sin a' the hirstle's fled the field   P166

Gin ye meet a bonny lassie   R53

Give ear O youth, and bow to truth   A340

Give me a genius, fill'd with soft delight   B527·4

Give me, ye sacred muses, to impart   P416

Glorious hero are you dead   C132

Glory by few is rightly understood   C411

Glory to god, author of Britains peace   T544

Glory to god on high, and peace on earth   G168

Glory to god who reigns on high   H473

Glowing, pure, with hallow'd fire   H217

Go, favourite man; spread to the wind thy sails   W256

Go, mighty prince, and those great nations see   S373

Go now my muse, on thy allegiance go   P24

Go on, little captain, stick close to Sir Bob   O184

Go on O worthy Prætor, nor refuse   P559

Go, says the centaur to Pelides, go   C418

Go shameful model of a cursed w-----e!   F84

God bless our gracious sovereign Anne   M32

God did his throne forsake   W569

God grant us grace and courage to defend   N142

God! great and just, omnipotent and high   H136

God is the bless'd foundation sure   H463

God of truth and power and grace   W315

God prosper long our gracious k—g   C195

God prosper long our gracious queen   H45

God prosper long our king and queen, and the wise parliament   N225

God prosper long our noble king   E560, F295, I71, L265, N59, P524, R311, S780, W376, W539

God prosper long our noble peers   M199

God prosper long our noble queen   L2

God prosper long our patriot cause   B39

God prosper long the commonweal   B42

God prosper long this free-born isle   N85

God prosper the king and the king's noble sons   A292

God save brave Vandeput   N210

God safe's is this auld Reeky's bard   H2

God-splut-hur-nails! Shall hur sit dumb and mute   S393

God the first poet was, and poets made   E145

God with us a glorious motto   N121

God wott, great cause I have to weep   A271

Goddess of beauty, have a care   T399

Goddess of numbers, and of thoughts sublime!   H375

Goddess of the brave and wise   T103

Goddess, whom antient Athens knew   H387

Goddolphine Stygem potas et Averna fluenta   P363

Goff, and the man, I sing, who, em'lous, plies   M137

Going to mass the other day   V107

Gone! and no comet to portend thy fall?   E204

Gone! and no omen to portend thy fall   A2

Gone, with a paunch stuff'd out with arrogance   T23

Good Christian people all, I pray   O274

Good Christian people, now be pleas'd to mind   T567

Good English folk, come shake both sides and head   E211

Good folks, I pray, have not you heard   N73

Good folks of this isle,/Pray listen a while   I61

Good lord! I'm undone, thy face I would shun   S589

Good morrow gossip Will   P713

Good-morrow, Guzzle, what, to work at five?   N296

Good morrow Thyrsis. May Aurora prove   M40

Good morrow to thee: how dost do?   B608

Good-morrow Tom; if not in haste   W387

Good news is arrived/Duke William the glorious   S548

Good people all, both low and high   R128

Good people all, I pray attend   T428

Good people all I pray draw near   N206

Good people all I pray give ear   G204

Good people all we pray give ear   N196

Good people attend, while I sing you a song   A131

Good people, come heark, and a story I'll tell   T584

Good people draw near,/And a tale you shall hear   W364

Good people draw near and lend me your ear   N82

Good people draw near,/To my ballad give ear   S204

Good people! flock here in a throng   P997

Good people give attention, and hear the bailiffs praise   T438

Good people give attention now   C204

Good people, give ear, and I'll tell you a story   P2

Good people give ear, I'll declare to you all   F24

Good people, I, El'sabeth dowager Ad-ms   B617

Good people, I pray ye attend and draw near   T9

Good people I say,/Come listen I pray   N227

Good people of England! give ear to my song!   C325, N160

Good people of England, I pray ye draw near   E599

Good sir, I pardon beg for this address C225
Good sir, in such a leaden age as this S67
Good Sir R——t serene B47
Good sir, sin the queen has done with addresses A52
Goupy, my brother, in virtù G310
Grace this my theam, ye muses, and combine N168
Græce loqui, & Latine K73
Grand Lewis let pride be abated D543
Grand-mothers, mothers, aunts, and sisters dear S415
Grandia, magnanimis stipulantur fata Britannis M419
Grant aid to me, Jehovah, I require C238
Grant me, great love, that gen'rous fire to know T360
Grave sir, if I am not mistaken T543
Great A—— be cautious and beware T400
Great A stands for army and B begins battle K49
Great Albion's genius, from her ease profound T101
Great Alderman Parsons now is chose W441
Great bard! in whom united we admire D384
Great Beelzebub, patron of whiggs H427
Great, brave, and faithful! let the proud disdain E428
Great Britain, I invite you to repent A149
Great Britain now hath baffled France and Rome G264
Great-Britain, styl'd from military deeds P1060
Great Britain's warlike arms do loudly ring H363
Great Britain's worthy patriots will excuse M564
Great cry and little wool – is now become S413
Great Devonshire is dead!---How dire the sound? P604
Great Duke! from conquests here retreat C326
Great, glorious man! Thus after clouds more bright T364
Great god almighty did at first decree O201
Great god how shall my trembling tongue declare E151, E197, E228, E255
Great god of truth, direct my muse S696
Great, good, and just; and no less brave and wise! B233
Great, good and just was once apply'd T334
Great Hamilton and Scot of royal blood D58
Great Harrison is dead, lament Hibernians all E144
Great hope of Britain! – Here the muse essays S102
Great, inexhausted source of day P280
Great monarch, hasten to thy native shore E323
Great monarch! sprung from ancient British kings J109
Great Neptune, jealous of his rival's pow'r M500
Great Newton's dead, – full ripe his fame R69
Great Orkney's dead, what news is this we hear E205
Great pox, thou noble sire of the gout A262
Great princess, 'tis decreed! --once ev'ry year S113
Great princess welcome to your native land P39
Great revolutions crown this wond'rous year F64
Great sir, a welcome, equal to our joy W280
Great sir, (as great as Cæsar's son) E360
Great sir, if your highness is pleas'd to peruse A60
Great soul! who no disguise, no changes knows T353
Great things, fates promise to th' brave British land M419
Great Upton to the highest bliss is born E461
Great Walpole once the blithest of the train L324
Great William, to the shades of death confin'd? O43
Great wretched man, whom cares of state distress S733

Greet a ye bairns and bearded fo'k H1
Griev'st thou, my friend, that harmony has foes? A82
Grim cruel death, how fatal is thy blow E88
Grizel, thou charmer of our isle C244
Guardian of our happy isle O62
Guide me, O Venus, darling of mankind B560
Gun is discharg'd of life, death was much quicker T511

H

Ha! young sedition: how does treason sell? T435
Hac Christus jussit se nostram sumere formam P358
Hac Christus voluit patrio se reddere coelo P378
Hac Jovis Hammonis cineres conduntur in urna P370
Hac volvente die, quanto pæane, Britannos S245
Hactenus æstatis brumæq; reciprocus ordo W571
Hactenus Aonides cecinerunt omnia læta K78
Had Athens all the Grecian sence engross'd P1022
Had beauteous Eve, fair mother of mankind O244
Had fate propitious made it mine K36
Had great Apelles once beheld that face B179
Had I but, sir, ability and skill H191
Had I deserv'd to be severely curst H308
Had I Heraclitus his faculty C228
Had I! O had I! Batt, thy face and throat S634
Had I the parts of Pope or Swift H291
Had I the power to will or to indite S80
Had I with Plato's eloquence been fill'd S110
Had not the sov'reign of the globe took care S7
Hæc domus augusta est, magni nam conscia partus I31
Hah! young sedition: how does treason sell? T435
Hail, all-victorious sister! we rejoice S632
Hail ancient book, most venerable code T300
Hail! ancient gentry, nature's eldest line D114
Hail angry maid! – at sight of this don't frown E377
Hail bard triumphant! whose poetick fire T355
Hail beauteous goddess! hail harmonious pow'r L169
Hail Belgian prince, we joy to see you in our isle V30
Hail, bless'd abode! thou mansion of repose P442
Hail! blessed queen, the guardian of our laws B585
Hail blest Elizium! sweet, secure retreat M249
Hail, bright Cecilia, hail! B373
Hail Britain's queen, and empress of the sea! R322
Hail Britannia, queen of isles F234
Hail, British fair ones, who in silence sit E514
Hail Bury! loveliest spot I ever found W531
Hail! busy motion, of a prating world N291
Hail! chair of state; thy praise I sing H456
Hail, Cynthia, silent empress of the night S191
Hail! doughty chiefs, great props of trade H390
Hail, fair Augusta, thro' the world renown'd S240
Hail! fairest wells, tho' late the muses deign H31
Hail faithful pilot of the British state P546
Hail, fragrant May, thou glory of the spring P461·5
Hail gen'rous masters all, I thus you greet M155
Hail, gentle purse! that erst wert lib'ral wont E306
Hail, glorious day! Does yet my life remain C303
Hail glorious man! the muse her tribute brings H246
Hail glorious off-spring of a glorious race! E500
Hail glorious youth! the wonder of the age T342
Hail goddess Poverty, my suit regard H236

INDEX OF FIRST LINES

Hail goddess to our isle propitious   J73
Hail god-like youth! whom Britain's angry stars   A97
Hail! great Cecilia! Hail, hail! patroness divine!   O54
Hail great Eugenius! more renown'd   H71
Hail, hail, auspicious Eugen, whose brave hand   L162
Hail happy Albion! Thou art strangely blest   O223
Hail! happy bard, who durst explore   P544
Hail! happy Child! thrice happy be the day   C348
Hail happy day, on which pleas'd heav'n doth smile   P150, P591
Hail happy day! that bless'd the earth   T331
Hail happy day,/When thy beams thou dost display   O51
Hail, happy fabrick, whose auspicious view   W567
Hail happy morn! Auspicious day   S616
Hail, happy queen! born to heal and to unite   N162
Hail, happy saint! from mortal woe set free!   M401
Hail happy Scotland! Bless the long'd for day   P575
Hail heav'nly muse, prepare, prepare   H166
Hail hi'roglyphick state machin   D115
Hail! hoary'st of Apollo's sons; permit   M566
Hail! holy tribe, nor let the impious brood   P85
Hail image, of th' eternal mind   D110
Hail learning's Pantheon, thou, the lovely prize   S282
Hail liberty! thou beatific grace   L170
Hail liberty! whose presence glads th' abode   R206
Hail March! who, on thy downy wings, dost bring   N48
Hail masonry! thou craft divine!   D190
Hail mighty Anne! may thou be ever blest   S468·7
Hail mighty Brunswick, in whose glorious veins   P671
Hail mighty fabrick! England's magazine   B227
Hail! mighty genius of this fruitful isle   T513
Hail mighty hero of the British race   P41
Hail mighty monarch, glorious king of kings   K9
Hail mighty monarch, welcome to the throne   E454
Hail miracle of monarchs who resigns   P169
Hail, noble artist! nature's rival, hail!   M331
Hail noble lord! my knife had err'd indeed   G311
Hail noble lord of parts immense   D148
Hail, noble sirs! may mirth your banquet crown   S7·5
Hail pious days! thou most propitious time   O219
Hail queen of islands! hail illustrious fair   D355
Hail radiant off-spring, emanation bright!   B252
Hail reverend tripos! guardian of the law   G311
Hail! royal maid, divinely fair and good   V8
Hail, royal maid! divinely good and great!   U11
Hail sacred art! thou gift of heaven, design'd   P585
Hail sacred day, distinguish'd by the birth   P1046
Hail sacred king, now wars and discord cease   E307
Hail sacred majesty: serene and great   R312
Hail sacred muse, and vocal shell   H50
Hail! sacred name! who kindly live   S362
Hail! sacred nymphs, whose influence inspires   S58
Hail! sacred peace, thrice happy are those climes   N141
Hail sacred peace! thrice welcome to our isle   O217
Hail sacred princess! Hail Great Britain's glory!   S947
Hail, sacred solitude! from this calm bay   S801
Hail! sacred sons of wisdom! whilst I choose   C293
Hail sacred spirits of ætherial frame   A228
Hail, saint triumphant, in whom earth did see   P538
Hail Sion's friends, to you glad news I bring   S469
Hail sons of war, accept the muses praise   B527
Hail! Stephen Duck, with praise around begirt   D422

Hail subtile heat! which pleasure brings   S155
Hail! thou great engine that for shew   C237
Hail thou resplendent source of high-church light!   H454
Hail thought inspiring plant! Thou balm of life!   T404·5
Hail to the day, that crown'd with David's name   G295
Hail to the lov'd, returning, glorious day!   E496
Hail to thee glorious rising year   R298
Hail tricking monarch! more successful far   B548
Hail, venerable shade, to whom   H471
Hail, victory! thou stranger to our land   D123
Hail wond'rous being, who in pow'r supreme   S495
Half tir'd with drinking, dull-plays, and the rest   T488
Hanno nos visit Syracusis nuper amice   P344
Han't you heard of a fortress, renowned in fame   B33
Happiest of the spaniel-race   P678
Happy are you that breathe the Hampton air   L186
Happy are you, whom Quantock overlooks   D291
Happy Britannia! Io pæan sing   M308
Happy queen, in whose calm bosom   I4
Happy that author, whose correct essay   D307
Happy the maid, who from green sickness free   B392
Happy the maid, whose body pure and chaste   F235
Happy the man, and worthy so to be   C398
Happy the man, who, free'd from vain desires   R167
Happy the man, who void of care and strife   B506
Happy the man, who void of cares and strife   P246
Happy the man, who, when he goes to stool   S206
Happy the man who with such ease   E361
Happy the man, whose tender care   H440
Happy the people where no priest gives rules   G311
Happy the people, who, tho' keen   T255
Happy the youth, whose nobly thinking mind   H182
Happy! thrice happy is his fate!   D19
Happy was I, before I knew to sin   W98
Happy was man, when first by nature made   A182
Happy were man, when born as free as air   F128
Hard fate! O Gauls! how soon our triumphs cease   S46
Hard fate that I should banish't be   E586
Hark, Britain, hark! The loudest trump of fame   W21
Hark, hark, brave boys do ye hear the report?   N228
Hark! hark the noise, the sorrows, and the eccho!   E162
Hark how the bells his fatal loss deplore   E240
Hark how the voice of joy breaks through the air   P288
Hark, I hear the cannon roar   B453
Hark! o'er Hesperian Midia's plains around   G3
Hark the bells ring, hark the bells ring   C337
Hark! ye citizens of London   H36
Harley at length has reapd the fame   D235
Harley, the nation's great support   S891
Harmonious maid, whose tuneful ear   O72
Harry Gambol at last, is gone packing his ways   A78
Has death at last or'ecome that libral soul   E207
Has earth no judge? Or has that judge no rod   S148
Has then the villain's neck deceiv'd our hope   E135
Has winter drawn thee, say, poetic friend   B436
Haste, great commander, to our longing isle   T336
Haste, O my soul, and let thy winged speed   W566·7
Haste, O my soul, and wing thy course away   W566
Haste, Polyhymnia, haste; thy shell prepare   T146
Hast, potent genius, hast away!   H70
Have all thy bards, Britannia, spent their vein   B254

Have I my fingers? and have I my eyes? S453
Have ye heard of a plot to destroy the poor king M132
Have you heard of late,/How affairs of state F251
Have you heard the report,/Quoth D'Anvers, at court F283
Have you not heard of a pious fray B424
Having giv'n all the whores a touch D536
He lands----the pious fears Britannia bore S367
He that in satyr dips his angry pen D144
He that owns with his heart, and helps with his hand H124
He that wou'd sail in troubl'd seas L238
He who attempts to sing the glorious deeds P705
He who his freedom cou'd, by wit command P515
He who with Homer dares engage the field N20
He's base, who wou'd degrade what's truly fine M489
He's come! now tory ministers avaunt N332
He's gone! But, still shall nature stun'd A151
He's rash and base who do's at arts repine M496
Health! good supreme! offspring of heaven! divine B10
Health, happiness, contentment, to my friend M504
Health, to his dear Maria, Rupert sends M509
Health to my spouse, and may that health I send P1041
Hear, all ye friends to knighthood S717
Hear, fair Belinda, hear thy suppliant's cry P60
Hear me ye Hockley valleys make my moan B124
Hear now, O heavens, and thou, O earth, give ear S530
Hear O celestial hosts that shine so bright S457
Hear, Phœbus, source of light, heav'n's brightest grace! D512
Hear, thou vile scribbler! of the rhiming trade G203
Hear us, O god! this joyful day H376
Heark! heark! the trumpet sounds, the court is met! G138
Heark, how the muses call aloud T78
Heaven bless great George, long may he be T113
Heav'n gives the needful, but neglected, call Y50
Heavens! are we such a servile nation grown F188
Heav'ns! to what height our follys now arise B127
Hectoris exuvias indutum cernite Mosen P371
Hei mihi! perpetuæ lachrymæ, sine fine dolores L6
Hei mihi quod non sum permagnos aptus ad ausus A222
Hélas! il ne vit plus, ah! perte irreparable E41
Hence airy empty pleasure A167
Hence all ye poor weak-minded fools O75
Hence courtiers and slaves, who no doubt are content N75
Hence from my breast I banish every joy L231
Hence goes a lamp of light, a son of thunder S169
Her heavenly form shall with Belinda's live D514
Her self half dead, to find her queen expir'd T71
Her soul's above, her mortal part's here laid E445
Her watry walls, a barrier all her own S236, S238
Here all thy active fires diffuse M129
Here an old bawd a girl draws in P1105
Here be de ver pretty show, as ever was seen O1
Here be de var pretty show just come from Parrie R122, R126
Here drawer, bring us t'other quart S2, W76
Here first come de Zew, who did bite all de varle R127
Here god by Moses gave to man B213
Here, in cold earth, wrapt in eternal sleep E438

Here interposing, as the goddess paus'd, – T198
Here is a loss to church state & to all E70
Here is a penyworth of wit C160
Here is news upon news boys come from Giblatore [!] S472
Here lies a horse beneath this stone S776
Here lies a prophet, who, as people say E443
Here lies an old man of seventy-seven E439
Here lies stoick John,/Born since forty and one T573
Here, loyal subjects, I am come C143
Here melting mix'd with air th' ideal forms T194
Here poesy – O lend thy aid divine S512
Here Scotus lyes, of late as wise W112
Here, wife, let's see my slippers, cap, and gown W129
Here will I first invoke the sylvan muse G5
Here will I sport a while on native plains H400
Here you see, without delusion S767
Heres a health to Queen Anne boys R310
Here's a health to the king and speedy peace B157
Here's a health to the knight H125
Here's a health to the noble and valiant Argyle J90
Here's a health to the p-----te, whose excellence reaches W393
Here's a health to the queen and her faithful adviser Q9
Here's a health to the queen, who in safety does sit on Q12
Here's a health to the tackers, about let it pass S783
Here's a health to the tackers, my boys H126
Here's a house to be let D463
Here's a story reviv'd from twelve hundred & two L198
Here's a whim wham new come over A353
Here's work, alas! for mourners, to deplore S420
Hermotimus, you're newly come abroad G229
Hero! sprung from antient blood! S505
Heroa quem nunc, Uranie, canes? L315
Heroes, and dreadful arms, and bloody fields M394
Heroes like stars when single radient shine S133
Heu dolor anxietas! Suspiria rumpite pectus C529
Heu! jacet indigna Hamiltonus cæde peremptus I27
Hey day, what's this? 'Tis very strange D439
Hibernia droops her flag now waves in air I62
Hibernia hard beset with gloomy cares B403
Hibernia now condole the fatal stroke I57
Hibernia! raise again thy drooping head I63
Hibernia's sons unprejudiced attend R139·2
Hic Belus abscondor caput objectare periclis P382
Hic est ille tuus natalis, septime, qui te P383
Hic jacet ereptus medijs, proh fata! trophæis C135
Hic regina jacet, nec magnis regibus impar I23
Hic ubi sublustri sylvae nutantis in umbra D390
High art thou rais'd (tho' short of thy desert) M437
High church ne'er claim'd a right divine from Jove H194
High, in thy starry orb H213
Highmore, you grant, that in the painter's art B519
Him, who reviles your muse, pronounce at sight F50
Him, whose sad absence thou hast long condol'd B417
Hirco, an old, but amorous blade L90
His aim (as by his notions plain appears P273
His good performance let no mortal boast W553

His grace Duke Cumberland must go   G293
Historians relate that in Afric are bred   C212
Hither, all ye heav'nly pow'rs   W358
Hither from farthest east to west   T587
Hither from Mexico I came   T390
Hoc saxum mihi filij induerunt   P382
Hogarth, by merit of your own   M331
Hogarth to virtue and to truth a friend   S78
Hollis, tho' long the conscious muse has stay'd   R327
Honoured friends, we are undone   T314
Hora dum nondum sonuit secunda   A177
Horace advises bards in vain   D523
Hosier! with indignant sorrow   P1045
Hover no more, my muse! o'er idle themes   H222
How are the mighty fallen!   S593
How are we pleas'd, when from the distant shore   I20
How beauteous does the azure skies appear   W203
How charm'd! with leading-strings   C497
How comes it, Daphnis, that our nymphs and swains   H47
How conqu'ring Greece, by heav'n's assisting care   M193
How does thy wond'rous art our eyes deceive   H101
How doth the city solitary sit   B516
How doubly blest was man in paradise   F86
How early did love's flame inspire   F85
How easy 'tis to prove that all is vanity   C387
How few surviving mortals warning take   E92
How few with serious joy behold the train   H418
How fierce a flame did Italy o'er-run   O286
How frail, how vain, momentainous man?   E106
How greatly, by our modern poets rage   O183
How happy a state did Britain once enjoy   P714
How happy a state did the miller possess   M232
How happy a state did the Spaniard possess   E335
How hard, my lord, is it to find   J42
How heav'n, provok'd, an awful look assumes   M312
How high our reach, how far our talent goes   M441
How is the anxious soul of man betray'd   E534
How is the great oppressor ceas'd?   P57
How jolly a patriot's life passes   J89
How justly now might I aspire   T48
How long, dear Puss, how long, how long   L15
How long may Heaven be banter'd by a nation   D145
How long must ye be deaf and blind?   O19
How many winters have I watch'd in vain?   N129
How mimic realms, and pageant hosts engage   P1158
How much, egregious Moore, are we   P978
How much, O pastor, do we owe   R32
How now Mr. Kite it is very well seen   N58
How now, sad soul! what means this constant moan   T256
How oft from trifles, hints we take   P261
How oft in these misjudging times   G179
How often do's Dame Fortune man beguile   C113
How pleasant is it, when the sun displays   S419·5
How sad of late is grown an author's case   M272
How shall I now the nine invoke   W448
How shall I paint the man my soul doth love?   R148
How shall I the nine invoke   W447
How shall my muse express thy pow'r or praise   B530·6
How sly the dissenters have acted of late   H192

How strange a thing, ye pow'rs is beauty grown!   B133
How strange an aukward thing is man   P487
How strangely times are alter'd, Hall!   D259
How strangely woman kind did first begin   F94
How stronge's thy sense! How charming are thy strains!   S167
How stupid, jackish, and how vile, at best   D538
How sweet, how charming is this place   H437
How sweet's the love which meets return   R92
How this fantastick world is chang'd of late   T495
How this sad change of state Apollo tell   L229
How (under heav'n) to make with little toil   G129
How unhappy are we, by this unjust decree   L33
How vain are mortal man's endeavours   P518
How vain, delusive, and how transitory   E126
How vain is grief, amidst the pomps of woe   D433
How vast's the power of all-commanding fate   H168
How very wicked have I been   L34
How will the grateful senate praise!   O37
How wond'rous fickle is the world!   J8
Howe'er I turn, or whersoe'er I tread   S534
Howe'er important in the high debate   A152
Howe'er impossible the feat may seem   C320
Howe're, some men accounted wise   P202
Huc adsint sacræ, mœstissima turba, sorores   E32
Huc ferte gressus, culmina linquite   C538
Huc, huc adeste, quotquot a sacris sibi   M408
Huc inculta veni, qualem decet esse dolentis   M409
Huc, venerande! tuæ mihi pervenere tabellæ   C428
Humanæ gentis fundebat talia pulchra   T132
Hunc, Benedicte, tuo cineri Pitcarnus honorem   P306
Hymen, disturb'd his song was disallow'd   C508
Hymen, Minerva, and celestial choir   S183

I

I am a famous scribbler   N54
I am a man just come from Fraunce-e   M412
I am a poet by my trade   N127
I am a sturdy beggar   L239
I am a swell'd-cheek ale-wife   G308
I am a thing--- esteem'd by all   D208
I am a turnip ho-er   E558
I am Ormond the brave, did you never hear of me?   S591
I am told my honest friend Tom Hogg   E149
I am very much concern'd to find   S627
I ask not, lovely virgins, why you weep?   P105
I ask not Phoebus, nor the fabled nine   B369
I beg your attention for I design to write   M547
I bring you news. – From Rome   H202
I can't forbear--- not tears alone shall flow   E217
I feel an impulse from the muse   P1112
I find I was a fool to mock the laws   F197
I follow fancy through her wanton maze   P63
I grant th' enormous vices of the age   M18
I hate the spring, I turn away   Y69
I hate the vulgar with untuneful mind   P70
I have a heart for love, and love   D301
I have (already) nam'd the pulpit-fool   D539
I have heard my dear daughters, a story of late   U19

I have such dread when I should die   C279
I have ten merks, nae mere, nor less   M3
I, he whose infant muse did heretofore   W568
I hear a horse race lately run   P640
I hear, my Cælia, you must be a wife   G223
I hear, my Lesbia, you must be a wife   G219
I heard, dear friend, this morn by crony Tom   A101
I heedless bless'd the flatt'ring wind and tide   P600
I hope there's no soul/Met over this bowl   W452
I humbly request who am cited as wencher   A272
I intend to give you a relation   D34
I Jocky Bell o' Braiken-brow lyes under this stane   P382
I lately read, and read in print   E611
I leave mortality's low sphere   H374
I loved no king in fortie one   E551, T557, W154
I much have wondred what they mean   H294
I must confess that we all lamented   P1148
I need no art to set a' needless gloss   W450
I never din'd with Dennis or with Pope   D42
I never meddl'd with intreagues   T533
I never slept on fam'd Parnassus head   C139
I now have an ambition   E578
I now in Bristol had regardless stay'd   J20
I nunc, disce moras & tædia longa dierum   D347
I often try'd in vain to find   S409
I often wish'd, I had a farm   D519
I own dear D—— your tale is true   E608
I Philip the king, and Queen Betty my wife   H245
I Pluto king of the dark regions   L140
I pray draw near and you shall hear   R1
I pray now come listen to me   W398
I question now, so well you act your part   E362
I raise the strain – genius of verse draw near   B180
I reach all things near me, and far off to boot   D205
I read, sir, your polite epistle   E371
I repent, that, my wisdom hither should bring me   L59
I rise about seven, and read till tow'rds nine   B405
I salutatum propere virorum   P405
I sang the exit of the best of kings   P263
I saw, one day, as people pass'd   D75
I should have dy'd silent, as flow'rs decay   B162
I sing a base with topping voice   M76
I sing a linen vail, the direful cause   J26
I sing a man of merit great   S448
I sing a prelate good, unbodied now   W354
I sing a prig, read it who list   W277
I sing a subject sung by no man   W554
I sing a virgin's smock, the direful cause   J23
I sing a winged army, and the train   P1179
I sing an old proverb that's very well known   L255
I sing no foreign bloody wars   I10
I sing no songs of Alexander's   H54
I sing not chiefs associated of old   G16
I sing not of affairs of states   R30
I sing not of battles, nor do I much chuse   D421
I sing not of battles that now are to cease   P46
I sing not of Bellona's praise, or war   B530·2
I sing not of great Cæsar's might   C147
I sing not of Jove's mighty thunder   N16
I sing not of the Draper's praise, nor yet of William Wood   S846

I sing not old Jason, who travell'd thro' Greece   P1072
I sing of a batter'd old knight   F26
I sing of a hero, whose fame and repute   N56
I sing of a parson, and Archy by name   R222
I synge of a sermon, a sermon of worth   E589
I sing of beauty, O! ye gods inspire   J17
I sing of bodies shap'd to various forms   I8
I sing of electors, but not of a king   E30
I sing of fashion: come, ye modish throng   F67
I sing of jolly Bacchus, and the wine   B498·5
I sing of neither Hogan Mogan   W141
I sing of Ratho. Help me to relate   M324
I sing that graceful toy, whose waving play   G47
I sing the assembly's rise, encrease and fame   B257
I sing the bard, whose merry strains   W96
I sing the bold man, that sleeps in his boots   H152·5
I sing the Briton, and his generous arms   B266
I sing the Briton mountain swain   M550
I sing the buzzing follies of the town   H89
I sing the causes of a troubled reign   W27
I sing the doughty blades of dauntless might   L200
I sing the faith, which all must once confess   H266
I sing the famous city   W561
I sing the founder of the British throne   J29
I sing the harmless pipe, the fragrant herb   B209
I sing the hero, who by right of arms   L215
I sing the loves of John and Betty   J68
I sing the man, of courage try'd   B270
I sing the man, that Britain's crown now wears   K10
I sing the man, who left fair Albion's shore   B240
I sing the man, who n'ere distinction knew   T518
I sing the man, who, when he takes the field   G185
I sing the man whose warlike force subdu'd   H275
I sing the man with shallow head   G316
I sing the natives of the boundless main   O236
I sing the pleasures of the nuptial bed   C4
I sing the pleasures of the rural throng   C327
I sing the potent herb, and sweet repast   P482
I sing the praise of heroes brave   H467
I sing the praises of a fart   P49
I sing the pride of Albion, and the pow'r   B527·1
I sing the prince, the scourge of Gallick power   T386, T589
I sing the rancour of a knight   T420
I sing the rape of an old woman   R119
I sing the wiles that artless lovers cheat   C548
I sing the youth, by envying brothers scorn   R269
I sing who's who in this our generation   H272
I sing you a song, of a right noble -----   P144
I sought a patroness, but sought in vain   Y136
I stood amaz'd at first, I could not bear   R306
I synge of a sermon, a sermon of worth   E589
I tell not, as whilom did merry Mat. Prior   B105
I tell the deeds of great bravadoes   A250
I thank you, sire, and triumph much to see   S632
I that e'erwhile, from lonely cottage sprung   P577
I the dapper spark, so smart   C35
I think Auld Reikie's now grown daft   S789
I thought to have sent/My due compliment   T358
I wairn ye a' to greet and drone   R46
I warn you a' wi' mony a groan   E252
I was the man, oh! cruel change of fate   S443
I who, e'er while, unequal numbers chose   F222

I who have sung, how from the realms of night B268
I wou'd, by heav'n, abolish public wrong F47
I'll ne'er dissemble, 'tis in vain! P27
I'll read no more, but catching from his lays S201
I'll sing you a song of what happen'd of late O112
I'll tell ye all P284·5
I'll tell you a fine tale of note W287
I'll tell you a story, a story anon L184
I'll tell you a story, a story most merry C494, E536
I'll tell you a story, a story so merry P1042, S669
I'll tell you a story, and warrant it true E450
I'll tell you a story as strange as 'tis new L64
I'll tell you a story, how lately Sir Blue S478
I'll tell you a story of lawyers right stout P710
I'll tell you a story that happen'd of late N102
I'm nor high church, nor low church, nor tory, nor whig M361
I'm one of those who in Basse Isle D434
I'm sorry, madam, at my heart to see C470
I'm sure you'le think it strange Dr. Dolly L50
I'm thinking, now the ceremony's over N140
I'm told, for we have news among the dead D102
I've often heard an antient story P1170
I've often wish'd that I had clear S860
I've travel'd far and near A339
Iambe noster, sive tarde, seu celer V100
If a painter should the fancy take H313
If a truth may be ask'd, sir, pray what did it mean? D353
If ancient sages well advise H30
If Anne thou wilt but be so kind M392
If any good Christian, or pagan, or Jew H359
If any line I write's a hobler L118
If Ariconian swains with pleasure see H141
If augurs can foresee, a wretch is come G41
If bards of old we may believe T10
If brave heroic acts a place can claim B164
If C--bb--r's odes disgrace the laurel'd muse M298
If conscious of thy ancient fire D524
If, dearest Dismal, you for once can dine S911
If e'er I forget/How much I'm in debt W411
If e'er in thy sight I found favour, Apollo D525
If e'er soft numbers grac'd the royal hearse E218
If English folk should laugh, and god should speak C441
If ever England mourn'd for man of sence E238
If ever grief was great without disguise E219
If ever statesman melted at distress B198
If fell corruption in each scene appears M63
If for a while you can sit still D66
If, for thy breach of sense and truth T474
If from the beauteous Bandon's side P124
If god almighty be a spirit D317
If grief, or dear respect, have made me slow T139
If, Hammond, I know who, and what you are R105
If heav'n the grateful liberty wou'd give P722
If heav'nly truth on her etherial throne M402
If his abused case revenge doth crave F194
If Hogarth a Change stock-jobber should draw A327
If human ills, which thou too well hast known R250
If I crave the assistance of any one muse N154
If I live to be old, for I find I go down P994
If I live to grow old,/(for I find I go down) P993

If I mistake not, sir, there was a time D286
If I no falshood in my life design'd L7
If I, O Steele, presumptuous shall appear R273
If I was by misfortune sent F83
If I, who wont to sing (supinely laid C432
If in a picture (Piso) you should see D309
If in this world, where dangers daily spring W221
If joy which now presents before mine eyes B452
If kings are gods, as scripture say they be C123
If ladies weep when petted lap-dogs die E163
If love and beauty can inspire the tongue H420
If man the greatest brute on earth was made F97
If master prove much kinder than his word S787
If men are deem'd for loyalty F221
If M——h would curb the king of France N331
If muses may direct the mind of man W515
If Pope his muse to Burlington shou'd raise O83
If prudence were the parent of success N278
If right of birth is wont to name an heir M142
If running the nation in debt W394
If Sapho can believe her time well spent N282
If sighs could soften, or distress cou'd move W434
If so! good angels! take his precious soul! E160
If some great artist in whose works conspire M251
If tea tables, b' allow'd for summer's noise N238
If tears can ever be a duty found R101
If th' old Samian doctrine of spirits be true D210
If the possession of imperial sway O194
If there be any, whether maid or wife L16
If there be truth in what you sing S841
If there on earth be one that has not met F134
If they did Dorcas for her thrift bemoan E112
If thou can'st lay aside a spendthrift's air J69
If thou from heav'n art sacredly inspir'd L153
If to a human face Sir James should draw B383
If to subvert, destroy, if to confound H262
If to the priest's ideal schemes we trust I70
If twice man's age, you would fulfil B110
If violated leagues for vengeance call W401
If virtue ever were the poets' care B52
If wanton leisure, and a cool recess V28
If we into our selves, or round us look P536
If we look back with retrospective eye S187
If we may credit what royal David said E167
If we, O Dorset, quit the city throng P211
If what the Tower of London holds O205
If, yet, confin'd within thy walls O chief L128
If yet, dear friend, the goddess fans the fire B173
If yet, great sir, your heart can comfort know C233
If yet, oh gen'rous Boyle! the tide of grief P655
If yet thou any memory retain S380
If yet unmindful of Ramillia's field N251
If you a painter, Piso, busy saw H314
If you great guardian of Britannia's fate E471
If you, ye virtuous fair, will fire my breast R191
Ill fare the miscreant, who, to mischief prone M327
Ill fate, thou wandering, unseen, shapeless foe P623
Ill-fated Albion! once the happy seat C103
Ill nature strange reigns in this age W1
Ille ego sum Plutus, cujus moderamine justo M24
Ille qui terris latitat Britannis P402
Illustre infortuné, le ciel enfin te vange L158
Illustrious C——l, ancient Scotia's boast H318

Illustrious monarch, but permit my song   S781
Illustrious pair! the blessing of this isle   P203
Illustrious peer, whose friendly mind   V101
Illustrious Pollio! were thy friend adorn'd   K70
Illustrious prince! by heav'n design'd   D471
Illustrious prince, forgive the feeble lay   D473
Illustrious prince of high renown   C9
Illustrious prince we'r come before you   S633
Illustrious prince! who best your martial race   O248
Illustrious queen! the loyal zeal excuse   B409
Immortal bard! for whom each muse has wove   L331
Immortal bard! that on Italian plains   D316
Immortal bard! thou fav'rite of the nine!   C288
Immortal genius! that alone inspires   L113
Immortal gods, shall woman still invaid   F32
Immortal maid, fair daughter of the skies!   B358
Imperial jugler of the state!   P1023
Imprimis, there's a table blotted   L155
In a calm season of the year   W47
In a council of state,/Was a mighty debate   S579
In a dark corner of a silent grove   P121
In a dark vale, where melancholy yew   B175
In a fair island, in the southern main   P279
In a lone vale, which nature made   E485
In a May-morning, on a meadow green   F116
In a tempestuous battle's raging heat   M499
In a wild corner of the world   W282
In Abram's life we see a plan   P1155
In Æsop's days, when birds and beasts could speak   P756
In Æsop's days when birds could prate   S586
In aged times when nations waged war   S62
In ages past when men did prize   C478
In amaze/Lost, I gaze!   S356
In an old author once I found   L251
In an old rock, as stories go   W527
In ancient days (as authors speak   S402
In antient days as poets tell   K92
In antient days, as sages write   S127
In ancient days, had Roman rage run down   B281
In ancient days when birds cou'd speak   T27
In ancient days, when times were good   P197
In ancient honest days, e'er factious pride   T406
In ancient legends we may find   G133
In ancient Rome thus great Augustus rose   N269
In antient times, a prince of matchless fame   T437
In ancient times, and long before the flood   Y5
In ancient times, as bards indite   D203
In ancient times (as stories tell)   T540
In ancient times, as story tells   S800
In antient times, before this isle was known   B418
In ancient times, ere bribery began   D234
In ancient times, e're wealth was learning's foe   M54
In antient times the wise were able   S796
In antient times when Britain's warlike sons   B289
In ancient times whilst sublime arts did ly   D402
In April, when the vernal skies, serene   P100
In Arthur's court Tom Thumb did live, a man of mickle might   T157
In barren soil, and damp unwholsome air   T137
In Beath once dwelt a worthy wife   N240
In bloody town of Newbury   B32
In blooming youth and virgin beauty gay   L45

In Britain's lamentation   D398
In Canaan dwelt one Jacob call'd by name   S154
In Charles the second's golden days   V85
In Charles the second's golden reign   V84
In clouds let sorrow sit, on ev'ry brow   R310·5
In compensation of your vademecum   E447
In Cornwall once, or somewhere else   S57
In days of old, so poets feign   B501
In days of old, when beasts in regal state   M522
In days of old when curs did bark   H188
In days of old, when ignorance prevail'd   R213
In days of yore as Æsop tells   P178
In days of yore, as antient legends speak   D211
In days of yore there liv'd a stately dame   W259
In days of yore, when beasts and birds   C281
In days of yore, when beasts could speak   A65, H326
In days of yore, when maiden-heads   V108
In days of yore, when old folks tell us   T534
In days of yore, when statesmen wore   G124
In days of yore, when vertue was in vogue   B530·8
In dead of night appear'd a form, tho' fair   I59
In dubious times, when plots so num'rous grew   U35
In due obedience to your sacred will   E354
In each ambitious measure crost!   J65
In eastern courts (from Britain's gentler sway   F145
In Eden's garden Adam fell   P745
In Edina's fair city, you have heard how of late   H251
In elder times when vice was young   P1024
In ev'ry field, on ev'ry wave   B590
In fair Hesperia's utmost southern shore   B420
In fair Tyrone, for fruitful fields renown'd   D199
In fickle days, when grave divines   L241
In Florence, far renown'd about those times   U5
In Florence liv'd a venerable sage   H135
In full flowing bowls while the liquor does smile   T514
In gayer hours, when high my fancy ran   S90
In George the first and second's reign   M38
In good faith Mr. H---p   I17
In good King Charles's golden days   V87
In good King G---'s golden days   B157
In Hedden fields, for curious pasture fam'd   D513
In Heriot's-Walks as I was roving   R26
In holiday-time, when the ladies of London   W200
In Homer's Iliad, and Odysses   T109
In Idumea's land, or Uz by name   G118
In Italy there is a town   N301
In jealous regions where the heat   W103
In Lancashire there liv'd a lord   L41
In lofty strains, ye grateful Britons sing   H451
In lofty verse, who would a master be   M380
In Lombardy there dwelt a wealthy knight   P1052
In London late a person did   T493
In London late happen'd a pleasant discourse   D270
In London liv'd, some years ago   P278
In London stands a famous pile   W177
In London Teutsch? – Verhasste Muse, still!   W276
In long vacation, when gay cit's repair   J19
In me, my friend, you'll call it madness quite   R140
In meditation wrapp'd! absorb'd in thought!   D326
In modern days it is become no crime   B19
In Munster once, as legends tell   D233
In northern climes when furious tempests blow   D97
In northern climes, where tides uncertain roll   S609

In northern hights, where Nature seldom smiles   D90
In old, and modern fables I have read   B530·3
In one great now, superior to an age   P1089
In one short now, superior to an age   P1089·1
In our unhappy days of yore   C18
In Oxford bards there are most sad ones   O268
In Paradise, by one man's sin   P744
In patriam, dux magne, tuam redis unus in ore   A21
In pious all-reforming times   M214
In pious times, e'er heaven's fav'rite nation   D289
In pious times, e'er priest-craft did begin   D448
In pious times when great divisions   H131
In pious times, when soul-physicians   W90
In popish and illit'rate times   N323
In reading your letter alone in my hackney   S899
In sable weeds let widdow'd Albion mourn   N134
In Sampson's days, the foxes they   O113
In seventeen hundred and fifteen years   C270
In 17 hundred and forty-five, as plainly did appear man   H204
In sight of treacherous Goodwin's faithless sands   D76
In silence to suppress my griefs I've try'd   B275
In silent shades, upon the bank of Thames   S163
In silent waiting while I muse   E10
In sixteen hundred sixty eight   D64
In slavish times when Peter rul'd the roast   W123
In some far country, now unknown   T31
In sonnet slee the man I sing   R49
In sorrow's gloomy vale, where mournful yew   T67
In spiteful times when humane folly   W193
In statione fuit classis; fusisque per auras   B331
In strains-majestic, and with heavenly fire   P196
In striving sir her to expose   S54
In summer's season, at the noon of day   E374
In Syrian pastures, on a flowery bank by a fountain   I49
In that dull time of recreation   W117
In that fair isle, the garden of the main   C420
In that kind season of the year   C29
In that most pious and as happy time   P270
In that soft season when descending showers   P974
In that soft season when each hedge and field   P1026
In that soft season, when the blushing rose   R199
In that soft time when nature youthful grows   D48
In that still hour of calm delight   V106
In the ages of old,/When of silver and gold   W128
In the beginning did th' all-high create   W328
In the beginning, the almighty god   H212
In the cool ev'ning of a summers day   S525
In the court of requests, I was yesterday walking   S482
In the days of Æsop, as we do hear   T30
In the dull time of long vacation   R245
In the holiday time when those evils betide   H289
In the island of Britain I sing of a k----t   K97
In the last of October, the first of November   R235
In the Milk-lane a house to be let is   P1007
In the reign of Queen Anne   N217
In the smooth dance to move with graceful mein   J59
In these deep solitudes and awful cells   P801
In these great rites assist ye sacred nine   S338

In these sad rites assist ye sacred nine   S296, S333
In these unhappy and more wretched days   F136
In this auld year, whose end is near   E597
In this great year our master Pope   A370
In this inspired sacred text   P743
In this rank age with mad ambition fir'd   C127
In this rude age, where vice triumphant reigns   N38
In those blest days, when Ahasuerus, the son   O107
In those cold climates, where the sun appears   S390
In thy calm intervals of social peace   E426
In time's remembrancers we find   K96
In time's wide wasting walk with backward tread   J93
In times e'er faction did embroil the state   L307
In times of libelling and squabbling   W155
In times of old, immortal Homer sung   B183
In times of old, when beasts could prate   F30
In times of old, when beasts were wondrous wise   P431
In times of yore, when brutes were speakers   B530·1
In times tyrannic, when despotic pow'r   C437
In times when dire Erinnys only reigns   P592
In times, when faction plumes her drooping wing   A192
In times when sordid int'rest rul'd the roast   A119
In troth, brother Lewis, who ever denies   K52
In two large columns, on thy motly page   V39
In vain, dear Jack, dost thou employ thy youth   D409
In vain did bounteous heaven bestow   O73
In vain, fair libertine, with wit misplac'd   T532
In vain Great Britain sues for Knight's discharge   V119
In vain I oft have try'd to find   S410
In vain of the battle we boast   D26, 45
In vain thy lawless fires contend with mine   F270
In vain we forge coercive chains, to bind   D467
In vain were all the forts we w——s could use   W261
In various forms, we ladies of the stage   P611
In various shapes religion has been drest   R153
In Virgil's sacred verse we find   P1070
In virtue's cause our old comedians wrote   F215
In W——d a while ago/Was rara s——t and rara show   F211
In western isle renown'd for bogs   H162
In Westminster lived a baker by trade   W38
In wicked times, when wanton wives   W72
In William's reign, when faction raged   T436
In Windsor forest, before war destroy'd   H334
In wretched times, when men were given   W53
In yonder grave a druid lies   C294
In your proceedings with the royal-youth   T356
In youth exalted high in air   D207
In youth no parent nurs'd my infant songs   S115
Incipe virgineum, Solymæ chorus! incipe carmen!   O235
Inclyta doctiloqui Solomonis cantica regis   T470
Inclytus hæc fudit Solomon Proverbia, natus   T470
Indulge no more (dear angry friend) the spleen   E365
Indulge one labour more, my drooping muse   T64
Indulge this favor, Merlin, and impart   O101
Indulgent pow'r! whose all-surveying eyes   M146
Industrious, unfatigu'd in faction's cause   C119
Influenced by the vile unchristian jars   S554

Inform me, Murray, by what wondrous skill   T350
Inform me, reason, what the cause may be   O84
Ingenious George, at last alace thou'rt gone   G169
Ingenious Lister! were a picture drawn   K55
Ingenious Stanhope, if you can, excuse   A331
Ingenious Stitch, I've read your rhymes   B602
Ingens artis opus manus est aggressa, parentem   D520
Inscrib'd to thee, and to eternal fame   P590
Insigne victis hoc super hostibus   B325
Insignis clericus, patriæ pater atque columna   D59
Inspire me every muse, and every grace   R190
Inspire my muse ye sons of sparkling wit   M554
Inspire us, genius of the day   M534
Inspir'd by you, what can our thoughts restrain?   V90
Inspir'd with your applause, the daring muse   T333
Instead of a song, if 'twill make you amends   H59
Instructing satyr, tune thy useful song   D128
Insuper immensi myrias cum subdita regni   S253
Into a fair morning, for fresh recreation   B237
Into a place in Argile shire   A12
Intriguing arts I sing, let none disdain   A320
Invading fleets affright us now no more   P1009
Invoke no muse, but the cœlestial king   T542·5
Ireland is now our royal care   B75
Iris, a tender soft believing maid   P9
Is it a time to melt at languid strains   O182
Is it not meet, my soul, some time to pause   M558
Is justice dead, or gone astray?   H293
Is Merry dead, his active spirit flown?   E190
Is S———'s ingratitude proclaim'd again?   A237
Is then, alas! Britannia's genius fled   P201
Is there a Briton hopes to see   G135
Is there a man, whose genius and whose fate   M87
Is there a traitor, whoremonger, or thief   M328
Is there but one so grateful as to tell   P669
Is there, in friendship, yet, a dearer name   D412
Is there on earth a torment can exceed   T155
Is there, or do the schoolmen dream?   N343
Is there, who breathes on this terraqueous ball   I69
Is this, O man, thy boasted excellence?   H387
Is this the spring renown'd for radiant dames   B94
Is this the vast advantage we propos'd?   C31
Is worthy Whitehead dead, that godly seer?   E274
Is't the reward of the ungrateful age   E245
Isacidæ proles, si Mosem planxerat olim   M167
Isis, quæ fluvios prona dea fundis ab urna   B232
It always has been thought discreet   P1068
It happen'd on a winter's night   W535
It is not certain what deliverance made   B226
It is not good to raise the dead   C32
It is the statute law of heav'n above   A314
It must be so — on terms so slight   P691
It so befell: a silly swain   C372
It was a most unfriendly part   S863
It was in August, on a night   F22
It was my hap spectator once to be   D44
It was, my lord, the dextrous shift   S498
It's finish'd – lo the long predicted year!   M261
It's sweet to stand about a dying-bed   G323
It's true, Tallard, when fickle chance deny'd   L146
Italian Mary's prayers were heard   M411

J

Jack met his friend Dick, and some compliments past   U4
Jam te, dive, tenent Homius, sapiensque Stevinus   P384
James, by the grace of Mar, the thing   P1035
Jane bifrons, priscos a tergo respice lapsi   D295
Jane, senex optat Pitcarnius esse velitis   P316
Jane, tui sexto mihi filia prodijt Agnes   P318
Janus, did ever to thy wond'ring eyes   S514
Janus, your silly goat (I see) looks thin   B207
Je chante ce héros, qui règna dans la France   V112
Je consacre, Daphnis, ma verve, & mon repos   V15
Je viens de rencontrer au milieu de la ruë   D281
Jehovah here of nothing all things makes   H259
Jehovah, whose almighty will   C267
Jenny come here: I'm told that you have been   B616
Jersey and Guernsey, who so near the Gaul's   S233
Jesus the faithful sheepherd of the flock   P158
Jews, Turks, and Christians, hear my song   D547
Job silent stood, when from a thick'ning cloud   T168
John Pryer's dead; dead! oh the cutting sound!   P553
John the quaker, did invent   W452
Jove once, in humour, fix'd an hour   S504
Joy of my heart, and comfort of my life   F191
Joy of my life, whose wit my soul inspires   O97
Joy to the bridegroom, prince of Clyde   R66
Juni, te regem jam mensibus esse fatetur   P328
Juni, te regem nunc annis esse jubemus   P327
Juno potens uteri, ad mortales non voco nixus   B314
Juppiter arripuit sibi me, Junone relicta   P388
Juppiter est hominis facie te fallere passus   P301
Jure dicat tibi navis iter, qui cinxerat orbem   V20
Just as he liv'd, he dy'd: 'twas sympathy   O227
Just as my restless mind began to please   S294
Just as revolting angels did resign   L189
Just as the sun shone on our hemisphere   G182
Just broke from school, pert, impudent and raw   J63
Just heaven at length, indulgent to mankind   E216
Just o'er the eastern hills the blushing morn   P119
Just ripe for vengance, and diviner wrath   E123
Just so the beauteous flow'r   T383
Just was the sun in his swift chariot hurl'd   E26
Just when emerging from that gloomy shade   J55
Justice and honour, who have taken wing   R152

K

Ken ye, sirs, for as much as some small differences   C402
Kerrorum soboles avita, supplex   K19
Kilmallock, my dear, neighbour town   L183
Kind friend, with whom I sip, and smoke   M375
Kind heav'n at length, successfully implor'd   H51
Kind heav'n, avert the threatned stroke, and take   S522
Kind heav'n has granted   S752
Kind reader, pray, my heat excuse   A64
King tender hearted people all   C506
Kind Venus goddess of the Paphian grove   B71

Kindly accept what kindly I indite   E359
King Cock-lorrel once, had the devil his guest   D40
King Edward, who lately at Windsor had been   S171
King of the British isles, from heroes sprung!   F138
Kings, arms, and empire, common themes! The muse   L313
Kings without scepters, a pretended heir   P1061
Kneller, with silence and surprize   A41
Know all men by these presents, death the tamer   S836
Know all men by these presents, that this indenture   N52
Know all men by these, that a grand preparation   I51
Know all men in the name of god   E118
Know all thou canst, nor timorously go   A377
Know all ye judges of the earth!   P55
Know then thyself, presume not god to scan   P833
Knows not your grace, when merit soars too high   I12
Knowst thou, my child, thou wert baptiz'd of old   W443

L

La passion dans laquelle je me trouve...   Y21
Ladies and gentlemen – I beg you'd stay   O224
Ladies and gentlemen, my lord of flame   M187
Ladies, our master chose a dreadful play   S416
Ladies, since you the knot of union wear   U12
Ladies, to you a suppliant lo I come   A56
Ladies, ye stare as if ye knew me not——   P1133
Lætitia plausuque urbem populumque frementem   R271
Lafeinte, a true sprout of the hipocrite race   D349
Lament, good Christians, when you hear this thing   G114
Lament, lament, for learned How that's gone   E150
Lament, lament, ye champions of the laws   E103
Lament my muse, beneath thy mournful weeds   E226
Lament you muses, mourn you sacred sheed   E214
Lamentor Mavortium peremptum: periit Cathcars   H408
Lampoon'd and hiss'd, and damn'd the thousandth time   F186
Large is the fame, great hero, thou hast won   T376
Last even'ing toil'd with dull fatigue of life   P159
Last morn young Rosalind, with laughing een   R70
Last night, as I lay tossing on my bed   A107
Last night my hours on friendship I bestow'd   M527
Last week as I was walking   E588
Lately I walkt towards the Colledge-green   S620
Laura, thy humours so perverse   E609
Laurus cruentas, & faciles nimis   T448
Le crime assez longtems gouverna⟨it⟩ l'Angleterre   C383
Leader of the nuptial band   O49
Learn Dulness, learn! "The universal cause   P840
Learnedly wise, and prudent as the rest   L77
Leave for a while, my lord, th' affairs of state   A369
Leave off your railing, you old envious wretch   I14
Leave, teizing principle, my breast   D423
Leixlip! thy devious walks, thy vary'd views   S400
L'Estrange departed! and no mourning muse   E179
Let all bold soldiers far and near   L32

Let arms and warriors other poets fire   W353
Let banter cease, and poetasters yield   H8
Let bards invoke the sacred nine t' inspire   C278
Let B——ks and H——r vend their cloudy wines   W149
Let Britain now a grateful homage pay   B223
Let charity be now the muse's care   B132
Let Christians all with one accord rejoice   N120
Let Christians now with joyful mirth   T520
Let disobedient youths I pray draw near   N204
Let each great genius of the tuneful nine   E202
Let England's church her sinking state deplore   T377
Let every Brittish heart rejoyce   C456
Let every mortal Christian now awake   E316
Let fair Augusta raise her drooping head   P256
Let fortune do whate'er she will   R227
Let Gallic bards, inspir'd with genuine wines   C185
Let gaudy mirth, to the blithe carrol-song   S107
Let great men loll ingloriously in state   S728
Let grief no more our English hearts untune   E338
Let hakney poets draw their pen   P40
Let haughty victors boast of conquests won   E466
Let, heav'nly muse, enthusiastick fire   B249
Let him that would his doubting thoughts convince   F305
Let hireling poets ply their venal lays   N10
Let holy guides prevail on tim'rous fools   W101
Let Israel now her grateful trophies raise   T46
Let jarring realms, and Europe's doubtful state   B55
Let knaves and fools lament   S130
Let lovers now bless their perplexing chains   H307
Let men of wit and foplings of the town   P1055
Let muses mourn, and physitians condole   E215
Let news-boys cry the scandal through the crowd   V83
Let no adult'rous love pollute thy soul   H92
Let not the news in Gath be told   C181
Let observation with extensive view   J87
Let other bards another subject chuse   S714
Let others boast of an unlawful flame   L283
Let others muse, in numbers sing   L268
Let others paint the terrors of the plain   P1012
Let others sing how Dettingen records   B8
Let others sing of arms, of lawrels bought   B140
Let others sing the hero bold, as great   F201
Let others swell their mercenary lays   B141
Let others with loud Iö's fill the skies   C352
Let passive-slaves contented be   F59
Let peasants rise at morn, 'tis more polite   F76
Let plodding cits, great sir, indulge their vein   W463
Let plodding cits, my lord, indulge their vein   W461
Let poet's fam'd and poet's laureat sing   D321
Let P——y speak, or Caleb write   N107
Let quakers weep and builders now rejoice   E268
Let rakes for ever rail at rules   R150
Let Scotia's sons in sable weeds appear   P156
Let Scotland mourn, the state and church have lost   S170
Let solemn grief in every face appear   P651
Let that majestick pen that writes   S639
Let the approaching holy time   H439
Let the aspiring few, who pant for fame   T363
Let the smiles, and the loves, and the muses draw nigh!   L13

Let the soldiers beware/How they're caut in a snare T396

Let the soldiers rejoyce,/With a general voice B204, E564

Let those grave bards Apollo's aid demand N37

Let those that love Helicon sip at the stream T512

Let treach'rous Demas never more pretend D212

Let us sing to the mem'ry of glorious Queen Bess Q8

Let venal annals boast a Cæsar's reign M386

Let wine turn a spark, and ale huff like a Hector S592

Let's joy in the medal with James the IIId's face W278

Let's melt the sullen world with sounds harmonious S215

Let's remember the men, that go with us again N320

Let's see the wondrous charge fix'd on Lorrain R154

Let's sing the new m——y's praise T119

Lewis our common lord's compassion L275

Life of your country's hope! the bard, whose strain M344

Life was inspir'd, the first life was divine H413

Life's but a burden when confin'd S451

Lift up thy hoary head, and rise E497

Lift up your heads, ye lofty gates H432, 433

Light of my solitude, I see W28

Like the meridian sun tho' merit shines L304

Like the unhappy Israelites distress'd F231

Like to the thunder-bearing bird W297

Like wretches thrown on Greenland's fatal coast L102

Listen ye fair! to love's prevailing sway M472

Litera, si præeat vocalis, pura vocatur B598

Little B—, who writes (and who doubts his ability?) K73

Little charm, of placid mien P208

Little girl in swadling cloaths Y108

Little lads of Dublin town A71

Loe! Charles at length is dead; and James proclaim'd C489

Lo! I that earst the glory spread W343

Lo! Moses wrapt in Hector's skin P371

Lo! sable night ascends the dusky air R18

Lo, the bless'd morning is begun C262

Lo! the mild sun salutes the opening spring S116

Lo! the tall column lifts its head A15

Lo! westward the church which incumbers the street M459

'Load, load the pallet, boy!' hark! Hogarth cries W414

Loaded, my lord, with cares of state S500

Locks, bars and walls too weak to bind E446

Lolling upon the ground, as stragglers do G93

Long after Merlin had strange things foretold G111

Long did Hibernia's isle in vain deplore N144

Long did my muse expectant wish to see E456

Long, Dodington, in debt, I long have sought Y128

Long ere physicians knew the healing art C480

Long had Bellona rais'd her furious hand B364

Long had Britannia mourn'd her native isle P275

Long had Britannia, plung'd in vice and ease P682

Long had I languish'd in continual night G167

Long had th' affrighted world with loud alarms P1132

Long had the mag-pies and the daws T29

Long had the rebel monster strove to rear E22

Long had this nation been amus'd in vain D151

Long had usurping George in council sate R212

Long has injurious satyr vex'd the town E309

Long has the city been the scene of vice B530·95

Long has the dreadful tempest rag'd S158

Long has the poet's lawful claim been known E414

Long has the world impatient with desire M267

Long hast thou reign'd, Sir R---n, uncontroul'd O184

Long have I seem'd to serve thee, lord W319

Long have I study'd for some mighty name O210

Long have I wish'd renowned heroe's praise L276

Long have our arms each others arms withstood T585

Long have the bards profan'd the British stage N176

Long I continued mute, and fear'd to sing R185

Long I depended with full hope P1036

Long I liv'd in dark privation D350

Long in a baleful cave, by nature made D544

Long in Augusta's courts had Venus reign'd D446

Long in suspence the tattling gossip stood C236

Long life to the queen, and a prosperous reign T401

Long our divided state S390

Long since, a merchant, where St. Dennis lies J9

Long since the pacquet brought the dismal news E251

Long time, by court tricks, had poor Grinsted been charm'd G299

Long time had discord reign'd thro' all the world P1132

Long time the scriblers of the town have try'd S44

Long thy return thy Hatfield wish'd in vain P599

Long waiting, when some poet's manly page M377

Long was this art to Britain's sons unknown S444

Long with licentious pow'r and gen'ral sway F176

Longitude, in the world, it's she that bears the sway T510

Lonsdale! thou ever-honour'd name N345

Look down, thou ever-chearful cherub, hope M439

Look here, immortal queen of beauty, rise M42

Look round, Alexis, see the gloomy shade W468

Look through all nature, this one maxim's plain F203

Lord, give the queen thy saving health H436, H473

Lord, in this parable, I see P738

Lord, what is man! a sigh a cry G309

Lorenzo! to recriminate is just Y47

Loud, and more loud, ye Britons shout, – 'tis he S712

Love is a passion, by no rules confin'd H229

Love like a tyrant whom no laws constrain P573

Love, like a tyrant with superior sway P565

Love once was nature, artless and untaught H13

Love's queen, yet not the Cyprian Venus sprung T66

Lov'd Britannia! Heav'n allows thee E317

Lovely babe of maid of honour O180

Lucifer, nam te docilis magistro P372

Lucinda the lovely,/The joy of her swain C392

Luget heu Arctos quia Phœbus Austrum K27

Lux optata nitet, quæ soles noctibus æquat P381

Lux tua splendescat latum, reverende per orbem P177

M

M'Intosh is a soldier brave   B448
M'Leod, you vild adulterous jad   L125
Mad actions to describe, lo! I prepare   P715
Madam, amidst the numerous crouds that wait   J71
Madam, attending providence, we do   T123
Madam, look out, your title is arraign'd   F36, W390
Madam, to all your censures I submit   G52
Madam, to you I send these lines   P534
Madam, what muse can speak, what pen display   C92
Madam, you're right, the q——'s a knowing man   P566
Mæcenas! sprung from royal blood!   T131
Maecenas volui grates tibi solvere, musa   P354
Magna quidem, non grata tamen, phantasmata Morpheus   P1156
Magna sequor tenuis, tenerisque per æthra nitor   T312
Magnanimis Scotisque atavis dignissima vixti   P300
Magne Harlæe, tibi meritum gratamur honorem   N311
Make de Spanish step   C497
Malice, no more, thy conduct shall upbraid   L228
Man was an embryo in great chaos' womb   C438
Man's life's a flying vapour, which doth rise   E48
Mane sub auroram, fessos complectitur artus   M207
Mankind can never live at ease   B215
Mankind must die; nor good from ill can save   B413
Manners, a satire, stroling hawkers cry   M189
Marcellus, too tedious have been our discourses   G240
Marino! -- welcome from the western shore   B306
Mark well our sad and dismal tale   G242
Matron of arts, and to the british youth   A199
May each new year some new perfection give   B67
May heav'n preserve our good Queen Anne   R223
May heaven shine upon our parliament   I19
May't please your grace, in your recess   T337
May't please your wors——ps, craving your permission   P277
May it please thee to admit me   L93
May it please you dread sir, we the clerks of Virginia   L296
May Marlborough such loud acclamations see   D565
May sprightly Venus with her watchful eye   H320
May such be crost, if not be curs'd who's zeal   T431
May this years influence, the nation bless   N245
Me brevis mimum peragente vitæ   P356
Me great Gambrivius inspire   H303
Me send you, Sir, one letter   D541
Me vis Dupplinii divinas dicere laudes   P341
Meikle sorrow dole and care   H3
Melazzo! Thou lasting monument of fame   H83
Melleus hic situs est Meldrumius, ore disertus   S149
Melpomene assist my doleful song   T259
Melpomene, thou patroness   B235, C531
Melpomonie, come and inspyre my quile   W449
Men who are out, hate those in play   R220
Mens domino benedic mea, mi pater alme, deusque   H143·5
Merridieth's gone, but where there's none can tell   E189
Merry was he, for whom we now are sad   N148
Methinks I see, beneath an arbor's shade   S549
Methinks I see Britannia's genius here   P1131

Metre, than prose, we evidently find   H208
Mi Bennette, tuus jacet sodalis   K18
Mi rure detento/Ah! cursu quam lento   W517
Midas, we are in story told   S847
'Midst all the clamours, noise, and false alarms   C148
'Midst home-bred feuds and foreign nurtur'd jars   T537
Mighty nonsense, the goddess that reigns o'er the stage   D427
Mild charity-----best blessing of the blest   P1107
Mild rose the morn, the face of nature bright   S105
Militis infesti me vis urgebat inermem   P355
Mine's the first note, I sound the whig's knell   N295
Minerva has vow'd since the bishops do slight her   O230
Mirror of wit! Mirror of loyalty!   O59
Miss Danae, when fair and young   P1076
Miss Molly, a fam'd toast, was fair and young   A158·5
Model of Venus! and most fam'd of any   F31
Modest, engaging, innocent and fair   C207
Molle id tempus erat crebris quo lapsibus imbres   G4
Mon frere, auriez vous crû que parmi les chrétiens   D280
Mon frere, enfin, je viens vous demander pardon   D279
Monarchs beware, your titles they disown   W390
Money, thou universal Indian curse   W50
Monsieur so long the cards had play'd   R318
Monsieur the revd. dean will write   O263
Monticolam Britonem, qui primus vincula Muri   H279
Mortal, thou betrayed to us   S619
Mortalis ævi gaudia lubrica   B185
Most authors chuse to celebrate   N232
Most bounteous queen, my grateful thanks I pay   D477
Most gracious king, the nation's father   L235
Most gracious sovereign lord, may it please   S12
Most gracious sovereign lord, our king   S13
Most happy day, the glorious peace is sign'd   T544
Most justly now 'tis ev'ry muse's theme   W25
Most learned and reverend, with humblest submission   O13
Most men have an ambition   E579
Most mighty lord/I'm come on board   L197
Most noble prince, Hibernia welcomes thee   N169
Most pious sir, complaint to you I send   C550
Most reverend dean, good Mr. Smedley   O261
Most reverend dean, pray cease to write   S509
Most reverend sir, and *quondam* chum   C530
Most true it is, I dare to say   D328
Mother of arts, delight of men and gods   O275
Mother of musings, contemplation sage   W246
Mount, mount thy silver streams, Idalia, fair   C436
Mountown! thou sweet retreat from Dublin cares   K63
Mourn, Albion, mourn; Astræa's now no more   T140
Mourn all who do the use of numbers know   P598
Mourn all ye city patriots, Verdoen's dead   E265
Mourn all ye loyalists in Britain's isle   E91
Mourn all ye nobles! at that rigid fate   L312
Mourn all ye wits, who suck the purer air   P1025
Mourn all you whigs, with deepest anguish mourn   E121
Mourn! Britain! mourn! thy captain general's fled   E73

Mourn Britains, mourn, your careful doctor's gone E272

Mourn each dissenting babe of grace B574

Mourn, England, mourn, since Kneller is no more S224

Mourn England mourn, the loss is great indeed E326

Mourn, hapless Caledonia, mourn S535

Mourn, mourn ye Britons all, for cruel death E287

Mourn! mourn! ye nine your Echlin now is gone E109

Mourn, mourn, ye presbyterians, all undone E264

Mourn! – mourn! you booksellers, – for cruel death B512

Mourn northern parts of the Great Britain's isle E250

Mourn, O! North Brittian! and ye judge's all E47

Mox me poenituit, sed vos non poenitet esse P395

Much honoured trade, I greatly am to blame M445

Multa tulere sacrae, te, rex, absente, columbae P392

Multa tulere tuae, te, rex, absente, columbae P391

Musa gemens hæret, (nil mirum) dira verendi I28

Musæ, noster amor, Lilliputides hoc mihi carmen P688

Muse, bid the verse in plaintive numbers flow V62

Muse, if thou can'st a while assist D245

Muse, leave a while soft Venus and her joys D52

Muse sing the British mountaneer, who told Q15

Muse sing the Brittain, who on mountains liv'd W283

Muse, sing the man, for various wiles renown'd T145

Muse, sing the mountaineer, the Briton T3

Muse, thrice invok'd, to Celsus speed the verse O91

Muse, voici le jour où nâquit nôtre reine L5

Muse will have her song; hark! she merrily sings S11

Musick soft charm of heav'n and earth O34

Musing one night in bed what I shou'd do F115

Must he then alass depart N2

Must I be silent still, and still be teaz'd M230

Must nature's vast profusion be in vain? O196

Must smiling innocence, and well-try'd worth C399

Must then my heart, familiar long with grief B354

Must we to further mis'ries still be brought G249

Mute with conceal'd distress, joy-widow'd long B533

My anxious soul is tore with doubtful strife H18

My birthright's privilege is sure but small P1122

My bony dear soney L300

My brother poets and physicians A259

My children dear, mark well my words H405

My country dear I have forsook N124

My countrey men come here I'le tell C340

My countrymen who do intend S165

My dear Amintor, on a summer's day T433

My dear, and only joy, I pray G238

My dear and only love I pray G236

My dear Lavinia, once the only joy W70

My dear loving country-men listen a while E583·5

My dear Pall-Mall, I hear you're got in favour W478

My dear, what makes my lord his visits pay W133

My dearest friend M.B. I hope thou'lt excuse L124

My friend, (a privilege with pride I claim N242

My friend D—y be not vain S555

My friend! I've heard you often plight your faith D331

My friend! what can we do? with stubborn will O87

My Grubstreet bard, your reasons nought avail A240

My honest friend, I'll tell you news C133

My honour'd friends, in senate now assembl'd H318

My humble muse no hero sings T579

My infant muse, assist my tender pen A344

My lads, what do you mean? I1

My l--ds and gent--men to you H249

My little book, go view imperial Rome O254

My lord, finding your lordship's letters on a stall D77

My lord, I just receiv'd, I own L202

My lord m—r and his a--n and c--n c--l too N96

My lord, my love upon the stage P750

My lord! sprung from the antient race divine K19

My lord, your sermon, preach'd at Bow H169

My lords and gentlemen, I meet you again T560

My lords and gentlemen to you H249

My lords and lairds wha represent G307

My master, sir, I must obey T372

My masters, and friends, and good people give ear S510

My masters tho' my muse be dull S722

My mournful muses guide this pen of mine E105, E208

My muse attempts no vain heroick skill B530·4

My muse/Infuse W10

My muse, let sacred truth be now thy guide O44

My muse, proceed, and reach thy destin'd end Y125

My muse, thy ambition cease; beware C180

My muse to Chesterfield directs her strains L320

My Nan she was good S585

My old acquaintance, and my dearest friend O9

My sacred liege, if sorrow cease to flow P128

My scheme's turn'd topsy turvy P1117

My silence, pardon, dearest Jo L129

My six and twenty join as evidence M300

My son, if to a courtier's life inclin'd W45

My son who now art in thy prime O126

My song is of Sawny, the poet of Windsor O165

My subject's too sublime for common pen P527

My tender muse pray don't be in a rage S66

My time, O ye muses! was happily spent D406

My tow'ring muse, by his great actions fir'd P638

My verse is satire; Dorset, lend your ear Y122

My weeping muse proceed with murnful tone E142

My Westminster friends/Now we've gained our ends I34

My young esquire by mamma sage G122

Myra, reverse thy suit; it cannot be R328

Mysterious fate how canst thou reconcile M546

N

Natali vestro, lacrymis jejunia pascunt P320

Natura omniparens cunctis præfecta creandis F80

Naturæ ambages, physicæ spectacula scenæ N330

Nature demands it from us all E94, F289

Nature on all some gift bestows L253

Nature, which purest prospects gives C265

Nature while Tempest liv'd, by her took aim C540

Natus patre pio, patrem sequitur sua proles I18

Nay, now forbear, for pity's sake give o're E146, E260

Nay, 'tis the same with all th' affected crew S493

Nay whigs since you're resolv'd you'll ne'er be wise W237

Near a fair, ancient, rural seat R134

Near Albion's clifts a pleasant vale there lies P622

Near barren fields, where honour dwells   W56
Near Essex, fost'ring nurse of Lion   M78
Near Grant's fair walls a stately city reign'd   T442
Near Jordans fertile streams in grandure stood   S543
Near Saint Jame's a young lady   L281
Near St. Sepulchres stands a building   P175
Near T----b---r, as stories tell us   D508
Near that proud dome where Mars his worn-out race   S269
Near the cool verge of that delightful strand   S192
Near the hundreds of Drury a monster was shown   D444
Near the silver sands wher Forth doth pass   P589
Near to a certain pound a church there stands   H105
Near to a parks delightful grove   T8
Near to an ancient country seat   T24
Near to the ruines of an ancient seat   S674
Near to the sacred and immortal frame   N13·5
Near Wantage, where our learned king   W460
Near winding Boyn, a chapel stands   S20
Ne'er more is Satan pleas'd, malicious toad   V105
Nequiter, ut medicam praxen, temerare suesti   P537
Never cry, popes and tyrants all go to the devil   F182
Never, dear Faz, torment thy brain   P1166
Never was creature plagued so   P1008
New revolutions, new alarms   O264
New scenes of pleasure now your joys invite   P1127
Next to those men, who, with their lutes, did call   T588
Nine taylors make a man, the muses nine   T6
Nine tripled and two are the years   H261
Nine years consum'd, in noise, and follys   C435
No airy theme my pensive muse employs   H90
No common height the muse must soar   N275
No common sorrow swells our brimful eyes   P672
No doubt, my readers, ye have heard at last   N293
No doubt you've heard, his excellence   C385
No fabling song, my mournful heart, essay   W355
No greater comfort to well-minded men   S650
No kingdom's free from scourge where sin abounds   P1001
No longer contemplation dwell   H14
No longer muse, no longer take thy flights   B218, F298
No longer now the criminal of state   E449
No longer, O thou god of heav'n and earth   H60
No more!--- Alas, that bitter word, no more!   E101
No more as pædagouge, but friend   T328
No more by fame mislead or glory fir'd   D424
No more, great rulers of the sky, ye awful pow'rs, no more   O55
No more I write of war and arms   S152
No more, illustrious chief! disclaim   G297
No more, my muse, let worldly toys   C335
No more, my Thyrsis, lay thy pipe aside   C88
No more, O muse! delight in trifling strains   P706
No more of bottles, or their corks   G277
No more of courts, of triumphs, or of arms   B242
No more our proud neighbours shall tell us with scorn   Y178
No more shall Scotland now in sadness mourn   H260
No muse I seek, but summon to my aid   H145·5
No, no; the left-hand box, in blue   M431
No, no, vain world, thy joys are frail   M157
No, not one word, can I of this great deed   W458·5

No packet arriv'd? and the wind still at east---   C152
No respite from my tortures can I have?   B146
No! sacred pages, never more repine   E83
No sooner does a maid arrive to years   W445
No sooner has Aurora shed her rays   A123
No sooner Satan in the mist withdrew   S172
No sooner there came/From Kingston on Thame   L92
No sooner youth throws off his infant plays   F131
No thanks to our foes, our cause it is clear   E571
No, 'tis in vain, not all their factious arts   P443
No usual flight of verse   M287
No voice more soft than thunder can express   P686
No wonder P—s, F—ch and Sh—r   Y11
No writer of scandal doth Caleb excell   B65
Nobile carmen habes, merito cui cantica cedant   K20
Nobile si carmen mihi musæ, quale Maroni   K66
Nobilis en ortu, ac illustris Ogilvius heros   N312
Noble Britons raise your voice   B457
Non, ego, Cæsareas acies; non arma virumq;   S613
Non merito irascar cum tot prurigine Famae   S38
None mourn his death whom living all admir'd   A122
Nor all deserve the biting satyr's sting   H32
Nor arms I sing, nor of adventurous deeds   C493
Nor reigns ambition in bold man alone   Y134
Nor shall they fall unmourn'd---Nor dare we pry   E120
Nor songs, nor tales of love delight the muse   F266
Nor turkey fat, nor goose from country-hut   L157
Nor wars alarms, nor falling states I sing   T268
Nor war's alarms, nor raging pow'r   S552
Norris, renown'd for actions good and great   F224
Northward a county lyes (in which does stand   U25
Nos vœux sont accomplis: vous brillez, heureux jour   N302·5
Not a mile from an oak in the island of Coss   W467
Not all the threats and favours of a crown   M415
Not all the threats or favours of a crown   B43, M68, M416
Not asking, nor expecting ought   P557
Not far from Trent's fair stream, and fruitful soil   S647
Not from eternity, mysterious name!   H264
Not light from darkness differs more   P81
Not long ago in Dorsetshire   U3
Not many days since   S129
Not marry! friend? why 'tis the life of life   M138
Not rival chiefs engag'd in bloody strife   D36
"Not to admire, is all the art I know   P965
Not twice a twelvemonth you appear in print   P932
Nothing so true as what you once let fall   P917
Now, after the Norfolk dinner was over   S786
Now all danger's over   C68
Now all was wrapt in dark mid-night   M62
Now all you good Britains from Dover and Fife   C34
Now are our noble representers met   S145
Now, barbers, bakers, coblers, buyers, sellers   L116
Now brave Captain Gordon's come   C30
Now Britain, now hold up thy head   E537
Now Britains mourn,/Your liberty's torn   B30
Now Briton's rejoice, and chear up your hearts   B568
Now C---b ceas'd and Molly rose   M572
Now could I wish for that fam'd golden lyre   C521
Now crimson blushes stain'd the western sky   C330
Now Daniel De-Foe, now run for thy life   H352

Now did the bag-pipe in hoarse notes begin   G50
Now do I find to death I'm near   L316
Now do I press amongst the learned throng   R75
Now Dunkirk's surrendred no room's left to fear   F261
Now England be merry, and ever rejoyce   G263
Now fame began abroad to spread   N241
Now for a landlord, who to let us know   V5
Now for a while aside I'll lay   D366
Now for these forty years in Great Britain's land   R162
Now frae east-nook of Fife the dawn   R40
Now from thy riot of destruction breathe   P415
Now great Augusta, whilst within thy walls   S227
Now had Apollo heard in verse and prose   C429
Now had imperial Rome confirm'd her sway   C56
Now had th' archangel trumpet, rais'd sublime   E528
Now had the son of Jove, mature, attain'd   L293
Now had those fleets once rivals in dispute   F62
Now, happy spring, retrieve thy sinking name   S425
Now high-church rejoyce at this turn of the state   O267
Now, honest friend, would'st thou, I shew   P475
Now John what makes thee look so shan   M302
Now lend your lugs, ye benders fine   R63
Now let all true loyal subjects rejoice   H189
Now let me begin with a noise and a pother   P1053
Now let salt tears run down our cheeks   E76
Now like themselves again the archers raise   R74
Now maidens all, pray lend an ear   S720
Now men with an unblushing face begin   C271
Now mourn, each peer, renowned knight   D57
Now muse, grown acquainted with country air   T487
Now night retires, and, glorious, breaks the day   P580
Now, now comes on the glorious year   R121
Now, now is come the glorious year   G183
Now now the queens health   V7
Now, now the whigs shall all go down   T425
Now Phœbus did with frowns the world survey   A3
Now ponder well my neighbours all   M1
Now ponder well you ladies fair   V103
Now ponder well you merchants all   H362
Now, satyr, raise thy forked sting, strike deep   D1
Now since the force of rude rebellion's fled   E348
Now sing, my muse, the noble patriots fame   T502
Now sirs y' ave seen this bug-bear of a play   P1121
Now sparks of light shoot streaming thro' the air   B319
Now surly winter shews his furrow'd face   C134
Now tete a tete, prepar'd for chearful chat   P101
Now that the days go smoothly on   V1
Now the active young attornies   H139
Now the day is almost peeping   C170
Now the long wish'd for morning gilds the east   J30
Now the whigs and their friends are confounded   W391
Now things are to the last decision bent   P131
Now through the welkin wide the rosy morn   B506
Now to the utmost southern goal   O177·5
Now vill—ns weep! since you have lost your head   E241
Now wat ye wha I met yestreen   R108
Now welcome, dear Xantippe, prithee tell   F196
Now, when fierce discord rages, and the sword   B475
Now Woods and his half-pence are all gone to pot   E541·5
Now you, my Delius, are dismiss'd the schools   H26
Now Zion bid thy lucid fountains flow   R326

Num, male scribendo, censendone, proditur artis   G6
Nunc age, siquid habes, mea musa, O nobile carmen   H277
Nuper Hamiltonus vacuæ pertœsus Edinæ   P305
Nuptial joys the song inspire   O79
Nympha, Peterboreis quæ nunc fæliciter ausis   C14
Nymphlings three, and three, and three   N1

O

'O' *see also* 'Oh'; the original spelling has been followed, regardless of grammar.

O! a masquerade's a fine place   L288
O A---a! think, thou poor unhappy qu---   A98
O Addison! were none your worth to sing   C266
O all ye nymphs, in lawless love's disport   K12
O all ye nymphs! who wait both day and night   M6
O all ye works of the almighty king!   F226
O am not I a weary wight   E544
O Anna! think, thou poor unhappy queen   A98
O assist me, ye powers that have rhimes at command   S9
O Bacchus, with thy noble juice   W57
O Bartledom fair/Since thy lord mayor   C41
O be my son, the mother cries   O111
O Bernard! could these notes of mourning lays   S383
O best of sovereigns! if you kindly hear   P526
O blessed life, where gospel-light   D416
O born by heaven's providential care   P610
O born for nations! Britains joy confest!   W296
O brave England's forces!   S458
O brother Tom, do you hear the event?   C369
O Caledon, O Caledon/How wretched is thy fate   S595
O Cannigate! poor elritch hole   R46
O cease ambition to molest   H157·2
O Cestrian dames, your humble servant   L182
O Chesterfield! my patron and my pride   C52
O Clio, shou'dst thou think to mount   S22
O could my muse in nervous numbers draw   R99
O C——r darling of the tuneful nine!   H462
O cruel death! can neither youth nor age   D82
O curs'd Atropus cruel wife!   E206
O curs'd Atropus, thou cancard wife   E183
O death, why tyrranisest thou in thy might?   E115
O decus Angliaci nautæ, pulcherrima sylvæ   D296
O Dieu, dont tous les cieux racontent les louanges   T107
O dool! and am I forc'd to die   R64
O drop drop briny tears from pious eyes   G321
O Dublin is a fine town   E593, U20
O fair Britannia! genius of this isle   H328
O fair Britannia! lovliest of the sea   W51
O fam'd and celebrated Allan!   R51
O fatal death! thou many methods takes   E231
O for a hundred pair of brazen lungs   B435
O! for a muse like his, that mourn'd in strains   D442
O for a muse of flame, the daring fire   T84
O for that heav'nly voice, that pierc'd so high   W305
O Garth! to whom thy own Apollo gave   E412
O generous Varus, happy and admired!   W291
O gloomy day! O melancholly scene!   O204

O glorious show! See England's queen appears   H149
O glorious youth! 'tis evidently plain   P521
O goddess! from whose name the month proceeds   N39
O! goddess of the dirty hue!   P539
O goddess! sing Achilles' choler   D485
O good neighbours have you not hear'd the news   G272
O gosh! what will come o' us now?   E220
O Grafton, Suffolk's lord, who are   B320
O great, eternal, high and mighty one   E97
O great Jehovah! lord of heav'n and earth   P625
O gulph of horror! O profound abyss!   F43
O happy shade! if thou can'st now attend   E182
O happy time!/'Tis no more a crime   U30
O harmony, to thee we sing   C370
O harmony where's now thy pow'r   T79
O heavenly Father, from thy mansions bright   C264
O heavens! inspire, O angels! now indite   M544
O Hel---m! blest, belov'd abode!   P1160
O! how d'ye do? I'm glad to see you well   M285
O Jesu! – Coz! – why this fantastick dress?   B20
O Jonathan of merry fame   O264
O king live thou for ever, and assure   H389
O! lend, Pierian virgins, lend your aid   B315
O let him seal his lips on mine   S746
O let me strike my boldest lyre!   L218
O liberty! the tribute of a breast   L172
O London is a brave town   C106
O long with me in Oxford-groves confin'd   Y90
O lord I know, thou know'st me well   P59
O magnanimity! uplift my muse   M397
O magnifie the lord of hosts with me   Q14
O may I, fam'd delicious villa, be   H70
O may the nine from Helicon inspire   P1039
O money, O money, where hast thou been   E304
O mortal man, who livest here by toil   T181
O muse the mournful scene   E285
O muse, to laureat Cibber dear   C346
O muse unfeign'd! O true cælestial fire   H382
O muse, who chief of the Castalian choir   H183
O! my Alexis, prithee tell   A154
O my blood boiles, my spirit's all in fire   P283
O my lamented Susan, while with thee   A328
O my lamented Talbot! while with thee   T186
O my little F——y, sweet F——y   L322
O my Mecænas, sprung of royal race   V38
O my sweet J——n——n, J——n——n   L321
O! now my muse dramatick stand aside   P629
O Partridge! art thou gone, and we in tears?   E209
O Phœbus! father of immortal verse   G289
O Phœbus, Phœbus, whether now employ'd   P1000
O Polly, speak thy resistless charm   L151
O qui recisæ finibus Indicis   P244
O qui salutem rite sciens, manu   H34
O Ranelagh's a fine place   L290
O rev'rend dean, since death has been so kind   E85
O sacred James, listning with ravish'd ear   E448
O say, when William from Bovinda's flood   F267
O seed divine, by heavn's great sower sown!   L73
O ship new billows which around thee roar   H317
O somne, blandum numen amantibus   D368
O son of Galen, lend your friendly aid   E416
O spring, thou fairest season of the year   W263
O S——t! why shou'd you who art wiser indeed   A73

O Strephon, (if that title please your ear)   M565
O teach me, my muse, a strange tale to rehearse   W453
O! tell me who's this lovely child?   B380
O! that it was but the laws of the land   H297
O that thou would'st the heavens rend!   W321
O the mighty fishery!   L211·2
O! thou cool traytor! Why am I reproach'd?   L282
O thou design'd by nature to controul   J45
O thou Eternal! (hallow'd; wond'rous name!)   T458
O thou, great chief of physic and grimace   M173
O thou great patron of mysterious fame   T368
O! thou, in ev'ry science skill'd   L225
O! thou my muse, that's now bedew'd with tears   E64
O thou renown'd in war, whose godlike deeds   G131
O thou supreme, whom gods their god confess!   S601
O thou that art the lord alone knows what   F268
O thou that hangedst on the tree   W317
O thou, to whom ten thousand altars smoak   A322
O thou, to whom thy poet pays   T351
O thou, truth's fairest off-spring! Heav'nly bred!   B17
O thou, who in eternal light, unseen   B366
O thou, who on thy flaming chariot rid'st   T91
O thou, whom all the cherubims adore   H457
O thou! whom heav'n's propitious pow'r   B408
O thou, whose soul with ev'ry virtue fraught   V88
O thou, whose virtues Albion's sons can trace   B351
O thou, whose wings, by night, by day   T35
O thou, with temper form'd to bless mankind   T254
O Tickell, greatly fated to inherit   B583
O Toland! mighty friend to nature's laws   E256
O toy que la raison, que l'instinct même adore   L93·5
O tyrant death! O hard result of fate   E122
O weep Britannia and lament   B468
O were an ancient bard to raise his voice   R241
O were my muse, inspir'd with sacred flame   P150
O what a change hath death in few days made!   E279
O what a change in few days hath death made   E194
O what a sad age of corruption we live in   M389
O what is the matter? this noise and this clatter?   N195
O! who their eyes from weeping can refrain?   E54
O who wou'd boast himself of royal birth?   M210
O why are we afraid of man   L178
O wisdom! now thy helpful hands extend!   O169
O wondrous man! of all the works of nature   M540
O ye Britains draw near   D85
O ye c——s and p——s, who are bound by your pay   S624
O yes, if in country or town   D392
O yes, O yes, both young and old   P161
O yes, O yes I cry   L71
O yes, O yes, I want to know   D320
O! yes, O! yes, if any man or woman   D5
O yes! O Yes! thrice and again – O yes!   R135
O you the monarch's bliss, the muse's friend!   D472
Observe that arch, the firmament above   N170
Occasionally as we discourst   S138
Octavus Martis te jussit, filia, nasci   P330
October one day, with mournful tune   Z1
O'er Calydonia's ruder alps   P564
O'er gracious spirit – sadness that is spread   E284
O'er Isis blooming banks with busy care   W251

O'er some dead worthy's grave our sweets to strow S230

O'er some dead worthy's grave the sweets to strow S228, S237, S297

O'erwhelm'd in grief, with horrid thoughts opprest D404

Of a worthy Dublin Drapier S406

Of æther pure, and distant spheres of light S4

Of all Great Britain's losses, this alone C333

Of all inhabitants of earth D206

Of all morality these are best plan S188

Of all our antick sights, and pageantry D460

Of all roots of H——r T571

Of all terrestrial kingdoms and abodes T93

Of all that fought about the fire N94

Of all that heightens, or formations mirth B347

Of all the blue bonnets, that came on the stage C314

Of all the booby's call'd a beau O110

Of all the cheats and shams that have of late G273, M396

Of all the days in the year E540

Of all the delicates which Britons try B418

Of all the engines humane wit can boast C272

Of all the evils that befal mankind C291

Of all the factions in the town G109

Of all the jobbs that e'er have past W481

Of all the jolly sights the town has shown W545

Of all the kings, or old, or new, that bear such mighty fame K47

Of all the passions, love we find K11

Of all the pirates I've heard or seen M192

Of all the plagues with which poor England's curst D24

Of all the simple things I know R9

Of all the sports beneath the sun L119

Of all the torments, cares and plagues that wait T150

Of all the trades of Dublin C549

Of all the trades of London S777

Of all the youths, whom Munster's fruitful soil B425

Of all things that are known in nature B566

Of all those sins that heat our northern clime K105

Of arms, devote to heav'n's eternal king B488

Of arts I sing; mysterious things explore I41

Of Belgian provinces by unions pow'r D220

Of birth obscure, his soul ingrate, uncouth P1003

Of Britons second conquest, and the man P65

Of Carlisle siege, that dreadful scene S459

Of Chloe all the town has rung S809

Of conquering faith, my pen attempts to tell G210

Of days with pain acquainted, and of nights T173

Of doubtful race was Georgy E565

Of English tipple, and the potent grain F104

Of ev'ry realm how hard's the fate C182

Of evil times if any do complain K26

Of female wiles I sing, their subtle art P25

Of glorious arms, and of their blest effects J101

Of hail, and snow, and stormy rain M91

Of happiness terrestrial, and the source G89

Of harmony, and her cœlestial pow'r C427

Of heart so dauntless, of such firm good-will, G128

Of heav'ns and earth O blessed be/the supreme lord and head H426

Of kicks and cuffs, of wounds and wars P1042

Of knights and squires of low degree S639

Of labours in vain many stories are told I73

Of late a rude and helpless mass I lay M406

Of late, as they say,/On a Christmas day E563

Of late our fields wore sick and pallid looks P152

Of late there is nothing at all will go down K101

Of late within a northern town J56

Of Leinster, fam'd for maidens fair T290

Of man, his progress, and his end F205

Of man's first crime, and that forbidden tree H342

Of man's first disobedience, and repast J10

Of marriage, love, contention, joys and woes J9

Of martial tribes in arms, of growing fear P51

Of mighty deeds, by doughty heroes done T127

Of my dear flock one more is gone D61

Of mystic visions, and th' illusive scenes P45

Of noble B——m, in metre known W302·5

Of old Augustus the king N110

Of old, in April, martial Rome O42

Of our ancestors brave true, ancient Scots H20

Of piety's unfeign'd delights I sing P505

Of quarrels, and changes, and changelings I sing S597

Of reason and of virtue born C414

Of religion and broils, and bold hardy deeds P1147

Of revolutions in that state I sing D363

Of rival theatres the mighty fall M197

Of spirit high, and matchless might H325

Of superstition such the case is M292

Of that fam'd British structure fain I'd write M104

Of these, dear friend, you have enjoin'd P50

Of things in which mankind does most excel S388

Of this lethargick age to lull the brain P29

Of time's effects, assist me muse to sing D191

Of tribes in arms, encroaching fear H132

Of trivial rhimes enough! – let's now E27

Of two battalions set in rank and file B174

Of wasteful havock, and destructive fate P627

Of woman's disobedience, and the fruits L204

Offspring divine! parent of peace and love! E191

Offspring of heav'n, celestial flame D30

Oft as the sun returns the circling year P1126

Oft Bardus to Apollo pray'd B310

Oft has the muse, on this distinguish'd day S118

Oft has the muse, with mean attempt, employ'd M56

Oft has this thought perplex'd my wav'ring mind C231

Oft' hast thou told me, Jack, in friendly part A212

Oft have I deeply, and with wonder thought M276

Oft have we reason'd much and long P20

'Oh' see also 'O'; the original spelling has been followed, regardless of grammar.

Oh all you statesmen now at court S792

Oh! at a lucky hour for Britain born F236

Oh! Betty, Betty I'm undone F181

Oh! blackest day that e're the sun 'rose on E174

Oh Blackmore! why do'st thou alone refuse E411

Oh, born to chasten, and to banish pain! P421

Oh! brave brother John, now it's plain N123

Oh! brother Tom, dost know the intent E591

Oh Chesterfield! to thee an Irish muse W269

Oh! Conaught, dear Conaught, how it grieves me to tell D420

Oh! cruel death can nothing stop thy rage E80

Oh! cruel death we know that thou E257

Oh cruel death, what's thy rage or intent? E230
Oh cursed fate those sacred books are burnt F144
Oh daring Industry! inspire my muse V121
Oh! death, thou conquerour of men E60
Oh! Edinburgh the muses seat E79
Oh! E—g—d attend whilst thy fate I deplore H158
Oh fam'd Britania, whither wilt thou run? E324
Oh father of the field! whose artful strains O168
Oh fortune! fortune, thou hast done thy worst E119
Oh happiness! our being's end and aim P845
Oh! happy F——ck, thou alone art he W551
Oh happy hour, when the unshackled soul A337
Oh! how chang'd is the gay scene L220
Oh, how sweet must the meditation be C144
Oh Joye! thy name I never knew C97
Oh learned Curll! thy skill excells M423
Oh! let the conqueror stop his swift career B238
Oh! may the fear of heaven's avenging hand E246
Oh! mornful muse, let me with tears rehearse E201
Oh muse! my only, and my last relief! L164
Oh my Belinda! prithee tell me true A96
Oh name it once again, will William come? S443
Oh! Oh! did ever any hear L55
Oh! rash, unhappy, and too thoughtless love! L287
Oh reason, with thy well-discov'ring light M477
Oh! St. James's is a lovely place C39
Oh! say, thou dear possessor of my breast! H21
Oh! Sion, how thy beauty fades away L31
Oh stubborn mobbs that ever did me hate H361
Oh supple bard! thy gentle muse delight's M480
Oh! that I had ne'er subscribed C313
Oh! that I had the pinions of a dove C169
Oh! that it were with me as in L39
Oh! that the voice of grief had pow'r to raise C322
Oh! the sad and dismal story U8
Oh! there was a jovial wedding, a jovial wedding I trow M562
Oh, thou, long trusted with each gift divine D334
Oh! thou Pretender stop thy swift career F170
Oh! thou supreme of things, whose great command N254
Oh! thou to shades of Prior Park attend O88
Oh thou! who from an ancient race O21
Oh thou, who lately by this silver stream O166
Oh, thou, who'rt sprung of pure thick blood! G99
Oh, thou! – who-ere, what-ere, where-ere, thou art H216
Oh, thou, whose bold and penetrating eye E470
Oh! unlucky bank, art thou now condemn'd E175
Oh! vain pretender, you are come J58
Oh! what convulsions seize my tender breast E165
Oh! what fine stories/Display the gay tories R158
Oh! what's this I hear, that disturbs my ear N193
Oh! when together will one age afford C334
Oh! where art thou, St. Taffy? N55
Oh! why dost thou forsake us thus? E573
Oh wicked whigs! What can you mean? P514, T589
Oh! wofull news, O most unhappy day H171, I56
Oh worthy Homer! from the Stygian coast M496
Oh Wotherspoon! just object of regret P1028
Oh ye muses I 'nvoke, now I sing the law scheme H310

Oh you! at once my Venus, and my muse V27
Old battle-array, big with horror is fled B520
Old Bung a second summons sent B567
Old Chiron to his pupil thus began J31
Old England attend, whilst thy fate I deplore H159
Old Eng----d mourns her past disgrace C347
Old Florio pore'd with eager eyes A372
Old Homer sounds Achilles' rage S487
Old I--y to show a most elegant tast B402
Old Latimer preaching did fairly describe S794
Old Ocean's praise/Demands my lays Y94
Old stories do tell, and the scripture does shew N318
Old stories tell how Hercules S769
Old surly Ben, to night, hath let us know P7
Old Zoilus, the sourest Dame Critice bore S225
Oldfield's no more! ------ And can the muse forbear P666
Omnia nox tenebris, tacitaque involverat umbra B333
On a fair mead a dunghill lay B499
On beds of roses, Pyrrha, say P1181
On closing flow'rs when genial gales diffuse W247
On Faughan's banks a little village stands C282
On Friday last, as we were at dinner B610
On Gallia's shore we sat and wept H16
On Good-Friday last (which the learned have told W75
On lofty Cooper's hills aerial brow A316
On Monday, August twenty-seven C205
On new-year's-day our blessed lord began G164
On publick virtue if the lyre be strung S651
On the Castalian banks the sacred nine S278
On the green borders of the silver Tweed A6
On the shore of a low ebbing sea R87
On the very last day of last Michaelmas term M228
On th' oozie bed among the scaly fry P149
On their Castalian banks, the sacred nine S267
On their Pernassus brow the sacred nine S300
On this last labour, this my closing strain Y132
On this returning happy day H429, T330
On Thursday next, sir, I expect W252
On Twit'nham's banks the nine now pensive sit P752
Once and again, the fault'ring muse has try'd C283
Once I had thought from writing to refrain M507
Once in a certain family D391
Once in a morning, e'er the circling sun H137
Once in a morning (when the sun did rise D219
Once mighty Rome, the ruling sceptre sway'd E193
Once more brave boys let us proclaim V33
Once more, by you inspir'd, my muse C64
Once more, great prince, in shining arms appear S376
Once more, great prince, permit an humble bard S569
Once more kick'd out and hurried to her grave E58
Once more, my muse, a generous offring make P451
Once more my muse these dark designs declare S439
Once more, O Pope, I take the pen in hand W431
Once more, O saviour prince, thy bard inspire W331
Once more our London muses pleas'd, repair T455
Once more our most dear indulgent heaven D568
Once more, stern god of war, once more inspire B153

Once more, the ever-circling sun C198
Once on a day, for so report T43
Once on a time, a righteous sage B221
Once on a time as ancient stories tell P68
Once on a time by stress of weather F2
Once on a time, in farmer's yard F60
Once on a time, near Channel-row T498
Once, on a time, Queen Hecub's boy C115
Once on a time some old wives met P1057
Once on a time, when the ague was brief P675
Once Pallas did her form disguise D209
One and twenty and six-pence, not three weeks ago E552
One cloudy day, a drop of rain B179
One day, as I sat musing, all alone D430
One day, as is his wont, the Dean A282
One ev'ning e'rst the moon unveil'd her light P254
One ev'ning fair, fast by the Bird-cage side B415
One morn serene, ere Phœbus had display'd C149
One morning as Chloe the prude lay a-bed S399
One morning, in his Twickenham grott S126
One morning taking pen and ink L232
One night extended on my downy bed B4, M21
One night when that salubrious cordial, wine L76
One Rhodilard by name,/A cat of wond'rous fame C317
One summer evening, when the wearied sun D551
One that had in her infant state B125
Oppress'd with cares, fatigu'd with labours G158
Opprest with grief, distrest with mournful groans W516
Or who the writer? or whence comes th' address? Y23
Oras per Anglorum undique fertiles B194
Ormond's glory, Marlbrough's arms S515
Où va cet aigle magnanime? O58
Oui, Damis, il est vrai, pour dix méchans auteurs R228
Our anchors weigh'd, a fair auspicious gale M501
Our brethren of E----nd who love us so dear S843
Our brewers alledge they have suffer'd much some years past G100
Our father, which in heav'n art, most high S181
Our fears for Townshend now are gladly o'er H333
Our floating isle allmost an age has spent D564
Our flocks at feed, and we devoid of care M569
Our glorious monarch's come H123
Our gracious sov'reign condescends H250
Our granums of old were so piously nice O206
Our great fore-fathers in poetic song H371
Our merchants and tarrs a strange pother have made N18
Our old friend, as I've heard, is now pretty hoddy B610
Our parents first rebellious sin, gave death M518
Our present state, and all things we survey T313
Our selves we're all deceiving W458
Our tongues are loos'd, and our restorer's come T446
Our troops of Great-Britain are now gone from home E318
Outliv'd in splendor, by the subsequent F28
Oxford, to you, my secret muse inclines M273
'Oyez' see 'O yes'

P

Painter, display, in honour of the state G184
Painter: your colours and your pencils get D319
Painting and poetry two sisters are C324
Painting and poetry, you know A83
Pale her locks, and clad in mourning E314
Pallas, immortal maid, thy succour bring D394
Pallidi vivis bene spretor Orci P343
Pamper'd in Kentish meads with pickled feed R168
Pande, anima, ignotas causas cui mystica sedes S749
Pangite, quæ Solymam colitis, jam carmina, musæ G4
Pannels, you are indicted as rascals W550
Paphos, was once bright Citherea's court P43
Paplet lov'd (ah lov'd too well!) P1175
Par le zéle inspiré je vais dans la carriere I67
Par quel pouvoir divin se ranime ma voix? V79
Pardon, from one scarce known, this rude address E381
Pardon, good god! that I should lightly spend M13
Pardon, great duke, if Britain's stile delights C233
Pardon great princess, this liberty I take C499
Pardon, illustrious prince, if in these times S706
Pardon me, madam, if in humble strain P662
Pardon the bold intrusion of a swain K13
Pardon th' officious muse, my lord, whose strain T45
Parent of all things! Cause supreme! B446
Parent of arts, whose skilful hand first taught L330
Paris Gazette say/tho' 'tis not your way P64
Parnassus February the twenty-seventh D202
Pars immortalis, deserta carne, Georgi B442
Pass by a tavern-door, my son S447
Patron of the tuneful throng T332
Patron of verse, O Halifax, attend P206
Patrons of men, my decus & tutela M422
Paul Meagre, you thin-gutted whelp, what a pox-is F287
Peace brother Jack, I'm glad to see ye D261
Peace is the joy of heav'n, the happiness R15
Peintre, pour bien tracer, la gloire de la France G184
Pensive, in sable weeds, Britannia sat P133
Pensive, where Vaga's current murm'ring glides P44
Pensively musing on the wayward fate D425
People may make reflections on a whore T148
Per fess sable and gules in chief he bears J53
Perlege versiculos, charitum pulcherrima, nostros P191
Permit an humble muse to sing thy praise P31
Permit, my condescending friend, permit C513
Permit, my lord, a grateful muse to sing B537
Permit, my lord, me to contgratulate T397
Perniciosa movet dum febris membra tumultus M328
Pernicious peace! fair but illusive syren C395
Perplext in thought, as young Alcides lay L79
Perusing the list of the tackers in print O276
Phillis, 'tis own'd, I am your slave V58
Philosophers, unpolish'd creatures, foes B193
Philosophers, who peep and pore O246
Phoebe pater, manes non hic vexare sepultos P332
Phoebe pater, tremulis qui primus carmina nervis T129
Phœbus and Cæsar once conspir'd to grace R297
Phoebus descend, on thy own Richmond shine R202

Phoebus! great sire! from whom harmonious sprung T129

Phœbus now shortning every shade S798

Phœbus! thou radiant honour of the sky H322

Phoebus, whose charriot ne'er stands still W533

Phospher, drive on, and usher in this day C355

Physicians, and surgeons, and midwives draw near S18

Physicians hold evacuation/Is very proper on occasion S655

Pierian daughters of immortal Jove R331

Pierian madams (no offence) M233

Pitcarni quereris quod nullo carmine laudem P354

Pitcarnus sophiæ est cultor amabilis K40

Pity my mournful case, you ladies fair L18

Plague of all cow'rds, I say – Why, bless my eyes – F102

Plaints, unattempted yet in bill or court T116

Planets and aspects I will sour A255

Pleasure but cheats us with an empty name P11

Pleridum sacrata cohors canit ore rotundo C227

Ploro, musa, viri casum: cadis inclite Cathcars! H408

Pluck'd from an angel's wing give me a pen P190

Pluribus ambigitur, num vere inscitior audit K88

Poets and poetry, in spight of fate G267

Poets before, have brought upon the stage A349

Poets have hitherto mistook O179

Poets, my lord, by some unlucky fate W440

Poets, when they some glorious theme design S243, S342

Poets, who mean to soar no common height H117

Poets whom truth inspires, and genius draws H214

Politeness is my theme – to you I write M255

Poor Buckinger at last is dead and gone E67

Poor Comi Willie, that good father's son P269

Poor England's condition/By sons of perdition E584

Poor, hapless bird, who haunt'st the vale below J48

Poor monsieur his conscience preserv'd for a year E594

Poor relict of my once known yellow store L51

Poor Scotland the seat of war is become C339

Poor Tom an honest country swain D251

Pope I ne'er grudg'd his own Pierian stream E132

Pope, to whose reed beneath the beachen shade L333

Pope wrote a satire, --- took it in his pate O233

Porrigat ætheras, mihi porrigat angelus alas P190

Portglasgow thou's e'en left a lean T583

Posthabitis, ultra quos non tulit Anna, duobus M407

Power, o'er ev'ry power supreme P208

Pox on these senseless, whining sonneteers C365

Praeclarum specimen nuper dedit insita virtus A22

Præda sui nuper Batavis ac hostibus Anglis M404

Præstigius Legerdemain, with strange artificial slights H200

Pray, catch the foxes, cubs of lesser size H392

Pray come you here the fight to shun N181

Pray gentlemans come now and zee my vine zhow N89

Pray isn't it queer/That a wild peer V98

Pray lend me your ear, you who've any to spare M359

Pray lend me your ears if you've any to spare J6

Pray, madam, let not India boast L286

Pray, sir, who are you A242, N64

Pray vat be dis vine show we gaze on? M355

Pray, what is this bank of which the town rings? B60

Prayer! thou vehicle of words, that shew N11

Preach concord to the winds. – I plainly see T257

Prepare, Britannia, now thy thoughts employ N40

Prepare, my muse, a country-seat to sing H300

Prepare, my muse, the wond'ring world to tell F209

Prepare th' harmonious lyre W514

Presumptuous arrogance! inhumane rage! E134

Presumptuous poet, could you dare S795

Pretty Polly say,/When did Jo--y G-- N64

Pride of the world, permit an humble muse H221

Primam hominis noxam, vetitaque ex arbore fœtus D344

Prime poëtarum, præclara gente Frohocka C78

Primum hominis lapsum, vetitaque ex arbore fructus T449

Primus ego his arvis musam meditabar agrestem B88

Prince Frederick, and then for a' L67

Princes, my fair, unfortunately great D361

Princesse vous pleurez vôtre deüil est extréme E40

Principio Jani fit circumcisio Christi S485

Prisca pharetratis quae fulsit gloria Scotis P401

Prisca redit virtus, pietasque refulget avita P396

Prithee! adventrous Jac――n stay S426

Prithee, Belinda (for thou know'st I'm young L9

Prithee, dear D---, what statesman now F137

Prithee, dear Harry, be sincere P1157

Prithee, old granny, hold thy jarring tongue W135

Prithy Robin say, make no more delay G124

Pro met with Con: ----- says Con to Pro P1102

Proceed my pen and reach the glorious end A343

Proclamas omnes papistas esse fugandos P345

Product of earth, by genial heat of sun M299

Proh dolor! Extincta est Malburgae gloria gentis C54

Proper, slender, not too tall S53

Protect our state, and let our Marlbro' thrive F142

Proud and imperious fate, what is thy hate? E282

Proud, lazy, lustful, ignorant and vain C207

Provock'd at length by such unhumane spite L25

Pythagora jactat Samius se fundus alumno P397

Q

Qua celebrem te, diva, lyra? Quo carmine pangam H276

Qua plangam tua fata lyra? Queis prosequar umbras H278

Quacks set out bills, Jack-Pudding makes harangues P1125

Quæ juvet, & lætas faceat quæ cura columbas V15

Quæ nova naturæ facies, qui lumina terrent N270

Quæ Paridi quondam spondebant numera divæ M207

Qualem ministrum numinis alitem M35

Qualis ambabus capiendus ulnis A177

Quam te prisca cupit gens Grampia, sancte, redire! P409

Quando prisca fides, omnes & Apollinis artes D55

Quandoquidem celebres regiones tum boreales K25

Quantum possideat quivis, cognoscere ferme S39

Quantus erat Mariae vindex Havartus, Elisae P362

Quarta dies abijt te salvo, Magne, Novembris   P315
Quatuor Europæ charissima flumina cœlo   V21
Que tu sçais bien, Kneller, à l'aide des couleurs   A48
Que veut dire ceci? quelle ville est la nôtre?   F183
Queen of my heart, dear charmer of my soul   E407
Queen of sweet numbers and resistless sound   J100
Queen of the gloomy king, whose awful sway   C534
Quel bruit entends-je? Que veut dire cet appareil   P48
Quel bruit étonnant nous menace?   V80
Quel est le triste sort des malheureux François   S46
Qui ferant fulmen creat ales acer   D54
Qui mihi combibulus puer es, cupis atque jocari   E483
Quicquid deorum, motibus inclytis   C15
Quid frustra erepti fatis quæramus, amici   R329
Quid juvat densis glomerata turmis   V117
Quid te, Pitcarni, juvat has nunc linquere terras   K24
Quis canat arma, viros? Ranas cecinisset Homerus   K17
Quis fidibus sociæ monstravit munera vocis   P1016
Quis fuero, cum tu Jacobe redibis in urbem   P313
Quis puer obscuro jacet, hospes amabilis, antro?   M271
Quite tired with the projects of the town   T482
Quo non cruentos papicolas agit   A20
Quo primævus Adas temerato fœdere numen   B312
Quod non quinta dies potuit patrare Novembris   P298,
   P323
Quod repetita sequi nollet Proserpina matrem   P336
Quod solium tandem inconcussum habet Anna, secundum
   M410
Quoth Daniel the doctor, to Daniel d'Foe   L62
Quoth Hal to Will the other day   P713
Quoth Stephen D--k to Tom of K--w   C543

R

Radiant sovereign of the day!   P260
Raise high my muse, bold soar thy tow'ring wing
   B348
Rare virtue, who forsook the town with you   T564
Rash author, 'tis a vain presumptuous crime   S540
Rat too, rat too, rat too, rat tat too, tat rat too   C3
Read o'er these lines, O fairest of the graces!   P191
Read o'er these lines, the records of my woes   A178
Read, sirs, away – I teach to kill dull time – N308
Reading the sordid lines that you have writ   T572
Reason, tho' bright, yet when survey'd with pride
   B169
Reason's bright power exalts us from the ground   B169
Rebellion has broken up house   E595
Rebellion, offspring of the Romish whore   N321
Receive, great sir, with a propitious smile   C353
Receive, lov'd prince, the tribute of our praise   M58
Rehearse, my muse, the solemn rites of love   S422
Rehearse, O muse, the deeds and glorious death   G190
Rejoice, brave prince! Perfection pure   O20
Rejoyce successless youths, and love-sick swains   U33
Rejoyce ye good writers, your pens are set free   P1161
Religion having suffer'd long   C318
Remember, Damon, you did tell   R28
Remote from liberty and truth   N339
Renown'd in arms, when mighty heroes rise   B555
Renowned Jesus, hast thou stood   P751
Res rebus quantum distant! Sunt, quæ penes ipsos   I74

Resolv'd to sing the midnight sport   M131
Respecting man, things are divided thus   W13
Restor'd to ancient rule begin my verse   B536
Restrain thy tears! the pious son   O68
Restraint and fear alike destroy   T390·5
Retire ye graces, quit the flowery plain   E261
Retir'd from business in a dark alcove   E187
Retiring to a cool retreat   V25
Review, my Litchfield, with regret mankind   R170
Revolving time in circling years does show   A120
Rich freedom's joys I sing; unparallel'd   B438
Ride now triumphant through the sky   C519
Right reverent fathers her nain-sell did hear   H205
Ring your bells, beat your drums   F81
Rise gentle satyr,/In modest lines the mystery reveal
   O242
Rise gracious muse! Harmonious numbers find
   M475
Rise happy morn, fair sun arise   W253
Rise, lawrell'd shade, from peaceful seats   V22
Rise sacred queen, Apollo's darling muse   J110
Rise sweet, Aurora, rise; propitious morn   F279
Risit Apollo tuo felici fidere fratri   P329
Robert and William both were jolly swains   B467
Robert the douse, by a' the swains rever'd   R88
Robin, by some misterious fate   T33
Robin-red breast, that long   S702
Romanæ scabies linguæ, teterrima Pindi   V100
Room room for the post, who, with zeal for the queen
   M531
Round some fair tree th' ambitious woodbine grows
   Y130
Rouse, drowsy muse, how you provoke me   P692
Rouse lab'ring weavers, never be dismay'd   G104
Rouse now my muse, surely in such a cause   W383
Rouze, rouze dear Britons, is it time to slumber
   G255
Rouse! rouse! my muse, in justice let me say   E140
Rouze satyr, take thy pen, nor dormant lie   S6
Rouse up my British muse, and sing once more   B526
Rowse up, old genius of my fruitful isles   B471
Rouze up, ye drowsie mortals! at the call   C217
Rouzed by the inchanting sounds of joy   A366
Rous'd from a lethargy of hundred years   F195
Rous'd from the grave by the loud cries   G250
Rules were by coxcombs made to cramp the mind
   M187
Run, run, the levee opens, cry the slaves   E464
Run, tell my lord mayor   P1032

S

S * * whose love indulg'd my labours past   P877
Sacra coronatum præit Autarcheia monarcham   S387
Sacra deo magno, multos venerata per annos   A14
Sacra dies olim Marti Caroloque fuisti   P386
Sacred, O Glotta, be the following strains   A281
Sacred to beauteous virtue be the lay   B192
Sacred to Britons be the happy day   O175
Sacred to thee, permit this lay   B48
Sad stupid age! alike in church and state   M231
Sad times! sad times! are coming on   N83

INDEX OF FIRST LINES

Sad turn! when these, whom noblest passions join'd P665

Sad was the hour, the sadder morn began H67

Sæpe revolvi animo, quis primus numine plenus N297

Safety attend the ship that brings O39

Saint Patrick, guardian of this isle R165

Salopian plains, those shady green retreats W242

Salve, chara dies, redeuntis tu decus anni! E496

Salve, dignus avis, exoptatusque Dromondis P312

Salve nympha oculos molles dejecta, humerosque O65

Salve pater patriæ, summorum gloria regum C486

Sanglant théâtre de la guerre C131

Satan, to ruin mankind in the root P163

Satan's first-born, vers'd in his parent's skill R192

Satire! ascend, with good intention fir'd F35

Satyr, audacious G——n's wiles reherse B302

Satire! be mute, decline thy baneful views S518

Satyr once more my towring muse sustain S442

Satyr proceed, raise thy poetick rage L230

Satyr sing Lachrime, thou'rt dead in law D102

Satyr, you can't be too severe H140

Satire's my verse; my lord, a friendly ear S164

Satyrick muse, who knows so well P180

Saturni infausta, cras signo ad sacra vocandus I26

Saunt'ring in an ev'ning's walk S654

Savage, I blame not your ambition S88

Sawney, a mimick sage of huge renown R21

Saxonas ac Anglos olim Germania fudit P404

Say, Britains! felt you nothing in your souls D106

Say, Cadmus, by what ray divine inspir'd P585

Say, curious friend, who rome'st from pole to pole! O92

Say drudging slave, the happiest of thy kind S615

Say, gen'rous parent of the vine E499

Say gentle Hymen, god of chaste delights F156

Say, gentle muse, whence all this mighty care H107

Say, goddess, for 'tis you can tell T554

Say, goddess muse, for thy all-searching eyes S427

Say, goddess muse, what caus'd that fatal day D39

Say, gods! how shall heroic souls behave M7

Say, great Pythagoras of our happier days K1

Say, heav'n born muse, (for who can better tell S5

Say, Lælius, by what power you claim V99

Say, Maija's son, by whose intriguing aid S197

Say, muse, how Damon, in St. James's Park B128

Say muse, how shall I sing the lovely pair B343

Say, muse, if sighs will give thee leave M89

Say, muse! what has the largest share C151

Say muse, what next, what high immortal theme D9

Say, muse, what pow'r unseen does vertue guide P136

Say, my dear count, and, with thy solemn face E400

Say, my dear friend; for you without disguise H177

Say, my Toupet, whence all this grief appears? C10

Say oh! my muse, the glorious cause declare D445

Say, Orrery, for this I long to hear O105

Say, queen of harmony, celestial muse H244

Say, rare machine, who taught thee to design? V57

Say, Robin, what can Traulus mean S914

Say sacred goddess, say, for no retreat N13

Say, shall the brave like common mortals dye C406

Say, sov'raign queen of awful night W379

Say, ye recording nine! blest maids that rove B82

Says Juvenal, 'In every clime, and state C128

Says my uncle, I pray you discover G59

Scaliger, quo nil voluere musae P325

Scandit odoratum quando Phœbeius ales B324

Scarce did the grey ey'd dawn appear M205

Scarce had the bells the news began E61

Scarce had the burning Phoebus roll'd his carr B91

Scarce had the curate made an end W111

Scarce had the ghosts of Pluto's gloomy shade R217

Scarce had we time allow'd our thanks to yield C249

Scarce in Parnassus shall we find one peer A325

Scipio and Lelius by the muse rever'd W274

Scire velim quare tota trepidatur in urbe R113

Scotland rejoyce, with a chearfull smile H248

Scotos pharetris quis sine gaudio K43

Skreen'd by a mountain, on the southern side R77

Scribogg vornou look about/The craps of Hoath are coming out A87

Search all the bright creation, you won't find M414

Sedition first and most accursed crime! S190

See a new progeny descends W484

See a young muse extend her callow wing P707

Se de great and mighty war F263

See, dearest Varus, at thy strange command A15

See fam'd Apollo and the nine L216

See how the new-born season springs! T80

See how the wrangling world in fumes arise O53

See Mira here, how atoms change P1019

See! Nature round a hoary prospect yields N270

See sirs, see here!/A doctor rare I39

See where our glorious William comes S600

See! Winter comes, to rule the varied year T211

Seeing our leisure serves us now O115

Seldom the man, whose word's sincere E308

Septem Pitcarni pro te cecidere lubentes P311

Seraphic brute! How else shall I address D554

Set the glass round/about you have a care sir D500

Seven and ten addyd to nyne S849

Seven planets they do grace the skies S352

Seven sages in our happy isle are seen S350

Seven sages in these latter times are seen S351

Seven years your levees I have haunted M343

Severe's the charge against all womankind A63

Shakespeare's receipt to tame a shrew N177

Shall all the battles, great Marlborough fought V24

Shall Anna's arms extend from pole to pole E420

Shall baleful hate unwearied vigour use E462

Shall blazing-stars, drop from their spheres V73

Shall Boulter die, and no memorial shew M8

Shall Britain and applauding nations round T62

Shall British glory rise again A160

Shall British honour be insulted so M382

Shall British senators permit the bays S56

Shall Britons still at feeble wishes stay J111

Shall Co——ey die, and yet not have E87

Shall every circling year M77

Shall every pension'd scribbler draw his pen G141

Shall feeble mortals in their low estate E181

Shall France triumphant over Europe ride C412

Shall Harley's sorrows then no limits know? V70

Shall heav'n too, make resumptions of its grants L305

Shall innocence by fatal rashness bleed P554

Shall knaves and fools command the world's applause W572

Shall letter'd spleen still grow upon our clime B139
Shall Marlbro' still new victories obtain? L149
Shall monarchy be quite forgot T530
Shall other climes incite poetic strains R260
Shall poets drive a mercenary trade P606
Shall Pope and Whitehead, with the rankest hate C129
Shall so much worth in silence pass away T393
Shall streaming tears a nations eyes o'erflow B368
Shall Strowan fall without the warrior's bays T381
Shall Temple beaus, or college smarts maintain P88
Shall the Englishman, Addison, sing a Campaign M254·5
Shall the gay beauties of this charming seat E358
Shall the great soul of Newton quit this earth T200
Shall then in vain such streams of sorrow flow D228
Shall then my kindred all my glory claim T390
Shall then the distant Indian coast N263
Shall Titchfield yet remain a name unknown M283
Shall Watts depart and quit the stage of life M282
Shalt thou, O bard divine, who e'rewhile sung O197
She comes! the fair deluder charms our eyes N50
She (for I know not yet her name in heaven) Y49
She's dead, alas! beyond recov'ry dead P690
She's dead! thanks to the jury's pious care P436
She-land, the praise of all the earth C158
Sherl--k, thy doom is sign'd, fate presses on A277
Shine forth, ye planets, with distinguish'd light P1083
Shou'd Addison's immortal verse S737
Should England's worthies from Elysium slide S784
Should Hogarth, with extravagant conceit E469
Shou'd hum'rous Hogarth, from a knavish plan M246
Should I invoke the antient Romans muse T504
Should I the language of my heart conceal D365
Should some strange poet, in this piece, affect D376
Should some unskilful painter undertake A179
Should the nine sisters from Parnassus high S184
Shou'd the old censor of imperial Rome G313
Should you, my friend, employ your time D470
Should you, my lord, a wretched picture view M503
Shut in a study six foot square R71
Shut, shut the door, good John! fatigu'd I said P802
Si ad præsulatum velles ascendere V82
Si non impediant lacrymarum flumina quicquid E39
Si senii descendam, & cœpi vergere, ad annos B334
Si vati faveas optima principum P526
Si vis ingenii, mihi si concessa potestas K68
Sicilian muse, exalt thy rural strain E36
Sicilian muse, from lofty flights descend L89
Sicilian muse, thy voice and subject raise G211
Sicilian muses, to a strain more noble ascend we I49
Silence ye cits, let patriots be dumb C464
Silence, ye jarring elements, be still H164
Silence, ye plaintiff instruments of woe! V72
Silent and grey the morning's dawn appear'd M98
Silvius upon me call'd, not long ago N303
Simple and plain, nor yet impress'd by vice R136
Simplicity of speech, and naked truth C73
Since all, in these harmonious times E433
Since all the din of war begins to cease R176
Since all the learned world agree W40
Since all the world's turn'd up-side down P506
Since antient fabulist this fancy had P42
Since Anna visited the muses seat P1096

Since bailiffs and mayors, to evade all objection T489
Since Britains seals to other hands are gone P528
Since charitable B---l--r's dead and gone P1054
Since Churchill's fame has thro' our regions run S737
Since Dismal became low, and D-----st high S729
Since disputations, wranglings, noise, and strife M443
Since epic strains no more are heard S503
Since evr'y scribbling Bays E550
Since fancy's in pleasure so strong R27
Since fate deceiv'd us both, in fear and hope R160
Since fate has robb'd me of the hapless youth P1120
Since furious Cam/Fam'd Isis does damn C6
Since, shentlemans, my rare show hit so pat S174
Since god decreed, all men shou'd turn to dust E108
Since good master Prior,/The tar water 'squire T39
Since great Apollo, with his harp in hand W188
Since heav'n propitious to our isle has sent H403
Since hir'd for life, thy servant muse must sing P1079
Since human folly first began K104
Since in such odd fantastick times as these C189
Since int'rest, vanity, and spite combine A171
Since it has lately pleas'd our new born state C433
Since its a fashion grown so common E56, E258
Since joking epilogues for current pass P1129
Since language never can describe my pain H157·5
Since letters are grown/So frequent in town L150
Since man is surely born to die C142
Since Maro in divine Augustus' days B531
Since men in faith were so divided D285
Since men like beasts each other's prey were made T76
Since men unite for to infect W389
Since monarchs by prerogative are wise M440
Since monarchs were monarchs, it never was known N103
Since most agree, that 'tis a crime O180
Since my weak voice in Congreve's praise preferr'd B315·5
Since Nassau bravely freed us H37
Since news at Paris grows so wondrous scarce L132
Since non but flatterers to —— resort G142
Since none have dar'd on this great theam to raise O7
Since none in virtue to perfection rise E346
Since nought can satisfy the wrath A11
Since one hath writ,/To thee, O P-tt! S452
Since one there is, who with uncommon art E434
Since our king to his German dominions is gone C101
Since people now with bus'ness mix L42
Since right and wrong, the stated case B69
Since save-alls are so much the mode of the nation A254
Since senates safe in legal rights rejoice V68
Since, shentlemans, my rare show hit so pat S174
Since so very impatient to hear of the doom P465
Since some with bare-fac'd impudence deny D67
Since sons of whores are noble men M559
Since tales are so much the new mode of the city C467
Since the black storms, which threat'nd hard our trade H5
Since the blissing fates W459
Since the business is over I'm glad there's an end on't S580

Since the Drapier's set up, and Wood is cry'd down S381

Since the metallick ages all are past W558

Sin' the queen has doon with addresses A53

Since the raign of King Solomon E177

Since the sad news has reach'd my ears E200

Since the sons of the church C176

Since the third Edward pois'd the vengeful lance L96

Since thou my soul, of pure celestial birth D192

Since troops of mad-men are in Bedlam pent M12

Since true content doth such a treasure bring F180

Since various subjects various pens employ C468

Since virtue first inspir'd harmonious lays A285

Since we can dye but once, and after death P733

Since we first fram'd that scale of various beings H130

Since we, good fellows both, here haply meet M521

Since we have gain'd what we attempted Q5

Since we have shun'd the hurry of the court O11

Since William the great,/The defence of the state B479

Since William's gone into the bright abodes P66

Since with the new year a new change hath begun W497

Since woolly Cotswold is no more in view B415

Since you, dear doctor, sav'd my life E437

Since you, dear Jon----an, alone best know G125

Since you, my friend, desire I should apply R203

Since you, my lord, did Europe's fate support T391

Since you, my lord, our glorious vice-roy reign G7

Since you, poor knaves, have scrap'd some pence and pity L134

Since you're resolv'd this dangerous state to try P626

Since your curiosity led you so far E369

Sincerest critick of my prose, or rhime C375

Sing all ye sacred heavenly choir P289

Sing Clio, the ador'd, the god-like youth B343

Sing great Anna's matchless name S216

Sing, heav'nly muse, in lays harmonious sing B178

– Sing, heav'nly muse, the Cambro-Britain, whose prolifick brain B176

Sing, honest muse, nor fruitless be thy song F58

Sing, muse, how rebel Titans rose B87

Sing muse (if grief allow) in softest lays E249

Sing muse, of hidden love the conscious flame C70

Sing muse, the Briton, who on mountains bred C250

Sing, muse, the conscious torch; whose friendly light S754

Sing, muse, the conscious torch, whose nightly flame E490

Sing muse, the glorious day, consign'd to fame T4

Sing, muse, the lamp that shed its conscious light B44

Sing muse the malice of that impious man A26

Sing muse, the progress of the patriot flame P1111

Sing, mystick muse, and with a fluent strain I3

Sing! O Britannia! do not cease! R240

Sing, O muse, Phœbus' wrath! Say what cause could persuade K79

Sing praise to our grac'ous Queen Anne E576

Sing, sacred prophet, the defeat of Saul L212

Sing, sing, O muse, the dire contested fray W412

Sing, sing, ye swains, in joyful strains express G261

Sir Gravity well grown in years B609

Sir, having nothing else to do L136

Sir, here's de express E313

Sir, I have long, and with impatience, sought Y99

Sir, in a garret near St. Martin's lane M511

Sir knight, who know with equal skill F107

Sir, may it please you but to hear H396

Sir, 'mong your gifts your candour's not the least S449

Sir Robert, tho' at your levee B301

Sir, since our Isis silently deplores S516

Sir,/Since the scum of these three nations C193

Sir, to your care we timely would commit S657

Sir, upon casting an attentive look B613

Sir, with submission, I humbly crave B525

Sister, I sometimes have complain'd T380

Sit deus ipse timor vester; quæ jussit, agatis B202

Sit down, sad muse! and thy free thoughts apply E124

Sly Mercury, once had a whim in his head C469

Smile (gentle Neptune) by Jove early sent L309

Smile, my Hephestion, smile; no more be seen W312

Smile, smile,/Blest isle C45

S—n and the man I sing who forc'd by age M224

So great, my lord, your worth, so bright your fame V123

So great your honour, so deserv'd your fame T7

So, having ended his campaigns in Gaul H64

So ho, who's there? Alas, where am I got? T409

So many have for a dinner or half crown M436

So much the creature his creator's care S251

So Orange fell, so Glo'ster went before W37

So slave! who owns those ragged journals there? T474

So! Sure as morning comes, the trade's the same B434

So the long absent winter-sun N77

So Tydeus look'd, when, single, he oppos'd C256

Social nuptial ties, 'tis said M110

Soft elegy, design'd for grief and tears D534

Soft Milton's charms in verse assist my pen P540

Soft Venus, love's too an anxious queen P218

Sol had just with-drawn his light O130

Sol's mannor was a pretty good house M217

Soldiers of Christ, arise W324

Sollicitos age falle dies vitæque labores B45

Some angry muse assist my nimble pen B186

Some angry muse direct my pen C125

Some bards of old times much delighted with sack F174

Some boutcher's wives got a fine soup L37

Some by the title led astray K100

Some call curiosity an evil F122

Some coblers turn poets, to serve their best friends C206

Some cocks of the game F5

Some crafty curs, who had abused their master A115

Some darling worthy t' an immortal crown S349

Some Eastern princes to be counted great W281

Some fourscore years ago, we plainly see P611

Some future Garth, brave chief, shall sing W297

Some happy souls who Jesus knew G209

Some husbands on a winter's day W347

Some in the ring delight to guide the rein S157

Some leagues remote from where fam'd Ganges flows H69

Some mighty genius now my breast inspire S445

Some people have pretended to talk of Sir William Butler's as the best colt in the town P755

Some poets court the airy praise of men P199

Some prelude here the muse advises B539

Some say, our states men now are very willing S945

Some say the weapons Levi wears P89

Some say their sires, the first made man O69

Some score of miles from town, as stories tell P82

Some things beyond our reach without us stand P998

Some think my satires (this is what I hear) F150

Some write of angels, some of goddess G123

Some years ago from Norfolk S730

Something so mournful is in what I'd write N138

Sometimes you tell me I am pert and proud W113

Somewhere about the sun, as I have read B530·9

Sons of the Thunderer, and Bellona's care D268

Soon as Aurora'd left old Tithon's bed P255

Soon as bleak northern winds had froze the air W288

Soon as bright Phœbus with revolving light O6

Soon as the dreadful busy search was o'er C473

Soon as the iron age on earth began D482

Soon as the sun began to peep C448

Soon as these lines salute thy piercing eye S553

Sorrowing I catch the reed, and call the muse M124

Sound the shril trumpet, fill it's silver womb P1138

Spectators of all ranks, come and behold G300

Speak, goddess muse!/As wond'rous news E298

Speak, goddess muse, in soft description tell U6

Speak, goddess! since 'tis thou that best canst tell G21

Speak, grieved muse, alarm the world, and read T382

Speak satire for by thee alone W470

Speak, satyr; for there's none can tell like thee D153

Speak satyr quickly, we have theames enough N180

Speak thou sweet solace of my vacant hours B2

Speed and the games I sing, where counties meet D8

Spes erat nuper mihi te videndi A176

Spieghiamo i vanni, io dissi al alma un giorno R186

Spight of Dutch friends and English foes S895

Spirit of Sternhold me inspire K67

Spread forth thy wings, I to my soul once said R186

Staff, mitre, and purse, made a damnable rout N57

Stand off! and hold your dull impertinence I43

Stars, robes, and the various colour'd strings F48

Start not, ye sons of crape --- nor think I mean A89

Start up my muse, shake off thy sable gloom B212

Stately stept he east the wa W213

Stay, friendly swain, and hear a lover's woe P104

Stay, sacred goddess, we thy aid implore H40

Stay, stay a while my faithful servant yet P1002

Steeds and the man I sing; the man S762

Stemmata quid faciunt? Quid prodest sanguine longo P186

Stern Æole of late G207

Stiff as I am, worn out with age S37

Still fond Calypso, pensive and forlorn A68

Still injur'd, still forgiving hero, where C514

Still let low wits, who sense nor honour prize S99

Still was the night, serene and bright W457

Still we do find, black cloth wears out the first E278, G139

St---ng with courage fresh assail D43

Stockell is dead, no more you hear his groan E247

Stop passenger, until my life you read E442

Stop, stop, my steed! hail Cambria, hail H346

Stote tuae moerens astat Pitcarnius urnae P297

Stout Jason's golden fleece, the sacking Troy T422

Stoutly fought, and bravely won! C510

Strange uproars shook the regions all below D244

Strange! who can call the course their home? H354

Stranger! this stately monument contains E440

Stretch'd in a lonesome vale (where spring decays T59

Stretch'd on the plain I grasp the slender reed W570

Strike, strike the lyre, the nuptial morn O80

Strike the deep note, the concent swell W306

Strike up, my unambitious lyre L217

Stripp'd now of ev'ry vain, fantastick air P611

Struck with the rising scene, thus I amaz'd T196

Studious and grave has ever been thy mind C415

Studious, the busy moments to deceive P366

Sublime attempts above our strength receive their value still S180

Sublime themes do to epic strains belong F238

Such a sad tale prepare to hear B607

Such always was the nature of a fool A252

Such desperadoes sure were never known C116

Such eyes as Somerset's; imperious dame! E375

Such harmony, as crowns th' Olympick revels U15

Such has been this ill-natur'd nations fate D132

Such is the course of providence below H337

Such is, yee fair, your universal sway P1124

Such was our builder's art, that soon as nam'd G39

Sue Lackit, of the London mould O114

Sunt queis displicuit Miltonis Epistola; quippe K75

Sunt quos Pelidis stomachum cecinisse juvabit S768

Superiour bards, the pride of ancient days B263

Superior powers that bieds aboon T583

Superiour qualities alike will raise T565·5

Suppliant your pardon first I must implore H157

Suppose Belinda painted to a hair G320

Sure I have read of many wonder C145

Sure of all arts that ever were invented S41

Sure there are poets which did never dream D214

Sure there are poets who never did dream O11

Sure there are times when bards may venture praise P1010

Sure there's a fate in excellence too strong S377

Surprizing dangers apt to startle more E114

Swains of Britannia's happy, gladsome isle S35

Sweet as it is to view our dangers past C117

Sweet charming muses, teach me how to raise P567

Sweet doings truly! we are finely fobb'd! J85

Sweet poplar shade, whose trembling leaves emong P1004

Sweet, pretty pratler of the c---t T322

Sweet rural scene!/Of flocks, and green! Y94

Swift as his fame, o'er all the world he flies W576

Swift, swift, good John, another bottle--fly- D305

Swift too, thy tale is told: a sound, a name T175

Swords, and the swords-men, muse, I sing C230

Sylvestrem qui primus aprum mira arte subegit R195

INDEX OF FIRST LINES

T

'T has been observ'd of human nature   B487
Taff boasted not of learning much, or arts   H107
Take a nuckle of veal   P952
Take (if you please) for nothing my advice   W241
Take of every thing odious that's under the sun   I40
Tancred, the ruler of Sicilia's land   H146
Te placidus vidit sol nasci, filia, luce   P321
Te poetarum coluere regem   P309
Te quoque sol vidit nascentem, filia, luce   P325
Te sequor læta calidus juventa   H148
Tea is the sparkling subject of my song   C11
Tea, thou delightful innocent repast!   I32
Teach me my muse to check with keenest pen   A166
Tears must succumb, where sullen grief abounds   T265
Tedious have been our fasts, and long our pray'rs   P253
Tell me, Apollo, for thou best dost know   D332
Tell me dear Owen what surprize of late   O11
Tell me (for sure some devil did)   E432
Tell me great fabrick! tho' our distance seems   E13
Tell me, Lucretius! was it chance that made   P699
Tell me, my muse! (if thou wilt deign to lend   D60
Tell me no more of purling streams   T469
Tell me no more who is my freind   B440
Tell me, proud insect, since thou can'st not fly   W148
Tell me, Review, what hast thou late survey'd   G42
Tell me, thou unknown something, that resid'st   S749
Tell me unthinking giddy nymphs   T380
Tell me, you glorious shades, where I may trace   O163
Tellurem fecere dii, sua littora Belgæ   P369
Telorum siluere minæ, redivivaque terris   S217
Term-time at hand, I, hit or miss it   S748
Terras purgabam monstris: fatalia terris   K24
Tertia Septembris vos orbi misit ovanti   P373
Teutonicas acies, supremaque Cæsaris arma   P407
Thalia anes again in blythsome lays   R80
Thalia, ever welcome to this isle   R104
Thalia, tell in sober lays   S861
Thames, when of late his swelling tide   O36
Thank heav'n! at last our wars are o'er   E530
Thank ye, most great and martial sir   T587
Thanks and renown be ever thine   R32
Thanks to the gods, who've crown'd my elder days   C1
That all is vanity below   L141
That day, when golden trumps awake the dead   B562
That glorious great and memorable day   L263
That gods sometimes, incognito   J105
That Græcian bard who sweetly sung of old   H77
That high-church have a right divine from Jove   H196
That I thus prostitute the muse   R93
That lowly vicar may in order rise   B530
That man is made by nature free   M82
That many gross deceits are rife   P1110
That muse that lately sung, in mournful strains   M316
That Observator whom you name   E322
That pretty little gaudy fly   P659
That subjects love from rev'rence, hate from fear   D86
That virtue Scotia's sons doth own   A22
That whereas your petitioners forlorn   T385
That your petitioner being about twenty-five years of age, has never yet been a bride   D337

The airy chariot breaks the azure roads   M269
The ancient poets, when they undertook   R314
The art of converse, how to sooth the soul   S757
The baneful yew erects its head   P80
The bard who sought e'erwhile in sportive strains   L179
The battle had never been gain'd   D26
The beardless actors of this favourite play   M346
The beasts with indignation warm'd   P435
The beauty new of Edinburgh town   W265
The being that's omnipotent, and said   H388
The birds reduc'd once to a pop'lar state   T11
The blackbird who had waited long   S675
The blackbird whose incessant care   S685
The bloom of youth upon his cheek is seen   P1113
The bold attempt, and vain, perhaps, essay   S30
The bold encroachers on the deep   S900
The brave Duke Hamilton, alas is kill'd   G163
The bright Astrea now no longer driven   A362
The British birds of late call'd over   L180
The British mountaineer, who first uprear'd   M551
The British muse in Chaucer first began   D27
The business of the drama being done   P1129
The cabinet, summon'd, in council conven'd   M450
The Ca——l has got a scoup   C36
The call when to consummate virtue given   S281, S298, S345
The Calv's-head brawny c—— leads the van   P453
The candid muse, ambitious to record   D515
The captains take their seats, the soldiers stand   T49
The chaos lay in wild confusion hurl'd   A108
The chaiplain and the teacher that's confin'd   E607
The chace I sing, hounds, and their various breed   S562
The chearful morn adorn'd each purple cloud   F223
The Chevalier being void of fear   B103
The chief and highest end of man   S527
The choice of anthems exquisite   E457
The christ'ning was not yet begun   E541
The Christian hero's martial looks here shine   O187
The Christian world's redeemer blest we see   H417
The chronicles of Florence tell   B184
The clan being turn'd out of places of power   O116
The clock had struck – and eager to be drunk   S486
The commons once destroy'd the church   S783
The conflict youthful Hercules endur'd   M313
The counsels of a friend, Belinda, hear   L328
The country girl that's well inclin'd   W475
The country 'squire that wants to be undone   W257
The court was met; the pris'ner brought   M433
The crown is fallen from our head   S559
The cruel taunts, the dire revengful flame   Q7
The cunning wiles of all the saints   R316
The curse, Apollo, why wilt thou prolong?   B478
The cushion dance had clos'd the ball   V23
The day draws near, the joyful day   H434, T330
The day is come, and freedom is betrayed   P613
The day was come, and all the birds   S695
The day was come when all the folk in furs   E29
The Dean wou'd visit Market-hill   S868
The debt which man by birth contracts, he must   M420
The defunct has obtain'd a name   E148

41

The dire misfortunes of a youthful swain   N300
The distant muse with filial duty fir'd   G43
The disturbance we have in our nation of late   N156
The doctor, in a clean starch'd band   M416·5
The doctrines which our Saviour taught   R7
The dolphin's race had govern'd long   P432
The doom on parents for orig'nal sin   B569
The Drapier I swear,/I love and revere   D428
The eager merchant does in vain sail o'er   D238
The eastern breeze, fresh harbinger of dawn   B490
The eternal god, at first by power divine   M135
Th' Eternal, who the fates of empires weighs   W332
The ever shining charioteer of heav'n   S248
The everlasting charioteer of Heav'n   S250
The excrements which they void all men are dust   S72
The fair, the bright, the great, alas! are fall'n   T174
The fam'd Columbus his proud sails unfurl'd   S274
The farmers of England say   N122
The fidler h's lost his fiddle, – hoe   F117
The feilds [!] no longer husbandry confess   R240
The finish'd mind in all its movements bright   R55
The fruit was tasted, and the threat fulfill'd   G298
The gently warbling lyre no more I string   C136
The genuine off-spring of a worthy sire   I18
The gleamy morn had scarcely shook off night   B472
The globe with wond'rous pains men traverse o'er   C95
The gloomy horrors of the night   P292
The glorious day is past for which we pray'd   T82
The godlike man who dares   M103
The gods and the goddesses lately did feast   B336
The gods, one day, to heaven's imperial court   P632
The gods resolv'd a master-piece to show   E444
The gods were round imperial Jove   C56·5
The golden age is now again restor'd   B284
The gout I think, remains as yet unsung   I37
The grateful tribute of these rural lays   D476
The grateful Trojan when kind fortune bore   H301
The great apostle, in his ravish'd breast   T459
The great reputation/You have in this nation   O15
The grey-ey'd morn, now, eastward breaks its way!   L161
The greyish dawn had scarce o'ercome the night   P281
The happy muse, to this high scene preferr'd   C378
The haughty Gaul, in ten campaigns o'erthrown   T303
The hawks were once at mortal jars   O190
The heav'n doth now put forth her smiling flag   P684
The heavenly contest, and award of Jove   M112
The hero feels a fertile skull   C104
Th' heroick youth, whose spear and batter'd helm   P1171
The highest pitch of sorrow swells my heart   P155
The horrid horses and sulphureous car   H368
The hue and cry we had of late   W444
The humble petition of the ladies, who are all ready to be eaten up with the spleen   L247
Th' immortal youth had newly left the day   S943
Th' impious quaff off sin, ev'n till they burst   B515
The inquisiter gen'ral resigning his place   M446
Th' insidious art, and the alluring snare   S464
The Jacobites, their insurrections   T556
The judges sat, and jury call'd   T472
The Juncto has broken up house   E595
The king, in each anticipating thought   B489

The king whom thy support has blest   H449
The labour of a Dublin day   D73
The land, the praise of all the earth   C159
The lark, while she her gratitude to prove   C96
The lasses of Dublin, in sorrowful dumps   B206
The last time I came o'er the moor   R90
The learned hold, that worms in time   D369
The learn'd inventers of each lib'ral art   J98
The life of man to represent   P1169
The like complaints, in Rama's vale were heard   E172
The lion having held the reins   P427, P454
The lion, 'tis no matter how   L191
The Lord himself, the mighty Lord   P96
The lord of light, and charioteer of day   O222
The Lord will yet on Jacob mercy show   P52
The lordly lion, by mishap   H357
The Lawland lads think they are fine   R58
The Macedonian youth, whose mighty name   F216
The maid is blest that will not hear   P953
The man for senates and for councils form'd   S652
The man is blest that doth provide   P91
The man is blest that hath not lent   C458
The man that fell by faction's strife   P571
The man that loves his king and nation   H372
The man that's obstinately just   C56·7
The man that's resolute and just   W33
The man who dotes on gold, how curs'd his fate!   W55
The man, who stedfastly adheres   C59
The man whom heaven has dispos'd to bless   D563
The man, whose life by virtue's model fram'd   C528
The man's auspicious conduct, that subdu'd   L68
The mighty Shamgar dy'd, Shamgar the brave   D84
The modest muse presumes not to enquire   T49·5
The moon was pendulous above   C484
The moral lay, to beauty due   M424
The morning's up, the sun prepares   C260
The mountain-dwelling Briton who design'd   L165
The muse a brutall battle shall recite   T95
The muse an exile from her once lov'd lyre   P703
The muse forgetting, by the muse forgot   P548
The muse of good patriots now virtuously sings   M379
The muse that by your victory's inspir'd   D95
The muse that oft, with sacred raptures fired   A41
The muse, that once in raptures us'd to pay   G137·2
The muse, that trac'd thee in far distant climes   E509
The muse, tho' conscious of her feeble lays   L103
The muse, tho' late, to thee, the muse's friend   S497
The, muse, who, near thy Britain's watry bounds   M532
The muse who sung the flight at Dettingen   D37
The muse, who touch'd with Catalonia's wrong   E408
The muses having lately met   C397
The muses now send forth their sonnets   W43
The nation had always some token   N5
The naturalists most aptly do compare   K2
The need of grace (a solemn theme) I sing   G234
The news from abroad does a secret reveal   M30
The night, in clouded majesty array'd   A229
The night is past. – Once more I homage pay   M469
The ninth of last came hot from Rome   I72
The noble Tamworth dead, th' harmonious nine   S271

The nume'rous rhimers of the age   P717
The nymph who wrote this in an amorous fit   R144
The old whiggish sages, we plainly do see   W385
The papists and tories do openly boast   P179
The patten, fan, and petticoat   A185
The pearl of Caledon is gone   E224
The pencil's glowing lines and vast command   A204
The physitians of late/Held a learned debate   E568
The picture strikes. – 'Tis drawn with wondrous art!   B78
The pious armies, and the chief I sing   H302
The plot is spoild and we are all undone   E203
The poets praise those most who need it least   C362
The pointed satyr, and the genial fire   K51
The pow'r supreme, creator of mankind   H340
The powerful monarch of the flood salutes   N35
The pow'rs above on fair Britannia smile   E15
The pride of France is lilly-white   S793
The princess somewhat in disorder   P1063
The prize which worth deserves, when worth receives   T370
The prologue over, few regard the play   L54
The roaring dons of Greece sat down   B430
The rod was but a harmless wand   S935
The rosie morning with prevailing light   F273
The rough designs in gentle bosoms cloak'd   G120
The rout and slaughter of that savage band   M136
The rovers and the butts you saw   R72
The royal harp, unstrung must ever lye   F290
The rustick muse thus having chang'd the scene   E355
The sable mantle of the low'ring night   T570
The sacred dawn of this auspicious light   B437
The sacred nine despise a cuckold's name   R131
The sacred nine, your aid once more impart   M119
The sages, lest you might their meaning find   S716
The Samian sage, who first maintain'd   P712
The sand-ridge baron now doth stand   N243
The schemes of our kirk are much better supported   S584
The scourge of heav'n, the prophet's lifted rod   P469
The shades of waning night had now begun   D29
The shape alone let others prize   F270
The shepherds and the nymphs were seen   S814
The silent night her sable robe had spread   T117
The son of god, who rules the pregnant earth   O245
The son of man transfigur'd, and the light   R198
The soul that's fill'd with virtue's light   P93
The sovereign beeing who doth beeing give   E244
The sov'reign lord of heav'ns and earth   D417
The Spanish dons, as authors tell us   E339
The spring's a coming   A354
The stage has been, and yet improv'd shall rise   P446
The statesmen in or out declare   D440
The story of King Authur [!] old   G303
The summer sun had half perform'd his race   O164
The summons were sent, and without more ado   P508
The sun appears to take a farewell view   S379
The sun full half his daily course had run   P630
The sun now chasing from our sight   W122
The sun was my mother, and bore me at night   S508
The sun without a rival guides the day   C410
The sweets of nature, – the disclosing spring   B188

The tack of old,/was thought as bold   O124
The taking one poor town in ten years time   M105
The tea was drank and ta'en away   C39
The tea was sip'd, Ocella gone   N246
The tears scarce dry'd, we for thy brother shed   O193
The tenant of a hut that fac'd the sea   F71
The theme's resolv'd: the glittering files appear!   H132
The thimble's first original rehearse   H112
The things that make a virgin please   S831
The thirsty tyrant, active in our woe   A355
The time of elections is now drawing near   R249
The times were come which bards of old   L326
The town and nation know Camilla   F284
The town being full of confusion   N159
The town has been so plagu'd of late   B483
The town is alarm'd and seems at a stand   A245
The tragick muse, sublime, delights to show   P1120
The tribe of templars, play'rs, apothecaries   P968
The Trojan swain had judg'd the great dispute   P1082
The Trojan tongues now, after feast   S517
The truth of womankind is all a cheat   F88
Th' unnumbred charms that in thy person shine   L147
The various scenes of vicious loves I sing   B426
The vast extent of empire is too large   P683
The verdant Hackney with her rural bow'rs   S335
The victor death, who will no mortal spare   P668
The vocal picture, and the pencil's speech   W273
The volume, sir, so kindly lent by you   F151
The voyage round the world is thought your due   V20
The weary sun had ta'en his leave of day   C471
The wight an' doughty captains a'   F184
The wind blows a loft boys   E341
The winter night I think it long   A225
The winters storm of civil war I sing   B129
The wise and great of every clime   A137
The wisest are by narrow bounds confin'd   E388
The witling of the witty race   N166
The wits are jarring, and the witlings strive   S153
The wolves, as 'tis said, in politicks deep   T535
The woman marry'd is divinely blest   F135
The wonders of god's ancient love   D560
The world I don't question has heard of the trial   T26
The world's and heaven's eternal foe   M495
The worlds pomp, is an ambitious state   H353
The year of wonders is arriv'd   A126, W557·5
The youthful muse that long unmark'd has play'd   C310
Thee, Bath, and flutt'ring belles and beaus I sing   B93
Thee sacred prophet I invoke   B68
Their harts mun be as hard as stean   E239
Then if by chance I could   A261
Then it is done! the wond'rous work compleat!   T451
Then must it thus, ye heavens for ever be   A183
Then struck up a smart with a soldierly air   M461
There are few unacquainted with th' old Palace-Hall   M457
There are (I scarce can think it, but am told)   P886
There are some things are counted real   W260
There are (whate'er you think sir) I am told   J116
There came a Scot of late I hear, to wait upon Tom Double   D274
There goes a tale of antient date   K53
There is a place in London-town   F4

There is no cause why ye so much admire   V109
There is no truth more evident to sense   E199
There liv'd a great and mighty prince   C202
There liv'd in Derby, near the Peak   M104
There liv'd i' th' west a squire, so great   P1106
There liv'd, no matter when, or where   O132
There was a fellow hard at work a sowing   P449
There was a fig-tree on a rising ground   P459
There was a fight which held out very long   A8
There was a great lord, came from a strange land   N154·5
There was a housewife kept a cock   F8
There was a monarch, whose imperial sway   A116
There was a simple Adamite   D53·5
There was an old woman that had a bee-hive   O131
There was once a glorious q——   N328
There's a thing in the east, that inhabits the south   S508
There's M——y the neat   V94
There's ne're a thriving trader   S581
There's never scarce a party-martyr   P284
There's scarce a bard, that writ in former time   F65
There's some say that we wan, some say that they wan   R2
These few evacuations   D358
These nations had always some tokens   A124
These sheets primeval doctrines yield   G280
These to my blyth indulgent friends   R33
They call me Bourn-bank/A bloody murthering cheet   S606
They who have best succeeded in their rhimes   H477
They're come, ———— alas! those days are come, wherein   O173
Think, Glaucus, you were once a fishing swain   D294
Think not your friend Le H--p to free, sir   L94·8
Thirsting for fame, at the Pierian spring   R86
This alderman in pomp of late   H351
This book contains a full relation   H61
This cloak was cut out in old Oliver's days   M203
This day for solemn sorrow set apart   C178
This day I am ordain'd to die   C440
This day when Phœbus, with his ruddie rays   C226
This day, with joy may Brittish hearts abound   S468·5
This evening, Thyrsis, with it's sultry heat   T154
This Indian weed now wither'd quite   E456
This is the day/Our glorious Anne was crown'd   L299
This is the most joyful time   E20
This is the song most excellent   S467
This is to give notice, I Tom the great scribler   T412
This long vacation how we've thrash'd in vain   E352
This month begins our year, god send it good   M198
This morn the god of wit and joke   S856
This mortal state is full of care, and of perplexity   C305
This motly piece to you I send   G283
This nations sins are many fold   K102
This new-years day, lord, take away   P751
This new year's paper comes to kiss your hands   H110
This noble princess of immortal fame   E137
This once the grateful muse presumptive sends   P532
This princess rare, of ancient pedigree   E235

This rise is made, yet! and we now stand, rank'd   J99
This sacred Song of Songs was penn'd   C229
This sentence, which I introduce   R320
This silver head call'd t' an immortal crown   S337
This song of triumph now I send   S473
This world's a tennis-court, and man's the ball   G239
Thornhill, what miracles are to be wrought   S363
Those British bards appears to me to have sunk   D226
Those stars, and this our elemental earth   M484
Though all the actions of your life are crown'd   D213
Tho' bold the muse, yet scarce she dares assay   T366
Tho' Britain on to ruin runs   E545
Though Britain's hardy troops demand your care   P204
Tho' by birth I'm a slave, yet I'm seldom confin'd   R205
Tho' Dame Religion's such a beauty   O270
Tho' death has done his worst you cannot die   E192
Tho' Europe groans, distress'd with clam'rous din   G214
Tho' fashions in apparel change   D335
Tho' Flandria calls our glorious chief away   L142
Tho' fuddl'd o'er night, the next morning we found   W150
Tho' gloomy thoughts disturb'd my anxious breast   P732
Tho' god a paradise had given   E330
Tho' god in wrath did first a king ordain   C114
Tho' great George be gone o'er, yet to shew his love to us   B23
Tho' great of birth, tho' none can higher trace   W30
Tho' greater stars, plac'd in a higher sphere   B530·5
Tho' grief and fondness in my breast rebel   J76
Tho' Homer in heroic sings   H410
Tho' human pleasures finite are   O237
Tho' long in rural shades retir'd   O31
Tho' money thus reigns ———— as by title divine   C141
Tho' muses court the shady groves and greens   G216
Tho' my affairs, good Master Evans   N317
Tho' my almighty hand sustains in being   S210
Tho' Ovid has given us so many relations   E569
Tho' Phœbus bright, ascended from the sea   N32
Tho' Phœbus does his kindlier warmth refuse   B514
Though Pope has said it, must the world submit   A375
Tho' proud Del—ne, for nameless, partial ends   A198
Tho' rhyme serves the thoughts of great poets to fetter   B76
Tho' sable woe o'ercast the mournful soul   V66
Tho', sacred nymphs, you're free from fond desires   C4
Though Sh---d---n will/Be Sh---d--n still   W143
Tho' strength of genius, by experience taught   D371
Tho' the fam'd errant bard of old   T94
Tho' the hoarse accents of the trumpet's voice   A79
Tho' the martin is a summer bird   M117
Tho' the ungodly senate has decreed   T581
Tho' Trentham's exalted to be a fine lord   N198
Tho' 'twas thy luck to cheat the fatal tree   A158·5
Tho' William was the care of providence   M72
Tho' with Herculean toil a wit   F213
Tho' wond'rous things the female saints pretend   M496
Tho' you conversant are at court   D293
Three buxom dames, of portly size   B68

Thro' all the changing scenes of life   H448

Thorough Bruges and Ghent   N310

Through dreary realms, and shores bereft of light   M34

Through the dark storm, and angry tide   N280

Thro' the wild maze of life's stil-varying plan   N336

Thro' those dread realms, encompass'd round with night   N313

Through winter streets to steer your course aright   G81

Thou art the seed, of a seditious weed   A150

Thou azure god, that dost the trident guide   O27

Thou best of lords, and thou of mortals best   E81

Thou best of poets, and thou best of friends   C78

Thou blest with ev'ry choicest gift in life   A321

Thou chief companion of my cup   E483

Thou city whose aspiring turrets rise   D267

Thou dome, where Edward first enroll'd   T291

Thou enemy, who e'er thou art   B163

Thou evangelic glory quickly dawn   S288

Thou fair fore-runner! of the sun's up-rise   M474

Thou first born sister of the sacred nine   D56

Thou, for whose view these numbers are design'd   W333

Thou, furnish'd with a great sagacious mind   P522

Thou globe of fire intense, amazing vast   E14

Thou god, to whose great memory   N7

Thou grand disposer of all humane things   C555

Thou great disturber of heroick songs   G101

Thou great preserver of men's fame   H458

Thou heav'nly muse, who kind assistance lent   P624

Thou merry muse, that didst of yore   N315

Thou mighty Sol, who in the east ascend   N25, N28

Thou more than awful house, where crouds resort   F125

Thou most distress'd, infatuated town   B571

Thou muse of state hast mourned a banish'd race   H465

Thou, on whose praises I delight to dwell!   L223

Thou Pope; oh popery burning hot   A235

Thou pride of villages whose ponds and groves   E286

Thou sacred queen of Helicon descend   F28

Thou scoundrel dunghill, hence, avaunt   B203

Thou Stanhope, whom no earth cou'd bear   E35

Thou! the bright judge of learning, and the friend   T566

Thou! the polite Tibullus of the age!   O103

Thou tuneful choir whose province 'tis to sing   P593

Thou virgin, heav'nly train, descend and sing   O61

Thou! who dost every thought and wish controul   H42

Thou, who the pangs of my embitter'd rage   E28

Thou wise and learned ruler of our ile   D196

Three dames, when wine, at a collation   H401

Three jolly lads as ere was seen on earth   F132

Three jolly lasses strapping brisk and gay   F133

Three mariners from diff'rent sees   M347

Three times the carline grain'd and rifted   R60

Three weeks, three melancholy weeks had past   B415

Three winters Cambria had with pleasure view'd   D234

Thrice did I hear Britannia's genius shriek   D438

Thrice glorious sir, our sov'reign, lord, and king   P147

Thrice hail great sir, thrice welcome to the land   A157

Thrice happy barque, to whom is giv'n   H49

Thrice happy Job long liv'd in regal state   Y100

Thrice happy swains! stretch'd in this silvan cave   P110

Thrice happy, who free from ambition and pride   B517

Thrice happy yet, (if they the blessing prize,)   G218

Thrice has the spring beheld thy faded fame   A136

Thrice holy lanthorns, whose transcendent light   P1140

Thrice welcome home, thou mighty conqueror   H247

Thrice worthy Bedford, Roxborough, and Fane   O207

Thus anxious for her lord's return   H311

Thus beauty, mimick'd in our humbler strains   B493

Thus do we sailors spend our merry lives   C277

Thus does the maz'd inexplicable round   B492

Thus far of plains manur'd, and heav'nly signs   B196

Thus far, with arms triumphant, have we gain'd   E315

Thus in a Grub Street state, how happy I   D509

Thus in my humble state how happy I   I44

Thus in the triumphs of my pow'r I reign   T501

Thus Kitty, beautiful and young   P1093

Thus nature's frame, and nature's god we sing   B495

Thus Rochester's song,/Which he prophecy'd long   F256

Thus said,/The son of god bows down his awful head   S27

Thus sets the shining planet of the day   E152

Thus spoke the goddess of the fearless eye   T191

Thus spoke to my lady the knight full of care   S904

Thus, Venus once bespoke her son   P82

Thy aid divine, Apollo I implore   D266

Thy bounties, love, in thy soft raptures when   A303

Thy charms, O sacred indolence, I sing   M303

Thy deeds are such, illustrious youth!   O66

Thy forest, Windsor, and the dreadful day   C408

Thy forests, Windsor! and thy green retreats   P987

Thy furrow'd brow, my Pylades, unbend   F98

Thy long neglected voice, sweet Clio, raise   O28

Thy muse, O bard, that wonders tells   A247

Thy son, Melpomine, inspire   B556

Thy virtues O Geneva! yet unsung   B304

Thy volume, Cibber, Iv'e perus'd with care   T128

Thy works, eternal power by whom she sings!   B11

Thy younglings, Cuddy, are but just awake   G69

Thyrsis adest, Meliboe; venit quoque ab urbe Menalcas   G1

Thyrsis, the darling of the fair   W309

Tickell, whose muse ambitious sings   S368

Till now of late, we thought the loud report   B551

'Till now, 'twas thought Sir Isa'c Newton   D300

Time no doubt, all things wears out   L63

Time-comforts are like grass; death hath bereav'd   E196

Timely blossom, infant fair   P217

Tir'd nature's sweet restorer, balmy sleep!   Y24

Tir'd with my spleen tho' with thy numbers pleas'd   E392

Tir'd with the busy follies of the town   M36

Tyr'd with the nauseous follies of the age   G151

Tir'd with the noysome follies of the age   F248

'Tis all a libel – P-xt-n (Sir) will say   P938

'Tis done! – and fate has giv'n the final blow! –   S753

'Tis done: death, stern destroyer, wins the day   L201

'Tis done! the glorious lamp of Britain's fled   W560

'Tis done! ----- Thou awful shade of Britain rise   O203

'Tis done, 'tis finish'd. – This he scarce had said   S28

'Tis even so, the false Hamilla's gone   F271

'Tis granted, sir, you've basely been accus'd   H106
'Tis hard for man, bewilder'd in a maze   R23
'Tis hard my lord that every flirt   L196
'Tis hard to say, if greater want of skill   P806
'Tis needless the records of time to explore   M69
'Tis never in list among miracles put   M275
'Tis no wonder if all honest men should be sower'd
   E557
'Tis not enough in secret to lament   E510
'Tis odd to conceive what a war has been wag'd   W367
'Tis plain the great or rich no power have   N137
'Tis said Poeta nascitur non fit   P476
'Tis so long since from me you have heard, that, God-
   wot   A269
'Tis strange! Must nonsense flow without constraint?
   B300
'Tis strange that protestants of any sort   O169
'Tis strange the miser should his cares employ   P908
'Tis strange to think what multitudes of men   T176
'Tis strange, while all to greatness homage pay   F123
'Tis sweet, when furious storms plough up the mayn
   D189
'Tis the twenty-ninth of May   N233
'Tis to your credit much, my dear, to praise   W134
'Tis true! Great losses for amazement call   P439
'Tis true, I said in amorous rhymes   B51
'Tis true, my friend, what busy fame has told   T591
'Tis true, the wretch that dares to write   L166
'Tis true---when death, fate's minister does call   E155
'Tis well and wisely done, my muse   B318
'Tis well we live in such a fickle place   F29
Titiro, tu d'un faggio ampio al coperto   R254
Tollite cuncta ---- caeptosque auferte labores   P299
T----m H----d awake! and listen well my tale!   A10
To a certain old chapel well known in the town   U2
To a hussar no room was by Charon allow'd   P129
To a thick shade, but such as ne'er inspir'd   H78
To all forreign nations now under the sun   D498
To all freeholders now I write   O262
To all his brethren, whether sitting   L60
To all loyal subjects glad tidings I bring   E567
To all my holy sisterhood, these do with greeting come
   D343
To all nice beauxs, and nicer ladies, who   S74
To all that virtue's holy ties can boast   T345
To all the clergy in this land/Eleven bishops write
   P112
To all the hobling generation   B538
To all the lovers in the city   A323
To all those liv'ry-men of London   L262
To all ye merchants now at land   S16
To all you tories far from court   N125
To arms, to arms, to arms, to arms   O239
To balderdash his old Falernian   B498·5
To Bath the queen a golden charriot draws   P184
To be discarded is indeed an evil   V76
To British ancestry I trow   S770
To change! What is it but to live?   T558
To charm the sense with beauteous scenes of art
   N305
To cure the nation from relaps   H298
To cure the nation of the rot   B295
To cut the teeth, you use a coral   M398

To day a mighty hero, comes to warm   G37
To day as great a soul is fled   E72
To day before a learn'd audience comes   S412
To day ye tunefull nine, who dwell upon   A342
To draw a tinker, esquire and an ape   T519
To dupes I write that stay home   W523
T' exalt the soul, or make the heart sincere   H98
To fabled deities, the dreams of men   S219
To fair Fidele's grassy tomb   C300
To faithless English, and the Dutch a prey   M405
To fill my rising song with sacred fire   P73
To fill the realm with fears of coming woe   W380
To genuine worth, to Parsons let the muse   V51
To get a good peace and a flourishing trade   P754
To give the last amendments to the bill   E479
To god, the world's great patron, first   H445
To guide the wand'ring step, and sketch the plan
   B439
To Hartford, and his learned friends   R89
To heaven altars, men most justly raise   P1123
To heights untower'd, through paths untrod before
   T250
To his dear vassals of the north   P1037
To hush the melancholy voice of war   C366
To Jacob god commandment gave   H446
To jealous love, and injur'd honour's ear   B135
To John Caswal esquire, so brisk and so bold   T343
To joy, to triumphs dedicate the day!   H377
To judge, my lord, from what you've writ   M390
To lean on common oak cou'd Jocelyn bear   O94
To let you know I am your friend   A72
To Lewis, my most Christian son   F272
To lift the low, the proud depress   L17
To list'ning crowds, in former ages   L3
To live secure from party rage and want   P125
To lonely shades and discontented groves   L195
To lonely vales and deep sequester'd woods   O192
To lordings proud I tune my song   D502
To lovers all, in town or city   A324
To-morrow (heav'n permit) I'll steal away   R189
To mourn the loss of a departed friend   Q17
To mournful plaints Brittania turn your muse   E212
To one fair lady out of court   P762
To open all your eyes, and let you know   H295
To our mayor 'twas bruited   B62
To paint the various charms, of various fair   I13
To paths untrod our humour leads   F172
To pay a glorious subject its just right   S328
To please two punks, who freely share their bounties
   T494
To Preston's solemnity many repair   H4
To read these lines a pensive eye prepare   E380
To science sacred, muse, exalt thy lays   J94
To scourge the riot and intemperate lust   D387
To search for times in dark oblivion cast   E333
To shun the jarring tumults of the town   L209
To sing Augusta's glory in extreme   D553
To sing of Albion's great and happy isle   G215
To sing of those blest days when providence   S42
To sink that state the senate does support   B159
To snuff the muse her grateful homage brings   A287
To Sol's bright temple paved with gold   P709
To suit this worthy and judicious age   W553

To take a superficial view of things   P704
To the church and great Anne   B279
To the great dead we shrines and altars give   S340
To the kingdom's content   N79
To thee, auspicious prince! I sing these lays   M147
To thee, blest guardian of the British world   S704
To thee, blest nymph, whom princely courts refine   D522
To thee, dear Dick, this tale I send   W552
To thee, dear James, my lover and my friend   A194
To thee, dear Mac! whose ev'ry wish succeeds   E401
To thee, dear rover, and thy vanquish'd friends   T272
To thee, dear Swift, these spotless leaves I send   T390
To thee, dear youth, in sacred wedlock ty'd   B541
To thee, dear youth, in wedlock ty'd for life   L121
To thee, great author of my infant muse   L174
To thee, great master of the vocal string   W360
To thee great West our isle this tribute send   P631
To thee, I send, my Polyarchus, this   C443
To thee! lov'd maid, with whom I joy to share   A90
To thee, my Arcas, on the rural plain   O231
To thee, my friend, though now perhaps disgrac'd   L126
To thee, my Snape, in these reforming times   A188
To thee O D——n, be these truths addrest   D7
To thee, O father of mankind   H423, H444, H450
To thee, O lord, our god and king   H438
To thee, O lord, we chearful praises sing   B80·5
To thee, O ——, my greatest, cruell'st foe   F33
To thee, Oh knight! in hopes of aid, I send   E413
To thee once more, by duteous raptures prest   E420·5
To thee, rude warrior, whom we once admir'd   C93
To thee, sweet Fop, these lines I send   B326
To thee, sweet songster, my advice I send   S179
To thee, the happy fav'rite of the nine   D383
To these our days, from days of old   P198
To think on our ancestors brave   K28
To this new ballad lend an ear   A263
To toast the fair of Britain's isle   T404
To trivial nymphs while Oxford's tasteless swains   W251
To view this wretched town, what man can live   S705
To wake the soul by tender strokes of art   E386, E406
To warm the mind by virtue's brightest fires   W205
To what a dull and dismal pass   F286
To what a height, O Britain, grew thy fame   B466
To what exalted heights doth heav'n intend   W529
To what intent and purpose was man made   O178
To Whitton's shades, and Hounslow's airy plain   T311
To win the fair, whom most the fair approve   W547
To win your hearts, and gain inglorious praise   L206
To worthies dead for offrings at their urn   S239, S279
To you, dear brothers, we complain   S547
To you, dear brothers, who in vain   S546
To you, dear Damon, long my faithful friend   B605
To you, dear Ormond, cross the seas   B582
To you, dear topers, at the court   C458
To you fair ladies of Dublin   M291
To you, fair nymphs of Venus' train   F73
To you fair traders now a shore   M33
To you, fine folks, at Marlbro' House   N219
To you, German sir, a petition I bring   P194
To you, great sir, in character and fame   E394

To you, great sir, the humble muse presumes   M467
To you in Pæan's fire and virtue's strong   M553
To you my dear friend I this ballad indite   M560
To you my friends, this book is recommended   K9
To you, my lord, whose goodness could excuse   A279
To you, my lords, whase elevation   R100
To you, O Vernon, whom a patriot zeal   B470
To you, right worshipful the brewers!   V2
To you sad wights of Crown and Fleece   F285
To you this humbly I address   C460
To you two 'squires whom we have sent   I47
To you, who know, as yet, no anxious hours   E435
To you who love to range the sylvan scene   G148
To you, ye tories, I address   A102
'Today' see 'To day'.
Tom and Harry and Kentish Tottie   L199
Tom is a fellow to be sure   W472
Tom solemn toll'd ----- the college bells around   S31
Tom was a little merry grig   T318
Tom, when the heat of battle's over   P479
'Tomorrow' see 'To morrow'.
Tonald Bayn her nane dear shoy   H206
Too long I have delay'd, most patient god   T251
Too long, illustrious prince, does Britain moan   N15
Too long provok'd, immortal muse! forgive   H209
Too long provok'd in these censorious times   F177
Too much my heart of beauty's power hath known   O177·5
Too well before thy arm has fought   N260
Too well these lines that fatal truth declare   H21
Touch, my muse, the jarring string   J72
Transient, and vain is fickle fortune's smile   F301
Transported with the muses softer charms   C483
Traulus of amphibious breed   S916
Treason too long contriv'd, too late believ'd   S146
Tremble, ye guilty! Tremble, ev'n the good!   T460
Tremendous Mars! thou awful source of war   T115
Tres quinquaginta, ac sexcentos circiter annos   C301
Tristia cum nati ploraret funera Phœbus   A224
Tritonia! goddess of the newborn skies   B491
Triumphal notes and hymns of joy   H435
Triumphant nine, prepare your cymbals, raise   E222
Troth, gentlemen, few know you better   M524
Troth, master, nothing could have pleas'd me more   H274
Trudging once thro' Temple-Bar   T248
True Britons come hither, let's all join together   E325
True churchmen all pray lend an ear   L314
True English boys be merry   T99
True grace and vertue are such special things   E154
True to thy motto glorious city hail!   I54
True, wou'd but all with thee, my Lollius, join   E387
Trust not, fond maids! those who adore   R252
Tu Sternholde, mi adspira!   K67
Tu suaves mirare modos, numerosq; decentes   D227
Tune ev'ry string, your voices raise   H12
Tuneful Alexis, on the Thame's fair side   H230
Tutela nostræ, qua patet, insulæ   N34
Twa mice, full blythe and amicable   P1073
'Twas at a time when bribery bore the sway   M229
'Twas at the dark and silent hour   S132
'Twas at the dawn, when dreams are sacred held   T144
'Twas at the gates of Calais, Hogarth tells   F198

'Twas at the joyful season of the year   N44
'Twas at the proctor's feast from folly won   G318
'Twas at the silent midnight-hour   L277
'Twas at the silent solemn hour   W503
'Twas at the time, when new returning light   C379
'Twas at their own Apollo's rising dawn   S326
'Twas Heav'n's decree----'tis seal'd----the moment's past   E429
'Twas in St. Edward the confessor's days   D275
'Twas in that season when you've seen   C495
'Twas in that welcome quarter of the year   V104
'Twas in the midst of a dark gloomy night   L259
'Twas in the midst of night, when Joan   P1062
'Twas in the solemn silence of the night   F262
'Twas in the town of London   M154
'Twas near his Sandwich, in his rural seat   S231
'Twas night, as on my bed I waking lay   M362
'Twas not the talent of the sot   S446
'Twas now high noon,/The sun in all his warmer glories shone   D437
'Twas on a joyful day; the gorgeous feast   D47
'Twas on the fatal day that claims a sigh   D483
'Twas on their own Castalian flowry plain   S325
'Twas said of old, deny it now who can   W439
'Twas summer, and, with sultry heat opprest   P8
'Twas thus, of old, the bearded awful sage   B434
'Twas well, when our forefathers did agree   C255
'Twas when the bright guide of day had driv'n   O168·2
'Twas when the swains, to shun the scorching beam   R237
'Tween Britain's wall and Troy's huge wall around   R210
Twelve times hath Sol his annual race begun   D481
Twenty conundrums have o'-late   S775
'Twere well, my Lælius, if I could pursue   D469
Twice has the muse to Walpole told my case   M321
Twice sixteen years hath over past   W446
Twice twenty tedious moons have roll'd away   S112
'Twixt Sally born in Lambeth town   E546
Two against one, when well agreed   J51
Two British wits conspir'd   H9
Two college sophs of Cambridge growth   S809
Two dogs from diff'rent litters come   F7
Two doughty ——s the other day   F140
Two good-natur'd wou'd--be's (two state politicians)   M204
Two kings of great honour, Georgius and Phillip   N183
Two men to Jove their prayers made   A109
Two or three visits, 2 or 3 bows   D208
Two potent heraulds joyntly do proclaim   O199
Two sea-port cities mark Britannia's fame   S100
Two sister springs, from the same parent hill   S578
Two sisters, young and gay, yet chaste   C434
Two weasels had once got an egg by a wile   A113
'Twould seem a little strange, I must confess   P607
Tyrant! if man cannot thy power asswage   B447

U

Ubique gentium & terrarum   M223
Ulysses fled, the darling of her breast   M83
Uncertainty of human fate   M159
Unde novus vates deserta per ardua Pindi   U26
Unde repentino luimus commissa dolore?   C17
Under a lonely yew as Thyrsis lay   G202
Under a myrtle, by fair Isis side   P201
Under the notion of a play you see   S408
Under this stone/Lies a reverend drone   E441
Under this stone, lies Dicky and Dolly   S831
Ungrateful death! an apple gave thee birth   E59
Unhappy fate, and woful time   F169
Unhappy man! by nature made to sway   S663
Unhappy man, thro' life's successive years   O240
Unhappy man! Traitor, I dare not say   T371
Unhappy man! whose ever changing mind   N117
Unhappy man! yoak'd with a wanton wife   F126
Unhappy me amongst the birds of prey   R239
Unhappy minute to us, 'twas that sent   B577
Unhappy prince! born to be fortunes jest   H254
Unhappy ship, thou art return'd in vain   S859
Unhappy state of all things here below   B441
Unkindly leaving the delightful plains   M485
Unskill'd in painting, vain were my essay   M331
Untaught and artless muse arise   O47
Untinsel'd be this verse, nor tagg'd with rhime   F237
Unto my sad complaint give ear   E572
Unto prelatick order you'd ascend   V82
Unto you wanton Edinburgh sparks   E16
Unworthy as I am, how must I boast   H76
Up, rouze your selves, ye nations, praise the lord   D222
Upon a time (ev'n so my nurse   M330
Upon a time, not long ago   S610
Upon a time the fairy elves   F37
Upon a time there was a lord   W559
Upon a time, when poets durst not sing   I5
Upon that happy nation lies a curse   A9
Upon the borders of eternity   A273
Upon the evening of a summers day   S662
Upon the fruitful banks of Thame   S687
Upon the Lord thy burden cast   C146
Upon the mossy grave I sat reclin'd   P656
Upon the southern end of that great hall   D242
Upon the twenty eight of January   E532
Upon this mountain, Lord, of thine   P741
Urania, fairest of the sacred nine   S329
Uranie, puerum memora pietate parentis   L315
Urg'd by the growing vices of the time   A172
Usque adeo insano juvat indulgere labori?   H104

V

Vain are these pomps, thy funeral rites to grace   P670
Vain cares of man! All earthly things how vain!   B432
Vain carnal men make carnal policy   E475
Vain restless man, insatiate in desire   G245
Vain were the task to give the soul to glow   V69
Vandomus Gallorum acies, arma arma frementes   W518
Vario, no more thy sacred skill prophane   A84
Vat be dat machine do make de folk groan-é?   G302
Vaunt not thyself, good Capt. Plume   E371
Vejovis est hominis facie te fallere passus   P304
Ventus, hyperboreo qui congeminatur ab axe   C257
Venus! call'st thou once more to arms?   P897

Venus of love and beauty queen L27
Vestros ante pedes, lacrymarum flumine largo L318
Vext with damn'd law-suits all my abject life B586
Vice once with virtue did engage W511
Victorious heroe's, learned bards excite B341
Victorious Sir, still faithful to thy word P148
Vidimus hæc pueri, juvenes hæc vidimus arva P335
View here the pourtrait of a factious priest V92
View here three brethren in iniquity T253
Virgins of Albion, ye fair female kind C520
Virtue or piety is all a cheat F99
Virtue's the mind's direction – and defence M490
Vis amor est animi, quam lex non ulla coercet H229
Visum est grammaticæ metricis lenire laborem B592,
    B597
Vive diu felix, et laetos redde parentes P296
Vive, Pitcarni, columen camænis O18
Vocalem breviant alia subeunte Latini P1142, V18
Voila vos inspirez qui sans l'avoir predit D284
Vouchsafe, distinguish'd poet, to excuse G130
Vous avez trés-bien fait, mon frere, & sagemēt D282
Vow Allie, what's come ore ye now B286
Vow, sirs, what's a this now come amang us G292
Vulcan my muse to me describe O260

W

Waes me, auld Reikie, we man part P151
Wake all thy fire, celestial muse H65, H75, H364
Wake Britain, 'tis high time to wake T69
Wake! m' ambitious soul awake! P1059
Wake sprightly muse, wake sweetly warbling lyre B342
Wake the British harp, again P210
Wake vocal shell, awake melodious muse B345
Walking in Saturn's goodly fane one morn P998
Waller, as sweet a bard, as ever sung! C75
Walliwafaw your fingers, death P157
Walpole, who com'st of ancient race M91
Wandring I went alongst a river side P118
Wanton loves, around me sporting S214
War happens not among the great M330
War, horrid war, his brazen throat extends P560
War is my theme; celestial maids! retire B89
War may bring better times B292
Warm'd by th' ethereal ray th' indulged muse P1144
Was ever a nation besotted like this P135
Was ev'ry Christian's conduct open laid F39
Was ne'er in Scotland heard nor seen R37
We address you to day in a very new fashion A55
We all the drunkards of the nation P160
We are of new false prophets warn'd P658
We are told by the town, that a man of great note
    O279
We are told of a sphinx who in ages of old M388
We Cupid, king, whose arbitrary sway S372
We had great wars with France and Spain G235
We have no great cause to be vaunting P183
We have not yet forgot sir D419
Wee have too kinges; the one is true P1034
We loyal hearts of Dublin C-----e, P1
We loyal subjects, may it please ye T427

We may reasonably fear a sad turn in the nation W404
We Mohocks rule the world by night M395
We must resign (heav'n his great soul does claim) E69
We Persians like, the rising sun adore C487
We read, in profane and sacred records M121
We receiv'd your advice as good daughters should do
    U17
We saw great sir, when every year you wore W280
We sing the man, who from clove-pudding D395
We slept: that was the hour th' almighty took M97
We that farm your honours ground H414
We the hundred and fifty elect of the gown L233
We, the long heads of Gotham, o'er our merry cups
    meeting B507
We the lord mayor of —— town I48
We trace war's image thro' its various scenes E460
We, who not long ago profest B567
We who were never yet at quiet W392
We'll fix King George upon the throne E586
We'll remember the men H125
We're a nation of fools, who are govern'd by knaves
    T263
Wearied by continuous strife M321
Wearied with long attendance on the court B80
Weary'd with vain pursuits, and humble grown M329
Weary of life, with restless thoughts opprest, T531
Wedlock, oh! curss'd uncomfortable state L290, P488
Weep all you passive slaves, no more repine E147
Weep, all you schismaticks, since he is gone S671
Weep ev'ry eye, and ev'ry tongue deplore P107
Weep, Scotland, weep! great cause thou hast to mourn!
    E49
Weep ye mountains and ye vallies E125
Weeping o'er thy sacred urn P217
Welcome brave monarch to this happy isle G132
Welcome brave warrior, welcome to the name C351
Welcome, dear friend, the joy of ev'ry heart P168
Welcome dear madam to our gloomy shead C312
Welcome genial day! S590
Welcome great George, unto the British crown E297
Welcome great hero from the Belgick plains D501
Welcome, great hero! from the best of queens C364
Welcome great hero to our British shore R209
Welcome, great monarch, to th' imperial crown R221
Wellcome home, from wars alarms H122
Welcome my bosom-friends, once more we're met
    S477
Welcome, my lord, heav'n be your guide R45
Welcome, my lord, thrice welcome from afar B171
Welcome my Thyrsis to thy native plains P461
Welcome, nice artist, to these learn'd retreats E513
Welcome, O welcome, thou celestial maid P134
Wellcome October, wellcome twenty day P674
Welcome the day which gave the hero birth E343
Welcome the month whose kalends bring B393
Welcome, the returning brave! M533
Welcome, thou brave defender of our right C172
Welcome thou friendly earnest of fourscore F112
Welcome! thou guardian genius of our isle C350
Welcome, thrice welcome most illustrious day P679
Welcome to Scotia's plains, dear injur'd youth P1058
Welcome to town, thou most esteem'd of friends M133
Welcome to us great prince, welcome I say P646

Welcome, welcome, brother debtor W469
Welcome ye shades, and ev'ry darker grove L286
Wellcome ye zephyrs from your southern shores! S785
Well Ch--pp---n, is it come to this B236
Well fare the hand which to our humble sight O220
Well fare thee, Allan, who in mother tongue R86
Well! – has your spite broke out at length? S137
Well! I confess it, I have said the play'rs P484
Well, if it be my time to quit the stage P898
Well, laureat, was the day in clover spent? O100
Well met Alexis! 'tis a glorious day B498
Well met, old friend! Time was when thou and I P69
Well met, right noble sir: what do you ail? J53·5
Well, now I see a man may be mislead O5
Well -- of all plagues which make mankind their sport W417
Well play'd, my dear friends, (for the catholick cause) F253
Well Ralph, howe'er your pleas'd to strive T413
Well, since my venerable dad is C98
Well – since we are met, our business is to try P446
Well! Sm-----y, since thou wilt expose O77
Well! thanks to my stars! I'm at last all alone S602
Well then it's o'er, and all the tricks undone D81
Well then th' expected hour is come at last M500·5
Well, Tickell! thou has found it out B584
Well, 'tis as Bickerstaff has guest S832
Well, 'tis as learned Coats has guest S834
Were I at rhyme as great a witch A251
Were I dear madam, who am none S70
Were I, dear M-----w, who am none L156
Were I Sir Robert, in your station M307
Were I some raking wit, whose talent lyes E533
Were tunes but such as in preceding days N173
Westward from fair Augusta's city, lies C541
What a bustle is here/About Madam Cadiere M280
What a bustle we make about high-church and low-church? W74
What a cursed crew have we got N185
What a diverting sight it wou'd have been L154
What a pother you keep about Molly M561
What a race were you running from bad into worse N178
What a racket is here V6
What ails thee Forbes that thou canst not bear A165
What all concerns I advertise C99
What am I? how produc'd? and for what end? A290
What, and how great, the virtue and the art P893
What? are at length the doubtful nations freed? S371
What! are the muses dumb, when 'tis agreed P693
What art divine the shining thimble found H113
What art thou, spleen, which everything dost ape? F141
What awkward judgments must they make of men H156
Vat be dat machine do make de folk groan-é? G302
What! Billy, still alive, who thought to meet G8
What blessed legacy was this B456
What Booker doth prognosticate L310
What bounds to sorrow shall the muse propose C188
What! brib'ry still! What! brib'ry still your theme! M284
What bright empyreal scene is this! N348

What can so many heavy deaths portend! B170
What can the British senate give C247
What care and industry the dove requires D315
What child has not heard of a conquering tour S599
What clamour's here about a dame W486
What, Clifford dead! no poet to rehearse E86
What contradictious notions now are spent W268
What could our young dramatic monarch mean W310
What crowns the fruitful marriage bed with joy R280
What culture best the flow'ry race improves G13
What curious webs the well-fed worms enclose S462
What cursed planet rul'd when I was born O266
What, dames, who so well the world has known M109
What dark and dismal shade is this B378
What diff'rent subjects diff'rent poets move! S25
What din and noise is this I hear C32
What dire offence from am'rous causes springs P941
What direful, dismal, mourning's this doth fill E281
What dismal news? what sad allarms do sound? S143
What dismal sound strikes mine affrighted ears! E133
What dismal tydings is this now I hear N202
What do me see! what do me read! A312
What doctor, if great Carteret condescends L138
What! durst the Frenchman such a sentence breathe P257
What ecstasies her bosom fire! G79
What Europe owes to Marlborough's martial flame M84
What eyes o'reflow with tears! that he is gone E156
What favourite muse shall I invoke H201
What former friend may ease my troubled thought M95
What frantick madness has possest mankind O2
What frenzy has of late possess'd the brain G18
What gars thee look sae dowf, dear Sandy say R82
What generous warrior of distinguish'd fame? O52
What gentle muse, Shall I use I2
What gives the maiden blush its loveliest dye D381
What god, what genius did the pencil move P977
What grief and wo do's now my soul oppress E63
What has this bugbear death to frighten man D458
What haste! young man, why up so soon i' th' morn? D277
What hideous shrieks are these, which pierce mine ears C388
What hurricanes disturb our isle? O257
What is greater joy and pleasure S15
What is it to be rich and great? W190
'What is nobility?' – Wou'd you then know D15
What! is the parliament dissolv'd at last? F297
What is the thing our natures doth require C502
What! is there yet a place below A364
What joy did England once receive M543
What kings henceforth shall reign, what states be free T310
What lust of malice, what malicious spite P1135
What madness, Britons, to suppose O70
What madness, countrey-men, inspires? H315
What makes a happy bridal; from what seed O142
What makes an English sat'rist loosely write E336
What makes thee look so sad? Dear Sandy say R86
What man are you that dares to come this way sir? S1

What man renown'd! what British worthy's praise Y2
What man? What heroe praise attains C62
What man with thirst of glorious acts would burn E8
What may delight the plains, beneath what signs B195
What mean these horrid visions of the night? P650
What mean these loud aërial cracks I hear? B155
What mean these sad looks and this sighing B556
What means my dearest, my sweet lovely creature G113
What means that quick repeated sigh? A76
What means the warlike Mars thus to appear E107
What means this dismal sound, that march so slow J92
What means this dreadful bustle on the shore D396
What means this mingled pomp on sea and land? T339
What means this secret, yet insulting pride P634
What means this solemn damp quite thro' the land W24
What means this tyrant, death, to trample down E55
What measures shall affliction know? P897
What melancholy rumour's this I hear? H233
What monsters nature does afford! R214
What moonshine or trade-wind hath blown thee here G15
What mournful muse, who knows so well E233
What mournful scene is this which doth appear? F306
What mournful sound is this doth reach mine ears E234
What muse shall I invoke, to help me sing E273
What must I do alas? I am undone! F252
What! must poor harrass'd Britain never rest D323
What mystic arts support a female reign T269
What nation e'er can hope for happiness W562
What news from London, says my friend? T271
What news is this flys up and down E327
What news, my friend, from your serene retreat R264·5
What noise is this? Sure 'tis Wood's dismal knell F304
What noise is this, that interrupts my sleep? B527·2
What num'rous blessings does god's law bestow A365
What object tempts my serious friend to smile? A267
What old Menalcas at his feast reveal'd S571
What place is this I've fixt my feet upon? E62
What pleasing harmony invite's the ear B411
What pow'r of words can equal thy renown O46
What pow'rs of nature, and what wond'rous arts P1159
What profit is in parentage? what good P188
What raskal's this dar be so bold G253
What riddles are the favours of a crown? S291
What rumour's this, as does our ears amuse? E157
What rumour's this that does our ears amuse? E159
What sacred pomp is this invades my eye E42, E229
What say you to our schemer fine? G178
What senseless scribler, did presume to write A95
What, shall a saucy rhyming dunce, sirs A57
What, shall Bellona bid her thunder cease T81
What, shall I always hear, and never write? L139
What! shall one man the nation's genius raise P615
What, shall the croud his injur'd name blaspheme G105
What sighs, what groans, are those I hear always? S529

What sight is this does every one behold? N29
What silly Murtagh wrap't in livid gloom? S45
What silly numbskull was't that did indite S55
What! Sinai's thunders on our pentecost? W556
What soil the apple loves, what care is due P237
What spatious veins inrich the British soil Y3
What! still be plagu'd and never take the scourge S725
What! still intent on bus'ness, books, and rhimes? N272
What strange disorder often springs T373
What strange impetuous storms of state V63
What stranger's this? and from what region far? G128
What strange confus'on at this time G217
What stile, what language, suits the poet's lays T563
What sudden damp has seiz'd upon my soul D224
What sudden heat inspires my lab'ring mind? M122
What sullen planet rul'd the direfull day M545
What swain is he, who merits double praise A164
What tender language, can my fancy find? H167
What thanks to thee, supreme above H425
What the dire itch of scribbling can restrain? C311
What thing is this I see and hear R224
What tho' but rais'd from dust, thou human mould S272, S323, S324, S327, S341, S347
What tho' I am a courtly lass D325
What tho' my name is toss'd about D464
What tho' no fabl'd deities are found M153
What tho' no pious tears nor vows can save E74
What! though we justly fun'ral pomp disuse E292
What thought, far less expression, can I find C304
What tongue can tell or pen express the pain C461
What tribute to thy temple, Lord H442
What true born Scot, but will be glad to see K46
What uncouth ardour in my bosom grows? H181
What various arts attempt the am'rous swain R207
What various styles to diff'rent strains belong D11
What various wiles, what diff'rent schemes are try'd A329
What weighty charge, O Mirza, 'mongst these towers A291
What well-wrought webs the reptile race infold R264
What wild opinions have possest mankind W63
What will the world at length come to S68
What, William dead! – Unthinking man forbear F163
What with new charms the flow'ry race improves G11
What wou'd my humble comrades have me say? P1084
What yet in tears? The fair Amestris still C496
What's this I hear, great De Veil breath'd his last E99
Whate'er to private offices we owe E425
Whatever calm retreat you chuse N267
Whatever person draws an ace N51
Whatever schemes in politicks arise O241
Whatever wicked atheists teach us G232
When a holy black Suede, the son of Bob S938
When a true son of church, and Tom-a-Becket Y14
When abandoned mockers and scriblers conspire A239
When Abrah'm, full of sacred awe H421
When Æsop's eldest born, first took his birth L190
When all the kingdom wanted grace P1146
When all was wrapt in dark mid-night M60

When all was wrapt in one continued night P54
When all was wrapt in sable night G96
When angry death glares in your face L148
What Anna and the Stuarts were? Their names P137
When Anna first (the glory of our isle) H10
When Anne, a princess of renown G181
When any great and famous man does die E168
When arts and sciences look low'ring down P87
When as Aurora did dispel F169
When as Qu---- A---- of great renown N90
When as Queen Robin rul'd this land N186
When, at the first, good heav'n created man M151
When at the first I step'd upon the stage S661
When awful Johnson on th' improving stage S81
When Bajazet was quell'd by Tamerlane S455
When beasts could every office do G243
When beasts could speak in times of yore C367
When beasts could speak, the learned say S804
When beauty shines with a triumphant air F227
When Bion, gentlest bard! resign'd his breath P1040
When blazing stars, or comets in the skies E262
When Blenheim and Ramellies wond'rous fields O226
When blooming youth, and rosy health combine R22
When B----n will not with the laws dispense C331
When bounteous heaven with such a lib'ral hand A367
When boys at Eton once a year S366
When B---- perceiv'd the beautiful dames N113
When bright Apollo, exil'd from the sky J9
When bright Apollo's flaming car had run C287
When bright Aurora shone with ruddy hue W10
When Britains bulwarks humbles Britain's foes N114
When Britain's isle was over-run B404
When Britain's lyon lull'd supinely lay H119
When Britannia, bright and gay P252
When British horse, but chiefly blue B38
When brooding fates design'd to bless the earth B199
When by th' assistance of some heavenly ray B316
When by the help of canvas wings I'd flown W201
When Charles, from anarchy's retreat C194
When Charles the fifth, so glorious for renown F69
When Charly of late in a damnable fright P470
When church was prov'd to have no pow'r S23
When Churchill on Onarda's plain W296
When circling time more sprightly grows R230
When Clayton, call'd to an immortal crown S343
When conquering Spain before the Indians stood W401
When covenanted reformation P588
When crowding thoughts no utterance can find T527
When Cutts is dead, shall none but ballad verse E473
When Dædalus of old with wings display'd H66
When dames of Britain shall espouse P1136
When daring poets would encomiums raise W8
When dawning nature in the world's first age T405
When death appears, the stoutest man's a coward H296
When death, great Charles the second's head, laid low O250
When death prepares to strike his fatal dart E266
When deeds like thine our just encomiums raise T352
When dread Tiberius sway'd the Roman world L270
When England was not safe in its own strength at home L208

When England's peace was threatened with a war S648
When Europe's peace was basely bought and sold O76
When Europe's sav'd, in silence can we sit? R240
When evening shades invite to open fields E531
When faction late Britannia's isle o'erspread A234
When faction loud was roaring N223
When fair Astræa to the earth descends W296
When fam'd Augustus did Rome's empire bless D552
When fam'd Augustus rul'd the Roman state B408
When fate some mighty genius has design'd H86
When female fury reunites it's force S51
When female virtues make the world admire W406
When, fir'd by novelty, and beauty's eyes R117
When first Britannia's slavish chain was broke W7
When first omnipotence his pow'r display'd P267
When first poetick broils grew high B104
When first religion triumph'd o'er the mind J49
When first the law of god was given P746
When first the muses deign'd t' inspire E421
When first the pow'r eternal brought to light F210
When first the 'squire, and tinker Wood S898
When first the Tatler to a mute was turn'd T60
When first the world from the black chaos rose S193
When first this doubtful task I did engage S662
When first this duel reach'd the tender ears C444
When first Ulysses from Calypso fled A69
When flagrant scandals o'er the world prevail T432
When flesh and blood are in their prime K35
When foes are o'ercome, we preserve them from slaughter S902
When foes obdurate grow, and treaties fail M349
When fools and knaves in scandals do unite L8
When for our fathers sins, by angry heaven F299
When France near pierc'd the empire to the heart H271
When from dark nothing heaven the world did make A253
When from his breast, brave Harley drew the knife T394
When, from unruly passions, women rail L273
When full 'tis round, when empty long W164
When furious Gauls attempted to consume A359
When Gaul with force and fraud was making way M542
When genial beams wade thro' the dewy morn R41
When George, the great elector of Hanover D558
When George with all his noble train P1116
When glorious Anna's happy reign began B80·5
When god almighty had his palace fram'd D540
When god at first was Israel's king F169
When god created th' earth, and ev'ry thing A314
When god decreed the higher orbs above E283
When god first, temp'ring mortar, moulded man M149
When god in Eden's happy shade D562
When good old Saturn banished from above P1038
When good Queen Bess did rule this land N88
When gracefull Judith, conscious of her charms P259
When Grantown and Bathon, as story records M462
When grave divinity thought fit T324
When great Anna rul'd the nation R155

When great Apollo's learned fav'rites dye   L319
When great Augustus govern'd ancient Rome   P1081
When great Eliza fill'd the British throne   B338
When great men dy'd the custom was of old   S689
When Greece, my lord, with tides of glory swoll'n   A168
When Greece, the muses native soil   M195
When grief intrusive does thy peace invade   S673
When guilty consciences do knaves accuse   H358
When Hangie saw death drawing near   P162
When happy plenty, the effect of peace   C61
When he that ought the halcyon laws to guard   I9
When heaven afflicts man must complain   N131
When heav'n corrects, shall man complain   E143
When heav'n has once with rich profusion join'd   H404
When heav'n incens'd with-held his rain   V52
When heaven reveals it self to mortal eyes   B349
When her Britannia wept Eliza's doom   S489
When her nain shell to Edinburgh went   J70
When his lov'd Germans George was forc'd to leave   L117
When Homer's gods together fight   P699
When honour'd heads call'd t' an immortal crown   S346
When Horace so divinely sings   T395
When I beheld the royal martyr slain   F57
When I beheld the sad procession go   E131
When I, in feeble verse, essay'd   D473
When I my exit from the world had made   O265
When I took in hand a pen for to write   H198
When in some curious gallery we stand   D51
When in sweet slumbers on my bed I lay   B4
When in the rites to the great dead we joyn   S265
When injur'd heroes suffer in their fame   H211
When injur'd honour bids its vengeance rise   E363
When Israel's army pass'd the dreadful stream   D109
When it was grown to dark mid-night   M59
When Janny Geddes, well did mark   H258
When Jemmy the second, not Jemmy the first   N200
When John the Baptist had prepar'd the way   M557
When Jove had measur'd out the spacious earth   C500
When Judah's stubborn race disdain'd to own   H165
When Juno, Pallas and the Cyprian queen   D466
When Juno, Venus, Pallas, strove   D2
When justice holds no more the scales   C57
When Keen and Quadra club'd their wits   E24
When kind informers new chimeras start   R24
When last I parted, tho' I seem'd t' agree   L284
When last we met, you sir, thro' manly pride   S168
When learning's triumph o'er her barb'rous foes   J85
When Lewis strove as all agree   P643
When Lewis the great/Had heard of the fate   F255
When Liffey backward rolls her muddy streams   G227
When lordly witlings bounce and chatter   T328
When loud-tongu'd vertue calls for our applause   P448
When lovely Cælia had resign'd   K37
When Lowbred of Rochdale, good people, sat down   B618
When lust and rage usurp'd the human breast   P1134
When luxury and lust cou'd once enslave   M365
When Mago, learn'd in deep deceit   W311
When man became impure and fell   B540
When many shams and tricks beside   M160

When Maro's lyre was in fame's temple hung   D71
When matters grew ripe for grave consultation   L1
When men, for want of courage and of sense   K16
When men of high-rais'd merits are to die   M470
When men of mettle thought it nonsense   R96
When men of parts, with indignation fir'd   R333
When men were taking pains to please their wives   S772·5
When midnight's silent, solemn hour   P761
When 'midst the myriads of his angel train   S253
When mighty chiefs, for mighty deeds renown'd   S175
When mony, and manners, were both a decaying   P486
When music, heavenly maid, was young   C295
When Naboth's vineyard look'd so fine   G10
When nature had drest up the trees alamode   S747
When nature prompts, and all the world's on fire   C164
When nature yet in embrio lay   M319
When noise and clamour gets the upper hand   A248
When numerous prodigies prevail   O30
When old King Harry youthful grew   W207
When on my mind I turn my studious eye   P200
When on some antique medal's dimner brass   V36
When on the royal head the crown devolv'd   S249
When on the stage Bayes bids th' eclipse advance   P1006
When on us heav'n show'r'd blessings down   F207
When Orpheus, as old poets tell   O251
When ought such observation draws   L123
When our gallants are preparing   D237
When party-rage o'er silent truth prevails   P547
When passions sleep, and every care's at rest   P576
When patriots fall, the most degen'rate age   S715
When Phebus shon with warmest rays   S222
When Phæbus with enliv'ning warmth prevails   P23
When Pierce Renegado came first to the town   B54
When pious Joshua Israel's people led   B530·7
When pious spleen, and godly jar   P120
When poignant satire lash'd a guilty age   P271
When Poll first mounted on the stage   P716
When pompous luxury and lazy pride   F277
When pop'ry was pull'd down in days of yore   P170
When popish priestcraft in a cruel reign   W80
When power divine, the earth and sea had fram'd   S52
When press'd by fate inferior mortals bow   B372
When princes, charm'd with peace, enjoy the throne   M39
When princes, fam'd for birth and merit, climb   N46
When proud fanaticks bore the sway   T500
When punch, that inspires us with wit and with gladness   W163
When purpled monarchs fall, the sons of verse   V61
When radiant Sol in occident declines   A7
When raging vice and restless discord reign'd   C517
When rebellious usurpation   D87
When Robin rul'd the British land   L94·3
When rogues of all sorts are thus fairly discarded   H416
When Rome, my lord, in her full glory shone   Y72
When Rome took thought, and her no god nor man   C490
When Rome was lash'd by Juvenal's sharp lines   A86

INDEX OF FIRST LINES

When Rome was rising into pow'r and fame A286
When Rome was Rome, and in its glory L181
When royal Anne resign'd her breath M519
When royal James in long process R211
When royal Jason and the Aragonauts A360
When, royal youth, must we be blest again I21
When sable clouds on racking winds do fly C356
When sable fame great Anna's death declar'd P680
When sad Britannia fear'd of late O181
When saints depart, and leave their earthly bed E90
When satyrs daily lash with honest rage S75
When savage Goths from Rhine return P1137
When Saxon princes England's sceptres bore A373
When scorching Phœbus had half run his course P258
When scribes to reason said good night W97
When sea and land shall disagree D494
When seventeen hundred is join'd to two ones M106
When shrewd star-gazers chance to spy C214
When silent show'rs refresh the pregnant soil R34
When Sol with his beams, had the meadows adorn'd, L29
When some by fraud and some by stealth W122
When some illustrious nuptial Gordian's tyed S242
When sorrows in the soul tempestuous rage S557
When souls are struck with beauteous heav'nly forms D359
When sovereign commons princes made N4
When spoil, corruption, every nameless lust V55
When Sultan Mahomet Han the scepter sway'd M357
When swift wing'd Time his circle had begun V118
When the almighty, from his heav'nly throne B134
When the almighty went out of his place C488
When the best of all queens that e're fill'd a throne W555
When the bright flame, that fires the patriot heart R262
When the bright world was fram'd, and all things plac'd H409
'When the cock crew, he wept' – Smote by that eye Y32
When the first sparks, at the creator's call O32
When the good man was won to so gracious a deed D89
When the grand p——er arriv'd in town N334
When the grave saints had wisely fix'd on three C554
When the great founder this vast pile began S301
When the great Julius on Britannia's strand E495
When the great three, the highest heav'ns dread lord S275
When the rebellious rout their god assail'd R142
When the Reverend Paul M296
When the spring of the year had arriv'd at its prime T490
When the sun darting gentle western light M14
When the twenty brave pleaders, cull'd out of the throng N98
When the whole sacred choir, the virgin nine S264
When th' world was so wicked that drinking and roaring T96
When these my doggrel rhimes you chance to see R8
When thro' the Ram, Sol takes his swift career B153
When time had freed me from my childish years W267

When Titan with his splendid rays had blest C319
When to my house you come dear Dean S418
When to retrieve the glory of our crown W4
When to that dear, but inauspicious bow'r B356
When to the temple we repair H430
When Torrington, to save our fleet L257
When travelling up and down my lane P642
When tuneful ladies strike the trembling lyre F143
When two brother starlings shall piss in a quill W410
When two forlorn st----tmen, by accident met N83·5
When two great friends are once to passion prone J21
When universal nature I survey B131
When verdant honours crown a publick head O238
When virtue from the busy world retires C422
When virtue in her infancy appear'd S354
When vertue's standard ecclesiasticks bear S98
When we reflect what desolation M140
When we the tidings eagerly receiv'd N6
When weekly bills increase, and here, and there Z2
When whimsy got into the head C12, H475
When will corruption cease? the nation cries G247
When winter's midnight darkness spreads the skies G327
When with attentive thought and curious eye C425
When women deviate from strict virtue's rules F91
When W——on cants, and L——g bauls B21
When worldly cares my pensive soul opprest W69
When worth, like yours, with native candour join'd M88
When you have a fat parson that's fleshy and new R145
When youth or beauty perish e'er they bloom S460
Whence comes it, *** that each pretending fool D385
Whence comes it, Walpole, that a soul, like thine M86
Whence did this dreadfull monster come? S144
Whence is the cause Britannia droops her head? H306
Whence is't, Mæcenas, that so few approve S158
Whence, madam, all this indignation now? L19
Whence sprung this glorious frame? or whence arose M188
Whence this sad pomp? the mighty cause declare P555
Whence this tumultuous noise? these dire alarms? V56
Whence this unwonted transport in my breast? A133
Whence, Windsor, this diffusive grace B143
Whene'er my muse attempts to sing E399
Whene'er you fought the haughty foes were broke T347
Whenever the all-gracious providence S348
Where Avon rolls its brown unsettled flood B451
Where bold and graceful soars, secure of fame T296
Where can the muse a sure protection find H43
Where erst Knight-Templars made their fam'd abode C390
Where gentle Thames thro' stately channels glides D236
Where Hermus' waters wash the Lydian strand W435
Where is our Lord! – 'twas here our Lord was laid L40
Where is th' asswaging pow'r that verse is said E374
Where is the tuneful tribe that sang so well S741
Where is your mourning, Tholsel, where is your sable hue F291

INDEX OF FIRST LINES

Where is't thou darling of the world   H453
Where Isis's streams in pleasing murmurs glide   A217
Where Kensington high o'er the neighb'ring lands   T288
Where Kensington's inviting structures lie   T486
Where lillies were growing   P84
Where Memphian tombs their royal mummies keep   P468
Where now be dose brag-boasters   E342
Where Paris boasts her polite scrapes   W408
Where patriot-hearts once naked to your sight   T516
Where proud Augusta, empire of the great   H111
Where Thames profuse, and lavish of his charms   A313
Where Thames with pride beholds Augusta's charms   S111
Where, where, degen'rate country-men – how high   G17
Where wholesom pot-herbs flourish all around   B287
Where's now the venerable oak   G302·5
Whereas a tribe of young backbitters   I53
Whereas good learning was design'd   P1103
Whereas, in late King George's reign, it was our fate to miss   M332
Whereas some friends of mine, confess'd   D526
Whereas the nation has address'd   P694
Whereas you were never marry'd, tho' come to the years of five and twenty   R169
Where-e'er Hibernia's tuneful lyre is strung   S401
Wherein, great Jove, have we thy anger mov'd   I58
Whether by fame or inclination drove   H115
Whether, possess'd of Circe's art   P122
While, active for the public weal   D529
While all the world to this day   B165
While anxious Europe trembled with alarms   B83
While at thy table, Lord, I sup   P739
While baleful fever, with progressive rage   M328
While bards renown'd dire feats of arms rehearse   T108
While beauty claims the love-resounding shell   P570
While blooming spring descends from genial skies   S394
While born to bring the muse's happier days   C300
While bravely single in fair virtue's cause   M165
While Bribewell every art with Jobson us'd   C535
While brick-layers hail thee, in the throng   W270
While Britain hears the trump of fame   B591
While Britain mourns, and pays her grateful tears   E405
While Britain's monarch does her state support   T61
While British crowds their loyal tongues employ   E503
While busy mortals, with the worthless crowd   B90
While calmer C–bb–r ceases dire debate   O89
While Cam and Isis at your royal feet   P5
While Charles, with his youthful charms   O221
While cringing crowds at faithless levees wait   W426
While crouds of nobles fill the royal dome   P649
While crouds of princes your deserts proclaim   A27
While, D****! here you prop our falling state   R157
While dear Alexis strives in tuneful strain   L279
While disappointed Caleb swells with rage   C442
While distant climates mourn their fate   C22
While dull poetasters are chiming   E549
While Europ's menac'd with disputes & jar   I65
While Europe's various realms your virtues own   N271

While ev'ry British heart a tongue employs   E507
While faction rages with envenom'd spite   C349
While faction with its baleful breath proclaims   S121
While factious feuds, loud strife and fierce debate   P1128
While fame no more his bosom fires   N276
While fanaticks, and papists, and quakers agree   C175
While fancy leads her gayer sons astray   H144
While flying o'er the golden strings   N275
While from their lays our modern bards exclude   C221
While frowning Mars our smiling isle surrounds   C200
While gloomy winter the sad muse forbids   V54
While Gothick arms begin t' infest the times   E504
While half the globe is shook with wars and arms   A190
While homeward bound brave Peddie makes his way   M118
While in the realms of everlasting night   L135
While kings and nations on thy counsels wait   R301
While life rolls on, to chace dull cares away   M506
While, mad with vengeance, on th' Albanian hills   B230
While many a bard of Phœbus' warbling throng   V74
While much distinguish'd you, my lord, support   E399
While my dear master, far frae hame   M404
While my sad lines in mournful numbers flow   P117
While Nassau's most auspicious name   D229
While no repulse thy courage can abate   H184
While none more gratefully embrac'd   M498
While now four lusters at the helm of state   M85
While other poets, hir'd to sing   G137
While others sing the fortune of the great   Y109
While others, soaring on a lofty wing   D22
While over arts unrivalled you preside   W289
While, own'd by you, with smiles the muse surveys   C299
While Oxford's name from clouds of danger breaks   C66
While peace, and war, and turns of state   S474
While poets sing of doves, and Philomel   T36
While pow'r triumphant bears unrival'd sway   F40
While Pult'ney still the publick cause sustains   P519
While rival queens disturb the peaceful stage   E379
While Rome, her genius to enflame   N264
While sable night on the star sprangled skies   H207
While Scota's tribes, on hills, in glens complains   P525
While shepherds watch'd their flocks by night   H447
While some for int'rest plough the foaming deep   T499
While some in odes their tuneful tribute raise   M510
While some in tuneful numbers sound the praise   G291
While some their spoils from battle bring   P633
While some with Cæsar's praise defile the page   C394
While Stanhope's praise I try to sing   T478
While still your rural scenes your eye delight   N285
While strife subsists 'twixt Cibber and the pit   W298
While swarms of panegyricks on thee pour   M190
While the amazed world, admiring, sees   P561
While the amazing deeds my soul pursues   N327
While the full breast swells with unutter'd woe   P691
While the great-vulgar shine with borrow'd rays   A215
While thousands, crowding with a grateful strife   S403
While threaten'd with ruin at home and abroad   M567
While thy epistles, to reform the age   S21
While thy most fruitful labours pass about   B476

55

While to new honours you, unenvy'd, soar   E492
While tow'ring bards the fate of heroes sing   W564
While venal pens and factious scribes   F46
While vice and folly bear imperial sway   D465
While, Walpole, thou'rt engag'd in Britain's cause   S40
While wanton love to others is a theme   P1178
While we to Anna's urn the tribute bring   P584
While widow'd nations your protection court   H243
While wild ambition dictates lawless claim   W272
While with a strong, and yet a gentle hand   W23
While with our names the world's so free   E367
While, with the public, you, my lord, lament   T208
While yet expecting the returning day   S442·2
While you, alone, the reins of empire hold   T440
While you and I were cordial friends   D272
While you, dear Paulus, sacrifice your rest   G147
While you, dear sir! from marriage bonds enlarg'd   C345
While you, dread sir, whom partial heav'n denies   A193
While you, great author of the sacred song   O67
While you, great patron of mankind, sustain   P881
While you, great sir, our sovereign's counsels share   H348
While you, in fair Augusta, justly great   E404
While you in town your precious moments spend   H175
While you, my dear, with philosophic eyes   D407
While you, my friend, the noisy town approve   M487
While you, my Lollius, amidst cares and strife   D324
While you, my lord, amidst a chosen few   N346
While you, my lord, bid stately piles ascend   G88
While you, my lord, for others welfare born   Y71
While you, my lord, from Britain's coasts retire   W204
While you my lord the rural shades admire   A39
While you, my lord, with an extensive hand   T338
While you on Liffy emulate Saint-James   O104
While you, perhaps, sage Littleton explore   E384
While you require, I dare not, sir, refuse   L130
While you with Lady Betty drank Bohee   W12
While you with lenient hand, around impart   T165
While your comrades abroad/Are plowing the main   B40
While your dul lines in senseless numbers flow   T361
While youth your poet once inspir'd   N262
Whilome a merchant at St. Dennis liv'd   M104
Whileom I sung two memorable men   B578
Whilom in Oxford, an old chuff did dwell   C245
Whilom in strain Miltonic Christ-Church bard   D533
Whilst bloody wars by myghty chifes [!] ware wag'd   I55
Whilst British council, steer'd with arduous care   S161
Whilst careful crowds your levees wait   W293
Whilst cool philosophy sat musing   C239
Whilst doubty Bob with muckle might   C367
Whilst Drake from darkness labours to retrieve   M152
Whilst early larks soar'd up on high   R265
Whilst Europe round us pants with dread alarms   G128
Whilst Europe trembling for its doubtful state   B151
Whilst Europe, waiting for the great event   M144
Whilst fierce Bellona threatens loud alarms   C285
Whilst F——r without slumber lay   D429

Whilst guardful Britain with majestic care   S159
Whilst great Argyle, allur'd with worthy views   C359
Whilst heav'n alone, which laid the prosp'rous train   A227
Whilst I, a foe to stocks and bubbles   F54
Whilst I, unequal, tempt the mighty theme   H102
Whilst I was darling of your breast   N304
Whilst impotent, tho' fill'd with rage   T547
Whilst in her cell sad Eloisa mourns   B81
Whilst numbers, to destructive pleasures prone   L224
Whilst on Parnassus top, inthron'd you sit   E395
Whilst on the canvas, by your matchless hands   D520
Whilst on the crowded beach the rabble stand   P721
Whilst other poets female charms admire   P1030
Whilst other theams superior bards employ   D80
Whilst others sing the various chance of arms   D414
Whilst others think, more bright their numbers shine   O213
Whilst others write of heroes and renown   A341
Whilst out of town, strange news alarm'd   W175
Whilst peace is brewing, like good strong beer   L163
Whilst princes give thy art applause   N265
Whilst restless kings ambitious of renown   E364
Whilst rich in brightest red the blushing rose   R304
Whilst rude of numbers, artless I attempt   R335
Whilst sacred friendship, I thy virtues sing   E474
Whilst Saturn rul'd the awful world in peace   P1115
Whilst Sol with jocund toe doth trip upon the misty mountains' top   H461
Whilst some affect the sun, and some the shade   B271
Whilst streaming tears thro' half a nation flow   P657
Whil'st such as would all order disapprove   C302
Whilst tears o'erflow the royal widow's bed   D339
Whilst the bold muse, by great examples taught   T503
Whilst the glad muse exults her strains   B532
Whilst thick to court transported tories run   T392
Whilst thou, great soul, pursu'st thy airy way   H103
Whilst thou my friend with sails unfurl'd   B308
Whilst Troy's defensive arms Minerva crown'd   P550
Whilst venal poets in unbidden lays   E424
Whilst we, illustrious child, attendance pay   J88
Whilst weeping Europe bends beneath her ills   G36
Whilst William's deeds and William's praise   W492
Whilst Wimple's dome its envy'd guest resigns,   B152
Whilst you and I were cordial friends   D243
Whilst you at Twick'nam plan the future wood   Y117
Whilst you, dear Harry, sweat and toil at college   E390
Whilst you, great Walpole, bare the weight   P79
Whilst you, my friend, with anxious cares attend   C107
Whilst you, my lord, acquire a deathless name   H402
Whilst you, my lord, adorn that stately seat   T299
Whilst you, my lord, forsake, a while, your seat   H332
Whilst you, my lord, such various toils sustain   J62
Whitie what gars ye hing your lips   L38
Who be dat de box do sit on?   M525, R137
Who be de noble lady dere   P1145
Who be he dat stand alone-a   A17
Who can be silent, when the jovial round   W529
Who can but ly in sable weed   E127
Who can condole this hero's loss? who can?   E185
Who can keep silence that doth see   W240
Who can sufficiently approve   W266

Who can with so much envy be possest   K43
Who can with thee, oh! bard immortal! joyn?   M471
Who could believe the town should prove so witty!   R188
Who could suspect his fate so hard should prove?   D44·5
Who dares affirm this is no pious age   S838
Who durst have said some time agoe   N234
Who envies fair prosperity or fame   M479
Who e'er thou art, who tempts in such a strain   A54
Who hopes to rival Milton's flame   D473
Who made the world, and everything therein?   G166
Who mounts the loftiest dignitys   N218
Who see my raree shew, come from Prague   C498
Who shall decide, when doctors disagree   P923
Who that e'er felt the poet's sacred fire   C292
Who woman would debar from ill   D441
Who wou'd be proud of being made a tool?   Y23
Who wo'd not both this age and country dread   E169
Who'll see my gallantee show?   R130
Who's that in melancholy dumps?   C386
Who's this I see,/That walks so sad   H407
Who's this? what! Ha----y the lyrick   J61
Whoe're attempts men's morals to reclaim   F280
Whoe'er he be that to a taste aspires   B396
Whoe'er thou art, tho' hating rigid rules   B564
Whoe'er thou art, who, without grace of god   F269
Whoe'er ye be, that scribling can't refrain   A326
Whoever has a cause dependant   N3
Whoever hopes, fair peace! to see thee more?   C211
Whoever knows not what it is to love   K60
Whoever they be, they're the weakest of fools   N201
Whom now, of all the world calls great   W451
Whores, cutpurses and men of fashion   W473
Whoso is wise amongst the people   R132
Why all mankind to death should subject be   H343
Why am I limited to place   T590
Why, Celadon, so museful and so still   M145
Why dies the trumpets sound? strike every string   T555
Why droops the head? Why languishes the eye?   H114
Why, envious age, wilt thou with lingring pain   I14
Why, Faulkner, shou'd you be surpriz'd   G317
Why, foolish woman, are you so enrag'd   G231·5
Why, Gr-----ill, is thy life confin'd   A54
Why, hark ye me, sirs, – if the rumour holds true   T484
Why, how now friend, I prithee of what church   D265
Why how now Pas--- since the last election   D262
Why in complaints shou'd mortals wast their breath   N136
Why is great Phœbus stil'd the god of lays   N175
Why is it in our nature to be poor   H114·5
Why, madam, must I tell this idle tale?   C112
Why now so melancholy Ben?   L159
Why rage the papist thus combin'd   B416
Why rest the sons of fortune not content   M270
Why righteous heav'n an angry face puts on   M309
Why shou'd the bells in merry peals thus roul?   O218
Why silent Clio dost the pomp dispise?   A347
Why sleep the silent powers, that guard the stage   H210
Why sleeps the bard? Why hangs the lyre unstrung   P533

Why sleeps the muse, whilst blund'ring Dorus lives   C382
Why son of -------- shou'd thy metre   E431
Why sounds the plain with sad complaint?   R68
Why stands so long the nation in amaze   A147
Why, Strephon, why, do you desert the plain?   G116
Why swells my heart? Why flows the painful tear?   E93
Why those disputes about the publick good?   O85
Why thus disguis'd? Ah! why's thy lovely face   C384
Why Tom, since thou cam'st last to town   O117
Why wears my pensive friend that gloomy brow   H161·5
Why weeps Mylindor in this gloomy grove?   A219
Why weeps Melindor in this sullen grove?   P172
Why when the spring renews the rising year   P111
Why whigs can't you be easy   P90
Why, why dull poets of this canker'd age   E130
Why will Florella when I gaze   N216
Why with such care will poor deluded man   P414·5
Widows all of Dublin town   S385
Will not the fi'ery chari'ot come   S735
Will then the muse, the great Priorian muse   C515
William, that name's joy's essence, pleasing sound   H147·5
William the brave, a fav'rite name   C326
William was he whom god's decree did send   U21
Wilt thou peruse what I indite   E410
Wise Caleb and C--t, two birds of a feather   W494
Wise Rochefoucault a maxim writ   S884
Wise Thales the father of all   W185
Wise was that Spartan lawgiver of old   W357
Wise was the clown who, when he first descried   K15
Wisely an observator said   E320
With all the charms of France and Rome   F282
With an old song made by an old ancient pate   O108
With bleeding heart and melting eyes   T477
With bleeding heart and weeping eyes   M549
With brisk merry lays/We'll sing to the praise   D428
With care what you collect, injoy with ease   O106
With crowns and orbs beneath your feet   N213
With drooping head I now bemoan   E267
With every honour grac'd, thy youth appears   N277
With faint essay, I on the trembling string   M405
With favour and fortune fastidiously blest   S830
With floods of tears we cannot but deplore   T388
With gen'ral sadness Albion mourns   M221
With grace peculiar, and severely bright   M268
With greatest respect and most awful submission   D65
With grief, resentment, and averted eyes   M15
With half an eye/Your riddle I spy   D205
With heavy heart and trembling hand   P1119
With his great fathers when great Brunswic slept   E510
With indignation let my muse exclaim   S131
With invocations some their breasts inflame   Y86
With Irish assurance let England no longer   E554
With joy great Swift, we view the breaking morn   A346
With joy we see the times, most gracious queen   B233
With joy we see this circle of the fair   P1124
With kisses of his mouth, let him kiss me   B280
With longing arms, while grateful Albion stands   W538
With moral tale let ancient wisdom move   P77

With more than usual brightness S209
With muse invok'd, and solemn proem R10
With my whole heart, my god and king P92
With noise of cannon, and of rattling drums T448
With pious thoughts, do thou begin the day C220
With pleasure, muse, did we the picture view T64
With rosy fingers, see the morn D287
With singing of ballads, and crying of news D530
With some, there seems a doubt, how first began B621
With streaming eyes, and with dejected mien V12
With sullen spleen devour'd, and gloomy thought F95
With the sad tidings of the day opprest P597
With this diversity of view R226
With utmost diligence I sought to find H41
With what amusement shall we crown the day T126
With what attractive charms this goodly frame A139
With what impatience merit waits S220
With woful phyz, and doleful greeting A265
Within a grove, the muses calm retreat M474
Within a grove, whose trees and fruitful soil V124
Within the confines of that dreary cell E319
Within the space of less than half a mile C391
Withoutten preface or preamble R87
Woman's prerogative, the theme I chuse C472
Women, e'er since their mother Eve W456
Wonder not Blount, whose magick hand A196
Wonder not, Nick, whose magick feather E368
Wond'rous the bard, whose happy tragic vein P1122
Would Denham's muse revisit earth again R14
Wou'd our druid but lend me C284
------, wou'd/You be good? T586
Would you be happy and continue so C138
Wrapt in one common wish three nations lay O23
Wrapt in the pleasures of a country seat S364
Wright-craft, this art who rightly would define D401
Writing a satire?/If I am, what then? E601
Wrongs to redress, and justice to maintain C201
When on the stage Bayes bids th' eclipse advance
  P1006

Y

Y Cymru Mwynion Medrys, mewn donniau dawn a
  dysc A278
Ye authors sage of every coat N222
Ye bards! of shallow sence, but specious sound M483
Ye bards of small desert, but vast conceit M481
Ye bards that glow with sacred fire P126
Ye bards! who in immortal lays N306
Ye beaus, who all hear my sad ditty W220
Ye beauteous youths to happiness design'd S29
Ye beaux and ye belles, both in court and in city C536
Ye beaux, and ye belles of the town and the city M352
Ye belles and ye beaus for a moment attend N80
Ye blades of our shire L101
Ye bold offenders, quick atone S756
Ye bold presbyterians what is it you mean D88
Ye brave Britons all to my ditty attend O25
Ye brave Britons all,/Who rejoice to be told of your
  country's fame F178
Ye British fair! whose charms outshine M372
Ye British maids with British beauty blest M23

Ye British sons, and all ye tuneful nine H6
Ye Britons, delighted attend to my theme F257
Ye Britons give ear/To my story, and hear O109
Ye Britons! who hate to be led by the nose A163
Ye Caledonian beauties, who have long R97
Ye circum, and uncircumcis'd D545
Ye citizens of Westminster E543
Ye coblers, and taylors draw near S384
Ye commons, and peers,/Pray, lend me your ears
  C269, J1
Ye commons and peers, who are bound by your pay
  S626
Ye commons and peers,/Ye've heard with your ears
  N71
Ye commons of England, who are on the scent A104
Ye courtiers and patriots, ye statesmen and wits T541
Ye cucolds all of fam'd Cheapside N106
Ye damnable dunces, ye criblers what mean ye A246
Ye daughters of Jerusalem P742
Ye Dettingen heroes, regard what I say Y16
Ye dippers and quakers N78
Ye distant spires, ye antique towers G254
Ye Dublin ladies that attend P516
Ye English sages grave and wise A270
Ye fabled deities, and fictious train K90
Ye fellows of Newgate, whose fingers are nice N288
Ye famales [!] of Dublin make haste, and repair P193
Ye folk of the town/From the peer to the clown N208
Ye fools in Great-Britain, repent in your folly B553
Ye fops of light heels without one grain of sense
  T115·5
Ye freeholders most dear/Of Cardigan-shire D393
Ye freemen so wise/Now open your eyes T528
Ye friends of the state S583
Ye furies dire who tread the Stygian sand N167
Ye gallants, come listen a while N72
Ye gallants of Dublin, come listen a while E555
Ye gen'rous fair by whom our house is grac'd P1133
Ye gentlest powers! of musick, who inspire F55
Ye gods! dear friend, where have you been? O129
Ye good Christian poeple, I pray you draw near N319
Ye grateful patriots, who this day revere N174
Ye great divinities above! P285
Ye green-rob'd dryads, oft' at dusky eve W243
Ye guardian gods! who wait on kings Y81
Ye guardian pow'rs! that ether rove S117
Ye heav'ns! To what a boundless theam T407
Ye high commissioners of death S640
Ye hours that with the circling sun O64
Ye hov'ring zephirs/To climes etherial S211
Ye human offsprings! of distinguish'd birth B496
Ye husbands, draw near, while I sing you a ditty
  W239
Ye impious Britons, whether will ye fly? I50
Ye injur'd females see W549
Ye injur'd sons of Grubstreet, all combine H360
Ye jolly ladds! how fair do's now the sky appear? S8
Ye knaves and ye fools, ye maids, widows and wives
  B462
Ye ladies and lasses that live in Great Britton P140
Ye ladies fair, of Britain's isles A92
Ye ladies fair who live remote P903
Ye ladies of Drury now weep M523

Ye ladies of Munster, come listen a while E542
Ye ladies that in Y---- street dwell B293
Ye lads and ye lasses that live at Longleat B41
Ye lads and ye lasses that live in Great Britain P139
Ye lasses and lads, if to listen you'll come C345
Ye learn'd adepts, in wond'rous secrets skill'd P1139
Ye learned doctors, on whose brows sits grief E95
Ye liquid streams, which thro' our sluces glide B92
Ye living heroes, who with grief o'erspread N279
Ye lords and ladies of this isle B26
Ye lords, and ye commons, give ear to my ditty P510
Ye lovers of physick, come lend me your ear N188
Ye lovers of your freedom L211
Ye loving Hibernians come listen a while D403
Ye loyalists your weeds put on E184
Ye maidens and wives,/Who lead honest lives L26
Ye marry'd men, who think ye lead sad lives T580
Ye martial breasts, the pride of Scotia's plain B363
Ye medley of mortals that make up this throng W563
Ye men of might, and muckle power A49, W397
Ye merry hearts that love to play P1048
Ye moral cattle of my plains D352
Ye muses all, and pitying virgins come P654
Ye muses nine, put on your sable dress E50
Ye muses now assist my vent'rous pen P67
Ye muses strike the trembling string E110
Ye neighbours and friends of Jesus draw near W323
Ye nine of Hippocrenes streams P192
Ye northern blasts, and Eurus, wont to sweep G197
Ye nymphs who in Fifes highest mountains dwell E476
Ye old whigs, met here my new honours to grace G270
Ye patriot crouds, who burn for England's fame J83
Ye patriots, who twenty long years W494
Ye pedants, quacks, block-heads, and coffee-house smarts M114
Ye peers, and seers; of gracious ears D25
Ye people at home/Who H---n---r hate I15
Ye people of Ireland both country and city I66
Ye people of Ireland, how comes it to pass M301
Ye Persian maids, attend your poet's lays C298
Ye pert buffoons of France P143
Ye plaids and greens, now in this place H150
Ye powers of song, my voice inspire O41
Ye pow'rs who watch o'er sublunary things F264
Ye princes, that on thrones do dwell T105
Ye rebels all, you're quite undone N158
Ye regents, non-regents, and men of the gown C7
Ye roundheaded tories, and longheaded Jacks D41
Ye rulers all, both great and small C323
Ye sacred dryads, who adorn the woods C89
Ye sacred muses! now inspire my quill R313
Ye sacred muses whose exalted lays B106
Ye sacred nine, can sorrow tune your choir S268
Ye sacred nine, can sorrows tune your choir S270, S339
Ye sacred nine, from Helicon D418
Ye sages that would have both law and good conscience B53
Ye satirical wits, who can make a great joke R31
Ye senseless mutineering crew W397
Ye shades, where sacred truth is sought P876
Ye sisters nine, assist my quill T414

Ye slaves who make it your pretence B34
Ye sober sad and merry dames G305
Ye Solymean muses change the strain R336
Ye sons of Athens, grant me one request H138
Ye sons of Levi, church divines O258
Ye sons of my church who were ever of such O170
Ye sons of old Crispian, a saint and a king T398
Ye sons of riot and imprudence come P21
Ye sons of sacred truth exalt your lays C167
Ye sons of women hither throng D534
Ye sons that at my altars fall C179
Ye subjects of true British race G265
Ye swains of Solyma! where-e'er ye lead B485
Ye tender fair, with streaming eyes N163
Ye tender nymphs who strive to please the town E195
Ye toping cits, by morn who whet F100
Ye tories for shame,/Give over your game T426
Ye tories of Britain, if you think it fitting T411
Ye Trojan nymphs and goddesses, who bring R118
Ye true-born Englishmen proceed B34, Y7
Ye true-hearted Britons, draw near to my ditty B458
Ye tuneful nine, that drink the purling stream C187
Ye tuneful nine, your poets mind inspire N22
Ye venerable sages of the schools B122
Ye waggish whigs, who raise your heads S536
Ye weavers all of Spittle Fields E547
Ye weeping muses with sad pomp attend M573
Ye Westminster boys,/All sing and rejoice T525
Ye Westminster boys/By your freedom of choice I35
Ye Westminster boys,/With one common voice I33
Ye whigs sing Te Deum, ye Jacobites fret S202
Ye whimsical people of fair London town L57
Ye who by merit, love and duty sway'd P1027
Ye who in constant hallelujahs join M194
Ye wise astronomers that pry H356
Ye wise philosophers explain S810
Ye writers of satire, ye whips of the times G319
Years have their glory, ages have their fame G173
Yes: all, my lord, usurp fair honour's name B504
Yes, cries John Calvin's Boanerges T149
Yes, glorious being, humbly I adore S761
Yes, G----n! when once virtue quits the earth T44
Yes, I will write. And let them laugh who will P474
Yes, I will write, O would the muse inspire S201
Yes, yes, my friend, disguise it as we will W244
Yes, you condemn those sages too refin'd M164
Yes, you despise the man to books confin'd P920
Yes – you, my lord, can stand the test of wit W536
Yet, yet a moment, one dim ray of light P787
You ancient bards, who Britain's glory wrote T52
You ask me, madam, if the muse D16
You ask me, sir, why thus by phantoms aw'd W438
You bakers of England both country and citty W262
You brave loyal hearts ev'ry where N155
You citizens all pray lend me an ear L81
You citizens of London N205
You, Damon, in your tender bride's embrace H44
You Englishmen draw near a while P760
You fair ones all at liberty W543
You gallant freeholders, now lend us a hand F239
You have, my dear coz (as now 'tis the fashion) B610
You Highlandmen with tongue and pen K39
You honest hearts, that wish'd fair play B294

INDEX OF FIRST LINES

You know, dear friend, and doubtless do lament   L145
You ladies fair, in pity with me join   L18
You lovers that are passing by   Y20
You loyal church-men far and near   W275
You loyal subjects now draw near   R317
You maidens who intend to wed   F68
You may expect, my friend, that I should be   L137
You may talk of haughty France, and boast of Spain   F124
You men of quick sight,/That pretend to new light   C532
You merchants of Britain who've nothing to do   M156
You people of zeal that love your poor souls   S69
You pinacle flyers, where would you advance   A238
You puts that have land, and you cits that have none   C203
You sacred sisters nine, my breast inspire   N30
You sacred sisters nine my theme attend   N31
You scorn, my Lollius, if I know thy heart   M165
You sons and daughters view my hoary head   A130
You sons of faction, who from truth dissent   E111
You sorry lousy taylors all   S79
You students of the Temple, now bewaile   E98
You subjects of Britton now you may rejoice   N194
You subjects of Ireland come all and rejoice   E570
You talk of your high-church addresses   A91
You tell me Dick you've lately read   E478
You tell me of a female pair   L94
You tender parents all both far and near   L56
You that are loyal churchmen smile   N209
You that at ev'ry trifling cross repine   B9
You that have courted women-kind   C332
You that oppress the captive African   P477
You that pretend my friend to be   W375
You that wish your country's peace   W371
You, Tityrus, canopy'd by a broad beech, softly reclining   I49
You true-born Englishmen proceed   C492, Y11
You Westminster boys so hearty and tight   W373
You, who can musick's charms inspire   O24
You who, like Proteus, in all shapes appear   J28
You, who the sweets of rural life have known   G66
You! whom I chose, and whom I still wou'd chuse   O93
You widdows, orphans, and each needy soul   E213
You wives that are lately married   J106

You wonder friend! that I, by nature mild   M491
You write so seldom, and are so severe   E345
You're welcome, Woolrich, from Dunfermline fair   G206
You've wondered, perhaps, and been in great rage   L246
Young, beauteous pride of a long-glorious race   E512
Young Damon, once upon a time   P478
Young Flash, a bard, and eke a beau   C407
Young heroe, whose fair virtues early rise   S751
Young lovers pray be of good chear   H195
Young man attend a while to what I say   G156
Young men and maidens all give ear   B201
Young men and maidens all, I pray you now attend   B85
Young Perkin's lately come over   N14
Young Slouch the farmer had a jolly wife   K65
Young Tityrus, thoughtful, mus'd along the plain   P116
Young youth, O tell me! whither art thou bound?   A106
Your aid, ye heav'n-born muses, hither bring   W342
Your cheese we have eat, and a toast with it drank   D557
Your consort grieves at slow Ulysses' stay   E436
Your deep observers of mankind   W347
Your duteous subjects, sir, and loyal   T424
Your friends receiv'd with aking hearts   A232
Your honour I court/For a timely support   P1100
Your house of hair and lady's hand   R204
Your laddy can't fight, but your laddy may sing   L297
Your leaving our gates, to shake off the dust   B571
Your man of bus'ness is your idlest ass   W574
Your pencil, Bindon, like the poet's quill   P661
Your sacred anthems, pious hymns, and psalms   T375
Your sad complaints no sooner I receiv'd   A230
Your sage and moralist can show   W341
Your shining conquests, madam, still maintain   R168
Your soldier, taking courage from his coat   S544
Your spleen is vain! take counsel of a friend   G150

Z

'Z—nds what a bustle is here between kings   A330

CHRONOLOGICAL INDEX

This index contains first editions only. It should be stressed that while publication is dated as precisely as possible from the evidence collected, these dates should not be considered definitive. In particular, for the years 1714–17 and 1723–50 when monthly catalogues are available, the month only is given unless more precise dates came to hand; I have not searched the newspapers for those years. Even when the day of the month is given it is usually only the earliest date that has been found. There are many possible causes for error in the dates given, some of which are discussed in the Introduction, I. xvii–iii; the year itself may be incorrect when a poem is printed late in one year but with the following year in the imprint.

[17––]

Astrea's commission to the complaining ghost. A363

The common-hunt, or, the pursute of the pope. C318

The Dutch bribe, a ballad. D557

The election. To the tune of the Cobler. E30

Gill, T.   A poem upon the apparition and ascension of our blessed saviour. G165

Joy upon joy: or, here's all in a hurry... J106

The kirk and covenant, with light foot... K84

A new ballad... N106

The old and new courtier. O108

Seguin, J.   An acrostick upon the name of Mrs Elizabeth Ball. S195

Seguin, J.   To Mrs Elizabeth Ball. S196

Seward, B.   A hymn. S361

[Ward, E.]   The tippling philosophers. W183

[17––]: SCOTLAND

[Davidson, —.]   The taylor's vindication. D53·5

An elegy on Mr. George Lauder. E176

[Graham, J. *marquis*.]   I'le never love the emore... G236

The merchants and hammer-mens complaint against the taylors... M185

The original of government, and duty of magistrats... O245

The picture and history of W-----m F-----ce... P269

The rake in fetters: or, the marriage mouse trap. R9

[17––]: IRELAND

An hymn to the great creator. H461

[170–]

The British ode: to...the Duke of Marlborough. B480

Hartlib, J.   To Mr. Samuel Moore, on his arch-types... H101

A hymn for Christmas. H422

The ladies tutor: or, the art of visiting. L16

The lady's ramble: or, the female night-walker. L29

Love for love... L283

A new song. Vote and be merry... N227

The oracles for war... O239

A poem on the taking St. Mary's. P643

[Pope, W.]   The old man's wish... P993

A prediction, said to have its rise from Scotland... P1018

Reflections upon the glorious victory over the French. R149

Sheeres, P.   A new year's gift... S387

A short dehortatory poem to a claret-prone kinsman... S447

A step to the d---l's exchange: or, the humours of the Wells, &c. S747

To Mr. Thomas Murray, on a celebrated picture... T350

The unfortunate fortunate marry'd-man. U4

[Wright, J.]   Burley on the Hill... W567

[170–]: SCOTLAND

The advocats complaint... A107

Captain Gordon's welcome home... C30

An epithalamium on the jovial nuptials of Capt. James Donaldson... E447

In memoriam...Roberti Gardiner... I24

John High-land-man's remarks upon the ladyes of Edinburgh... J70

Monteith, R.   To the most noble...Patrick, earl of Marchmount... M421

[Pitcairne, A.]   Gualterus Danistonus, scotus, Sannazario veneto propriam quietem gratulatur. P369

The unbyassd patriot. A poem on...James duke of Hamilton. U1

[170–]: IRELAND

A poem in Latin, on the wonderful conversion of Dr. Shea. P537

1701

Jan   [Defoe, D.] The true-born Englishman. D153

3 Jan   Paul Diack: or, the chat of the gods... P129

14 Jan   Æsop in Spain... A116

31 Jan   An answer to...The true-born Englishman... A233

Feb   In honour to the king and parliament... I19

5 Feb   The vestry: a poem. V78

8 Feb   The election. A poem. E29

18 Feb   Tate, N. A congratulatory poem on the new parliament... T52

20 Feb   A word of advice to the male-contents. W562

22 Feb   [Chudleigh, M., *Lady*.] The ladies defence... C172

26 Feb   The English gentleman justified... E333

27 Feb   The fable of the cuckoo... F6

1 Mar   Shenkin ap Morgan. The true-born Welshman... S393

13 Mar   An account of a great fight, between the Christians, and the quakers... A8

15 Mar   [Froud, J.] The grove... F275

3 Apr   An elegy on...Henry duke of Norfolk... E201

7 Apr   Minerva's remonstrance to Great Britains genius... M269

12 Apr   The fatal union of France and Spain. F69

22 Apr   The Dispensary transvers'd... D332

29 Apr   The beau in a wood... B127

May   [Brown, T.] Advice to the Kentish long-tails... B507

15 May   Christus natus est... C171

17 May   English men no bastards... E336

22 May   A whip for the Spaniards... W401

24 May   An elegy on...William Kidd... E168

24 May   Of war. A poem... O90

28 May   Spite and spleen: or the doctor run mad... S657

June   On the tenth of June... O222

June   'Ye true-born Englishmen proceed...' Y7

27 June   The ballad...answered stanza by stanza... B34

2 July   An elegy upon...Aaron Smith... E241

4 July   [Settle, E.] Minerva triumphans...to the honour of...the Cotton Library... S282

5 July   The dissertator in burlesque. D335

10 July   The town display'd... T433

16 July   The Kentish men. A satyr... K16

19 July   [Pomfret, J.] Two love poems... P736

30 July   The effigies of the Legion. E22

31 July   [Pittis, W.] Chaucer's whims... P431

1 Aug   Tate, N. The Kentish worthies. T62

5 Aug   The pleasures of a single life... P488

20 Aug   Articles of peace... A330

20 Aug   The sylvan dream... S943

20 Aug   [Tutchin, J.] The apostates. T574

27 Aug   [Ward, E.] Battel without bloodshed... W49

1 Sept   Tom of Bedlam... T409

4 Sept   [Settle, E.] The scaffold lately erected in Westminster-Hall. S291

8 Sept   An elegy on...King James... E157

16 Sept   The triumph of the great L——d S——. T501

18 Sept   A rod for Tunbridge beaus... R245

20 Sept   The art of love. Paraphrased from Ovid. A323

23 Sept   The generous muse...in memory of...James the II... G105

23 Sept   A satyr on the Kentish-men... S56

2 Oct   A dialogue between the cities of London and Paris... D267

6 Oct   A new satyr against the French king... N180

9 Oct   An ode on the death of the late King James... O44

14 Oct   [Ward, E.] The revels of the gods... W163

17 Oct   An historical poem upon...James II. H254

20 Oct   Advice to Great Britain... A80

21 Oct   Yalden, T. A poem on the mines late of Sir Carbery Price... Y3

27 Oct   [Hopkins, C.] A satyr against confinement. H308

30 Oct   A consolatory poem in praise of retirement... C387

Nov   England's late jury: a satyr. E320

Nov   A song on the king's birth-day... S590

Nov   [Ward, E.] The character of a covetous citizen... W55

6 Nov   The king of St. Germains... K52

6 Nov   The last new prologue and epilogue... L54

7 Nov   The heaven-drivers. H131

14 Nov   The visions of Dom Francisco de Quevedo... V107

15 Nov   [Tutchin, J.] The British muse... T577

20 Nov   The grand affairs of Europe, discuss'd... G240

25 Nov   Tate, N. A monumental poem in memory of... Sir George Treby... T64

27 Nov   The lawyer turn'd butcher... L76

27 Nov   The Prince of Wales: a poem. P1061

4 Dec   Wedlock a paradice... W267

5 Dec   A satyr on mankind... S52

6 Dec   An elegy on...Sr. Bartholomew Shower... E238

8 Dec   Vox britannica: or, the state of Europe. V118

9 Dec   Advice to whiggs... A105

16 Dec   The excellency of a holy life... E534

22 Dec   Funeral discipline... F287

23 Dec   [Harris, J.] Leighton-stone-air... H70

An answer to the Pleasures of a single life... A253

[Billingsley, N.] Carmen lugubre... On the death of... Grace Billingsley...B216

Dibben, T. Carmen sæculare to the king. D295

An elegy on the death of James the second... E155

An elegy upon his late majesty James II... E160

Epilogue. The last comic epilogue... E352

Exaltatio cleri... E533

Harris, J. A congratulatory poem...to...Duke of Queens-berry... H66

Hogg, W. Ad virum nobilissimum...Robertum Harlæum... H277

The Jacobites lament for...the late King James... J53·5

Λιτανεια τεσσαρακοστη. Or, a lenten litany... L193

The nuptialls of the lamb... N348

An ode: or elegy on...James the second... O53

On the death of King James. O194

Perkins, J. Elegia in obitum...Henrici ducis de Beaufort ... P186

A pindarick ode, occasioned by the death of the late lord chief justice Treby. P286

The piss-pot... P293

A poem on the death of...the Duke of Gloucester. P597

A satyr, on a true-born Dutch-skipper... S50

[Tate, N.] The humble address of the muses to his majesty. T61

Trapp, J. Ædes Badmintonianæ... T443

A true character of the Prince of Wales's poet... T518

The weaver turn'd devil... W262

Wesley, S. The history of the new testament... W325

[*1701?*]

A dialogue between Pasquin and Morforio... D262

[Ward, E.] The insinuating bawd: and the repenting harlot. [1701/–] W98

1701: SCOTLAND

An advice to young-men... A106

The believer's farewel to the world... B170

Campbell, K. In obitum...D. Georgii Campbell... C17

Dick, D. True Christian love... D301

Elegie on the death of Mr. George Campbell... E75

An elegie on...Lord Basil Hamilton... E138

Elegie on...Lord Basil Hamilton... E139

An elogie on ...James the seventh and second... E156

An elegie upon...James VII... E161

Elegie on the death of Mr. Gilbert Rule... E232

A facetious poem in imitation of the Cherry and slae... F22

[Gibson, W.] The damneds doom... G138

In obitum...D. Georgii Campbelli... I28

1701: Scotland (*cont.*)

The mournful muse...to the pious memory of...Lord Basil Hamilton... M545

On the dreadful fire, in the land market of Edinburgh... O201

On the much lamented death of...James, VII. & II...O212

On the...death of...Lord Basil Hamiltoun... O227

A panegyrick on...Anna dutches of Buccleugh... P39

A pastoral poem to the memory of...Lord Basil Hamiltoun... P118

[Simson, P.] The Song of Solomon... S467

[*1701?*]

Truth's champion or an elegie. On...Alexander Shields. T542·5

1701: IRELAND

Smith, D. The shepherds jubilee, or, a pastoral welcome to...the Earl of Rochester... S513

Williams, B. Congratulatio Roffensis...on the arrival of ...Lawrence earl of Rochester... W474

[*1701?*]

A poem, occasioned by the hangings in the castle of Dublin... P557

1702

Jan	Prince Perkin the 2d... P1062
Jan	Tate, N. An ode upon the assembling of the new parliament... T69
Jan	[Yalden, T.] Æsop at court... Y1
6 Jan	[Pittis, W.] The patriots... P451
7 Jan	Sedley, *Sir* C. The happy pair... S193
19 Jan	The blasted laurel. B281
5 Feb	The French tyrant, or the royal slave... F262
14 Feb	Protestant divisions... P1146
16 Feb	To the honoured Cavendish Weedon... T375
19 Feb	The modern whig dictator... M387
Mar	[Harris, B.] Brittania's tears...In an elegy... [on] William III... H60
12 Mar	The tavern hunter... T96
13 Mar	An ode on the death of King William III. O43
13 Mar	Smith, M. A pindarique poem sacred to... William III. S524
14 Mar	The mournful congress...on the death of... William III... M542
16 Mar	Britannia's loss... B469
16 Mar	Phillips, S. England's happiness...on the present parliament. P256
16 Mar	[Settle, E.] Spes Hunsdoniana: a poem on... Matthew Bluck... S294
19 Mar	An elegy, from the mercers...upon the death of the late King William... E280

19 Mar Hext, F. A pindarique ode, sacred to the memory of William III... H168

23 Mar A congratulatory poem on the happy accession ...of...Princess Anne... C356

23 Mar Settle, E. Carmen irenicum. The happy union of the two East-India companies. S243

31 Mar Batavia in tears: or, an elegy from the Dutch... B92

Apr Smith, M. The vision, or a prospect of death ... S525

2 Apr Oldmixon, J. A funerall idyll, sacred to... William III. O166

9 Apr Albina: or a poem on...William III. A154

9 Apr The English muse...upon her majesty's accession... E338

16 Apr Walter, T. A poem dedicated to the memory... of...William the third. W37

21 Apr The solemnity of the muses, at the funeral of King William III. S549

22 Apr The church of England's joy on the happy accession... C180

22 Apr Phillips, S. England's glory: a congratulatory poem on the coronation... P255

24 Apr [Barbon, —] Magna Britannia triumphans... B80·5

24 Apr England's triumph in the joyful coronation... E328

24 Apr A pindaric ode dedicated to... William III... P285

28 Apr Albina, the second part. Or, the coronation... A155

28 Apr The loyalist...in memory of William III... L305

May Phillips, S. The German Cæsar... P257

1 May Dyke, A. The female muse. A poem on the coronation... D568

7 May Albion's glory: a pindarique ode on the... coronation... A156

8 May Park, H. The mourning curat: a poem occasion'd by the death of...William III... P66

9 May Burridge, R. A congratulatory poem, on the coronation... B585

12 May [Defoe, D.] The mock mourners... D132

14 May [Stennett, J.] A poem to the memory of his late majesty... S741

21 May [Daniel, R.] The dream: a poem occasion'd by the death of...William III. D431

1 June Hughes, J. The house of Nassau. H375

3 June England's triumph...on the happy coronation ... E329

16 June [Prior, M.] To a young gentleman in love. P1088

18 June Dennis, J. The monument...to the immortal memory of...William the third... D224

18 June A satyr against dancing. S41

19 June Phillips, S. The grove, or, muse's paradice... P258

July Jackson, J. A funeral tear to the pious memory of...William Russel... J11

4 July Satira in poetastros O-c---enses. S38

10 July Manning, F. The shrine...to the memory of King William III. M90

21 July The ladies choice: a poem. L9

23 July Suffragium: or, the humours of the electors... S784

27 July The history of the famous may-pole at Ewelm ... H256

4 Aug A hue and cry after the Observator... H359

Sept An essay on Prince Eugene's success in Italy... E466

Sept [Pittis, W.] Jest and earnest... P432

1 Sept The heroe in miniature: or...Prince Eugene. H153

3 Sept Good advice to the ladies... G219

Nov [Defoe, D.] The Spanish descent... D151

Nov The innocent lampoon... I43

19 Nov A poem on the late glorious success of...the Duke of Ormond at Vigo. P622

21 Nov Harris, J. Luzara...on prince Eugenius of Savoy... H71

23 Nov [Ward, E.] Bribery and simony... W50

27 Nov The retrievement... R168

Dec The condemn'd bridegroom...Mr. Hogan Swanson... C332

Dec Denne, H. Love alone: or, the star that leads to Christ... D217

Dec Polsted, E. Cambria triumphans... P717

7 Dec [Blackmore, Sir R.] A hymn to the light of the world... B252

10 Dec Congreve, W. A hymn to harmony... C370

15 Dec Anna in anno mirabili... A226

19 Dec Hob turn'd courtier. H263

30 Dec Thura Britannica. A congratulatory poem... T267

An answer to the Mock mourners... A252

[Bold, M.] Paradisus amissa... B312

'Burnet, G.' An elegy on the death of...William the third... B579

The city madam, and the country maid... C207

Coney, T. A pindarique ode upon her majesty's happy accession... C335

[Defoe, D.] Reformation of manners... D145

Elegie sur la mort du...Guillaume III... E41

Fleming, R. Fame's mausoleum...to the glorious memory of William... F163

Great Brittain's joy for...Queen Ann... G263

Harris, J. A poem...to the pious memory of...William III. H77

Her majestie's welcome to St. Paul's cathedral. H149

Hogg, W. Ad augustissimam, serenissimamque Annam ... H276

Hogg, W. In obitum...Gulielmi tertii... H278

In obitum...Guilielmi III... I30

Lewis in a sweat... L162

Lewis, E. The weeping muse...to the memory of his late majesty. L164

The loyal address of the clergy of Virginia. L296

The miseries of England... M278

The mournfull muse, an elegy on...William IIId... M544

The mournful poem, on the royal funeral... M546

A poem on the death of Tho. Cholmondeley... P607

The poet's address to...King William... P693

The poet's address to the ensuing parliament. P694

Prince Eugene; a pindarique. P1059

The protestant queen... P1148

Pugna navalis inter Anglos & Gallos... P1156

The restauration; or: a change for the better... R163

The royal court in mourning... R307

The royal hero...William III... R310·5

The royal progress... R317

The sailors account of the action at Vigo. S11

Scandalous Fuller rewarded... S130

Settle, E. Eusebia triumphans. The Hannover succession ... S253

Some verses on...King William... S559

Sorsoleil, J. B. Columna votiva regi. S608

[Stennett, J.] A poem to the memory of Mr. Nathanael Taylor... S745

Tate, N. A poem upon tea... T72

The tavern query, or the loyal health... T99

Te deum...pour les glorieux succez des armes... T107

A tribute of tears...for the death of William the third... T477

The Vigo victory... V96

Waller, W. On the death of king William IIId... W24

[Waring, H.] The coronation... W221

Wedlock vindicated: or, the ladies answer... W268

[1702?]

A congratulatory poem to...Sir E.S. C362

Phœnix moriendo revixit... P263

The seamen's sorrow...on the...death of Admiral John Benbow...[1702/03] S162

[Smith, E.] Ode. [1702/03] S515

The muse's address...in behalf of insolvent prisoners for debt. [1702/14] M564

An ode pindarick on Barbadoes. [1702/14] O55

On man. A satyr. [1702/14] O178

A satyr against hypocrites... [1702/14] S42

1702: SCOTLAND

Ad illustrissimum...Jacobum Hamiltoniæ ducem... A21

An elogie on...John Hamilton... E141

An elegy on...the Countess of Leven... E180

An elegie on...Sir John Shaw... E236

Elegie on the death of...King William. E281

Elogie on...William, the third... E282

The last speech and confession of Jannet Riddle... L55

Monteith, R. Augustissimæ, serenissimæ, lectissimæ, Annæ... M417

A poem upon...Prince William... P682

Poems on her sacred majestie. P689

Porterfield, J. God's judgements against sin... P1001

Porterfield, J. A relation of the late misfortune at Leith ... P1002

A pyramid to...William the second... P1180

A threnodie...on the decease of...William... T265

To the most serene and potent princess, Ann... T388

To the truely noble, James marquess of Montrose... T397

[Williamson, D.] A mournful poem on...King William ... W516

[1702?]

Poverties coat turn'd by a taylor in Hamilton...[1702/14?] P1008

1702: IRELAND

Englands sorrow...for the loss of...William the IIId... E326

[Stearne, J.] The death and burial of John Asgill... S735

Upon...King William the III. U21

[1702?]

An ode for St. Cæcillia's day...[1702/14] O24

A poem occasion'd by the city of Dublin's repairing the statue of William the IIId...[1702/14] P550

1703

2 Jan   Tate, N. The song for new-year's-day, 1703... T78

15 Jan   Shute, J. A pindarick ode, upon...sending... the Duke of Marlborough to...Holland... S457

15 Jan   [Tooke, C.] To the right honourable Sir George Rooke...at his return from...Vigo. T418

30 Jan   [Bryan, —] The temple of fame, a poem occasion'd by the late success... B551

Feb   Tate, N. Portrait-royal. A poem upon her majesty's picture... T74

6 Feb Wall, T. An ode for an entertainment of musick on her majesty's birth-day... W21

8 Feb An anniversary ode on her majesty's birth-day... A228

16 Feb [Harris, J.] Anglia triumphans... H64

23 Feb Hughes, J. An ode in praise of musick... H380

25 Feb Hell upon earth: or, the character of the Poultrey compter. H134

Mar Elegia in præmaturum obitum...Johannis, marchionis de Blancford... E32

9 Mar [Mandeville, B.] The pamphleteers. A satyr. M72

23 Mar Astrea triumphans...to his grace the Duke of Ormond... A362

13 Apr Britton's consort: or, the musick-meeting... B482

21 Apr The satyrizer satyriz'd: or a defence of Mr. Britton's musick-meeting... S85

30 Apr The scriptural history of Joseph and his brethren... S154

May [Mandeville, B.] Some fables after the easie and familiar method of Monsieur de la Fontaine. M73

20 May [Brown, T.] The mourning poet: or the unknown comforts of imprisonment... B514

5 June The wonderful pentecost...on Whit-Sunday last. W556

26 June A satyr against love. S43

29 June The hypocrites: a satyr. H477

July [Trapp, J.] A prologue to the University of Oxford... T455

2 July Congreve, W. The tears of Amaryllis for Amyntas... C379

15 July A new prologue relating to the Act at Oxford... N173

16 July Defoe, D. More reformation. A satyr upon himself. D144

26 July A prefatory prologue... P1022

2 Aug [Defoe, D.] A hymn to the pillory. D115

12 Aug A hymn to Tyburn... H471

24 Aug [Pittis, W.] The true-born-Hugonot; or, Daniel de Foe. P456

1 Sept [Brown, T.] An elegy upon the lamented death of Edward Millington... B512

8 Sept Spooner, L. A looking-glass for smoakers... S661

2 Oct A hymn to the funeral sermon. H458

2 Oct [Pittis, W.] The last new prologues and epilogues... P446

9 Oct Remarks on the author of the Hymn to the Pillory... R154

11 Nov The players turn'd academicks... P486

12 Nov The fable of the beasts and their king... F3

Dec Religio poetæ... R153

Dec [Ward, E.] In imitation of Hudibras... W97

Dec Wesley, S. The history of the old testament in verse... W328

16 Dec [Pomfret, J.] A prospect of death... P733

18 Dec Phosphorus. Or, the church of England the best of all protestant churches... P265

Bilcliffe, J. The holy Bible...Done into verse... B213

Burridge, R. The recantation. B588

Claridge, R. Carmen spirituale: or, Christian counsel to youth. C218

The counterpart of the Elegy on the Philadelphian society... C441

Crauford, D. Ovidius Britannicus: or, love-epistles... C496

An elegy, upon the Philadelphian society...with the false oracles, last speech, and confession. E211

An elegy on...Lady Grace Pierpoint... E213

An excellent new copy of verses...for the loss of... Thomas Cooke... E572

Froud, J. Musa gratulatrix or a congratulatory poem to her majesty... F276

The golden age from the fourth eclogue of Virgil... G211

The holiday ramble: or, a walk to Pancridge. H289

Lacaux, P. Charles I. martir, poëme. L4

The ladies answer to the True born English-woman... L8

Motteux, P. Words sung before her majesty on her birth-day... M534

A new dialogue between the horse at Charing-cross, and the horse at Stocks-market. N129

Nine satyrs, or moral poems... N303

A poem on the late violent storm... P625

Pride's exchange broke up: or Indian calicoes and silks expos'd. P1051

A prologue, sent to Mr. Row, to his new play... P1125

[1703?]

Spencer, R. A congratulatory line: to the right honourable the Lord North and Grey... S648

Advice to the true representatives of old England. [1703?/04?] A104

Bragge, F. The passion of our saviour...[1703/–] B378

The clergyman and goldsmith, in the trap...[1703/–] C237

1703: SCOTLAND

[Clark, J.] The wise or foolish choice... C229

[An elegy] on the death of...Archibald duke of Argyle... E48

[An elegy] on the death of...George Earl of Southerland... E242

1703: Scotland (cont.)

An elegie upon the...death of...George earl of Souther-land... E243

[Symson, D.] A poem on her sacred majesty Q. Anne... S947

[*1703?*]

Denneston, W. Mytilopolis sive Musselburgi...elogium. D219

Illustrissimo ac nobilissimo heroi Georgio comiti de Cromartie...[1703/04] I6

1703: IRELAND

A congratulatory poem; on his grace the Duke of Ormond ... C352

1704

7 Jan	Prologue for the musick... P1124
18 Jan	Crabb, J. A poem upon the late storm and hurricane... C488
18 Jan	Hopkins, C. The art of love... H307
20 Jan	Advice to the saylors... A101
5 Feb	[Ward, E.] The libertine's choice... W101
12 Feb	[Prior, M.] Prologue...on her majesty's birth-day. P1083
4 Mar	A letter of advice to a friend in London... L137
6 Mar	Tutchin, J. A poem in the praise of folly and knavery. T579
13 Mar	The prologue and epilogue to the...Albions queens... P1121
16 Mar	[Wycherley, W.] The folly of industry... W574
21 Mar	Freke, J. A poem on the safe arrival of the Spanish monarch, Charles III... F250
Apr	[Cobb, S.] A psalm of thanksgiving to be sung by the children of Christ's-Hospital... C258
Apr	Faction display'd. The second part. F25
4 Apr	A step to the lobby. S748
5 Apr	An address to our sovereign lady. A55
5 Apr	The negative prophesy... N16
10 Apr	Uvedale, T. The remedy of love, in imitation of Ovid. U33
15 Apr	[Mandeville, B.] Typhon: or the wars between the gods and giants... M76
22 Apr	Faction display'd, in answer to Faction display'd. F24
22 Apr	Ormondus redux... O248
May	The locusts: or, chancery painted to the life... L229
18 May	The seven wise men. S351
23 June	[King, W.] Mully of Mountown. K63
4 July	Yalden, T. An essay on the character of Sir Willoughby Aston... Y2
6 July	A trip to the devil's summer-house... T490

11 July	[King, W.] The fairy feast. K62
12 July	A new prologue spoken at the theatre in Lincoln's-Inn-fields... N175
20 July	A prologue spoken by F---ny L--e...on a dray-horse... P1129
27 July	The picture of the Observator drawn to the life. P273
29 July	Cælias complaint: or, love's looking-glass... C90
4 Aug	Tutchin defended: or, an answer to the Picture of the Observator. T572
8 Aug	The tryal of skill: or, a new session of the poets ... T475
12 Aug	A congratulatory poem to...the Duke of Marlborough... C361
14 Aug	T--ch--n touch'd to the quick... T104
15 Aug	[Defoe, D.] An elegy on the author of the True-born-English-man... D102
16 Aug	[Ward, E.] The dissenter. W63
19 Aug	Clare, R. The English hero: or, the Duke of Marlborough... C217
29 Aug	Defoe, D. A hymn to victory. D123
31 Aug	Æsop the wanderer... A118
Sept	The royal conqueress... R306
7 Sept	The royal triumph... R322
14 Sept	[Ward, E.] All men mad: or, England a great Bedlam. W43
16 Sept	Johnson, C. A congratulatory verse, to...the Dutchess of Marlborough... J71
16 Sept	A poem to...the Dutchess of Marlborough... P662
18 Sept	The victory a poem... V90
30 Sept	[Prior, M.] A letter to Monsieur Boileau Depreaux... P1079
24 Oct	Arwaker, E. An embassy from heav'n... A334
24 Oct	Epinikion Marlburiense Bleinhemianum... E356
31 Oct	[Steele, R.] An imitation of the sixth ode of Horace, apply'd to...the Duke of Marlborough ... S737
2 Nov	The leaden-age. L89
2 Nov	[Ward, E.] A journey to h-ll... W100
6 Nov	[Browne, J.] Albion's naval glory, or Britannia's triumphs... B527·1
7 Nov	[Ward, E.] Helter skelter: or, the devil upon two sticks... W76
9 Nov	The Observator's, or, commonwealth-man's pedigree and coat of arms. O4
21 Nov	Denne, H. Marlborough. An heroic poem. D218
21 Nov	[Ward, E.] A satyr against wine... W172
23 Nov	[Pittis, W.] A hymn to Neptune... P443
28 Nov	Dennis, J. Britannia triumphans... D222

28 Nov [Wine, J.] A welcome to victory... W529

30 Nov Le feu de joye... F115

Dec An elegy on the...death of the bill to prevent occasional conformity... E58

Dec An elegy on the...death of Sir Roger L'Estrange ... E179

9 Dec Deborah and Barak. D84

14 Dec Addison, J. The campaign... A27

14 Dec Beauty's advocate... B134

14 Dec A glimpse of hell: or...the common side of Newgate. G179

15 Dec A hymn to money. A satyr. H453

20 Dec Cobb, S. Honour retriev'd... C249

20 Dec Γλυκοπικρα: or, miscellanies melancholly and diverting... G202

21 Dec Robins, J. The hero of the age: or, Duke of Marlborough... R240

27 Dec A Te deum for Lewis le Grand. T105

28 Dec [Smallwood, J.] A congratulatory poem to... the Duke of Marlborough... S488

The address. A49

Advice to Mr. Vario the painter... A84

Æsop at Portugal... A110

Æsop in Scotland... A115

Britain's joy, for the noble victory... B453

[Brown, T.] The last Observator: or, the devil in mourning... B513

The church of England's address... C179

Cobb, S. The Portugal expedition... C257

The confederates joy, for the taking of Landau... C337

Dux Britannicus, or the Duke of Marlborough. D565

An elegy on the...death of Mr. Benjamin Keach... E165

Fatal love or, the young maiden's tragedy... F68

The French king distracted... F252

Hullin, —. Discours chrêtien contre les impies... H385

The second part of the Locusts... L230

[Mainwaring, A.] This history and fall of the conformity bill... M32

Mr. P-----d's elegy on the death of Mr. John Gadbury ... M297

The Observator's recantation and confession... O5

A paraphrase upon the golden verses of Pythagoras. P62

Perkins, J. Ad serenissimam Annam...ad Thermas iter facientem. P184

Pix, M. A pastoral elegy on...the Earl of Burlington. P461

[Pix, M.] Violenta, or the rewards of virtue... P463

The planter's charity. P477

The queen's thanksgiving hymn, in St. Paul's Church, for the glorious victory obtained at Blenheim... Q14

Settle, E. Augusta lacrimans...to the memory of...Sr Thomas Crisp. S226

Settle, E. A funeral tear, to the memory of...Charles, earl of Burlington. S264

The seven wise men. S350

[Shippen, W.] Faction display'd. A poem... S427

[Shippen, W.] Moderation display'd: a poem... S437

The whigs scandalous address answered stanza by stanza. W397

[1704?]

Et tu Brute? or, the m--'d c--l. E479

A health to honesty or, the tackers character. H124

[Buckeridge, B.] On her majesty's grant of Woodstock park, &c. to...the Duke of Marlborough...[1704/05] B555

Durston, J. Illustrissimo domino...duci Marlboriensi ...epinicium...[1704/05] D555

[Smith, E.] Janus, did ever to thy wond'ring eyes. [1704/05] S514

Pix, M. To the right honourable the Earl of Kent... [1704/06] P462

Hoffman, F. A poem on the mannour of Woodstock... [1704/-] H271

1704: SCOTLAND

[Allan, —] A curb for a coxcomb, or, an answer to the Renagado whip'd... A165

[Allan, —] A satyre on F----s of D---r, by way of return for his Essay on marriage. A166

Death to believers a passage to glory; or an elegie to... James Curry... D82

An essay, upon Polemo medinia... E476

Hill, A. To the memorie of Sir Charles Maitland of Pittrichie... H233

[Forbes, W.] An essay upon marriage... F185

[Forbes, W.] The renegado whip't. A satyre in answer to A----n's lybel... F194

[Forbes, W.] The true Scots genius, reviving... F195

A panegyrick on a noble peer and worthy patriot. P33

1704: IRELAND

Nov Cæcilia's song. C87

1705

Jan Albion's triumph: or, Roman bravery... A157

2 Jan Luctus Britannici, a poem, to the memory of Sir Roger L'Estrange... L319

2 Jan Oldmixon, J. A pastoral poem on the victories at Schellenburgh and Bleinheim... O168

2 Jan [Philips, J.] Bleinheim, a poem... P226

8 Jan Motteux, P. Words sung at the entertainment ...to his grace the Duke of Marlborough... M533

9 Jan [Defoe, D.] The double welcome. A poem to the Duke of Marlbro'. D95

9 Jan [Ward, E.] Honesty in distress, but reliev'd by no party... W82

11 Jan The monster: or, the world turn'd topsy turvy. M414

12 Jan Wright, S. A hymn to the incarnation. W569

13 Jan Deborah: a sacred ode. D83

16 Jan The battles. A poem... B106

18 Jan Tate, N. The triumph, or warriours welcome ... T84

19 Jan Wesley, S. Marlborough; or, the fate of Europe... W332

25 Jan The baboon a-la-mode. A satyr against the French. B2

29 Jan [Philips, J.] The splendid shilling... P246

1 Feb A trip to Nottingham... T488

6 Feb Arwaker, E. The birth-night, a pastoral. A333

6 Feb [Congreve, W.] Prologue to the court; on the queen's birth-day, 1704. C378

6 Feb A dialogue between the French standards in Westminster-hall, and the guns on the Tower-wharf... D268

6 Feb The sailor turn'd pyrate... S9

14 Feb An epilogue to the court, on the queen's birth-day. E355

14 Feb The hog toss'd in a blanket... H274

15 Feb Markland, G. A divine poem, in memory of the late high wind. M97

20 Feb Coppinger, M. A session of the poets... C429

1 Mar The broken-pipkin: a tale... B484

1 Mar A trip to Litchfield... T487

5 Mar The female monster...A satyr. F97

8 Mar [Coward, W.] Abramideis: or, the faithful patriarch... C475

15 Mar [Spooner, L.] Poetical recreations... S662

19 Mar Johnson, C. The queen: a pindarick ode. J72

26 Mar Fitchett, J. The hero reviv'd... F152

29 Mar [Browne, J.] Liberty and property. A satyr. B530·4

Apr [Cobb, S.] A psalm of thanksgiving to be sung by the children of Christ's-Hospital... C259

2 Apr [Mandeville, B.] The grumbling hive: or, knaves turn'd honest. M70

13 Apr Daniel the prophet no conjurer... D26

14 Apr The Coventry ballad, &c. H127

14 Apr Miscellanious poetical novels or tales... M275

26 Apr [Browne, J.] The fox set to watch the geese... B530·1

26 Apr The French king's advice to the late high-flying m--b--rs. F253

May A health to the Northamptonshire sneakers. H125

May Malet, T. The soldier's religion... M39

3 May A new translation of Æsop... N236

11 May The Perkinite Jacks: or, a new ballad on the tackers. P183

5 June Goldwin, W. Great Britain: or, the happy isle. G215

12 June A trip lately to Scotland... T483

19 June The grand mistake: or, all men happy if they please... G245

July The amorous nun... A217

July The church militant, or the whigs triumphant ... C176

July [Defoe, D.] The dyet of Poland, a satyr. D97

5 July Oliver Cromwell's ghost's advice to his friends. O170

6 July [Shippen, W.] The devil upon dun: or, moderation in masquerade. S442·2

10 July The Oxford treatment of their Cambridge friends, at the act... O275

12 July [Ward, E.] Fortune's bounty... W72

19 July Blackmore, Sir R. Eliza: an epick poem. B249

Aug The confederacy: or, a welcome to victory... C336

Aug Female apostacy: or, the true-born English-woman. F86

Aug [Oldmixon, J.] A chain of providence... O168·2

29 Aug [Ward, E.] Hudibras redivivus...Part the first. W90

Sept Miscellaneous poetical novels or tales...The second collection. M276

8 Sept The thanksgiving. A poem. T123

20 Oct [Ward, E.] A fair shell, but a rotten kernel... W68

22 Nov [Pittis, W.] A hymn to confinement... P442

29 Nov [Lenthall, W.] A trip to Leverpoole, by two of fate's children... L104

29 Nov [Ward, E.] More priestcraft... W123

Dec A net for the d---l: or, the town display'd... N37

Dec Splitter of freeholds. A satyr. S659

1 Dec Liberty. A poem. L169

18 Dec The dog in the wheel... D391

Æsop at Barcelona... A109

An answer to the Great noise about nothing... A248

[Betterton, T.] The royal conquest...As it was sung in the Prophetess... B204

Causton, P. Tunbridgialia: or, the pleasures of Tunbridge... C78

The c---y e---on... C554

The D---- deputies. A satyr. D1

[Darby, C.] The tackers. D45

The doleful complaint of Sir Humphry Mac-----h, on the loss of his election at Oxford. D393

An elegy on the burning of the Church memorial. E83

An elegy on...Captain Thomas Green... E134

An elegy on...Dr. John How... E150

An elegy on...Sir Roger L'Estrange. E178

An elegy on...Doctor Titus Oates... E203

An elegy upon...Dr. Titus Oates... E204

Epilogue: spoken by Mrs. Mountfort... E351

Froud, J. A prologue at the opening of the theatre in Bristol. F277

The gamster prosecuted... G8

[Garth, Sir S.] Prologue spoken at the first opening of the queen's new theatre in the Hay-market. G39

The Geneva ballad. G109

[Geree, J.] A poem to his grace the Duke of Marlborough ... G131

Good advice to beaus and batchelours... G218

A great noise about nothing: or the church's danger. G273

A health to the tackers. H126

His grace the Duke of Marlborough's welcome... H247

Hullin, —. Ode, sur les glorieux succés de monseigneur le Duc de Marlborough... H386

Korath: or the danger of schism. K105

Lacaux, P. Poëme pour le jour de la naissance de la reine. L5

The London ladies dressing-room... L238

The messenger defeated: or, the lawyer's escape... M205

Moderation display'd, the second part... M362

The Northamptonshire health. N320

The oculist...address'd to Sir William Read... O14

Oxfordshire. O276

[Pittis, W.] An elegy on the lamented death of poor Truth and Honesty... P434

[Pittis, W.] Fire and faggot or the city bonfire. P436

[Prior, M.] An English padlock. P1076

Pritz, J. G. De serenissima atque potentissima principe, Anna...poemation... P1101

Sadler, J. Loyalty, attended with great news... S7

[Shippen, W.] The sequel: or moderation further display'd... S442

Sir John Leake's fight with Admiral Ponty... S472

The Suffolk health. S783

The tacker's ghost... T1

Tate, N. On a new copy-book, entitl'd the Penman's magazine... T70

[Thompson, W.] Some fruits of solitude... T176

To my friend Dr. Tho. Clark... T352

[Trotter, C.] A poem on his grace the Duke of Marlborough's return... T509

The true Christian's jubile[!]... T520

The university answer to the pretended University ballad. U17

The university ballad... U19

The vision. V104

A whip for the whiggs. W404

[1705?]

The duumvirate. D564

The English padlock unlock'd. E339

A declaration without doors. D85

The picture of the first occasional conformist... P272

The quaker's song, sung by Mrs. Willis... Q6

[Rowe, N.] Horace, lib. ii. ode iv. imitated...[1705/07?] R291

The valliant souldiers and sailors loyal subjects health... [1705/07] V7

Rime and reason: or, a word in season... [1705/–] R188

1705: SCOTLAND

On the blessed day of our Saviours birth... O191

Bang the brocker, or Bully Pierce alias A-----n the turncoat... B54

Captain Green's last conference with Captain Madder... C31

Captain Thomas Green's last farewell... C33

A seasonable advice, to all who encline to go in pirrating ... S165

[Clark, J.] The cross and the crown... C226

A confession and lamentation, recomended to Mr. Madder... C340

Congratulation for the happy arrival of...the Duke of Argile... C343

[Forbes, W.] Mack-faux the mock-moralist or Pierce the traitor... F186

[Forbes, W.] A pil for pork-eaters... F188

The horrid murther committed by Captain Green... H323

The merites of piracie or, a new song on Captain Green ... M192

A new-years gift for the renegado... N244

Symson, A. Tripatriarchicon... S944

[Whyte, W.] Elegie on...Sir James Falconer of Phesdo ... W450

[1705?]

Campbell, K. Ad nobilissimos Anglos consolidantes. C13

Campbell, K. Ad serenissimam reginam. Ode. C14

Nobilissimo & illustrissimo Jacobo comiti de Seafield... Congratulatio. N312

1706

8 Jan [Defoe, D.] A hymn to peace... D110

12 Jan Æsop in Europe... A113

14 Jan [Prior, M.] The squirrel. A poem. P1086

26 Jan Oldmixon, J. Iberia liberata... O167

30 Jan [Browne, J.] The country parson's honest advice ... B528

7 Feb England's glory... E317

21 Feb [Fenton, E.] Cerealia: an imitation of Milton. F104

7 Mar The law corrupted; a satire. L73

14 Mar [Ward, E.] The rambling fuddle-caps... W150

16 Mar Harison, W. Woodstock Park. H51

26 Mar [Cobb, S.] A psalm of thanksgiving to be sung by the children of Christ's-Hospital... C260

Apr The description, or the matchless-fair-one. D238

3 Apr [Alsop, A.] Charlettus Percivallo suo... A177

3 Apr [Hoffman, F.] The pilgrim's progress...done into verse. H268

10 Apr The crafty courtier: or the fable of Reinard the fox... C493

20 Apr Against ingratitude. Satire the second. A122

27 Apr Goldwin, W. Europe. A poem. G214

30 Apr [Vernon, —] Corona civica. V36

May [Defoe, D.] An essay on the great battle at Ramellies. D106

2 May Joshua: a poem in imitation of Milton... J101

3 May [Walsh, W.] Horace lib. III. ode iii. imitated. W33

9 May [Browne, J.] The insect war... B530·3

11 May The country parson's advice to those little scribblers... C454

23 May Tate, N. Britannia's prayer for the queen. T48

31 May [Browne, J.] The royal prophetess... B530·7

June Defoe, D. Daniel Defoe's Hymn for the thanksgiving. D109

1 June An ode on the Duke of Marlborough. O46

10 June [Johnson, C.] Ramelies. A poem. J73

18 June A letter to Mr. Prior, occasion'd by the Duke of Marlborough's late victory... L149

25 June On the victory at Ramelies. O228

29 June The unfortunate lovers... U5

2 July [Fenton, E.] On the first-fit of the gout. F112

4 July Steele, R. Prologue to the University of Oxford. S740

4 July Wagstaffe, W. Ramelies: a poem... W3

6 July Bouchery, W. Hymnus sacer: sive paraphrasis in Deboræ et Baraci canticum... B325

6 July [Prior, M.] An ode, humbly inscrib'd to the queen... P1081

6 July [Ward, E.] The riddle, or a paradoxical character of a hairy monster often found in Holland... W164

10 July Cibber, C. A prologue in the opera call'd Camilla... C200

10 July A paraphrase on the fourteenth chapter of Isaiah... P56

16 July The high-church hieroglyphick... H193

18 July Gardiner, J. Rapin of gardens... G11

20 July [Defoe, D.] Jure divino: a satyr. D128

20 July An epistle to Sir Richard Blackmore... E411

23 July [Blackmore, Sir R.] Advice to the poets... B238

23 July A description of the play-house in Dorset-garden. D236

23 July An ode occasion'd by the battle of Rammelies. O37

Aug A cynic laughing: or, the gentleman in a garret ... C555

6 Aug [Phillips, J.] The vision of Mons. Chamillard concerning the battle of Ramilies... P254

10 Aug A panegyrick epistle...to S. R—— B——... P31

19 Aug Congreve, W. A pindarique ode...on the victorious progress of her majesty's arms... C376

26 Aug Hurst, B. A poem to Florinda singing. H412

29 Aug [Atwood, W.] A modern inscription to the Duke of Marlborough's fame... A365·5

5 Sept To his grace the Duke of Marlborough on his late successes in Flanders. T338

23 Sept Smithfield groans... S530

26 Sept Hampstead-wells. H31

10 Oct Hampstead-wells. Part II. H32

14 Oct Paris, J. Ramillies. A poem... P65

19 Oct [Bolton, —] Prince Eugene: an heroic poem... B315

24 Oct [Daniel, R.] The British warriour... D27

26 Oct The prologue spoken by Mrs. Babb... P1130

26 Oct The taylor turn'd poet... T6

30 Oct A hymn to St. Tack, sung at ...Oxford. H454

1 Nov 'Butler, S.' Dildoides. A burlesque poem. B607

5 Nov Tate, N. A congratulary poem, to...Richard earl Rivers... T49·5

7 Nov [Finch, A. countess.] The Tunbridge prodigy. F142

14 Nov [Tickell, T.] Oxford. A poem. T299

20 Nov Frowd, R. A poem on Prince Eugene's victory over the Duke of Orleans... F278

26 Nov [Clay, S.] An epistle from the elector of Bavaria to the French king... C233

Dec D'Urfey, T. A new ode. Or, dialogue between Mars, the god of war... D549

5 Dec   Neale, T. Ἐνύπνιον: or the vision... N13

14 Dec   Judoign. A poem on the late victory in Brabant. J110

17 Dec   Chase, J. An ode. On the success of her majesty's arms... C139

17 Dec   [Gould, R.] The poetess, a satyr... G231·5

19 Dec   A new ode...on the glorious successes of her majesty's arms... N162

24 Dec   D'Urfey, T. The trophies: or, Augusta's glory... D553

30 Dec   [Conduitt, J.] A poem upon the late glorious successes, &c... C334

30 Dec   Dennis, J. The battle of Ramillia... D220

31 Dec   A letter from the B. of S—— to the A.B. of Paris... L132

Baker, D. The history of Job... B9

The beggar on horseback... B161

[Cavendish, W. *duke*.] An allusion to the bishop of Cambray's supplement of Homer. C81

The Dutchess of C——'s memorial...D464

D'Urfey, T. Titus and Gissippus: or, the power of friendship... D552

An elegy on...James, duke of Berwick... E57

An elegy on...Mr. Benjamin Dod... E102

Farquhar, G. The prologue spoken...at the opening of the theatre in the Hay-market... F64

Feilding, R. General Fielding's answer to the Dutchess of C——'s memorial... F83

Feilding, R. Handsome Fealding's letter to his first wife... F84

The fifteen comforts of cuckoldom... F127

The fifteen comforts of matrimony... F128

The fifteen comforts of whoring... F131

The French king's rhodomontade... F256

The lawyers answer to the Country parson's good advice ... L77

A letter to Mareschal Tallard... L146

Lettre au Marechal de Tallard. L158

The mercury hawkers in mourning... M186

A new elegy on the death of trade. N132

Now is the time. N331

The Paris gazeteer... P64

Patience. A present to the Press-yard. P121

Pinkeman's company in mourning... P290

[Prior, M.] Pallas and Venus. An epigram. P1082

The royal gamsters; or the old cards new shuffled... R308

The royal health... R310

Settle, E. Thalia triumphans to the hond Saml. Barker ... S299

Spencer, R. An epithalamium upon the happy marriage of the...Earl of Orrorey... S650

Taubman, N. Virtue in distress... T93

The tripe club. A satyr... T495

[Trotter, C.] On his grace the Duke of Marlborough... T508

Vaticinium pacis... V21

The whores and bawds answer to the Fifteen comforts of whoring. W445

[1706?]

The batchelors and maids answer to the Fifteen comforts of matrimony... B5

Ode. [Carminum præses...] O17

A pindarick ode on his excellency John duke of Marlborough... P287

Tate, N. The song for new-year's-day, 1706... T79

A bridle for the French king... [1706/07] B447

Browne, J. 'Sir, with submission, I humbly crave' [1706/07] B525

The unfortunate family... [1706/12?] U3

1706: SCOTLAND

6 Aug   A pastoral elegy on...Christian Riddel... P105

Nov   [Defoe, D.] The vision, a poem. D185

Nov   [Hamilton, J. *baron*.] A Scots answer to a British vision. H9

Nov   [Defoe, D.] A reply to the Scots answer to the British vision. D148

Dec   Defoe, D. Caledonia, &c... D90

Dec   A second defence of the Scotish vision. S167

11 Dec   [Brown, T.] A dialogue between the pillory and Daniel Defoe. B511

19 Dec   A poem upon the union. P687

Campbell, K. Carmen Rammeliense. C15

Elegie on...Mr. David Williamson... E283

The man of honour... M68

A search after honesty a poem. S163

[Symson, A.] Unio politico-poetico-joco-seria... S945

Three poems, Mahanaim...Peniel...and the Triumph consummat... T256

[1706?]

[Hamilton, J. *baron*.] An equivalent for Defoe. H8

On the death of Sir William Sharp... O199

[Pitcairne, A.] Gualteri Dannistoni ad Georgium Buchananum epistola... P364

She put her hand upon his scull... S384

A voice from the north... [1706/07] V109

Monteith, R. To the...dean and faculty of advocates. [1706/10?] M422

1706: IRELAND

Marlborough: a poem... M105

The new idol, a poem... N144

1707

1 Jan [Walsh, W.] Ode for the thanksgiving day. W35

2 Jan [Wycherley, W.] On his grace the Duke of Marlborough. W576

6 Jan Rowe, N. A poem upon the late glorious successes of her majesty's arms... R301

11 Jan [Fenton, E.] An ode to the sun, for the new-year. F110

Feb 'Defoe, D.' The fifteen comforts of a Scotch-man. D107

4 Mar [Harris, J.] Marlborides, sive bellum Britannicum... H74

5 Mar Tate, N. The muse's memorial of the happy recovery of... Richard earl of Burlington... T67

7 Mar Great-Britain's happiness: a poem on the passing of the union... G261

7 Mar [Gardiner, E.] A poem occasion'd by the late thanksgiving... G10·5

13 Mar [Philips, J.] Honoratissimo viro, Henrico St.--John... P244

19 Mar The fifteen plagues of a maiden-head... F135

20 Mar The porch and academy open'd, or Epictetus's manual... P998

25 Mar Glanvill, J. A poem, occasion'd by the successes of the present war... G173

27 Mar Epinicion sacro nomini Annæ Magnæ Britanniæ... E357

27 Mar [Darby, C.] The union a poem... D46·5

27 Mar Vernon, —. The union. A poem... V38

7 Apr [Harison, W.] On his grace the Duke of Marlborough going for Holland... H49

8 Apr Maidwell, L. Comitia lyrica: sive carmen panegyricum... M24

29 Apr Dickinson, W. Ode gratulatoria, in Magnæ Britanniæ imperium... D302

May [Browne, J.] The British court: a poem... B527·4

1 May [Pix, M.] A poem...to the lords commissioners for the union... P461·5

1 May [Pomfret, J.] Quae rare, chara... P735

5 May Great Britain's joyful triumph, for the happy union... G264

14 May [Browne, J.] The patriots of Great Britain... B530·6

17 May Theobald, L. A pindarick ode on the union. T146

20 May [Dunton, J.] The pulpit-fool. A satyr. D538

22 May The several qualities of the British court... S360

31 May A satyr upon musty-snuff. S74

12 June [Rowe, N.] Unio. R304

26 June [Browne, J.] The London belles... B530·5

July Perkins, J. The poet's fancy... P191

8 July A pastoral essay lamenting the death of...Mr. Coke of Norfolk. P109

15 July [Dunton, J.] The second part of the Pulpit-fool ... D539

11 Aug Hymenæus, a poem. H420

19 Aug Grubb, J. The British heroes... G303

30 Aug The fair in an uproar, or, the dancing doggs... F29

25 Sept An elegy on Mr. John Tutchin... E263

7 Oct [Dunton, J.] The he-strumpets... D536

23 Oct To his grace the Duke of Marlborough. T336

31 Oct A poem of condolance on the loss of Sir Cloudesley Shovel... P562

8 Nov On the union of the two kingdoms... O226

27 Nov Aubin, P. The Stuarts: a pindarique ode... A367

27 Nov [Browne, J.] The Gothick hero...Charles XII ... B530·2

29 Nov [Darby, C.] A poem upon our unhappy loss of Sir Cloudesly Shovel... D44·5

29 Nov [Dunton, J.] Bumography: or, a touch at the lady's tails... D534

12 Dec A thundering poem to the swearer... T266

18 Dec [King, W.] The art of cookery... K55

23 Dec A funeral poem, on the death of...Sir Cloudesly Shovel... F300

24 Dec Hill, A. Camillus...to Charles earl of Peterborough... H211

24 Dec Pittis, W. A funeral poem sacred to...Sir Cloudesly Shovel... P439

Advice to the author of...The British court. A88

Advice to the ladies, or, an answer to the court and city beauties... A96

Ashby, R. A tender greeting and exhortation to youth. A340

The batchelor's choice... B3

[Brady, N.] A song compos'd by Mr. Henry Purcell... B373

Brookes, H. Daphnis. A pastoral poem... B498

[Browne, J.] The singing-bird's address to the eagle... B530·9

A character of a turn-coat... C123

The country vicar's address to her majesty. C460

The country-man and his wife Joan in mourning... C461

Cross-grove, H. Britannia. Anna's glory: or the happy union... C517

Dialogue entre deux freres, touchant les prophetes cevenois [and six continuations]. D278

The duty of a husband... D563

An elegy on...William duke of Devonshire... E101

An elegy on John Tutchin... E262

An elegy on...Mr. John Tutchin... E264

An elegy on...Mr. James Whiston... E272

An elegy on...Mr. Jeremiah White... E273

An epistle to...Charles Montague... E420

Fools have fortune... F180

The fifteen comforts of a Dutch-man... F124

The fifteen comforts of a lawyer... F125

The fifteen comforts of a wanton wife... F126

Gill, T. Instructions for children, in verse. G160

The glorious works of creation and providence... G182

Greene, T. Threnodiæ Britannicæ. A funeral poem to... John lord Cutts. G289

Hawke, E. A poem upon the law... H109

In imitation of Lucretius... I20

The infallible mountebank, or, quack doctor. I39

[Jackson, S.] The duty of a wife. J12

The maids vindication: or, the fifteen comforts of living a single life... M23

Massalina: or; the town mistris in masquerade. M133

A modern Latin ode attempted in English... M375

An ode in praise of musick... O34

A new elegy on...Sir Cloudesly Shovel... N134

A new elegy upon...the Lord Cuts... N138

On the marriage of...the lord-keeper to Mrs. Clavering. O208

A plain hymn to our redeemer... P472

Scrub, scrub: a poem in praise of the itch... S155

Settle, E. Augusta triumphans. Ramilly and Turin... S240

Settle, E. Carmen irenicum. The union of...Great Britain... S245

Settle, E. Virtuti sacellum...to the pious memory of... Sir Robert Clayton, kt. S343

Tate, N. The triumph of union... T82

Theobald, L. Naufragium britannicum...to the memory of Sr Cloudesly Shovel. T144

The true-born Britain... T513

A true caracter of the Bread-street tatlers... T517

Two kingdoms made one... T585

The union topknot... U12

[Ward, E.] A Good-Friday ramble... W75

The women-hater's lamentation... W549

[1707?]

A choice penny-worth of wit... C160

The church in no danger... C175

The duty of a husband... D562

Estcourt, R. Britain's jubilee: a new congratulatory ballad... E478

Fowler, J. On the queens most glorious victories over the French king. F216

The high-church bully: or, the praises of Mr. Higgins. H191

The Scotch lords welcome to England... S140

Tutchin's everlasting monument... T573

The prophets: an heroic poem... [1707/08] P1140

The battle of Almanza. [1707/–] B96

1707: SCOTLAND

Jan   A Scots poem: or a new-years gift... S145

23 Jan   A song on his grace the Duke of Marlborough's happy return into England... S587

Feb   The knights of the horn orders address... K102

Feb   A poem upon the most potent prince James duke of Hamilton... P681

Elegy upon...the Dutchess of Athol... E51

An elegy on...Mary Eriskine... E112

An elegy upon...Sir David Hume of Crossrig... E154

An elegy on...Lady Jean Ramsay... E224

An elegye upon the...ilustrious and venerable lady Princess Scocia. E235

Elegy on...John earl of Stairs... E244

An elegy upon...John earl of Stair's. E245

The moderate man's advice against extravagant drinking ... M360

Scotlands tears, or Scotland bemoaning the loss of her antient priviledges... S143

A short satyre on...the Albanian animal... S449

Waring, H. The divine or hypostatical union... W236

[1707?]

Campbell, K. Faciam eos in gentem unam. C16

A Scots excise-man described. [1707/–] S144

1707: IRELAND

An essay by way of elegy, on...Arthur Upton... E461

An essay to the memory of John, lord Cutts... E473

Ireland's prospect of happiness... I63

An ode on the queen's birth-day... O51

A poem on the happy union between England and Scotland... P619

1708

15 Jan   Cook, E. The sot-weed factor: or, a voyage to Maryland... C405

23 Jan   Mirth in ridicule... M272

24 Jan   A poem, shewing a plain and short way to be happy... P658

28 Jan   The merchants advocate... M184

29 Jan Hickeringill, E. A burlesque poem in praise of ignorance... H180

29 Jan [Philips, J.] Cyder. A poem. P237

29 Jan A poem inscrib'd to Lieut. gen. Ingoldsby... P543

2 Feb [Settle, E.] Honori sacellum...to the memory of William duke of Devonshire... S265

3 Feb Great Britains hope, in an address to my Lord Pembroke... G262

7 Feb The landlord's tale: a poem... L44

7 Feb The seditious insects...in convocation. S192

Mar 'Tis high time to make hast... T315

4 Mar Powell, J. A poem on the Earl of Peterborow and Monmouth... P1009

11 Mar The devil to do about Dunkirk... D245

12 Mar The pretended Prince of Wales's lamentation for the small pox. P1031

19 Mar Tate, N. A consolatory poem to...John lord Cutts... T59

29 Mar An elegy upon...Dr. John Partridgd [!]... E209

30 Mar [Swift, J.] An elegy on Mr. Patrige... S832

Apr [Browne, J.] The splitter of freeholds... B530·95

Apr King, W. The art of love... K60

3 Apr The cupulo...of St. Paul's... C541

26 Apr Hill, A. The invasion... H221

28 Apr The flight of the Pretender... F170

May The French prophet's resurrection... F260

May The plagues of Ægypt... P468

May Tate, N. The celebrated speeches of Ajax and Ulysses... T49

6 May Omega: a poem on the last judgment... O173

22 May [Blackmore, Sir R.] The Kit-Cats. B257

22 May [Gay, J.] Wine a poem. G89

29 May Demas chastis'd: or, the Buxsted advocate... D212

1 June Ozell, J. Boileau's Lutrin... O282

5 June The poet's paradise... P697

8 June [Browne, J.] St. James's Park: a satyr. B530·8

22 June The long vacation: a satyr... L243

24 June Iter boreale... I73

16 July Gaynam, J. Marlborough still conquers... G93

20 July The battel of Audenard... B98

21 July Gildon, C. Libertas triumphans... G153

26 July [Dunton, J.] Stinking fish... D540

31 July Windsor Castle: a poem... W525

Aug Almonds for parrots... A173

Aug Tate, N. A congratulatory poem to...Prince George of Denmark... T55

12 Aug The true state of mortality... T531

13 Aug Audenarde, a poem... A369

22 Sept [Ward, E.] Marriage dialogues... W113

25 Sept A long vacation prologue... L246

30 Oct An elegy on...Prince George of Denmark... E129

15 Nov [Pittis, W.] Æsop at Oxford... P422

16 Nov Dive, C. To the queen, upon the death of his royal highness. D339

16 Nov Welsted, L. A poem, occasioned by... Audenard... W305

17 Nov An ode to the queen, on the death of his royal highness George... O72

23 Nov [Holdsworth, E.] Muscipula... H279

Dec The great hero, and the little one... G268

Dec Newgate in tears. Being an elegy on...Richard Murray... N287

7 Dec [Wilson, B.] Aldenardum carmen Duci Malburiensi... W518

11 Dec A poem on the defeat of the French army at the river Schelde... P608

25 Dec Milton's sublimity asserted... M267

Abbott, W. An elegy on...Sir Walter St. John... A2

Abigal's lamentation for the loss of secretary H-----y... A3

Apotheosis basilike... A273

Aubin, P. The extasy... A366

Aubin, P. The wellcome: a poem, to...the Duke of Marlborough... A368

Burgundy bewitch'd: or, Vendome in a trance... B577

'Burnet, G.' A new elegy on...Prince George... B581

The chimney-sweeper in disgrace... C150

A condolatory poem...to her...majesty... C333

A dialogue between Windsor Castle, and Blenheim House ... D275

Dodington, G. B., baron. Ad somnum. D368

D'Urfey, T. The French pride abated... D543

D'Urfey, T. Honor & opes... D544

Elegie sur la mort de son altesse royale le Prince George... E40

An elegy on...Sir Thomas Rawlinson... E226

The French invasion... F251

A happy memorable ballad, on the fight near Audenarde... H45

The invasion; a satyr... I51

Jack Frenchman's lamentation... J1

'Maurus, R.' The Pretender's declaration... M140

Motteux, P. A song perform'd at the post-office feast... M531

The mourning court... M548

A new ballad. To the tune of, Chivy Chace. N88

A new song. To the tune of Lilly bullaro, &c. N217

Old England's new triumph: or, the battel of Oudenard. O109

The picture of a female favourite. P270

[Samber, R.] On the passion of our blessed Saviour. S27

The scrutiny... S157

The scrutiny: with the second ode... S158

Settle, E. Honori sacellum...to the memory of... Robert earl of Scarsdale. S266

Settle, E. Memoriæ fragranti...to the memory of... Viscountess Fitzharding. S278

Settle, E. Memoriæ fragranti...to the pious memory of ...Sr. E: Waldo kt. S279

Settle, E. Musa triumphans. To his grace the Duke of Newcastle... S287

Settle, E. Threnodium apollinare...to the memory of... Henry Hare baron of Colerane. S340

Settle, E. Threnodium apollinare...to the memory of Dr. Edward Tyson... S341

Speak truth, and shame the devil... S619

Tate, N. The Windsor muse's address... T88

The thanksgiving song... T125

Threnodia virginea: or, the apotheosis... T261

Tres libri Solomonis... T470

A trip to Dunkirk... T484

[Ward, E.] The wars of the elements... W201

The Welsh-monster... W282

[*1708?*]

[Alsop, A.] Charissimo suo duci de Vendosme. Tallardus. A176

England triumphant... E313

A poem on the defeat of the French army at the river Scheld... P609

Tate, N. The song for the new-year 1708... T80

Pomfret, S. Mr. Pomfret's hymn at the sacrament. [1708/09] P738

1708: SCOTLAND

25 Dec Pitcairne, A. Davidi Dromondio jurisconsulto... P356

The aged father's blessing... A130

[Brown, W.] The Lamentations of Jeremiah, paraphras'd. B516

An elegy on...John Hamilton lord Balhaven... E53

Elegy on...Lord John Hamilton of Balhaven. E54

Epitaph on...David Crawfurd of Drumsuy... E444

[Erskine, R.] The believer's dowry... E451

Pastora's lament for Adonis... P102

Whyte, W. Elegy on...Lord John Hamilton of Balhaven... W449

[*1708?*]

[Pitcairne, A.] Ad Georgium Kirtonum... [1708?/13] P305

Pitcairne, A. Q. Horatio Flacco... [1708?/13] P399

Pitcairne, A. Roberto Graio scoto... [1708?/13] P402

1708: IRELAND

An elegy, on...Edward earl of Meath... E187

Grant, J. Alpheus, or a pastoral elegy on...Prince George... G251

Ormsbye, R. Carmen heroicum... O249

1709

6 Jan   Carmen seculare... C55

29 Jan   [Wright, J.] Phœnix Paulina... W568

1 Feb   The eagle and the robin... E2

8 Feb   [Bellamy, D.] Taffy's triumph... B176

8 Feb   Celadon...on the death of...the P. of Denmark... C88

12 Feb   [Quincy, J.] The mouse-trap... Q15

12 Feb   [Ward, E.] The forgiving husband, and adulterous wife... W70

15 Feb   [Hill, T.] Nundinæ Sturbrigienses, anno 1702... H238

19 Feb   Expeditio militaris Addisoniana... E603

21 Feb   [Swift, J.] A famous prediction of Merlin... S849

22 Feb   An heroick essay upon the unequal'd victory... at Wynendale. H154

1 Mar   Gill, T. Advice to youth... G156

8 Mar   Scipio Britannicus: the scourge of France... S137.5

9 Mar   The beasts in power, or Robin's song... B125

10 Mar   [Blackmore, *Sir* R.] Instructions to Vander Bank... B254

16 Mar   The dream of the Solan goose... D434

18 Mar   Horneck, P. An ode. Inscrib'd to...the Earl of Wharton... H320

Apr   [Cobb, S.] A psalm of thanksgiving... C261

2 Apr   [Earbery, M.] The battel of Oudenarde. E8

7 Apr   Newcomb, T. An epistle from the Duke of Burgundy to the French king. N251

7 Apr   A poem occasioned by the death of Mr. Dent... P552

7 Apr   The progress of valour... P1115

13 Apr   [Rowe, N.] Epilogue spoken by Mrs Barry... R287

14 Apr   Coward, W. Licentia poetica discuss'd... C477

19 Apr   [Plaxton, W.] The Yorkshire-racers... P480

19 Apr   [Ward, E.] The vanity of upstarts... W190

28 Apr   Welsted, L. The Duke of Marlborough's arrival... W288

11 May   A translation of Mr. Hill's Nundinae Sturbrigienses... T442

17 May   Pittis, W. Nereo. A funeral-poem sacred to... Sir George Rooke... P448

19 May [Churchill, W.] A poem...to his grace the Duke of Marlborough... C187

23 May The mall: or, the reigning beauties... M42

24 May Alcander: a poem... A158

24 May Johnson, R. Cursus equestris Nottinghamiensis... J75

June An hymn for the charity-schools... H423

15 June Canary-birds naturaliz'd in Utopia. C18

22 June [Browne, J.] The circus: or, British olympicks... B527·8

6 July [Richards, T.] Χοιροχωρογραφια: sive, Hoglandiæ descriptio. R195

26 Aug Cupid in quest of beauty... C540

27 Aug The hunting after money. H409

1 Sept Taffi's master-piece... T3

3 Sept The amorous war... A218

8 Sept Cobb, S. The female reign... C247

20 Sept The unfortunate ramble... U6

Oct The servitour: a poem... S222

20 Oct A letter to a friend... L142

12 Nov [Hughes, J.] An ode on the incarnation. H364

21 Nov A thanksgiving, or the elect-lady upon the war... T124

6 Dec Butler, R. The British Michael... B605

23 Dec The priest turn'd poet... P1053

An agent turn'd inside out... A131

The bear-garden in mourning... B124

Bickerstaff, E. England's doom. A prophecy... B210

Cade, T. A divine poem on the redemption... C1·5

[Congreve, W.] A prologue spoken by Mrs. Bracegirdle... C377

The dog-kennel to be lett... D392

An elegy, on the death of the French king... E123

[Ellis, W.] The queen of Great Brittain's royal bounty to the distressed Palatines. E296

Feilding, R. An elegy on the death of the Dutchess of Cleveland... F82

The fifteen pleasures of a virgin... F136

[Finch, A. *countess*.] The spleen, a pindarique ode... F141

A funeral satyr in memory of...Anthony Bowyer... F305

The garden plot. G10

The glorious campaign... G180

High church, with a demonstration... H199

Love without affectation... L287

The mouse-trap... M552

Nugæ canoræ: or, the taste of the town... N335

[Reynolds, J.] Death's vision... R177

The royal shuffler... R318

The sacred parallel of royal martyrdom... S5

The Scheld: a poem on the late glorious victory... S133

Settle, E. Augusta lacrymans...to the memory of...Sr Charles Thorold. S227

[Settle, E.] Honori sacellum...to the memory of...Henry Thynne. S267

[Settle, E.] Thalia triumphans. To...James earl of Salisbury... S300

Settle, E. Virtuti sacellum...to the memory of...Sr. John Buckworth. S344

[Swift, J.] Baucis and Philemon... S800

The three champions. T253

To the Duke of Marlborough... T366

A warning piece... W238

A warning to lovers... W241

The Welsh mouse-trap... W283

[*1709?*]

The Duke of Anjous farewel to Spain... D498

The Duke of Marlborough's welcome... D501

To my lord bishop of R―― ――... T353

D'Urfey, T. The authentick letter of Marshal de Boufflers... [1709/10] D541

Pomfret, S. Mr. Pomfret's hymn at the sacrament... [1709/10] P739

Browne, J. To each gentleman soldier...[1709/11] B526

1709: SCOTLAND

Dowglass, R. An elegy upon...the Dutches of Queensberry... D415

Elegie on...Mr. George Meldrum... E188

An epitaph on the French prophet... E443

A rare new song, shewing the bravery of...the Duke of Argile... R121

Robin red-breast and the wren... R235

[Scott, *Sir* W.] Epitaphium viri reverendissimi D. Georgii Meldrumii... S149

Smith, R. An elegie upon...John marquis of Tullibardine... S529

To the memory of...George Meldrum... T384

[*1709?*]

In obitum...D. Gul. Crechton. I26

Pitcairne, A. Archibaldo Stevensono equiti... [1709/10] P343

1709: IRELAND

An elegy, on the death of the French king... E123

[Thompson, W.] Mendico-hymen: seu tuphlo-perogamia. T166

Williams, W. A poem on the piety and prosperity of... Anne... W515

Ireland (*cont.*)   [*1709?*]
Labour lost... [1709/10] L2

[171–]

[Bonwick, A.] To the memory of...Sir George Freeman ... B322

Cocken, D. To the worshipful Company of Frame-work-knitters. C272

A defence for the ladies... D87

The duties of servants to their masters... D559

Ellis, W. The true emblem of a sot... E294

An epitaph on Mr Samuel. Smith... E441

Gill, T. A new-year's-gift... G164

Gill, T. Thomas Gills...upon the recovery of his sight ... G167

Gill, T. Upon the nativity of our blessed saviour. G168

Guiscard's ghost to Lord B-------ke. G311

A hymn to be sung by the charity boys... H433

An hymn, to be sung by the charity-boys... H435

The lost maidenhead restor'd... L272

The loyal Irish man... L300

The Oxford riddle... O269

Ramondon, L. A new song, to an Irish coranoch... R28

A satyr: shewing, the nature and proceedings of the church of En----d. S69

A supplement to...The duties of servants... S787

The wanton baker of Westminster... W38

We've lost it at last. W261

[171–]: SCOTLAND

Acrostic. A18

Colme, J. De ætate, & vita humana... C301

Edinburgh's observator... E16

An elegy on Willy Bald... E52

An elegy on the great and famous Blew-stone... E62

An elegy on...Francis Masterton apothecary. E186

An elegy on...John Merry... E190

The grandsir's ghost... G250

Gray's ellegie, with his own conceity answer. G253

An humble address, to the...general assembly... H392

The lady's answer, to...satyres on the hoop'd petticoats. L25

A new proclamation concerning farthingales... N172

A new-years-gift... N245

A poem on the...death of Captain Chiesly... P629

A poem on the race of Leith... P640

A poem upon the noble company of young Archers... P684

Ramondon, L. A new song... R27, R29

[*171–*]: *Scotland* (*cont.*)
Ramondon, L. Victory and beauty, a new song... R30

The usurer... U30

Vindiciæ secundum Joannem Despauterium datæ. V100

[171–]: IRELAND

Oxinards's lamentation e're he hung himself... O266

1710

Jan	The trumpeter. A fable... T534	
Jan	[Ward, E.] Pulpit-war... W148	
24 Jan	[Evans, A.] The apparition. E517	
Feb	A poem on the queen's birth-day. P639·5	
16 Feb	Stanza's on King Charles the martyr... S718	
1 Mar	The tale of a nettle... T13	
2 Mar	Bragge, F. Two odes from the Latin of... Rapin... B380	
3 Mar	The projector, or Remarker remark'd... P1118	
7 Mar	Callipædiæ; or, an art now to have handsome children... C4	
7 Mar	[Oldisworth, W.] Callipædia: or, the art of getting pretty children... O142	
14 Mar	The encomium, a poem... E309	
25 Mar	An elegy on the death of high-church passive-obedience... E147	
4 Apr	The Oxfordshire election. O279	
5 Apr	Fair warning. F36	
6 Apr	[Ward, E.] Britannia: a poem... W51	
10 Apr	Captain Tom's ballad... C34	
24 Apr	The epilogue, to be spoken before the four Indian kings... E353	
26 Apr	Have at you blind harpers... H108	
26 Apr	[Ward, E.] Vulgus Britannicus...[Part 1] W193	
28 Apr	The credit and interest of Great Britain consider'd... C502	
28 Apr	The royal strangers ramble... R321	
May	The age of mad-folks. A124	
May	A hymn to be sung at the anniversary-meeting of the charity-schools... H429	
May	The idol of Paris... I3	
2 May	Stubbes, G. The laurel, and the olive... S773	
8 May	The save-alls. S121	
9 May	A trip to Kensington... T486	
9 May	The Westminster combat. W367	
12 May	Advice to the q--n. A98	
12 May	Tale of a tarr. T19	
13 May	The London tale... L241	
13 May	[Stacy, E.] The black-bird's tale. S679	
17 May	The perils of false brethren... P178	
18 May	The court lady's tale... C467	
22 May	Smith, E. A poem on the death of Mr. John Philips... S516	
22 May	A toast for all true hearts. T401	

23 May The Welchman's tales concerning the times... W287

30 May An elegy on the lamented death of John Dolben ... E103

1 June On the sentence...on Dr. Sacheverell. O219

3 June The wolf stript of his shepherd's clothing... W545

8 June Squire Bickerstaffe's elegy on...John Dolben ... S671

9 June High-church miracles... H196

10 June The birds and beasts, a fable... B219

12 June A coppy of verses writt in a common-prayer-book... C433

23 June Horace turn'd whigg... H315

28 June A receipt to dress a parson after the newest fashion... R145

30 June [Pittis, W.] The Sunderland tale. P455

1 July The play-house scuffle... P487

3 July A rary--show... R128

4 July [Pittis, W.] The seven extinguishers... P453

6 July [Stacy, E.] The black-bird's second tale. S685

10 July Ozell, J. La secchia rapita: the trophy bucket ... O286

11 July Good advice if rightly taken. G217

12 July Welsted, L. A poem to the memory of... Mr. Philips... W308

25 July The impeachment. I11

29 July A new extempore-prayer... N142

5 Aug The fickle courtier... F116

8 Aug [Ward, E.] The galloper... W74

15 Aug [Phillips, J.] Mr John Milton's satyre against hypocrites... P253

15 Aug [Pittis, W.] The fox unkenell'd... P437

16 Aug [Ward, E.] The tipling philosophers... W185

Sept She's her own woman again. S386

Sept Worcester dumb-bells; a ballad... W561

5 Sept [Garth, Sir S.] A poem to the Earl of Godolphin ... G36

16 Sept Honest Clodd's advice to his countrymen... H295

19 Sept A new and ingenious fortune book... N51

20 Sept The mad-mans hospital... M12

26 Sept The lunacy... L326

28 Sept An epilogue intended to be spoken by Mr. Estcourt... E347

2 Oct The new revolution... N178

3 Oct The glorious warriour...in praise of General Stanhope... G181

4 Oct To Mr. Stanhope... T347

7 Oct [Swift, J.] The virtues of Sid Hamet the magician's rod. S935

9 Oct A dialogue between Captain Tom and Sir H——y D——n C——t. D255

9 Oct A dream: or, the force of fancy... D437

9 Oct To the immortal memory of that renowned manager... T376

14 Oct The fair question... F30

26 Oct Monarchy and church, as explain'd by Dr. Henry Sacheverel. M396

2 Nov Bickham, G. A poem on writing... B211

4 Nov The devil a barrel better herring... D239

10 Nov [Stacy, E.] The tale of the robin-red-breast... S702

21 Nov Dickinson, W. Ode in artem anatomicam... D303

23 Nov Ward, E. The life and notable adventures of ...Don Quixote de la Mancha... Part I. W103

25 Nov Mr. Baron L------'s charge to the grand jury ... M289

28 Nov The new loyal health... N155

Dec Hymn, to be sung by the charity-boys of St. George's chapel... H434

11 Dec The roasting of a parson... R223

16 Dec Ward, E. Nuptial dialogues and debates... W129

An acrostick upon the name of Dr. Henry Sacheverell... A19

Adams, —. The brave Englishman... A25

The age of wonders... A126

[Ainsworth, R.] An epicedium sacred to...Thomas White... A132

All out at last... A161

An answer to High church loyalty... A238

An answer to the Six save-alls... A254

Belisarius and Zariana. A dialogue. B171

Blake, E. England's glory... B279

Britannia's summons to the old genius of the nation... B471

A new elegy upon the death of the late p——t... B574

The commoner, a poem. C319

Consolation to Mira mourning... C384

The court visit... C470

Curses against the stars... C550

The danger is over... D25

A defence of the church of England... D88

An answer to The tale of a nettle... D89

A dialogue between St. Peter and a low-church-man. D265

The dissolution. D336

D—n—l B—g—s his circular letter... D343

Dr Bungey's recantation. D350

The doctor militant, or church-triumphant... D354

Don Francisco Sutorioso. D395

The dream; the 24th. Sept. 1710... D438

England's passing-bell... E324

The English salours[!] triumph... E341

An excellent new ballad... E543

Exequiæ Carolinæ... E602

A farewel to passive-obedience... F59

Farquhar, G. Barcellona... F62

Fire and faggot... F144

High boys and low boys... H188

The high church health... H192

High church in its glory... H194

The high church lovers... H195

The high church spectakles... H198

A hymn to the scaffold, in Westminster-hall. H465

Jack Presbyter's downfal... J6

Jack Presbiter's triumphant rejoycing... J7

The junto. J112

The l——d m——r's farewel... L81

Leviathan, or, a hymn to poor brother Ben... L159

The London address. L233

Love and divinity united... L281

Malice's master-piece... M41

The medlers... M160

[Milbourne, L.] The moderate cabal... M230

The modern turn-coats... M385

The modest...petition of the w--ggs... M392

The nation run mad. N5

A new ballad on a late strolling doctor... N73

A new ballad, to the tune of Packington's pound N98

A new ballad, to the tune of the Black-smith. N103

A new elegy upon...Edward lord Griffin... N135

A new litany... N151

The new loyal members of parliament's delight... N156

The new wonder, or, a trip to St. Paul's... N241

The old pack. O118

A paraphrase on the fourteenth chapter of Isaiah... P57

[Pittis, W.] Kiss me if you dare... P445

[Pittis, W.] The L---d T——rs out at last... P447

[Pittis, W.] Out with 'em while you are about it. P449

[Pittis, W.] A story to the purpose... P454

[Pittis, W.] Vulpone's tale. P458

Sacheverell, and Hoadly... S2

Sarah's farewel to c-----t... S36

The screw-plot discover'd... S152

The second part of the Apparition. S172

Settle, E. Thalia lacrimans. A funeral poem to...Lytton Lytton. S296

[Settle, E.] Threnodia hymenæa...to the memory of... Thomas Thynne. S333

Some verses inscrib'd to the memory of...John Dolben ... S556

The sorrowful lamentation...of Daniel Damere... S603

[Stacy, E.] The black-bird's third tale. S686

The tacking-club... T2

A tale from St. James's. T8

The tale of a dolphin. T12

A tale of my L--d Wh--on... T23

A trip from Westminster-hall to Oxford. T482

The triumph of monarchy... T500

Trophaea marina. To Sir Charles Wager... T507·5

The tub and pulpit... T543

The upstart. A satyr. U25

'View here the pourtrait of a factious priest...' V92

Votum pro pace. V117

Ward, T. Englands reformation... W207

The wheedling gilts of White-Cross-street... W383

Wonders upon wonders... W557·5

Wright, T. Bruma, et vespera brumalis... W571

[1710?]

Æsop at Westminster... A112

A ballad on the Junto. B30

Ban----ry grumblers. B62

An elegy on moderation. E191

Ellis, W. A poem on...Dr. Sacheverell. E295

The Jacobites coat of arms. J53

The lawrel and the ox... L72

Minerva to Phoebus. M268

[Monsey, R.] Ad virum ornatissimum...Jacobum Astley ... M407

A new ballad. To the tune of Fair Rosamond. N90

News from Worcester... N295

O tempora! or a satyr on the times... O2

The tale of the cock-match... T26

Wild, J. Nottingham printing perfected... W458

An address of part of the Ch-sh-re grand-j——y... [1710/11] A52

Verses upon Dr. G--'s verses to the E. of G---n. [1710/11] V76

The whigs no plunderers. [1710/11] W394

Berington, S. To his most excellent majesty James III ...[1710?/16] B199

1710: SCOTLAND

June [Pitcairne, A.] Ad Josephum Scaligerum... P325

11 Oct [Pitcairne, A.] Ad G.B. P301

An alarm, to Scotland... A149

[Brown, W.] Impiety and superstition expos'd. B515

1710: Scotland (cont.)

An elegy on...Christian marchioness of Montrose... E194

Elegie on...William Rue... E231

In dolendum obitum...Joannis Cunninghamii... I18

[Pitcairne, A.] On...Sir Archibald Stevenson. P381

A second elegy on...David Blair... S169

Stanzas sacred to...David Blair... S719

To the ministers and elders met at Edinburgh... T385

[*1710?*]

Ode ad...Archibaldum Pitcarnium. [1710?/13] O18

Pitcairne, A. *For Latin verses probably printed between 1710 and his death in 1713, see P295–407 passim.*

1710: IRELAND

Feb   A serenata...on the birth-day of...Anne... S215

10 July   A poem on the late King William... P623

Curses against the stars... C550

The dissenters triumph... D333

An elegy on...R. Freeman... E122

A late dialogue between Dr. Burgess and Daniel d'Foe... L62

The mouse-trap... M550

The narrative of high and low. N4

[*1710?*]

The church of England martyr... C178

A dialogue between St. Peter and a low-church-man. D265

A dialogue between whigg and whigg... D274

[Percival, W.] Elegia. In obitum...Henrici Alderich... [1710/11] P177

The honest citizens wish. [1710/14] H294

1711

Feb   Tate, N.   The song for her majesty's birth-day ... T77

15 Feb   The fall and restoration of man... F42

22 Feb   [Stacy, E.] The picture of a church militant... S696

24 Feb   The state bell-mans collection of verses... S722

6 Mar   [Prior, M.] Horace lib. I. epistle the ninth... P1078

7 Mar   Free-thinkers... F247

15 Mar   The twelve blessings of a scolding wife. T580

16 Mar   The gates of hell opend... G42

16 Mar   The loyalist... L307

19 Mar   The (Latin) description of Hogland... L68

31 Mar   [Stacy, E.] An elegy...to the memory of Dr. Thomas Kenn... S689

Apr   A hymn to be sung in Poplar chappel... H450

6 Apr   [Blackmore, *Sir* R.] The nature of man... B263

10 Apr   [Prior, M.] To...Mr. Harley, wounded by Guiscard. P1089

11 Apr   [Stacy, E.] Assassination display'd... S674

14 Apr   High-church and the doctor out of breath... H189

21 Apr   The adventures of Esquire Twiford... A67

28 Apr   [Castleton, N.] To the right honourable Mr. Harley. C64

May   A hymn to be sung at the anniversary-meeting of the charity-schools... H430

15 May   [Pope, A.] An essay on criticism. P806

16 May   The fifteen plagues of a cook-maid... F133

16 May   [Hamilton, N.] The changes: or, faction vanquish'd... H10

16 May   Harison, W.   The passion of Sappho... H50

17 May   Nicols, W.   De literis inventis libri sex... N297

22 May   The story of Typhon. S770

22 May   [Trapp, J.] To...Mr. Harley, on his first appearing in publick... T466

25 May   The fifteen plagues of a coach-man... F132

June   The funeral-ticket of Mr. Hypocrite Low-church ... F307

1 June   The queen's and my Lord of Oxford's new toast Q9

2 June   Fenton, E.   An epistle to Mr. Southerne... F106

2 June   [Jonson, B.] Earl Mortimer's speech. J99

6 June   The whigs new toast to the B--- of S----y. W393

14 June   To his grace the Duke of Ormond... T339

15 June   To the...Earl of Oxford and Mortimer... T391

18 June   [Castleton, N.] To the...Lord Harley, on the promotion of his father... C66

23 June   [Pittis, W.] Æsop at the Bell-tavern... P425

27 June   The prince. An epigram... P1056

3 July   The loyal-wish. L303

11 July   Scotch-cloath, or occasional-conformity. S138

12 July   There's but one plague in England... T148

13 July   The farthingale reviv'd... F65

17 July   Chorley, J.   A metrical index to the Bible... C162

29 July   A noise about nothing... N317

18 Aug   The stumbling-block... S775

Sept   A welcome to the medal... W278

10 Sept   The whole duty of a Christian... W443

1 Oct   The butter'd apple-pye. B609

11 Oct   To the...lord high treasurer... T394

30 Oct   The peace-haters... P135

Nov   An hymn to be sung by the charity children of St. James Clerkenwell... H446

Nov   The Kit-cat clubs lamentation... K94

Nov   Queen Elizabeth's day... Q8

Nov   The thanksgiving... T119

12 Nov   A new copy of verses... N123

27 Nov   [Williams, D.] A pindaric on the nativity... W514

Dec   To be sung by the children of the Blew Coat school... T330

6 Dec   [Swift, J.] An excellent new song, being the intended speech... S844

8 Dec   [Russell, R.] The impeachment... R333

8 Dec   A toast for A--------e and Robbin... T400

24 Dec   [Swift, J.] The W--ds-r prophecy. S938

31 Dec   The character of a certain whigg. C119

Advice to the high-church. A91

Calidonia rediviva... C2

A choice new song, call'd, She-land, and robinocracy... C158

The complaint of the poor... C323

Dr. Radcliffe's advice to the ladies... D356

The E—l of G—d—n to D—ct—r G—th... E28

An elegy on the death of M. de Guiscard... E135

An excellent new song, called, An end to our sorrows... E576

An excellent new song call'd Loyalty restored... E577

An excellent new song, to the...tune of Lillibullero. E591

An excellent old ballad, made at the restauration of K. Charles II... E595

Forty one in miniature... F209

The French king's lamentation... F255

Gill, T. The blind man's case at London... G158

He's wellcome home... H122

A hue and cry after Daniel de Foe... H352

The husbandmens humble petition... H414

The lottery, a poem. L274

Loyalty display'd... L308

An elegy on...Wriothseley duke of Bedford... L312

[Mainwaring, A.] An excellent new song, called, Credit restored... M26

[Mainwaring, A.] The South Sea whim... M33

[Mainwaring, A.] An excellent new song, called, Mat's peace... M30

A mess for the devil... M204

[Monsey, R.] Viro honoratissimo... M410

More to be done yet... M437

A new ballad, shewing all shall be well... N83

A new ballad. To the old tune of Chevy-chase. N85

A new elegy upon...Sir Charles Duncomb... N137

Newcomb, T. The happy rival or Venus mistaken... N253

The Nottinghamshire ballade... N329

Now John's come, Robin must troop. N332

An occasional poem, upon the meeting of the Loyal Society... O7

The old medal new struck... O116

Oxford and Mortimer's vindication... O267

A panegyrick upon the English Catiline. P41

Perkins, J. A poem...on the death of...Thomas Kenn... P190

A poem...to...William lord Cowper. P528

The royal martyr... R316

A satyr on the stabbing of...Robert Harley... S64

Settle, E. Augusta lacrimans...to the memory of Heneage Fetherston. S228

Settle, E. Augusta lacrimans...to the memory of Sir Joseph Wolfe. S229

Settle, E. Augusta triumphans... S241

[Settle, E.] Honori sacellum... To the memory of... John duke of Rutland. S268

Settle, E. Memoriæ fraganti...to the memory of...Sir Richard Levet. S280

[Settle, E.] A pindaric poem, on the propagation of the gospel... S288

[Settle, E.] Threnodia apollinaris...to the memory of... Laurence earl of Rochester. S323

Some bold truths out at last... S554

The tale of a disbanded officer. T11

Tale of a Newcastle-salmon. T18

A tail [!] of J-n and S-h... T22

To the Duke of Marlborough, on the taking of Bouchain. T364

The tories triumph on the news of the Pretender's expedition... T425

A touch to the wheedlers... T431

The truth at last... T538

The vacation ramble: or, a view of Westminster. V1

When we shall have peace, the Lord of Oxford knows. W385

The Windsor prophecy, found in a Marlborough rock. W527

A wonderful new prophecy... W555

[*1711?*]

The apparition. A274

Ellis, W. The drunkard's looking-glass... E293

The fifteen plagues of a lawyer... F134

A new song... [1711/12] N189

Pomfret, S. Mr. Pomfret's hymn at the sacrament... [1711/12] P740

A whig-ballad: called, A safe peace, or none... [1711/12] W388

On her majesty's inauguration-day... [1711/14] O175

1711: SCOTLAND

Feb   Mary Queen, of Scots dowary... M122

An account of the...grave makers in Edinburgh... A13

Arnot, S.   A theoretick view of eternity... A314

The cardinal's coach couped... C36

Early soliloquies. E10

Elegie on...Sir William Anstruther... E47

An elegie upon...Adam Brown... E66

Elegy on...Thomas Wilkie... E279

Ker, R.   The true church of Scotland's lamentation... K29

[Monteith, R.] An elegy on...Thomas Fisher... M420

[Pitcairne, A.] Ad Homerum... P309

The XX Psalm, imitated from Buchanan. T581

[1711?]

Hepburn, R.   Ad Georgium Makenzium... H148

[Pitcairne, A.] Ad Jacobum Magnum. P315

[Pitcairne, A.] 'Carole Gothorum longe fortissime ductor' P346

[Pitcairne, A.] 'Carole, si similis fratris, similisve parentis' P348

1711: IRELAND

Feb   The universal applause of Mount Parnassus... U15

June   The funeral of the low-church: or, the whigs last will and testament. F297

Nov   Garth, Sir S.   A prologue for the 4th of November, 1711. Being the anniversary for the birth-day of the late K. William... G37

Nov   The shortest way to peace: or, an answer to a prologue that was to be spoke at the Queen's Theatre in Dublin, on Monday the 5th of November, 1711. S455

An account of Mr Guiscard... A9

An elegy on...Joseph emperor of Germany... E164

Loyalty honour'd, or a welcome to...James duke of Ormonde. L309

The r-----r's s-----ch explain'd. R323

The signior in fashion... S461

Some bold truths out at last... S554

A touch to the wheedlers... T431

[Trapp, J.] The church and monarchy secur'd... T446

[Ward, E.] The religious turn-coat... W154

[1711?]

The tinn-plate-workers complaint... T314

The new Kilmainham ballad... [1711/12] N145

1712

Jan   [Dibben, T.] Excellentissimo domino, domino Johanni episcopo Bristoliensi... D296

Jan   [Newcomb, T.] Bibliotheca... N246

2 Jan   A Bob for the court... B295

2 Jan   An excellent new song, call'd the Trusty and true Englishman. E584

15 Jan   [Fenton, E.] M. Manlius Capitolinus. F108

16 Jan   A fable of the widow and her cat. F13

28 Jan   The fable of the shepherd and his dog... F10

31 Jan   When the cat's away... W384

Feb   A hymn to be sung by the charity children of St. Dunstan's... H443

Feb   In palatium sancti Jacobi... I31

4 Feb   The grand enquiry... G243

5 Feb   The land-leviathan; or, modern hydra... L42

5 Feb   To be sung on Wednesday Feb. 6...being the birth-day. T331

6 Feb   Fenton, E.   To the queen, on her majesty's birth-day. F113

7 Feb   Dive, C.   On the Duke of Marlborough. D338

7 Feb   [Ward, E.] The quack-vintners... W149

8 Feb   On the death of Mr. Edmund Smith... O197

14 Feb   [Swift, J.] The fable of Midas. S847

21 Feb   The cuckold in purgatory... C537

21 Feb   Prince Eugene's welcome. P1060

23 Feb   The press restrain'd... P1025

26 Feb   [Pittis, W.] The fable of the cods-heads... P435

26 Feb   [Sewell, G.] The favourite, a simile. S366

28 Feb   Blackmore, Sir R.   Creation... B242

11 Mar   Æsop at Utrecht. A111

11 Mar   The true copy of a paper stuck upon the D. of M-----'s gate... T521

12 Mar   Brooke and Hellier... B487

15 Mar   [Diaper, W.] Nereides: or, sea eclogues. D294

20 Mar   An elegy on the royal family of France. E120

Apr   [Cobb, S.] A psalm of thanksgiving... C262

Apr   Honest Tom's resentment of a pamphlet... H298

5 Apr   A miscellaneous poem... M273

8 Apr   [Gill, T.] Useful and delightful instructions... G162·5

17 Apr   The K-ntish spy... K104

18 Apr   The old wives tales... O130

22 Apr   The epilogue to...James Duke of Ormond's last speech... E354

15 May   A plot or no plot. P508

22 May   [Plaxton, W.] Advice to new-married husbands... P479

24 May   Goldwin, W.   A poetical description of Bristol. G216

24 May   The retirement. R167

19 June   Grandsire Hambden's ghost... G249

23 June   Rowe, N.   Callipædia... R280

25 June   Stoppage no payment... S769

26 June   [Swift, J.] T--l--nd's invitation to Dismal... S911

27 June   Sewell, G.   The patriot... S369

30 June   A funeral poem upon...Lieutenant-general Wood... F304

10 July   [Swift, J.] Peace and Dunkirk... S895

16 July   Nobilissimo domino Roberto domino Harley... N311

17 July   Cobb, S.   The mouse-trap... C250

17 July   Whiggism laid open... W391

1 Aug   The adventures of Telemachus... A69

26 Aug   Motteux, P.   A poem upon tea. M528

2 Sept   The shining sisters... S425

2 Sept   [Watts, I.] Stanza's. To my Lady Sunderland... W255

6 Sept   Tate, N.   The muse's memorial... T68

16 Sept   [Browne, J.] Britain's palladium... B527·2

2 Oct   [Prior, M.] Earl Robert's mice... P1073

13 Oct   Rose, W.   The history of Joseph... R269

28 Oct   Tickell, T.   A poem, to his excellency the lord privy-seal... T303

Nov   [Hughes, J.] On November 4. 1712... H366

Nov   The Lord M--n's ghost to the D---- of R---nd... L259

1 Nov   [Sewell, G.] To his grace the Duke of Marlborough... S373

3 Nov   [Morrice, B.] An essay on the poets. M481

8 Nov   [Crispe, H.] Some verses sent to...the Earl of Oxford... C514

12 Nov   Ellwood, T.   Davideis... E299

13 Nov   [Stacy, E.] The parliament of birds. S690

20 Nov   The garter... G16

27 Nov   [Hughes, J.] An ode to the creator of the world... H382

Dec   An hymn to be sung by the charity-children of St. Giles Cripplegate... H445

Dec   An hymn to be sung by the charity-children of the parish of St. Bride's... H447

11 Dec   A satyr upon old maids. S75

23 Dec   The British censor. B476

29 Dec   Diaper, W.   Dryades... D292

The address to Mr. G-- Gr--n--ll... A54

As bob as a robin... A335

Brooks and Hellier... B498·5

The Canterbury tale... C29

Carthage reveng'd. C56

The Christian's exercise. C169

Cobb, S.   The carpenter of Oxford... C245

[Cobb, S.] A poem on Prince Eugene. C256

The congratulation...to...the Duke of Ormond. C344

A congratulatory poem, on...James, duke of Ormond... C351

The consultation. C393

Crispe, H.   To the honourable Matthew Prior... C515

The D--- of M----- turn'd conjurer... D2

The description of Dunkirk... D235

The devil in a whirl-wind at Westminster-hall... D242

Dunkirk deliver'd... D532

The Dutch are come in at last... D556

Fire and faggot... E84

England's surprize... E327

An excellent ballad of the Lord Mohun and Duke Hamilton... E535

An excellent new song, call'd, The full tryal...of John duke of Marlborough. E578

A fable of the housewife and her cock. F8

The fable of the lyon and the fox. F9

The French preliminaries... F258

The general casher'd... G101

Gill, T.   Questions and answers in verse... G166

Hill, A.   The book of Ecclesiastes paraphrased... H234

An hymn, to be sung by charity-children in St. Bride's church... H432

The impeachment of his grace the D. of Marlboro'... I12

Kirkham, C.   Philanglus and Astræa... K85

Lloyd, R. L.   To King William... L208

The loyal trimmer. L302

Marlborough remov'd... M106

The Mohocks... M394

The Mohocks revel... M395

[Montagu, C. earl.] The honest man at court. M415

A new litany. N150

A new-years gift for the plunderers of the world... N243

An ode...sung at the sheriffs-feast... O57

The old tack, and the new. O124

On the jewel in the Tower. O205

A paraphrase on part of the fourteenth chapter of Isaiah... P52

A peace, a peace, a glorious peace... P131

Perkins, J.   An elegy on...William Grahme... P189

Physick. A poem. P267

[Pittis, W.] The Windsor prophecy. P459

A poem on the death of Mr. Peter Molineux. P598

Poor England bob'd at home and abroad. P754

The portraiture of Oliverus secundus... P1003

The queen's and the Duke of Ormond's new toast. Q12

The reward of ambition... R173

Scandalum magnatum... S131

Settle, E. Augusta lacrimans...to the memory of... Charles Baynton. S230

Settle, E. Augusta lacrimans...to the memory of...Sir Henry Furnesse. S231

Settle, E. Honori sacellum...to the memory of... Thomas earl of Coventry. S269

Settle, E. Threnodia apollinaris...to the memory of Dr. Martin Lister. S324

Settle, E. Threnodia hymenæa...to the memory of... Sir Henry Atkins. S334

Settle, E. Threnodia hymenæa...to the memory of... George Carter. S335

Settle, E. Threnodia hymenæa...to the memory of... Mrs. Anna Raymond. S336

Settle, E. Threnodia hymenæa...to the memory of... Frances viscss. Weymouth. S337

Settle, E. Virtuti sacellum...to the memory of...Sir Edmund Harrison. S345

Shute, J. A sacred poem of the glory & happiness of heaven. S456

The soldiers lamentation for the loss of their general... S546

[Southcott, T.] Monsieur Boileau's epistle to his gardiner. S615

The speech of Oliver's ghost to the protesters against a peace. S631

The state weather-cocks... S729

[Tate, N.] An epigram on the Spectator. T60

They are all mad and bewitch'd... T149

'Tis pity they shou'd be parted...T316

To his grace the Duke of Marlborough... T337

The triumphs of the lady of the ocean. T507

The tr—us treaty... T535

Truth in disguise... T540

The ungrateful world... U7

Vaticinium, or the prophecy... V20

A vindication of the Duke of Marlborough. V97

Vulpoon in the snare... V111

Waring, H. The dark penitent's complaint... W233

A well-timber'd poem, on her sacred majesty... W281

A whip and a bell. W400

The White-hall prophecy... W410

[1712?]

The ass age... A349

Beelzebub's advice to his club at the Devil. B159

The Barkshire tragedy... B200

[Craggs, J.] King Edward's ghost... C494

The Duke of Marlborough's delight... D500

Elegy on the death of handsome Fealding... E113

The fable of the cocks and ganders. F5

French sincerity exemplified... F261

Gill, T. Lamentation on the death of his grace Duke Hamilton. G163

The loyal Calves-head-club... L298

'Near to the sacred and immortal frame' N13·5

The pigs petition against Bartholomew Fair... P277

The second part of King Edward and the cobler... S171

[Stacy, E.] The parliament of birds. The second part. S695

Pasquin at Paul's. [1712/13?] P97

Pomfret, S. Mr. Pomfret's hymn at the sacrament. [1712/13] P741

A trip to Germany...[1712/13] T485

Browne, J. To each gentleman soldier in the company of Captain Samuell Robinson...[1712/14] B527

Duke Hamilton and Lord Moon. [1712/–] D496

1712: SCOTLAND

Nov [Pitcairne, A.] Ad Calvini discipulos. P298

Nov [Pitcairne, A.] Ad Jonathanem ----------------Novembris anni MDCCXII. P324

Nov [Pitcairne, A.] Elisae Havartae principi Gordoniae...s.d. P362

Dec [Pitcairne, A.] Die XXV. Decembris anni MDCCXII. P358

Dec [Pitcairne, A.] Die XXX Novembris... P360

Dec [Pitcairne, A.] In Jacobum principem Ham tonium... P374

5 Dec A huy and cry after George Macartney... H353

Donaldson, J. A panegyrick upon the...art of weaving. D400

Donaldson, J. A panegyrick upon the...art of malting and brewing. D402

An epitaph on his grace James Duke of Hamilton... E440

In obitum...Jacobi ducis de Hamilton... I27

Ker, R. A short but true account of the nobility...of Scotland... K28

[Pitcairne, A.] Ad Johannem Calvinum. P323

[Pitcairne, A.] Ad Junium anni MDCCXII. P327

[Pitcairne, A.] In Maij vigesimam nonam... P378

[1712?]

A balsom for backsliders... B46

Pitcairne, A. *For Latin verses probably printed between 1712 and his death in 1713, see P294–406 passim.*

The turncoat... [1712/14] T557

1712: IRELAND

Feb   A serenata theatrale... S212

Marlborough remov'd... M106

The state weather-cocks... S729

[1712?]

An answer to the letter... A251

A dialogue between the miller and his dogg. D269

A letter to the reverend Mr. M---w F----h... L156

The song. Doctor Higgins's deliverance... S580

1713

6 Jan   Tate, N. The muse's bower, an epithalamium on the...Marquis of Caermarthen... T66

7 Jan   [Crispe, H.] An epithalamium...Marquess of Carmarthen... C510

10 Jan   A poem on the civil-wars of the Old-Baily... P594

12 Jan   Yarhell's kitchen... Y5

13 Jan   A paraphrase on the xxixth psalm... P61

15 Jan   Gay, J. Rural sports... G66

17 Jan   Flora triumphans. Wanstead garden... F173

17 Jan   [Oldisworth, W.] A pindarick ode, to the memory of Dr. William King... O156

2 Feb   A poem on the memorable fall of Chloe's p--s pot... P627

5 Feb   [Harris, T.] An hymn to the redeemer. H81

12 Feb   The Olympick odes of Pindar... O171

13 Feb   The blue garter... B289

23 Feb   [Crispe, H.] The antidote... C508

24 Feb   A short account of the expiring parl--m--nt. S445

Mar   The Br——sh embassadress's speech to the French king. B548

7 Mar   Pope, A. Windsor-Forest... P987

10 Mar   Young, E. An epistle to...Lord Lansdown. Y72

26 Mar   [Parnell, T.] An essay on the different stiles of poetry. P70

31 Mar   Deal in an uproar... D76

Apr   [Cobb, S.] A psalm of thanksgiving... C263

Apr   De pace...carmen gratulatorium. D74

Apr   [Dibben, T.] The young club... D298

4 Apr   Serenissimæ...reginæ...epinicium. S217

5 Apr   [Reynardson, F.] The stage... R176

9 Apr   [Parnell, T.] The horse and the olive... P77

9 Apr   [Trapp, J.] Peace. A poem... T451

14 Apr   [Brereton, T.] Charnock's remains... B413

23 Apr   A poem dedicated to the queen... P526

25 Apr   [Reynardson, F.] An ode to the Pretender... R175

28 Apr   Higgons, B. A poem on the peace... H184

28 Apr   Smith, M. On the peace... S520

May   A hymn to be sung by the charity children of Popler... H438

14 May   Ovid's Tristia... O254

22 May   Anna triumphans... A227

2 June   Bookey, S. In congratulation to Sir John Lake ... B323

25 June   [Evans, A.] Vertumnus... E530

July   An hymn to be sung by the charity-children at Bath... H436

July   A poem on the peace, sung...in Bath... P633

7 July   Adams, —. To the queen upon the peace... A24

7 July   Crispe, H. A poem on...the promotion of... Lord Keeper Harcourt... C513

14 July   Young, E. A poem on the last day. Y109

16 July   Pope, A. Ode for musick. P904

16 July   Tate, N. The triumph of peace... T81

17 July   Crispe, H. On the...commissioners of her majesty's Custom-House... C511

21 July   [Newcomb, T.] Pacata Britannia... N269

1 Aug   Quincy, J. A poem to the memory of...Joseph Stennett. Q17

3 Aug   Tickell, T. The prologue to the university of Oxford... T310

4 Aug   [Hinchliffe, W.] Stanza's to the lord treasurer, upon the peace. H244

3 Sept   [Centlivre, S.] The masquerade... C95

9 Sept   Tucker, N. A new poem on the ratification of ...peace... T544

28 Sept   A poem to the memory of...Joseph Stennett. P669

20 Oct   [Ward, E.] The field-spy... W69

23 Oct   [Swift, J.] Part of the seventh epistle of the first book of Horace... S891

28 Oct   [Bingley, J.] The fair quakers... B217

10 Nov   The statutarian... S734

1 Dec   [Croxall, S.] An original canto of Spencer... C522

8 Dec   Gay, J. The fan... G47

12 Dec   The second part of the Fair quakers... S173

16 Dec   [Crispe, H.] An elegy on the...late marchioness of Carmarthen... C509

Æthiops: a poem. A119

Æthiopides: a poem... A120

Anderson, J. In...obitum...Henrici, episcopi Londinensis... A222

A bowl of punch upon the peace. B336

Brady, N. Proposals for publishing a translation of Virgil's Æneids... B374

The candidates. C22

[Castleton, N.] An ode to the...high-treasurer of Great-Britain. C62

The country courtship... C449

Dr. Pepusche's song... D355

Duke H——ton's ghost to the Duke of Sh----ry. D497

An elegy on the death of Mr. Joseph Fuller... E124

An excellent new ballad...how a noble lord was robb'd of his birth-day cloaths... E547

An epistle from Sempronia to Cethegus... E375

Female folly... F94

[Forbes, W.] The rattle-snake, or a bastonado for a whig. F192

A full and true account of a dreadful fire...in the Pope's breeches. F284

A hymn to be sung by the charity children of Popler... H439

Lewis upon Lewis... L163

The merchant a-la-mode... M174

The merchant a-la-mode, &c... M183

[Mortimer, J.] An essay, to the pious memory of... George Trosse... M518

A new elegy upon...Daniel Burgess... N136

A new song. To the tune of, Marlborough push 'em again. N218

Nothing but truth... N328

The optics... Inscrib'd to Roger Grant... O238

The pedlar... P139

The plot discover'd... P507

The raree show. R122

Sage, C. The loyalists... S7·5

[Settle, E.] Irene triumphans... S275

Settle, E. Memoriæ fragranti...to the memory of... Margaret Woolfe. S281

Settle, E. Thalia lacrimans...to the memory of... Edward Godfrey. S297

Settle, E. Threnodia hymenæa...to the memory of the ...earl of Kingston. S338

Settle, E. Virtuti sacellum...to the memory of Mrs. Kath. Richards. S346

Sir Roger's speech to his mercenary troops... S477

Spencer, B. The benefactress...the Dutchess of New-castle... S647

A tale of Sir John Cass... T25

A tale of the mag-pies and jack-daws. T29

A tale. Robin's tame pidgeons turn'd wild. T33

[Trapp, J.] Dr. Crofts's exercise... T448

A trip to the masquerade... T492

The triumph of virtue... T502

Two poems. Viz. I. Plot upon plot... T589

The vanity of free-thinking... V16

Waller, W. Peace on earth... W25

[Ward, E.] The history of the grand rebellion... W80

Wesley, S. An hymn on peace... W331

[1713?]

Brown, T. Tom. Brown's letter from the shades... B514·5

A dialogue between Martin Luther, and Jack Calvin. D261

The em..ss....ss's sp..ch to the Fr..ch k..g. E307

An excellent new ballad, called Illustrious George shall come... E545

The notable dialogue which passed yesterday... N326

O raree show, O brave show!... O1

Libertatis amator; a litany. [1713/14] L167

Pomfret, S. Mr. Pomfret's hymn at the sacrament... [1713/14] P742

Second thoughts... [1713/14] S176

1713: SCOTLAND

Mar [Kincaid, T.] In Regiam Sagittariorum Scotorum Cohortem. K43

Apr Pitcairne, A. Ad Jesum Christum dei filium... P320

Apr [Sinclair, Sir A.] To the queen... S468·7

May Pitcairne, A. Ad Jacobum Dromondum... P312

May Pitcairne, A. 'Dum tibi laudatur Maij vigesima nona' P361

May [Pitcairne, A.] Margarita regina et diva Scotorum ... P386

May [Sinclair, Sir A.] On the twenty third day of April 1713... S468·5

June [Pitcairne, A.] Ad Archibaldum Reidium... P296

July [Pitcairne, A.] Presbyteri Scoti Petro. P395

July [Pitcairne, A.] XXV Julii MDCCXIII. P409

Oct Davidson, G. Joanni Voluseno...de morte Archibaldi Pitcarnii Scoti. D55

Oct Pitcairne, A. Ad Gulielmum Benedictum... P306

Nov [Ker, J.] Pitcarnium morientem. K24

Nov Ruddiman, T. In obitum Archibaldi Pitcarnii ... R329

Anderson, J. The winter night... A225

Donaldson, J. A panegyrick upon the...art of wright-craft. D401

Elegy on...Archibald Pitcairn. E214

Elegie on...Archibald Pitcarne... E215

An elegie, on...Sir James Stuart... E250

A hymn preparatory to some electors... H427

Killychrankie... K39

Kincaid, T. In Archibaldi Pitcarnii medici dissertationes & poemata. K40

1713: Scotland (cont.)

In obitum...D. A. Fountainhall... I29

[Pitcairne, A.] Ricardio Stilio anglo... P400

Pitcairne, A. Roberto Fribarnio... P401

[Ramsay, A.] A poem to the memory of...Archbald Pitcairn... R78

A second elegy upon...Sir James Stewart... S170

To the memory of Sir James Steuart... T382

Wilson, J. To Dr. David Dickson... W521

[*1713?*]

[Kincaid, T.] In D. Archibaldi Pitcarnii...bibliothecam instructissimam. K42

[Pitcairne, A.] Calderus Visharto... P345

The highland reformation. [1713/14] H207

A poem on the Royal Company of Scottish Archers. [1713/–] P641

1713: IRELAND

June An idylle on the peace... I4

June A prologue to Peace-triumphant... P1132

A congratulatory poem, upon the safe arrival of...Duke of Shrewsbury... C364

The dreamer's dream. D439

The speaker. A poem inscrib'd to Alan Brodrick... S620

[*1713?*]

An elegy on eighteen aldermen... E111

The Dublin intelligence. D463

A panegyrical epigram. P42

To the most illustrious hero George Lewis... T386

Warning; once warning. W237

The Dublin-ballad. [1713/14] D462

The hue and cry, or Ox---ds farewel to Ireland... [1713/14] H361

A letter to the author of the Speaker. [1713/14] L154

1714

Jan An hymn to be sung by the charity-children of St. Brides... H441

7 Jan [Swift, J.] The first ode of the second book of Horace paraphras'd... S854

18 Jan A fable translated out of Phædrus... F19

19 Jan The maypole's new-years-gift... M155

2 Feb Diaper, W. An imitation of the seventeenth epistle of the first book of Horace... D293

2 Mar Burchett, J. The ark... B569

4 Mar Pope, A. The rape of the lock... P941

9 Mar The congress... C366

16 Mar Tate, N. A congratulatory poem, on her majesties happy recovery... T50

Apr Three verses of the 78th psalm... T258

8 Apr To the right honourable the Lord P---m... T395

14 Apr The crisis upon crisis... C507

15 Apr Gay, J. The shepherd's week... G69

20 Apr Hill, A. The dedication of the beech-tree... H213

27 Apr John Dennis...to Richard Steele... J69

29 Apr An ode...to...John, lord bishop of London. O31

May An hymn to be sung by the charity children of St. George... H444

May Tomkins, T. A tale of Midas the king... T414

14 May [Pearson, T.] Hester, a poem. P136

14 May A prince and no prince... P1057

25 May Young, E. The force of religion... Y74

June Henley, J. Esther queen of Persia. H144

June Hughes, J. The rape of Proserpine... H368

June An hymn, to be sung by the charity-children of St. Brides... H442

June A town eclogue... T435

16 June Price, F. Wales: a poem. P1038

25 June An epistle from an half-pay officer... E365

14 July The constable's trip... C391

15 July Eusden, L. Verses at the last publick commencement at Cambridge. E514

22 July Long, R. The music speech... L247

28 July Lacy, J. The Steeleids... L7

30 July A change at court... C113

Aug A copy of verses...to the Duke of Cambridge ... C430

6 Aug Smith, M. A pastoral sacred to the glorious memory of...Queen Anne... S522

14 Aug [Turner, P.] A pindaric ode upon the death of ...Queen Anne... T570

19 Aug A letter from Mr. Jacob Bickerstaffe... L130

24 Aug An elegy on the death of...Queen Anne... E44

24 Aug An essay on the death of our...queen. E467

24 Aug [Needler, H.] The fifth ode of the fourth book of Horace imitated... N15

24 Aug Theobald, L. The mausoleum... T140

Sept Daniel, R. God the creator, and the preserver. D30

Sept Fishery, a poem... F151

Sept [Hinchliffe, W.] An ode presented to the king... H243

Sept An hymn to be sung by the charity-children... H449

1 Sept Philips, A. An epistle to...Charles lord Halifax... P206

1 Sept Turner, P. Augustus. A poem on the accession... T569

6 Sept A genuine epistle from M—w P—r... G125

11 Sept Piers, S., *Lady*. George for Britain... P275

13 Sept The arrival... A315

13 Sept [Ward, E.] The mourning prophet... W125

14 Sept Janus. A tale. J56

15 Sept The motto. An elegy... M538

15 Sept Perkin's-cabal... P180

16 Sept Meditations on the fall of Bob and Harry. M159

17 Sept Young, E. On the late queen's death... Y99

18 Sept Chapman, R. Britannia rediviva... C114

21 Sept A poem on the arrival of the king... P584

21 Sept [Ward, E.] The Hudibrastick brewer... W96

24 Sept [Steele, R.] The prologue at the opening of the Theatre-Royal... S739

25 Sept The arrival of the king... A316

Oct Centlivre, S. A poem...to his most sacred majesty George... C96

Oct Magdalen-grove... M14

Oct Oldmixon, J. Britannia liberata... O164

1 Oct A poem on the arrival of...King George. P580

2 Oct Dennis, J. A poem upon the death of...Queen Anne... D226

5 Oct Croxall, S. An ode humbly inscrib'd to the king... C521

8 Oct [Sewell, G.] A poem upon his majesties accession... S371

12 Oct Eusden, L. A letter to Mr. Addison... E492

14 Oct Centlivre, S. An epistle to Mrs. Wallup... C92

14 Oct Trick for trick; or, the hasty cuckold... T479

15 Oct Rowe, N. Mecænas...the Earl of Hallifax. R297

18 Oct The state gamesters... S724

21 Oct The coronation. C437

Nov An elegy on the heroic poem lately publish'd... E145

Nov Verses written to the Duke of Marlborough... V77

6 Nov A poem upon...his majesty's coronation. P679

20 Nov [Gay, J.] A letter to a lady... G52

20 Nov Welsted, L. An epistle to Mr. Steele... W291

27 Nov Smalridge, G. A poem on the death of...Queen Anne... S489

Dec An ode...on his majesty's happy accession. O28

3 Dec The Jacks put to their trumps... J8

Advice to a poet... A74

Advice to the tories... A102

Æsop in mourning... A114

[Allett, T.] Oxford act... A168

A ballad on Lord Pelham's birth-day... B29

Belphegor: or the marriage of the devil. B184

A city intrigue... C205

Cobb, S. News from both universities... C255

The country peoples recreation... C456

[Croxall, S.] Another original canto of Spencer... C527

Dartington. A poem. D53

A dialogue between Hermodactyl and Gambol... D259

An elegy on...Queen Anne... E43

An elegy on...Queen Anne... E45

An elegy on the...death of Harry Gambol... E126

Ellis, W. A welcome to the high and mighty hero George... E297

An essay upon friendship... E474

[Evans, A.] Præ-existence... E528

An excellent new ballad. E537

An excellent new hymn... E573

A glance upon his spent time. G170

A great overthrow at court. G275

Harris, J. A congratulatory ode, on...George Augustus... H65

Harris, J. A funeral-pindarique ode, sacred to...Queen Anne... H67

Harris, J. A funeral poem on...Elizabeth countess of Bridgewater... H67·5

Harris, J. Great Britain's glory... H68

Harris, J. An ode...to the queen's most excellent majesty... H75

A health to be sung and drank by all honest Britons... H123

A holy poem: or Christmas carrol... H292

[Hughes, J.] An hymn to be sung by the work-house children. H376

In Magnæ Britanniæ reginæ mortem. I23

Instructions to a painter. I45

The lamentation of a sinner... L34

The last will and testament of the High-German doctor... L61

The life of Cato the censor... L181

A mournful copy of verses on...Queen Anne... M543

The mourning court... M549

A new ballad, call'd the Greenwich hunting-match. N59

A new ballad. To an excellent French tune. N83·5

A new lord to the old lordship... N154·5

A new song, warbled out of the oracular oven of Tho. Baker... N228

The origin of the whale bone-petticoat... O242

The ox roasted and the bull baited... O264

[Perkins, J.] Britanniæ lætantis ex-altatio... P185

A pindaric essay on the arrival of his majesty King George. P284·5

The Pretender's declaration... P1036

The second part of the Rare show. S174

Settle, E. Augusta lacrimans...to the memory of...Sir Wm Hodges. S232

Settle, E. Augusta lacrimans...to the memory of...John Seale. S233

Settle, E. Augusta triumphans... S242

[Settle, E.] Carmen natalitum...to...Thomas lord Pelham. S248

Settle, E. Honori sacellum...to the memory of...Henry duke of Beaufort. S270

Settle, E. Honori sacellum...to the memory of... Robert ld. Tamworth. S271

Settle, E. Thalia lacrimans...to the memory of... Baptist earl of Gainsborough. S298

Settle, E. Thalia triumphans...on the happy marriage of...Lord Dunkellin. S301

Settle, E. Threnodia britannica...to the memory of... Anne queen... S329

Settle, E. Threnodia hymenæa...to the memory of... Lady Mary Chamber. S339

Settle, E. Virtuti sacellum...to the memory of...Sir Charles Hedges. S347

Smut's epistle to the whigs. S536

The succession... S781

To Robert earl of Oxford... T358

To the king. T379

The trifle, a new song... T480

The turn-coats... T558

A voyage to the court of Neptune. V122

[Young, E.] An epistle to the lord Viscount Bolingbroke... Y71

[Ward, E.] The republican procession... W155

The weeping church-men... W275

The welcome... W280

[Welsted, L.] The prophecy... W311

The whigs address to his majesty. W392

[1714?]

Advice to Dr. Harry Gambol... A78

The country squire's ditty... C458

The German doctor's cure for all diseases. G132

Illia's plain: or the happy-flock. I5

A new song. N186

On the Duke of Marlborough's restoration... O202

On the rejoycings on the first of August... O218

Perkin's farewel... P182

A plot discover'd against the trade and industry of Great Britain. P506

Strange news from St. James's... S772·5

Whig and tory. W387

The coffee-women turn'd courtiers...[1714/15] C275

The Duke of Marlborough and the court's new toast. [1714/15?] D499

The Dutch embassy. [1714/15] D558

The glorious year...[1714/15] G183

Let each have their own. [1714/15] L117

A new ballad alluding to two modern vile histories... [1714/15] N57

A new ballad. To the tune of Dear catholick brother. [1714/15?] N89

The new court... [1714/15] N125

The old woman and her bee hive. [1714/15?] O131

A poem on his grace the D. of Or---d. [1714/15?] P567

Pomfret, S. Mr. Pomfret's hymn at the sacrament. [1714/15] P743

Savage, R. To his most sacred majesty... [1714/15] S110

To his m----y, the loyal address of the tories. [1714/15?] T341

The vagabond tories...[1714/15?] V6

Horace's allegorical advice to the people of Rome... [1714/17] H317

England's...address to her lawful sovereign... [1714/18?] E323

The character of a turn-coat... [1714/20?] C125

Spencer, R. A congratulatory poem on the...princess of Wales... [1714/20] S649

A letter to Sir R— W—... [1714/41] L152

Bellows, T. To each gentleman soldier... [1714/-] B183

'Garth, Sir S.' A prophecy written in the Roman language... [1714/-] G41

The Hanover gardiner. [1714/-] H35

A prophecy. [1714/-] P1136

The vicar of Bray. [1714/-] V84

1714: SCOTLAND

Mar   [Meston, W.] Mob contra mob... M214

May   In obitum...Jacobi Steuarti... I25

July   Ker, J. Ad cives Edinburgenses, de pompa Regiorum Sagittariorum... K17

24 Sept   [Clark, J.] Gratulatio Britannica... C227

Britains rejoiceing at the coronation... B456

Dionysius Cato his four books of moral precepts... D317

The down-fall of Cockburn's meeting-house... D419

An elegy on...John Murray lord Bowhill... E64

An elegy on...George earl of Cromarty... E91

[Erskine, R.] A congratulatory poem upon the coronation... E454

Glasgow's parrad... G176

The Hannoverian torrie and whig at their bottle... H37

Monteith, R. Augustissimo, serenissimo, invictissimo, Georgio... M419

A pastoral elegie on...the Earl of Cromarty... P106

[Pennecuik, A.] An address to his majesty King George. P147

1714: Scotland (cont.)

A poem, to...George Lewis... P671

The poor widows mite in seven meditations... P758

Roch, W.   The Christians A.B.C.... R243

A wedding song, on the marriage of John Brown... W265

[*1714?*]

Elegy upon the...death of Lucky Law. E177

Cock, J.   A prophesie for the year one thousand seven hundred and fifteen years. [1714/15] C270

The humble address of the quakers in Scotland... [1714/15] H389

The humble address of the wives of the bow... [1714/15] H391

1714: IRELAND

Feb   A serenata. To be represented on the birth-day... S216

Advice from the stars... A72

Britannia's tears... B472

The morning's salutation... B608

A dialogue between a secretary of state and a Connaught squier... D254

An elegy. On...Ma----w Fr----ch... E121

Greer, J.   A poem upon...Allen Broderick... G291

A litany for lent. L194

Morphett, R.   The general loss...to the memory of... Sir Francis Hamilton. M470

Leigh, —.   An epilogue, to...the Dutchess of Shrewsbury... L102

A poem upon the happy arrival of...King George. P680

Polyphemus's farewel... P721

A short answer to a late scurrilous libel... S446

Tit for tat: or an answer to the Dublin ballad. T321

Whalley, J.   A decree of the stars for Cornelius Carter. W375

1715

Jan   A hymn, to be sung on the thanksgiving day. H451

Jan   [Somervile, W.] An imitation of the ninth ode of the fourth book of Horace... S577

24 Jan   Paine, J.   Instructions to free-holders... P24

Feb   Brereton, T.   George: a poem... B417

1 Feb   Pope, A.   The temple of fame. P974

Mar   The resolution of a layman in times of peril. R161

Mar   Theobald, L.   The cave of poverty... T137

10 Mar   Æsop at the bear-garden... P1026

25 Mar   [Stacy, E.] The blackbird's song. S675

Apr   Ivie, E.   Epicteti Enchiridion latinis versibus adumbratum. I74

1 Apr   Honesty the best policy... H300

6 Apr   The scamperer... S129

29 Apr   England's exhortation... E316

30 Apr   A poem in memory of Robert Nelson. P538

May   The eclipse, a poem... E14

May   An hymn, to be sung by the charity-children... of Farrindon within... H437

May   The Lord Bol------ke's epistolary canto... L258

May   The miller of Trompington... M233

May   Philips, E.   A pindarique ode on the birth-day... P225

May   The rooks and crows... R265

5 May   [Garth, *Sir* S.] Claremont... G18

11 May   The dream, a poem... D430

21 May   Four hudibrastick canto's... F211

June   The birth-day. June 10, 1715. B223

June   An evening thought. E531

June   A merry letter from the Ld. Bol----ke... M201

June   The report or a hymn to the tories. R158

June   The song of the robin-redbreast... S586

7 June   Tickell, T.   The first book of Homer's Iliad. T281

15 June   [Stacy, E.] The tale of the raven and the black-bird. S700

July   [Stacy, E.] Britannia's memorial... S687

6 July   Croxall, S.   The vision. C528

14 July   [Defoe, D.] A hymn to the mob. D114

14 July   The tory's downfall... R303

16 July   [Tooly, T.] Homer in a nutshell... T420

29 July   The country hobb upon the town mobb... C450

Aug   [Burnet, *Sir* T.] The flying general... B582

9 Aug   To the E. of O----d... T368

16 Aug   The patriot... P123

25 Aug   [Sewell, G.] An epistle to Joseph Addison... S365

10 Sept   A letter to Mr. Prior... L148

27 Sept   [Sewell, G.] Verses to...the Duke of Marlborough... S376

Oct   [Hughes, J.] An allusion to Horace, book I. ode xxii. H372

Oct   [Morrice, B.] Verses to Mr. Tickell... M500·5

22 Oct   The Bath toasts for the year 1715... B94

Nov   The plain truth. P473

Nov   [Tickell, T.] An imitation of the prophecy of Nereus... T283

Nov   The woeful treaty... W539

4 Nov   An English-man's thought on the fourth of November. E343

21 Nov   [Duckett, G.] The Northumberland prophecy ... D486

Dec   A congratulatory poem to...the D. of Argyle...
C359

Dec   [Edwards, T.] A Christmas carol... E20

Dec   Pygmaïogeranomachia... P1179

1 Dec   Some verses occasion'd by the late death of an
Irish nobleman... S557

20 Dec   [Addison, J.] To...the Princess of Wales...
A41

23 Dec   [Crabb, J.] A tale, and no tale... C490

26 Dec   A new copy of verses, on the nativity... N120

29 Dec   [Samber, R.] An ode on Christmas-day. S26

The apparition... A276

The blessings attending George's accession... B284

Catcott, A. S.   The poem of Musæus, on the loves of
Hero and Leander... C70

A certain dutiful son's lamentation... C98

Comberbach, R.   A poem, upon...King George...
C310

The council of hell. C439

An epitaph on Bona-fide. E439

The fox unkennel'd... F221

A funeral poem...to the memory of J..n B....y...
F298

A halter for rebels... H7

[Hinchliffe, W.] An epithalamium address'd to Mrs. Cox
... H242

His majesty's request. H250

Histrio theologicus... H262

Homunculus: or, the character of Mezereon... H293

Honesto Willo... H299

A hue and cry after the Lord B-k... H358

The impartial satyrist. I10

The Leicestershire freeholder's song... L101

The lion's proclamation. L191

The meditation, a cantata... M157

Memoriæ sacrum...D. Gilberti Burnet... M167

Merit and gratitude conjoin'd... M191

A most gracious speech paraphras'd... M519

Mother Hubbard's tale of the ape and fox... M522

The mouse-trap... M551

Nero the second. N36

A new court ballad. N124

A new toast... N233

A new toast, to...James duke of Ormond. N234

A new tory health... N235

On the thanksgiving day. O223

Ormond's vision... O247

Pasquin to the queen's statue... P98

Paul, W.   A pindarique ode sacred to the memory of...
Queen Anne. P130

Perkin redivivus... P179

A poem sacred to the immortal memory of...Anne...
P650

Poor Teague... P757

The Pretender is coming... P1032

The regular physician... R152

Revolution upon revolution... R172

Right Brunswick-mum... R209

Robin-red-breast's answer to the Black-bird's song. R238

The royal martyr... R313

Settle, E.   Carmen natalitum...to...the lord Viscount
Townshend... S249

Settle, E.   Threnodia apollinaris...to the memory of...
Charles E. of Hallifax... S325

Settle, E.   Rebellion display'd... S290

A song. S579

The speech of his grace, the Duke of M---... S627

To the K---g's most excellent m——y... T377

The tory hero... T426

[Ward, E.] The Lord Whiglove's elegy... W112

[1715?]

Ar ddydd-gwyl Ddewi, ag ar anedigaeth Twysoges
Gymry. A278

The complaint of a family, who...turn'd away a good
steward... C321

The landing. L43

The Lord Bollingbroke prov'd guilty of high-treason.
L257

Loyalty reviv'd, a song. L310

[Meston, W.] Cato's ghost. M208

A new song. N185

A new song between Ormun and Malburor. N192

A new song on St. George's day... N209

Nostradamus's prophecy. N325

The princess's lock: a merry tale. P1063

The siege of Cales. S458

Song for his majesty's birth-day. S582

Song in commemoration of royal Nann. S585

Pomfret, S. Mr. Pomfret's hymn at the sacrament...
[1715/16] P744

An epistle to Sir. Scipio Hill... E413

An excellent new ballad. To the tune of, A begging we
will go, &c. [1715/20] E558

An excellent new ballad. To the tune of D'Urfey's Fart.
[1715/20] E563

The history of the bob tails... [1715/20] H255

The history of the Guelphs... [1715/20] H257

The turnip song: a Georgick... [1715/20] T571

The loyal church-man's triumph... [1715/-] L299

The moderate man. [1715/-] M359

A new ballad. [1715/–] N55

The old woman spinning of thyme. [1715/–] O133

The plagues of Nod. [1715/–] P469

A song on the late Duke of Ormond. [1715/–] S591

1715: SCOTLAND

Feb   An excellent new ballad, intituled the New way of the turn coat... E551

Mar   The church of Scotlands lamentation... C181

Elegy on...Gilbert Burnet... E70

Elegy on...the Earl of Forquar... E117

An elegy upon...Samuel Murray... E196

An hundred godly lessons... H405

Merrie Andrews remarks upon the...ensuing year... M198

Ramondon, L.   In Heriot's-Walks... R26

[Ramsay, A.] On this great eclipse. R75

Steddy, J. A trip to Bar-le-Duc. S736

[1715?]

The Cameronian address to King George. C9

A conference in rime... C339

A dialogue between...the Duke of Argyle, and the Earl of Mar... D260

The Marquis of Huntly's retreat from the battle of Sheriff Moor. M107

A poem to the praise of the Voluntier company. P674

[Meston, W.] To the memory of...John earl of Strathmore... [1715/16?] M221

Elegy on the death of Hary Ormiston... [1715?/22] E206

The sorrowful lamentation of Herrie Ormistoun... [1715?/22] S605

The clans lamentation... [1715/–] C216

A new Scotch song... [1715/–] N181

A panegyrick on the vintners... [1715/–] P40

A race at Sheriff-muir... [1715/–] R2

1715: IRELAND

May   Fortune not blind: a serenade... F206

1716

Jan   Welsted, L.   An ode on the birthday of...the Prince of Wales... W296

Jan   Player, H.   Tobacco... P482

Jan   [Wogan, C.] The Preston prisoners to the ladies ... W543

3 Jan   Rowe, N.   Ode for the new year MDCCXVI. R298

25 Jan   Gay, J. Trivia... G81

25 Jan   The Pretender's declaration... P1035

Feb   Horneck, P.   A votive ode for the happy delivery of...the Princess of Wales... H322

2 Feb   An epistle to Sir Samuel Garth... E412

14 Feb   The tories address to King G----e... T424

Mar   [Crow, I.] A psalm of thanksgiving to be sung by the children of Christ's-Hospital... C518

Mar   An hymn, to be sung by the charity-children of the parish of St. Brides... H448

Mar   Love verses... L286

16 Mar   An epilogue recommending the cause of liberty ... E348

24 Mar   Two poems: one on the royal family... T588

Apr   Burchett, J.   Strife and envy... B572

Apr   Hughes, J.   An ode for the birth-day of...the Princess of Wales... H377

Apr   Morley, R.   A pindarick ode upon the death of ...Anne, countess of Sunderland... M468

2 Apr   The fate of traytors... F74

12 Apr   A poem to the memory of Thomas late marquiss of Wharton... P670

12 Apr   To his grace the Duke of Argyle... T335

14 Apr   Taurus in circo... T95

18 Apr   A tale of the finches. T27

28 Apr   [Baynard, E.] Health; a poem... B110

28 Apr   A poem on the death of the Countess of Sunderland. P601

3 May   Pope, A.   To the ingenious Mr. Moore... P978

17 May   Moore' worms for the learned Mr. Curll... M423

19 May   A poem on the drawing room... P611

26 May   [Oldmixon, J.] The catholick poet... O165

26 May   Worlidge, E.   The resurrection. W564

29 May   [Duckett, G.] Homerides... D485

June   Brown bread and honour, a tale... B501

June   [Fenton, E.] A letter to the knight of the sable shield. F107

20 June   [D'Anvers, A.] Academia... D34

23 June   The pleasures of piety. P505

28 June   [Chute, F.] The petticoat, an heroi-comical poem. C189

30 June   Pope, A.   A Roman catholick version of the first psalm... P953

12 July   Some verses on the king's going to Hanover... S560

14 July   [Ward, E.] St. Paul's church... W170

19 July   [Tunstall, W.] St. Cyprian's Discourse to Donatus... T548

25 July   Chute, F.   Beauty and virtue... C188

26 July   Parson Paul's speech, translated into English metre. P86

Aug   Eternity: a poem. E482

7 Aug   The bishop of Ely's thanksgiving-sermon... B226

31 Aug   [Bisse, T.] Microscopium, & Certamen glaciale. B232

Sept   Brereton, T. An English psalm... B416

Sept   Thornycroft, J. A poem on the complete victory gain'd over the Turks... T250

Nov   [Brereton, J.] The fifth ode of the fourth book of Horace... B408

Nov   The gentleman commoner... G122

Nov   An heroi-comical epistle from a certain doctor ... H155

Nov   Rebellious fame... R142

Nov   The way of the town... W257

6 Nov   Dotage. A poem... D412

16 Nov   Purney, T. Pastorals... P1172

20 Nov   Theobald, L. The Odyssey of Homer... T145

Dec   Morrice, B. A voyage from the East-Indies. M501

[Garth, Sir S.] An appeal to the people of Great Britain ... G17

Harris, J. On the anniversary of...K. George's coronation... H76

Hesperi-neso-graphia... H162

Keinton, M. A poem. K10

Mr. Paul's speech turn'd into verse... M296

[Nevil, H.] The first of August... N40

[Nevil, H.] A poem, occasion'd by the birth-day of... King George... N44

On Dr. Paul and Justice Hall... O174

On Mr. Walpole's recovery. O181

On the first of August, 1716. O204

The Oxford tragedy... O274

A poem on Mr. Paul. P571

Poor Robin's song... P756

A prologue...on the anniversary of the king's coronation ... P1126

A prologue...on the birth-day of...the Prince of Wales ... P1127

Rolli, P. A. All'augusta imperadrice Elisabetta Cristina ... R253

Rowland, D. A true copy of...the Welshman's... prophesy... R305

Settle, E. Augusta lacrimans...to the memory of... Caesar Chambrelan. S234

Settle, E. Augusta lacrimans...to the memory of... Sir Sam. Moyer. S235

Settle, E. Virtuti sacellum...to the memory of...Sir Stephen Fox. S348

Tate, N. A poem sacred to the glorious memory of... Queen Anne. T71

[Tunstall, W.] From W.T. in the Marshalsea to C.W. in Newgate... T546

[Tunstall, W.] From W.T. to C.W. The second part. T547

[Tunstall, W.] W.T. to fair Clio... T552

[Tunstall, W.] W.T. to Mrs. M.M.... T553

Waldron, G. An occasional poem on the death of... Anne countess of Sunderland... W5

[Wesley, S.] Neck or nothing... W343

[1716?]

The conjuring whig... C381

Directions to a painter. D319

The masquerade plot. M132

Motteux, P. A. To the king on his majesty's landing in Holland. M532

A new song... N223

A poem to the praise of...King George... P673

The Pretender's letter to the tories... P1037

Randolph, H. Chichlæus. R111

Pomfret, S. Mr. Pomfret's hymn at the sacrament... [1716/17] P745

A prophecy, by Merlyn...[1716?/18?] P1137

In imitation of the 5th ode of Horace. Lib, 4. [1716/20?] I21

On the sight of his majesty's picture. [1716/20] O220

Threnodiæ britannicæ... [1716/20] T263

1716: SCOTLAND

Advice to the muse, on the king's landing. A97

Colme, J. A poem on the blessed nativity... C302

[Colme, J.] A poem on the 30th of January 1716. C304

A dialogue betwixt Satan and a young man... D277

An elegy upon...Anne dutches of Hamilton... E137

Elegy on...Patrick Hamilton... E142

An elegy upon...Janet Hill... E148

An elegy upon...Commissioner Kello... E166

An epistle to Mr. Pope... E404

The experienc'd student... E607

The famed hero, or, the Duke of Argyll's welcome... F52

The jolly soldier... J90

The lamentation...of Serjeant William Ainslie... L32

A lamentation over the sad changes incident to believers... L39

On the most noble Lord Kenmure... O210

A poem on self-denial and resignation... P576

[Ramsay, A.] The battel: or, morning-interview. R34

Skene, R. Immobilia sanctorum festa... S485

[1716?]

A copy of verses sent in a letter... C432

An excellent new song lately composed... E586

[*1716?*]: *Scotland* (*cont.*)

The black-bird, or the flower of England flown. [1716/19] B237

Brigadier M'Intosh's farewel to the highlands...[1716/–] B448

[Robertson, A.] Str-------'s farewell to the hermitage... [1716/–] R226

1716: IRELAND

May A serenata theatrale, to be represented on the birth-day... S213

Buggin, R. The inchanted garden, a vision. B560

A full and ample explanation, of one King James's declaration. F282

In imitation of Ovid Metamorphosis... I8

The Pretender routed... P1033

The speech of the p—st of T—y C—ge... S633

1717

Jan Britain's joy; or, King George return'd... B454

Jan Daniel, R. A poem on the return of...King George from Hanover... D31

Jan The soldier's loyalty... S54

15 Jan [Prior, M.] The dove. P1070

15 Jan [Tickell, T.] An epistle from a lady in England... T272

22 Jan The Drury-lane monster... D444

24 Jan A satyr upon the present times. S77

31 Jan Markland, G. Pteryplegia: or, the art of shooting-flying. M98

31 Jan Pope, A. The court ballad... P762

31 Jan Robinson, —. A poem occasion'd by the king's arrival... R241

Feb [Breval, J. D.] The art of dress. B418

Feb [Bulkeley, J.] The last day. B561

Feb [Crabb, J.] A poem to the king. C487

Feb Griffith, N. The leek. A poem on St. David's day... G295

Feb Lock, —. The temple of love. L209

14 Feb Purney, T. Pastorals... P1175

18 Feb Gay, J. Two epistles... G88

21 Feb [Wyvill, C.] The parson's daughter... W578

Mar [Behn, A.] The land of love. B162

Mar [Centlivre, S.] An epistle to the King of Sweden... C93

Mar Holt, —. A fairy tale... H290

Mar [Morrice, B.] Love and resentment... M485

7 Mar [Welsted, L.] Palæmon to Cælia, at Bath... W303

Apr [Amhurst, N.] An epistle from a student at Oxford... A193

Apr [Beckingham, C.] Monsieur Rapin's...poem on Christ's-passion... B140

Apr Eusden, L. A poem on the marriage of...the Duke of Newcastle... E504

20 Apr [Ward, E.] British wonders... W53

May [Wren, J.] The country life... W566

16 May [Parnell, T.] Homer's battle of the frogs and mice... P73

22 May The protestant toasts... P1151

23 May [Ward, E.] A seasonable sketch of an Oxford reformation... W175

30 May A poem on the...birth-day of...King George ... P577

3 June [Robethon, J.] Essai sur la critique... R228

4 June [Jacob, G.] A journey to Bath and Bristol... J19

24 June An answer from the King of Sweden... A231

29 June Brereton, T. A day's journey, from the vale of Evesham to Oxford... B415

8 July Mandragora; or, the quacks. M78

23 July The British court... B477

23 July Newcomb, T. An ode sacred to the memory of...the Countess of Berkeley... N261

23 July Wicksted, —. An ode for the year MDCCXVII. W451

25 July [Churchill, W.] October...inscrib'd to the fox-hunters... C185

10 Aug [Amhurst, N.] A congratulatory epistle to... Joseph Addison... A190

10 Aug A view of the Duke of Marlborough's battles... A215

13 Aug [Breval, J. D.] Mac-Dermot... B425

27 Aug Bartholomew Fair... B90

27 Aug A night's ramble... N300

27 Aug Savage, R. The convocation... S98

19 Sept Belgrade. A poem. B164

27 Sept [Bockett, E.] Aminadab's courtship... B298

18 Oct [Glanvill, A.] The rake reform'd... G171

22 Oct Philips, A. An epistle to the honourable James Craggs... P204

29 Oct [Ward, E.] The tower of Babel... W189

Nov [Fox, J.] The publick spirit. F222

14 Nov [Breval, J. D.] Calpe, or Gibraltar. B420

18 Nov Sewell, G. The proclamation of Cupid... S372

21 Nov The town assemblies. T432

23 Nov Biddle, E. A poem on the birth of the young prince... B212

25 Nov Eusden, L. A poem to her royal highness... E507

28 Nov An epistle to young gentlemen... E435

6 Dec Ames, H. A poem on the birth of the young prince. A181

9 Dec   An answer from the Lord ***** in Ireland... A232

10 Dec   An ode on the birth of the young prince. O40

16 Dec   Little Preston... L200

[Bockett, E.] The author of a Character... B300

[Bockett, E.] A character. B302

[Bockett, E.] A character defended. B303

[Bockett, E.] A return to the author of a Letter... B307

[Boldero, J.] In illustrissimum infantem nuper natum. B314

The Br—d-street patriots... B404

Catcott, A. S. The court of love... C69

Catherall, S. Εἰκων Σωκρατικη... C73

[Dry, J.] Merton walks... D446

An epistle to...Joseph Addison. E420·5

[Gildon, C.] Canons: or, the vision. G151

The faction... F23

Faith and practice... F39

Harris, J. An Indian pastoral eclogue. H69

The hero in blue... H452·5

Huddesford, W. A congratulatory letter...to...Joseph Addison... H348

The invasion... I50

[Jacob, G.] The rape of the smock... J23

Jones, R. Britannia triumphans... J97

A letter to the author of A character. L153

Marchetti, A. Di Tito Lucrezio Caro Della natura delle cose... M93

[Nevil, H.] A poem on the birth-day of...the Princess of Wales... N48

[Nevil, H.] A poem on the birth-day of...King George. N49

Nicols, W. Περι ἀρχων libri septem... N299

On the nativity of...Jesus Christ... O213

[Rutter, J.] Bethlem Hospital... R335

[Samber, R.] On the passion of our blessed Saviour. S28

Settle, E. The eucharist... S251

Settle, E. Honori sacellum...to the memory of... Clement Pettit. S272

[Smedley, J.] Smoke the doctor... S510

A touch of the times... T430

Two poems. Viz. The retreat... T590

Waldron, G. A poem, humbly inscrib'd to...George, prince of Wales. W7

A walk from St. James's to Convent-Garden... W12

[1717?]

'Baker, Sir J.' Horace, epod. IV. imitated... B15

An excellent new ballad. E540

The history of the 29 years rebellion and usurpation... The loyal resolution &c. L301

Waldron, G. The regency and return. W9

An elegy upon the young prince... [1717/18] E288

An excellent new ballad. [1717/18] E541

An excellent new ballad on the fall of guinea's. [1717/18] E552

The falling out... [1717/18] F44

A new ballad. [1717/18] N53

A new song... [1717/18?] N224

Pomfret, S. Mr. Pomfret's hymn at the sacrament... [1717/18] P746

The Pretender...[1717/18] P1034

A song to the Old Britons, on St. Taffy's day... [1717/18] S593

A song. To the tune of, Dear catholick brother... [1717/18] S597

To the soldiers of Great Britain... [1717/18] T396

Ker, J. Excellentissimæ regis majestati, petitio. [1717/21] K25

The mock senator... [1717/22?] M357

1717: SCOTLAND

Arbuckle, J. Snuff a poem. A287

[Colme, J.] A poem on the blessed nativity... C303

Davidson, G. Georgius Davidsonus Comiti Aboinio... D54

An elegy on...Charles Dunbreck... E107

Elegy on...loyal Margaret... E184

On the death of Mr. Brand... O196

Preston, W. The saints rich treasure. P1029

A wedding song upon...William Mitchel... W266

[1717?]

Charmion, J. Æ. M. S....D. Ebenezræ Pembertoni... Epitaphium. C135

Dickson, D. Georgio dei gratia... [1717/–] D304

1717: IRELAND

May   A serenata da camera...on the birth-day... S211

The Frenchman's lamentation for the loss of the Earl of Gallway. F264

1718

8 Jan   [Amhurst, N.] Congratulatory verses to Edward Biddle... A191

21 Jan   Bewick, W. Faustus, Fortunatus, and Amyntas ... B208

29 Jan   The royal martyr: or, fanatick piety. R314

30 Jan   [Amhurst, N.] The resurrection. A204

4 Feb   A lash for the laureat... L48

18 Feb   [Sewell, G.] Verses to...the Princess of Wales ... S375

25 Feb   Austin, and the monks of Bangor. A373

4 Mar   The art of intriguing... A320

22 Mar   Shepheard, J. An hymn to the...trinity... S397

Apr   [Crow, I.] A psalm of thanksgiving... C519

Apr   An epistle to R--- W--... E408

8 Apr   Upon Lady Katherine H-de's first appearing at the play-house... P1093

22 Apr   [Amhurst, N.] Protestant popery... A200

29 Apr   Shelvocke, G. Divine love... S392

2 May   Bond, W. The third book of Tasso's Jerusalem ... B319

20 May   [Pittis, W.] Æsop in masquerade... P426

28 May   [Gaynam, J.] The tories looking-glass... G95

28 May   [Smedley, J.] On...the Earl of Cadogan's publick entry at the Hague... S507

29 May   [Amhurst, N.] A congratulatory epistle from... the Pope... A188

1 June   [Morgan, H.] Cynegetica; or, the force and pleasure of hunting... M443

17 June   Tickell, T. An ode. Occasioned by...the Earl Stanhope's voyage to France. T293

18 June   [Morrice, B.] Three satires... M496

24 June   [Burnet, *Sir* T.] The tickler tickell'd... B584

5 July   The impotent lover describ'd... I14

8 July   [Burnet, *Sir* T.] A second epistle to Mr. Tickell ... B583

15 July   Trapp, J. The Æneis of Virgil... T444

19 Aug   Hell in epitome... H133

2 Sept   Dart, J. The complaint of the black knight from Chaucer. D48

13 Sept   Taswell, E. Miscellanea sacra... T46

Oct   [Purney, T.] The Chevalier de St. George... P1171

Nov   Great-Britain's welcome to...King George... G266

9 Dec   Pandora's box: a satyr against snuff. P29

16 Dec   Pack, R. The nooning... P8

17 Dec   I'm a fit fellow to ask questions indeed... I1

20 Dec   [Breval, J. D.] Ovid in masquerade... B430

28 Dec   The art of beauty... A317

30 Dec   Amhurst, N. An epistle from the Princess Sobieski... A194

[Amhurst, N.] Strephon's revenge... A207

The apparition... A277

The Barnard-Castle tragedy... B85

The bed-tester-plot... B154

Bewick, W. Alphus: or, the fourth eclogue... B207

The following address, from the hundreds of Drury... C193

A congratulatory poem, on the anniversary-day... C355

The discarded country gager... D321

A divine poem on the creation... D341

An epistle from an English Jesuit... E364

Foster, R. The restauration. F210

[Goatley, J.] To the author of the panegyrick on the Canterbury ladies. G203

Hell upon earth... H135

Hill, A. The northern star. H225

Jacob, G. The court beauties... J17

Jones, S. Whitby... J98

Keimer, S. A search after religion... K9

Love's invention... L288

[Nevil, H.] A poem on the anniversary of his majesty's birthday. N45

[Newcomb, T.] Two poems viz. I. On the deluge... N275

An ode, perform'd on St. Cecilia's day... O54

A panegyrical poem on the...beauties in...Canterbury. P43

A pindarique ode on the arrival of...Sir Nicholas Lawes ... P288

The politicks and patriots of Jamaica. P715

The saints congratulatory address... S23

Settle, E. Augusta lacrimans...to the memory of... Sir James Bateman. S236

The sorrowful lamentation...of John Price... S604

The tale of my lord the owl... T24

Taubman, N. The British nations tribute of loyalty and duty... T92

Waldron, G. A poem on the parliament. W8

[1718?]

Britannias lamentation for the loss of Mustapha... B468

A dialogue between the old black horse at Charing Cross ... D270

Eelbeck, H. Epinicion anglicanum ad...D. Georgium Bingium... E21

An excellent new ballad. To the tune of Chivy Chace. E560

An excellent new ballad. To the tune of, Let the soldiers rejoyce, &c. E564

An excellent new ballad. To the tune of, Of noble race was --. E565

King Theodore's defeat... K54

The petition... P194

Pomfret, S. Mr. Pomfret's hymn... P751

A speech deliver'd by the High-German speaking-dog... S621

The Swedish lamentation... S792

Charles of Sweeden. [1718/19] C132

A fable of an old woman and her doctor. [1718/19] F1

[Meston, W.] An elegy on the King of Sweden. [1718/19] M210

Pomfret, S. Mr. Pomfret's hymn at the sacrament... [1718/19] P747

A prophetick congratulatory hymn to...King James the III... [1718/19] P1138

[Ker, J.] Serenissimo et invictissimo...Georgio... [1718/20?] K27

1718: SCOTLAND

May The cloak's knavery. C240

Nov [Ramsay, A.] Edinburgh's address to the country. R44

[Cheyn, W.] The friendship of Christ... C144

Cheyn, W. God's glorious perfections... C145

An elegy on Lucky Gibson... E130

An elegie, upon...Colonel Sara... E234

Luckie Gibson's latter-will... L316

News from Bathgate... N293

Pennecuik, A. Britannia triumphans... P150

Ramsay, A. Christ's kirk on the green. R37

Ramsay, A. Elegies on Maggy Johnston, John Cowper, and Lucky Wood... R46

[Ramsay, A.] Lucky Spence's last advice. R60

Ramsay, A. Scots songs. R90

[Ramsay, A.] The scriblers lash'd. R93

Ramsay, A. Tartana: or, the plaid. R97

The true Scots mens lament... T530

The wedding song of Gibbie and Marjorie... W264

The white regiment's lament for...Captain Sarah. W407

The whores of Edinburgh's lament for...Luckie Spence. W446

[1718?]

[Cheyn, W.] Some pressing motives, to the cheerful performance of these four Christian dutyes... C146

1718: IRELAND

An elegy on...Jenny the fish... E163

A poem on the Pretender's birth-day. P634

1719

Jan [Harris, T.] The fox, a fryar... H80

Jan 'Pope, A.' News from court... P903

1 Jan Elegiae tristes, ad pudicitiam adhortantes. E39

9 Jan A mock epithalamium upon the fictitious marriage of the Pretender... M351

24 Jan Harris, T. A poem on the death of the king of Sweden... H85

31 Jan An answer to Mr. Pope's ballad... A241

Feb [Breval, J. D.] The church-scuffle... B424

5 Feb The Oxford cricks. O268

10 Feb Young, E. A paraphrase on part of the book of Job. Y100

17 Feb The Rochester pad... R244

20 Feb Mr. B-----ll's farewel to the ladies of Dublin... M291

21 Feb [Harris, T.] Melazzo, and its brave defence. H83

23 Feb [Bond, W.] A description of the four last things ... B316

10 Mar Rowe, N. Lucan's Pharsalia... R292

19 Mar Keimer, S. The platonick courtship... K8

23 Mar [Smedley, J.] An ode to the...Earl of Cadogan. S505

2 Apr The ode-maker... O77

21 Apr [Amhurst, N.] The protestant session... A202

5 May Gagnier, J. Carolina. Ecloga... G1

11 May Sewell, G. An epistle from Hampstead, to Mr. Thornhill... S363

16 June Tauronomachia... T94

25 June A hymn to the victory in Scotland. H467

18 July Young, E. A letter to Mr. Tickell... Y90

30 July Ramsay, A. Richy and Sandy... R84

Aug The D...s hue and cry after an old turnip man. D5

Aug A letter to Mr. William Whiston... L150

1 Aug [Peck, F.] Sighs upon the...death of Queen Anne... P137

8 Aug The royal invitation: or, Britannia's glory. R312

10 Sept On the ladies hoops and hats now worn. O206

13 Oct Pope, A. Eloisa to Abelard. P801

16 Oct A fable of the dogs. F7

Nov A congratulatory poem upon his...majesty's happy arrival... C363

Nov Old Mother-Money's farewell... O117

Nov A poem on the happy return of...King George ... P618

23 Nov An ode on his majesty's return. O39

28 Nov A consolatory epistle to the Jacks of Great Britain... C385

Dec Eubulus Oxoniensis discipulis suis... E483

12 Dec Crabb, J. In Georgium reducem carmen... C486

15 Dec Bulkeley, J. The last day. B562

15 Dec [Morrice, B.] Astræa...and Composition. M474

An answer to the Hymn to the victory in Scotland. A250

Arbuckle, J. An epistle to...Thomas earl of Hadington ... A279

A ballad in honour of the present regency. B23

Forty-one. F207

Foxton, T. The night-piece. F225

[Gent, T.] Teague's ramble. G119

The happy conquest... H41

Harris, T. A pindarique ode, on the...death of... Madam Howland... H84

Harris, T. To her royal highness, the Princess of Wales ... H88

Massey, W. Synopsis sacerrima... M135

[Monsey, R.] In diem illum auspicatissimum... M408

[Nevil, H.] A poem on the...birth-day of his majesty King George... N46

A new ballad, to the tune of King John, and the Abbot of Canterbury. N95

The ninth ode of the third book of Horace... N304

A pastoral letter... P112

Peck, F. Verses to the...Lady Elizabeth Cecil... P138

A poem on the nativity... P630

Prior, M. Verses spoke to the Lady Henrietta-Cavendish Holles Harley... P1096

Prosodia Alvariana... P1142

Rightful monarchy, and revolution tyranny discuss'd... R211

Settle, E. Augusta lacrimans...to the memory of... Sir Daniel Wray. S237

Settle, E. Threnodia apollinaris...to the memory of... Joseph Addison. S326

The seven wise-men of England... S352

The trinitarian combat... S705

Tolson, F. Octavius prince of Syra... T406

A true touch of the times... T533

[Waldron, G.] Christianity without persecution... W4

Waller's ghost to the modern poets... W22

The Welchman-s last will and testament. W284

Whiggery display'd... W389

The whole tryal, examination, and conviction of the turnip-man... W444

[1719?]

An epithalamium on the king's marriage. E448

His highness's speech to his mirmidons. H249

A new song concerning two games of cards... N199

A new song, made on the intended invasion... N203

Pope, A. To Sir Godfrey Kneller... P977

A new song sung by a Spaniard... [1719/20] N213

Pomfret, S. Mr. Pomfret's hymn at the sacrament. [1719/20] P748

1719: SCOTLAND

Dec [Mitchell, J.] Verses spoken after the performance of...the Orphan... M346

[Cockburn, R.] Vice triumphant... C271

Cogitations upon death... C279

An elegy on...Joseph Foord... E115

1719: Scotland (cont.)

[Harvey, J.] To the memory of...William, late earl of Kintore... H103

Mitchell, J. Melpomene...to the memory of Mr. Joseph Foord. M316

Ramsay, A. Content. A poem. R41

[Ramsay, A.] Familiar epistles between W-- H--- and A-- R--. R51

Ramsay, A. Richy and Sandy... R82

[Wardlaw, E., *Lady*.] Hardyknute, a fragment. W213

[1719?]

His grace the great Duke of Argyl's welcom... H248

A poem on the great Mr. Law. [1719/20] P616

1719: IRELAND

May A serenade to be represented on the birth-day ... S207

A pastoral in imitation of the first eclogue of Virgil... O9

[172–]

The battle of the colliers... B105

The crab-tree, a tale. C484

The curious females, a tale. C546

Damocles. D19

Dodd, J. Tragedy speeches burlesqu'd. D360

An epistle from a merchant's clerk to his master... [172–/3–?] E360

An excellent new ballad...of a terrible fray that happen'd lately at Squire --------'s... E546

Hoffman, F. The creed of Francis Hoffman... H266

[Hoffman, F.] The new theory of the orbs of heaven... H267

Hoffman, F. The real door... H272

[Lamboll, W.] A lamentation over Sion... L31

A new ballad. To the tune of Hey boys up go we. N93

The prison groans...of Elizabeth Forister... P1099

The progress: or, the unfortunate knight. P1116

Some verses on the advantages of a fishery... S558

A song entitl'd a satyr on a trades... S581

[172–]: SCOTLAND

A block for Allan Ramsay's wigs... B286

An elegy on...Cathcart... E79

Elegie on John Pringle... E220

An elegy on the death of John Wat... E267

The Gillmertoun Vulcan gone... G169

The lamentation of the butchers wives in Musleburgh... L37

[Pennecuik, A.] The criminal stirling imprisoned... P153

[Pennecuik, A.] Elegy on...Maggie Wilson... P157

[*172*–]: *Scotland* (*cont.*)

[Pennecuik, A.] The last speech...of John Dalgleish... P162

Pennecuik, A. Rome's legacy, to the kirk of Scotland... P170

[Ramsay, A.] Fy gar rub her o'er wi' strae... R53

The restoration of famous Cathcart... R162

A satyr upon Allan Ramsay... S73

[172–]: IRELAND

An account of the dreadful apparition of Mr. G------e... A10

Dr. Anthony turn'd poet and astrologer. A255

Doctor Anthony's last will... A259

[Ashton, R.] A satyr on the journey-men taylors. A347

The barbarous and bloody murder of Mr. E—re... B63

The distress'd maid being put to her last shift... D337

The doctor's decade... D358

The fair sex turn'd Amazons... F32

Ireland's lamentation, or, a new ballad on Capt. Mooney... I61

The mantua-makers a poem. M92

A new L.E.G. on John Tissey... N148

Oxenard reviv'd... O265

A petition to the ladies of Dublin... P193

A poem in a letter from a young lady in Mary's parish... P534

A poem on Captain F-rr--r's travelling... P564

The reformation: a satyre. R150

The revd. Dr. S---- answer to the distress'd maids petition... R169

A riddle, in answer to the hairy monster. R205

A satyr on Madam Cut-A—e... S51

A satyrical poem on the society of journey-men taylors.

[Swift, J.] Apollo outwitted... S798

1720

6 Jan   Eusden, L. An ode for the new year... E497

6 Jan   [Gay, J.] Daphnis and Chloe. G44

18 Jan   Catherall, S. An essay on the conflagration... C76

18 Jan   Cobden, E. A poem on the death of...Joseph Addison. C266

19 Jan   A ballad, upon a gentleman's sitting upon the Lady W-----'s Cremona fiddle. B41

23 Jan   Welsted, L. An epistle to his grace the Duke of Chandos. W289

26 Jan   [Hill, A.] Gideon, or the restoration of Israel. H217

Feb   [Rowe, E.] An expostulatory epistle to Sir Richard Steele... R273

Feb   [Smedley, J.] A familiar epistle to...the ld. bp. of Bangor. S503

16 Feb   [Prior, M.] The conversation. P1068

20 Feb   Pack, R. Religion and philosophy... P9

22 Feb   Hamilton, N. The power of musick... H12

25 Feb   Hill, T. Stoic philosophy... H236

8 Mar   [Beckingham, C.] Christus patiens... B141

10 Mar   [Prior, M.] Prologue to the Orphan... P1084

17 Mar   A poem humbly inscrib'd to Sir John Norris... P531

22 Mar   [Newcomb, T.] Scating: a poem. N270

25 Mar   The compleat art of painting... C324

25 Mar   [Congreve, W.] An impossible thing. C372

2 May   May-day: or, the original or garlands. M153

11 May   An elegy on the death of trade. E259

17 May   Hughes, J. The ecstasy. H374

19 May   [Jacob, G.] A poem on the happy reconciliation... J21

24 May   [Croxall, S.] The fair Circassian... C520

26 May   [Tickell, T.] An ode inscribed to...the Earl of Sunderland... T291

2 June   Eusden, L. An ode for the birthday... E494

3 June   [Sewell, G.] An ode to Mr. Tickell... S368

9 June   Mitchell, J. Jonah: a poem. M309

17 June   A vade mecum for malt-worms... V2

July   The lecturers combat for the parish of St. Andrew Holborn... L92

4 July   Ramsay, A. A poem on the South-Sea... R106

29 July   Eusden, L. To her highness the Princess Anne... E512

1 Aug   Amhurst, N. An epistle...to Sir John Blount... A196

2 Aug   Hill, A. The creation... H212

2 Aug   Ramsay, A. Patie and Roger... R77

4 Aug   Mitchell, J. The dolefull swains... M304

6 Aug   An epistle to William Morley... E433

15 Aug   Duke upon duke... D502

22 Aug   An answer to Duke upon duke... A235

23 Aug   To Robert Ch-ster, esq... T357

30 Aug   [Smedley, J.] A familiar epistle to...Charles earl of Sunderland... S500

31 Aug   An irregular ode... I68

1 Sept   [Ward, E.] The delights of the bottle... W57

2 Sept   Amhurst, N. A familiar epistle from Tunbridge-Wells... A198

9 Sept   The last guinea; a poem. L51

15 Sept   The weaver's new ballad on the S—h-Sea... W262·5

20 Sept   [Morrice, B.] Astræa: or, the composition.

20 Sept   [Newcomb, T.] An ode to...the Duke of Richmond... W263

22 Sept A guide for malt-worms. The second part... V5

26 Sept A familiar epistle to Mr. Mitchell... F54

12 Oct The hasty wedding... H105

25 Oct The fifth ode of the fourth book of Horace... F138

26 Oct [Morrice, B.] Two odes of Horace... M498

31 Oct Ramsay, A. The prospect of plenty... R81

31 Oct Stanhope, H. An epistle to...the Prince of Wales... S706

7 Nov Sewell, G. An ode on his majesty's happy arrival... S367

8 Nov A poem occasion'd by...South Sea stock... P561

11 Nov Arundell, —. The directors... A331

12 Nov Verses on the king's return. V63

19 Nov An ode upon the times... O76

26 Nov Stanhope, H. The governour... S712

Dec Foxton, T. Jesina: or, delusive gold... F223

Dec [Jacob, H.] The curious maid. J34

5 Dec [Bockett, E.] The yea and nay stock-jobbers... B308

6 Dec [Randolph, H.] Commercium ad mare australe. R113

12 Dec [Sewell, G.] Carmen seculare, for the year 1720. S362

Anti-priapeia... A265

The celebrated beauties... C89

Centlivre, S. A woman's case... C97

Crambo's elopement... C495

D'Urfey, T. The hubble bubbles... D545

An emblem of the South Sea... E304

The High German doctor... H200

Lincolnshire. A poem. L186

The Lord's day... L263

Monsey, R. In obitum...Clementis Herne... M409

The nature...of publick and private prayer... N11

[Nevil, H.] A poem in honour of the birth-day of...King George... N43

Patricius to Manlius. P122

A poem on the death of Robert Keck... P600

Price, H. A copy of verses occasioned by the death of...George lord bishop of Bristol... P1040

Rosse, A. Andreæ Rossæi...Glottiades... R271

Settle, E. Augusta lacrimans...to the memory of...Sir William Ashurst. S238

Settle, E. Virtuti sacellum...to the memory of...John earl of Dundonald. S349

Tolson, F. A poem on...the South-Sea bill. T407

Tom of Bedlam's new medley. T411

Vézian, A. L'anniversaire de la naissance du roy. V79

[Ward, E.] A South-Sea ballad... W177

[1720?]

The honest man is worth a kingdom. H297

It's come home to him at last... I71

Newcomb, T. Carmen seculare... N250

Patch work or the comprehension... P120

The truth found out at last... T539

Gent, T. God's judgments shewn unto mankind... [1720/21] G114

Pomfret, S. Mr. Pomfret's hymn at the sacrament... [1720/21] P749

An epitaph upon the late Mrs Ann Hales... [1720?/22] E446

1720: SCOTLAND

May Ramsay, A. Edinburgh's salutation to the...marquess of Carnarvon. R45

June Ramsay, A. Wealth, or the woody. R104

Sept Ramsay, A. An ode...on the marriage of...earl of Weemys... R70

Oct Ramsay, A. To the royal burrows of Scotland... R80

Ariel and Mirza: an eclogue... A291

Elegy, upon...Sir Robert Blacwood... E60

An elegie on...William Delape... E97

An elegy on...Geo: Drummond... E106

Elegy on...Margaret Hall... E136

Elegy on...Alexander Ross... E230

An elegy on...William lord Strathnaver... E249

Elegy, on...David earl of Weems... E269

Elegy, on...James Whetty... E271

Elias and Enoch... E289

An exact list of the battle of Dyesart... E532

[Meston, W.] Phaethon... M217

A poem to the pious memory of...Alexander...bishop of Edinburgh. P672

[Ramsay, A.] Patie and Roger... R76

Ramsay, A. To Mr. Law. R99

[Ramsay, A.] The young laird and Edinburgh Katy. R108

The South Sea ballad... S611

Threnodia...to the memory of...James Webster... T259

To the memory of...William Dunlop... T383

[Watson, J.] 'On Thursday next, sir, I expect' W252

[1720?]

Allan Ramsay metamorphosed to a hather-bloter poet... A164

'Couper, J.' Bag-pipes no musick... C463

[Ramsay, A.] Bessy Bell and Mary Gray. R36

[Ramsay, A.] Grubstreet nae satyre... R56

The raree show ballad: or, the British Missisippi... R127

[1720?]: Scotland (cont.)

A poem upon a lady's being offered a purse... P676

[Meston, W.] A tale of a man and his mare... [1720/21] M218

[Ramsay, A.] Scots songs, viz. Mary Scot... [1720/21] R92

An habbyac on the death of Allan Ramsay. [1720/25?] H2

1720: IRELAND

July   [Swift, J.] An elegy on...Mr. Demar... S836

[Concanen, M.] A match at foot-ball... C327

[Concanen, M.] Meliora's tears for Thyrsis... C330

A familiar answer to a familiar letter. F53

Hibernia's lamentation... H174

[Sheridan, T.] The invitation in imitation of Horace's epistle to Torquatus... S407

[Sheridan, T.] Prologue spoke at the Theatre-Royal... S413

[Swift, J.] Run upon the bankers. S900

1721

2 Jan   [Swift, J.] The bubble: a poem. S810

4 Jan   Johnston, —. A poem...to the Lord Sunbury on his birth-day. J88

9 Jan   [Morrice, B.] The present state of poetry... M491

10 Jan   [Jacob, G.] Human happiness... J18

11 Jan   [Jacob, H.] Apollo's stratagem, or Button unmask'd. J27

11 Jan   Samber, R. The paradox... S29

14 Jan   An epistle from Dick Francklin... E368

Feb   Hoffman, F. The true protestant director... H273

3 Feb   Welsted, L. A prologue to the town... W310

6 Feb   [Pitt, C.] The plague of Marseilles... P414·5

10 Feb   Mitchell, J. An ode on the power of musick. M319

11 Feb   An answer to the Curious maid. A247

13 Feb   [Prior, M.] Colin's mistakes... P1065

17 Feb   Stanhope, H. Verses sacred to the memory of... James earl Stanhope... S715

21 Feb   [Philips, —.] The romance of the rose... P202

23 Feb   The peeper: being a sequel to the Curious maid. P141

24 Feb   Chamberlen, —. News from hell... C103

28 Feb   [Gay, J.] A panegyrical epistle to Mr. Thomas Snow... G64

28 Feb   Hughes, J. Verses occasion'd by reading Mr. Dryden's Fables... H371

Mar   The lady of Brumpton and knight of Malta. L20

9 Mar   Hill, A. The judgement-day. H222

11 Mar   Love drowned in the South-Sea... L282

13 Mar   Pitt, C. A poem on the death of the late Earl Stanhope... P415

20 Mar   The platonic. A tale. P478

21 Mar   The longitude found out... L253

22 Mar   Theobald, J. Albion, a poem. T129

25 Mar   Sewell, G. Verses to...the Lord Carteret... S377

28 Mar   The curious maid, continu'd. C547

31 Mar   The leaky vessel, a tale. L90

Apr   Downes, J. A pindarick sacred to the memory of...James earl Stanhope... D418

13 Apr   The bauble, a tale. B108

25 Apr   Æsculapius: a poem... A108

28 Apr   [Dart, J.] Westminster Abbey: a poem. D52

15 May   [Markland, J.] Three new poems... M104

26 May   Browne, M. The throne of justice... B536

26 May   Richmond or Richmount... R202

6 June   Duncombe, W. The Carmen saeculare of Horace. D512

30 June   Morrice, B. An epistle to Mr. Welsted... M480

4 July   Illustrissimo...Jacobo duci de Chandos... I7

14 July   [Rooke, J.] A true ecclestical history... R264·5

12 Aug   Lloyd, J. Deus. Poema. L205

Sept   A tale of the lady's bodkin. T28

28 Sept   A town eclogue...on the death of Matthew Prior. T434

7 Oct   Catherall, S. An epistle...to the university of Oxford... C75

11 Oct   Ramsay, A. Robert, Richy and Sandy... R88

12 Oct   Beckingham, C. Verses on the death of Mr. Prior... B152

24 Oct   Morrice, B. An essay on the poets. M483

4 Nov   Pomfret, J. Dies novissima... P730

17 Nov   Congratulatory verses to...Thomas Wharton ... C365

21 Nov   Mitchell, J. The charms of indolence. M303

25 Nov   [Tickell, T.] Kensington Garden. T288

27 Nov   [Sewell, G.] An epistle from London, to Richardson Pack... S364

Dec   Verses to the memory of Matthew Prior... V70

13 Dec   [Pack, R.] An epilogue spoke to a play call'd the Alchymist. P7

16 Dec   Browne, M. The Richmond beauties... B532

18 Dec   Mitchell, J. An epistle to...John earl of Stairs... M305

19 Dec   The nightingale. A tale. N301

[Aston, A.] The pleasures of the Bath... A354

The bublers medley... B553

An elegy on...Andrew Giffard... E131

Eusden, L. An ode for the birthday... E495

Eusden, L. An ode for the new-year... E499

Harris, T. Augusta lachrymans, or Belvoir in tears... H78

Harris, T. The skreen, detected... H87

The Hell-fire club... H136

Honesty yet to be found... H301

Instructions to a painter... I46

The pillory scuffle... P284

Settle, E. Honori sacellum...to the memory of...Sr John Shaw... S273

Settle, E. Honori sacellum...to...William lord North and Grey... S274

[Ward, E.] The merry travellers... W117

[Ward, E.] The northern cuckold... W127

[1721?]

Aston, A. A new South-Sea ballad... A353

The co-gr-ss of asses. C281

Wilde, S. The weavers humble offering... W459

An epitaph upon Mrs. Frances Kentish... [1721/22] E445

Pomfret, S. Mr. Pomfret's hymn at the sacrament. [1721/22] P750

The unhappy voyage... [1721/22] U8

1721: SCOTLAND

Jan [Ramsay, A.] An elegy on Patie Birnie... R49

20 Mar The highland-man upon the overture, called negative. H205

May Vox populi or; the general cry. V119

Arbuckle, J. Glotta... A281

[Boyse, S.] To the memory of...John Anderson... B368

[Clarke, J.] The practical atheist... C228

Pennecuik, A. An ancient prophecy concerning stock-jobbing... P149

[Pennecuik, A.] Elegy on the death of Nicol Muschet... P155

[Pennecuik, A.] The mock magistrates... P165

Ramsay, A. The rise and fall of stocks, 1720... R87

Scotland's tears. An elegy...Sir David Dalrymple... S142

The sorrowfull lamentation of Nicol Mucshet... S607

The women's indictment against Burnbank... W550

[1721?]

Robert the rymer's hue and cry after the flying man... R224

Elegy on the mournful banishment, of James Campbell... [1721/22] E76

Pennecuik, A. Elegy on...John lord Belhaven... [1721/22] P156

[Pennecuik, A.] Huy and cry for apprehending George Fachney... [1721/22] P161

[1721?]: Scotland (cont.)

The supplication and lamentation of George Fachney... [1721/22] S788

1721: IRELAND

Mar An elegy on...Denis Daly... E96

Mar An elegy on...Sir John King... E170

Mar [Swift, J.] Epilogue... In the behalf of the distressed weavers. S838

Apr The puppet-show, a poem. P1169

May A contest between Mars and Jupiter... C395

June A new song, call'd the Twitcher... N197

Oct Ireland in universal mourning... I57

Oct A new prologue... N174

Oct Philips, A. An epilogue...to...the Duke and Dutchess of Grafton... P203

Dec The bank thrown down. B60

Dec S——'s master piece... S1

The ancient philosophers vindicated against tipling. A220

The character of a Welsh-man... C126

[Delany, P.] News from Parnassus. D202

[Delany, P.] To...Arthur, earl of Anglesey... D210

An elegy on...Sir Toby Buttler... E72

An elegy made on the Last speech and dying words of the ...Bank of Ireland... E175

An elegy on...Thomas Putland... E223

[Helsham, R.] D-----n S------t's prologue to Hyppolitus... H138

Hortensius sibi constans. H327

Sheridan. T. Mr. Sheridan's prologue to the Greek play... S408

[1721?]

A letter to Tom Punsibi... L157

[Swift, J.] The journal. [1721/22] S861

An ode...to...Charles duke of Grafton... [1721/24] O27

1722

16 Feb The spunge. A new song... S660

21 Feb The Westminster bubble... W364

2 Mar Cornwall, C. Homeros, Homoros... C435

3 Mar The Richmond maidenhead, a tale. R201

27 Mar An elegy upon...Mr. Toland. E256

30 Mar [Ward, E.] The parish gutt'lers... W136

13 Apr The Middlesex patriots... M229

May A school-boy's elegy upon...the Earl of Sunderland. S136

7 May Blackmore, Sir R. Redemption: a divine poem... B268

10 May Welsted, L. An epistle to...the earl of Cadogan. W293

2 June The dancing-master. D24

7 June   Monsieur Thing's origin. M413

3 July   A ramble thro' Hyde-Park... R24

3 July   Welsted, L. The genius, an ode... W294

7 July   An epistle to Archibald Hutcheson... E394

11 July   Gay, J. An epistle to...Henrietta, dutchess of Marlborough. G45

Aug   Cooke, T. Marlborough, a poem... C416

7 Aug   Amhurst, N. The British general... A187

8 Aug   An epistle to Mr. Pope... E405

11 Aug   [Jacob, G.] Britain's hero... J16

13 Aug   The adventure of the bee and the spider... A65

30 Aug   [Ward, E.] The wand'ring spy...Part II... W122

Sept   The subscribers... S780

3 Sept   Belsize-house. A satyr... B186

9 Oct   The plotters... P515

10 Oct   Dart, J. A poem on Chaucer... D51

15 Nov   Eusden, L. Three poems... E509

16 Nov   A serio-comical elegy, on...Matthew Buckinger ... S218

16 Nov   Verses to the Lord Carteret... V68

6 Dec   Jacob, H. Bedlam, a poem. J28

6 Dec   The parson and his maid... P82

8 Dec   [Settle, E.] Minervæ sacellum... S285

14 Dec   Welsted, L. An epistle to the late Dr. Garth... W292

18 Dec   [Bacon, P.] The kite... B6

28 Dec   The eagle, a fable... E1

[Bourne, V.] Corydon querens... B329

An elegiac pastoral on...the Duke of Marlborough... E36

An elegy...upon...John duke of Marlebourgh. E185

Eusden, L. The parallel... E502

A funeral poem, sacred to...John Churchill, duke...of Marlborough... F302

[Gent, T.] The forsaken lover's letter... G113

Harris, T. The pomp of death... H86

Lodge, E. A funeral poem...Mr. Saml Pomfret... L231

The London clergy's petition...answer'd... L236

Luctus Aulæ Westmonasteriensis obitum...Joannis ducis Marlburiensis. L318

[Morrice, B.] The unequal enemies... M499

Newcomb, T. Verses to the...Earl of Cadogan... N279

Oppian's Halieuticks... O236

The parsons compassion... P89

A poem on the modern Arians. P628

Prat, D. An ode to Mr. Handel... P1017

Rightful monarchy: or, revolution tyranny... R212

Settle, E. Augusta lacrimans...to the memory of...Sir Thomas Abney. S239

Settle, E. Carmen natalitum...to...Brownloe, earl of Exeter... S250

Settle, E. Threnodia britannica...to the memory of... John duke of Marlborough. S331

[Sewell, G.] Verses written on the morning of the Duke of Marlborough's funeral. S379

The soldiers elegy on...John, duke of Marlborough... S545

[Tickell, T.] To Sir Godfrey Kneller... T311

Union...on the meeting of the parliament... U10

Virtue in danger... V103

[Wren, J.] Retirement: a divine soliloquy. W566·7

[1722?]

A new ballad...to John Higden... N62

The old t---p m---'s letter to his son... O127

To Venus, upon the charms of music... T399

1722: SCOTLAND

23 Feb   Burnbank and George Fachney's last shift... B578

Amyntar: a pastoral elegy... A219

Cogitations upon death... C280

The Edinburgh cuckolds... E15

Hamilton, W. A new edition of the life...of...Sir William Wallace... H20

Lintoun's lamentation, occasioned by the death of... Mr. Alexander Pennicuick... L189

[Ramsay, A.] A tale of three bonnets. R96

[Ramsay, A.] To the honourable, Sr. John Clerk of Pennycuik... R101

Sutherland's lament, for the loss of his post... S789

[1722?]

A dialogue between George Fachney and Alexander Pennicuik. D258

[Pennecuik, A.] Burnbank's farewel to Edinburgh... P151

The sorrowful lamentation, of James Campbell of Burnbank... S606

1722: IRELAND

Jan   A new song call'd the Sorrowful lamentations of Anthony Bulger... N196

Feb   An elegy on...Richard Delemar... E98

June   Tom Pun-sibi's resurrection disprov'd. T413

3 Aug   Upon the fringes... U20

Dec   An elegy on...Capt. Edward Charleton... E82

Advice to the ladies of Michael's parish... A95

[Brown, N.] The north-country-wedding... B506

An elegiack ode on...James, earl Stanhope. E35

An elegy on...Matthew Buckinger... E67

1722: Ireland (cont.)

An elegy on...Thomas Sheridan... E237

Ane elegy, occasion'd by...Alexander Sinclare... E239

An elegy on...Charles earl of Sunderland... E251

In Johannem Churchill ducem Marlburiensem epitaphium. I22

The late English p----t's elegy. L63

The Munster wedding... M562

A new ballad, occasion'd by the Pretenders declaration... N71

A new ballad on the dispute between the quakers and anabaptists. N78

A new litany... N153

[Percival, W.] A description in answer to the Journal. P175

A poem being an answer to the Ladies libraries... P520

A poem inscrib'd to the memory of...King William. P545

A poem occasioned by the funeral of...John duke of Marlborough. P555

A poem on...the Prince of Wales's birth-day... P569

A poem on Tom Pun----bi... P647

The prude, a tale. P1153

The robin-red-breast... R237

A satyr on the author of the Ladies-library. S55

The soldiers lamentation, for the loss of their general... S547

The drinking match... W376

[*1722?*]

A character. C118

The lady's watch. L30

Via ad episcopatum. V82

The bishop of Rochester's case... [1722/23] B227

1723

Jan   Cooke, T. A poem occasion'd by the late conspiracy. C421

Jan   [Crabb, J.] Quadriennium Jacobi, sc. secundi... C489

Jan   Pope, A. First chorus. Of Athenian philosophers... P876

21 Jan   The rape of the bride... R119

23 Jan   The bawdy-house: a poem. B109

4 Feb   An epistle to...Doctor W--d----d... E416

7 Feb   The louse-trap a poem. L276

12 Feb   The natural philosophers; a tale. N9

14 Feb   The ghastly wound. A tale... G133

15 Feb   The free masons... F244

19 Feb   Baker, H. An invocation of health. B10

19 Feb   Button, and button-hole... B610

28 Feb   A tale of a bottomless tub. T10

Mar   The ball; or, un passo tempo... B19

Mar   Markland, J. An ode on...the young princess... M103

Mar   The pettifoggers. A satire... P197

Mar   Roman courage display'd in English bravery... R263

4 Mar   Ridotto: or, downfall of masquerades... R208

5 Mar   Prior, M. Down-Hall: a poem. P1072

6 Mar   Newcomb, T. The last judgment... N254

Apr   A ballad...on occasion of a duel... B42

1 Apr   The first of April... F149

3 Apr   [Kennett, W.] Armour. A poem... K12

25 Apr   Britons thanksgiving... B481

May   Amhurst, N. The conspiracy... A192

May   The ascent of the separate soul. A337

May   The deluge: or, cautious old-woman. D211

May   An epistle from an half-pay officer... E366

May   Eusden, L. The ode for the birth-day... E496

May   An ode humbly inscribed to the king. O30

May   Prior, M. The turtle and the sparrow. P1090

May   Silk-worms: a poem... S462

May   Wilkes, T. The golden farmer... W460

June   Morrice, B. An address to Homer. M471

July   Blackmore, *Sir* R. Alfred, an epick poem. B240

Aug   The rival politicians... R216

29 Aug   [Hauksbee, F.] The patch... H107

Sept   Davies, J. Bury-fair... D60

Oct   King Satan... K53

Dec   Bond, W. An odaic essay in commemoration of the nativity... B318

Dec   Philips, A. An ode...on the death of... William, earl Cowper. P210

6 Dec   [Le Pla, M.] A paraphrase on the Song of the three children. L105

Carmen elegiacum in mortem...ducis Malborough... C54

Councillor Layer's last farewell... C440

Dawson, W. The atheist... D71

An elegy, sacred to...George Whitehead... E274

[Ellis, W.] A divine poem...to the memory of...Richard Claridge... E292

The fable of the blackbird and kite. F4

A fight and no fight... F140

[Ker, J.] Serenissimo et clementissimo principi Georgio... K26

[Nevil, H.] A congratulatory poem, on the...birth-day of...King George. N39

A poem...to the gentlemen of the Oxfordshire society. P532

Settle, E. Threnodia apollinaris...to the memory of...
William earl Cowper. S327

Settle, E. Threnodia apollinaris...to the memory of...
Sir Christopher Wren. S328

Settle, E. Trophæa marina. To...Captain Ogle... S342

Sherburn, W. The fourth book of Virgil's Æneid... S404

Tunstall, —. Carmen genethliacum...to...Sir Thomas
Parkyns. T545

Waldron, G. An ode on the 28th of May... W6

[Wesley, S.] A new ballad. W344

1723: SCOTLAND

July　Ramsay, A. The fair assembly... R50

An account of...Alaster Mackalaster... A12

An elegy upon...Mrs. Mary Gordan... E133

The highland man's lament, for the death of Donald
Bayn... H206

[Meston, W.] The knight. M211

[Pennecuik, A.] Corydon and Cochrania...on the nuptials of...James duke of Hamiltoun... P152

[Pennecuik, A.] The melancholy muse... P164

[Pennecuik, A.] Muschet revived... P167

A poem on the South-Sea... P642

Ramsay, A. Jenny and Meggy... R59

Ramsay, A. The nuptials: a masque... R66

[1723?]

[Mallet, D.] William and Margaret... M59

[Ramsay, A.] The highland laddie. R58

[Ramsay, A.] A new song. To the tune of Lochaber no
more. R65

1723: IRELAND

Mar　A prologue to the Conscious lovers... P1133

26 Mar　Orpheus redivivus: a poem on the Irish harp...
S738

May　A contest between Marsyas and Apollo...
C396

Oct　An elegy on...Sir Constantine Phipps...
E212

The butchers letter of advice to the weavers. B603

[Coffey, C.] Temple-Oagg: or, the spaw-well. C278

[Delany, P.] To the Dutchess of Grafton. D209

[Fitzgerald, —.] Mendico-hymen...The beggar's match.
F156

Ireland's happiness compleated... I60

Jove's ramble... J105

A paradox. The best perfume... P49

A poem on the Princess of Wales's birth-day... P638

[Sheridan, T.] A prologue design'd for the play of
Oedipus... S412

[1723?]

[Swift, J.] The first of April...[172 3/24?] S856

Ireland (cont.)

The quaker's petition to the h------ of c——. [1723/30?]
Q5

1724

4 Jan　Withers, J. An epistle to...Robert Walpole...
W538

9 Jan　[Morrice, B.] The amour of Cytherea... M472

Apr　The confessor. A tale. C342

Apr　Dawson, W. The British swain... D72

Apr　An epistle to Mr. Handel... E402

Apr　Heydegger's letter to the bishop of London.
H169

Apr　Merrivale, T. The necromancer... M197

Apr　Philander and Sacharissa. A novel... P201

May　[Benson, W.] Virgil's husbandry... B196

May　The masquerade. A poem. M131

May　The session of musicians... S223

June　The ball... B20

July　[Amhurst, N.] Oculus Britanniæ... A199

Nov　Female piety and virtue. F99

Nov　Hatton, H. C. An occasional satyr. H106

Dec　[Earle, J.] Umbritii Cantiani Rus... E9

[Anderson, J.] In luctuosum...obitum...Gulielmi, archi-
episcopi Eboracensis. A224

[Bell, B.] The osiers... B173

[Bennison, J.] Ode ad...Thomam Parkyns... B194

Bockett, E. A poem to the memory of Aquila Rose...
B306

[Bourne, V.] In obitum Roussaei... B332

A congratulatory poem on...King George's...return...
C353

A congratulatory poem on the translation of...Edmund
...to the see of London. C358

Diamond cut diamond... D289

An epistle from S------o, to A------a R------n. E377

Greer, J. Ad Cæsarem britannicum...redeuntem ode.
G290

The invincible hero Arthure Dillon's sword... I55

Mitchell, J. Ode on Buchanan. M318

A poem on the death of...William earl Cowper. P606

St. Taffy's day... S22

[Ward, E.] The dancing devils... W56

[1724?]

[Wesley, S.] The battle of the sexes... W333

Newgate's garland... [1724/25] N288

The triple alliance. [1724/27] T498

1724: SCOTLAND

Jan　A garland for a fraudulent bankrupts brow...
G15

1724: Scotland (*cont.*)

An elegy on...James Bathgate... E55

An elegy to... William Nisbet... E199

[Forbes, W.] Xantippe, or the scolding wife... F196

Gibson, W. An elegy upon...John Wilson... G139

The grievious complaint of the beaux and the bads... G294

The groans of the people... G301

An habbiack elegy on...Robert F------s... H1

Margaret Dickson's penetential confession. M95

A mournful song, upon the breach of...covenant... M547

[Pennecuik, A.] The shepherds tears...to the memory of ...William Nisbet... P172

Ramsay, A. Health: a poem. R57

[Ramsay, A.] Mouldy-Mowdiwart... R64

[Ramsay, A.] An ode sacred to the memory of... Anne dutchess of Hamilton. R68

[Ramsay, A.] On pride... R71

[Ramsay, A.] On seeing the archers... R72

[Ramsay, A.] On the Royal Company of Archers... R74

[Ramsay, A.] The poetick sermon... R79

[*1724?*]

An habby on the death of Mis. James Cruickshanks... H3

Pennecuik, A. A panegyrick on Philip king of Spain... P169

Pennecuik, A. Dialogue betwixt a Glasgow malt-man... [1724/25] P154

[Ramsay, A.] The monk and the miller's wife... [1724/26] R63

1724: IRELAND

Jan   A poem address'd to the Quidnunc's... P518

25 Mar   [Tisdall, W.] Tom Pun-sibi metamorphosed... T318

May   A serenade to be represented on the birth-day ... S208

17 Sept [Swift, J.] A serious poem upon William Wood ... S902

Oct   To the citizens. T362

Nov   An express from Parnassus... E610

Nov   [Swift, J.] An excellent new song upon...our good lord archbishop of Dublin... S846

Nov   [Swift, J.] Prometheus, a poem. S898

Dec   A moral poem on the middle state of life... M436

An address to the ladies of St. Warborough's parish. A56

All prophecy's at an end... A162

The bridge of life... B441

The Drapier anatomiz'd: a song. D428

An elegy on my lord New Town Butler... E71

An elegy on Alderman Constantine... E89

1724: Ireland (*cont.*)

An elegy on Sir John Rawdon... E225

An elegy on...Henry Sacheverell... E233

An elegy on the hon. —— Talent... E253

An excellent new ballad against Wood's half-pence... E541·5

An excellent new ballad upon the new half-pence... E570

An excellent new ballad upon the present grand-jury. E571

An excellent new song...against Woods's brass half-pence... E588

An excellent new song upon the declarations...against Wood's half-pence... E593

An excellent new song upon the late grand-jury. E594

Hibernia resurgens. To my lord bishop of Derry... H173

Ireland's warning...upon Woods's base half-pence... I66

Kennedy, H. The comical revenge... K11

The lamentations of Mary Magdalene... L40

A letter from a cobler... to Jet Black. L118

A letter from a young lady, to the revd. D----n S----t. L123

A letter from Aminadab Firebrass...to M.B. drapier. L124

A new epilogue to the Conscious lovers... N140

A new poem ascrib'd to...the late grand-jury. N165

A new prologue to the Conscious lovers... N176

Owens, S. A petition...to...King George... O257

Owens, S. A poem, or advice to the authors of a satyrical poem... O258

Owens, S. Remarks upon the report of the committee of the lords... O260

A paraphrase on part of the book of Joshua. P51

A poem in praise of nastiness... P539

The presbyter unmask'd. A tale. P1024

Punch's petition to the ladies. P1167

The rivals. A poem... R220

[Smedley, J.] An epistle to...the Duke of Grafton... S498

[Swift, J.] An elegy on Dr. John Whalley... S834

[Swift, J.] His grace's answer to Jonathan. S858

To his grace the arch-bishop of Dublin... T334

The true and genuine elegy of Matthew Gun... T511

A true character of the wooden monster... T519

[*1724?*]

Damon's case and resolution... D21

A hue and cry after the eclipse... H356

A letter from the Quidnunc's at St. James's coffee-house ... L136

Mr. Woods to all the people of Ireland. M301

Modern wit; or twelve celebrated beauties... M388

[*1724?*]: *Ireland* (cont.)

An ode...to the honourable William Con——ly. O29

A rebus written by a lady... R144

The wonderfull man... W554

An excellent new song call'd the Irish-man's joy...
[1724/25] E583·5

1725

25 Jan   [Young, E.] The universal passion. Satire I.
       Y122

Feb   [Barford, R.] Abelard to Eloisa. B81

Feb   Bewick, W. A poem on tobacco... B209

Feb   Musidora; a pastoral elegy on...Mrs. Bowes...
     M569

Feb   The phantom. P198

26 Feb   Pitt, C. Vida's Art of poetry... P416

Mar   Beckingham, C. Verses occasion'd by the death
     of the Czar of Muscovy... B151

Mar   The creation of women. C500

Apr   'Vigaeus, T.' Actum fidei... V95

Apr   [Wesley, S.] The pig, and the mastiff. W347

Apr   [Young, E.] The universal passion. Satire III.
     Y128

2 Apr   [Young, E.] The universal passion. Satire II.
     Y125

May   [Cooke, T.] The battle of the poets... C408

12 May   [Gay, J.] To a lady on her passion for old china.
     G79

June   [Benson, W.] Virgil's husbandry... B195

June   Griffith, N. An ode to...Sir William Morgan.
     G297

June   Mitchell, J. Two poetical petitions... M344

June   [Savage, R.] The authors of the town... S89

18 June   [Young, E.] The universal passion. Satire IV.
     Y130

July   Eusden, L. The origin of the knights of the
     Bath... E500

July   Weighley, alias Wild... W277

Sept   Catherall, S. Cato major... C72

Nov   An ode to the grand Khaibar. O69

Nov   Pope, T. The Stamford toasts... P992

Nov   A session of painters... S224

Dec   [Dodington, G. B., *baron*] An epistle to...Sir
     Robert Walpole. D371

Dec   Eusden, L. To Mr. John Saunders... E513

Dec   Morrice, B. An essay on the universe. M484

Dec   Welsted, L. Oikographia... W302

An epistle to Ge--ge Ch--ne... E398

The female worthies... F103

[Merrick, J.] Heliocrene a poem... M195

[Mitchell, J.] The sine-cure... M329

Newcomb, T. An ode on the general conflagration...
N259

Rooke, J. The silk-worms... R264

Somervile, W. The two springs, a fable... S578

[Taswell, W.] Muscipula: or, the mouse-trap... T47

Vanière, J. Columbæ... V15

[*1725?*]

Hannes, W. Ode ad...Matthæum Frampton. H34

The tale of the robbin... T30

The maiden's dream. [1725?/–] M21

1725: SCOTLAND

13 Mar   [Pennecuik, A.] Groans from the grave... P159

8 May   To the worshipful, cordners of the West-port...
     T398

Aug   [Pennecuik, A.] A huy and cry after Sir John
     Barlycorn... P160

Ker, J. Ad D. D. Gul. Bennettum de Grubbet... K18

Ker, J. Donaides...de eximia Jacobi Fraserii... K22

Mallet, D. A poem, in imitation of Donaides. M54

The mourner. A funeral poem...James Brisbain... M541

A poem upon the tragedy of Thorn. P685

[*1725?*]

The grief and lamentation of Auld-Reeky... G292

The lamentation of the fruit wives... L38

[Meston, W.] Viri humani...Gulielmi Sutherlandi...
M223

The taverners answer to the drunken wives lament...
T100

Pennecuik, A. Old-Reekie's loud and joyful acclama-
tion... [1725/26] P168

[Ramsay, A.] The general mistake...[1725/26] R55

1725: IRELAND

Jan   An elegy on...Serjeant Fitz-Gerald... E114

Mar   A funeral elegy on...Jacob Peppard... F291

Apr   Elegy on...John Harding... E143

Apr   An elegy on...Thaddeus Mc.Dermot... E182

May   A prologue for his majesty's birth-day... P1123

May   A serenade to be represented on the birth-day...
     S209

21 May   Ireland's universal loss...of Allan Broderick...
     I65

June   A poem upon R—r a lady's spaniel. P678

July   [Nelson, H.] A new poem on the...journey-men
     taylors... N26

22 July   A poem on the new lord chancellor. P631

Aug   An elegy on...Alderman Ford... E116

Aug   [Nelson, H.] The Dublin-jubilee... N20

Sept   An elegy on...Dean Clayton... E85

1725: Ireland (cont.)

Sept An elegy on...visc. Tullemoore... E261

Sept On wisdom's defeat... O230

Oct Ashton, R. A poem in honour of the...journey-men shoe-makers... A344

Oct An elegy on...Aaron Crossly... E92

Oct The last speech of Wisdom's defeat... L59

Nov An elegy on...Nicholas Dalton... E95

Nov An elegy on...Sir Henery Echlin... E109

Nov An elegy on...— Worth esq... E286

Nov A poem by Doctor Young, on Miss Harvey... Y108

12 Nov A cruel and bloody declaration... C529

Dec [Davys, E. *viscount.*] A poem delivered to... Doctor Swift... D64

[Arbuckle, J.] A new prologue... A285

Ashton, R. A congratulatory poem to...Dean Swift. A341

The bachelor's dream. B4

[Barber, M.] To his excellency the Lord Carteret... B78

[Barber, M.] The widows address to the...Lady Carteret. B80

The birth of manly virtue from Callimachus. B221

The blacksmith's recreation... B269

A blott is no blott... B288

The boarding-school... B293

A call to the guard by beat of drum. C3

[Carey, H.] Namby Pamby... C49

A Christmas box for Namby Pamby... C170

[Coffey, C.] A prologue...on the 22d of April... C277

A congratulary poem on Dean Swift's return to town. C350

D'Anvers, A. The funeral... D36

Davys, E. *viscount.* To his excellency our Lord Carteret... D65

The death and burial of the new coin'd half-pence. D81

The Donore ballad... D403

An elegy on...Charles Campbel... E74

Elegy on...Ch-----les Co-----ey, the poet. E87

An elegy on...Mr Harrison... E144

An elegy on...Jaquo' the monkey... E162

An elegy on...Robert lord vis. Molesworth... E192

An elegy on...Jo. Poe... E216

England's ingratitude: or, Jonathan Wild's complaint. E319

An epistle from Jack Sheppard... E369

Hue and cry after them brewers... H360

[King, W.] The old cheese... K65

A lady's answer to Mr. Ambrose Philips. L21

A new ballad, or, the lamentation for Miss P—p... N82

A new London poem on the procession of the journey-men taylors... N154

A new poem ascrib'd to the lady who wrote the answer to Mr. Philips's poem... N166

1725: Ireland (cont.)

Nick and froth or... N296

No-body turn'd some-body... N314

Old Tom the tooper's last advice... O126

The old woman's tale. O134

On the works of Humpus, town-poet. O229

[Owens, S.] A scourge for the author of the satyr, gibing on Trinity College... O261

[Owens, S.] Trinity College vindicated... O263

[Philips, A.] The following poems... P208

Philips, A. Poems by Mr. Philips, &c. P217

Philips, A. To the honourable Miss Carteret. P221

[Pilkington, M.] A pastoral elegy on...a lady's canary bird... P281

[Pilkington, M.] The progress of musick in Ireland... P282

A poem inscrib'd to...Lord Carteret. P542

A poem inscrib'd to the author of The birth of manly virtue. P544

A poem on the birth-day of...King George... P591

A poem on the Drapiers birth-day... P610

A poem to D--------- S--------. P660

A satyr. Ascrib'd to...L— C——t. S44

A satyr satiris'd... S68

A second poem, to Dr. Jo—n S—t. S175

[Shadwell, C.] A second song, sung at the club at Mr. Taplin's... S381

[Sheridan, T.] The Drapier's ballad... S406

'Shippen, W.' Tyburn's courteous invitation to William Wood... S443

[Smedley, J.] A Christmas invitation to the Lord Carteret. S497

[Smedley, J.] A satyr. S509

[Swift, J.] A letter...to D. S—y. S876

Swift, J. Sphinx... S910

The taylors answer to Vulcan's speech... T7

[Tickell, T.] Lucy and Colin, a song... T290

To the honourable Mr. D.T.... T373

Tom Punsibi's farewel to the muses. T412

Vel, S. The troopers elogy... V24

Vulcan's speech... V123

Whiteacre's glory: or, the drubbing of Seignior Stopha... W409

Wit upon crutches...to...Mr. Arbuckle... W537

[*1725?*]

[Barber, M.] Apollo's edict. B75

The brazen age banish'd. B403

The double-shaver, or, an advice to the barbers. D413

The humble petition of a beautiful young lady... H394

The Munster combat... M560

The new b— —p's complaint... N113

[*1725?*]: *Ireland* (*cont.*)

Owens, S.   Remarks on the young ladies petition... O259

The p—— and s—— fe——s of T——y C——e... P1

A paraphrase on the lxxxii psalm... P55

A poem on the erecting a groom-porter's-house... P614

The conclave dissected... [1725/26] C331

Namby Pamby's answer to Captain Gordon. [1725/26] N1

To Mr. Philips, on his late poetry in Ireland. [1725/27?] T344

[Whyte, L.] The broken mug. [1725?/27] W447

The ship's mate and the parson... [1725/29] S426

A poem by Namby Pamby. [1725/–] P523

[*1725/30*]

Dr. Anthony's petition. A261

Doctor Anthony's poem in praise of the pox. A262

Ἀστραῖος: humbly dedicated to...Lord Carteret. A361

Birkhead, M.   The enter'd prentices song... B220

The butchers answer to the taylors poem... B602

Delafaye, C.   The fellow crafts song. D190

A dialogue between the brogue-makers and journey-men shoe-makers. D266

The expostulation or the disconsolate shepherd. E609

Helter skelter, the devil in a frying-pan... H140

A last farewell, to Dolly. L50

⟨   ⟩ made on the...twenty four corporations... M11

Neptune to Lord Carteret. N35

A new ballad intituled the Freeman's advice... N69

A new ballad, on a mock duel... N74

A new poem on the beauties of the universe. N170

An old fashion song... O110

Pancharilla, from Bonefonius... P27

'Philips, A.'   The tea-pot... P218

A poem in praise of the journey-men taylors. P540

A poem to the memory of...Henry Piercy. P668

The reformer's ghost... R151

Remarks upon remarks, on a certain lady... R156

A riddle by Dr. S——t, to my Lady Carteret. R204

A satyr on Miss Ga—fny... S53

A satyr, on the town-poet's... S67

A short state of the case, to the vicar of N—. S450

The stumbling-horse... S776

[Swift, J.] A riddle by Doctor R——e. S899

The Temple-Oge ballad. T115·5

To the honourable Master Henry Barry... T372

The tradesman's hue and cry after the bumb-bailiffs... T438

'Wimble, W.' The character of a certain f—w of T—y C—e... W522

1726

Jan   [Bowden, S.] A poem on the new method of treating physic... B335

Jan   Cooke, T.   The bath... C406

18 Jan   [Morrice, B.] Verses on the king... M500

21 Jan   [Young, E.] The universal passion. Satire the last. Y132

Feb   Beckingham, C.   The lyre... B139

Feb   Part of the XLI psalm, to be sung by the British charity-children... P91

Feb   Welsted, L.   An ode to...Major-General Wade... W297

12 Feb   Hypocondria. A poem... H475

Apr   Mitchell, J.   The promotion, and the alternative... M321

29 Apr   Thomson, J.   Winter. A poem. T211

May   Human passions: a satyr... H387

May   The longitude discover'd; a tale. L251

May   Services and sufferings... S220

May   Wesley, S.   The Iliad in a nutshell... W342

10 May   [Carey, H.] Faustina... C42

13 May   Barford, R.   The assembly... B82

June   Beckingham, C.   An ode to...Sir Robert Walpole... B143

11 June   [Carey, H.] Mocking is catching... C47

July   Young, E.   The instalment. To...Sir Robert Walpole... Y86

20 Aug   Foxton, T.   The tower. A poem. F227

Sept   Mawer, J.   The progress of language... M149

Oct   [Byrom, J.] Tunbridgiale, a poem... B620

Nov   [Boyd, E.] Variety... B347

Nov   The nocturnal... N315

Dec   [Curteis, T.] Genethlia... C553

Dec   [Welsted, L.] A hymn to the creator... W295

20 Dec   The discovery: or, the squire turned ferret... D328

Εἰκόνες ἰατρικαι... E26

[Ellison, C.] A most pleasant description of Benwel village... E298

Eusden, L.   An epistle to...Sir Robert Walpole... E488

[Gay, J.] Molly Mog... G59

Menalcas, or a pastoral... M171

Newcomb, T.   Verses to...the Duke of Richmond... N277

[Thirkeld, T.] A Sunday evening's conversation at Benwell... T154

Threnodia Cestriensis... T260

Verses occasioned by the judgment passed on John Ward... V55

Ward, E.   News from Madrid... W126

[1726?]

The picture of pictures...[1726/30?] P271

Pope, A. A receipt to make a soop...[1726/–] P952

1726: SCOTLAND

Feb   Ramsay, A. A Scots ode, to the British antiquarians. R89

Aug   [Pennecuik, A.] A lecture to the ladies... P163

A funeral poem occasion'd by...those noble martyrs... F299

[Pennecuik, A.] The faithful sheepherd...to the memory of...Thomas Paterson... P158

Pennecuik A. The mournfull sheepherds...to the memory of Sir Francies Grant... P166

1726: IRELAND

Jan   An elegy on...Thomas Hogg... E149

Jan   A generous exhortation to undertakers and journeymen-weavers, &c. G104

Apr   An hymn to be sung by the charity-children, of St. Andrew's parish... H440

Apr   [Swift, J.] Cadenus and Vanessa. S814

May   A serenade to be represented on the birth-day... S210

June   Dalton, O. An elegy on...James Fitzsimons... D17

July   An elegy on...Viscount Charlemont... E80

July   An elegy on...Viscount Charlemont... E81

July   An elegy on...Viscount Longford... E240

July   [Nelson, H.] A poem, in the honour of the...journey-men taylors... N30

Aug   An elegy on...Sir. Samuel Cook... E90

Aug   A funeral elegy, on...Sir Samuel Cooke... F293

Oct   Ashton, R. A poem in honour of the...journeymen shoe-makers... A345

Dec   Elegy on...Richard West... E270

Advice from fairyland... A71

Dr. Anthony's lamentation for the loss of all his patients. A258

The apothecary in the sheet... A271

The apothecary's petition to a canonical judge. A272

Ashton, R. A new elegy on...Henry Nelson... A343

The blunder of all blunders... B290

The catch sung by the journey-men weavers... C68

[Delany, P.] A riddle... D205

[Delany, P.] A riddle... D206

[Delany, P.] A third riddle. D207

[Delany, P.] A fourth riddle. D208

The departure. To...Lord Carteret. D228

A dialogue between two sisters and a certain apothecary. D273

1726: Ireland (cont.)

An elegy on...Earl Cadogan... E73

An elegy on...Dennis McCarthy... E181

An elegy on... W—— T——r, an attorney... E258

An epistle in behalf of our Irish poets... E383

An excellent new ballad. E536

An excellent new ballad, shewing how Mr. Mor—cai Ad—d—m's... E556

An excellent new song, to a good old tune. E589

The fable of Bubo and Turturella... F2

The fair court... F28

The fairy-king, a poem. F37

The geneology, a poem... G99

[Hervey, J. *baron*] Monimia to Philocles... H157·5

Hewitt, —. Alexis to Celia... H167

Hye, for cakes and ale... H170

The history of the old and new testament... H259

An infallible cure for the gout. I37

[Jacob, H.] The members to their soverain. J45

A letter to the bishop of M. by Dr. Sw—t... L155

M. Ad----m's lamentation... M1

[Mitchell, J.] Poltis king of Thrace... M320·5

Myrtillo. A pastoral poem... M573

Namby Pamby's lamentation... N2

A new ballad in praise of...Londonderry. N63

A new ballad on the dissolution of the poor-house... N79

A new song to the honourable Miss C—— —— ——t. N216

[Ogle, G.] The Liffy: a fable... O97

A pastoral on St. Patrick's-day... P114

'Philips, A.' A new poem. P209

Philips, A. To his excellency the Lord Carteret... P219

A poem...to...Thomas Tickell. P533

A poem on a lady's bed. P563

A poem on Mrs. M—t A—s. P573

A poem on the dean of St. Patrick's birth-day... P596

A poem on the journeymen taylors... P639

A poem to a widow... P659

A poem to the whole people of Ireland... P675

The prisoner's petition to his patron. P1100

A satyr on the author of She would if she could. S54

A satyr on the poets of the town... S62

A satyr. To Miss M—y W—t—n. S70

A satyr. To the author of Namby Pamby... S71

She wou'd if she cou'd... S385

[Sheridan, T.] A true and faithful inventory... S419

The squirelin. A tale. S672

Starrat, W. A pastoral in praise of Allan Ramsay. S721

Thompson, W. A poetical paraphrase on part of the book of Job... T168

1726: Ireland (cont.)

The triumphant taylors... T504

A vindication of the Duke of Wh——n's answer to the Quaker's letter. V98

A warning to Ireland... W240

A young lady's complaint for the stay of Dean Swift in England. Y22

[1726?]

Doctor Anthony's new year's-gift. A260

[Barber, M.] The prodigy: or, the silent woman... B76

An excellent new ballad in praise of Monaky Gall... E549

Horse and away... H324

A hue and cry after a c-----y m---------te. H351

A hue and cry after M——k... H355

The infallible Dr Anthony. I38

A new ballad on the departure of Miss B——ll G——m-b——ll. N77

A new gingle/On Tom Dingle. N143

A new poem, in commemoration of the 10th. of June... N167

A poem on the thirtieth of October... P646

The printers petition to the poetical senate... P1064

Helter skelter, or the hue and cry after the attornies... [1726/27?] H139

A new poem in honour of the journey-men taylors. [1726?/27?] N168

[Smedley, J.] A riddle... [1726/27?] S508

Captain Wel——he's answer to Miss Molly War---r-t--on. [1726/28] C35

1727

Jan	[Hawling, F.] The signal... H115
21 Jan	Robin-Hood and the Duke of Lancaster... R232
Feb	Bond, W. Verses sacred to the memory of the ...Duchess of Grafton... B320
Feb	Folly. A poem. F176
Feb	An occasional poem. O6
Feb	Ralph, J. The tempest... R22
Feb	St. A-d-è's miscarriage... S18
Feb	[Young, E.] The universal passion. Satire V. Y134
20 Feb	Thomson, J. Summer. A poem. T220
Mar	An answer from S——a F——a to S——r S——o. A230
Mar	[Carey, H.] The Grumbletonians... C43
Mar	The discontented virgin. D325
Mar	An epistle from S——r S——o to S——a F——a. E379
Mar	[Wesley, S.] To the memory of...Francis Gastrell... W354

16 Mar	[Mitchell, J.] The Totness address, versified. M333
23 Mar	[Stanhope, P. D. *earl.*] The Cambro Briton robb'd of his bauble... S717
25 Mar	The address, a new ballad... A50
28 Mar	The poets address. P708
Apr	The circumvention... C202
Apr	Mottley, J. Verses to...Sir Robert Walpole... M537
Apr	An old maid's fortune... O114
May	[Cooke, T.] Philander and Cydippe... C420
May	[Mitchell, J.] A tale and two fables in verse... M330
May	Two Lilliputian odes... T586
4 May	Several copies of verses on occasion of Mr. Gulliver's travels. S356
8 May	Thomson, J. A poem sacred to the memory of Sir Isaac Newton. T200
June	A ballad: occasion'd by some ladies wearing ruffs at court... B26
June	Collins, R. Nature display'd C293
June	[Davys, J.] The art of decyphering discovered ... D66
June	Laugh and be fat... L71
June	Mitchell, J. The judgment of Hercules. M313
June	Overton, J. David and Goliah... O253
June	Robin's pathetick tale... R239
June	Savage, R. A poem, sacred to...King George ... S107
June	[Young, E.] Cynthio. Y69
July	[Browne, M.] Verses to...the Earl of Scarborough... B537
July	Coffee: a tale. C274
July	A new Lilliputian ballad on the appearance of their majesties... N149
July	The Templer's bill of complaint... T116
18 July	Pattison, W. An epistle to his majesty... P128
Aug	An elegy on...King George... E128
Aug	Mitchell, J. The shoe-heel... M327
Aug	Mitchell, J. To their most excellent majesties ... M332
Oct	Dunton, J. King George for ever... D537
Oct	Pack, R. A congratulatory poem to his majesty ... P5
Oct	A poem; occasion'd by reading Shaftesbury's Characteristicks... P549
Oct	[Roach, R.] Carmen coronarium... R221
Oct	Stacie, ——. Consolatory verses to a lady... S673
Oct	[Watts, I.] An ode on the coronation... W253
Nov	Ames, H. A new translation of Horace's Art of poetry... A179
Nov	Curteis, T. Eirenodia... C551
Nov	Eusden, L. Three poems... E510

Nov A poem on the coronation... P595

Nov Woodward, G. A poem to the glorious memory of...King George I. W560

7 Nov Hog-land: or a description of Hampshire... H275

10 Nov Fielding, H. The coronation... F119

Dec The martin and the oyster... M117

Dec Mawer, J. Liberty asserted... M146

Dec Mr. Addison's fine ode to Dr. Thomas Burnet ... M287

[Anderson, J.] In luctuosum...obitum...Georgii Ludovici... A223

Beckingham, C. A poem on...King George the second ... B144

Bellamy, D. An elegiac poem, in commemoration of... King George. B175

Bordman, T. In obitum illustrissimi Georgii I... B324

Bridge, W. In obitum regis Georgii I. B442

Bung's address... B567

The contre temps; or, rival queans... C400

An epistle from Signora F----a to a lady. E376

F——na's answer to S——no's epistle. F175

Foxton, T. A poetical paraphrase on the...Benedicite. F226

The hawkers new-year's gift... H110

Hereditary right exemplified... H151

In answer to the Le H——p's ballad... I17

Kiss my a-se is no treason... K92

Le H-----p at Hanover. A new song. L94·3

Le H——p's epistle to P. F——k. L94·8

Little-John's answer to Robin-Hood and the Duke of Lancaster... L198

Love and courtship, a poem. L280

Mawer, J. The coronation... M141

Mawer, J. An epistle to the king... M144

A poem, sacred to the birth-day of...George... P649

The saylors address to his majesty. S12

Selbey, W. The temple of Venus. S197

A shorter and truer advertisement...or, Dr D--g--l--s in an extasy... S453

The Totness address transversed. T427

A trip to the pillory... T493

Uvedale, T. The death-bed display'd... U31

Vézian, A. Ode au roi... V80

Weichmann, C. F. Etwas Teutsches zur Verteidigung der Teutschen... W276

[1727?]

The maids christmas box. M22

A new ballad. To the tune of, London is a fine town, &c. N96

A song, on the confession...of William Stevenson... S589

To the...Earl of Oxford... T392

Lord upon knight; and knight upon squire. [1727/28] L261

A new ballad. Tune of, To you fair ladies now at land. [1727/28] N107

The equivalent for fasting... [1727/30] E450

The political pair; or, the state gossip... [1727/–] P713

1727: SCOTLAND

16 Feb A letter from Doctor Dalgleish to...Mrs. M'Leod... L125

May The apparition. A275

An account of...Mrs. M'Leod. A11

Clark, H. Meditations upon the love of Christ... C222

An elegy on...Mirs. M'Leod... E183

Ker, J. Cantici Solomonis paraphrasis gemina... K20

The last farewel...of Mrs. M'Leoid... L49

Mrs. M'Leod's last farewel to John Gibson. M302

Ramsay, A. An ode to the memory of Sir Isaac Newton ... R69

Smith, R. The Assembly's shorter catechism... S527

[1727?]

A pastoral poem, sacred to the memory of...King George. P116

R------ P------s complaint of his hard fate... [1727/–] R1

1727: IRELAND

Apr An elegy on...Sir John Eccles... E108

May An elegy on...Henry Moore, earl of Drogheda ... E105

May An elegy on the...Lord of Howth... E152

May Heaven invaded... H130

June Hibernia in universal mourning... H171

June Hibernia in universal mourning... H172

June A new song. Made on our late soverin lord King George... N202

July An elegy on...John Parnel... E208

July Nelson, H. A new poem on the procession of journey-men taylors... N27

Aug Elegy on...William Whitshed... E278

Sept An elegy on...Doctor Trever... E260

Sept A new elegy...on the death of Dr. Traver's... N131

Oct Ashton, R. An historical poem in honour of the ...journeymen shoemakers... A342

Oct An elegy on...Robert Rochford... E229

Oct A serenata theatrale, to be represented on the birth-day... S214

Nov An elegy on...the Lord Altham... E42

Dec An elegy on...Robert Fortune... E118

1727: Ireland (cont.)

Dec   An elegy on...Robert Fortune... E119

Dec   An elegy on...'Squire Roberts... E228

Apollo's advice to all freeholders... A269

Ashton, R.   A poem on the birth day of...Queen Anne ... A346

Aston, M.   Hibernia out of mourning... A358

Aston, M.   Peace and plenty... A359

Aston, M.   Virtue and industry... A360

Ballad made on the present election... B25

The bridegroom at his wit's-end... B440

[Carey, H.] A Lilliputian ode on King George... C45

[Coffey, C.] The bason: a poem... C276

A commendatory poem to the...city of Dublin... C316

Creagh, *Sir* M.   Poem presented...to their present majesties... C499

Curry, J.   Courtship... C548

An elegy on...George Curtis... E94

An elegy on...the passau countess of Kerry... E167

Elegy upon the death of Mrs. Motly. E195

An elegy on...Viscount Nettervill... E197

An elegy on...Charles Proby... E222

An elegy upon Tiger... E254

An epistle to a worshipful gentleman... E389

⟨   ⟩ for the death of Mr. Curtis... F181

The Grubstreet cavalacade... G305

An hoop for the broken mugg. H303

The intended city's address paraphras'd. I48

Liberty: a poem. L170

The Little Beaus speech... L197

Munster Juggy preferr'd... M561

A new song made on the...society of scriblers... N206

A new war between cakes and ale... N238

O'Brien, W.   A epick poem. On...William Leigh... O3

A pastoral elegy upon...Mr. Allan Ramsy. P108

A poem on the approaching coronation. P578

A poem on the journeymen sheermen, and dyers. P621

A poem upon the news of...Lord Carteret's return... P683

A satyr on the lawyers... S57

[Sheridan, T.] To...Viscount Mont-Cassel... S417

[Sheridan, T.] Tom Punsibi's letter to Dean Swift. S418

A Spanish farst. S618

Warning to coucolds... W239

[1727?]

Dr. Anthony's description of the coronation. A257

'Anthony, *Doctor*.' A satyr on a clyster-pipe... A264

The auricula. A372

A committee of rats, on the down-fall of catts. C317

The devil to do on the death of Old-Nick. D247

[1727?]: Ireland (cont.)

A diverting dialogue between a state black-a-more and a young lady... D340

The elections... E31

An elegy on...Jack Clifford... E86

Elegy on...Mr. No Body. E200

Epilogue. Designed to be spoken by Alonzo... E346

An excellent new ballad, to a new tune. E557

An excellent new ballad to the tune of You cut purses all, &c. E568

Great cry and little wooll... G267

The lady's letter to the freeholders... L28

Limerick to Kilmallock; sendeth greeting... L183

The Little Beau's lamentation... L195

The mock-patron... M356

A new British prophecy... N114

A new dialogue, between a wolf, and shepherd's dog. N128

A paraphrase on the seven penitential psalms... P60

To the college poets... T363

The vulture and eagle... V124

1728

9 Jan   An epistle from Sapho to Philenis... E374

23 Jan   Liberty: or, the meeting of the parliament. L172

30 Jan   [Fielding, H.] The masquerade... F122

31 Jan   Ralph, J.   Night: a poem. R18

Feb   An epistle to...Sir Robert Walpole. E424

Feb   Part of the 112th psalm...to be sung by the charity-children... P93

15 Feb   Desaguliers, J. T.   The Newtonian system of the world... D234

20 Feb   [Newcomb, T.] An ode to the queen... N266

21 Feb   Edwards, S.   The Copernican system... E19

24 Feb   [Young, E.] The universal passion. Satire VI. Y136

29 Feb   Colin Clout's madrigal... C284

29 Feb   Frowde, P.   Verses on her majesty's birth-day. F279

1 Mar   Bellamy, D.   Two court fables... B179

10 Mar   Two new ballads. T587

19 Mar   Bisset, W.   Verses compos'd for the birth-day ... B233

20 Mar   [Byrom, J.] A full and true account of an horrid and barbarous robbery... B614

21 Mar   [Mallet, D.] The excursion. M50

21 Mar   Nature in perfection...to Mrs. Bret... N10

22 Mar   A new ballad, inscrib'd to Polly Peachum... N64

26 Mar   Nixon, J.   An ode to the queen... N306

30 Mar [Zinzano, N.] Paradice regain'd: or, the art of gardening. Z2

2 Apr A letter to Polly... L151

18 Apr Savage, R. The bastard... S90

20 Apr Fatio de Duillier, N. Neutonus ecloga. F80

23 Apr [Lyttelton, G., baron.] Bleinheim. L330

29 Apr Mitchell, J. Ratho: a poem to the king. M324

30 Apr Pitt, C. An essay on Virgil's Æneid... P410

1 May Prologue, and epilogue, to the Orphan... P1122

1 May The speech of Marius to the people of Rome... S630

10 May Garbott, W. New-River... G9

15 May [Bourne, V.] Thyrsis & Chloe... B333

15 May Le Pla, M. The song of the three children paraphras'd. L107

18 May Flint, G. The lunatick... F172

18 May [Pope, A.] The Dunciad. P764

24 May Howard, L. A poem sacred to the memory of King William III... H333

29 May Seagrave, R. The state of Europe... S161

30 May Budgell, E. A poem upon his majesty's late journey... B557

5 June Thomson, J. Spring. T227

8 June [Young, E.] Ocean. An ode... Y94

20 June Polly Peachum on fire... P716

26 June [Ralph, J.] Sawney... R21

July The belief of the divinity of Jesus Christ... B169

2 July Marriage; a satire... M109

18 July [Smedley, J.] The metamorphosis... S504

16 Aug Madness: a poem... M13

21 Aug Ralph, J. The muses' address to the king. R15

3 Sept [Broxholme, N.] A letter from a lady to her husband abroad. B541

21 Sept L-- H---p's embassy to H----r... L1

11 Oct A funeral poem; sacred to...the late Earl of Lincoln. F301

15 Oct [Broome, W.] The oak, and the dunghill. B499

16 Oct Ralph, J. Zeuma: or the love of liberty. R23

16 Oct Vanière, J. Apes. V14

29 Nov The English beautys. E330

Dec The Norfolk congress versified... N318

6 Dec The dunghill and the oak... D513

12 Dec The better sequel better'd... B203

12 Dec [Ward, E.] Durgen... W66

16 Dec The hunter hunted... H406

18 Dec Quadrille to perfection as play'd at Soissons... Q3

19 Dec [Beckingham, C.] Sarah, the quaker, to Lothario ... B146

21 Dec The congress of beasts... C367

23 Dec A poem on the arrival of...Prince Frederick. P581

[Besse, J.] A spiritual poem... B202

An answer to Polly Peachum's ballad... A242

Bourne, V. Votum Dris Gualteri Pope latinè redditum. B334

Dotage. A poem... D410

[Howard, L.] Greenwich-Park... H332

Humphreys, S. Cannons... H402

The livery-man's answer to a letter... L202

The lord and no lord, and Squire Squat... L255

Smith, —. The invitation... S512

Voltaire, F. M. A. de. La Henriade. V112

[1728?]

A hymn to the birth-day. H455

[Floyd, P.] Prosperity to Houghton... [1728/29?] F174

A supplement to the Norfolk congress... [1728/29] S786

[Yonge, Sir W.] The Norfolk garland...[1728/29?] Y19

1728: SCOTLAND

10 Apr A pil to Tonny Ashton or the play-house puld down. P283

16 Apr A merry dialogue...betwixt Tonny Ashton, and John Curry. M200

7 June Verses to the memory of...James Peadie... V73

The forger's doom: or, John Currie's last speech. F197

The last speech of Thomas and Robert Moore's... L58

[Ramsay, A.] On the death of Lady Margaret Anstruther. R73

The speech of John Curry... S629

[1728?]

[Blair, R.] A poem dedicated to the memory of... William Law... B275

1728: IRELAND

Mar Gale, O. Oliver Gales, speech... G7

Mar A pastoral elegy on... Peter Finall... P107

25 Mar The Little Beaus petition... L196

8 Aug A poem on the art of printing. P585

Sept An elegy on...Francis Higgin's... E146

Sept [Sheridan, T.] Ballyspellin. S405

Nov An elegy on...Joseph Boyss... E65

Aston, M. An heroick poem, on the...art of brewing... A356

[Barber, M.] A tale being an addition to Mr. Gay's Fables. B77

The black procession... B235

Black upon blue... B236

1728: Ireland (cont.)

[Choppin, R.] A just character of the revd. Mr. Boyce. C161

[Cowper, J.] Τεχνηθυραμβεια or, a poem upon Paddy Murphy... C482

Crumbs of comfort... C531

[Dunkin, W.] Τεχνηθυραμβεια... D527

An elegy on...a fur-bush... E125

An elegy on...William Howard... E151

An elegy on...John Stoyte... E248

An excellent new ballad inscrib'd to the Irish Polly Peachum... E550

An honest elegy. On...Councellor Howard. H296

An iambick ode, upon an iambick match... I2

The last speech to the election... L60

Miss Gall's letter to a certain c-o-1-l beau. M281

On state affairs. Four fables... O190

Opputtinomtompi: or, the parson married. O237

The parliament of hell; or the marriage of the devil. P68

A pindarick ode, on the resurrection... P289

Silva to Strephon... S463

Spuddy's lamentation for the loss of her collar... S666

Sterling, J. The loves of Hero and Leander... S754

Swaddling John's address to the publick. S790

[Swift, J.] An answer to the Ballyspellin ballad. S797

[Tickell, T.] A poem in praise of the horn-book... T300

[*1728?*]

A crutch for a lame conscience... C532

Ecclesia & reformatio... E13

The ladies opera. L15

To my worthy friend T--- S--- D.D... T355

Fanatical doctrine... [1728/29] F57

Nelson, H. The order of the procession of the journey-men builders... [1728/29?] N28

The new epilogue spoke and sung by Polley Peachum... [1728/29] N139

A new poem on the order of the procession... [1728?/29?] N171

A prologue upon the beaus... [1728/29?] P1134

[Swift, J.] On Paddy's character of the Intelligencer. [1728/29] S887

1729

4 Jan   Savage, R. The wanderer... S119

9 Jan   Freeman, I. Æsop at St. James's. F243

15 Jan   Humphreys, S. A congratulatory poem... to...Frederick, prince of Wales... H403

21 Jan   [Thomson, J.] Britannia. A poem. T177

22 Jan   Eusden, L. A poem...to...Prince Frederic ... E503

23 Jan   Le-Hunt, A. Verses on the safe arrival of his royal highness... L99

27 Jan   [Jacob, H.] The silent flute... J46

27 Jan   [Ralph, J.] Clarinda: or the fair libertine. R14

3 Feb   The church too hard for the state... C182

10 Feb   Lothario's answer to Sarah the quaker... L273

27 Feb   The levy-haunter, a satire. L161

Mar   Congreve, W. A letter...to...Viscount Cobham. C375

Mar   [Hetherly, S.] A psalm of thanksgiving to be sung by the children of Christ's Hospital... H164

1 Mar   An epistle from Matt of the Mint... E372

4 Mar   The banish'd beauty... B55

8 Mar   [Jenyns, S.] The art of dancing... J59

13 Mar   [Pope, A.] The Dunciad, variorum. P771

17 Mar   The parrot and the owl. P80

25 Mar   The female faction... F92

1 Apr   [Breval, J. D.] Henry and Minerva. B424·5

1 Apr   A satyrical poem: or, the Beggar's-opera dissected. S80

7 Apr   Fraser, P. Iniquity display'd... F231

16 Apr   [Bockett, E.] Geneva: a poem... B304

17 Apr   A poem on the death of Mr. Rich Shales... P599.

18 Apr   [Browne, M.] Piscatory eclogues... B531

24 Apr   God's judgment upon hereticks... G204

27 Apr   [Meredith, A.] The prologue and epilogue to... Hurlothrumbo... M187

3 May   The loss of liberty... L270

8 May   [Smith, J.] The British worthies. S518

9 May   [Mallet, D.] A poem to the memory of Mr. Congreve... M56

13 May   The beau-thief detected... B128

14 May   [Henley, J.] Tom o' Bedlam's Dunciad... H145·5

15 May   [Lowth, R.] The genealogy of Christ... L292

15 May   [Wesley, S.] The prisons open'd... W353

16 May   The Dulcinead variorum... D508

31 May   Mottley, J. Verses addressed to...Sir Robert Walpole... M536

June   England in miniature... E311

June   The handsome Arabian... H33

6 June   A sequel to the Dunciad... S206

19 June   The Christian priest... C167

19 June   Verses on the death of Dr. Samuel Clarke. V61

20 June   [Jortin, J.] A hymn to harmony. J100

20 June   Lucifer's defeat: or, the mantle-chimney... L313

21 June   A poem on the death of the late Duke of Devonshire. P604

2 Aug The pacifick fleet... P2

7 Aug [Ward, E.] Apollo's maggot in his cups... W47

15 Aug Three Belgic fables... T252

18 Aug Stephens, H. An epistle to...Frederick, prince of Wales. S751

26 Aug Bartholomew-fair... B91

19 Sept The adventures of Telemachus... A68

20 Sept [Dodsley, R.] Servitude: a poem... D388

27 Sept Tea. A poem... T109

30 Sept Mitchell, J. The monument... M317

1 Oct [Stammers, W.] Liberty... To the queen. S704

1 Nov Panthea. An elegy on...Viscountess Scudamore ... P44

4 Nov An epistolary letter from T----- H----- to Sr H-----s S------e... E437

Dec Rolli, P. A. Del paradiso perduto... R255

5 Dec Mottley, J. An epistle...to...Sir Robert Walpole... M535

8 Dec [Bramston, J.] The art of politicks... B383

11 Dec A poem sacred to the memory of...Lady Aber——ny... P654

12 Dec [Beckingham, C.] An epistle from Calista to Altamont. B135

12 Dec [Pulteney, W. earl.] The honest jury... P1161

20 Dec The Oxford sermon versified. O270

24 Dec The new dozen at Westminster... N130

31 Dec The Cambridge election... C7

Belhaven's vision... B165

The country vicar, or, Alkibla burlesqued. C459

The Craftsman's business... C492

An elegy on...Elizabeth Staples... E246

Great-Britain's glory. Or, the stay-at-home fleet... G257

King John: a poem... K51

Le-Hunt, A. Verses occasioned by the death of... William duke of Devonshire... L98

The Lilliputian widow... L182

A medley on the times. M161

Mr. Whiston's erroneous principles... M300

Thomas redivivus... T157

Tilly, W. Beata Maria virgo ab angelo Gabriele salutata ... T312

Vézian, A. Vers a Monsieur Pelham... V81

[1729?]

Houghton hare-hunting... H331

[Campbell, A. duke.] A pastoral elegy on the death of the Lady Hilaretta... [1729/30] C10

Chaloner, T. The true Briton... [1729/36] C101

Hall, J. The marshal's humble offering to each gentleman soldier... [1729/37] H5

Bambridge and H--g---n's petition... [1729/-] B47

An epitaph on Mrs. Marjory Scott... [1729/-] E442

1729: SCOTLAND

14 May A ballad by J-----n B-----s. B21

23 May J-----n B-----s's ballad continued. B22

16 June An answer to John Brigs's ballads. A239

An elegy on...Lord Pencaitland... E210

Harvey, J. The life of Robert Bruce... H102

The Latin dedication of the honourable Mr. Alexander Hume-Campbell... L67

[1729?]

An answer to the Assembly of bum-bees. A244

The bum-bees assembly: a poem. B566

1729: IRELAND

Jan An elegy on...Edward Winfield... E285

Jan [Swift, J.] The journal of a Dublin lady... S863

1 Jan Durgen, a satyr... D554

Feb Sheridan, T. An ode to be performed at the castle of Dublin... S411

Mar A poem by D—— S——. On the scheme propos'd to the people of Ireland... P522

May An elegy on...Sir Daniel Dowdwel... E104

May An elegy on...William King... E173

May A new song call'd Ireland's universal loss... N193

June Ware, H. An eligiaick song. On the death of... Mary Wall... W220

July Nelson, H. A poem in praise of the...journeymen taylors... N29

Aug An elegy on...Madam Bently... E56

Oct An elegy on...William Connelly... E88

Nov An elegy on...Richard Nuttley... E202

Doctor Anthony's advice to the Hibernian Æsop... A256

Aston, M. An elegy on...John Mullen... A355

The character of a master of a vessel. C122

The coachman's wish... C244

[Delany, P.] An epistle to... John lord Carteret... D196

An elegy on...William late lord archbishop... E171

An elegy on...William King... E174

The general assembly of the brewers. G100

A hue and cry after the Letter to the lord-mayor... H357

Ireland in mourning: or, a funeral elegy on...William King. I56

The journal of a Dublin beau. J102

A letter...to the...lord mayor... L119

The logico-astrologico-physico-mathematician... L232

Nelson, H. A poem on the procession of journeymen smiths... N31

1729: Ireland (cont.)

Nelson, H. A poem on the procession of journeymen taylors... N32

Nelson, H. The speech of the first stone laid in the parliament-house... N33

A new and mournful elegy, on... J—— S——wll... N52

[Owens, S.] Sr. Tubal Cain's advice to the free-holders ... O262

The paper kite, a fable... P47

A pastoral poem to a lady in St. P--- parish... P117

A poem occasion'd by the lord mayor's reducing the price of coals... P559

A satyr on the taylors procession... S66

[Sheridan, T.] Prologue spoken before a Greek play... S415

[Sterling, J.] A funeral poem on...William Conolly. S753

To his excellency John, lord Carteret... T332

To the author of a late lampoon. T361

[Welsted, L.] The power of love... W309

[*1729?*]

A commical dialogue between R. F--------ne, and Madam B-------ly... C312

A comical sonnet,/On Ch-------s blue bonnet... C314

King Cock-lorrel's treat... D40

An elegy on...Alexander Montgomery... E193

A merry new joke,/On Joseph's old cloak. M203

The new weather-cock's song, at the castle. N239

Towzer, a tale. T436

A young Frenchman's lampoon... Y21

[173–]

Belvedere: a poem. B187

Carey, H. A pastoral. C53

Chicken, E. The collier's wedding. C147

Chloe monita. C157

The cobler of Gloucester... C264

A cure for the cow... C545

A flight from Westminster... F168

Gutteridge, T. The universal elegy... G327

[Mawer, J.] The happy reign... M145

Micah, vi. 8. Do justice, &c... M227

The miller of Essex... M232

The monkey and the hounds. M398

[Morris, R.] An enquiry after virtue... M504

A new copy of verses compos'd on a certain young lady... N118

A rhapsody upon the marvellous. R187·5

A sacred ode on the passion... S4·5

Sedgwick, R. A divine poem: or, a paraphrase on the Lord's prayer. S181

Sedgwick, R. A metaphisical essay... S184

Sedgwick, R. A paraphrase...of the apostles creed... S186

Sedgwick, R. A paraphrase...of the ten commandments ... S187

Sedgwick, R. A paraphrase on the second table of the ten commandments... S188

[173–]: SCOTLAND

The country lamentation. C451

The moderate man's confession. M361

An ode, to Alexander Robertson of Strowan... O59

The poor client's complaint... P753

[173–]: IRELAND

An advice to Scribogg hare... A87

Beware of lakey vessels... B206

An exelent [!] new ballad ascrib'd to the ladies of Munster. E542

The goose pye, a poem. G227

A new ballad on the game of bragg... N80

A satyre upon a monstrous peruke gown and band... S72

[Wesley, S.] The cobler, a tale. W341

1730

8 Jan	The barber turn'd packer... B65	
11 Jan	Harte, W. An essay on satire... H98	
21 Jan	[Gay, J.] The mad dog, a tale. G58	
26 Jan	[Young, E.] Two epistles to Mr. Pope... Y117	
27 Jan	[Bockett, E.] Blunt to Walpole... B301	
31 Jan	The robin. A poem. R230	
2 Feb	An epistle to...Sir Robert Walpole... E428	
12 Feb	Claudian's Rufinus... C231	
14 Feb	Bl--ke--y's prologue and epilogue... O224·2	
19 Feb	Dr. Croxall to Sir Robert Walpole. D353	
19 Feb	The saylors song, or, Dunkirk restored... S16	
2 Mar	An epistle from Altamont to Lorenzo. E363	
2 Mar	The memorable British sh——rs... M166	
2 Mar	The rape...to Colonel Francisco. R117	
4 Mar	Atwood, G. The CXIXth psalm paraphras'd ... A365	
13 Mar	An epistle from Jonathan Wild to Colonel Chartres. E370	
17 Mar	[Carey, H.] Blunderella... C39	
Apr	[Bond, W.] Cobham and Congreve... B315·5	
Apr	An epistle to MacD——d... E401	
Apr	An epistle to...Sir Robert Walpole. E425	

Apr Hay, W. Mount Caburn... H117

Apr The reprieve: an epistle...to C-----l C--------s. R160

2 Apr The rival lap dog and the tale... R214

2 Apr [Young, E.] Imperium pelagi... Y82

4 Apr [Hill, A.] The progress of wit... H230

15 Apr Barford, R. An epistle to the...Earl of Chesterfield... B83

28 Apr [Welsted, L. & Smythe, J. M.] One epistle to Mr. A. Pope... W302·5

May An epistle from the late Lord Bo---ke to the Duke of W----n. E380

May The London address... L235

May Savage, R. Verses, occasion'd by...Viscountess Tyrconnel's recovery... S111

May Thurston, J. The toilette. T269

May Vaslet, L. Emmanuelis Alvari Regulae de syllabarum quantitate... V18

8 May The fidler's fling at roguery... F117

13 May [Savage, J.] Horace to Scaeva... S88

June Brice, A. Freedom: a poem... B438

June The happy bride... H39

June Rudd, S. An elegiac essay on...John Noble... R326

June [Thomas, E.] The metamorphosis of the town ... T158

June Thomson, J. The seasons. T236

June Watts. I. To his excellency Jonathan Belcher ... W256

25 June [Newcomb, T.] Blasphemy as old as the creation ... N248

30 June [Lyttelton, G., baron.] An epistle to Mr. Pope... L331

July The fatigues of a great man... F76

July Le-Hunt, A. A poem...to the Lord and Lady Brudenall... L95

July The looking-glass... L254

July The noble duellists... N313

14 July Taylor, J. The music speech... T103

23 July Lockman, J. An ode: inscrib'd to...the Duke of Buckingham... L217

Aug Samber, R. Epithalamium on...Lord Brudenel ... S25

Sept [Hawling, F.] The Richmond beauties... H114·5

Sept Turner, J. Almeria. T563

Oct Augusta: or the city's triumph... A371

Oct Duck, S. Royal benevolence... D477

Oct Littlemore, S. A poem on the death of... Mrs. Oldfield... L201

Oct Morrice, B. Dissectio mentis humanae... M477

Oct A poem to the memory of Mrs. Oldfield... P666

Oct Verses inscribed to...Humphry Parsons... V51

Oct Ward, E. To...Humphrey Parsons... W188

Nov Boyd, E. Verses...to...King George IId. on his birth-day. B349

Nov Farmer, P. A new model for the rebuilding masonry... F61

Nov Morland, —. A poem to his majesty... M467

Nov A pastoral elegy on the death of Calista... P104

12 Nov Mainwario's welcome to Ophelia... M34

17 Nov A new Norfolk ballad... N160

Dec [Cooke, T.] The candidates for the bays... C409

Dec A hymn to the new laureat. H462

Dec The Lincoln's-Inn 'squire... L184

Dec The lunatick...to John Sh——r... L327

Dec [Morrice, B.] The religion of reason. M493

Dec The squire and the cardinal... S669

Advice to the ladies of Great Britain... A92

[Boyd, E.] A poem on the arrival of...William earl Cowper... B343

[Boyd, E.] To...William lord Harrington... B344

The court spy; or the starling's song... C469

The duck drowned in Parnassus... D466

[Free, J.] The story of Susanna. F238

The Hebrew campaign... H132

[Howard, W.] The good stewards... H337

The humble petition of...Ph——p d. of Wh——n... H396

Le-Hunt, A. A poem address'd to...Richard, earl of Burlington... L96

Lloyd, J. The play, a satire... L206

Mother Needham's elegy... M523

A new song made on...Humphrey Parsons... N205

Taperell, J. A pastoral in memory of... T38

Two excellent new ballads... T584

[Wesley, S.] Verses on the death of Mrs. Morice. W355

[*1730?*]

An historical ballad... H252

A hymn to Alderman Parsons... H428

Trouat, L. The best discovery in a new-year's gift. T510

[Ward, E.] The ambitious father...[1730?/31] W45

1730: SCOTLAND

19 Dec The last speech...of Thomas Vert... L56

A pastoral in imitation of Virgil's first eclogue. P110

Two elegys, the first, on wanton Watty M'Aulay... T583

1730: IRELAND

Feb An ode, to be perform'd at the castle of Dublin ... O60

1730: Ireland (cont.)

2 Feb   [Swift, J.] A libel on D-- D-----... S877

Apr   [Swift, J.] Traulus... S914

May   An elegy on...Daniel Kimberly... E169

Sept   An elegy on...Richard Hoyle... E153

Dec   A funeral elegy on...Mr. Richard Johnson and Mr. John Porter... F289

Dec   A paraphrase on the CXXXIX psalm... P59

12 Dec   A new song made on...Mr. John Porter, and Mr. Richard Johnson... N204

Advice from C----b S------y to his daughter. A70

Advice to a certain dean. A73

'Anthony, *Doctor*.' Pride will have a fall... A263

'Blackwell, J.' A friendly apology for a certain justice of peace... B270

The Colcannen match... C282

A conference concerning transubstantiation... C338

Cowper, J. Technethyrambeia: or, a poem on Paddy Murphey... C483

[Dalacourt, J.] Abelard to Eloisa... D6

[Delany, P.] The pheasant and the lark. D203

'Drake, J.' The complaint... D423

Dulness cherish'd... D509

[Dunkin, W.] A vindication of the libel... D530

An elegy on...Mother Blackham... E59

An elegy on...Francis Burgersdicius... E69

An elegy on...James duke of Ormonde... E207

An epistle to a certain dean... E386

An epistle to D——n S——t... E396

An epistle to Mr. Thomas Elrington... E406

An excellent new ballad on the wedding of pritty Miss S--lly... E555

A funeral apotheosis on the Tribunes... F286

[Gahagan, U.] Palæmon... G5

The goddess Envy to Doctor D--l--y. G205

'Gulliver, M.' The Asiniad... G312

'Gulliver, M.' The Censoriad... G313

'Gulliver, M.' The Heraldiad... G316

'Gulliver, M.' A letter...to George Faulkner. G317

'Gulliver, M.' Threnodia... G319

'Gulliverianus, M.' The art of beauing... G320

[Hervey, J. *baron*.] A satyr. In the manner of Persius... H161·5

Huy, A. A new year's gift... H417

The imperious beauty... I13

The inspir'd poet... I44

Ireland's black day... I58

[King, W.] An ode to Mira. K71

A letter from a friend to Miss M---y S----y. L120

A letter of advice to the revd. D--r. D—la—y... L138

A letter to Miss S------y. L147

1730: Ireland (cont.)

The metamorphose of a certain Dublin beau's-head... M224

A modest defence of Mr. Gr--n... M389

A modest praise of pritty Miss Smalley. M393

M---y S----y's answer to her father's advice. M572

A new opera-epilogue... N163

A panegyrick in answer to a libel... P32

A panegyric on the Reverend D--n S----t... P36

The parson bewitch'd... P84

[Poekrich, R.] The Temple-Oge ballad. P516

A poem on Dr C——d, and the three rival sisters... P565

A satyr. By way of reply, to Martin Guilliver... S45

Some seasonable advice to Doctor D——n——y. S555

[Swift, J.] An answer to Dr. D-----y's fable... S796

[Swift, J.] An apology to the Lady C——r——t... S799

[Swift, J.] An epistle upon an epistle... S842

[Swift, J.] An excellent new ballad: or the true En---sh d---n to be hang'd... S843

[Swift, J.] Horace book I. ode XIV... S859

[Swift, J.] Lady A——s——n weary of the Dean. S868

[Swift, J.] To Doctor D-l---y, on the libels writ against him. S913

[Swift, J.] Traulus. The second part. S916

The tea-kettle... T112

A translation of Horace's epistle to Augustus... T440

A trip to Temple-Oge... T489

A view of the Irish bar... V94

'Wagstaff, H.' The Dullardiad... W1

The wonder of wonders... W551

[1730?]

An answer to the Christmas-box... A246

[Dalacourt, J.] The match, a poem. D8

'Gulliver, M.' The proctor's banquet... G318

Venus reveng'd: or, Cloe triumphant. V26

1731

Jan   A poem in answer to a lampoon...on the Cambridge ladies. P535

7 Jan   Cibber, C. An ode to his majesty... C198

16 Jan   A dialogue between...Sir Robert Walpole, and William Poultney... D272

Feb   An answer to...The countess's speech... A234

Feb   On the modern incendiaries. O209

1 Feb   The duel... D488

1 Feb   An epistle from little Captain Brazen... E371

4 Feb   The countess's speech to her son Roderigo... C444

5 Feb [Miller, J.] Harlequin-Horace... M251

9 Feb [Morrice, B.] An epistle to Mr. Pope... M479

9 Feb Sir Robert Brass... S474

11 Feb The parson hunter. P85

13 Feb Mitchell, J. Three poetical epistles... M331

15 Feb Drury, R. Pulteney: or, the patriot. D445

18 Feb The progress of patriotism... P1111

27 Feb [Dodsley, R.] An epistle from a footman... D383

9 Mar The devil knows what... D243

11 Mar Rudd, S. A poem on the death of...Thomas Hollis... R327

13 Mar The deist's creed... D189

13 Mar Hill, A. Advice to the poets... H209

16 Mar Lord Pole translated... L260

Apr A new Norfolk ballad... N159

Apr Samber, R. To the memory of Edward Russel... S30

May The Chelsea monarch... C141

May First oars to L--m--th... F146

May Human wisdom displayed... H388

1 May [Mawer, J.] Verses to...Edward, lord bishop of Durham... M150

5 May Peace. A poem... P133

26 May The mitre. A tale... M347

29 May Adams, G. Vera fides... A26

29 May South Britain: a poem... S609

3 June Remarks on the life of Japhet Crook... R155

17 June The knight and the cardinal... K96

18 June The statesman... S730

24 June A poem, address'd to...William Pulteney... P519

July A new state picture. N230

Aug Pitt, H. Verses...to his majesty... P421

19 Aug Mr. Bowman's sermon...versify'd... M292

Sept A poem sacred to the memory of...Dan. Poulteney. P653

16 Sept The hunting of the stag. H410

23 Sept A dialogue in burlesque verse, between Parson Betty and Parson Bowman... D285

Oct Cibber, C. An ode for his majesty's birth-day... C194

5 Oct [Bockett, E.] The annotations of the Grub-street society on Mr. Bowman's sermon... B299

9 Nov [Wesley, S.] The parish priest... W345

19 Nov Miss Cadiere's case very handsomely handled... M280

19 Nov Spiritual fornication... S655

13 Dec Pope, A. An epistle to...Richard earl of Burlington... P908

14 Dec The ladies frolick: or the spy in armour... L13

Anderson, J. Ad reverendissimum...archiepiscopum Cantuariensem... A221

Bourne, V. Gulielmus Susannæ valedicens. B331

Boyd, E. Verses congratulatory, on...Lady Diana Spencer... B348

[Chamberlen, P.] The perspective, or Calista dissected. C104

Chapman, R. The new-year's gift... C116

A congratulatory poem...to...Francis Child... C348

Costeker, J. L. Κοστιαχον: or, wit triumphant over beauty. C438

A new ballad. By Caleb D'Anvers... D41

[Hill, A.] The picture of love... H229

The journalists displayed... J103

The Lancashire garland... L41

A new express from the dead... N141

Parsons's triumph. P90

Phillips, T. To the...religious Dame Elizabeth Phillips... P259

Price, H. Shalum and Hilpa... P1043

The rape of Helen... R118

Sir Blue blu'd... S471

The temple of war ...T115

[*1731?*]

An ode for the new year. Written by Colley Cibber... C195

Horler, J. Hymn on the nativity... H319

Pope, A. On Charles earl of Dorset... P931·5

[Swift, J.] Confondant du passé le leger souvenir... S830

The toasts. A new ballad... [1731/35] T404

1731: SCOTLAND
[*1731?*]

Mons Alexander in Struani domini sui reditum. [1731/32] M404

1731: IRELAND

Mar An elegy on...Frances countess of Tirconnel ... E255

Nov [Swift, J.] The place of the damn'd. S897

An answer to the Band-ballad... A245

The band... B53

Death. A poem. D80

An elegy on...Paeter Verdoen... E265

An explanation of a tale of a tale... E608

The most renown'd history of Pope Joan... M520

A new opera-epilogue... N164

A new poem made on the safe arrival of the...Duke of Dorset... N169

A panegyrick on...John Baptist Girard... P38

[Percival, W.] The college-examination. P173

1731: Ireland (*cont.*)

The Phœnix of Claudian... P264

Poema in Richardum Sadlerum... P688

Sharp, J. The lawyer's tears... S383

[Shepherd, S.] Pallas and Venus reconcil'd... S402

A tale in allusion to a certain tale. T9

Tankerville, E. An elegiack poem, on the death of a lady's sparrow... T36

Tracey, M. The critical minute... T437

Treason against the ladies. T469

[*1731?*]

A new ballad. N54

The prologue and epilogue of George Barnwell... P1120

Webb, G. Batchelors-Hall. W263

1732

1 Jan	Cibber, C. An ode to his majesty... C199
3 Jan	Welsted, L. Of dulness and scandal... W298
11 Jan	A character of Anselmus... C127
11 Jan	Seagrave, R. The peace of Europe... S159
12 Jan	[Swift, J.] A soldier and a scholar... S904
13 Jan	[Weston, J.] The assembled patriots... W374
14 Jan	Humphreys, S. Malpasia... H404
17 Jan	[Budgell, E.] Verres and his scribblers... B559
20 Jan	War with priestcraft: or, the free-thinkers Iliad... W40
22 Jan	Of good nature... O82
24 Jan	The beauties of the universe. B131
27 Jan	[Turner, J.] An epistle to Mr. Pope. T565·5
28 Jan	Malice defeated... M40
3 Feb	Welsted, L. Of false fame... W301
7 Feb	[Vaughan, J.] An ode. Occasion'd by rejecting the proposal for erecting a statue of King William III... V22
8 Feb	On P——e and W——d... O183
26 Feb	Don Francisco's descent to the infernal regions ... D396
26 Feb	Thurston, J. The fall. T268
Mar	Part of the 23d psalm...to be sung by the charity children... P96
1 Mar	Savage, R. The volunteer laureat... S112
4 Mar	Love after enjoyment... L279
9 Mar	Of modern wit... O83
16 Mar	Taste and beauty... T45
17 Mar	[West, G.] Stowe... W360
25 Mar	[Lyttelton, G., *baron*.] The progress of love. L333
3 Apr	[Delany, P.] Longford's Glyn... D199
18 Apr	Duck, S. To...the Duke of Cumberland... D481
27 Apr	The harlot's progress... H54

9 May	The dramatic poetaster a vision... D425
9 May	Theobald, L. An epistle...to...John, earl of Orrery. T139
11 May	The progress of a rake... P1106
20 May	A hymn to the chair... H456
25 May	Jacob, H. Chiron to Achilles. J31
26 May	The merry campaign... M199
3 June	[Newcomb, T.] An ode to...the Duke of Newcastle... N262
12 June	Vanella in the straw... V8
17 June	The natural history of the arbor vitæ... N7
17 June	[Swift, J.] The lady's dressing room... S869
22 June	Rudd, S. Zara. An elegiac pastoral on... Sarah Abney... R328
23 June	[Bancks, J.] The royal guardian. B52
23 June	Ridotto al fresco. R207
6 July	The christening. A satirical poem... C164
18 July	[Lockman, J.] Henriade... L215
18 July	The progress of divine love... P1108
20 July	Dyer, R. An epistle...to...Elizabeth Trevor ... D567
Aug	Phino-Godol... P261
Aug	[Swift, J.] Annoque domini 1732... S794
28 Aug	Savage, R. An epistle to...Sir Robert Walpole ... S99
Sept	Part of the song of Deborah and Barak... P95
12 Sept	Castle-Howard... C61
27 Sept	A congratulatory poem on his majesty's safe arrival... C354
30 Sept	Mitchell, J. The royal hermitage... M326
Oct	Ode after the manner of the first of Horace... O21
11 Oct	Collier, W. A congratulatory poem on his majesty's happy return... C292
Nov	[Price, H.] – Risum teneatis? amici... P1042
6 Nov	Phillips, E. An ode on the birth-day. P251
16 Nov	Trick upon trick. T479·5
20 Nov	[King, W.] The toast, an epic poem... K79
Dec	Alma mater: a satirical poem... A171
Dec	To Nicholas Harding... T356
Dec	Wisdom revealed; or, the tree of life discover'd ... W533

[Adee, S.] The Craftsman's apology... A60

The bed of honour... B153

Colpas, A. A brief rhythmical composition... C305

An elegy on...Mathias Merrideth... E189

A guide from the cradle to the grave... G309

[Howard, W.] The universal doom... H343

Letter of thanks...to the honest-jury of Guilford... L140

The line of beauty... L188

The little junto... L199

Maxwell, S. Eboracum. M152

Mitchell, J. Transportation: or, the tower... M343

The modern fanaticks characteriz'd... M370

Musick...to Mr. Robert Lympany... M566

The original of apparel... O244

Poems on the death of...Henrietta Hamilton, countess of Orrery... P691

Rowe, N. The golden verses of Pythagoras... R288

A young distracted lady. Y20

[*1732?*]

Diaper, W. Brent a poem. D291

[Mawer, J.] An epistle...to...the Earl of Oxford... M142

1732: SCOTLAND

Oct [Boyse, S.] Verses occasioned by seeing the palace and park of Dalkeith... B369

Lauder, W. A poem of Hugo Grotius on the holy sacrament... L69

[Preston, W.] An epistle to the heritors of the West-kirk parish... P1027

[Preston, W.] On the death of...Patrick Wotherspoon... P1028

[*1732?*]

[Robertson, A.] To the anonymous author of a Latin ode, &c. R227

1732: IRELAND

Apr An elegy. On...Mr. T------r, the famous occulist... E257

[Amhurst, N.] The bottle-scrue... A185

An answer to Hamilton's Bawn... A237

[Belcher, J.] A cat may look upon a king... B163

Bœoticorum liber. Or, a new art of poetry... B310

[Carthy, C.] An ode...to the city of Dublin. C56·7

[Dalacourt, J.] The progress of beauty. D9

Fear and interest makes the harvest... F81

The gentleman's study, in answer to the Lady's dressing-room. G123

The lady's last shift... L27

A prologue, spoken at the opening of the new play-house ... P1128

The remonstrance... R157

Richardson, L. The transfiguration. R198

[Shepherd, S.] Chloe surpriz'd: or, the second part of the Lady's dressing-room... S399

[Sheridan, T.] A new simile for the ladies... S409

[Sheridan, T.] A prologue to Julius Caesar... S416

The spleen: a poem... S658

[Sterling, J.] The alderman's guide... S752

[Swift, J.] An elegy on Dicky and Dolly... S831

1732: Ireland (*cont.*)

Thomson, J. A specimen of thought upon the gloomy region... T248

[*1732?*]

Gay, J. On Monday next...will be perform'd...the following ode...[1732/–] G63

1733

Jan Britannia excisa: Britain excis'd... B459

Jan The happy life... H43

Jan A sequel to Britannia excisa... S204

15 Jan Pope, A. Of the use of riches... P923

Feb The congress of excise-asses... C368

Feb A full and true account of a curious dialogue... F283

Feb He, who worst, may still hold the candle... H121

Feb Sad pretext: or, divine love ill-requited... S6

Feb Tobacco, a poem. T404·5

13 Feb Cloe convinc'd: or, seeing's believing... C156

13 Feb Good goose don't bite... G225

15 Feb Pope, A. The first satire of the second book of Horace... P886

20 Feb [Pope, A.] An essay on man... Part I. P822

21 Feb The happiness of retirement... H38

22 Feb Price, H. The antediluvian novel... P1044

24 Feb [Chandler, M.] A description of Bath... C107

27 Feb 'Jones, J.' The secret history of bubbies... J95

Mar Sappho to Adonis... S34

Mar Sirs, are ye mad? S482

5 Mar [Bramston, J.] The man of taste... B396

6 Mar The sequel of Mr. Pope's law-case... S203

8 Mar Savage, R. The volunteer-laureat...Number II ... S113

8 Mar Verses address'd to the imitator of the first satire of the second book of Horace. V39

12 Mar [Lyttelton, G. *baron.*] Advice to a lady. L328

13 Mar [Bancks, J.] The Bacchanalians: or, a midnight modern conversation... B48

20 Mar Beauty and proportion. B133

20 Mar The knight and the purse... K100

21 Mar Lumley, G. The royal hermitage... L325

28 Mar [Hammond, J.] An elegy to a young lady... H21

29 Mar [Pope, A.] An essay on man... Epistle II. P833

30 Mar An epistle to the little satyrist of Twickenham. E415

31 Mar [Morrice, B.] On the English translations of Homer... M489

Apr The city triumphant: or, the burning of the excise-monster... C212

Apr The countryman's answer to the ballad, call'd, Britannia excisa. C462

Apr Directions how to gain by losses... D318

Apr An excise elegy: or, the dragon demolish'd... E599

Apr The fair suicide... F33

Apr A just imitation of the first satire of the second book of Horace... J116

Apr Polymnia: or, the charms of musick... P720

Apr The projector's looking-glass... P1119

3 Apr A proper reply to a lady, occasioned by her Verses address'd to the imitator... P1135

5 Apr The excise sermon versified. E600·5

12 Apr Swift, J. The life and genuine character of Doctor Swift. S884

13 Apr Advice to Sappho... A86

16 Apr [Mallet, D.] Of verbal criticism... M51

16 Apr Sedition. A poem... S190

18 Apr An essay on the universe... E470

May The mock marriage... M352

May The sailor: or a sketch of the seaman's art... S8

1 May [Breval, J. D.] The lure of Venus: or, a harlot's progress... B427

1 May A song sung before King Charles the IId... S592

4 May Stanhope, H. The patriot... S714

5 May The classic quarrel... C230

8 May [Pope, A.] An essay on man... Epistle III. P840

10 May Of publick good... O85

22 May [Manning, F.] The British hero... M84

29 May The neuter: or, a modest satire on the poets of the age... N38

31 May Mr. Taste's tour from the island of politeness... M299

31 May The wrongheads: a poem... W572

June The blazing star. An ode... B283

June The fourth satire of the first book of Horace... F215

June [Newcomb, T.] The manners of the age... N256

June News. A burlesque poem... N291

June A satyr on the New Tunbridge Wells... S59

June Upon the poet laureat's being expelled the house of lords. U23

2 June [Newcomb, T.] The woman of taste... N282

7 June The satirist... S81

7 June [Whitehead, P.] The state dunces... W426

8 June A poetical essay on vulgar praise and hate... P705

9 June The London merchants triumphant... L239

15 June Advice to an aspiring young gentleman of fortune... A77

22 June A friendly epistle to the author of the State dunces. F269

July Brewster, T. A translation of the second satyr of Persius. B437

July The citizen's procession... C203

2 July The theatric squabble... T127

6 July [Whitehead, P.] The state dunces... Part II. W431

7 July The counterpart of the State-dunces. C442

7 July The female dunces. Inscrib'd to Mr. Pope. F91

12 July The excise-bill versify'd... E598

12 July [Newcomb, T.] The woman of taste. In a second epistle... N285

Aug The quack triumphant... Q2

Aug Tickell, T. On her majesty's re-building the lodgings of the Black Prince... T296

11 Aug Lloyd, J. The blanket... L204

14 Aug The Tamiad: an heroic poem... T35

23 Aug The wooden age... W558

Sept [Bowyer, W.] The beau and the academick... B337

Sept Kick him Jenny. A tale. K32

Sept The man-midwife unmasqu'd... M69

Sept A new crop of blockheads... N127

10 Sept Robin and Will... R231

20 Sept Mother Osborne's letter to the protestant dissenters... M524

25 Sept [Hasledine, W.] Bellus homo et academicus... H104

Oct The happy marriage: an eclogue... H44

Oct A pastoral poem. P115

Oct The theatre turned upside down... T126

Nov The gods in debate... G207

Nov The lady's decoy: or, the man-midwife's defence... L26

Nov A poetical description of the life...of that noted actress Melissa... P700

Nov Stirling, J. A system of rhetoric, in a method entirely new... S763

1 Nov The art of scribling... A326

1 Nov The union, a poem... U11

3 Nov The muse in distress... M563

5 Nov [Pope, A.] The impertinent... P898

6 Nov The Parsoniad; a satyr... P88

9 Nov A poem on the intended nuptials of Anne princess royal... P620

10 Nov [Hervey, J. baron.] An epistle from a nobleman to a doctor of divinity... H157

13 Nov An essay on faction. E462

15 Nov [Swift, J.] An epistle to a lady... S841

22 Nov   Sanderson, T.   Three odes... S32

Dec   Geneva. A poem in blank verse... B554

Dec   An epistle to Eustace Budgell... E397

Dec   Oysters. A poem. O281

Dec   The pike: a tale. P278

19 Dec   [Morrice, B.] On rural felicity... M487

27 Dec   [Malden, —.] The Maldon ballad... M38

31 Dec   [Swift, J.] On poetry: a rapsody. S888

The accomplish'd leader... A7

Barrett, M. & Rayner W.   An ode...to...the Prince of Orange... B86

Britannia excisa... Part II... B462

Chapman, R. An essay on the judgment of Paris... C115

The disappointed marriage... D320

A funeral tear, to...Daniel Wilcox... F306

[Green, M.] The grotto... G282

Gutteridge, T. An elegy, in memory of...Daniel Wilcox... G321

Hamilton, T. Sanguine lovers... H13

The happy nuptials... H47

Lee, J. A love-letter... L93

Motteaux before the eight copies of verses... M539

[Newcomb, T.] Verses to the injur'd patriot. N278

Odell, T. An ode sacred to the nuptials... O79

On reading a certain speech. O184

On the excise-scheme being dropt in the house of commons. O203

The players: a satire. P484

The progress of a harlot... P1105

The projector in the dumps... P1117

R--b--n in the suds, or, a hue and cry after the bill of excise. R135

R--b--n's progress; in eight scenes... R136

Sedgwick, R. An epithalamium on the marriage of... the Prince of Orange... S183

Silvester, T. Piscatio. Or, angling... S464

The sturdy beggars. S777

To the fore-chairman that carried her majesty... T371

Verney, R. *baron.* Dunces out of state... V28

Verney, R. *baron.* A poem on the safe arrival of the Prince of Orange... V30

[*1733?*]

Flavia to Fanny... [1733/34] F162

1733: SCOTLAND

Hunter, J. The wanderer and traveller... H407

Morgan, J. A poem on the taylor craft... M445

Preston, W. To the divine majesty. P1030

1733: IRELAND

Feb   An ode, to be performed at the castle of Dublin ... O61

June   An elegy on...Christian Borr... E63

The adventure of a German knight... A64

Astræa's congratulation. An ode upon Alderman Henry French... A364

[Barber, C.] To the...Lady Elizabeth Boyle... B67

[Carthy, C.] The gift of Pallas... C56·5

[Chamberlaine, W.] The three travellers. C102

An epistle to a friend. E388

A funeral elegy on...John Farquarson... F292

The grunters' request, to take off the test. G307

The Kerry cavalcade... K30

[Lawson, J.] The upper gallery... L74

On Miss Vane's f—t... O180

A poem on the nuptials of Anne... P632

Saint Patrick's Well: a tale. S20

A satyr on the Mall in Great Britain-street. S58

[Swift, J.] An answer to a scandalous poem... S795

To the reverend Doctor Swift...on his birth-day... T390

To the right honourable Lady Mary... T390·5

Turco-judaeo-machia... T554

Verses inscrib'd to...Col. Boyle... V49

The visit. Or, the lady in the lobster. V108

Waldron, J. A poem upon music. W10

Waldron, J. A satyr against tea... W11

[*1733?*]

Dalacourt, J. A prospect of poetry... D11

A hue and cry...after the downfall of B—— and —— bank... H362

1734

Jan   [Browne, I. H.] On design and beauty. B519

Jan   Fashion: a poem. F67

Jan   Jacob, H. Hymn to the goddess of silence. J44

Jan   A lecture in verse... L91

Jan   The Norfolk gamester... N319

Jan   Poor land's ruin;/Is it Robin's doing?... P755

Jan   A rap at the rapsody. R116

Jan   Ter-Horst, J. H. Augustissimo...domino Georgio secundo... T118

12 Jan   [Manning, F.] The muse an advocate for injur'd merit... M86

14 Jan   A tryal of skill between a court lord, and a Twickenham 'squire... T473

16 Jan   Pope, A. An epistle to...lord visct. Cobham. P920

17 Jan   Advice to the clergy... A89

17 Jan Duck, S. Truth and falshood. D482

17 Jan The tryal of skill between 'Squire Walsingham and Mother Osborne... T474

24 Jan [Pope, A.] An essay on man... Epistle IV. P845

26 Jan Tit for tat... T322

31 Jan [Dodsley, R.] The modern reasoners... D385

Feb The dependant... D229

Feb Fagg him Salley... F26

Feb [Stanhope, P. earl.] The state screen display'd... S716

2 Feb [Bellamy, D.] Back-gammon... B174

8 Feb The labyrinth. A tale... L3

8 Feb [Montagu, Lady M. W.] The Dean's provocation for writing the Lady's dressing-room. M416·5

14 Feb The court monkies... C468

14 Feb Gerard, —. An epistle to the egregious Mr. Pope... G130

Feb [Bramston, J.] The gardener's congratulatory poem to the Prince... B393

Mar The c---- unmasqu'd... C1

Mar The dutchess's epistle to her son Don Pedro... D465

Mar An epistle from the platonick Madam B---ier ... E381

Mar The false patriot... F50

Mar Kick him Nan... K35

Mar The knight and the prelate... K97

Mar The ladies of pleasure... L14

Mar Phillips, E. On the nuptials of...the Prince of Orange... P252

Mar A satire. S40

Mar Savage, R. The volunteer-laureat. S114

Mar The state weather-cocks. S728

Mar A poem on the approaching nuptials of Anne... P579

12 Mar The hyp-doctor in tune... H474

13 Mar A poem...to...the Prince of Orange... P527

14 Mar An epistle from a gentleman at Twickenham, to a nobleman at St. James's... E359

15 Mar Duck, S. A poem on the marriage of...the Prince of Orange... D473

Apr Baker, H. The universe. B11

Apr The complaint of Job. C322

Apr [Morrice, B.] A satirical essay on modern poets. M494

Apr The patriots triumph... P126

Apr Priestcraft: or, the way to promotion... P1055

Apr The secret history of an old shoe... S177

11 Apr [Mallet, D.] Verses presented to...the Prince of Orange... M58

27 Apr D'Anvers, G. M. Persius Scaramouch... D42

May Lord Wharton's puppies... L262

May Terpsicore à Londres. T118·5

3 May Modern patriotism, a poem. M377

10 May [Arbuthnot, J.] Γνωθι σεαυτον. Know yourself. A290

June Discontent the universal misery... D324

June Dr. Codex's fifth pastoral... D352

June The humours of a country election... H398

June The parson and his clerk... P81

June [Turner, J.] An epistle to Dr. Young. T564

July The dramatick sessions... D427

July Savage, R. On the departure of the Prince and Princess of Orange. S105

4 July Pope, A. The first satire of the second book of Horace... P893

Aug Richmond Park: a poem. R203

Sept [Chandler, M.] A description of Bath... C108

Sept The mist clear'd up at the Nore... M286

Oct Ayre, W. The saint: a tale. A374

Oct Of superstition... O87

Nov Campbell, D. A poem upon tea... C11

Nov Dodsley, R. An epistle to Mr. Pope... D384

Dec Darius's feast... D47

Dec Female chastity, truth and sanctity... F88

Dec [Trapp, J.] Thoughts upon the four last things ... T456

Dec Ward's downfal... W42

5 Dec [Swift, J.] A beautiful young nymph going to bed... S809

21 Dec [Pope, A.] Sober advice from Horace... P968

The Billingsgate fray... B215

A collection of state flowers. C285

Dawley, D'Anvers, and Fog's triumph... D69

Dobson, W. Solomon de mundi vanitate... D346

Dutton, A. A narration of the wonders of grace... D560

[Forbes, W.] The patriots, a satyr... F187

Gent, T. The pattern of piety... G118

[Howard, W.] The happy government... H340

Kitty and Dick: or, the nightingale... K95

Love-letters between a nobleman and his sister... L284

Merrick, J. Messiah. A divine essay... M194

The modern patriots... M379

An ode on the marriage of...the Duke of Portland... O49

Part of the CXIIth psalm...to be sung by the charity-boys... P94

[1734?]

La belle assemblée; or, the Tinmouth bathers... B180

The bishop or no bishop... B228

Gutteridge, T. The royal wedding... G326

The knight outrid... K101

Sedgwick, R. A cheirological essay on the royal family...
S180

The stocks: or, high change in 'Change-alley... S767

[Barber, M.] Verses occasion'd by seeing the captives...
from Barbary. [1734/35] B79

1734: SCOTLAND

Blair, T. Gibbie and Wattie... B276

[Boyse, S.] An ode, inscribed to the Royal Company of
Archers... B363

The faithful few... F40

La parade des archers écossois... P48

1734: IRELAND

Feb   Dunkin, W. An ode, to be performed at the
castle of Dublin... D524

Oct   Pilkington, M. An ode to be performed at the
castle of Dublin... P280

25 Oct   A poem on the...journeymen shoemakers...
P593

The battle of the bards. B104

[Dalacourt, J.] The Chevalier de St. Patrick... D7

[Dunkin, W.] An account of a...apparition lately seen in
Trinity-College... D514

Dunkin, W. The lover's web... D522

[Dunkin, W.] Mezentius on the rack. D523

[Dunkin, W.] The poet's prayer. D525

'Dunkin, W.' A proclamation from Parnassus... D526

An elegy on...Brice Blare... E61

An epistle to the Rev'd. ---... E419

The Kaven-bail poem... K1

A libel upon the Dublin dunces... L166

The patriot, an ode... P124

A poem on the marriage of...Viscount Mountjoy. P626

The vision: or, virtue in danger... V106

The Whitehaven garters. A ballad. W411

[1734?]

Aston, M. An heroick poem on the weaving trade...
A357

An inventory of the manuscripts...of the Chevalier de
St. Patrick's study... I53

A lullaby for the d--n of St P-t-k's... L321

An huze: or, the d--n's answer to the lullaby. L322

The scall'd crow's nest... [1734/35] S127

1735

Jan   [Brooke, H.] Universal beauty. B491

Jan   The countess's epistle to her lover... C443

Jan   [Melmoth, W.] Of active and retired life...
M164

Jan   Moncrieff, R. Magnanimity... M397

Jan   [Young, E.] The foreign address... Y81

2 Jan   Pope, A. An epistle...to Dr. Arbuthnot. P802

6 Jan   [Dodsley, R.] Beauty: or the art of charming.
D381

11 Jan   Thomson, J. Antient and modern Italy compared... T186

20 Jan   [Paget, T. C. baron.] An essay on human life.
P11

24 Jan   [Manning, F.] Of business and retirement...
M87

27 Jan   The cause of liberty... C77

Feb   The loyal worthies... L304

Feb   [Minshull, —.] The miser, a poem... M270

Feb   [Trapp, J.] Thoughts... Part II. Judgment.
T458

4 Feb   An epistle to Alexander Pope... E392

6 Feb   Thomson, J. Greece... T191

7 Feb   [Harte, W.] An essay on reason. H93

7 Feb   Pope, A. Of the characters of women... P917

Mar   [Brooke, H.] Universal beauty... Part II. B492

Mar   The connoisseur. A satire... C382

Mar   Duck, S. A poem on her majesty's birth-day.
D472

Mar   Hetherly, S. A psalm...Christ's Hospital...
H165

Mar   Of power. A moral poem. O84

Mar   Satyrae quatuor. S39

Mar   Savage, R. The volunteer-laureat... S115

Mar   Tit for tat. Part II... T328

Mar   True popery no foppery... T529

20 Mar   Ogle, G. Epistles of Horace imitated... O93

21 Mar   The woman's man. W547

23 Mar   Thomson, J. Rome... T194

Apr   [Brooke, H.] Universal beauty... Part III. B493

Apr   The happy courtezan... H42

Apr   [Manning, F.] Of levity and steadiness... M88

Apr   Mitchell, J. A sick-bed soliloquy to an empty
purse... M328

Apr   The modern poet. A rapsody. M380

17 Apr   Savage, R. The progress of a divine. S109

May   Dobson, W. Solomon... [Book II.] D347

May   An epistle to Sir J--r--y S---b----k. E410

May   Isidora to Casimir: an epistle. I70

May   [Jacob, H.] A genuine epistle...to the late
famous Mother Lodge. J43

May   Parnassus to be sold... P69

May   The secrets of a woman's heart... S179

2 May   [Jacob, H.] An epistle to a person of quality...
J42

13 May   Somervile, W.   The chace. S562

17 May   The truth. A poem. T536

June   [Brooke, H.] Universal beauty... Part IV. B494

June   An epistle to the author of the Essay on reason. E414

July   [Brooke, H.] Universal beauty... Part V. B495

24 July   The rake's progress... R10

Aug   The chace... In heroick verse. C136

Aug   Munns, N.   Horneck's Fire of the altar versified ... M558

Aug   Stockton, W.   Cursus venaticus leporinus. S768

Aug   [Trapp, J.] Thoughts... Part III. Heaven. T459

Sept   [Dorman, J.] The female rake... D407

Sept   The female speaker... F101

15 Sept   A hymn to the pope... H463

Oct   Drake upon Duck... D422

Oct   Horace Of the art of poetry... H313

Oct   Mitchell, J.   A familiar epistle to...Sir Robert Walpole... M307

Oct   The prospect: a divine poem... P1144

Nov   Carey, H.   Of stage tyrants... C52

Nov   Danvers, J.   Tipping tipt justice... D43

Nov   Higgons, B.   A poem on nature: in imitation of Lucretius... H183

Nov   Jacob, H.   Brutus the Trojan... J29

Nov   Mitchell, J.   The plea of Parnassus... M320

Nov   Ogle, G.   The second epistle of Horace imitated ... O103

Nov   True taste: or, female philosophy... T532

3 Nov   [Dorman, J.] The rake of taste... D409

12 Nov   [Miller, J.] Seasonable reproof... M258

Dec   [Brereton, J.] Merlin: a poem... B409

Dec   The female proselyte a sad back-slider... F100

12 Dec   [Trapp, J.] Thoughts... Part IV. Hell. T460

The clergyman's daughter's new annual book... C238

Codrington, S.   The beatific vision. C273

The fate of courtezans and their enamerato's... F73

[Gilbert, T.] A view of the town... G148

[Green, M.] A copy of verses...occasion'd by his reading Robert Barclay's Apology. G280

The lion and fox... L190

Luck, R.   Abramis: carmen heroicum... L315

Munns, N.   The great example... M557

[Newcomb, T.] An ode to...the Duke of Richmond... N264

Phelips, P.   Of man's chief happiness... P199

Randolph, —.   On the much lamented death of...Lady Oxenden... R110

Samber, R.   Cassandra. A pastoral eclogue... S24

Shooting flying, a poem... S444

The speech englished, a new ballad. S624

Suffolk and Norfolk... S782

The true Britons. T516

[1735?]

[Carey, H.] The downfall of Bartholomew fair... C41

Leucifer's grand emesarys found out... L314

Carey, H.   A new song in the Honest Yorkshireman... [1735/–] C51

Swift, J.   The furniture of a woman's mind... [1735/–] S857

1735: SCOTLAND

Feb   A new ballad, to the tune of the Abbot of Canterbury. N102

May   [Ramsay, A.] An address of thanks from the Society of rakes... R32

Boyse, S.   Retirement: a poem... B366

Boyse, S.   Verses, sacred to the memory of...Charles, earl of Peterborough. B372

Don Poetastro's epistle to J--n B--ggs... D397

A hymn on the sufferings and death of...Jesus Christ... H426

1735: IRELAND

Oct   Victor, B.   An ode, to be performed at the castle of Dublin... V89

Dec   David Mullan's petition to...the counsellors, lawyers, &c... M554

An alarm to the wits... A151

Alma's complaint... A172

Arbuckle, J.   Momus mistaken... A282

The Dean's answer to David Mullan's letter. D78

Dick, or devil, or the devil upon Dick... D300

Dunkin, W.   The vice-roy: a poem... D529

An elegy on A—r—n W—e... E268

A fable; with a word of advice... F20

Humphreys, S.   The amorous groom, and the gossips wager... H401

A letter from the city mumpers... L134

A letter of serious advice to a young poet. L139

Morrice, B.   The country-house. M476

Morrice, B.   The successful fisher... M495

David Mullan's letter to Dean Swift. M553

Novæ bibliothecæ S.S. Trin. Coll. Dub. descriptio... N330

Reason's tribunal... R139

The sham author; or, the English rap... S382

Verses on a certain young lady... V58

The wishing-maid... W535

1736

Jan   [Bennet, P.] The beau philosopher... B193

Jan   [Blyth, F.] Advice to a friend on his marriage. B291

Jan   An epistle to John James H--dd--g--r...E400

Jan   Lockman, J. An ode to the memory of...the Duke of Buckinghamshire. L220

Jan   Parratt, W. Carmen seculare... To the king... P78

Jan   Savage, R. A poem on the birth-day of the Prince of Wales. S106

15 Jan   [Browne, I. H.] A pipe of tobacco... B520

15 Jan   Thomson, J. Britain... T196

Feb   De la Garde, M. An essay on real felicity. D192

Feb   [Moore, E.] Yarico to Inkle... M434

Feb   Nixon, J. Merlin. A poem... N305

10 Feb   Thomson, J. The prospect... T198

Mar   [Brooke, H.] Universal beauty... Part VI. B496

Mar   Georgia, a poem... G128

Mar   [Nugent, R. earl.] Political justice... N346

Mar   Cousteil, I. Woman's prerogative... C472

2 Mar   [Armstrong, J.] The oeconomy of love... A303

16 Mar   [Dalton, J.] An epistle to a young nobleman... D15

31 Mar   [Bridges, —.] Divine wisdom and providence... B443

Apr   The character of a freeman. C121

Apr   An elegy on...Madam Gineva... E132

Apr   England's doom... E315

Apr   An epistle to...the Duke of Grafton... E399

Apr   Hetherly, S. A psalm...Christ's Hospital... H166

Apr   Erskine, W. Scacchia ludus: or, the game of chess... E460

Apr   A gratulatory poem on the happy prospect of peace. G252

Apr   [Lockman, J.] David's lamentation over Saul and Jonathan. L212

Apr   Odell, T. An ode sacred to the nuptials... O80

Apr   Sedition: a poem... S189

7 Apr   [Melmoth, W.] Two epistles of Horace imitated. M165

May   [Bancks, J.] Nature will prevail... B50

May   Bounce to Fop... B326

May   [Jacob, H.] The prude's purgatory. J50

May   Mawer, J. Oppian's Cynegeticks... M147

May   Mitchell, J. Gratulatory verses to Britannia... M308

5 May   [Bramston, J.] Ignorami lamentatio supra legis communis... B394

6 May   [Budgell, E.] Desolation: or, the fall of gin... B556

June   Frederick and Augusta... F234

24 June   Tale of a tub bottled off and moraliz'd... T21

July   A cure for a scold. C544

July   [Rowe, E.] The history of Joseph... R274

July   [Walpole, E.] Sannazarius on the birth of our saviour... W29·5

July   A voyage from the East-Indies. V121

1 July   Jeffreys, G. Father Francis and Sister Constance... J57

Aug   The tribe of Levi... T476

Sept   Discontent; or, an essay on faction... D323

Sept   Price, H. Batrachomuomachia... P1039

Nov   Four satires... F213

Nov   Modern matrimony... M376

Nov   Origines Bathenses... O246

Dec   Marsh, C. A poem on Christmas-day. M115

23 Dec   The sailor's lamentation. S10

The Beeriad or progress of drink... B160

Cooke, T. An essay on nobility... C411

De la Garde, M. The adventures of three hundred years ... D191

Dobson, W. Solomon... [Book III.] D348

The doctor and Bess. A satyr. D349

The forsaken fair... F199

[Free, J.] Advice to the fair-sex... F235

In praise of tea... I32

A new song upon a new subject... N225

[Notcutt, W.] The history of Joseph... N327

The old man's legacy to his daughters... O115

A pastoral lamenting the death of...viscount Howe... P111

Savage, R. The volunteer laureat... For the year 1736. S116

The tattoo: a poem... T91

Theobald, J. The second book of Virgil's Æneid. T134

Vanella's progress. In eight scenes. V13

Verses to the memory of Mrs. Elizabeth Frankland. V72

[Whistler, A.] The shuttlecock... W406

[1736?]

[Boyle, J. earl.] Verses by a young nobleman... B354

On the death of John Wagstaffe... O193

1736: SCOTLAND

Boyse, S. The tears of the muses... B367

Erskine, R. A paraphrase...upon the Song of Solomon ... E457

Lachrymæ Academiæ...in obitum...Jacobi Smithæi... L6

1736: Scotland (cont.)

A letter to a member of the town council of Edinburgh. L145

A poem, occasioned by the death of the persons unfortunately killed and wounded in the Grass-market... P554

A poem, sacred to the memory of...James Smith... P657

[*1736?*]

The flight of religious piety from Scotland... F169

The history of the secret expedition. H260

1736: IRELAND

Feb   [Shepherd, S.] An ode, to be performed at the castle of Dublin... S401

A brush to the Curry-comb of truth... B550

The chamber-maid's policy... C105

The devil upon two sticks... D251

[Dunkin, W.] A curry-comb of truth for a certain dean... D516

The dunoscope... D533

An elegy on the...Countess of Neuburgh. E198

An essay on preferment. E464

The fresh-man's entry into the university... F265

Hammond, W. Advice to a son. H26

Jackson, W. Maxims for the conduct of life... J15

A letter, from J—n W—d, to J— L—n. L129

A modest enquiry, address'd to the Bishop of Cloyne. M390

The Munster and Conaught attorney's... M559

A new ballad by way of dialogue between a kite, and a crow... N58

The old woman and her goose... O132

Proposals for the erecting a protestant nunnery... P1141

A rapsody on the army. R187

This is to give notice...of...a new and diverting puppet shew... T156

Vanella: or, an elegy... V12

The wonder: or, the devil outwitted. W552

The wonderful bard... W553

[*1736?*]

The general deception... G102

1737

Jan   [Hyde, H. *viscount.*] An ode to the Earl of Chesterfield... H419

13 Jan   [Jacob, H.] Patriotic love... J48

Feb   The diseases of Bath... D331

Feb   [Dorman, J.] Folly. A poem. D408

Feb   Fra Cipolla. A tale... F228

Feb   Green, M. The spleen... G283

Feb   A poem occasion'd by the death of Charles Talbot... P551

Feb   [Stillingfleet, B.] An essay on conversation. S757

Feb   The true great man... T527

4 Feb   Jacob, H. Donna Clara to her daughter Teresa ... J40

26 Feb   [Jacob, H.] The unequal match... J51

Mar   Albania...to the genius of Scotland... A152

Mar   Boyle, J. *earl.* A poem... to the memory of Edmund Sheffield... B354·5

Mar   [Boyse, S.] The olive... B364

Mar   Savage, R. The volunteer laureat...for the year 1737. S117

Mar   The session of the critics... S225

Mar   Ward, J. Happiness: a poem. W205

Mar   The year of wonders... Y14

6 Mar   [Nugent, R. *earl.*] An essay on happiness... N336

9 Mar   Pope, A. Horace his ode to Venus... P896

29 Mar   Glover, R. Leonidas, a poem. G190

Apr   [Bancks, J.] The game of put... B49

Apr   [Beach, T.] Eugenio... B122

Apr   The false patriot's confession... H157·2

Apr   The prophetic physician... P1139

28 Apr   Pope, A. The second epistle of the second book of Horace. P955

May   The contrast to the Man of honour. C399

May   The cur and the lap-dog... C542

May   [Manning, F.] An essay on the vicious bent and taste of the times... M85

May   Order, a poem. O240

9 May   Mother Gin, a tragi-comical eclogue... M521

20 May   [Pope, A.] The first epistle of the second book of Horace, imitated. P881

June   The art of life... A321

June   [Kirkpatrick, J.] An epistle to Alexander Pope ... K88·5

June   Of the use and improvement of the stage... O89

June   [Ogle, G.] Of legacy-hunting... O101

June   The poet and the muse. P692

1 June   On the much lamented death of...Queen Anne... O211

17 June   Thomson, J. A poem to the memory of... Lord Talbot... T208

25 June   Savage, R. Of public spirit... S102

Aug   A trip to Vaux-hall... T494

Aug   Welsted, L. A poem to...the Princess of Wales... W306

Sept   [Amhurst, N.] The test of love. A212

15 Sept [Maittaire, M.] Carmen epinicium... M35

1 Nov Ogle, G. The miser's feast... O100

5 Nov [Hill, A.] The tears of the muses... H231

Dec Duck, S. The vision... D483

Dec A poem sacred to the memory of her late majesty, Caroline... P651

Dec The sighs of Albion... S460

Dec Verses on the...death of...Queen Caroline. V65

28 Dec [Paget, T. C. *baron.*] An epistle to Mr. P——... P10

Boyd, E. The happy North-Briton... B342

The city ramble... C210

[Cooke, T.] Essays. I. On nobility... C412

An epistle to a young student... E390

An excellent new ballad... E569

[Hawling, F.] Verses upon...Queen Caroline... H116

An introduction of the ancient Greek and Latin measures into British poetry... I49

Jacob, H. The progress of religion. J49

The last speech of the statue at Stock's-market... L57

Lumley, G. Frontello and Dorinda. L323

The man of honour. M63

[Nicoll, J.] Hodge and the devil... N296·5

Tomlinson, M. An ode sacred to the memory of her late majesty. T415

The widows and orphans triumph... W452

[1737?]

The beauty and excellence of charity... B132

Purver, A. Counsel to Friends children. [1737/-] P1176

1737: SCOTLAND

Aug Ramsay, A. To the honourable Duncan Forbes ... R100

[Brodie, J.] Le repos. An epistle to the publick. B483

An elegy on...the Earl of Orkney... E205

The eucharist. A poem. E484

Godly Sarah, or, the sighing sister... G206

[Hamilton, W.] The eighteenth epistle of the second book of Horace... H15

A poem on the banks of Forth. P589

The vision of the two brothers... V105

[1737?]

The history of...Janny Geddes. H258

1737: IRELAND

Oct [Wilkes, W.] Tom in the suds... W470

The alderman's advice to his daughter... A158·5

Arbuckle, J. A poem inscribed to the Dublin Society. A286

1737: Ireland (cont.)

The art of wenching... A328

An excellent new ballad, on the...bankers... E554

A friend in need is a friend in deed... F266

A funeral elegy on the...Countess of Antrim... F294

[Gahagan, U.] An epithalamium...on the marriage of Robert Rochfort... G3

The grunting ale-wife... G308

Ireland's mourning flagg. I62

[Ward, J.] An address...to...the Duke of Devonshire... W204

[Wilkes, W.] The humours of the Black-dog... W464

[Wilkes, W.] The humours of the Black-dog continued... W466

[Wilkes, W.] The third part of the Humours... W467

1738

Jan [Bancks, J.] Love atones for little crimes... B51

Jan [Barber, J.] The farmer's daughter... B68

Jan The dream...to the...memory of her late majesty Queen Caroline. D433

Jan Guido's ghost: a tale. G310

Jan [Manning, F.] On the late queen's sickness and death... M89

23 Jan Pope, A. The sixth epistle of the first book of Horace imitated. P965

27 Jan Brooke, H. Tasso's Jerusalem... Book I. B488

30 Jan Hooke, T. The Jerusalem of Torquato Tasso. [Book 1.] H302

Feb [Manning, F.] The two first odes of Horace imitated. M91

Feb Ogle, G. The eleventh epistle of the first book of Horace imitated. O92

10 Feb [Barber, J.] Tom K----g's: or, the Paphian grove... B71

28 Feb [Sterling, J.] An ode on the times... S756

28 Feb Swift, J. An imitation of the sixth satire of the second book of Horace... S860

Mar [Barber, J.] The law suit... B69

Mar [Gilbert, T.] The world unmask'd. G150

Mar Harrison, J. A poem, occasion'd by the...death of...Robert Bragge... H90

Mar Howard, W. A paraphrase in verse, on part of...Paradise lost. H342

Mar [Jacob, H.] Callista; or the prize of beauty. J30

Mar The tit-bit. A tale. T320

Mar Turner, J. The first epistle of the first book of Horace imitated. T566

Mar [Vievar, A.] What is man?... V91

Mar The young senator... Y23

2 Mar Savage, R. The volunteer laureat, number VII ... S118

7 Mar　Pope, A.　The first epistle of the first book of Horace imitated. P877

Apr　Advice to the fair... A90

Apr　Lumley, G.　The greatest statesman and the happiest fair... L324

Apr　The magistrate...to Sir John Barnard... M18

Apr　Ogle, G.　The second epistle of the first book of Horace imitated. O104

5 Apr　Brooke, H.　Tasso's Jerusalem... Book II. B489

18 Apr　[Dodsley, R.] The art of preaching... D376

24 Apr　[Miller, J.] Of politeness... M255

May　Cruttenden, R.　Pindar's ode to Proserpina... C534

May　The modern Englishman. M365

May　The negotiators. Or, Don Diego brought to reason... N18

May　[Seymour, F. *duchess*.] The story of Inkle and Yarrico... S380

May　[Walpole, E.] The sixth satire of the first book of Horace imitated. W30

13 May　[Johnson, S.] London: a poem... J76

16 May　Pope, A.　One thousand seven hundred and thirty eight... P932

June　Meredith, J.　An essay on the divine attributes... M188

June　The rival wives... R217

22 June　[Pope, A.] The universal prayer. P982

July　Achilles to Chiron... A16

July　An ode to...Viscount Townshend... O71

18 July　Pope, A.　One thousand seven hundred and thirty eight. Dialogue II. P938

Aug　August the second, one thousand seven hundred and thirty-eight... A370

Aug　A dialogue on one thousand seven hundred and thirty-eight... D286

Aug　The rival wives answer'd... R219

Aug　The royal sin: or, adultery rebuk'd... R320

18 Aug　Brooke, H.　Tasso's Jerusalem... Book III. B490

Sept　[Akenside, M.] A British philippic... A133

21 Sept　Three epistles in the ethic way... T254

Oct　The breeches, a tale... B407

Oct　False happiness: a satire... F45

24 Oct　[Newcomb, T.] A supplement to One thousand seven hundred thirty-eight. N272

26 Oct　Ogle, G.　The third epistle of the first book of Horace imitated. O105

Nov　Morrice, B.　The present corruption of Britons... M490

10 Nov　[King, W.] Miltonis epistola ad Pollionem. K68

12 Dec　Solitude. An irregular ode... S552

A battle fought with the boasters... B95

The constant lovers... C392

An elegy on the death of the Lady Walpole... E266

[Fry, J.] An essay on conduct and education. F280

Gent, T.　Pater patriæ... G116

Gordon, W.　Epistles translated from the French of Mr. Voltaire... G229

[Hall, D.] Upon the anniversary held at Preston... H4

Heany, J.　Oxford, the seat of the muses... H128

[Legh, G.] The clergyman's choice of a wife... L94

[Manning, F.] The adventures of Telemachus... M83

[Newcomb, T.] An ode to Mr. Ellis... N265

Ogle, G.　The fifth epistle of the first book of Horace imitated. O94

Richards, T.　Cambriæ suspiria in obitum...Carolinæ... R194

Time and eternity... T313

To Sylvia, a poem... T360

To the Earl of Essex, on his instalment... T370

Verses on the death of...Queen Caroline... V62

[*1738?*]

Great news from St. James's... G272

1738: SCOTLAND

4 July　His grace the Duke of Argyle's welcome... H246

Captain Porteous's ghost... C32

Knox, T.　Philopolites. His grace the Duke of Argyle's speech... K103

[Leslie, C.] The fall of virtue... L111

Marriage is honourable. Epithalamium... M111

1738: IRELAND

The humours of the present Irish clowns... H400

Ireland's blessing on her hopeful squires. I59

The muse's flight... M565

The pettycoat. A poem... P196

'Rattle, J.' The plot discover'd... R131

[Swift, J.] The beasts confession to the priest... S804

Thomson, J.　Sir Solomon Gundi... T247

Wilkes, W.　The mourning muse or, verses sacred to the memory of...Robert Craighead... W468

[Wilkes, W.] Tom in the suds... Canto the second... W471

[Wilkes, W.] Tom in the suds... Canto the third... W472

[Wilkes, W.] Tom in the suds... Canto the fourth... W473

[*1738?*]

An ode upon that execrable club...call'd the Blasters... O75

1739

Jan [Ellis, J.] The surprize... E290

Jan [Nugent, R. *earl.*] An ode, to his royal highness ... N341

Jan Raven and owl... R134

12 Jan Sir R----- triumphant... S473

19 Jan Swift, J. Verses on the death of Doctor Swift. S920

31 Jan Whitehead, P. Manners: a satire. W417

Feb Brereton, R. A dialogue, between Menalcas and Palæmon... B411

Feb A congratulatory poem...to...Sir Robert Walpole... C349

Feb [Cooke, T.] A rhapsody on virtue and pleasure ... C422

Feb [Gilbert, T.] A panegyric on a court. G142

Feb [Paget, T. C., *earl.*] A kind of a dialogue in hudibrasticks... P20

Feb Seventeen hundred and thirty-nine... S354

Feb The star-gazer: or, latitude for longitude. S720

6 Feb Sir * * * speech upon the peace... S478

12 Feb [Nugent, R. *earl.*] An ode on Mr. Pulteney... N339

Mar Brownsword, W. On prophecy... B540

Mar Dodd, J. The irresistible fair... D359

Mar Dudley, —. The first satire of Persius... D487

Mar Epidemical madness... E345

Mar The green-cloth: or, the verge of the court... G276

Mar L--d B-------ke's speech upon the convention... L80

Mar Meredith, J. Manners decypher'd... M189

1 Mar Characters: an epistle... C129

13 Mar Ayre, W. Truth... A375

15 Mar Ogle, G. The eighth epistle of the first book of Horace imitated. O91

Apr Grobianus; or, the compleat booby... B564

Apr An epistle in verse to a friend... E384

Apr [Pilkington, L.] The statues... P279

May Bridges, —. An hymn to the supreme being. B446

May Candour...on the abuse of wit and eloquence. C23

May The church yard... C184

May The methodists, an humorous burlesque poem ... M226

May The sixteenth epode of Horace imitated... S483

May Three odes from the second book of Horace imitated. T255

May [West, G.] A canto of the Fairy queen... W357

10 May An epistle to...Sir Robert Walpole. E426

June College-wit sharpen'd... C286

June [King, W.] Sermo pedestris. K75

June Ogle, G. Gualtherus and Griselda... O95

June The state of Rome, under Nero and Domitian ... S725

13 June Ayre, W. Truth... A377

28 June [Turner, *Sir* E.] An imitation of Horace's 16th epode. T562

July [Brownsword, W.] Laugh and lye down... B538

July A dialogue which lately pass'd between the knight and his man John. D287

July The pious youth... P292

July [Powney, R.] The stag chace in Windsor Forest. P1012

10 July The methodists, a satyrical poem... M225

Aug Collier, M. The woman's labour... C288

Aug An excursory view on the present state... E601

Aug The false patriot... F47

Aug Men and measures characterised from Horace ... M168

Sept Celibacy: or, good advice... C91

Sept Dr. Codex's pastoral letter versified... D352.5

Sept Hemp. A poem... H141

Sept To arms: or, the British lyon rouz'd... T329

10 Sept A satire in the manner of Persius... S49

12 Sept His catholic majesty's most Christian manifesto ... H245

Oct The champion's defeat... C106

Oct Miller, J. The art of life... M246

Nov A touch of the times... T428

Nov 'Wharton, P. *duke.*' The fear of death... W379

6 Nov Parratt, W. An ode, to...Sir Robert Walpole ... P79

10 Nov Glover, R. London: or, the progress of commerce. G197

15 Nov One thousand seven hundred thirty nine... O233

Dec Drake, J. The lover. D424

Dec E— — —h's instructions to their member. E24

Dec [Jackson, A.] Paradise lost...Attempted in rhime... J10

Dec The satirists: a satire... S83

Dec Strahan, A. The first Æneid of Virgil... S771

12 Dec Ogle, G. The twelfth epistle of the first book of Horace imitated. O106

Brailsford, J. Derby silk-mill... B382

Burch, J. The impartial Englishman... B568

The convention... C402

Cooke, T. Petworth... C419

Cooke, T. A cursory view of the creation... C425

Drive on coachman... D441

The English sailors resolution... E340

An epistle to Dean Swift... E395

A hopeful convention agreed upon... H306

The instructors instructed... I47

Lockman, J. An ode for St. Cecilia's-day. L216

[Morgan, D.] The country bard... M440

The mountain of miseries... M540

A new copy of verses... N122

An ode...to...the Prince of Wales... O35

Political madness. A new ballad... P711

A political touch of the times. P714

The popular convention. P997

Theobald, J. The fourth book of Virgil's Æneid. T136

The **** turn'd into English... T560

[1739?]

Advice to Mr. Handel... A82

A new song. N183

Who's afraid now... W442

Theobald, J. A new translation of the first ode of Horace ... [1739/46] T131

Theobald, J. Part of the fourth book of Milton's Paradise lost... [1739/46] T132

1739: SCOTLAND

Jan   [Leslie, C.] On the scarcity of the copper coin. L116

Apr   [Leslie, C.] Masonry: a poem. L113

Erskine, R. An elegy...on...Alexander Hamilton... E456

[Hamilton, W.] Three odes... H19

[Leslie, C.] An essay on design and beauty. L108

Verses sacred to the memory of...Alexander Stuart... V66

1739: IRELAND

Ballard, J. Honour. A poem... B43

[Hiffernan, P.] The enthusiasm... H181

[Hiffernan, P.] The poet. H182

The holy Parnassus... H291

Lonergan, E. The dean and the country parson... L242

[1739?]

An ode, address'd to all the freemen... O19

[174–]

Albertus the second: or, the curious justice. A153

The c----t candidate and the cobler. C535

England's glory... E318

England's resolution to down with popery... E325

[Gent, T.] The history of...Jesus Christ... G115

[Hawksworth, A. R.] The breathings of a pious soul... H114

The narrative. N3

An ode compos'd in the year M.DCCXX... O23

Tolson, F. Hermathenæ, or moral emblems... T405

The triumphs & excellency of faith... T505

Turner, N. The heathen's conversion... T567

[174–]: SCOTLAND

An alarm to the seceders... A150

[Davidson, W.] The Cuckow's song anent the election of peers. D58

A hymn, fit to be sung on days of humiliation and prayer. H421

A new song. N188

A new song... N222

A short hint of the life of Al--------r Scl-----r. S448

[174–]: IRELAND

The contest decided, address'd to Mrs. Woffington. C397

On Miss Death. O179

1740

Jan   Horace's instructions to the Roman senate... H318

Jan   [Newcomb, T.] Vindicta Britannica: an ode... N280

Jan   A poem occasioned by the present war with Spain. P560

Jan   A poetical essay on physick. P703

Feb   [Boyd, E.] Admiral Haddock: or, the progress of Spain. B338

Feb   [Boyse, S.] Deity: a poem. B359

Feb   A Chinese tale... C151

Feb   [Gilbert, T.] The first satire of Juvenal imitated. G141

Feb   The place-bill, a ballad... P465

4 Feb   Somervile, W. Hobbinol... S571

6 Feb   Parker, B. Money. A poem... P67

22 Feb   The soliloquy of a great man... S550

27 Feb   [Dyer, J.] The ruins of Rome. D566

Mar   [Dinsdale, J.] The dove-cote... D315

Mar   Tans'ur, W. Poetical meditations on the four last things... T37

Mar   [Wesley, C.] The taking of Jericho. W322

1 Mar   [King, W.] Milton's epistle to Pollio... K70

3 Mar   A seasonable rebuke to the playhouse rioters... S166

20 Mar [Lorleach, —.] The muff...a court tale... L268

25 Mar Plain truth, or downright Dunstable... P475

28 Mar [Brownsword, W.] Laugh upon laugh... B539

Apr Chase, J. The sixth epistle of the first book of Horace... C138

Apr Duck, S. Alrick and Isabel... D467

Apr A letter to a friend in the country. L141

Apr Loveling, B. The first satire of Persius imitated. L291

Apr A poem on the death of...Lady Elizabeth Hastings. P602

Apr The protestant knock... P1147

Apr The triumph of beauty... T499

14 Apr [King, W.] Scamnum, ecloga. K74

14 Apr [Lorleach, —.] A satirical epistle to Mr. Pope. L269

15 Apr A new ballad on the taking of Porto-Bello... N81

28 Apr Liberty regain'd... L174

May Satyrical and panegyrical instructions to Mr. William Hogarth... S78

May Seasonable admonitions. A satire... S164

May Wesley, C. The life of faith... W318

16 May Verses to the memory of...Lady Elizabeth Hastings. V74

21 May [Glover, R.] Admiral Hosier's ghost... G186

July The British admiral... B474

July Price, H. The spectre: or, Admiral Hosier's ghost... P1045

7 July The mock campaign; or, English bravery. M349

11 July The ghost and the miller. G134

Sept [Spiltimber, G.] The statesman... S652

26 Sept [Rogers, T.] An epistolary poem to a lady... R251

Oct The bench. An eclogue... B189

Oct The city struggle... C211

Oct Dinsdale, J. The modern art of breeding bees. D316

Oct [Gibbons, T.] The fox and monkey. G137·5

Oct Horace, book IV. ode v. imitated. H311

Oct The new amour... N50

Oct The progress of the war... P1112

Oct Spiltimber, G. To the king, on his majesty's happy return. S653

Oct The Torbay expedition... T422

Oct [Upton, F.] In laudem Edvardi Vernoni... U26

23 Oct [Miller, J.] Are these things so?... M234

Nov The fair thinker, or reason asserted... F35

Nov He has kept his word... H119

Nov They are not. T150

8 Nov [Morris, R.] Yes, they are... M511

13 Nov The whimsical age, or the political juglers. W398

15 Nov What of that!... W380

17 Nov [Cowper, A.] The faction, a tale... C478

18 Nov Spiltimber, G. The weather-menders... S654

19 Nov The popish impostor... F230

Dec [Boyd, E.] Truth, a poem. B345

Dec Come on then... C311

Dec [Morris, R.] Have at you all... M507

Dec The oddity: a poem... O15

Dec An ode to the Duke of Argyll... O68

Dec A poem on...Admiral Vernon... P615

Dec [Pulteney, W. earl.] An epistle from Lord L---l to Lord C---d. P1160

18 Dec [Miller, J.] The great man's answer to Are these things so?... M249

20 Dec [Newcomb, T.] A supplement to...Are these things so? N271

22 Dec Trapp, J. Johannis Miltoni Paradisus amissus latine redditus. T449

The city, in glory... C204

Denny, G. Sexus invicem depraeliantes... D227

The Englishman's answer to the magick lanthorn. E342

An epistle to the supposed author... E431

A father's advices to his children... F75

Flemyng, M. Neuropathia... F165

[Le Franc de Pompignan, J.-J.] La prière universelle... L93·5

A letter from a lady to her husband. L121

A letter from Don Blas de Lezo... L126

A letter from Don Thomas Geraldino... L128

A new camp song... N115

A new medley. N157

Occasion'd by the lamentable death of the Lady Pryce... O8

A poem occasioned by the death of Mr. John Pryer... P553

Ryall, C. The mourner... R336

Whittington reviv'd, or the city in triumph... W441

The widsom of religion... W532

Woodman, J. The rat-catcher at Chelsea College... W559

[1740?]

English courage display'd... E331

The English Haddock... E335

The fox in mourning... F220

The raree-show-man... R130

The true Briton's thought. T514

The younger brother's garland... Y178

A new song... [1740/41] N219

1740: SCOTLAND

Sept   [Leslie, C.] Mum. A political ballad... L114

An epistle address'd to a friend. E358

Ker, J. Ad illustrissimum...Robertum marchionem de Bowmont... K19

1740: IRELAND

Oct   An ode to be performed at the castle of Dublin ... O63

[Carthy, C.] An ode on the present war with Spain. C57

[Carthy, C.] The third ode, of the third book of Horace, imitated... C59

[Dunkin, W.] Epistola ad Franciscum Bindonem... D520

Elegy on the much lamented death of...the potatoes... E219

The Hibernian politicians... H175

The Hibernian politicians; part the second... H177

'O'Connor, M.' The petition...to the provost and senior fellows of Trinity College... O13

The resurrection of the potatoes... R165

[Shepherd, S.] A poem inscribed to...Lord Tullamoore ... S403

[1740?]

Bo---'s in disgrace... B292

1741

7 Jan   Fielding, H. Of true greatness... F123

8 Jan   [Nugent, R. *earl.*] An ode to mankind... N343

8 Jan   Pro and Con. P1102

13 Jan   An epistle from a n--ble l--d to Mr. P--y. E361

15 Jan   A ballad... B40

16 Jan   The Westminster justice. W372

20 Jan   A poem on the birth-day of...the Prince of Wales. P592

21 Jan   [Fielding, H.] Της Ομηρου Vερνον-ιαδος... F120

22 Jan   Whitehead, W. The danger of writing verse... W438

Feb   Characteristicks: a dialogue. C128

Feb   A preparative address to a certain great man... P1023

Feb   Reasons for writing verse... R140

Feb   Welsted, L. The summum bonum... W312

2 Feb   Balguy, J. The fast-day. B17

10 Feb   [Brewster, T.] The satires of Persius... Satire the first. B432

13 Feb   Duck, S. Hints to a schoolmaster... D470

17 Feb   [Cowper, A.] High boys up go we!... C479

21 Feb   The motion. M525

23 Feb   The reason. R137

28 Feb   The compleat history of Bob of Lyn... C325

Mar   Gilbert, T. The second epistle of the first book of Horace imitated. G147

Mar   [Lockman, J.] Verses to a lady of quality... L226

Mar   The new-year's-gift... N242

Mar   Rogers, T. Disease: or, the vanity and misery of human life... R250

Mar   Rogers, T. The royal pattern. Or, advice to the fair sex. R252

Mar   [Sacheverell, J.] The tempest: a poem. S4

Mar   The three politicians... T257

Mar   [Tibal, P.] The tell tale... T271

Mar   [Wallis, J.] The history of David's troubles... W27

5 Mar   The grand defeat... G242

7 Mar   The grounds. G302

10 Mar   Duck, S. Every man in his own way... D469

12 Mar   A paraphrase on the hundred and fourth psalm ... P58

19 Mar   The art of poetry. A325

19 Mar   Vindiciæ publicæ: an ode to the real patriot. V99

23 Mar   [Brewster, T.] The satires of Persius... Satire the second. B433

28 Mar   Mock masonry... M355

30 Mar   The acquital. A17

Apr   Boyle, J. *earl.* The first ode of the first book of Horace imitated... B351

Apr   Fables, in English and French verse... F21

Apr   The government of the human body... G232

Apr   [Joy, J.] Epistola ad amicum familiaris. J107

Apr   The polygamist: or, the lustful priest... P719

1 Apr   The funeral of faction. F295

7 Apr   The protest. P1145

21 Apr   Truth and moderation. T537

23 Apr   [Shenstone, W.] The judgment of Hercules... S394

May   Marsh, C. A poetical epistle... M116

May   [Morgan, D.] The country bard... Canto the second... M441

May   Patriotism. A satire. P125

May   Robinson, S. Cælia's revenge... R242

May   The Turkish paradise or Vaux-hall gardens... T555

June   A poem...on the success of his majesty's arms ... P546

6 June   Spanish courage. A satire... S617

27 June   [Williams, *Sir* C. H.] A dialogue between G--s E---e and B--b D---n. W478

July   The expedition. An ode... E605

24 July Bennet, G. Pamela versified... B192

Oct The c—rd—n—ls master-piece... C498

Oct The priest and the widow... P1052

Nov Bedlam: a poem on his majesty's happy escape ... B155

Nov The late gallant exploits of a famous balancing captain... L64

Nov [Miller, J.] The year forty-one... M261

Nov The true English-boys song, to Vernon's glory ... T525

7 Nov Consummation: or, the rape of Adonis. C394

28 Nov Boyle, J. *earl.* Pyrrha... B356

Dec The by-stander. B621

Dec [Jones, L.] Io! Triumphe! A poem upon Admiral Vernon. J96

Dec The sixteenth ode of Horace, book iii. imitated ... S484

Dec The statesman's mirrour... S733

Dec The independent Westminster choice... I33

1 Dec The medalist. A new ballad. M156

Army proceedings or the conjunct expedition. A312

An answer to Mr. Leech. A240

Britannia... A pastoral dialogue... B467

Britannia's precaution to her sons... B470

[Chicken, E.] No; -- this is the truth. C148

[Collier, J.] The black-bird: a poem. C287

English courage display'd... E332

The fatality of forc'd marriage... F71

The freeholder... F239

The French-man letter to his friend in England... F263

Full moon. A new city ballad... F285

Gutteridge, T. An elegy, in memory of...John Newman ... G322

An inventory of the goods and chattels of P---r W----s ... I52

Invictæ fidelitatis præmium. I54

Is this the truth? I69

A key to the whole state of Europe. K31

King Harry the eighth's ghost... K48

A letter from a member of parliament... L122

Lockman, J. An ode, to...Cardinal de Fleury... L219

[Martin, T.] Captain John Peddie... M118

No---- that's a mistake... N309

The N-rw-ch cav-lc-de and opposition... N334

Order in government: the British plan... O241

Paget, W. A voyage to Ipswich... P23

The pound for the Hereford freemen... P1007

A South-Saxon ode. S610

The theatrical volunteer... T128

To John Caswal esquire, so brisk and so bold. T343

To the right honourable the Lady Aubrey Beauclerk... T393

Vernon's glory... V31

Vernon's glory: or, the Spaniards defeat... V33

The Westminster election... W371

Westminster tryumphant... W373

[1741?]

Mr. Burchett's farewel to Sandwich. B571

A genuine copy of two excellent court ballads... G124

Grand sale at Westminster... G248

The Hanoverian leeches... H36

Pious exhortation of Sir Samuel Goodere... P291

[Bramston, J.] Scotch taste in vista's. [1741/42] B402

The independent Westminster electors toast... [1741/42] I34

1741: SCOTLAND

Davidson, W. Carthagena, a new poem... D56

Davidson, W. The Cuckow's lamentation for our loss at Carthagena. D57

[Drummond, T.] To the memory of Mr. David Drummond... D443

Hunter, R. Θρηνος ἐπικηδειος ἐπι τω θανατω του πανυ Καδκαρτος... H408

Melancholly sonnets... M162

Mundus delirans, or the infatuation. M556

1741: IRELAND

A comi-farci-operatical humorous and political burlesque scene... C315

The Hibernian politicians; part the third... H179

The lady and the linnet. L17

A letter from the late revd. Mr. Sewel... L135

Ormsbye, R. An heroic poem on the memorable battle fought at Bleinheim... O250

A poem occasioned by a view of Powers-court House... P548

1742

6 Jan [Collins, W.] Persian eclogues... C298

8 Jan [King, W.] Templum libertatis. Liber primus. K77

16 Jan Somervile, W. Field sports... S569

19 Jan [Martin, T.] A poem on the war in the West-Indies... M120

22 Jan Pyrrha a cantata... P1181

Feb The Christian test... C168

Feb Modern quality... M382

16 Feb Right triumphant, or the devil to pay... R210

18 Feb L'allegro ed il penseroso in sonno... A167

18 Feb The c—rd—n—l dancing-master... C497

23 Feb   [West, G.] The institution of the order of the Garter. W358

Mar   Gibbons, T. An elegy sacred to the memory of William Beldam. G137·2

Mar   The happy coalition... H40

Mar   Lady Mary: a dialogue... L19

Mar   An ode on Sir Robert Walpole's being created earl of Orford. O39·5

Mar   Woman in miniature. A satire... W546

18 Mar   The screen. A simile. S151

20 Mar   [Pope, A.] The new Dunciad... P787

23 Mar   The grand removal... G247

Apr   [Brewster, T.] The satires of Persius... Satire the third and fourth. B434

Apr   Ogle, M. Mordecai triumphant... O107

Apr   The old wife's tale... O129

Apr   The Sarah-ad: or, a flight for fame... S37

6 Apr   Morrice, B. To the falsely celebrated British Homer. M497

May   The dawn of honour... D70

May   The lucky mistake: or lady surpriz'd... L317

May   A wife and no wife... W456

8 May   Michaelmas term... M228

15 May   [Shenstone, W.] The school-mistress, a poem ... S395

31 May   [Young, E.] The complaint: or, night-thoughts ... Y24

June   The old fox chas'd... O112

June   A poem, inscribed to...the Earl of Orford. P547

21 June   A consolatory poem on the death of a young lady... C388

29 June   The Reports of Sir Edward Coke, kt. in verse... R159

July   Brickenden, F. Advice to a young gentleman. B439

July   An epistle to...William Pultney... E429

July   The temples of virtue and pleasure. T117

30 July   [Williams, Sir C. H.] The old coachman... W494

Aug   Merrick, J. The destruction of Troy... M193

Aug   The political padlock, and the English key... P712

3 Aug   [Williams, Sir C. H.] The country girl. W475

5 Aug   Ad versutum cardinalem... A23

24 Aug   [Hervey, J. baron.] The difference between verbal and practical virtue... H156

31 Aug   Sawney and Colley... S126

Sept   Boyse, S. The praise of peace... B365

Sept   [Wesley, C.] The paraphrase on Isaiah 14. W321

3 Sept   [Williams, Sir C. H.] A new ode, to a number of great men newly made... W484

Oct   The devil repriev'd from the jaws of death... D244

Oct   Female honour... F95

Oct   [Hyde, H. viscount.] The judgment of the muse ... H418

Oct   [Wesley, C.] The means of grace. W319

Oct   [Wesley, C.] Thanksgiving for the colliers. W323

2 Oct   The Scribleriad... S153

18 Oct   [Hervey, J. baron.] The patriots are come... H158

Nov   A clear stage, and no favour... C236

Nov   [Hammond, J.] Love elegies. H22

11 Nov   Beef and butt beer, against mum and pumpernickle... B157

16 Nov   [Warton, J.] Fashion: an epistolary satire... W244

25 Nov   [Morris, R.] The art of architecture... M503

30 Nov   [Young, E.] Night the second... Y32

Dec   [Carte, T.] The blatant-beast. C55·5

Dec   [Gent, T.] British piety display'd... G111

Dec   A poem to Francis Bindon... P661

Dec   [Wesley, C.] Hymn for the condemned prisoners. W317

16 Dec   [Young, E.] Night the third... Y36

17 Dec   The emulation of the insects... E308

Bob Booty's lost deal... B294

[Brewster, T.] The satires of Persius... Satire the fifth. B435

[Brewster, T.] The satires of Persius... Satire the sixth B436

The city lady's choice of a new standing member... C206

The defection: or, the patriot prostituted. D86

Dermot and Cicely: or, the Irish gimblet... D233

Don, a poem. D394

The false patriot... F48

The farce is over; or, the plot discover'd... F58

Gutteridge, T. An elegy sacred to...James Wood. G324

Hallam, I. The cocker: a poem... H6

[Newcomb, T.] An ode to...the E----l of O--------d ... N267

No screen! or, the masque remov'd... N308

On the death of Dr. Alured Clarke. O192

A poem. Canto I. P524

Rolli, P. A. La Bucolica di Publio Virgilio Marone... R254

Wesley, C. An elegy on the death of Robert Jones... W313

[1742?]

Antoeus. A tale. A268

The mayor and the mob... M154

The progress of charity... P1107

[Wesley, C.] The whole armour of god. W324

1742: SCOTLAND

Apr   Help to patience under affliction... H137

Oct   The zealous country-mens lament for the absence of Mr. George Whitefield... Z1

Ἐῐς την του Χριστου σταυρωσιν μονοστροφικα... E27

An excellent new ballad... E544

Groans from the grave... G300

A poem to the memory of Mr. Hugh Murray-Kynnynmound... P665

[1742?]

The life and history of Robert the raven. L180

1742: IRELAND

The anointment. A poem. A229

De la Mayne, T. H.   Love and honour... D194

To Mrs. Cibber, a poem. T351

[1742?]

An impartial narrative of the Pretender's god-son... I9

1743

Jan   Cooke, T.   An epistle to...the Countess of Shaftesbury... C410

Jan   A great man's speech in Downing-street... G270

Jan   [King, W.] Templum libertatis. Liber secundus. K78

Jan   Part of the CXXXVIIIth psalm... P92

Jan   [Williams, *Sir* C. H.] The wife and the nurse. W511

12 Jan   The difference between keeping and marriage ... D305

28 Jan   [Williams, *Sir* C. H.] Esq; S---ys's budget open'd... W480

Feb   [Hawkins, W.] The thimble... H112

Feb   J---l's wife. A new ballad... J67

Feb   The old fox and his son... O111

Feb   A short trip into Kent... S451

Feb   [Williams, *Sir* C. H.] S——s and J——l. W503

18 Feb   Mr. P—pe's picture in miniature... M298

19 Feb   Whitehead, W.   An essay on ridicule. W439

Mar   Blair, R.   The grave. B271

Mar   Lockman, J.   Pastoral stanzas... L222

Mar   [White, G.] The miraculous sheep's eye... W408

10 Mar   [Young, E.] The complaint... [Night the fourth.] Y43

25 Mar   [Cobden, E.] On Miss Forrester playing with her shadow. C265

Apr   Britain's wrongs... B458

Apr   Phelps, J. The human barometer... P200

Apr   Præ-existence and transmigration... P1019

4 Apr   Dorinda: or, the grove in tears... D404

7 Apr   The eagle, falconer, and hawk... E7

14 Apr   G----e and D----y... G96

14 Apr   Price, H.   Laodamia to Protesilaus... P1041

21 Apr   Drinking by authority... D440

23 Apr   Eugenio...on the death of Dorinda. E485

26 Apr   The Northumberland miracle... N323

30 Apr   Priest-craft and lust... P1054

May   An epistle to Mistress N---v---l... E407

May   [Hill, A.] The Fanciad. H214

3 May   A second dialogue between G--s E-e and B--b D-----n. S168

4 May   The wind in the east... W523

5 May   Grierson, G. H.   A prophecy and poem... G293

5 May   Whitehead, W.   Ann Boleyn to Henry the eighth. W434

June   Morell, T.   The Christian's epinikion... M438

June   A new song on the...battle fought the 16th. instant... N211

4 June   [Dering, H.] Reliquiæ Eboracenses. D232

July   [Morgan, M.] The Causidicade... M446

2 July   [Boyse, S.] Albion's triumph... B358

2 July   A joyful ode: inscribed to the king... J108

6 July   Tea, a poem. T108

9 July   Lockman, J.   Verses to...the Duke of Cumberland... L228

9 July   A new bloody ballad on the bloody battle at Dettingen... N110

11 July   Highmore, J.   Dettingen. A poem... H208

21 July   Monmouth-street in tears... M400

23 July   [Bettesworth, J.] The judgment of Paris... B205

Aug   Bally, G.   Solomon de mundi vanitate... B45

1 Aug   A poem on the battle of Dettingen. P590

4 Aug   The battle of Dettingen. An ode. B101

1 Sept   Edrisa: or, an elegiac poem... E17

Oct   An elegy on...the Duke of Argyle... E50

Oct   Sephalissa to Sylvius... S201

13 Oct   [Dodsley, R.] Verses on the grotto at Twickenham... D390

26 Oct   The yellow sash... Y16

29 Oct   [Pope, A.] The Dunciad, in four books... P796

Nov   A poetical thought on the creation. P707

Nov   Thoughts in sickness. T251

4 Nov   [Bramston, J.] The crooked six-pence... B392

6 Nov   British bravery... B475

15 Nov   Duck, S.   An ode on the battle of Dettingen. D471

16 Nov   The Jubilade. An ode... J109

18 Nov   Verses humbly inscrib'd to his majesty... V48

25 Nov   Dodsley, R.   Pain and patience. D387

26 Nov   Gawler, W.   Dorchester: a poem. G43

28 Nov   The trial of Roger... T472

29 Nov   [Dodington, G. B. *baron.*] An epistle from John More... D369

Dec   [Belsham, J.] Mors triumphans: ode lyrica. B185

Dec   [Collins, W.] Verses humbly address'd to Sir Thomas Hanmer... C299

Dec   A congratulatory ode...to a certain very great man... C346

Dec   Martin, T.   A poem on the late action at Dettingen... M119

Dec   Savage, R.   London and Bristol compar'd... S100

Dec   Whitehead, W.   Atys and Adrastus... W435

6 Dec   Doddridge, P.   The principles of Christian religion... D366

13 Dec   The machine: or, love's preservative... M6

16 Dec   [Young, E.] The complaint... Night the fifth. Y47

17 Dec   Morris, R.   Saint Leonard's Hill... M510

20 Dec   [Brown, J.] Honour... B504

23 Dec   [Wesley, C.] A hymn for Christmas day. W316

Amelia to Mallamour... A178

A ballad sung by the English grenadiers... B38

Boyd, E.   Glory to the highest... B341

Britain's triumph, or, Monsieur defeated. B457

Bromwich, J.   The good shepherd... B486

Collier, S.   On discontent. C291

Corona Cupidinis: or the effigies of love... C436

[Cowper, A.] The progress of physic. C480

A duel and no duel... D494

An elegiac poem to...John Hubbard... E38

An elegy on...Miss Edwards... E110

Gutteridge, T.   An elegy, sacred to...John Hubbard... G323

An hue and cry after M----- Y----h's white-horse... H354

[Kennicott, B.] A poem on the recovery of...Eliz. Courtenay... K13

Lockman, J.   To...the Dutchess of Buckingham: with the Jesuits travels. L223

Maxwell, J.   The reflection. M151

[Morris, R.] An enquiry after virtue... Part II... M506

No thing and no body... N310

The progress of methodism in Bristol... P1110

The progress of time... P1113

Psychomachia; the war of the soul... P1155

Smart, C.   Carmen...in S. Cæciliam... S 490

A song on the battle of Dettingen... S588

[Williams, *Sir* C. H.] Plain thoughts in plain language. W501

[*1743?*]

King Harry the IXth, teaching L——d C——t his political alphabet. K49

Lamentation from the Drury-lane play-house... L33

The old fox his legacy... O113

A new coppy of verses, on the present times... [*1743/45*] N121

Huggins, A.   To each gentleman soldier in the company of...Paul Ferris... [*1743/–*] H363

1743: SCOTLAND

May   [Mathison, T.] The goff... M137

25 July   [Lowth, R.] The judgment of Hercules... L293

Dowie, T.   The country man's companion... D416

[Drummond, T.] A poem to the memory of...Thomas Rattray. D442

An elegy on...John, duke of Argyle... E49

A letter to a friend... L144

[*1743?*]

An elegy on...James duke of Hamilton. E140

1743: IRELAND

Oct   Burroughs, L.   An ode, to be performed at the castle of Dublin... B589

The charmers... C134

D'Anvers, A.   A poem on the glorious victory... D39

The Richardiad. A satire... R192

The squib... S667

1744

Jan   [Miller, J.] The H------r heroes... M254·5

Jan   Ode on the incarnation... O48

Jan   Pamela: or, the fair impostor... P25

14 Jan   [Akenside, M.] The pleasures of imagination. A139

1 Feb   An essay on the soul of man. E468

11 Feb   The equity of Parnassus. E449

18 Feb   A poem...to Mrs. Deane, oculist... P541

Mar   The strolling hero, or Rome's knight errant... B604

Mar   Good-nature. A poem. G226

8 Mar   [Warton, J.] The enthusiast... W243

10 Mar   The jolly patriots... J89

30 Mar   [Young, E.] Night the sixth. The infidel reclaim'd... Y49

Apr [Hill, A.] The impartial... H220

Apr A paraphrase on the creation. P54

Apr A poetical and critical essay on Homer... P699

Apr Sophron... Occasion'd by the death of... Robert Wright. S601

Apr A wife and no wife... W453

4 Apr [Boyd, E.] Altamira's ghost... B340

10 Apr [Armstrong, J.] The art of preserving health. A296

24 Apr The St. James's beauties... S19

26 Apr Whitehead, W. On nobility... W440

27 Apr [King, W.] Antonietti, ducis Corsorum, epistola ... K66

May Clark, J. Bethlem, a poem... C225

May The Deviliad. D252

May Hart, J. Ποιημα νουθετικον... H92

3 May Verses occasioned by seeing proposals for founding an hospital... V52

8 May Theobald, J. A poem sacred to the king. T133

9 May Collins, W. An epistle: addrest to Sir Thomas Hanmer... C300

10 May A poet's impartial reply... P696

24 May [Moore, E.] Fables for the female sex. M424

June A congratulatory poem on the happy recovery of the Earl of Stair... C357

June From Pope Benedict XIV. to Lewis XV. of France... F272

June [Saunders, —.] An essay on calumny... S86

June [Whitehead, P.] The Gymnasiad, or boxing match... W412

5 June An elegy on Mr. Pope... E217

19 June Discord, or, one thousand seven hundred forty four... D326

22 June An elegy on...Alexander Pope... E218

5 July [Dance, J.] Cricket. An heroic poem... D22

23 July [Young, E.] The complaint... [Night the seventh.] Y50

28 July Elegeia Popi in memoriam infelicis nymphæ... E34

27 Aug An epistle to * * * * * *... E385

29 Aug A consolatory ode. Inscrib'd to the Marquis de la Chetardie... C386

Sept The female moralist. F98

Oct Pope's ghost: a ballad... P761

Nov The conspiracy... Part I. C390

Nov [Newcomb, T.] Verses left in a grotto in Richmond Garden... N276

13 Nov Barford, R. A poem on Knolls-Hill in Essex... B84

14 Nov [Akenside, M.] An epistle to Curio. A136

1 Dec Cannon, T. Apollo; a poem... C28

An essay on victory... E471

Godwin, E. A brief account of god's dealings... G208

Godwin, E. The death-bed... G210

[Hawkins, W.] The thimble... H113

Italian policy... I72

Peter. A tale. P192

[1744?]

Admiral Matthews engagement... A61

The loyal Britain: or, George forever. L297

A new song, call'd, the Observator of the times. N195

A new song of the warrs. N207

Walpole redivivus: or, a new excise. W29

Craft, J. The Saphirah in triumph... C491

[Wesley, C.] A hymn at the sacrament. W315

1744: SCOTLAND

Alexis...to the memory of Alexander Innes... A159

The Berkshire tragedy... B201

Davidson, W. In mrum. Georgium Livingston... epitaphium. D59

Meston, W. Ad consulem Abredonensem. M207

A poem on Dr. Taylor... P566

A poem on the election of a knight of the shire of Edinburgh. P613

The wonderful works of providence... W557

1744: IRELAND

Dunkin, W. An epistle to...James lord visct. Charlemont... D519

1745

Jan The art of love. A322

Jan The first ode of the third book of Horace... F148

Jan Friendship and love. A dialogue... F270

Jan The review... R170

Jan [Williams, Sir C. H.] Place-book for the year seventeen-hundred, forty-five. W497

15 Jan Voltaire, F. M. A. de. Lettre au roi de Prusse. V116

17 Jan In and out and turn about... I15

22 Jan [Morgan, M.] The Triumvirade... M462

31 Jan The fifth ode of the first book of Horace imitated. F137

31 Jan The seventh satyre of Juvenal imitated. S355

Feb British frenzy: or, the mock-Apollo. B478

Feb The French marshal catch'd in a trap... F257

Feb [Morgan, M.] The sequel... M461

17 Feb Morell, T. Hope: a poetical essay... M439

26 Feb Thompson, W. Sickness... Book I. T173

Mar Dalton, J. Two epistles... D16

Mar The Porcupinade... P1000

Mar [Warton, T.] Five pastoral eclogues... W245·5

7 Mar [Young, E.] The complaint... Night the eighth ... Y52

Apr Powney, R. Templum harmoniæ. P1016

Apr [Pulteney, W. *earl*.] An ode, imitated from ode XI. book 2d. of Horace... P1166

Apr [Reynolds, J.] Jesus. A poem. R185

Apr Wit, a poem... W536

10 Apr Grigg, J. The saviour... Book the first. G298

12 Apr Thompson, W. Sickness... Book the second. T174

22 Apr Veillée a la campagne... V23

24 Apr [Brown, J.] An essay on satire... B502

24 Apr Matrimony, pro and con... M138

May An epistle to...Philip earl of Chesterfield. E421

May Fontenoy, a new satiric ballad... F178

May An ode, to Mr. Handel. O67

May The Stilton hero. S762

May Tomlinson. M. The trinity. T416

June [Poole, —.] Advice to the ladies... P752

18 June The thirteenth satyre of Juvenal imitated. T155

July The discarded fair-one... D322

July From Cæsario to Hamilla an answer. F271

July Kirkpatrick, J. Celeberrimi Popii Tentamen de modis criticis scripta dijudicandi. K88

July [Nugent, R. *earl*.] An ode to...Viscount Lonsdale. N345

2 Aug War. A poem. W39

Sept The alarm... A147

Sept Music in good time... M567

Oct Cibber, T. The association... C201

Oct The first satire of the second book of Horace, imitated. F150

Oct The Hampstead congress... H30

Oct The Scotch mist clearing up... S141

11 Oct Britannia invicta... B466

23 Oct The parallel: an essay... P50

25 Oct Madden, S. Boulter's monument... M8

Nov Clancy, M. Templum Veneris... C215

Nov [Cobden, E.] A religious ode, occasioned by the present rebellion. C267

Nov [Cooper, J. G.] The power of harmony... C427

Nov Modern fashions... M372

Nov [Scott, T.] England's danger and duty... S146

4 Nov The baffled hero... B8

12 Nov King George for England... K47

18 Nov The rebel Scot. R141

20 Nov Campbell, D. *junior*. The Perkinade... C12

Dec Bishop Ridly's ghost... B230

Dec Gibbons, T. Britannia's alarm... G135

Dec [Hopkins, T.] The lawyers disbanded... H310

Dec The politic j-------ge... P710

Dec Price, J. A protestant king and the Bible. P1047

Dec A prologue spoken December 9, 1745... P1131

Dec Rules for a Christian life versified. R322·5

Dec The Spanish armada, an ode. S616

Dec [Williams, *Sir* C. H.] The heroes... W481

2 Dec Spiltimber, G. On public virtue... S651

12 Dec [Ridley, G.] Jovi eleutherio... R206

23 Dec Rosalind, a pastoral... R266

All hands to a court martial... A160

The Chevalier's market or highland fair. C143

Cooke, T. Immortality reveal'd... C415

The dead emperor: or, reviving peace... D75

The European mourners: or, the emperor's funeral... E487

The grove's complaint... G302·5

The highland invasion... H202

Jemmy's pedigree. J58

The national alarm... N6

Neck or nothing: or, the devil take the hindmost... N14

A new muster of Bays's troops. N158

A new song, proper for the times... N212

On love, an elegy. O177·5

Price, J. Christmas day. P1046

The quack-doctor... Q1

The re---cy. A poem... R148

Stephens, E. The dying heathen... S749

Verses occasion'd by the present rebellion. V56

Wallis, J. Reflections on a candle... W28

[*1745?*]

Great Britain in danger. G255

Newcomb, T. An ode inscribed to the memory of the late Earl of Orford. N258

Oldnall, E. Two essays, in verse... O169

Paget, W. The humours of the Fleet... P21

Roberts, —. England's glory. Or the French king strip'd ... R225

A new copy of verses concerning the late engagement... [1745/46] N119

On operas... [1745/46] O182

Dean Swift for ever... [1745?/–] D77

The humble address of the wine-merchants... [1745/–] H390

1745: SCOTLAND

A son altesse royale...le Prince de Galles. A1

The battle of Preston... B103

The birth-day ode. B224

The blockade of Edinburgh castle... B287

Charles Edouard en Ecosse... C131

Le conquerant d'Ecosse. C383

An elegy on...Colonel James Gardner... E127

An excellent song on the present times... E597

Henderson, A. Psalmi centesimi quarti paraphrasis poetica. H143·5

Les Irlandois. Poëme... I67

June 10th, 1745. Being the anniversary of his majesty's birth. J111

A new song entituled, the Warming-pan. N200

News from Borrowstounness... N294

Ode au prince conquerant d'Ecosse. O22

Ode sur l'entreprise du Prince de Galles. O58

An ode to his royal highness, Charles... O66

On the signal victory at Gladsmuir... O221

A poem on Prince Charles's victory at Gladsmuir. P575

A poem upon the 29th of May... P686

Prince Charles his welcome to Scotland. P1058

A song to the tune of the Abbot of Canterbury, &c. S599

To his royal highness, Charles... T342

[1745?]

An excellent new ballad... E567

[Hamilton, W.] An ode on the victory at Gladsmuir... H17

On seeing the prince's picture. O187

A poem by a lady on seeing...the prince regent. P521

A poem on the prince. P636

[Don, J.] Britain's lamentation, and hopes of triumph. [1745/46] D399

A new ballad... [1745/46] N94

L'ombre de Jacques II... [1745/46] O172

1745: IRELAND

Oct   Burroughs, L. An ode to be performed at the castle of Dublin... B590

Oct   A funeral elegy on...Jonathan Swift... F290

An allusion to the third ode of the first book of Horace... A170

The Draper's apparition to G-----e F------r... D429

An essay on the theatres... E469

The fate of an Hibernian muse... F72

A friendly admonition to all persons of the Romish persuasion... F267

[Jones, H.] The bricklayer's poem...to...the lord lieutenant... J91

1745: Ireland (cont.)

[Jones, H.] The bricklayer's poem to the Countess of Chesterfield... J92

Monsieur Pretendant, and Signioro Pretenderillo. M411

To the ladies of Dublin... T380

The triumph of wisdom... T503

Weeks, J. E. The Amazon or female courage vindicated ... W269

[Weeks, J. E.] The cobler's poem... W270

[Weeks, J. E.] Rebellion. A poem... W272

Weeks, J. E. The resurrection... W273

[1745?]

The mishap. A poem... [1745/–] M279

1746

Jan   The bellman of St. James's verses extraordinary. B181

Jan   The Royal Hunters... R311

Jan   The siege of Carlisle... S459

Jan   Volpone disappointed... V110

3 Jan   Hobson, T. Christianity the light of the moral world. H264

21 Jan   [Young, E.] The consolation... Y54

26 Jan   A poetical essay on...happiness... P704

Feb   The British heroe... B479

Feb   Ἑωσφορος: or, the morning star... H147·5

Feb   The female volunteer... F102

10 Feb   Marriage a-la-mode... M110

12 Feb   [Morgan, M.] The Processionade... M457

13 Feb   [Cooke, T.] An hymn to liberty. C414

13 Feb   Henry and Blanche... H146

14 Feb   Thompson, W. Sickness... Book the third... T175

22 Feb   [Pope, A.] Verses upon the late D——ss of M——. P984

22 Feb   Power and patriotism... P1010

24 Feb   An ode on the success of...the Duke of Cumberland. O52

Mar   [Jenyns, S.] The modern fine gentleman. J63

Mar   One thousand, seven hundred, and forty-five... O231

Mar   Short verses, in imitation of long verses... S452

Mar   [Williams, Sir C. H.] An ode from the E---- of B---- to ambition. W487

5 Mar   Horace Of the art of poetry, translated. H314

6 Mar   The Taffydeis... T4

13 Mar   An epistle to William Pitt. E434

30 Mar   An hymn to god. H452

Apr   The art of stock-jobbing... A327

Apr   Barrett, S.   Bucolica Alexandri Popii... B88

Apr   Glass excised... G178

Apr   Lockman, J.   To the...promoter of the cambrick and tea-bills... L224

Apr   Lockman, J.   To the...Earl and Countess of Middlesex. L225

Apr   Past and present... P100

Apr   Scott, T.   Reformation a poem. S148

Apr   The sequel of Arms and the man... S202

Apr   The unembarassed countenance... U2

Apr   [Whitehead, P.]   A new ballad on Lord D--n---l's altering his chapel... W425

7 Apr   [Fortescue, J.] An epistle with some odes... F200

28 Apr   Thompson, W.   An hymn to May. T171

30 Apr   Free, J.   The guardian... F236

30 Apr   The modern fine lady... M373

30 Apr   Orpheus and Hecate... O251

May   The battle of Culloden... B100

May   [Browne, I. H.] The fire side... B517

May   The horse and the flies. H325

May   The Northern monster... N321

May   The tribute of the muses... T478

6 May   On the death of...James Gardiner... O200

9 May   The aloe tree, a tale. A175

June   Adultery a-la-mode... A63

June   Chaucer's Farmer and fryar modernized. C140

June   Modern virtue. A satire. M386

14 June   Britain's ode of victory... B455

28 June   Love's invention, or, the recreation in vogue... L290

July   Barrett, S.   The battle of the giants... B87

July   Liberty: an ode... L171

July   Louis le rampant... L275

July   An ode sacred to...the Duke of Cumberland... O56

July   On the late...John Spencer... O207

July   Pastorella; or, the sylvan muse. P119

9 July   Past and present... Part II... P101

18 July   [Hill, A.] Free thoughts upon faith... H216

Aug   Lockman, J.   An ode, on the crushing of the rebellion... L218

Aug   Newcomb, T.   An ode, presented to...the Duke of Cumberland... N260

Aug   The progress of glory... P1109

Aug   [Smollett, T.] Advice: a satire. S531

Aug   The sugar plantation a poem. S784·5

20 Aug   Achates to Varus... A15

23 Aug   [Williams, Sir C. H.] An ode to the honourable H---y F--x... W488

Sept   H------ss----y to Sir C--- H---- W----s... H346

Sept   [Williams, Sir C. H.] An ode addressed to the author of the Conquered duchess... W486

25 Sept   [Walpole, H.] The beauties... W31

27 Sept   Williams, Sir C. H.   An ode to...Stephen Poyntz... W492

Oct   The country priest... C457

Nov   The compliment... C326

5 Nov   [Walpole, H.] Epilogue to Tamerlane... W32

7 Nov   Hill, A.   The art of acting. Part 1... H210

15 Nov   Chapman, T.   The winter campaign. C117

Dec   The curatical battle for Q. Chappel... C543

Dec   De la Garde, M.   The vision. A poem. D193

4 Dec   A new canto of Spencer's Fairy queen. N117

Arms and the man... A292

[Dering, H.] De senectute. D231

An elegy on...Sir Thomas De Veil... E99

An epistle from D--ct--r R--ck... E367

Fall, J.   The protestants charge against the church of Rome... F43

Godwin, E.   Christian tales... G209

The high mass. A poem... H201

John and Betty. A tale. J68

Macdonald, D.   The apparition of Donald Macdonald's ghost... M2

Macdonald, D.   The saddle put on the right horse... M3

[Maty, M.] Ode sur la rébellion... M139

Neoptolemus. Ode...N34

A new song. Call'd the Duke of Cumberland's victory... N194

Newcomb, T.   An epistle to...the Duke of Cumberland... N252

Nihell, J.   La bataille de Preston. N302·5

Pellieux, —.   Panegyrique de son altesse...le duc de Cumberland. P146

Schomberg, R.   An ode on the present rebellion... S134

The transactions of the Pretender's son... T439

Turnbull, W.   Some verses composed upon...the Jacobites... T556

[1746?]

Allt, W.   The Gibeonites of this day discover'd... A169

A poem on the late rebellion... P624

The Pope and Pretender in a quandary... P760

Rann, —.   A new song... R115

The soldiers praise of Duke William. S548

A song, for the thanksgiving night... S583

Taste. A satire... T44

Bishop, S. Ode...ad honoratissimum Stephanum Poyntz... [1746/50] B231

The heighland man... [1746/–] H204

Wagstaffe, J. A choice of life... [1746/–] W2

1746: SCOTLAND

June [Hamilton, W.] A soliloquy. H18

July 'Mirabello, *Comes de.*' De incarnatione. M271

Oct Graham, D. A full...account of the rebellion ... G235

Ad priscos Scotos...in praelia apud Gladsmuir... A22

Arms and the man I sing. A294

Britain made free... B452

[Dowie, T.] A poem on regeneration... D417

An elegy, inscrib'd to the Duke of Cumberland. E93

An excellent new song: being a brief account of the rebels ... E575

Henderson, A. Cumbrius triumphans carmen... H142

Henderson, A. Expeditio militaris, sive Britannia liberata ... H143

A humble advice to the loyal Scots and English... H393

The Lady Kilmarnock and Lady Balmerino's sorrowful lamentation... L18

A new ballad on the battle of Drummossie-muir... N76

An ode on the birth-day of...William duke of Cumberland. O42

The original and conduct to the Young Pretender... O243

Pibrach Chonald Dui: or Gard'ner's revenge. P268

The rebels bold march into England... R143

A song upon the late victory at Culloden... S600

Teakel, J. An excellent new song... T113

To his grace, James, duke of Perth. T333

[1746?]

A birth-day ode. B225

The contrast. C398

An ode, addressed to...William duke of Cumberland. O20

The sweet William. S793

[Smollett, T.] The tears of Scotland. [1746/50?] S535

A song, to the tune of Auld lang syne. [1746/–] S595

1746: IRELAND

Oct An ode to be performed at the castle of Dublin ... O64

Chivalrie, no trifle... C152

The Christian hero. C166

D'Anvers. A. The invasion, a poem... D37

The fourth ode of the fourth book of Horace... F214

[Jones, H.] Philosophy. A poem... J94

1746: Ireland (cont.)

The landscape. L45

Leixlip: a poem... L103

Merit. A satire... M190

A poem on Mr. Sheridan and Mr. Barry. P572

A serious address to Mr. Cinnick's followers... S219

A Tartarean tale... T43

Weeks, J. E. A rhapsody on the stage... W274

1747

Jan Bally, G. The loves of Hero and Leander... B44

Jan [Hawkins, W.] Female empire... H111

Jan [Ruffhead, J.] The passions of man... R331

Jan [Smollett, T.] Reproof: a satire. S534

Jan Tar water, a ballad... T39

Jan [Winter, J.] Bury, and its environs... W531

6 Jan The rise and progress of sacerdotal sanctity... R213

17 Jan Lucy, a pastoral... L320

Feb Advice to a widow. A76

Feb Aston, —. An eclogue after Virgil's manner... A352

Feb Britannia's triumph... B473

Feb [Fortescue, J.] The expedition... F201

Feb Plain truth: a satire... P474

Feb A poem on our war in Flanders... P574

Feb The vices of the town. V88

14 Feb The glory of France... G184

Mar [Barrett, S.] War, an epic satyr. B89

Mar Thompson, W. Ode brumalis... T172

Apr 'Douglas, W.' The resurrection... D414

Apr Masters, G. A poem...to...the Duke of Cumberland... M136

Apr A poetical representation of the passion of our blessed Saviour. P706

Apr Rich, E. P. Stinchcomb-Hill... R191

Apr Secretary Janus, a dialogue... S178

Apr [Warton, T.] The pleasures of melancholy. W246

2 Apr A poem to the king. P664

17 Apr [Mason, W.] Musæus: a monody... M124

17 Apr The pantheon: a vision. P45

27 Apr [Mallet, D.] Amyntor and Theodora... M44

May [Kidgell, J.] Table-talk. September 1745. K37

May Lovat's ghost... L277

May A panegyrick on the fair-sex. P34

May Plot or no plot... P510

30 May [Gray, T.] An ode on a distant prospect of Eton College. G254

June   Culloden, or loyalty triumphant. C539

June   The ladies choice for new members of parliament ... L12

June   An ode to the inhabitants of Great-Britain... O70

June   [Tattersal, J.] Winter, an ode... T89

June   Verax to Adamia... V27

June   Whitehead, P. Honour. A satire. W414

Aug   [Byrom, J.] An epistle to a friend... B612

Aug   An ode occasion'd by some late successes at sea ... O36

Aug   The solitary. An ode... S551

Sept   [Dodd, W.] Diggon Davy's resolution on the death of his last cow. D362

Sept   [Fortescue, J.] Nature, a poem... F202

Oct   Covent Garden in mourning... C473

Oct   The lord's lamentation... L265

8 Oct   [Johnson, S.] Prologue and epilogue... J85

15 Oct   The Litchfield squabble... L175

16 Oct   A ballad on the taking of Bergen-op-zoom. B33

17 Oct   A race for Canterbury... R7

30 Oct   [Lyttelton, G. *baron.*] To the memory of a lady lately deceased. L337

31 Oct   The accident, a pastoral essay. A5

Nov   [Cawthorn, J.] Abelard to Eloisa. C85

Nov   The downfall of Westminster-bridge... D421

Nov   [Jenyns, S.] An ode to the hon. Philip Y--ke... J65

Nov   On the nature of the most ingenious arts... O216

Nov   The plaid hunting... P470

Nov   Richmond. A vision. R199

Nov   Verses, occasion'd by the sight of a chamera obscura. V57

Dec   The amorous jilt... A216

Dec   The Fustiad; or, cudgel-match... F308

Dec   Gibbons, T. An elegy on...Peter Goodwin... G137

Dec   An ode to...Sir Peter Warren... O74

Dec   Potter, R. Retirement: an epistle. P1006

9 Dec   Dr. Woodward's ghost... D357

The court broker... C464

The cries of the oppressed... C506

Crumbs of comfort for a reverend...lover... C530

Dissenting piety. D334

For the fifth of November, 1747... F182

Gahagan, U. Tentamen de re critica... G6

The glory of...the Duke of Cumberland... G185

[Major, W.] The retirement... M36

The model, or the modern gentleman... M358

To Mr. S-------- M-----, on his turning evidence. T345

[Warter, T.] Shrewsbury Quarry... W242

[*1747?*]

Great Britain's union... G265

Here's coming and going... H150

A new song. On Miss in her teens... N208

A new system of rural politicks... N232

The sailors pleasure before the mast... S15

[Byrom, J.] A genuine dialogue between a gentlewoman at Derby and her maid Jenny... [1747/48] B616

1747: SCOTLAND

Feb   [Hamilton, W.] Contemplation: or, the triumph of love. H14

Don, J. Britain's consolation... D398

Hist: a ballad... H251

An ode on the birthday of...the Duke of Cumberland. O41

A poem, compos'd the second of November, 1747... P525

[*1747?*]

[Hamilton, W.] An imitation of the 137. psalm. H16

1747: IRELAND

Oct   Burroughs, L. An ode to be performed at the castle of Dublin... B591

A congratulatory letter from one poet to another... C345

A day spent in Dublin... D73

A description of the young A-------s cavalcade... D237

The down-fall of the counts... D420

Dunkin, W. Bœotia, a poem... D515

The farmer's yard... F60

The gentleman. An heroic poem. G120

Owens, S. An elegy on...John Lock... O256

A poem, sacred to...Lady Harriot Boyle. P655

The poet's dream. P695

The poets petitions... P709

Shepherd, S. Leixlip: a poem. S400

The swans: a fable... S791

Verses occasioned by the college examinations... V54

Virasel, S. An ode to...Philip earl of Chesterfield... V101

[Young, L.] Utopia: or, Apollo's golden days. Y177

1748

Jan   [Jenyns, S.] The embarass'd knight... J61

Jan   Layng, P. The judgment of Hercules... L79

Jan   [Newcomb, T.] The oracle, an ode... N268

Jan   [Wilkes, W.] Hounslow-Heath... W461

19 Jan Akenside, M. An ode to...the Earl of Huntingdon. A137

21 Jan Scott, T. A father's instructions to his son. S147

Feb Adollizing... A62

Feb Bath. A poem. B93

Feb [Morgan, M.] The 'Piscopade... M450

Feb Shiells, R. Marriage: a poetical essay. S422

Mar [Byrom, J.] Sir Lowbred O---n... B618

Mar Clio. A poem... C239

Mar Emma, carmen...latine redditum. E305

Mar The epistles of Penelope to Ulysses... E436

22 Mar Kenrick, W. The town. A satire. K15

Apr The accomplish'd hero... A6

Apr The after-thought: or, a review of the...fire in Cornhill... A121

Apr [Brecknock, T.] The important triflers... B405

Apr [Parnell, T.] The hermit... P72

4 Apr Provisions for the convent. P1152

14 Apr The courtship. A pastoral... C471

May The hoop-petticoat... H304

May [Morris, R.] Rupert to Maria... M509

May The pantin. A new ballad. P46

May The puppet shew... P1170

May A sorrowful ditty... S602

6 May Thomson, J. The castle of indolence... T181

26 May [Moore, E.] The trial of Selim the Persian... M433

June A hymn for the use of the m—d—n b—ds. H424

June Scelus's ghost... S132

July A syllabus of the animal œconomy... S942

Aug Advice to Mr L---------n, the dwarf fan painter... A83

Aug A congratulatory ode...to the statesman on his travels... C347

Aug The female apologist... F85

26 Aug A paraphrase on the book of Job... P53

Sept Harrison, H. A tragicomic...poem...on the hyperbole... H89

Sept [Kidgell, J.] An answer to the Advice to Mr. L—g—n... K36

10 Sept A poem on...the Duke of Cumberland. P568

Oct McKinstry, H. The glory of Spain subdu'd... M7

Oct The monosyllable If! M402

Oct Musidorus...to the memory of Mr. James Thomson. M570

Oct The peace: a poem... P134

Nov The morning: or, judgment. M469

Dec The art of courtship... A319

Dec The c——t sermon... C536

Dec An ode on the peace... O50

The all-devouring monster... A163

[Byrom, J.] Good people, I, El'sabeth dowager Ad-ms... B617

The congress of the beasts... C369

[Fortescue, J.] Nature a poem... F203

[Freeman, B.] Southampton; a poem... F242

On the peace proclaim'd... O217

Purver, A. A poem to the praise of god. P1178

Simmonds, J. The Wandsworth campaign. S466

The small-pox... S487

Sodoms catastrophe...S543

Stephens, E. A poem on the park and woods of...Lord Bathurst. S750

Venus and Ardelia, a tale. V25

[Wilkes, W.] The prisoner's ballad... W469

[1748?]

Sir Billy Tinsel... [1748/49] S470

1748: SCOTLAND

[Forbes, R.] Ajax his speech to the Grecian knabbs... F184

Ode to...Anne countess of Northesk. O73

[Ramsay, A.] The vision... R103

[1748?]

Ad Gulielmum Cumbriae ducem ode. A20

1748: IRELAND

Charley in the chair. C133

Chetwood, W. R. Kilkenny: or, the old man's wish. C142

The marrow of the Tickler's works... M114

An ode, in honour of his majesty's birth-day... O32

A poem, on Miss Bellamy. P570

A new ballad. [1748/49] N56

1749

Jan The hostages... H328

Jan [Hudson, T.] A naval panegyric... H350

Jan Loyalty triumphant in bonds... L311

9 Jan Johnson, S. The vanity of human wishes... J87

Feb The convent. A tale. C401

Feb England's alarum-bell... E314

Feb Gahagan, U. Mr. Pope's Temple of fame... G4

Feb   Grace. A poem. G234

Feb   Onely, R. Cl. Alex. Popi Messiah, ecloga sacra... O235

Feb   Wright, T. Four pastorals... W570

1 Feb   Gracchus. A poetical character. G233

2 Feb   [Jenyns, S.] Horatii ep. I. lib. II. ad Augustum ... J62

6 Feb   Mason, W. Isis. An elegy. M123

8 Feb   An apology to the town...by J. Nick-all. A270

10 Feb   Gibbons, T. An elegiac poem, to...Isaac Watts... G136

16 Feb   [Gilbert, T.] A satire on all parties. G143

25 Feb   [King, W.] A poetical abridgment... K73

Mar   A new ballad to an excellent old tune... N84

Mar   A tale of two tubs... T31

5 Mar   The magician, or bottle cungerer. M15

20 Mar   A companion to the bottle... C320

Apr   An accurate...encomium on the most illustrious persons... A14

Apr   Jones, H. On seeing a picture of...the Prince of Wales... J93

Apr   [Kirkpatrick, J.] The sea piece... Canto II. K89

Apr   Monsieur Ragoo; or, a squib for the grand f-re-w-rks. M412

Apr   An ode for the thanksgiving day... O25

Apr   An ode to evening... O65

Apr   A poem sacred to...Isaac Watts... P656

Apr   A satyr: in French and English. S46

Apr   Selden, A. Love and folly... S198

Apr   [Thornton, B.] An ode on Saint Cæcilia's day... T249

11 Apr   The Sappho-an... S35

20 Apr   Green, —. An ode to...the Duke of Cumberland. G279

26 Apr   Brown, J. On liberty... B505

May   Browne, M. Sunday thoughts. Part I... B533

May   The Green-park folly... G277

May   Missing, J. A poem to the memory of Isaac Watts. M282

May   Missing, J. Titchfield, a poetical essay. M283

May   Potter, R. A farewell hymne to the country... P1004

May   Rhapsody by John Baptist Felix Zappi... R186

May   Rolt, R. Cambria... R260

9 May   Jane Shore to the Duke of Gloster... J55

19 May   The world in disguise: or masks all... W563

June   Cam and Isis... C6

June   Collins, W. Ode occasion'd by the death of Mr. Thomson. C294

June   [Moore, E.] An ode to Garrick... M431

June   Solomon and Abra; or, love epistles. S553

June   [Tyrwhitt, T.] An epistle to Florio... T591

July   [Dodd, W.] The African prince now in England ... D361

July   Warton, J. An ode occasion'd by reading Mr. West's translation of Pindar. W245

July   [Warton, T.] Verses on Miss C-----s and W-----t. W251

6 July   [Wilmot, G.] Carmen rhythmicum, monachicum ... W517

Aug   [Byrom, J.] The bellman and the captain. B611

Aug   [Byrom, J.] An epistle to a gentleman of the Temple... B613

Aug   A poetical epistle to Miss C--h--y... P702

30 Aug   [Dodd, W.] Zara, at the Court of Annamaboe... D365

Sept   Characters in dancing... C130

30 Sept   A new receipt to tame a shrew. N177

Oct   [Fortescue, J.] A view of life in its several passions... F205

Oct   Rolt, R. A poem, sacred to...Sir Watkins Williams Wynne. R262

Nov   The artful priest... A329

Nov   A ballad. To the tune of Chevy Chase. B39

Nov   The triumphs of bigotry... T506

21 Nov   [Cooke, T.] An ode on beauty... C417

Dec   Mandey, —. A modest occasional ode. M77

Dec   [Missy, C. de] A dialogue between two free electors... M285

Dec   A new song concerning the Westminster election. N198

Dec   A poetic epistle, addressed to Sir George Vandeput. P698

Dec   A roast for a Scots parson... R222

11 Dec   [Jenyns, S.] The 'squire and the parson. J66

An address to the worshipful company of barbers... A57

The barber and fireworks. B64

The belvidere: a poem... B188

The Bristol-wells... B451

A comical history of the Bible and stick... C313

[Cooke, T.] The convert: a poem. C424

A copy of verses made on the publick fire-works... C431

An elegy on...Sir Watkin Williams Wynn... E287

The fan: a heroi-comical poem... F55

Folly triumphant... F177

Harte, W. Part of Pindar's first Pythian ode... H99

Manlius; or the brave adventurer... M81

Mason, W. Ode performed in the Senate-House... M129

A meditation in the fields... M158

No peace for the wicked... N307

An ode on the happy marriage of...Philip David Kræuter ... O47

A pastoral elegy... P103

A slight sketch of some insignificant characters... S486

The speech of...George I. to...Queen Anne... S632

The trimmer trimm'd... T481

[1749?]

A caution to the burgesses... C80

A certain proposal of a certain little tutor... C99

[Forrest, T.] The roast beef of Old England. [1749/–] F198

1749: SCOTLAND

Dec   Forbes, F.   Suite de la satyre de Boileau sur la ville de Paris. F183

Dec   A poem, on the associate synods procedure... P588

Babel inspected. B1

An elegy on the late Mass John T——... E252

[1749?]

Epitaph on Alexander Robertson of Struan. E438

To the memory of Alexander Robertson of Strowan. T381

1749: IRELAND

The chymerical patriot: or, Lucas awake. C149

Clancy, M.   A poem inscribed to...the Earl of Harrington... C214

Clarissa: or, the courtezan. C221

Cock-fighting display'd: or, Lucas cut down. C269

[Cooper, W.] Præhonorabili domino, ———... C428

Cullin, M.   Ode in pacem. C538

A curry-comb of truth for the a————n... C549

The country beau... C448

The extravagant wish... E611

The fire-works. A poem... F145

'Fitzcotton, H.'   A new, and accurate translation of the first book, of Homer's Iliad. F153

The freeman's litany. F241

The horse and the monkey... H326

[Pullein, S.] The eleventh epistle of the first book of Horace, imitated... P1157

A rod in piss for the a---m-n... R249

The school-master's letter... S137

A scourge for the incendiary. S150

The true patriot... T528

The universal coquet: a fable... U16

Virasel, S.   Philander and Aspasia. V102

[1749?]

A new ballad, on a late drubbing... N72

1750

Jan   Truth on all sides... T541

Feb   Kirkpatrick, J.   The sea piece... K90

Feb   A short critical poem on poets and poetry... P476

Feb   The power of beauty: a poem. P1011

Feb   Rams all... Addressed to the satirists... R31

1 Feb   [Jackson, A.] Matrimonial scenes...modernized from Chaucer. J9

9 Feb   [Coventry, F.] Penshurst... C474

12 Feb   Sion comforted; and the methodist reprov'd... S469

27 Feb   The Georgics of Virgil... G129

Mar   Advice to England... Occasioned by the late earthquake... A79

Mar   Age in distress: or, Job's lamentation... A123

Mar   Friendly advice to a child unborn... F268

Mar   [Missy, C. de] Bribery a satire. M284

Mar   The parson preferred. P87

Mar   The coquets: or, a convert and a half... C434

Mar   [Cooke, T.] An ode on martial virtue... C418

Mar   [Cole, J.] To the memory of...Mordecai Andrews... C283

Mar   A poem on the death of...Mordecai Andrews. P605

Mar   A proclamation, a poem. P1103

Mar   [Sampson, J.] The intrigue. A college eclogue. S31

Mar   Verses on the late earthquakes... V64

12 Mar   [Warton, T.] The triumph of Isis... W247

Apr   [Burgh, J.] An hymn to the creator of the world ... B575

Apr   The empty purse... E306

Apr   [Fortescue, J.]   Science: an epistle... F204

Apr   [Hamilton, W. G.] Four odes... H20·5

Apr   An hymn to the deity... H457

Apr   [Morgan, M.] The Scandalizade... M459

Apr   A philosophic ode on the sun... P260

Apr   St. Paul's Cathedral, a poem... S21

Apr   [Thompson, I.] Poetic essays... T165

7 Apr   [Johnson, S.] A new prologue spoken by Mr. Garrick... J83

12 Apr   The military prophet: or a flight from providence ... M231

27 Apr   Smart, C.   On the eternity of the supreme being. S495

May   Damon and Amarillis: a pastoral eclogue... D20

May   False honour: or, the folly of duelling... F46

May   Stillingfleet, B.   Some thoughts occasioned by the late earthquakes. S761

May   Verses to the memory of John Roydon Hughes ... V69

June   Browne, M.   Sunday thoughts. B535

June   An epistle from a royalist to a young lady... E362

June   The marriage of Venus. M112

June   A Newgate eclogue, in honour of...Squire Ketch... N286

June   The prodigal son return'd... P1104

18 June   [Smart, C.] The Horatian canons of friendship ... S493

July   The confession of Peter Hough... C341

July   [Dodd, W.] A new book of the Dunciad... D363

July   [Lockman, J.] Britannia's gold mine; or, the herring-fishery... L211

July   A new ballad, most humbly inscrib'd to a most hon. m——te... N70

July   A summer voyage to the gulph of Venice... S785

10 July   Arnold, C.   Distress. A poetical essay... A313

Aug   Ashwick, S.   The eighth book of the Iliad... A348

20 Aug   An infallible recipe to make a wicked manager of a theatre... I40

Sept   An epistle to...Tho. G-bb-ns, on his Juvenilia ... E418

Sept   The hard-us'd poet's complaint... H48

Sept   [Mendez, M.] The Battiad. Canto the first. M172

Nov   A hymn of thanksgiving for his m————y's return... H425

Nov   A new song sung Wednesday Nov. 16... N215

Nov   Parent, D.   Serious thoughts on death... P63

Nov   The Rosciad. A poem. R268

7 Nov   The quarrel between Venus and Hymen... Q7

22 Nov   [Mendez, M.] The Battiad. Canto the second. M173

27 Nov   Turner, D.   A poem to the memory of... Samuel Wilson... T561

Dec   An epistle to a fellow commoner at Cambridge. E387

Dec   Free, J.   Stigand: or, the antigallican. F237

Dec   The Grinsted ballad. G299

Dec   Newmarket. A satire. N290

Dec   Pandæmonium: or a new infernal expedition... P28

[Bentley, R.] A petition...in favour of Mr. Maclean. B198

Bland, J.   A grammatical version...of the Song of Solomon... B280

Dobson, W.   Paradisus amissus... D344

An elegy sacred to...Samuel Stockell... E247

An elegy sacred to...Samuel Willson... E284

Gutteridge, T.   An elegy sacred to...Mordecai Andrews ... G325

[King, W.] Elogium famæ inserviens Jacci Etonensis... K67

The life and actions of W.S... L179

A new ballad on subsidy treaties... N75

Of the characters of men... O88

Peg T——m's invitation to the...voters of Westminster. P143

Peg Trim Tram in the suds... P144

Peg Trim-tram's defeat... P145

A poem on the earthquake. P612

Rich, E. P.   A poem on Cheltenham beauties... R189

Rich, E. P.   A poem on the Bath beauties. R190

Taylor, C.   Britannia: a poem, inscribed to...the Duke of Cumberland... T101

[1750?]

Collins, W.   The passions, an ode... C295

A new song on the scrutiny for Sir George Vandeput... [1750/51] N210

[Davies, S.] The following verses were composed by a pious clergyman in Virginia... [1750/–] D61

Taylor, C.   The scale, or, woman weigh'd with man... [1750/–] T102

True blue will never stain. [1750/–] T512

1750: SCOTLAND

May   A new song for Thursday the 17th of May 1750. N201

May   A song, in answer to the first part... S584

Sept   Eusden, L.   Hero and Leander... E490

Erskine, R.   A short paraphrase upon the Lamentations of Jeremiah... E459

[1750?]

A monody in commemoration of the 10th of September 1750. M401

1750: IRELAND

Apr   Manners, H.   The linnet and goldfinch... M82

The antisatyrist. A dialogue... A267

Pullein, S.   Scacchia, ludus... P1158

Pullein, S.   The silkworm: a poem... P1159

INDEX OF IMPRINTS

This index includes not only those named in imprints, but also those referred to in bibliographical notes as having advertised books, having entered them in the Stationers' Register, *or having printed them in those cases where the fact has been established. I have added the note (printer) when it appears to be implied by the imprint or established from other sources.*

No attempt was made to record addresses in imprints, but an exception was made for those which seemed unfamiliar. It has therefore been possible to add the addresses of some persons not recorded in the Bibliographical Society's Dictionaries of booksellers and printers (referred to as Plomer), but I have not retraced my steps when I subsequently found that a bookseller or printer was not recorded. The lack of addresses also means that it has been difficult to distinguish persons with similar names and to attribute publications between them with certainty; the user is advised to check the addresses before accepting my identifications.

The dates under which books are entered are those that appear in the imprint, even when advertisements suggest a year later or earlier. In a few cases where the terminal date of a career is affected (as when a publisher died in November, having already issued books with the date of the following year) I have made the necessary adjustment.

Books giving only the place of publication have been excluded, as have those with no imprint but where a place of publication has been suggested; an exception has been made for provincial and foreign publications. Original Scottish and Irish editions (almost always printed at Edinburgh and Dublin) can be traced from those sections of the Chronological Index. Piracies and reprints published there are listed at the head of Scotland and Ireland below.

ARRANGEMENT

		page
London		
	'for the author'	151
	printers and booksellers	152
English provincial		
	'for the author'	184
	by towns	184
Scotland		190
Edinburgh		
	'for the author'	191
	printers and booksellers	191
Scottish provincial		
	by towns	193
Ireland		194
Dublin		
	'for the author'	194
	printers and booksellers	194
Irish provincial		
	by towns	200
Foreign		
	no imprint	200
	by towns	200

LONDON

No attempt has been made to list London editions with no imprint.

'For the author'

Only those works with the specific imprint 'for the author' are included here. Others were doubtless printed for the author, with such imprints as 'London, printed in the year . . .', 'London, printed by . . .', 'London printed, and sold by . . .', or with no imprint at all. The author's name or initials are given when known.

1701	A8 (T.H.), E533 (W.H.), P429 (W. Pittis)
1702	H278 (W. Hogg)
1703	H64 (J. Harris), H71–2 (J. Harris), H134, S457 (J. Shute), W556
1704	K63 (W. King), S226 (E. Settle), S255 (E. Settle), S264 (E. Settle)
1705	S7 (J. Sadler), S9, S258 (E. Settle)
1706	D109 (D. Defoe), U5
1707	D550 (T. D'Urfey), D553 (T. D'Urfey), S240 (E. Settle), S245–7 (E. Settle), S343 (E. Settle)
1708	A366 (P. Aubin), C88, C333 (T—s S—on), S279 (E. Settle)

London: 'For the author' (cont.)

1709 S133 (T. S—), S260 (E. Settle)

1710 F62 (G. Farquhar's widow and children), L178 (G. Liddell), S296 (E. Settle)

1711 S228–9 (E. Settle), S260·5 (E. Settle), S288 (E. Settle)

1712 P189 (J. Perkins), S230–1 (E. Settle), S269 (E. Settle), S324 (E. Settle), S334–7 (E. Settle), S345 (E. Settle)

1713 B374 (N. Brady), S75, S217, S275–7 (E. Settle), S281 (E. Settle), S297 (E. Settle), S338 (E. Settle), S346 (E. Settle), S520 (M. Smith), T66 (N. Tate), T502

1714 B375 (N. Brady), E474 (W.F.), H292 (K.A.), I45, S233 (E. Settle), S270–1 (E. Settle), S298 (E. Settle), S329 (E. Settle), S339 (E. Settle), S347 (E. Settle), S523 (M. Smith)

1715 R209 ('J. C. Whitelock'), R313, S290 (E. Settle), S325 (E. Settle), S678 (E. Stacy)

1716 E482 (T.R.), N40 (H. Nevil), N44 (H. Nevil), S234 (E. Settle), S348 (E. Settle), T548–9 (W. Tunstall)

1717 E604, L153, N41 (H. Nevil), N48–9 (H. Nevil), O213, S251 (E. Settle), S272 (E. Settle), S311 (E. Settle), T430, T550 (W. Tunstall)

1718 D341, H133, K9 (S. Keimer), N42 (H. Nevil), N45 (H. Nevil), O214, S236 (E. Settle), S312–13 (E. Settle), T46 (E. Taswell)

1719 D342, H84 (T. Harris), N46 (H. Nevil), P630, S237 (E. Settle), S314 (E. Settle), S326 (E. Settle)

1720 L263, N11, N43 (H. Nevil), P122, S238 (E. Settle), S315–8 (E. Settle), S349 (E. Settle)

1721 C103 (Mr. Chamberlen), H78 (T. Harris), H87 (T. Harris), I46, S239 (E. Settle), S252 (E. Settle), S274 (E. Settle), S319–20 (E. Settle)

1722 F302, H81·5 (T. Harris), H86 (T. Harris), O215, P628, S250 (E. Settle), S286 (E. Settle), S321 (E. Settle), S331 (E. Settle)

1723 B10 (H. Baker), D71 (W. Dawson), N12, N39 (H. Nevil), S322 (E. Settle), S327–8 (E. Settle), S342 (E. Settle)

1724 B306 (E. Bockett), G290 (J. Greer), N47 (H. Nevil), W120 (E. Ward)

1725/31 F172 (G. Flint)

1726 P992 (T. Pope), W126 (E. Ward)

1727 P649, U31 (T. Uvedale)

1728 G9 (W. Garbott), H406, Q3 (the hon. W.P.)

1729 C492, F231 (P. Fraser), F243 (I. Freeman), L264, P1161–2 (W. Pulteney)

173–? G327 (T. Gutteridge)

1730 H132, H337 (W. Howard), V51 (J.W.)

1730/31 W45 (E. Ward)

1731 C348, C444–7, D445 (R. Drury), H338–9 (W. Howard), T115

1732 B153, C354, H343 (W. Howard), O244

1733 A86 ('for the authoress'), H13 (T. Hamilton), H344 (W. Howard), N278 (T. Newcomb), P484, S183 (R. Sedgwick), S203, V29 (R. Verney)

1734 D560–1 (A. Dutton), G130 (Mr. Gerard), H340 (W. Howard), W42

1735 D43 (J. Danvers), G148 (T. Gilbert), H463, L190, M328 (J. Mitchell), M397 (R. Moncrieff), P69, S109 (R. Savage)

London: 'For the author' (cont.)

1736 B193 (P. Bennet), D191–2 (M. De la Garde), E315, O115 (N.T. deceased), S189, T134 (J. Theobald)

1737 B132, B342 (E. Boyd)

1738 B407, H342 (W. Howard), L324 (G. Lumley), T313

1739 A377 (W. Ayre), B411 (R. Brereton), B538 (W. Brownsword), B568 (J. Burch), C288–90 (M. Collier), C425 (T. Cooke), D359 (J. Dodd), M440 (D. Morgan), T136 (J. Theobald)

1740 B345 (E. Boyd), F75 (D.H.), J10 (A. Jackson), L214 (J. Lockman), L269 (Mr. Lorleach), P67 (B. Parker), W559 (J. Woodman)

1741 L226 (J. Lockman), M118 (T. Martin) M441 (D. Morgan), N334, P546 (C— H—), S4·1 (J. Sacheverell)

1742 D195 (T. H. De la Mayne), M497 (B. Morrice) O107 (M. Ogle), O112 ('Humphry Doggrel'), R210, W67 (false?)

1743 B341 (E. Boyd), C436, D404–6, S451 ('Phileleutherus Britannus'), S490 (C. Smart)

1744 E385, E471, P54, P541

1745 C415 (T. Cooke)

1746 A169 (W. Allt), L218 (J. Lockman), L224 (J. Lockman), L275, M442 (D. Morgan), O200, R331–2 (J. Ruffhead)

1747 C473, H341 (W. Howard), L175–7, M36 (W. Major), M136·1 (G. Masters), R191 (E. P. Rich), R213

1748 E436, W463 (W. Wilkes)

1749 A14

1750 A313 (C. Arnold), C283 (J. Cole), G325 (T. Gutteridge), H48, J9 (A. Jackson), S21, S469, S493–4 (C. Smart)

Printers and booksellers

A——, B——

1714 T480

Ackers, Charles (*printer*)

1728 P410, R18

1729 B531, L270, R20, R23

1732 P1108

1733 L271, S6, T35, W572

1738 V91

Adams, F.

1735 T516

Ager, Simon (near the Royal Exchange, Cornhill)

1707 E272

Alkin, John (Alkins in *Plomer*)

1702 P1148

Amey, Robert

1733 K100

1734 K101

1736 E315

1737 B364, P692

1740 H318

1742 C168

Andrew, Tom, *jun.* (pseudonymous?)

1749 P702

Applebee, John

1727 O114

1739 B338

London (cont.)

Arbor, John (in Fleet-street)
1711　T22

Aris, Samuel (*printer*)
1729　R255

Aris, Thomas (*printer*; at Birmingham, 1741–61?)
1739　T136

Ashburn, D. (near Fleet-street)
1736　V13

Astley, Thomas
1726　G29
1727　M327, M332
1728　T222
1729　P774
1732　D291, D425
1733　B133, S763, T35, W572
1735　M101
1736　S764
1740　S764·5
1742　M120
1750　S766

Atkins, Maurice
1708　T470
1709　T471

Atkins, Timothy (suggested to be pseudonymous in *Plomer*)
1729　O270
1730　D353, O271–2

Atkinson, J.
1709　H320

Atkinson, Thomas
1705　C429
1706　W3
1707　P735

Austen, Stephen
1727　B422, M99
1735　S768
1744　T450

Aylward, J.
1736　T91

B., A. (a fictitious imprint)
1732　Y20

B., E. (near Ludgate; apparently a pirate)
1706　C208, E102, R308, W151

B., J.
1708　T55

B., L.
1731　P1111

B., R.
1717　W327

B., S. (Briscoe, Samuel)
1711　S696–7

'Baalam, printed for, and sold by the tribe of Isachar'
1721　C281

Baber, John (possibly in error for John Barber)
1713　B289, S445

Baddam, B. (*printer*, with M. Carter in Well-Close-square)
1720　C495

Bagnall, John (near Fleet-street)
1709　W241

Baily (unidentified; probably a supplier to chapmen)
1737　W131

London (cont.)

Baker, John (in partnership with R. Burrough, 1707–8)
1702　S741, S744
1707　G10·5, M25
1708　O282, S157–8, T55
1709　H320, S746, T253
1710　C307, C433, D239, F30, F36, H108, H295, I3, L326, M396, N142, N178, P437, S386, S671, T347, T534, W148, W545
1711　C2, F65, N155, P135, P425,
1712　B476, B487, B498·5, C256, T68, V20
1713　B413, C22, D76, F284, P139, P594, P669, T29, T33–4
1714　D226, F151, L181, Q16, S176, T414, W311
1715　E14, S376, S687, T368, W208
1716　H162, H322, O165 (false), T95, W539–41
1717　J97

Baker, S. (apparently successor to John)
1717　A181, B90, B212, N300, T432
1718　A277, E408–9, G152

Baker, St. John (at Thavies-Inn-Gate in Holborn)
1712　W514

Baker, Samuel
1750　H48

Baker, T. (? Thomas)
1715　M500·5

Baker, W. (in the Strand)
1746　A293

Baldwin, Abigail (succeeded by James Roberts, Nov. 1713)
1701　A116, B507, C387, E168, E336, F69, H254, P286, S943, T61–3
1702　A324, B281, H70, H308, P66, P285, P693, P1061, P1156, S41, S294
1703　A362, M534, S661
1704　G202, O168, T105, W574
1705　C336, D84, M70, M533, O14, O168·2, S662
1705/10?　N237
1706　B530·7, F142, G214, P287
1707　E357, S265
1708　I73, O109, P1140, T261
1709　H154, P1115, S849, W288
1710　E347, E519, G217, H196, H315, O219, T19, T507·5, W308
1711　A67, L68
1712　L208, M481, P52, P1073, W384
1713　P627, Q17
1714　C522 (but published 1 Dec 1713; the second edition of 3 Dec published by James Roberts)

Baldwin, R. (possibly the printer in Jamaica, 1719)
1715　P225

Baldwin, R. (in partnership with T. Astley in St Paul's Churchyard; probably Richard senior)
1732　D291

Baldwin, R. (in partnership with J. Jeffreys; possibly Robert)
1743　W62
1746　A327

Baldwin, R., *jun.* (probably Richard Baldwin)
1750　S766

Ballard, Samuel
1704　T579
1705　M70
1718　P483

London (*cont.*)
Banks, A.
  1702 G240
  1707 M134
Barber, John (*printer*)
  1709 C261
  1711 P1089·1
  1712 C262
  1713 B289, C263, H184, S445, S891, T451–3
  1714 S854
  1716 C518
  1718 C519
  1723 P876
Barker, Anthony
  1706 O167
Barker, Benjamin
  1709 D339, W305
  1713 W331
  1720 B598
  1722 B329, B594
  1726 B330, W342
  1727 F176
  1728 B333–4
  1729 B599
  1731 B331
  1732 B595, P95
  1734 B600
Barker, B. & B. (clearly the successors to the preceding)
  1742 B601
  1743 B596
Barnardiston, Joseph
  1744 P54
Barnes, John (*fl.* 1688–1711)
  1705 F152
  1710 B211
Barnes, John (*fl.* 1749–53, at Charing-Cross)
  1750 B534–5
Barnet, C. (in Fleet-street)
  1703 E572
Barnham, Robert
  1701 E241, P293
  1715 S700–1
Baron, Thomas
  1741 S646 (possibly in error for 1751)
Barrington, M.
  1711 D356
Bartlett, M. (apparently Mrs Bartlett)
  1739 B338
  1740 F89
  1741 F90
Bassett, Richard
  1702 P451
  1704 C257
  1705 P443–4
Bateman, John
  1720 J88
  1721 P414·5, P415, W566·5
  1722 W566·7
Bates, Charles
  1702 P1149
  1705 B204
  1706 P64
Bathurst, Charles
  1738 S860

London: Bathurst, C. (*cont.*)
  1739 D201, S920–4
  1741 B351
  1742 K77
  1743 K78
  1744 P541
  1745 P1016, S355, T155
  1747 R191
  1750 S495
Batley, Jeremiah (also Bately, Battley)
  1720 D50, R282
  1721 D52
  1722 W122
  1724 B318, W56
  1731 H476
  1732 N262
  1733 L204, N256–7, N282–3, N285
  1735 N264
Battersby, Robert
  1704 J71
Battersby, Susanna
  1707 A183
  1708 S27
  1720 A184
Beets, A. (over against St. Clement's Church in the Strand; possibly fictitious)
  1729 B165
Bell, Andrew
  1702 D224, F163–4, H375, S524–5, S741, S744–5
  1713 P669
  1720 R282
Bell, E.
  1722 M305
Bennet, Charles
  1735 R257
  1736 R259
Bennet, Thomas
  1702 B130
  1705 P226–30, P247–8
  1706 F104–5
Benson, J. (in the Strand)
  1715 F221
Berington, B.
  1712 T68
Berington, E. (also Berrington; *printer* until 1716 and in 1729)
  1709 T366
  1712 T68
  1716 H155, T548–50
  1717 B561, P763
  1718 E364, F210, H225
  1719 H85, P603
  1729 S80
Berkley, S. (possibly error of transcription for Samuel Buckley)
  1734 F187
Bethel, J.
  1710 P487
Bettenham, James (*printer* from 1725)
  1718 A207–9, H133, P29, S397
  1719 A317, B111, K8, M80, P30, R315
  1725 B81
  1727 W276
  1728 P765, S161

London: Bettenham, J. (*cont.*)
1731	B331
1732	B595
1738	H302
1741	B432–3
1742	B434–6
1743	B596

Bettesworth, Arthur (from 1731–37 in partnership with C. Hitch)
1709	D569
1710	W103–4, W115, W129
1711	W105–9
1712	W110
1713	O254
1714	B267, H144, W116
1715	H145, Y111
1716	H369
1717	B162
1718	B246, J98
1720	C266, R282
1722	B268, W122
1723	W130
1724	W56, W120
1725	P416, Y112
1726	O255, W126
1727	B320
1728	P410
1730	Y171
1736	P411, Y171
1737	W131

Bevins, Edward
1744	P25

'Bickerstaff' (*printer*, at the Black-Boy in Fleet-lane)
1735/–	S857

Bickerton, Thomas
1707	H211
1708	H221, S278, S340–1, T49
1709	S267
1710	P1118
1716	W209
1719	F7, L150, P30, T94, W284
1720	H212, J21, V2–5
1721	A247, M480, M483, M498, M502, T434

Bickerton, Weaver
1729	V61
1730	G315
1734	D473
1743	S201
1744	B522–3, C357, D22, D252
1745	C201, D23, S141, S651
1746	M110

Bickham, George (the engraver)
1727	B175
1743	S451
1745	C143
1750	H48

Bill, John (*printer*, in the Strand; possibly pseudonymous)
1712	T317

Billingsley, J.
1716	W539–41
1718	E408–9
1720	B308–9
1724	F158
1725	F99

London (*cont.*)
Billingsley, S.
1728	R18
1729	R20, R23

Birt, Samuel
1737	P651–2
1738	R276
1740	U26
1742	M193, U27
1746	F200
1747	B89
1748	P568

Blackstone, James, *see* Brackstone
Bland, J. (*printer*, near Fleet-street)
1706	D549

Bland, N.
1725	M484

Bland, Thomas
1706	F84

Blandford, Nicholas (*printer?*)
1726	B143, C47, N315, S819–25, T211–14
1727	R221, S18
1729	S751, S829
1730	P37, T180, T223, T233

Blare, Elizabeth
1706/12?	U3

Blare, Jos.
1702	R307
1720	D505 (false imprint)

Bockett, Elias (*author*)
1730	B301

Bond, *Mrs* (next door to Old Man's coffee-house at Charing-cross; probably not a bookseller)
170–?	H422

Bonwicke, Henry
1705	A333

Boreham, W.
1718	N42, P426, S392
1719	C385, O10, O117, P618
1720	I68, T421
1721	H273, P478, S29

Boreman, Thomas
1734	P968
1735	C443, P969

Botham, W. (*printer*)
1723	B240

Boulter, A. (probably Mrs Boulter)
1713	M174
1714	G125–7, G132, P180, S781
1715	B582, C92, D114, H7, S129, T426
1716	T588, W539–41

Boulter, S.
1715	D114
1716	T588

Bouquet, J. (in partnership with J. Payne)
1749	B533, D361, D365
1750	B534–5, C434, D363, J83, P260, P1011, V64

Bowyer, Jonah
1705	P1101
1707	P244–5
1709	W17
1721	P202

Bowyer, William (*printer*; the work of the elder (who died

London: *Bowyer, W. (cont.)*
27 Dec 1737) has not been distinguished from that of his son who entered partnership 1722)

1706	G11
1710	W561
1711	C64, C66, F106, J99, S775, T467
1713	C62
1714	P275, P944, R297
1715	P946, P975
1716	B232, E348–9, F107, G81–3, T145, W18
1717	D31
1718	G13, O143, S397
1719	B111, P801, P991
1720	R84
1721	P817
1723	P876, P949
1727	S356–7
1728	V14, V113
1729	W353
1730	S88, T103
1731	D272, W345–6
1732	A289, B311, D10, D199, L215, R284, S869–70, S904–7, T479·5
1733	B337, B437, H104, L75
1734	S809, T118, T118·5
1735	J29, J42–3, M164, S562–4
1736	J50, W29·5
1737	J40–1, J48, J51–2, M35, W20
1738	F165, J30, K68–9, P10, T449
1739	B446, K75–6, T428, T562
1740	K74, S571–3, S924
1741	B351
1742	P789–90, S569
1743	P796–7, P865
1744	P819–20, R193
1745	C415, G298, P752, P867–8, S762, V23
1746	P871
1748	P872
1749	B505, P800, P1004
1750	H20·5

Boyd, Elizabeth (*author*; at a cook's shop, the sign of the Leg of Pork and Sausages in Leicester-street, by Swallow-street, St. James's)
1740	B339

Boydel, J.
1739	G276

Brackstone, James (or Blackstone)
1743	P707

Bradford, John (*printer*)
1701	C171
1703	B213, S154
1707	G304, N134, N138
1708	H46
1709	E4, G24
1711	F132–3
1712	A351, S691, S695

Bragg, Benjamin (or Bragge)
1702	A226, H73, H153, L9, R163, S784
1703	D217, F3, N173, 625
1704	C217, C361, D218, S488, T490, T572, V90, W101
1705	B134, B484, B527·1, B530·1, B530·4, C176, C429, D26, D95, D100–1, E355, F97, G40, G215, K105, M414, O168·2, O275, P246, P442, R240, S194, S439, T123, T509, U18,

London: *Bragg, B. (cont.)*
	V104, W68, W72, W82, W90, W123, W172, W575
1706	A113, A122, A177, B530·15, B530·3, D27, D130, D188, D220, D236, D238, E317, F64, H32, H193, J73, L149, O228, P31, P56, T49·5, U5, V21, W150, W164
1707	D536, D539, D550, D553, E263, H211, J110, O208, O226, S530, T67, U12, W91
1708	B530·2, C405, D44·5, E129, H180, J5, L44, S192, T531, W525
1709	C82, C187, M42, P424, P448, P999, S137·5
1710	E147, E353, P178.

'Braggs, B.' (deliberate mis-spelling of Bragg? cf. 'Breggs, B.')
1707	U13

Brasier, Charles
1749	S35

Bray, T.
1732	S794

Bray, William
1716	W209

'Breggs, B.' (deliberate mis-spelling of Bragg? cf. 'Braggs, B.')
1707	U14

Brett, George
1739	T329

Brett, John
1739	C349, D352·5, D441, D551, M226, W379
1740	F89, L291
1741	F90

Brewer, W. (near Thames-street)
1711	M437

Briggs, Richard (or Brigs)
1701	P490
1702	L162

Brindley, John ('James' in *Plomer*)
1729	B531, D411, L270
1730	L95, S88, T236
1731	D383
1732	H54–8, H456, P1106
1733	L325
1734	M377–8
1736	B354·5, H183
1737	C542, K88·5, O101, O240
1738	G310
1739	E345, O35
1744	P541
1745	M8
1747	D414
1749	T592
1750	A348, H48, S761

Briscoe, Samuel
1710	W193, W198
1711	S696–7, W199
1715	S700
1719	M474
1720	W57
1721	W59–60, W128
1722	W122, W136–7, W366
1723	W118–9
1726	W121

Bromage, J.
1749	M432

London (*cont.*)
Brome, Charles
  1703 S663
Brooks, A. (near St. Paul's)
  1730 H396
Brooks, J. (or Brookes, near Fleet-street; ? = James Brooke or Brooks in *Plomer*)
  1714 A114, S724
Brotherton, John
  1720 B141, C266
  1721 W310
  1723 W333
  1724 W56, W334
  1725 A38, W347
  1727 C420, W350
  1732 H54–7, H456, P1106
  1745 M8
Brown, C. (in the Strand)
  1740 H120
Brown, Charles (entry in *SR*)
  1712 C171
Brown, Daniel (or Browne; several persons may be included here; books of 1711, 1715, and 1746 are said to be printed by Brown)
  1702 D224, H375, S741, S744
  1710 W308
  1711 W385
  1712 M481
  1715 S677
  1730 H39
  1740 C138
  1746 P1109
Brown, J.
  175–? J26
Brown, John (*printer*, in the Strand)
  1729 L182
Brown, Jonas (or Browne)
  1714 B267, T140–2
  1715 B245, M233, T137
  1716 B416, H369
  1717 B561, P1172–5
  1718 O54, S372
Brown, Robert (*printer*)
  1747 R191
Browne, C. (near Moorfields)
  1732 B559
Browne, T. (*printer*, in partnership with John Darby)
  1727 B324
Brudenell, J. (*printer*, in Little-Britain)
  1707 S246
'B——tr, A, one who has had expensive experience of the doctor's barbarous practice' (fictitious)
  1714 A78
Buck, T. (in the Strand)
  1739 P711
Buckeridge, H. (*printer*)
  1727 H110
Buckland, James
  1738 V91
  1744 B185, S601
  1745 G135
  1749 G136, P656
  1750 K90

London (*cont.*)
Buckley, Samuel
  1711 B263
  1712 B242–4
  1734 F187(?)
Bullock, Thomas
  1708 G153
Bunchley, Samuel
  1707 B527·4–5, B530·5, B530·9, P191, S155, W75
Burgiss, E. (in the Strand)
  1744 N324
'Burgo, Hugo de' (*printer*, pseudonymous)
  c. 1730 F168
Burleigh, Ferdinando (buried 11 Sept 1714)
  1714 B569, E365, F19, G69–70, H368, O284, S541, T395, T435, T569
Burleigh, Rebecca (in Amen-corner; widow of Ferdinando, married William Graves 1718)
  1714 J8
  1714/17 H317
  1715 B218, C92, D486, H372, L258, P473, R158, S557, V77
  1716 B572, C188–90, D485, G73, H373, L286, O165 (false), P953, T250, T424, T588
  1717 B415, B418, H290, J23, M485–6, P762, P1151, P1172–4, R142, S544
  1718 B420 ('1708' for 1718; but Nov 1717)
Burrough, R. (in partnership with J. Baker)
  1707 G10·5, M25
  1708 O282, S157–8, T55
Bussey, S.
  1725 M569
Buttler, T. (or Butler, near Bernards Inn, Holborn)
  1724 B318
C., B. (in Paternoster Row), *see* Cowse, Benjamin
C., C. (near Fleet-street)
  1703 W50
  1707 J13
C., F. (Francis Clifton?)
  171–? D87 (near Black Fryars)
  1718 H135 (near Fleet-street)
C., T.
  1701 W262 (near Spitle-fields)
  1707 T146
  172– B105 (with H.D. in Fleet-street)
Cailloué, J. (libraire, au coin de Beauford-buildings, dans le Strand)
  1706 L158
Campbell, A. (*printer*; imprint always given as Westminster)
  1726 M321–3, M500
  1727 D328–30, U31
  1728 D234
  1729 B128, P654
  1730 V51
Carpenter, Henry
  1746 B517, C543, M442, U2
  1747 D421, P510
  1748 A83, C536, K36, M402
  1749 B39
  1750 N286, T541
Carpenter, J.
  1742 W484

London (*cont.*)

Carpenter, T. (used in a piracy: possibly pseudonymous)
   1740 H120

Carrett, J. (*printer*, near St. Paul's)
   1714 M14

Carter, Angell (possibly a pamphlet seller)
   1707 F135

Carter, M. (*printer*, in partnership with B. Baddam, in Well-Close-square)
   1720 C495

Carter, William
   1709 C477
   1710 P1118(?), W571

Castle, Edward
   1714 B569
   1716 B572

Catterns, J.
   1739 D487

'Caution, T., at Guild-hall' (pseudonymous)
   1714 T558

Cave, Edward
   1735 B409–10
   1736 E399
   1738 O71, S118
   1742 B365
   1745 M372
   1746 B87–8, L171
   1747 J85
   1750 J82

Chandler, Richard (after 1734 in partnership with Caesar Ward, with branches at York & Scarborough)
   1733 P1044
   1735 S768
   1737 T527

Chandler, Samuel
   1724 E9
   1725 V95
   1726 B335, P1143

Chaney, James (*printer*)
   1738 A133–4
   1746 A5

Changuinon, Francis
   1750 M284

Chantry, John
   1701 O90
   1703 C496
   1705 C475, S194
   1706 E411, T48

Chapelle, Henry
   1739 A377
   1743 L228
   1744 V48
   1745 F257
   1746 L218
   1747 B44, V27
   1750 B534–5, D20, H48

Chapman, Samuel
   1720 P561
   1721 B251, R202
   1723 E416
   1727 S107

Chapman, Thomas
   1707 T144

London (*cont.*)

Charlton, *Mrs*
   1734 M377–8
   1735 B291, T532

Charlton, R.
   1737 H157·2

Chartres, C. (possibly pseudonymous)
   1730 L235

Chastel, Moise
   1746 P146

Chettwood, J.
   1735 R10–12

Chetwood, William
   1713 P627
   1718 M443, P1093, P1171
   1719 B414, P618
   1720 B562, M444, P531, S503, W289–90
   1721 B251, C328

Child, Timothy (or Childe)
   1707 D302, M24
   1710 D303
   1714 W291

Chiswell, Richard
   170–? S639

Cholmondeley, Noah
   1732 P1108

Chrichley, J. (or Critchly)
   1731 C438
   1732 H57, P1106
   1734 C77, M377–8
   1736 C121
   1739 H141

'Church, A., in the Strand' (pseudonymous)
   1731 N141

Churchill, Awnsham & John
   1705 B249
   1706 B238–9

Clark, Allan (*printer*)
   1721 A108

Clark, J. (*engraver*)
   1720 D33

Clark, John (probably distinct from the John Clarkes below, but the division of their work is doubtful)
   1705 W569
   1709 H364, R178
   1714 E528
   1716 R181
   1719 B316–17, P1142
   1720 B265
   1725 R182
   1726 P1143
   1727 O253

Clarke, John (see also John Clark above)
   1722 B329
   1726 M149
   1728 K6
   1729 P774
   1732 C127
   1737 K7

Clarke, John (usually in association with Lawton Gilliver)
   1736 J57, K82
   1737 A321, M521, S757

London: Clarke, J. (cont.)
1738 M255–6, S552
1739 B540, H161·6
Clavel, Robert
1706 B9
Clay, Francis
1718 S372
1720 R282
1722 E405
1733 M84
Clayton, E. (in Goodman's-fields)
1713 M176
Cleave, Isaac
1706 F278
Clements, Henry (also in Oxford)
1708 A369, K61, W518
1710 W561
1711 N297
1711/14 O175
1713 B323, T451–3
1714 P136, Y110
1715 C70, I74
1716 N298
1717 C69, C73, D446–7, H348–9
1718 B319
1719 P137, P249
Clements, S.
172–/3–? E360
'Clevercock, Roger' (fictitious)
1734 K33·5
Cliff, Nathaniel
1714 B267
Clifton, Francis (*printer*)
171–? D87 (C.,F.)
1716 R305
1718 H135 (C.,F.)
1719 G119
1720 A236, D504, T411
Clifton, K. (in Hanging-Sword Court in Fleet-street)
1725 T30
1727 C44
Cluer, John
1713? H435
1714 H444
1717 F39
1720 V2
Cocks, J., *see* Cox, J.
Coderc, J. P.
1728 V114
Cogan, Francis
1732 A289
1736 H183
Cole, H.
1722 J16
Collicoat, J. (near West-Smithfield)
1712/13 E579–80
Collins, Arthur
1709 H320, W568
Collins, Freeman (also at Norwich)
1705 F115
Collyer, Joseph
1744 E465, W453
1745 B8, C12, F178, F257, K47, R141

London (cont.)
Combes, Thomas
1721 C75
1722 B329
Comyns, Edmund (also as Cummins)
1737 W131
1741 P1052
1742 A213
Coningsby, Christopher
1717 S517
Conyers, George
170–? S639
Cook, *Mr* (at the Royal Exchange; clearly related to E. Cook)
1750 B534–5
Cook, E. (or Cooke; apparently the Mrs Cook or Cooke listed separately by *Plomer*, for both are associated with Mrs E. Nutt and Mrs A. Dodd)
1733 F269
1734 K95, M377–8
1735 B291, C52, S179, T532
1737 O240
1739 B338, D359
1744 E449
1747 V57
1748 D181
Cook, F. (in Black-fryars)
1735 F73
Cook, H. (or Cooke)
1731 D285, M292–3
1732 S655–6
Cook, M. (almost certainly in error for E. Cook)
1735 K95
Cook, W. (in the Strand)
1746 L290
Cooke, E. *see* Cook, E.
Cooke, H. *see* Cook, H.
Cooper, Mr (at the Artillery Coffee-house in Chiswell-street; probably not a bookseller's)
173–? G327
Cooper, John (in Fleet-street)
1738 S380
1739 S473
1740 B95·5, C151, O233–4, P465
Cooper, M. (at the Globe in Pater-noster-Row; probably a false imprint and date)
1736 L187
Cooper, Mary (succeeded her husband Thomas who died 9 Feb 1743)
174–? S638
1743 B101, B271–2, B392, B504, C265, C299, D387, D390, D405–6, D471, E7, E17, E485–6, G43, H208, J108, M438, M400, M446–9, M510, P200, P796, P865, P1019, S567, T108, T251, W434, W439, Y41, Y43, Y47, Y55, Y57
1744 A136, B604, C300, C386, E34, E218, G226, H113, H220, J60, K66, O48, P54, P696, P819, S100–1, V52, W243, W412, W435–6, W440, Y35, Y42, Y46, Y48, Y50
1745 A147–8, A309, A322, B84, B230, C215, C267, D75, D322, E421, F150, F270–1, G135, G298, H24, H30, H146, M8, M138, M457–8, M461–6, N345, P752, R206, R266, S762, T173–4, V116, Y52, Y54

London, Cooper, M. (cont.)

1746 A5, B87, B455, B518, C117, C140, C326, C414, D38, D44, D193, E434, F236, H6, H111, H147·5, J63, L171, L218, L224, M373, M386, M457, N260, O52, O56, P50, P101, P119, P704, S459, S531, T4, T171, T175, W31-2, W492

1747 A76, A310, A352, B33, B44, B473, B612, C85, D362, F201-2, G6, G254, J85, K37, L320, L337-8, M124-6, O36, P34, P45, P474, P574, P664, S534, S551, T5, V27, W246, W414

1748 A137-8, A319, B405, B473, B618, C86, C239, F203, F230·2, H424, L339, M7, M127, M433, P1170, S147, Y61

1749 A311, B503, B505, C99, C401, C417, F205, G233, J55, J62, J87, K89, M123, M431, O235, S568, T103, T506, W563

1750 B575, C418, C474, E418, F204, F268, G129, K90, M112, M284, O88, P1104, Q7, S761, T417

Cooper, Thomas (succeeded by Mary, 1743).

1732 A60, W298-301

1733 A77, M563, P705, S204, S714

1734 B393, B554, D324, D352, L3, M416·5, R203, S40, T322

1735 B291, D472, E414, F100, M164, S562-4

1736 A303, B50, B326-7, D323, E132, M165, M308, N305, O246, V121

1737 A152, A212, A305, D408, F213, H419, I49, M376, O89, P877-8, P881-3, P1139, S225

1738 A370, C422, C534, D286, H129, H232, K68-9, M89, M365, P932-5, P973, S806-7, T320

1739 A306, B411, B446, B564-5, C106, C129, C184, C413, D424, G197-8, H228, K75-6, M168, M189, P20, P279, P997, T562

1740 C311, E361, F230, H311, K74, L141, M234-7, M249, M505, M507, M511-3, O68, P67, P615, P703, P1160, T151-2, T428, V74, W380-1

1741 A17, B356, B432-3, B621, C498, D375, E605, F295, G147, J107, M525, N242, N343, P58, P125, R137-8, R140, R242, S394, T257, T555, V99, W312, W438

1742 B434-6, B439, C388, E308, G247, H418, L19, M266, M503, O111-12, O129, P547, P787-90, P1015, S37, S395, W244, Y32, Y36-8

1743 C410, H22, M506, Y34, Y40

1747 T345 (apparently a false imprint)

Coram, Patrick

1741 W372

Corbett, Charles (or Corbet)

173-? M504

1733 P88

1734 L284

1734/- M378

1735 M380

1736 D191-2

1737 C542, K88·5, P551

1739 B338, E601, F47, H141, H245, M225, P79, S83, S725-6, T255, T302

1740 B345, D227, G134, H59, M349, N280, P1147, S166, S652-3, T37, T499

1741 C128, F120, F123

1744 B340, E449, I72

1746 H325

1747 O216, P706, R199, W461

London, Corbett, C. (cont.)

1748 A6, H304, O50

1749 B361, T249

1750 C481, E387

Corbett, M.

1709 D569

Corbett, Thomas (or Corbet)

1716 B226

1722 B563

1731 H388

1732 H456

Cowper, T., see Cooper, Thomas

Cowse, Benjamin (terminal date 1723 in Plomer; the later Cowse or Couse in Paternoster Row is possibly a descendant)

1715 W326, W329

1721 D418

1742 B157

1743 J109, Y16

1744 C390, D326, Y31, Y49-50

Cox, H. Shute (in partnership with Richard Manby)

1745 V23

1749 C294, P1004

1750 H20·5, P1005

Cox, J. (or Cocks)

1735 C11, M371

Cox, N. (in Story's Passage, going out of St. James's-Park)

1721 B108

1724 H169

Cox, Nicholas

1702 L305, O166

1704 U33

1705 J72

Cox, Thomas

1719 A279-80

1720 R282

1731 R327

1732 D425

1733 S6

Cramphorn, J. (or Cramphorne; printer, in Fleet-street, 1712; Snow-hill, 1714)

1712 D2

1714 T479

Creake, Bezaleel

1717 R142

1723 E416

1727 B347, F119

1729 C167, H403, S518

Critchly, J., see Chrichley, J.

Crokatt, James

1727 C293

Croskill, Richard

1706 L104

'Cross, C., near Westminster' (apparently Charing Cross; pseudonymous)

1714 A74-5, A315, D259, J56, M159, M538, P1036

Crouch, Samuel

1706 S634

1707 E420

1711 S636

1712 G216

Cruden, Alexander

1735 M307

London (*cont.*)

Cruttenden, R.
  1720 R282

Cuff, John (optical instrument maker)
  1747 V57

Cummins, *Mr*, *see* Comyns, Edmund

Curll, Edmund (also at Tunbridge Wells. His son Henry below apparently acted for him in 1727)
  1706 L149
  1707 B315, G289
  1708 B257, O282–3
  1709 H239, H285–6, H320, R287
  1710 D437, F42
  1712 C245, C250, C515, D338, M394, R280–1, R333, S369, T60, W110, W255
  1713 A24, H244, O171, O287, R176, S373–4
  1714 H144, O284, Y74
  1715 B94, H145, O288, R303, S489, S541, W208, Y76–7, Y111
  1716 F74, O165, P978–9
  1717 A190, A193, A215, B418–19, B425, B477, E420·5, J23, N261
  1718 A188, A200, A204–6, L288–9, N275, P1094, S375
  1719 A194, A202, B424, B430, P8
  1720 A331–2, B141, C97, C192, C251, C266, N270, P9, R43, R282, S706–10, S712–13
  1721 B431, F223–4, M104, S715
  1722 B532, P730, R264·5
  1723 C476, K12
  1724 D60, H107
  1725 Y112
  1726 P992
  1728 B169, S542
  1729 G204 (false imprint?)
  1730 B315·5
  1733 J116, R285
  1736 B524, J25
  1737 B142
  1741 C394, Y115
  1744 B191
  1746 A15

Curll, Henry (or Curle; the son of the preceding)
  1727 C274, F227, J24, P128, T427
  1728 H275 (for 1727)

Cuxon, J.
  1718 S23

D., B. (in Fleet-street)
  1702 R164

D., B. (Benjamin Dod)
  1738 R276

D., G. (*printer*)
  1735 S444

D., H. (with T.C. in Fleet-street)
  172– B105

D., J. (*printer*; John Darby?)
  1710 O286
  1714 H368
  1716 H369

D., J. (probably J. Dormer)
  1733 Q2

D., W. (*printer*; William Downing?)
  1706 L149

Darby, 'Captain'
  1701 D153

London (*cont.*)

Darby, John, *senior* (*printer*)
  1701 P597

Darby, John, *junior* (*printer*)
  1707 B498, H74
  1709 S746
  1710 E309, O286, T19
  1711 F65
  1713 P669
  1714 H368
  1716 D485, H369, R253
  1720 R282
  1727 B324

Darrack, Thomas (*printer*)
  1709 A218
  1710 M396

Davidson, Joseph
  1740 D315–16

Davies, Charles, *see* Davis, Charles

Davies, T.
  1738 M18–19

Davis, A. (near St. Paul's)
  1727 K92

Davis, Charles (or Davies)
  1729 V14
  1731 C141
  1732 L215
  1741 F21
  1744 R193
  1749 B505

Davis, D. (*printer*, in Fleet-street)
  1712 T523

Davis, J. (in 1749, near St. Paul's)
  1731 S475
  1749 B64

Davis, T. (despite the varying addresses, the works listed here are all of a similar popular style)
  1742 B158 (in Shorts Gardens)
  1743 D495, E50 (in Fleet-street), E110 (in Black-horse-alley in Fleet-street)

Davis, Thomas
  1706 H269

Davis, W. (*printer*, near Cornhill)
  1714/15 T341

Dawks, Ichabod (*printer*)
  1702 C356

Deacon, Bridget
  170–? P993
  1702 P1149–50, R317
  1708 M548

Deacon, S. (possibly successor to Bridget in 1708)
  170–? O239
  1708 D543

Deeve, John
  1701 C172, F273, F275

Delage, J. (? *printer* of French works, dans Stationer-Court)
  1702 E41, T107
  1703 L4
  1704 H385
  1705 H386
  1708 E40
  1717 R228

Denham, W. (*printer*)
  1713 S75

London (cont.)
Dicey, Cluer
  174–?   T567
Dickenson, J. (in Witch-street)
  1733   W427–8, W431
  1734   S177
Dickenson, W. (in Witch-street; his relationship to the preceding is obscure, and possibly this imprint is false)
  1733   W426
Dickinson, B. (or Dickenson; apparently specialized in engraved works)
  1732   B52, H54–7, H456, M199, P1106
  1733   B48
  1735   C136, F101
  1736   F199
  1747   C473, L175–7, R7
  1748   G4, P1152
  1749   A270, C137, C320, M15, M17, P22, R222
  1750   M231
Dicks, J.
  1731   C104, N159
Dilly, W.
  1749   P656
'Dob, A.' (false imprint, meant for Anne Dodd)
  1729   P774–5
Dod, Benjamin (or Dodd)
  1738   R276
  1741   R277
  1742   E429–30
  1744   R279
Dod, *Mrs* (at Westminster; possibly Anne Dodd, but this earliest appearance at Westminster is not recorded)
  1710   S172
Dodd, *Mr* (*printer*; probably Nathaniel)
  1722   G113
Dodd, Anne (It is not certain that this entry represents one person)
  1713   S891–3
  1714   B184, S854, T435
  1715   H451, P650
  1716   W258
  1717   F23, W259
  1718   G172, J98
  1719   R244
  1720   B265, B308–9, J34–5, M309–11
  1721   H136, J27, J36, W310
  1722   P1154
  1723   B10, B19, N9, P197
  1724   F158
  1725   B209, F99, F288
  1726   B143, C47, N315
  1727   A179, O114, S18
  1728   B541, F122, G223, L172, P764–8
  1729   B203, B544–7, C375, F243, P654, P771–3, P776
  1730   C39–40, D477, F76, L95, V51
  1731   C438, D383, D488–91, H462, O209, P85, P1111
  1732   H54–8, H456, O183, P1106
  1733   A326, B48, B86, C203, F78, N38, P886–7, R285, S81, T126–7, V39–41
  1734   D229, H474, K95, M377–8
  1735   B291, C11, C52, D409, G148, M270, P886, T532, V44–5
  1736   E399, H183, M381, S189

London: Dodd, A. (cont.)
  1737   G283, G285, O101, O240, P692, S460, V65
  1738   A133–4, G287, G310, P59
  1739   A377, B338, D359, E345, O35.
  1740   J10, P602
  1741   F90, M355, P592, P1052, S617
  1742   A213, B365
  1743   P590
  1744   C28, E449
  1745   H30, M372, S355
  1746   O207, O231, P100
  1747   C539, P574, P664
  1748   A62, D181
Dodd, Benjamin, *see* Dod, Benjamin
Dodd, N. (at the Peacock, without Temple-Bar; probably Nathaniel, husband of Anne)
  1717   M482
  1722   G113
Dodsley, Robert
  1735   E410
  1736   D15, L213, L220, S116
  1737   B122–3, G190, H116, O100, P877–8, P882, P955–7, S102, S460
  1738   B488–90, D376, G194–5, J76–9, O92, O94, O104–5, P938, P982, S118, S756, T254, V91
  1739   E426, G196, J81, N341, O91, O95, O106, S104, W417–18
  1740   N81, P412, W215
  1741   A325, B356, D469–70, G232, N343, P58, S394, W438
  1742   D387, M503, P418, S395, W244, W358, Y24–6, Y32, Y36–8
  1743   B45, B392, B504, C265, D390, D471, P414, W434, W439, Y28–30, Y34, Y40–1, Y43, Y47, Y55, Y57
  1744   A136, A139–42, B185, C300, E218, F98, V52, W243, W440, Y31, Y35, Y42, Y46, Y48–9
  1745   A322, B84, B502, C215, C267, C427, D16, H146, K88, M8, M439, N345, O67, R206, T173–4, T416, W245·5
  1746   C117, C414, E434, F236, H452, S491, T171, T175, W32, W492
  1747   D414, G254, J85, L320, M124–6, P45, R191, W246, Y59
  1748   A137–8, M127, S147, V25
  1749   B503, C417, J55, J62, J66, J87, M123, M130, W563, Y60
  1750   C474, G129, J82, S495, T417, Y64–5
Dormer, J.
  1733   F91, M69, N127, Q2
  1734   C285, C468, F26, N319, S728, T323, T473
Dormer, T. (*printer* in 1735)
  1732   L279, O82, W374
  1733   R136
  1735   P69
Dove, N. (writing-master, published his own work)
  1743   P1113
Downes, R.
  1735   C11
Downing, Joseph (*printer*)
  1709   H423
  1710   H429
  1711   H430

London Downing, J. (cont.)
  1712 G162·5, S456
  1713 H436
  1716 G162·6
  1717 N299
  1718 P483
Downing, William (*printer*)
  1704 D218
  1706 L149
  171–? C272
  1720 W58
  1721 W117
Draper, Somerset
  1744 P243
  1746 B88
  1748 E305
Drury, Samuel
  1702 J11
Du Bosc, Claude
  1741 F21
Duke, J.
  1733 H44
Duncan, John
  1743 B205, E407, S201
Dunoyer, H.
  1750 H48
Dunoyer, P.
  1717 R228
  1719 G1
Dutton, J. (*printer*, near Fleet-street)
  1708 N287
  1709 F82
  1710 N135
Edlin, Thomas (*printer*)
  1720 J35
  1721 B108, B536, J27, J36, L253, M502, P141
  1723 C54, J28, J39
  1728 H333
  1730 B343–4, B349–50, L96
  1731 B348
Edwards, David (*printer*)
  1701 B34–5, O44–5, P431
  1702 R163
  1704 E179
Edwards, Mary (in Fetter-Lane)
  1707 F300, J12
  1708 W85
  1710 W87
Eldridge, T. ('who frames and sells all sorts of map, prints, and almanacks')
  1746/– W2
Ellis, William (*author*, at the Queen's head, the corner of Crown-court in Grace-church-street)
  1709 E296
  1723 E292, R263
Evans, J.
  1746 E367
Everingham, Elinor (*printer*)
  1713 T544
Fabian, Mary
  1701 T574
Falstaff, William (possibly a pseudonym)
  1750 E362

London (cont.)
Farmer, Daniel
  1738 M365
Fawcet, Francis
  1705 B527·1
Fayram, Francis (or Fayrham)
  1723 W130
  1728 B334
Fayram, Robert (entry in *SR* only)
  1719 Y100
Feales, W.
  1732 R284, R288
Feltham, Anthony
  1706 L146
Fenner, Mary
  1743 B272, D366
Fisher, J.
  1735 V44
'Flame, *Lord*' ('at Hurlothrumbo's Head, in the Strand'; fictitious)
  1741 B156
Fletcher, Stephen (in Westminster Hall; also in Oxford)
  1727 D66
Flower, T.
  1735 W547
Ford, Richard
  1720 R271
  1735 R183–4
Foster, G. (at the White Horse, on Ludgate-Hill)
  1741 G302
  1743 D494, J67
  1747 S178
Foster, Mark
  1713 R175
Fournier, D. (*print seller?*)
  1747 G184
Fowler, William (in Hanging Sword Court, Fleet Street)
  1727 B27, L71
Fox, Joseph (from 1734 in parternship with his son, probably also Joseph)
  1707 E420
  1715 D114
  1716 T588
  1736 O80
  1744 C28
Fox, T.
  1747 A216, C464
  1749 H328–9
France, W. (near Leicester Fields)
  1737 K34
Francklin, Richard (or Franklin)
  1718 A207–9, L288–9
  1719 A317
  1720 A196–8, A210
  1721 C328
  1722 A187
  1723 A192
  1724 A199, A211, B318
  1725 M344
  1730 C469, T498, T510
  1744 M424
  1746 C414, M427
  1749 M428

London (*cont.*)
Freeman, A. (probably pseudonymous)
  1747 C154–5
Freeman, S. (possibly pseudonymous)
  1750 G299
Freer, George
  1746 S532
Friend, John (in Westminster-Hall)
  1711 L307
Fuller, John
  1750 A123
Fullum, T.
  1742 O39·5
G., J. (*printer*)
  1702 B312
G., P. (Gwillim, Philip)
  1710 C502
G., R.
  1708 E603
Game, Thomas
  1733 P720
Gardiner, S. (in the Strand; pseudonymous?)
  1733 D320
Gardner, D. (or Gardiner)
  1733 J95, P720
Gardner, E.
  1735 S24
  1749 G136, P656
Gardner, Thomas (engraver)
  1743 P1113
  1749 P1114
Gardner, Thomas (*printer*)
  1738 S756
  1739 D424
  1740 L127
  1742 D195
  1746 N34
  1748 W463
Gardyner, J. (*printer*)
  1704 P733
'Garlick Pinch, Mounsier de, at de Tree Flying Frog, in Spiter de Field' (fictitious)
  1708 E313
Gaylard, *Doctor* (*printer*, in Great-Carter-lane near Doctors-Commons; learned compositor with Bowyer, 1732)
  172– P1116
Gent, Thomas (*printer*; subsequently at York)
  1711 N123, R316
  1724 G290
Gibbons, Anthony (*printer*)
  1733 S203
Gibbs, Jacob
  1723 B109
Gilbert, Stephen (*printer*)
  1711 F132–3
  1722 S331–2
  1723 E274 (in partnership with R. Phillips)
Gilliver, Lawton
  1728 P1122
  1729 B383–7, J100, L313, P773, P777–9, P781
  1730 B83, H98, L217, N248, Y82, Y117
  1731 B391, H462, M251, P908–12
  1732 D567, L333–5, P923, W360–2

London: Gilliver, L. (*cont.*)
  1733 B396, L328, M51–3, P886–7, P920, P925–6, S34, S81, S113, W558 ('Gulliver')
  1734 D47, D384–5, M58, P802, P850–2, P893–4, P961, S105, S114, S841, T456–8
  1735 B496, C52, D381, H93–4, M253–4, M258–9, P785, P917, P964, S115, T459–60, Y81
  1736 B394, B520–1, D15, H97, H183, J57, K82, M147, M434, P411, P786,
  1737 A321, M521, P965, S460, S757
  1738 M255–6, S552
  1739 B538–40
  1740 D566
  1741 T449
  1744 E217
Glenister, Thomas (entered copies to Tonson in *SR*)
  1714 P206
  1715 T281
Goadby, Samuel (partner with Mrs Vertue)
  1750 C283
Godfree, J. (in Fleet-street, pseudonymous?)
  171– L300
Goodall, T.
  1706 P290
Goodwin, H. (*printer*, in the Strand)
  1711? F134
Goodwin, M.
  1701 A253
Goodwin, Timothy
  1705 L169
  1707 E420, I20
  1712 R167
Gorden, George (*printer* of a piracy)
  1729/– S866
Goreham, H.
  1740 G141, S78
  1742 L317
Gosling, Robert
  1712 C245, R333, T60, W110
  1713 A227, I41, N269, P526
  1714 O31
  1715 M551
  1716 W18
  1717 B377
  1720 H218
  1737 W20
Gouge, J. (or Goudge)
  1707 P998
  1709 W288
Gover, J.
  1733 K33
Graham, Josiah
  1738 M365
  1739 M540
  1741 B189–90
Grantham, J.
  1705 N37
  1706 B530·15
  1713 T502
Graves, *Mrs* (apparently succeeded John Graves)
  1728 G223
Graves, John (succeeded by Mrs Graves in 1728?)
  1711 P806
  1716 H369

London: Graves, J. (cont.)
1718   S507 (in St. James's Street)
1720   C266, S500
1721   B152, C328, E368, W310
1723   E496, F149
1725   M484
1727   A179
Graves, W. (in Paternoster Row)
1718   P1093, S507
Gray, John
1728   M324
1729   R14
1733   C107
1734   C108
1735   R183
Gray, Thomas (in Exeter-Change)
1738   M490
Green, C.
1704   F252
Green, Thomas
1728   N10
1733   H43
Greg, G.
1730   R214
Griffith, E. (possibly Elizabeth, partner of Thomas)
1722   P1154
Griffith, G.
1746   N232
Griffith, Thomas (or Griffiths, at the London Gazette, Charing-Cross)
1719   M291, S505
1720   S500
1721   M303
Griffiths, J.
1749   N177
Griffiths, Ralph
1748   A121, K15, M570, S422
1749   S553
1750   S31
Griffiths, T., *see* Griffith, Thomas
Guess, William (near Temple-Bar; pseudonymous?)
1734   E359
Guest, C.
1730   C231
'Gulliver, *Captain*, near the Temple' (pseudonymous; for Lawton Gilliver?)
1730   S883
Gulliver, L. (pseudonymous? – or in error for Gilliver)
1733   W558
Gunning, Richard (*printer*)
1713   F192–3
Gussen, J. (*printer*, in partnership with J. Haberkorn, in Gerrard Street)
1749   O47
Guy, Thomas
1709   R179
Gwillim, Philip
1710   C502
Gyles, Fletcher (also Giles, according to *Plomer*)
1729   V14
1732   M142
1734   P11
1736   M147, P13, P15
1738   P10

London: Gyles, F. (cont.)
1739   P20
Gyles, T. (in Holborn; probably in error for F. Gyles)
1733   N291
H., J. (*printer*)
1711   S636
1712   D294
1717   S517
H., J. (in Sword and Buckler Court, on Ludgate Hill; probably J. Huggonson)
1742   S126
H., T. (*printer?*, in Black-fryars)
1711/12   W388
H., T. (in West Smithfield; probably Thomas Harris)
1742   M154
H., W. (*printer*)
1711   T364
1716   P482
1720   E259
Haberkorn, John (*printer*; in 1749 in partnership with J. Gussen)
1749   O47
175–   P19
Harbin, Richard (*printer*)
1717   C185–6, M482
Harding, John
1711   W108–9
1712   W110
Harding, Samuel
1732   D425
1738   R276
1750   H48
Harper, Charles
1701   W325
1704   W328
1705   W332
Harper, John
1743   M400
Harris, Benjamin (*printer*)
1701   A233, H61
1702   B92, H60, S549, V107, W37
1705   K2
Harris, Benjamin, *junior* (*printer*, in Cornhill; succeeded by his brother Vavasour)
1711   N332
1715   H62
Harris, George
1712   A69
Harris, J. (near St. James's Bagnio)
1717   W578
1725   B209
Harris, James (*printer*, 'near Dr. Cimmons [!]')
1734   B229
Harris, Mary
1734   F88, G130
1735   W547
Harris, Thomas
1742   M154, W313
Harris, Vavasour (at the Golden Boar's Head, Grace-church Street; successor to Benjamin junior; previously in Bristol)
171–?   K4
Harris, W.
1730   D477–8, L95

London (cont.)

Harrison, J.
1715 D114, H451, S129
1716 H155, P505, T588, W539–41
1717 F23, H152·5, P1151, R142
1722 P1154

Harrison, Richard
1706 E317

Harrison, Thomas
1710 H197
1711 W278
1713 Q17

Hart, John
1746 H201

Hart, William (*printer*)
1713 B548, E581

Harvey, William
1708 P608

Hawes, William
1706 N13
1709 M267

Hawkes, Will. ('courier', with Tom Ponder)
1705 H125

Hawkins, E.
1701 A182
1702 B579

Hawkins, George
1735 M164, S562–4
1738 H302, K68–9
1739 W357
1740 K74, T428
1741 B351
1742 K77
1743 H22, K78, S567
1744 Y50
1745 H24, Y52, Y54
1746 B518
1747 N117, S551
1748 Y61
1749 S568, Y62

Hawkins, J.
1738 M188, W30

Haywood, Elizabeth
1744 E449

Hazard, Joseph
1741 P546

Head, M.
1731 R155

Heathcott, William
1710 W87

Henchman, William (also Hensman, Hinchman, according to *Plomer*)
1705 F115

Henry, David
1749 N177

Hett, Richard (in partnership with J. Clark, 1725–27)
1725 R182
1726 P1143
1727 O253
1735 C273, R183–4
1738 V62
1745 R332·5
1747 D414

London (cont.)

Hill, C. (in Cheap-side)
1726/30? P271

Hill, E.
1736 E400 (near St. Paul's)
1737 P899–901 (in White-Fryers, Fleet-street)

Hillier, Nathaniel
1707 S419·5

Hills, Henry (*printer*)
170– P726
1701 E155
1702 H149
1705 H247
1705/– R188
1706 B5, C209, D112
1706/08 B447, C235
1707 I39, T266
1708 B99, B259–61, B530·84, B577, D105, D121, D168, D449–50, F171, G90–1, G94, I51, L244, P239, P441, T57, T262, W84, W526
1708/09 P494
1708/10 S613
1709 A39–40, B177, B256, B262, B527·9, B530·86, B552, C19, C79, C83–4, C248, D113, D214–6, D307–10, D455, D458–60, E5–6, F141, F248–9, F274, G23, G92, G221, G230, H240, H287–8, H321, H334, H365, L245, M43, M267, O252, P234–5, P240–1, P481, P495–7, P536, R197, S222, S388, S390, S435–6, S441, S664–5, S801, S852, W23, W71, W102, W152–3
1709/10 P644
1710 A33–4, B129, B171, C319, C433, D213, D395, D461, E521, G231, H413, J53, P211–14, P690, R223, S540, S614, S641, S718, S802–3, T347, T497, T500, U25, W86, W148, W458·5
1711 L274, W278
1712 C351, W281

Hills, P. (in Cornhill)
170– L16
1706 D131

Hinchliffe, William (elsewhere as Hinchcliffe)
1714 H243, N15
1715 H367
1716 B408
1717 G295
1718 G296
1719 F225
1720 R273
1725 R182
1727 B324
1728 P410
1731 C438
1735 C11
1736 P411
1740 P412

Hinde, Andrew (or Hynde; *printer*, near Fleet-street)
1710 C467, L143, T482
1711 T148
1716 P756
1719 T533

Hinde, Luke (in partnership with T. Sowle Raylton)
1741 F281
1749 E303

London: Hinde, L. (cont.)

Hinton, John
- 1746 P1010
- 1747 G6, M136
- 1750 A79

Hitch, C. (from 1731–37 in partnership with A. Bettes-worth)
- 1731 Y171
- 1736 P411
- 1737 W131, Y171
- 1740 P412
- 1741 Y115
- 1743 P419
- 1744 R193
- 1750 T165, V69

Hodges, James (knighted 1758)
- 173–? P996
- 1737 W131

Hodgson, J. (*printer*, in Fleet-street)
- 1739 W421

Hodgson, Thomas
- 1702 L164

Holbeche, A.
- 1731 S609

Holder, P.
- 1734 K97, P126

Holland, James
- 1705 T84, T86
- 1713 T81
- 1714 T50

Hollingworth, Mary
- 17–– J106

Holloway, Edward (*printer*)
- 1718 B468 (near Fleet Ditch)
- 1734 A89, P755 (near Hungerford-market)

Holloway, N.
- 1733 P262

Holmes, John
- 1713 E375

Holt, Michael (*printer*, in Fleet-street)
- 1713 B289, S445, T25

Holt, S. (*printer*)
- 1716 K10

Hooke, John (also Hook)
- 1714 P1038
- 1715 W326, W329
- 1716 W330
- 1720 C192, R282
- 1722 W122
- 1723 N254
- 1728 G9
- 1730 F117

Hooper, J. (apparently fictitious; possibly a deliberate mis-spelling of T. Cooper, used in a piracy)
- 1740 W382

Horne, Thomas
- 1710 P994

Hotham, Matthew
- 1722 W122

How, John (*printer*)
- 1701 W49, W141, W163
- 1702 H153, L9, S784

London: How, J. (cont.)
- 1703 D217
- 1704 L137
- 1705 G245
- 1706 H193, U5
- 1709 C55
- 1710 W142
- 171– W143–4

How, L. (in Petticoat-lane)
- 174– T568
- 1750 E247

Howlatt, T. (*printer*, in Silver Street, Bloomsbury; probably the Howlett in *Plomer*)
- 1719 P630

Hubbard, J. H. (in the Old-Bailey)
- 1742 D244, P791–2

Huddlestone, S. (or Huddleston)
- 1719 A241, P903
- 1722 P1154

Huggonson, J. (*printer?*)
- 1733 S888
- 1734 T474
- 1736 B443
- 1737 B444, C412
- 1741 B155, L64–5, M156, M262, P1181, S484, S733
- 1742 C236, C497, D70, F95, H40, M382–3, S126, W456, W546
- 1743 N310

Hughes, Joseph
- 1704 T490

Hughs, John (*printer*)
- 1732 O82
- 1733 O79
- 1734 E397
- 1735 S39
- 1736 B313, T134
- 1738 B488–90
- 1742 P418
- 1743 P414

Hughs, W. (*printer*, in Fleet-street)
- 1743 B457

Hynde, Andrew, *see* Hinde, A.

Ilive, Abraham
- 1741 B192

Ilive, T. (*printer*)
- 1709 S419·6

Illidge, Samuel
- 1704 M76

Innys, John (1718–25 in partnership with William Innys)
- 170–? S639
- 1718 S397
- 1719 B111
- 1724 B196–7
- 1725 B195

Innys, William (1718–25 in partnership with John Innys)
- 1718 S397
- 1719 B111
- 1724 B196–7
- 1725 B195
- 1730 A365, V18

London: Innys, W. (cont.)
1733 B337, H104
1739 C425
Iorns, J., *see* Irons, J.
Irons, J. (also Iorns)
1733 S59–60
1734 C1
Isted, John
1704 S488
J., G. (*printer*)
1709 W568
1719 P249
J., R. (*printer*; possibly Richard Janeway)
1707 B530·6
'Jack-about, Will' (pseudonymous)
1713 B514·5
Jackson, Andrew (also as author)
1740 J10
1750 J9
Jackson, David
1714 B267
Jackson, E.
1708 T315
Jackson, J. (in St. James's)
1725 H106
1726 P992
1728 L172
1729 L292, S518
1730 F117, S16–17, T563
1731 C438, P421
1732 D481
1733 C107, L325, P620
1735 C52, D472
1737 D483–4
1741 P1052
1742 A213
1750 B534–5, H48
Jackson, J. (at the Golden Lion near St. Paul's)
1746 V110
James, George (*printer*)
1715 P538
James, J.
1735 H13·2–·5
James, W.
1732 C164, V8–10
1733 E598–600
Janeway, J.
1732 C354, M473
Janeway, Richard (*printer*)
1701 I19
1703 E32
1704 C361, S488
1707 B530·6
171–? G164
1713 T589
Jarriot, T. (*printer*)
1714 C391
Jauncy, Thomas
1720 F54, L51–2, M304, P242, R77, R81, R106–7, S362, S367–8
1720/21 R92
1721 B251, H222–3, J18, M319, R87
Jeeves, S.
1715 C98

London (cont.)
Jefferys, J.
1743 W62
1746 A327
Jeffries, Francis
1734 W61
1735 M557–8
Jenkins, J. (*printer?*, in the Strand, or near Ludgate)
1733 P1117, R135, U23
Jephson, Charles (*printer*)
1737 S460
'John of Gaunt' (near Charing Cross in the Strand; pseudonymous)
1749 A329
Johnson, J. (1715, near Charing-Cross; 1731, near London Bridge)
1715 M191
172–? C484
1731 D41, J104
1737 Y14
Johnson, Robert
1701 J53·5
Johnson, T.
1742 F48 (near Christ's Hospital in Newgate-street)
1746 N322 (in the Strand)
Johnson, Thomas (*printer*, near the Royal-Exchange)
1706 E57
Johnson, Tom. (on Tower-Hill)
1713 R124
Johnston, William
1749 S198–9
Jolliffe, John (or Jollyffe)
1731 D488–91, T115
1732 H54–8, H456, O183, P1106
1733 B48, B86, R285
1734/– M378
1736 D323
1737 S460
1748 P1152
Jones, *Mr* (named with Cooper & Woodfall; possibly J. Jones)
1746 C140
'Jones, and Whitherington, two statues in Rome' pseudonymous
1702 S130
Jones, David
1738 Y23
'Jones, Evan, near Shon ap Morgan Row' (fictitious)
1716 C381
Jones, H.
1741 O241
Jones, J. (*printer*, at Temple-bar)
1712 N243
1714 I45
Jones, J. (probably several persons are concealed here)
1727 R234
1737 E390
1739 R134, S720
1742 W496
1746 C140, R311
Jones, John (*printer*, in the Strand)
1742 B294
Jones, T. (near Smithfield)
1707 T517

London (cont.)

Jones, T. (*printer*, near Fleet-street)
1711 Q10
1715 S585

'Jump, *Squire*' (fictitious)
1726 D271

Keble, Samuel
1701 W13
1702 W15
1708 G89, T49, W16
1709 W17
1716 W18

Keimer, Samuel (*printer*; subsequently in Philadelphia)
1715 S129

Keith, George
1749 G234
1750 A348, P605, S21

Kent, Henry (*printer*)
1743 P1041
1747 N268, O74
1748 M7

King, Charles
1713 W331
1716 W343
1717 B162
1728 L172
1731 C438

King, I. (possibly a printseller, related to John below)
1710 B211

King, John (at the Bible and Crown in Little-Britain; probably the 1732 entry represents another man)
1709 S344
1710 S333
1711 S268, S323
1732 W139

King, John (*printseller*)
1741 T537
1749 P1114

King, M. (in Fore-street)
1749 G136

King, R. (at the Prince's Arms in St. Paul's churchyard)
1720 B562
1727 B324

King, R. (in Fore-street)
1745 G135

Knaplock, Robert
1719 E39
1723 R216

Knapton, James
1706 B325
1712 R269
1714 B267
1715 C70
1716 D34
1717 C69, C73, D446-7, H348-9
1718 A191
1719 E39
1720 C76
1721 C75
1723 B240, R216
1727 P5

Knapton, John & Paul
1738 S860

London: Knapton, J. & P. (*cont.*)
1740 P602
1745 P867-9
1746 P871
1748 P872-3
1749 P800

L., D. (*printer*; probably Dryden Leach)
1709 C174

L., F. (*printer*; probably Francis Leach)
1705 M533

L., J. (*printer*; possibly John Leake)
1708 O72

L., J.
1742 R13

Lacy, J.
1722 B329

Lathbury, Edward
1724 L105-6

Lawrence, John
1702 S745
1706 J101
1708 T261
1709 R178

Leach, Dryden (*printer*, son of the following)
1709 C174
1713 O238

Leach, Francis (*printer*)
1703 C258
1705 C259, G215, M533
1706 C260, D552
1707 D550, D553

Leake, John (*printer*)
1708 O72
1713 W331
1717 D412

Leake, John
1742 O107

Lee, R.
1744 F272

Lee, S. (*printer*)
1716 E482

Lewis, Edward
1710 B219, S685

Lewis, G.
1747 D414

Lewis, J.
1736 C544

Lewis, John (*printer*)
1745 H264
1746 A169

Lewis, William
1710 B605
1711 P806-8
1712 S615
1713 P810-12
1718 B319
1720 B141
1721 W310
1723 J28, J39
1729 P44
1735 J29
1736 W29·5
1737 J40-1, J48, J51-2

London: Lewis, W. (cont.)
1738   J30
1744   P761
'Lilliput, John, in the Little-Minories' (fictitious)
1729   K51
Lingard, Henry (*printer*, in Fleet-street)
1718   S604
Lintot, Bernard (or Lintott, until 1716)
1701   D335, P597
1702   M90
1703   H380
1704   N175
1705   E351
1706   C200, G11, P1086–7, S740, T93
1707   B498
1708   F170, K57, K60–1
1708/9   H279–81
1709   C174, H237
1710   E347, E517, O142, S516
1711   F106, J99, P1056, P1078, S775, T467, W105–6
1712   C245, D297, K59, P1060, S425, T331
1713   C95, D292, D299, P61, P904, P987–9, Y5–6, Y72
1714   C114, C521, G52–5, P275, P941–4, R297, S522–3
1715   O28, P946, P974–5
1716   B376, E348–9, E412, F107, G81–3, P813
1717   D31, G88, P73–4, T145, W451
1718   G13, P948
1719   O143, P816, P905
1720   G44, R84, P801, P991, V63
1721   G64–5, L205, R88
1722   P817, P906, W293–4
1723   P949
1726   B82
1728   G14, P818
1729   O144
1730   G86
Lintot, Henry (son of the preceding)
1732   K79, O83, P251
1735   O84
1742   R159 (as assignee of Edward Sayer)
1748   E305
1749   P821
Lion, G., *see* Lyon, G.
Litchfield, John (apparently pseudonymous)
1747   L265
Littleton, Jacob (in Fleet-street)
1739   L80
Lloyd, [Edward?] (publisher of *Lloyd's list* of shipping)
1750   S785
Lloyd, O.
1715   B245
Lloyd, William
1738   B407, R217–19, R320
1739   D287
Lock, Jacob
1739   S478–9
1741   C325
Longman, Thomas
1727   B324
1740   P602
1745   M8
1748   B93 (in partnership with T. Shewell)

London (cont.)
Longshaw, R. (near Charing-Cross)
1704   M297
Lucas, William
1705   N236
Lyne, Samuel (at the Globe in Newgate Street)
1744   C225
Lyon, A.
1734/–   M378
Lyon, D. (in partnership with James Woodman)
1728   V113
1729   V14
Lyon, G. (or Lion)
1743   B458, D440, M298
1744   T472
1745   M567
1746   L275
M., A. (near St. Paul's; probably for A. Moore)
1730   S670
1731   S475
M., B.
1716   O274
M., C. (in Fleet-street)
1702   W268
M., H. (*printer*; probably H. Meere)
1706   B238
1707   M24
M., J. (*printer*; possibly John Matthews)
1710   B380
1714   F151
M., N. (*printer*)
1717   D246
McEuen, James (also in Edinburgh)
1722   B268
'Mallard, W., near the May-pole in the Strand' (fictitious)
1719   A250
Mallet, Elizabeth
1702   B80·5, T576–7
1703   A117·2
Malthus, Sarah
1704   A84, A334, B2, E165, H453, K63, R322, W529
1705   A157, A217, F86, L319, N236, T483
'Man, A., near St. Clements' (pseudonymous)
1714   L34–5
Manby, Richard (from 1745 in partnership with H.S. Cox)
1739   C425
1744   W435–6
1745   V23
1749   C294, P1004
1750   H20·5, P1005
Marsh, Charles (also as author)
1729   C492
1741   M116
Marshall, John (in partnership with Joseph Marshall, 1710; the works listed under 1717 and 1724 name J. Marshall, and possibly Joseph is intended)
1710   L178
1717   T430
1722   L231
1723   H270
1724   D289–90
Marshall, Joseph (in partnership with John Marshall, 1710; see that entry for other possible works)

London: Marshall, J. (cont.)
　1710　L178
　1728　B179
Marshall, Mary (in Newgate Street)
　1743　W408
　1745　G135
'Mastiff, J., in the Mint' (pseudonymous)
　1713　N326
Matthews, Emanuel
　1714　C163
Matthews, John (*printer*)
　1707　D92
　1709　J75
　1710　B380, B605
　1714　F151
Mawson, Robert
　1710　B380
May, B.
　1733　H44
Mayo, John (*printer*; also Mayos)
　1703　P717
　1710　P1118
Meadows, William
　1715　C70
　1717　C69, C73
　1720　C76
　1721　C75, W310
　1726　B620
　1727　A179, B422, R22
　1728　F301, L107, R15, R20
　1738　V91
　1750　H457
Mears, William (also Meares, Meres, Meeres)
　1713　P627
　1718　S372
　1719　H83, H83·2
　1723　H370, N254, R216
　1725　H227
　1728　C284, E424
　1729　D411
　1732　T139
　1733　C442, J116, L325, P115, P485, S482
　1734　T564
　1735　M328
　1738　T565
Mechell, J.
　1738　G150
　1739　G142
　1745　H202
Meere, Hugh (*printer*; possibly of the Mears family)
　1705　B527·1, W68
　1706　B238
　1707　M24
　1708　T55
　1709　L287, W70
　1713　H244, I41, O156, P526, S7·5
　1714　D226, E43, W116
　1716　N40, N44
　1717　B162
　1720　P122
Meighan, P.
　1731　H186-7
　1736　H183

London (cont.)
'Merryman, *Mr*' (fictitious)
　1750　N215, P145
'Merry Wise, Mark'em' (fictitious imprint)
　1720　P120
Midwinter, Edward (*printer*)
　1705　L169
　1709　H409
　1710　B279, N51
　1711　D170
　1713　O1
　1714　B267, M543
Milbourn, Alexander (*printer*, in the Little-Old-Bailey)
　1702　M546
Milford, —
　1750　C341
Millan, John
　1726　B143, M321, M323, M492, T211-14
　1727　B422, B537, T200-5, T220
　1728　T216, T222
　1729　M56
　1730　T179-80, T217, T223, T233, T239-40
　1732　M40
　1734　T219
　1735　T225, T242
　1741　B40, P1023
　1750　H48
Millar, Andrew
　1728　T227
　1729　T229
　1730　S111, T236, T239-40
　1731　T230-1
　1735　T186-8, T191, T194, T242
　1736　A303, E460, T196, T198
　1737　T208
　1741　T207
　1742　A307
　1743　A178 (? in error for 1746)
　1744　A296, T243-4
　1745　A299, M8
　1746　S784·5, T245
　1747　A301, L337-8
　1748　A302, C239, L339, P1170, T181-2
　1749　H219
　1750　B534-5, M435, Y64-5
Miller, Isaac (entered copyright to Tonson in *SR*)
　1714　E514
Milles, B. (*printer*)
　1739/46　T131-2
Mills, Bryan
　1710　H315
　1715　D114
Mills, James
　1718　S392
Minors, Ralph
　1739　A375, A377
Monger, P. (in the Strand)
　1735　S782, T328
Montagu, Richard
　1732　H54-8, H456, P1106
　1740　H59
Montgomery, Hugh
　1712　T149

London: (cont.)

Moor, A., *see* Moore, A.

Moor, B. (apparently for A. Moore, which form appears in the advertisements)

  1720 A235

Moor, John, *see* Moore, John

Moore, A. (or Moor, More; *pseudonym*)

The first use seen in 1720 is 'A. Moor near St. Paul's', possibly intended in the same way as 'A. Man near St. Clement's'; subsequently the form is 'A. Moore', and there is some suggestion that Anne Moore is intended. Whether or not any such person existed, the imprint was regularly used, fictitiously; cf. a letter to Caleb d'Anvers of 1730 on the licentiousness of the press in Cholmondely (Houghton) MS. 74/34 at C: 'It must be premised that the name of the printer is on these occasions omitted & A. Moor near St. Paul's generally put where the law directs the printers name to be'.

Some of the other Moores below may also be pseudonyms.

  1720 A235, D502
  172- W165-6
  1722 D24, P515, S660
  1722/23 L237
  1723 B42, B610, D507, F140, F244-6, R208
  1727 B26, C202, C400, D325, F175, H151, I17, M117, P708, R239, S717
  1727/28 L261, N108
  1728 A242, B146-8, C367, D410, H152, H332, L151, L255, N64-6, N318, P716, S504
  1728/29 Q4, S786
  1729 B55, B135-7, B149, C7-8, C182, D508, E372, G204, G257-9, J46, L67, L273, N130, P2, S206, T252
  1729/30 C10
  1730 A92-3, A371, B65-6, C409, E370, E380, E401, G58, L201, N160, N313, R160, S669-70, S880-2
  173- C264
  1731 A234, B53 (Dublin), D488-92, E371, N230-1, S474-5
  1732 S908 (Dublin)
  1734 D427
  1737 T494
  1741 P645, P719
  1743 D387·2, G98, O113, W524
  1746 A292, B479, H346, W486-90
  1747 C465, J65
  1750 R31, S785

Moore, B. (? for A. Moore)

  1747 L277

Moore, E. (or More)

  1719 W210 (in Duke-street, near Lincolns-Inn-Fields)
  1723 P532

Moore, J. (near St. Paul's)

  1745/46 N119

Moore, James

  1730 L184

Moore, John (or Moor, More; 1715 near St. Paul's)

  1715 H262, S675-6
  1718 H133
  1723 F4

Moore, M. (or More, near St. Paul's)

  1745 W481
  1746 S452, W425

Moore, Thomas (*printer*)

  1704 C337

London: Moore, T. (cont.)

  1705 S472
  1706 R310
  1714 S76 (near St. George's Church, Southwark)

More, *see also* Moore

More, R. (near St. Paul's; possibly intended for A. Moore)

  1727 I17

Morgan, J.

  1737 C399

Morley, J.

  1723 A337

Morphew, John

  1706 C139, C555, F112, F143, H454, N162, T6, T508
  1707 A367, B3, B315, B530·6, D92, E478, F29, G175, G182, G231·5, G264, G303, H420, L132, M375, P461·5, T146, T585, V38, W576
  1708 A176, A368, B98, B530·8, C541, D245, D535, D540, F260, G93, G153, H45, J1-2, L243, L246, M272, O72, P439, P468, P543, P608, P658, P697, P1009, T55, T125, W83, W201
  1709 A158, A218, B125, B176, D339, D434, D569, E2, J75, L142, L287, M267, N335, Q15, S5, S722, T3, T442, W70, W113, W305
  1710 B171-2, B471, C4, C502, D255, E309, P253, P487, S686, S722, S935, W51-2, W74, W115, W193-8
  1711 C36-7 (false imprint), E135, E577, G42, H10-11, L307, P528, P806, P1089·1, S64, S674, S689, S696-7, S770, T339, T391, T394, T447, T466, W199, W443
  1712 A69, A349, B527·2, C510, C514, F13, F108, F173, F304, G16, L42, M273, N246, N311, O130, O197-8, P479, P1025, P1074, S690, S847, S911, T331, W149, W514
  1713 B217, B336, C63, C508-9, C511, C513, D74, E530, F193, H81, H184, O156, P70, P77, P526, S75, S891, T66, T81, V16, W25, W80
  1714 A168, C507, D293, E44, E467, H213, J69, L7, L247-9, M155, N15, P584, S173, S734, T50, T570, W69, W96, W111
  1715 C70, C98, E145, P1026, R161, S698-701, W81
  1716 B501, D34, E482, G122, O165 (false), W170-1, W257-8, W564
  1717 B140, C69, C73, C186, D246, L210, M482, S28, S77, S98, W53-4, W175, W259
  1718 D48, F210, H225, L48, M79, R314, T46, W189
  1720 C76, H218, T357, T407

Morrice, Arabella (or Morris, without Temple-Bar; probably a relation of Bezaleel Morrice the author)

  1717 C93, H290, J19, M485-6, M501, W12

Morris, J.

  1719 R312

Mott, Robert (*printer*, in Aldersgate-street)

  1712 T521

Motte, Anne (copyright entered to her in *SR* by Benjamin Motte: perhaps a present to a relation)

  1711 W443

Motte, Benjamin (*printer* in 1707)

  1707 H420
  1710 S935
  1711 W443
  1727 S356
  1728 B557

London: Motte, B. (cont.)
1729 L99
1730 T269–70
1732 T268
1734 S841
1738 S860

Mount, Richard
1701 A80

N., R., *see* Newcomb, Richard

Needham, —
1749 P698

Nevill, S. (Neville in *Plomer*)
1735 M320

New, Henry (owner of copyright in *SR*)
1749 N177

Newbery, John (formerly at Reading)
1750 N290, S493–4

Newcomb, *Mrs.* (at the Naked Boy, near Temple Bar)
175–? G87

Newcomb, Ann (probably wife of Richard; made entry for George Parker in *SR*)
1710 I11

Newcomb, Richard (*printer*)
170–? L283
1710 P455, R128, R145, T401
1711 N317, Q9, T580, W393
1712 D242, L259, Q12, S631
1713 B289, D497, F94, M174, R126, S445

Newman, Dorman
1712 A69

Nicholl, Sutton (engraver & printseller)
1710 H194, W557·5
1711 O116

Nichols, *Mr* (possibly Thomas)
1733 C368

Nichols, John (*printer*, near Charing-Cross)
1714 E126

Nicholson, John
1715 W81

Nickolson, J. (near West-Smithfield)
1712 E327

Nicks, John
1721 P414·5, P415

Noble, Francis
1739 G276
1741 I42
1750 H48

Noble, S.
1715 R313

Noon, John
1713 Q17
1716 P482
1718 P483
1722 S780
1724 D72, P201
1743 L223

Noorthouck, Herman
1727 B422

Norris, Thomas
1708 W83
171–? P995
1710 W103–4, W129
1711 W105–9
1712 C171, W110
1714 W116, W275

London: Norris T. (cont.)
1715 E316
1723 W130

Nortin, Mary (pseudonymous?)
1726 D271

Nut, S. (possibly Sarah Nutt, daughter of Elizabeth)
1723 B10

Nutt, Elizabeth
1726 B143, C47
1727 S18
1728 B541
1729 B203, B544–7, C375, F243, P599, P654
1730 L95
1731 D383, D488–91, H462, O209, P85
1732 H57–8, H456, O183, P1106
1733 B48, F269, P886–7, R285, S81, T127
1734 D229, K95, M377–8
1735 B291, C52, D409, M270, T532
1736 H183, S189
1737 O240, S460
1739 A377, B338, H141
1740 J10
1744 E449

Nutt, John
170–? H422
1701 A80, B127, D332, E22, E333, L54, O90, P488–9, P722, P736, S52, S282, V118, W267, W562, Y3–4
1702 A156, B469, C180, C207, C356, D29, D29·2, D568, E328, E338, F262, H168, I43, M542, O43, O166, P255–8, P492, P622, P1059, S193, S243, S253–4, T72, T375, Y1
1703 B512, B551, C441, G21, H380, P446, P717, R168, S457, T74, T78, W21, W50
1704 C90, C257, D123–4, D222, L230, M76, O248, P265–6, P463, P733, P1121, Q14
1705 B106, C249, D268, G39, G220, H125, M97, M275–6, T84–6
1705/07 R291
1706 B607, C493, D110, G22, L104, O167, P1082, V36–7

Nutt, M.
1747 B44

Oldcastle, J. (near St. Paul's)
1746 B181–2
1747 R213

Oliver, John (*printer*)
1747 D362

Onley, William (*printer*)
170–? P993
1702 E328

Osborn, John (or Osborne; partner with T. Longman from 1725, died 1734)
1713 R180
1714 B267
1716 H369
1724 E9
1727 B324

Osborn, John (father and son, formerly of Horsley Downs; from 1733 at the Golden Ball, Paternoster Row)
1737 W131
1740 B474
1743 H214
1746 H210, H216
1748 S533

London (*cont.*)

Osborn, S. (*printer*)
1739 N339

Osborne, Thomas (or Osborn, died 1743)
1707 T67
1711 P806
1723 P1091
1733 C230, N38, P1135
1736 M147
1740 E529

Osborne, Thomas (son of the preceding)
1747 B44

Oswald, John
1724 M312
1733 E470, H38, M489
1734 D561
1735 C11, R183
1738 H90
1742 E458
1743 E38
1745 S616
1748 G137
1749 G136, P656

Overton, Henry
1710 B211

Owen, Edward
1732 C61

Owen, William
1741 B470
1747 F308, O70, P470, S534, W531
1748 A319, C471, D94, M450–4, M469, S132, S410, S533
1749 C6, C130, F155, F205, G143–4, J93, K73, M282–3, M285, O65, R186, R260–2, W245, W251, W517
1750 E306, F204, G129, G146, H48, K67, L211, P28, P476, W247–9

P., E. (*printer*; possibly Edmund Powell)
1708 T470

P., F. (*printer*, near Fleet-street)
1707 F135

P., H.
171–? K4
172–? K5

P., H. (*printer*; clearly H. Parker)
1717 P1175

P., R.
1732 O183

P., S. (near Charing-Cross)
1702 T99

P., W. (*printer*)
1729 J59

Paine, Thomas, *see* Payne, Thomas

Palmer, Richard
1713 P627
1716 S26

Palmer, Samuel (*printer*)
1717 N41, N49, O213
1720 M309–11
1721 R88
1723 A337
1725 P416

Parker, Edmund
1708 O173

London (*cont.*)

Parker, George (entered copyrights in *SR*)
1710 I11, S702

Parker, H. (*printer*)
1717 P1173–5

Parker, John
1723 B10
1735 C11

Parker, William
1740 S867
1742 A23

Parkhurst, Thomas
1702 M544
1709 R178

Patterson, C. (in the Strand)
1738 C392

Payne, John (in partnership with J. Bouquet)
1749 B533, D361, D365
1750 B534–5, C434, D363, J83, P260, P1011, V64

Payne, Olive (Oliver in *Plomer*)
1734/– M378
1740 R251

Payne, Thomas (also Paine; 1723 near Stationers Hall)
1722 A65–6, C416, D51, E256, E394, M229, P82–3, R24–5, S136, S285
1723 G133, M103, W460
1724 B318, H226
1729 B304, E311, E437
1730 L250 (at the Crown in Ivy-lane)
1731 M150

Payne, Thomas (near the South-Sea House, Bishopsgate-street; the division of works with the preceding is uncertain)
1736 F234
1748 B365
1750 J9

Pearson, [William?] (*printer*)
1722 L318

Peele, John
1718 C5
1720 B562
1721 L205, M303, N301, R202
1722 C365, J16, M499, W292, W364–6
1723 A192, E366, O30, P210, R119–20, S462
1724 D289–90
1725 G297, H106, T47, W302
1726 S819–25, W297
1727 C43, M75
1729 S829
1733 E462

Pemberton, John (also in partnership with his son John)
1712 C245
1713 S373–4
1714 H144, O164, Y74
1715 H145, Y76–7, Y111
1718 B246
1719 S363
1720 N263, R77, R282, S362, S367–8
1722 S379
1723 E1, N254, R67, S404
1725 B195
1727 F226, P595
1729 S518
1732 L215

London (*cont.*)
Pemberton, John & John
  1736 B248
Pemberton, John & Henry
  1741 B17–18
  1744 C357
Penn, John
  1733 P278
  1735 M270
Penny, Robert (*printer*)
  1735 G148
Pepper, W.
  1727 A179
Pero, John
  1704 M76
Perry, J.
  1745 H310
Philips, J. (possibly Joshua, or perhaps identical with John below)
  1707 P562
  1714 Q16
Phillips, John
  1713 B217
Phillips, R. (*printer*, in West-Smithfield)
  1707 E264
  1721 H273
  1723 E274 (with S. Gilbert)
  1729/37 H5
  1746 M2–4
Philpot (near Charing-Cross; possibly pseudonymous)
  1711 F15
Pickard, John (*printer*)
  1717 M93
Pier, H. (or Piers?)
  1750 H48
'Pigmy, S.' (*printer* for Tom. Thumb; pseudonymous)
  1727 T586
Pike, M.
  1734 L262, P81
Place, John
  1701 P736
Playford, Henry
  1708 T59
Pollard, E. (at the Queen's-Head on St. Margaret's Hill, Southwark)
  1726 W121
Ponder, Tom ('courier')
  1705 H125
Pool, Edward (Poole in *Plomer*)
  1709 Q15
Popping, Sarah
  1710 A25, G181
  1711 T364
  1714 L130–1, P180, P580, P679
  1715 D114, D430
  1716 O165 (false), P482
  1717 F23, I50
  1719 C363
Powell, Edmund (*printer*)
  1708 T470
  1710 P253, S679–81, S684
  1715 C450, H293, R152

London (*cont.*)
Powell, Elizabeth (at the Prince of Wales's Arms, in Black-Fryars, near Ludgate)
  1714 I5
Prevost, Nicholas
  1728 V114
  1730 V18
  1732 M142
Price, A. (probably fictitious according to *Plomer*)
  1749 E314
Price, A. *junior* (probably fictitious like the preceding)
  1749 T31
Prince, Samuel
  1723 N9
'Proctor, Caveat, near Doctors' Commons' (fictitious)
  1734 B228
Proud, A. (in the Old Bailey, near Ludgate)
  1749 G277–8
Purser, John (*printer*; the first may be the work of James who died in Feb 1738. See *Library* V. 23 (1968) 243–7)
  1729 M535
  1738 F45
  1741 T449
  1744 T450
  1745 K88
  1748 J61
'Querit, T., in the Strand' (pseudonymous)
  1743 H354
'Quibus' (fictitious imprint)
  1738 G272
R., D. (in Half-pav'd Court, Salisbury-court; almost certainly D. Richmond)
  1707 C461
R., R. (*printer*)
  1708 T59
R., W. (possibly William Rayner)
  1728 D513
Ramsay, Patrick (possibly pseudonymous)
  1739 E24
Ranger, J. (possibly pseudonymous)
  17—? P1050
Rawlins, J. (*printer*)
  1703 T74
  1705 T84–6
Raylton, Tace Sowle (at the Bible in George-yard, Lombard-street. For works published before her marriage in 1706, see Sowle, Tace. Other works produced after her marriage were issued as 'by the assigns of Jane Sowle')
  173–? C503–4
  1735 G280
  1735/40? G281
  1737/– P1176–7
  1741 F281
  1749 E303
Raylton, Thomas, *see* Sowle, Jane, assigns of
Raymond, L.
  1746 A292
Rayner, E.
  1731 D243, M347–8, P519
Rayner, William
  1728 D513
  1729 W285
  1733 B86, T322

London (cont.)
Raynolds, T. (deliberate misprint for T. Reynolds)
  1733 B461
Read, George
  1728 L1
Read, James (*printer*)
  1702 B585, G263
  1705 E150, T520
  1707 E101, F135
  1708 B581, B581·5, D448·5, P609
  1709 E3, T76, W520
  1709/- P498
  171-? O269
  1710 E353, O2
  1711 N137
  1712 D556, M415
  1712/13 T485
  1713 E307, M175, N136, T492
  1714 E45, P1057
  1725 B209
  1727 B144
  1730 R117
Read, Thomas (*printer*)
  1729 B56–8, F232, M536
  1730 E363
  1732 V22
  1737 F228, W168–9
  1739 C91, G224
Read, W. (assigns of, in a partly pseudonymous imprint)
  1730 O224·2
Reade, J.
  1709 S227
Reason, *Miss* (at the Wells; possibly related to W. Reason)
  1733 B283
Reason, Jeremiah (in Flower de Luce Court, Fleet-street, the same address as W. Reason below)
  1748 D357, S487
Reason, W.
  1735 D475
Redmayne, Elizabeth (*printer*)
  1702 B592, B597
Redmayne, J. (*printer*, apparently successor to P. Redmayne)
  1722 B594
  1724 B332
Redmayne, P.
  1720 B598
Redmayne, R. (*printer*)
  1718 D48
Redmayne, William (*printer*)
  1712 F173
  1713 S217
Reeve, William (possibly the William Reeves in *Plomer*)
  1749 P1114
  1750 H48
Reilly, R. (*printer*)
  1736 V121
Reinshau, T. (near St. James's)
  1733 L239, L240·2
Reynolds, T.
  1733 B459, C212, M352–4, P1105
  1733/34 F162
  1734 B228, D465, K35, T324–5

London: Reynolds, T. (cont.)
  1735 L304
  1739 C402–3, S354
  1744 M6 (in Fleet-street)
Richards, R.
  1740 H119
Richardson, Samuel (*printer*)
  1722 C435
  1725 C72, H227, M569
  1726 C406
  1727 M333–8
  1728 M50
  1729 B7, B424·5, S119, T177
  1730 H117, H230, T236, W302·5–6
  1731 H209
  1732 W298–301
  1733 S204
  1734 C108, T219
  1735 B491, B494–6, O84, T225
  1736 C109, N346
  1737 D484, H231, N336
  1738 C110, Y23
  1739 H228
  1740 D467
  1741 C111, D469, M116, W312
  1743 H214
  1744 H220, Y50
  1745 M8, Y52, Y54
  1746 H210, H216
  1747 L337, T39
  1748 L339, Y61
  1749 B613, H219
  1750 Y64
Richardson, William (*printer*)
  1720 T539
Richmond, D. (in Half-pav'd Court, Salisbury-court)
  1707 C461, D562
Rivington, Charles
  1720 B141, B562, R282
  1730 F117
Rivington, John
  1742 M193
  1744 P541
  1745 P1047, R185
Rivington, John & James
  1749 T249
Roberts, James
  1714 A316, C205, C255, C366, C430, C437, C524–5, C527, S371, T140–2, V122
  1715 C490, E20, E343, E531, F211, G20, H300, H451, L148, M233, P123, P1179, R265, S365, S376, S586, T137, T283–4
  1716 B110, B226, B408, B416, D173, H155, M468, M501, O165 (false), P86, P505, P601, P611, P1035, S26, S560, T27, T285, T546–7, T552, W543
  1717 A231, B164, B298, B454, B561, C93, C487, D444, G151, J19–20, L200, M98, O40, P1070, T145, W12, W303–4
  1718 A232, A373, B583–4, E364, E435, G95, M351, P483
  1719 A241, F225, H80, H80·2, H83, H83·2, M291, M474, M496, O206, O268, S505, U35

London: Roberts, J. (cont.)

1720 B41, B308–9, B421, C372–3, D545, E433, E483, F138–9, H236, H374, M153, M309–11, M475, O76, P531, S362, S368, S500

1721 B152, C103, C547, E368, H136, J18, J36, L20, L90, L282, M491, R88, S810, V70, W192, W310

1722 B178, C435, C489, N279, P1154, R201, S218, W294

1723 C421, D211, E416, P1072, P1090–1, R216, T10, W333

1724 B20, B113, C342, C358, E402, F158, K53, L105–6, M131, M197, P606, W334

1725 B151, C72, C408, E398, F99, F288, M484, P198, P222, S89, S224, S578, W277, W347, Y122–30

1726 B143, C42, C47, B330, C406, E488–9, H387, L251, M321, M323, M492, O69, S220, S816–18, T211, T260, W342, W354, Y132

1727 A179, A230, B422, B485, D537, E379, E510–11, F119, F176, H115, M146, M315, M330, O6, P549, R232, S107, S673, T200, T220, W253, W560, Y69, Y134

1728 B179, B233–4, B499, B541, B614, D234, E330, F122, H333, H402, L330, M13, M109, N10, N306, P581, R21, S512, Y136, Z2

1729 A68, B55, B91, B424·5, B544–7, E503, F92, F233, H403, J59, L98, L161, M317, P80, P604, S704, T109, T312, V61, W353

1730 D35, E428, H114·5, L95–6, L331, M467, P37, P666, R230, R326, S111, T563, W302·5–6

1731 A26, B114, D189, D383, L13, M280, P421, R118, S30, W435

1732 B131, B311, C199, C292, D10, D199, M326, P251, P1042, R207, R328, S99, S159–60, S869–70, S904–7, T45, T356, V22, W40–1, W346

1733 A86, B337, B437, C107, D318, F67, F215, F283, G207, H21, H157, L75, L271, M84, M524, P1044, S8, S190, S592, S884, U11, V46

1734 A374, B519, D13, D69, D229, F50, H398, L14, M86, M377–8, P527, R116, S809

1735 C11, D422, H42, H313, H463, I70, J42–3, L315, M88, P78

1736 B116, B193, B443, B556, D349, F234, G128, G252, M115, S106, T21

1737 A321, B444, D331, D433, D483–4, J49, M85, P896

1738 B359, G229, M83, M91, N272, T565–6

1739 C288, P292

1740 B117, B360, C478, D467, N271, P475, S164, S654, T150

1741 B17–18, C479, D469–70, G232, G242, H399, P1102, R250, R252, T271

1742 A23, A167, B118, C298, H156

1743 C480–1, H112, M119

1744 C28, E217, E472, N276, P25, S86

1745 Q1, W39

1746 A175, N321

1749 B120

Roberts, John (fictitious?)

1741 L122

Roberts, T. (near Warwick Lane; fictitious?)

1730 D466

Robins, Thomas (Plomer suggests the imprint is fictitious, but it appears to be genuine)

London: Robins, T. (cont.)

1740 C211, F35, L115, N50, O15, P1112, S550, T422–3

Robinson, Jacob

1738 A16, B71, B73, M365

1739 E384, H161·6

1741 M261

1742 A213, C55·5

1743 B358, B475, L228, M368

1744 E468, F98, H92, P699, S19, T133, V48

1745 B466, B478, F148, H203, K88, W536

1745/– D77

1746 C457, H314, O200

1747 B44

1748 E436, H89, P53, S543

1749 T591–2

1750 H48, K90, R268

Robinson, Jonathan

1706 A365·5

1707 W549

1709 S419·6

Robinson, M. (on Saffron Hill)

1728 A243

'Roger, Honest, country-man to the Observator' (pseudonymous)

1705 H274

Roger, Robert (dans les Black-Fryers, prés de l'Imprimerie royale)

1705 L5

Rogers, D. (printer)

1708 G93

Rogers, G. (stationer, just within Bishopsgate)

1717 L153

Rogers, J. (in Fleet-street; possibly John, subsequently in Shrewsbury)

1707 M23

Rogers, T. (in Fleet-street)

1709 B210

Rogers, William

1701 T52–4

Roper, Abel

1704 P662

1705 C475

1710 A4, W74

Round, J.

1709 H320

Russel, William

1745 T463

1748 T464

1749 T465

Russell, P.

1746 L218

S., E. (printer; possibly Edward Say)

1733 S637

S., J. (printer?, near St Paul's)

1743 Y17

S., S. (possibly Samuel Sturton)

1706 D238

Sackfield, John

1717 S28

1718 I14

Sambroke, P. (under the Piazza's, Covent Garden)

1741 B74

London (cont.)

Sandby, William
  1742   T117
  1750   B534–5

Sanger, Egbert
  1706   O46, T338
  1707   B315, G173, R304, T299
  1708   B257, O282–3, S157–8
  1709   B254, H285–6, H320, R287, T366
  1710   O286, S773
  1712   C250, D294, R280

Sare, Richard
  1705   D83
  1711   C64–6
  1713   C63
  1715   P538

Sawbridge, George
  1704   P62
  1712   P267
  1715   W93

Sawyer, T. (near Ludgate-hill)
  1706   M186

Say, Edward (*printer*)
  1722   B329
  1728   L107
  1733   S637
  1735   L315

Sayer, Edward
  1742   R159

'Seeker, Serious, and Company, at the sign of the Looking Glass opposite to the Cameleon in Little Britain' (fictitious)
  1720   P120

Senex, John
  1702   P1059

Sharp, E. (in Holborn)
  172–?   P1099

Sharpey, T. (in Cheapside)
  1716   P482

Shaw, E. (*printer*)
  1730/31 W45

Shaw, W.
  1732   W533
  1733   C156, G225

Sheepey, Marshall
  1749   A213, H350
  1750   A348, F237

Sheron, J.
  1732   L140

Shewell, Thomas (in partnership with Thomas Longman)
  1748   B93

'Shon ap Rice, at the sign of the Goat in Rixham Row' (fictitious)
  1701   S393

Shropshire, Walter
  1739   D424
  1750   J9

Shuckburgh, John
  1729   S518
  1735   C52
  1738   S806
  1739   P1012
  1740   P1014
  1744   H113
  1748   E305

London (cont.)

Simson, Jane (made entry in *SR* to Symon Sympson)
  1710   T376

Slater, [Henry?]
  1741   I42
  1750   H48

Slow, S. (or Sloe)
  1731   S730
  1732   C164, D396
  1733   J95, L26, M299, P700
  1734   L91, S716
  1735   T532
  1736   C472

Smith
A number of Smiths were in business in Cornhill and the Royal Exchange, and may well have been related; they appear to include A., B., E., & M. Smith. A., E., and M. Smith are associated with E. Nutt. Some of these imprints may be false.

Smith, A. (in Cornhill, 1717; at the Royal Exchange, 1729)
  1717   P763
  1729   B203, F243

Smith, B. (near the Exchange)
  1727   S12

Smith, D.
  1732   E189

Smith, E. (in Cornhill, 1716; at the Royal Exchange, 1730; possibly Elizabeth)
  1713   P507
  1716   M423
  1717   R335
  1719   F7
  1728   G223
  1730   C232, L95

Smith, G.
  1750   B198, M172–3, M459–60

Smith, H. (*printer*, in Holborn)
  1711   L308

Smith, J. (*printer*, in Cornhill)
  1714   S772·5

Smith, John (near Fleet-street, or in the Strand: both addresses are found in 1711)
  1709   C377
  1710   E341, F63, H188, P447
  1711   F132–3, L312
  1715   N234

Smith, Joseph (possibly some entries refer to John above, or are pseudonymous)
  1726   N96–7
  1727   A50–1, P708, S717, T493
  1731   T115

Smith, M. (in Cornhill)
  1724   E377, S223
  1727   S18
  1728   M212–13

Smith, R. (probably at least two persons, possibly identical with the following Richards)
  1705   G220
  1715?   N209
  1734   E381

Smith, Richard (*printer*, at Charing-Cross)
  1712   W400

Smith, Richard (in Pater-Noster-Row)
  1715   P538

London (*cont.*)
Smith, T. (in Fleet-street)
  1710 T26
Smith, W. (seller of Oxford publications)
  1717 D446–7, H348–9
Smith, W. (musician, at Corelli's Head against Norfolk-street, in the Strand)
  1730 F117, R214
  1734 F118
Smith, W.
  1738 B68
Smyth, Alex.
  1734 W61
'Sow, L.' (apparently for S. Slow; a piracy)
  1731 S732
Sowle, Jane (*printer*)
  1707 A340
  1709 W238
Sowle, Jane, assigns of (i.e. Thomas Raylton (until 1723) and Tace Sowle Raylton)
  1712 E299
  1715 A339
  1716 C220
  1719 M135
  1727 E302
  1728 B202
  1738 F280
Sowle, Tace (subsequently Tace Sowle Raylton; for works published by her as 'by the assigns of Jane Sowle', see the preceding; and for other works after her marriage, see Raylton, T. Sowle)
  1703 C218
  1705 T176
Sparkes, W.
  1715 T420
Spavan, George
  1738 B69, B73
  1739 B70
  1743 N323
Spavan, R.
  1749 B613
  1750 H48
Speed, Thomas
  1701 D67
Spoorn, J. (near the Strand)
  1710 D350
Sprint, John & Benjamin
  1709 C1·5
Stagg, John
  1716 H155
  1717 B561
  1725 F99, M484, P198
  1728 E19, L172
  1729 P774
  1730 H117
  1732 H54–8, P1106
  1736 H183
  1740 S571–3
  1742 S569
  1743 C480–1, S567
  1744 P541
  1745 M8
Standen, John
  1739 S483

London (*cont.*)
Standfast, Richard
  1710 F63
  1713 S7·5
'Standfast, Thomas, at the Guardian Angel, near Westminster-Hall' (fictitious)
  1749 N84
Steen, Meshach
  1740 P560
Steidel, G.
  1745 F270, V116
  1746 O207
Stephens, J. (*printer*)
  1727 W350
  1728 S630
Stibbs, H. (near Cornhill)
  1748 F85
Still, John (*printer*)
  1707 M133
Stokes, Charles
  1722 C435
Stokoe, Luke
  1716 H155
Strahan, George
  1720 H218
  1728 T227, Z2
  1736 H183
  1739 S771
  1744 P541
  1747 D414
Strahan, William (*printer*)
  1740 D315–16, G137·5, W318–19
  1741 L226–7, S4
  1742 B282, E458, G137·2, W317, W320–3
  1743 B205, E407, L222, L228, V48, W316
  1744 B185, P54
  1745 R332·5
  1746 L218, L224, L225, S784·5
  1747 A301, V27
  1748 A302, C239, S533
  1749 G136
  1750 B534–5, C434, L211, V64
Sturt, John (in Golden-Lion Court in Aldersgate Street; a printseller)
  1703/– B378
Sturton, Samuel
  1706 A122, D238, L73
Swan, J. & R. (probably John (below) and Robert)
  1750 S469
Swan, John (near St. Martin's Lane, in the Strand)
  1748 A121, M37
  1750 A313, P63
  175–? J26
Symon, Edward
  1713 B217
  1716 C359
  1720 R282
  1726 B139
Sympson, Symon (owner of copyright entered in *SR*)
  1710 T376
T., J. (possibly Jacob Tonson)
  1705 R8
T., R. (*printer*; possibly R. Tookey)
  1719 C363

London (*cont.*)

'Tanteribobus' (*printer*; fictitious)
  1738 G272
Taylor, *Mr* (possibly T. Taylor)
  1735 T532
Taylor, B. (*printer*, near Fleet-street)
  1709 D498
Taylor, John
  1707 E23
Taylor, T.
  1735 T532
  1741 B467, I52, J96, T128, W478–9
  1742 M228
Taylor, William
  1708 K61
  1709 R178
  1711 P806, W105–6
  1714 B267, D30, G71
  1715 C70
  1716 H369
  1717 C69, W566
  1720 C192, H200
  1721 C75
'Telltruth' (fictitious)
  1750 N70
Thomas, R. (behind the Royal Exchange, or in Fleet-street; probably the same man)
  1719 D5, H467, W444
Thomas, R.
  1746 A63
Thompson, *Mr* (*printer*; mentioned by one of Harley's informers)
  1706 L104
Thompson, J. (in the Strand)
  1729/– B47
  1731 F146, P90
Thompson, R.
  1738 N18–19
Thorpe, J.
  1720 E259
Tibbitt, T. (possibly pseudonymous)
  1733 P1119
Tilly, J. (*printer*)
  1735 S768
Tinney, John (engraver, at the Crown in Great East Cheap, Cannon Street)
  1730/– B379
  1741 P1145, T537
'Tinpan, Henry, near the Strand' (fictitious)
  1748 P46
Tomlinson, J.
  1748 S602
'Tompson, Jocab' (false imprint for a piracy of a publication of Tonson)
  1705 P1077
'Tomson, J.' (reported printer of a libel)
  1711 S844
Tomson, R. (or Thomson, near Cheapside)
  1722 M413
'Tonpson, J.' (false imprint for Dublin publication)
  1729 D40
Tonson, Jacob. (The business appears to have been transferred to Jacob II, the nephew, in 1718)

London: Tonson, J. (*cont.*)

  1701 D295
  1702 P1088, T64
  1703 B252, C370, C379
  1704 P1079, P1083, P1124, Y2
  1705 A27–30, C378, P1076, R8(?)
  1706 C233, C376, H51–3, P65, P1081, T495, W33, W35
  1707 C334, F110, H49, R301
  1708 P237
  1709 H238–9, N251
  1710 C4
  1711 H50, P1089
  1712 B242–4, M528–30
  1713 A36, G66–8, H382–4, T303–8, T310
  1714 B266–7, E492, E514–16, G25, G47–9, G69–71, P206, S739, T309, Y99
  1715 B245, B417, C528, G18, S577, T281
  1716 A41–5, H377, P670, R298, T335, W296
  1717 E504–6, H348–9, P204, R241, T272–8
  1718 C5, E507, G27, R292, T293
  1719 P1096, Y90–2, Y100–2
  1720 E494, E497, E512, G44, H12, O39, P242, P1068, P1084, P1098, T291, V79
  1721 E495–6, E499, G74, P1065, S377
  1722 E502, E509, G45, P1017, R296, S364, T288, T311, V68
  1723 E496, W538
  1725 A38, E500, G79, Y122, Y125, Y128, Y130
  1726 G29, Y132
  1727 V80
  1728 G75, Y169
  1729 V81
  1730 Y171
  1732 R288
  1733 T296
  1734 A290
Tonson, Jacob III & Richard
  1741 G32, Y173
  1742 G78
  1743 B45
  1744 P243
  1746 B88
  1748 E305
Tooke, Benjamin
  1702 T267, T418
  1705 M39
  1711 F106
  1712 F113
  1713 P70
  1721 S810
Tookey, Robert (*printer*)
  1704 A84, E165, R322
  1705 A157, L319
  1706 H268–9
  1708 D540
  1719 C363
  1724 C353
Torbuck, John
  1738 B51, B68, B73, C252
  174–? C253
  1741 W46·2
Towers, J.
  1732 P261

London: (cont.)
Towers, T.
  1733 H121
Tracy, Ebenezer (at the Three Bibles on London Bridge)
  1702 T477
  1714 W111
Tracy, Han. (successor to the preceding)
  172–? K5
Travis, Nath.
  1717 A231
Trott, J.
  1745 P710
Trott, W.
  1728 E374
  1730 M34, P104
  1742 D233
'Trowel, Andrew' (*printer* in Grub-street; fictitious)
  1730 O224·2
'True, James, auctioneer' (fictitious)
  1741 G248
'Trueman, Charles, near St. James's' (fictitious)
  1749 M77
Trye, Thomas
  1742 W313
  1747 R191
  1750 B534–5
Turbutt, Robert (Turbot in *Plomer*)
  1735 C382
Turner, M. (at the Post-office, corner of Bow-street, Covent-garden)
  1729 H145·5
Turner, T. (in the Strand)
  1720 L92
Turner, William
  1701 G105–7
  1704 Q14
  1705 C249
  1706 P254
  1707 P109
Turnham, John (near St. Paul's Church-yard)
  1711 T400
Type, A. (near Cheapside; probably fictitious)
  1750 F46, H425
Vaillant, Paul
  1740 L93·5
  1743 B45
  1747 M44
  1748 M48–9, P1006
Vandenhoek, Abraham
  1729 J100
Varnam, Thomas
  1713 R180
  1714 B267
Vernon, Thomas (*printer*, near the Temple)
  1714 P182
Vertue, *Mrs* (in partnership with Samuel Goadby)
  1750 C283
Viney, Robert
  1735 C11
W., H. (*printer*; possibly Henry Woodfall)
  1733 H47
W., J. (in Fleet-street; possibly Jeremiah Wilkins)
  1701 E352

London: (cont.)
W., J. (*printer*)
  1730 W188
W., T. (*printer*)
  1723 D211, E416
W., W. (*printer*; William Wilkins)
  1718 S507
'Wadham, J., near the Meeting-house in Little Wild-street' (fictitious)
  1739 C286
Walker, Robert (*printer*, at the White Hart, without Temple Bar)
  1728 D513
  1729 C492, H33, M187, P599, P1161, T157
  1730 C409, L95, L201, N160, O224·2
  1731 C444–7, D445, K96, P133, S731, W286
  1732 D396
Walker, W. (near Holbourn)
  1710 S603
Walkwood, David (near Fleet-street; probably fictitious)
  1711 W386
Waller, T.
  1746 T171
  1747 T89–90, T172
  1749 W570
Walter, J.
  1708 M548
  1709/10 D541
  171–? P995
  1714 M549
Walthoe, John (the first entry clearly refers to the father, the others may be to father or son)
  170–? S639
  1723 P210
  1725 W302
  1726 D371–3, Y86
  1727 M537, N266, T116, W295
  1728 M50, S755
  1729 B7, S119
  1730 E425
  1736 N346
  1737 N336, W306
Ward, Aaron
  1719 P1142
  1724 M312
  1726 P1143
  1730 R326
  1731 R327
  1733 A7
  1743 T108
  1746 F43
Ward, Caesar (in partnership with Richard Chandler, with branches at York & Scarborough)
  1735 S768
  1737 T527
Ward, John
  1749 G136 (in Little Britain)
  1750 T561
Ward, R. (*printer*, in the Strand)
  1714 W392
Ward, T.
  1737 H231
  1747 C530

London (cont.)

Ward, Thomas
  1709 L142
  1717 W327

Ware, Richard
  1732 H54–6
  1737 W131

Waring, W.
  1733 G207

Warner, John
  1744 C346, R193

Warner, Thomas
  1713 A35
  1717 P577
  1718 A320, B207–8, B319, I14, J17, P715, P1094
  1719 G266, H85, O77, P603, R244, T406
  1720 C324, H105
  1722 B186
  1723 L276, M471
  1724 H34, M472, S22
  1725 B81, C500, L24
  1726 E26, H162, H475, O99, S826
  1727 B144, B347, D328–30, M287
  1728 L172
  1729 M300, T177, W48, W66
  1730 M477
  1731 B299, H209, L260, M478
  1732 L172, M343, U34, W46

Warner, W.
  1736 D323

Wates, S. (in Fleet-street)
  1707? C160

Watkins, T.
  1750 B587

Watson, James (*printer*)
  1729 P774

Watson, M. (*printer?*, next the King's Arms tavern)
  1739 C23–6, H306

Watts, John (*printer*, though rarely acknowledging the fact; at first in partnership with the Tonsons as a printer, by 1720 a copyright owner also)
  1711 P1089 (entry in *SR*)
  1719 G1, S363
  1720 C520
  1721 D512, H371
  1723 H370
  1726 G59
  1728 F279
  1729 R20
  1731 C194, C198, M331
  1732 H404, J31, S112
  1734 D482, J44
  1735 M87
  1738 M83
  1739 M246–8

Waugh, James
  1745 S146
  1746 S148
  1748 D367
  1749 B274

Webb, *Mr* (near St. Paul's; compare W. Webb below)
  1740 G186

Webb, A. (near St. Paul's; compare W. Webb below)
  1744 R170

London (cont.)

Webb, J. (near St. Paul's; compare W. Webb below)
  1745 F137

Webb, W. (1733 'near the Royal Exchange'; 1741 'near' or 'over against St. Paul's'. Mrs Lois Morrison has suggested that this is a fictitious imprint, like A. Moore)
  1733 R231
  1741 M526
  1742 C206, D86, H158, P712, S153, W475–6, W494–5
  1743 D305, D369, G96, G270, K49, N110, P1054, S168, W480, W501, W503–6, W511, W523
  1744 J89, M254·5
  1745 E487, I15, P1000, P1166, W497
  1746 G178, O251, P984, S202
  1747 J86, L12, T39–40, V88
  1748 C347, T346
  1750 N75, P1103

Webb, W., *junior* (near Temple-Bar; if W. Webb is a fictitious imprint, clearly this is also)
  1748 M509
  1749 A329, O25

Webster, T.
  1742 N308

Webster, W. (near St. Paul's)
  1743 B205

Wellington, Richard
  1703 M73
  1704 H307, M74
  1705 R8

Wellington, Richard (son of preceding)
  1733 A171, F33–4
  1734 C322, P252
  1746 P1109, T478

Wells, John
  1701 B37

Whiston, John
  1745 M8
  1750 P1158

White, R. (near Smithfield Bars)
  1738 E266

White, T. (*printer*, in Chancery-lane)
  1727 L198, R233

White, William (near Fleet-street)
  1715 P757

'Whitherington & Jones, two statues in Rome' (fictitious)
  1702 S130

Whitridge, Henry (also Whithridge, Whittridge)
  1725 F99
  1726 N315
  1727 M333–9
  1730 R326
  1732 T565·5
  1745 M8
  1748 M469

Wickins, John
  1705 D268

Wilcox, J.
  1709 S300
  1717 P577
  1721 R202
  1735 B491–6, C11
  1737 S460

Wild, Joseph (or Wilde, as *Plomer*)
  1702 A154–5

London (*cont.*)

Wildbore, T.
1736   T476

'Wildfire, Will., at the Powder-Mills near Temple-Bar' (fictitious)
1749   M412

Wilford, John
1721?   D175
1722   W94
1725   T551
1729   S80, S865
1730   B301, B558, D531, F61, H230, M166, M493, T158–9
1731   D68, D178, D383, H410, M479, P535, S609, T160
1732   M370, T301
1733   B427, E415, H104, M416, M487, O85, P484, P620, P822–7, P833–4, P840, P898, S32
1734   B174, B215, D42, M377–8, M494, O87, P579, P845, P1055, S841
1734/35   P839, P844
1735   D407, E392, P832
1736   P1039
1737   W205
1738   A90
1743   T163
1744   T164
1748   D122, D181

Wilkin, R. (probably Richard below, or his son)
1728   C551

Wilkin, Richard
1702   C335

Wilkin, W. (at the King's Head in St. Paul's Church-yard, like the two preceding)
1727   C553

Wilkins, Jeremiah (*printer* of elegies, near Fleet-street)
1701   E157, E201, E238, E352
1702/03   S162
1703   E213

Wilkins, William (*printer*)
1714   N154·5, P284·5, P584, T569, W159
1717   G295
1718   G296, S507
1719   S505
1723   A192, O30
1726   W297, Y105
1735   O93, O103
1738   S760

Wilkinson, J. (near Charing Cross)
1732   N7

Williams, E. (near Charing Cross)
1743   N211

Williams, J. (*printer*, in Southwark)
1703/–   C237

Williams, J. (*printer*, in the Strand)
1715   C321

Williams, J. (near the Strand)
1727   M340

Williams, John
1720   P561

Williams, Robert (near the Temple)
1701   O53

Williams, W. (near St. Paul's)
1744   W454

London (*cont.*)

Willis, John
1701   B127

Willock, Robert
1741   S4
1748   S942

Willoughby, Robert
1717   L209–10

Wilson, John (*printer*, at the Turk's-Head in Gracechurch-street)
1738   N273

Wilson, R. (*printer*, near Ludgate Hill)
1707   S156

Wilson, Thomas
1704   O5

'Wink-a-pinka, E.' (fictitious)
1750   P143

Wise, Will (*printer*, in Fetter-lane)
1710   E103, L241, L281, R321, W287

'Wiseacre, Peter, in the Old-Baily' (fictitious)
1731   J103

Wiseman, John (near the Royal-Exchange)
1704   F68

'Witford, J.' (deliberate mis-spelling of Wilford for piracies)
'1736'   P17, P855–9

Withers, Edward
1746   D193
1750   P87

Wood, John (in partnership with C. Woodward from 1739 until his death in 1741)
1735   N264
1741   T449

Wood, John (under the Royal Exchange)
1748   L46

Woodfall, George
1745   H30, K47, N6
1746   C140, D38, L218, O207
1747   B44, P664
1748   P134
1749   G279, J93, L311
1750   E306, H48

Woodfall, Henry (*printer*; the work of the two Henrys, father and son, has not been distinguished)
1723   K26
1733   H47
1734   T219, T231
1735   T186–8, T191, T194
1736   T196, T198
1737   P881–3
1740   L214, L268–9, O8, P475
1744   T243–4
1746   T245

Woodman, James
1721   C328, E368, I7
1723   B10
1728   V113
1729   V14

Woodward, C. (in partnership with John Wood)
1741   T449

Woodward, James
1709   C247, L287, W70, W113
1710   C307, W103–4, W129, W185–6, W193–8
1711   W105–9, W199

London: Woodward, J. (cont.)

1712 G249, W110
1714 L181, W69, W111, W116, W125

Woodward, Thomas

1715 C96
1723 P210
1725 W302
1728 V113
1731 D272
1733 R284
1735 M164, S562

Worrall, John

1742 R159
1746 B12
1746/- B13

Worrall, Thomas

1727 B422, T170
1728 L107, S90–4, Y94
1729 D388
1730 D389
1732 B371
1733 F67
1734 B11
1736 R274
1737 O211, R275
1738 B445, R276

Wotton, Matthew

170–? S639
1702 E466

Wotton, Thomas (or Wooton)

1732 O21

'Would-have-all, *Sir* John, in Fleet-lane' (fictitious)

1720 E304

Wren, John (near Great Turnstile, High Holborn)

1750 B280
175–? W95

Wright, John (*printer*, behind the Exchange)

1727/- P713
1729 H164, P771
1732 P923, W362
1733 B396, P925–6
1734 P802, P850–2, T458
1735 H93–4, H165, P917, P964, T459–60
1736 H97, H166
1737 P896
1738 P932
1741 P546
1742 P787

Wyat, John

1704 C488
1707 D46·5, P472
1718 P483

Wyatt, W.

1735 C11

Wygate, J.

1738 B407

York, J. (near Temple-Bar)

171– G311

Young, E.

1717 S98

ENGLISH PROVINCIAL

'For the author'

The following poems printed for the author are listed together here as well as under the appropriate towns.

1703 F276 (J. Froud)
1704 R306 (N.B.)
1707 C517 (H. Cross-grove)
1712 K85–7 (C. Kirkham)
1713 A119–20
1718 B85, G203 (J. Goatley), P43 (T.H.)
1720 L186
1724 B173 (B. Bell)
1730 B438 (A. Brice)
1731 H319 (J. Horler)
1732 C305 (A. Colpas), M152 (S. Maxwell)
1736 I32
1737 L323 (G. Lumley)
1738 G116 (T. Gent), H128 (J. Heany)
1739 B382 (J. Brailsford)
1740 F165 (M. Flemyng), R336 (C. Ryall), T37 (W. Tans'ur)
1741 C287 (J. Collier), P23 (W. Paget)
1742 G111 (T. Gent)
1743 B486 (J. Bromwich), G112 (T. Gent), S490 (C. Smart)
1745 G302·5, O169 (E. Oldnall), P21 (W. Paget), P1046 (J. Price)
1746 J68, P624, T556 (W. Turnbull)
1747 F308
1748 S750

See also W225–35 for poems by Henry Waring printed for the author at unnamed but probably provincial towns.

By towns

Alcester

Keating, J. (also at Shipston & Stratford)
1749 P103

Alnwick

1745 W28

Barnes

'*Sold by the author*' (William Tans'ur)
1740 T37

Barnstaple

Gaydon, John
1735 L315

Bath

1713 H436, P633
1738 W337

Farley, Felix (later at Bristol)
1732 L188
1733 M539, T371

Frederick, William
1741 B433
1742 B434–6
1749 B451

Leake, James
1733 C107

English provincial: Bath: Leake, J. (cont.)
- 1734 C108
- 1735 C52
- 1736 C109
- 1738 C110
- 1740 P412
- 1741 B433, C111
- 1742 B434–6
- 1744 C112
- 1748 B93
- 1749 F205
- 1750 F204

Lobb, Samuel
- 1733 C107

Birmingham

'For the author'
- 1743 B486 (J. Bromwich)
- 1745 P21 (W. Paget)
- 1749 C424 (T. Cooke), P103

Printers and booksellers

Aris, Thomas (*printer*, previously at London)
- 1743 B486
- 1745 P21
- 1749 C424, P103

Warren, Thomas
- 1745 O169
- 1749 P103

Bridgnorth

Haslewood, Benjamin
- 1745 O169

Bristol

No imprint
- 1705 F277
- 1714 P185
- 174– H114
- 1741 P291

'For the author'
- 1703 F276 (J. Froud)
- 1704 R306 (N.B.)

Printers and booksellers

Bonny, William (*printer*)
- 1701 P186–8
- 1702 P263
- 1703 F276
- 1704 R306
- 1711 O7, P190
- 1712 W233
- 1715 H451·2

Cadell, Thomas
- 1749 B451

Cossley, William
- 1731 P1043

Farley, Felix (*printer*; earlier at Bath)
- 1742 W313
- 1744 G208, G210
- 1748 W314

Farley, Samuel (*printer*)
- 1720 W182

English provincial: Bristol: Farley, S. (cont.)
- 1721 A354
- 1731 P1043

Farley, Samuel & Felix (*printers*)
- 1748 P1178

Greep, Henry (*printer*, in Lewin's-Mead)
- 1721 E131

Harris, Vavasour (in Wind-street; son of Benjamin Harris, senior; later in London)
- 1702 S549

Lewis, Martha
- 1731 P1043
- 1748 B93

Penn, Joseph (*printer?*)
- 1712 G216
- 1720 C89

Watts, J. (*printer*)
- 1743 P1110

Wilson, John (recorded by *Plomer* at Bath)
- 1742 W313

Buckinghamshire

'printed at the Catherine-wheel, for the right worshipful the mayor of Chipping Wiccomb' (fictitious)
- 1705 W404–5

Bury St Edmunds

'For the author'
- 1720 L186

Printers and booksellers

Baily, Thomas, & Thompson, William (also at Stamford)
- 172–? B514, W71, W89, W163, W165, W174
- 1721 W88–9

Cambridge

False imprints
- 1710 A238, H192, T13–14
- 1712 N150

No imprint
- 1730 P907
- 1733 B437, S32
- 1749 S632
- 1750 B587

'For the author'
- 1724 B173 (B. Bell)
- 1743 S490 (C. Smart)

Printers and booksellers

Bentham, Joseph (*printer*)
- 1743 B45, S490
- 1746 S491
- 1749 M129–30
- 1750 S495

Crownfield, Cornelius
- 1714 L247–9
- 1719 E39, P1096
- 1723 E496
- 1727 P5
- 1736 B193
- 1740 P412

Crownfield, Cornelius & John
- 1743 B45

English provincial: Cambridge (cont.)

Jeffery, Edmund
  1706 B325

Thurlbourn, William
  1727 M146
  1730 L250, T103
  1733 S464
  1736 B193
  1737 A321
  1740 P412
  1741 B433
  1742 B434–6
  1743 B45
  1746 B88
  1749 M130
  1750 S495

University Press
  1702 B130
  1706 B325
  1723 E496
  1724 B173
  1728 E19
  1736 P111
  1743 B45, S490

Canterbury
  1720/22 E446
  1721/22 E445
  1722 T399

'For the author'
  1718 G203 (J. Goatley), P43 (T. H.)
  1736 I32

Printers and booksellers
Abree, James (*printer*)
  1718 C355, P43
Smith, T.
  1747 B89

Chester
  1715 C310
  1748 B617 ('printed by a true blue')
Verité, *Monsr.* (a printseller?)
  1750 I40

Cirencester
  1745 S749
'For the author'
  1748 S750

Derby
Allestree, Henry
  1714 W280
Fox, Samuel
  1742 T117
Fox, Stephen
  1742 T117

Durham
  1745 W28

Eton
Pote, Joseph
  1743 B45

English provincial: Eton: Pote, J. (cont.)
  1746 C326
  1748 L79
'typis Savilianis'
  1712 S366

Exeter
'For the author'
  1730 B438 (A. Brice)

Printers and booksellers
Bishop, Philip (*printer*)
  1714 D53
Brice, Andrew (*printer*)
  1730 B438
Brice, Andrew & Sarah (*printers*, at the sign of the Printing-press in Gandy's Lane)
  1743 K13
Farley, Mark (*printer*)
  1746 G209
Farley, Samuel (*printer*, over against the New-Inn in the Fore-street)
  1702 S11
  1704 P184
  1713 M518
Marsh, John
  1713 M518
Score, Edward
  1735 L315
  1737 P651–2

Gosport
Philpot, James
  1736 B160

Hereford
  1739 E395
  1741 A240, I54, P1007, T343

'For the author'
  1746 J68

Printers and booksellers
Hodges, P.
  1745 O169
Smith, Willoughby (*printer*)
  1746 J68
Wilde, James (also at Ludlow, and perhaps Kidderminster)
  1745 O169

Hexham
  1745 W28

Hinckley
Palmer, R.
  1746 A169

Hull
Ryles, Thomas
  1732 M142

Ipswich
'For the author'
  1741 P23 (W. Paget)

English provincial: Ipswich (cont.)
Printers and booksellers
Bagnall, John (*printer*)
  1736 N327
Craighton, William (*printer*)
  1741 P23

'Isle of Man' (possibly a false imprint)
  174– N3
  1740 H175–6
  1741 H179
  1743 S667
N., C. (*printer*; equally likely to be fictitious)
  1740 H177
  1741 H178

Kendal
  Ashburner, Thomas (*printer*)
    1723 E276

Kidderminster
  Moseley, H.
    1749 C424
  Wilde, *Mr* (possibly James Wilde of Hereford who also
  had a shop at Ludlow)
    1745 O169

King's Lynn
  Garratt, William (*printer?*)
    1740 P1045

Lichfield
  Bailey, Richard
    1749 C424

Ludlow
  Robinson, Edward
    171–? S787
  Wilde, James (also in Hereford)
    1745 O169

Manchester
  1731 L41
  '*For the author*'
    1741 C287 (J. Collier)
    1746 P624

  Printers and booksellers
  Clark, Abraham
    1750 L179
  Whitworth, R. (*printer*)
    1742/– B119
    1746 P624
    1750 L179

Morpeth
  1745 W28

Newcastle upon Tyne
  1740 M239, W532
  1741 C148
  1744 A144

English provincial: Newcastle (cont.)
  '*For the author*'
    1718 B85
    1737 L323 (G. Lumley)
    1746 T556 (W. Turnbull)
  Printers and booksellers
  Akenhead, Robert, *junior*
    1750 T165
  Gooding, John (*printer*, on the Side)
    1745 W28
  Goolding, T. (*printer*, on the Side; possibly related to
  the preceding)
    1715 H299
  Lane, Isaac, & Co. (*printers*, at the head of the Side)
    1734/36 B180
  Umfreville, Thomas, & Co. (*printers*)
    1737 L323
  West, Joseph (in the Groat-market)
    1741 I69, N309
  White, John (*printer*)
    17–– B214
    1711 W457
    1712 H234
    172– C242
    1720/– R39
    1726 E298, T154
    173– C147

Northampton
  1731 D476
  Dicey, William (*printer*)
    1723/– M61
    1735 P199

Norwich
  1705 H127 (false imprint?)
  '*For the author*'
    1707 C517 (H. Cross-grove)
    1713 A119–20
  Printers and booksellers
  Burges, Francis (*printer*)
    1702 P725, W24
  Carlos, James
    1749 F55–6
  Chase, William (*printer*)
    1711 C162
  Collins, Freeman (*printer*; also at London)
    1712 G138·5
  Collins, H. (*printer*, near the Red-Well)
    1715 I10
  Collins, Susanna (*printer*, successor to Freeman)
    1713 A119–20
  Cross-grove, Henry (*printer*)
    1707 C517
    1709 E8, E8·1
    1710 M407
    1711 M410
    1719 M408
    1720 M409
    1729 E246
  Goddard, Thomas
    1711 C162
    1714 C163

English provincial: Norwich (cont.)
Oliver, Samuel
1702 W24

Nottingham
'For the author'
1739 B382 (J. Brailsford)
Printers and booksellers
Ayscough, George (*printer*)
1739 B382
1740 E431–2
Ayscough, William (*printer*)
1710 W458
Collyer, John (*printer*)
1714 W280
1719/20? R85
1723 T545
1724 B194
Collyer, Thomas (*printer*)
1739 I47
Ward, William
1713 S647

Oxford
False imprints
1705 H126
1710 D89, E324, G110
1714 C113
1749 N307
No imprint
170– B232
1704/5 D555
1706 O17
1707 B373, O34
1708 D368
1710 E519, E522–3 (possibly false)
1713 D355, T448
1716 R111
1720 T129
1727 B442
1733 B437
1733 S191
1749 A57–9, B64, T481
1750 B587, C295
'For the author'
1738 H128 (J. Heany)
Printers and booksellers
Barrett, John
1750 W248–9
Broughton, *Mr* (possibly not a bookseller)
1738 H128
Clements, Henry (also in London)
1707 G303
Clements, Richard
1730 T103
1740 P412
1741 B433
1742 B434–6
Fletcher, James
1737 A321
1741 J107
1743 B45

English provincial: Oxford: Fletcher, J. (cont.)
1746 C389
1747 F202
1748 F203, H304
1749 F205, W517
1750 F204
Fletcher, Mary
1733 S464
1744 E34
Fletcher, R. (possibly in error for James)
1746 B88
Fletcher, Stephen (also in London)
1709 M267
1713 E530
1723 I75
1727 D66
Hayes, William
1748 F242
Kibblewhite, Stephen (or Kiblewhite)
1718 A191
Lichfield, Leonard (*printer*)
1709 S800
1710 E517
1713 E530 ('by L.L.')
1717 C73
1719 C486
1722 B6
1723 R216
1724 H34
1733 S464
1736 W406
1738 H128
1741 T271, W27
1748 F242
Parker, Sackville
1741 T271, W27
1746 B88
1747 B89
1750 K67
Peisley, Anthony
1710 E517
1715 C70
1717 C69, C73
1720 C76
1721 C75
Royce, W. (in St Clements)
1712 B200
Stephens, John
1709 H286
University Press ('at the Theater' or 'e theatro Shel-doniano')
1713 Y109–10
1715 C70, I74
1717 C69, H348–9
1720 R113–4
1721 C75
1722 O236
1723 I75
1728 F80
1734 D346
1735 D347
1736 D348
1742 M193

English provincial: Oxford: University Press (cont.)
    1747 K14
    1750 D344
Whistler, Edward
    1713 Y109–10
    1717 D446–7, H348–9
Williams, T. (*printer*)
    1718 I1
Wilmot, Samuel
    1723 R216

Preston
    1750/– T102
Hopkins, John
    1743 G112
Stanley, James, & Moon, John
    1748 O217
    1750 T101

Reading
    172–? L31
    1737 W44, W79
Ayres, W. (or Eyres, *printer*, in the Market-place)
    1734 M194
Henry, David
    1739 M225
Kinnier, D. (*printer*)
    1725 M195
Newbery, John (also in London), & Micklewright, C.
    1742 C388
    1744 M196

Salisbury
'For the author'
    1731 H319 (J. Horler)
    1745 G302·5, P1046 (J. Price)

Printers and booksellers
Collins, Benjamin (*printer*)
    1742 M120
    1745 G302·5, N212, P1046
Collins, William
    1731 O209
    1732 D291
Easton, Edward
    1731 O209
    1743 M119

Scarborough
Gent, Thomas (*printer*; also at London & York)
    1734 G118
Ward, Caesar & Chandler, Richard (also at London & York)
    1732 M152
    1737 T527

Sheffield
Lister, Francis (*printer*, near the Shambles)
    1746 N194
Turner, Joseph
    1701 S943
    1709 C1·5

English provincial (cont.)
Sherborne
'For the author'
    1740 R336 (C. Ryall)

Printers and booksellers
Goadby, Robert (also at Bath & Yeovil)
    1741 B470

Shipston
Keating, J. (also at Alcester & Stratford)
    1749 P103

Shrewsbury
Cotton, John
    1745 O169
    1749 C424
Cotton, John, & Eddowes, Joshua (*printers*)
    1749 E287
Jones, Thomas (*printer*)
    1704 D565
Lathrop, Richard (*printer*)
    1738 R194
    1747 W242
Rogers, John
    1709 R177
    1713 R180

Southampton
Fifield, Mary
    1733 S637

Stamford
    1721 H301

'For the author'
    1712 K85–7 (C. Kirkham)

Printers and booksellers
Howgrave, Francis (*printer*)
    1742 H6
Palmer, Edmund
    1726 P992
Thompson, William
    1726 P992
Thompson, William, & Baily, Thomas (*printers*, also at Bury St Edmunds)
    172–? W174

Stratford on Avon
Keating, J. (also at Alcester & Shipston)
    1749 P103

Taunton
Chauklin, Sarah
    1742 U27

Tunbridge Wells
    1705 C78 (at the end of the Upper Walk, Mount-Sion)
    1706 H412
    1749 C130
Curll, Edmund (also at London)
    1712 W255

English provincial (cont.)
Wellingborough
  Middleton, Benjamin
    173–? C503

Westminster
  A. Campbell (1726–30) *see* London

Winchester
  '*For the author*'
    1732 C305 (A. Colpas)
  Printers and booksellers
  Colson, William
    1705 M97
  Greenville, William (*printer*)
    1750? C296
  Philpot, Isaac (*printer*)
    1732 C305

Windsor
  'printed for Timothy Star at the Blue Ribband' (false imprint)
    1741 K48

Worcester
    171–? D559
  '*For the author*'
    1745 O169 (E. Oldnall)
  Printers and booksellers
  Bryan, Stephen (*printer*)
    171–? S787
  Olivers, Thomas (*printer*)
    1745 O169

Yeovil
  '*For the author*'
    1747 F308
  Printers and booksellers
  Goadby, Robert (also at Bath & Sherborne)
    1747 F308

York
    173– M145
    1745/– H390
  '*For the author*'
    1732 M152 (S. Maxwell)
    1738 G116 (T. Gent)
    1740 F165 (M. Flemyng)
    1743 G112 (T. Gent)
  Printers and booksellers
  Gent, Thomas (*printer*; also at London & Scarborough)
    1732 M142
    1736 M147
    1738 G116
    174– G115
    1742 G111
    1743 G112, M151
  Hammond, Thomas, *junior*
    1718 J98
  Hildyard, John
    1732 M142, M152

English provincial: York: Hildyard, J. (cont.)
    1736 M147
    1740 P602
    1743 D232
    1746 D231
    1750 S495
  Ward, Caesar, & Chandler, Richard (also at London & Scarborough)
    1737 T527
    1740 F165
    1743 D232
  Ward, Robert (*printer*, in partnership with John White junior)
    1725 F103
  White, Grace (*printer*, widow of John White senior)
    1718 J98
  White, John, *senior* (*printer*)
    170–? P1018
  White, John, *junior* (*printer*, in partnership with Robert Ward)
    1725 F103

SCOTLAND

No attempt has been made to list Scottish editions with no imprint, most of which originated in Edinburgh. First editions can be identified from the Scottish sections of the Chronological Index; the following list is an attempt to supplement that with Scottish reprints and a number of poems of doubtful origin which may be Scottish.

  17–– G237
  1701 B510, D160, E158, P724, Y13
  1703 D143
  1704 D127, E481, S431
  1704/05 W78
  1705 A31, P232, S438
  1706 D187, M68
  1707 L133
  1708 J3, S833
  171– E441
  1711 C36–8, F66, N329, S723, S940
  1711/– T582
  1712 P509, R174, S912, T524
  1714 A249, C526, G176–7, G274, K44–6
  1715 M108
  1715/16 M222, T286
  1715/– N182
  1716 E350
  1716/– B449
  1717 P759
  1718 R38, R61–2, R94
  1719 H469–70
  1719/20 P617, R47, R52
  172– R54
  1720 A266, D547, R109, W178
  1721 M219, W187
  1721/22 E77–8
  1722 E12, E68, M306, R102
  1723 S421
  1724 H63, S903
  1725 Y138, Y140, Y142–5
  1726 S828, Y139, Y146

1727   L53, M341, Y147
1728   P769, W377, Y141, Y148
1729   L67
1729/30 P1164
173-   F191
1731   M215, P216
1732   B167, B370, E221, P915
1733   B399, C213
1733/-   P836
1734   B277, F41, K98
1735   S565
1737   G284, P897, P958
1738   D377, M216, P879, P966
1739   C404, D288, E25, E427, G199, M169, N342,
        S480, S727, W423
1740   L127·5, M238, P466, S574
1741   B155·5, E606, W46·5
1742   A214, P793, W477, W485, Y27, Y33, Y39
1743   Y18, Y45
1744   A143
1745   O188-9, P636, W500
1745/46 D399, W483
1746   A294, E575, J64, M5
1746/-   S596
1747   D398, L267, M45, P471, P513, T41, W415
1748   M571, S423, T184
1749   M430, O26, S47, W437
1750   B121, J84, P863, W250, Y116, Y176

EDINBURGH

No attempt has been made to list Edinburgh poems with no imprint; see the note under Scotland above.

'For the author'

1705   S944 (A. Symson)
1706   S945 (A. Symson)
1718   C144 (W. Cheyn), P150 (A. Pennecuik), R37,
        R40, R46, R90, R97 (A. Ramsay)
1719   A288 (J. Arbuckle), R35, R41-2, R91, R98 (A.
        Ramsay)
1720   R95, R99 (A. Ramsay)
1720/21 R92 (A. Ramsay)
1721   R87 (A. Ramsay)
1722   E15
1723   R59 (A. Ramsay)
1724   P171 (A. Pennecuik), R57 (A. Ramsay)
1727   K20 (J. Ker)
1732   L69 (W. Lauder)
1734   B276 (T. Blair)
1738   M111
1743   D416 (T. Dowie)
1745   N294

Printers and booksellers

Adams, William, *junior* (*printer*)
1715   H405
1716   S485
1718   C240, R37, R44, R46, R60, R90, R97
1719   P676, R35
1723   P152
1729   E210

Edinburgh (*cont.*)
Alison, Alexander (*printer*)
1735   H426
Anderson, Andrew, heirs and successors of (*printers*)
1702   A21, B580, M417
1705   C226
1706   D90, D150
1709   K3, T384
1714   M419
Balfour, John (in partnership with Gavin Hamilton)
1746   E93
1747   H14
Brown, Robert (*printer*)
1706/-   F130
1714   D317
1717   D174
1718   C144, P728
1719   C279, E11
1720   E452
1721   P729
1725   M541
1733   M445
Brown, William (*printer*, in partnership with John Mosman)
1716   E607
1717   T279
1718   P150
1721   P149
Brymer, Alexander
1739   L113
Catanach, John (*printer*)
1729   H102
Cheyne, William (*printer*)
173-   P753
1733   W429, W432
1734   B363, F40, P127
1735   B372, T189
1737   M66, Y15
1740   M350
1741   M263
Cochran, James (*printer*, in partnership with Alexander Murray?)
1739   L113
1743   M137
Crawford, Gideon
1736   E457
Davidson, Alexander
1721   S142
1732   P1027-8
1733   P1030
Dickie, William
1715   S736
Drummond, R. (*printer*, in the Swan-close; the works of 1741, 1744 and 1749 only bear this address, and may not be his work)
1741   D56
1744   W557
1747   B273
1749   B278
Duncan, David
1739   E456
Fleming, Robert (*printer*)
1730   D479, T234

Edinburgh: Fleming, R. (*cont.*)

1731	M294
1732	L69
1733	O86, W433
1734	D386, F79, P921, S889, T326
1735	G149
1737	T210
1738	L111–12
1739	L108–9
1743	D370, W502
1745	R171
1747	S135
1750	F183

Freebairn, David

1705	S944

Freebairn, Robert (*printer*, from 1706?; 1715–16 at Perth)

1705	S944
1712	P358, S692
1712/13	P307
172–?	M214

Hamilton, Gavin (*printer*, in partnership with John Balfour 1746–47)

1734	P127
1746	E93
1747	H14

Hart, Andrew (*printer*)

1713	R78

Jaffrey, George (*printer*)

1702	P1002
1704	E477
1705	C33, C343
1706	E283

Keed, John

1744	B201

Kincaid, Alexander

1738	L111–12
1739	L108–9
1742	A307

Knox, Henry

1705	S944

Lumisden, Thomas (*printer*, in partnership with John Robertson to 1746; 1748 as Thomas Lumisden & company)

1727	S527
1729	S528
1736	E457
1743	D416
1746	D417, P268
1748	C224

McEuen, James (also in London)

1719	A280, A288, M316

McEuen, James & company (*printers*)

1719	A288, M316

Mackie, John (or Macky)

1718	C144

Martin, John

1718	P150

Moncur, John (*printer*)

1707	M360
1708	B516, E451
1710	B515
1711	H190
1712	D400, D402, H353, P132
1713	D401

Edinburgh: Moncur, J. (*cont.*)

1723	P642

Mosman, John (*printer*, in partnership with William Brown; 1721 as J. Mosman & company)

1716	E607
1717	T279
1718	P150
1721	P149

'Murchieson, Donald' (fictitious)

1749	M81

Murray, Alexander (*printer*, in partnership with James Cochran?)

1739	L113

Paton, John

1721	S811
1725	P685

'Philabeg, Fergus' (fictitious)

1749	M81

Ramsay, Allan

Ramsay published all his own poems in Edinburgh; they are not included here. It also seems probable that he took a major part in the production of Edinburgh piracies of London editions.

1720	C463
1723	M59
1724	W214
1726	S827
1732	J33
1734	P803

Reid, John (*printer*)

1701	M545
1708	E53–4, W449
1711	K29

Reid, John, *junior* (*printer*)

1704	E476
1708	G268
1709	R235
1710	A129

Reid, John, III (*printer*; 1713 in Liberton's Wynd, the address of his father who died in August 1712; 1714–18 in Pearson's Closs)

1713	H473, K39
1714	E454, R243
1715	R26, R236
1716	D277
1718	T530

Reid, Margaret (*printer*; widow of John Reid junior)

171–	E441, H392
1719	R83

Robertson, John (*printer*, in partnership with Thomas Lumisden)

1727	S527
1729	S528
1736	E457
1743	D416
1746	D417, P268

Ross, James (*printer*)

1727	A275

Ross, John (or Rosse)

1750	E490, G33, M435

Ruddiman, Thomas (*printer*. In association with his brother Walter, who had been apprenticed to Robert Freebairn, he started a printing house which worked for Freebairn until 1715; a co-partnery between the brothers

Edinburgh: Ruddiman, T. (cont.)
was drawn up in 1719, but it was not until 1727 that they
became full partners)
 1712 P307, P358–9, P362, P374–5, S692
 1713 D55, K24, K40–1, K43–4, P306, P312, P320,
    P400, R329–30, S468·5, S468·7
 1714 K17, M214
 172– R53
 1720 R272
 1723 E417
 1725 K22
 1727 K20
Ruddiman, Thomas & Walter (*printers*)
 1729 B388
 1731/2 M404
 1732 J32–3, P927
 1733 L329, M52, P828–9, P835, P841, P890, V42
 1734 P803, P846, P962
 1735 P12, P918, P970
 1736 P657
 1737 E484, N337, P884, S758
 1738 J78, P936, P939, P983, S808
 1739 S925, W424
Ruddiman, Thomas, Walter, & Thomas (*printers*)
 1740 R289, T429
 1741 D443, H408, L66, N344, S932
 1742 E27, F49, H160, P665
 1743 G271, H23, W507, W513
 1744 D327
S., *Mr* (*printer*; possibly Matthias Symson)
 1701 O227
Sands, William
 1739 L113
Spottiswood, John (*printer*)
 1706/– M422
Stewart, George
 1716 R34
Swanstoun, William
 1704 D82
Symmer, Alexander
 1734 P127
Symson, Andrew (*printer*; see Matthias below)
 1705 S944
 1706 S945
 1708 A130
 1711 A314
Symson, Matthias (*printer*; said to have set up a printing
shop in 1700, and then to have left it to his father Andrew)
 1701 O227, P723
Traill, John
 1734 P127
Vallange, John
 1710 B515
Wardlaw, James
 1703 C229
Watson, James (*printer*; 1701 printed in Glasgow)
 1701 S467
 1702 E180, P1001
 1703 C229
 1705 C31, F188–90
 1706 P105, P364–5
 1709 E443, P727, P731–2, P737, S853, W114
 1710 S125, S683, S936

Edinburgh: Watson, J. (cont.)
 1711 C308, T468
 1712 E440, I27
 1713 N152
 1714 P147–8
 1715 R75
 1719 W213
 1720 W252

SCOTTISH PROVINCIAL

By towns

Aberdeen
 Chalmers, James (*printer*)
  1744 A159, M207

Balfron (near Glasgow)
 Smith, Walter (chapman)
  1749 P588

Coupar, Fife
 Henderson, Robert
  1735 H426

Dunfermline
 Beugo, James
  1736 E457

Glasgow
 1714 E455
 1717 A287
 1719 A288
 1721 H205
 1727 C222
 1728 L58, V73
 1731 B166
 1733 H407
 1737 V105
 1738/– D378
 1740 C223
 1749 B1
 Brown, Hugh (*printer*)
  1714 C227
 Duncan, James (*printer*)
  1722 C280
  1746 G235
 Duncan, William (*printer*)
  1721 A281, B368
  1722 H20
 Foulis, Robert (*printer*)
  174– H421
  1743 L293
  1744 I76
  1745 W216
  1748 A20, W218
 Foulis, Robert & Andrew (*printers*)
  1750 E490, G33, M435, P875, R290, Y174
 Mathie, Alexander
  1717 T279
 Miller, Alexander (*printer*)
  1739 V66

Scottish provincial: Glasgow (cont.)

Newlands, John
1750 E459

Sanders, Robert (*printer*)
1701 A106
1705 N240
1713 A225
1716 L39, S468
1723 E453

Stuart, James
1705 C226

Watson, James (*printer*, in the Gorbals; subsequently at Edinburgh)
1701 S467

Leith

Yetts, William (on the pier)
173– M361

Perth

Freebairn, Robert (normally at Edinburgh)
1716 A97

IRELAND

No attempt has been made to list Irish editions with no imprint. First editions can be identified from the Irish sections of the Chronological Index: the following list is an attempt to supplement that with Irish reprints and a number of poems of doubtful origin which may be Irish.

1701 D264, G108, W403
1701/02 T578
1702 D134
1704 D104
1705 D99
1707 D108
1709 T354
1710 C550, D241, D265, E525, H316, N179, P529, P1049, R129, R147, S937, T349
1711 F12, N146, S941, T340, T365, W396
1712 C344, F17–18, P514, T16, T122
1714 M182, P181, R125, W160–1
1715 M209
1716 P981
1719 O78, S506
172– C241, C485, C533, N21–5, W167
1720 D548, S837, W180–1
1721 B61, B608·5, J38, S812–13, S839
1722 C374, P176, S862
1724 S499, S835, W336
1725 B586, C50, C246, G80, L22–3, P224
1726 C407, D374, E590, S815
1727 S359, W254
1728 B28, K93, N67, P586–7
1729 C183, J47, P4, P783–4
1729/30 P1165
1730 A94, D198, D204, F77, H397, L207, N161, S878–9
1730/31 L185
1731 S476
1732 A186, K81, N8, S871–2, V11
1734 K99

Ireland (cont.)

1735 B28
1736 D518, P142
1737 M67, P972, W465
1738 M391, N274
1739 E291, M367, S481
1740 M241–3, M245, M250, M515–17
1741 F121, M264–5
1742 A268, A308, F96, M384
1743 E18, P26, W508
1744 W455
1746 L295, W491
1747 C153, G121
1748 M455–6, S128
1749 G145, T32
1750 P951

DUBLIN

'For the author'

1709 W515 (W. Williams)
1720 C327 (M. Concanen)
1730 H417 (A. Huy)
1732 T248 (J. Thomson)
1738 T247 (J. Thomson)
1740 O13 ('M. O'Connor')
1741 L17
1742 D194 (T. H. De la Mayne)
1746 M190, W274 (J. E. Weeks)
1748 C142 (W. R. Chetwood)
1750 P1158–9 (S. Pullein)

Printers and booksellers

Afleck, John
1728? E13

Anburey, William Shaw (*printer*; in partnership with J. Watts, 1730)
1727 P108
1730 G320

Bate, Edward (*printer*)
1743 S97
1745 A170
1746 S219

Benson, Thomas
1728 P289, P770, S96

Bentley, W. (opposite the Sun in Pill-lane; engraver?)
1725/30 O110

Bowes, Phillip
1744 P798

Bradley, Abraham
1730 D6
1731 M295
1735 T190, T193
1736 H26, H28

Brian, Ed.
1728 I2

Brocas, John (*printer*)
1701 S513, W474
1702 D29·5
1705 A32, P233

Brock, Stearne
1729 B389

Dublin (*cont.*)
Bruce, W.
 1737 G192–3
Butler, Thomas
 1744 W413
Campbell, Patrick
 1702 W14
Carr, J. (or Car, in Silver Court in Castle-street)
 1726 E556
 1728/29 N139
Carson, James (*printer*)
 1717 D32
 1719 O9, R294, Y104
 1720 H174, S413
 1722 N71, P555
 1723 E417·2, P1133
 1724 A338, H163, H173, N140, N176, O257, P518, S498, W145
 1725 A285
 1729 E171–2, T332
 1731 D80
 1734 E61, P963
 1735 M476
 1737 E554
 1740 O63
 1740/41 O16
Carter, Cornelius (*printer*)
 1702 L306
 1708 G251, G269
 1711 Q11, S139
 1712 B527·3
 1713 S693–4
 1714 A72, S216
 1720 J22
 1721 C126, N197
 1725 B80, D403, E74, E85, E116, E261, F291, N26, P610
 1726 E181, F293, N30, P114
 1727 A346
Cotter, Joseph
 1747 P695
 1749 S150
Crampton, Philip
 1727 C548·5, M100
 1728 P770, S96
Crooke, Andrew (*printer*)
 1728 S754
Dalton, James
 1739 L285
Dalton, Samuel (*printer*)
 1738 W468
 1739 B43
Dickson, Christopher (*printer*)
 1727 A360, S14
 1729 B150
 1730 H417, W551
 1733 V43
 1734 P593
 1743 D39, N112
Dickson, Elizabeth (*printer*; widow of Francis)
 1713 E582, T387
 1714 P680

Dublin (*cont.*)
Dickson, Francis (*printer*)
 1702 E326
 1707 D93
 1711 E164, L309
Dickson, Richard (*printer*; 1725 with E. Needham, 1726 with Gwyn Needham)
 1724 B441, T519
 1725 M560, P223
 1725/29 S426
 1726 A71, D208, D228
 1727 E31, E568
 1728 E550
 1729 B59, D554, T110
 1731 S383
Dobson, Eliphal, *junior*
 1710 D542
 1716 A47
Droghedy, Paddy ('and sold at his lodgings opposite to Madam Violante's booth in Dames-street'; fictitious?)
 1732 C243
Dugan, Patrick
 1719 Y93
 1725 G28, W138
Durneene, J. (*printer*)
 1728 M281 (in Pembroke-court)
 1729 N52 (next door to the Waly's head, in Patrick's-street)
Esdall, James (*printer*)
 1745 T380, W269, W273
 1746 W274
 1747 L278
 1748 C142
 1749 H330
 1750 D364
Ewing, George
 1725 Y149–50, Y152–3, Y156–7, Y160
 1726 Y154, Y158, Y163
 1727 B247, Y151, Y161, Y165
 1728 B77, B543, R19, T228, Y155, Y159, Y162, Y164, Y166–8, Y170
 1729 G77, S108
 1730 G31, O62, O273, O285, S411·5, T218, T224, T235, T241, Y84–5, Y97, Y114, Y120
 1731 Y172
 1732 Y107
 1733 O61, P830, P843, P849, P929, S82
 1734 D524, P280, P831, P838, P848
 1735 V89, Y80
 1736 S401
 1737 A286
 1738 P940, Y89
 1740 O63, T226, T232
 1742 P795, S570
 1743 B589
Ewing, George & Alexander
 1744 P799
 1745 B590
 1746 O64
 1747 B591
 1748 C142, T185, Y121

Dublin (*cont.*)

Exshaw, Edward
173– W341
1733 P632
1735 D382, M488, W352
1739 B428–9, W206

Exshaw, Edward & John
1747 H25
1748 L47, M128

Fairbrother, Samuel (*printer*)
1714 M470
1717 C94
1722 E301
1724 W19

Faulkner, George (*printer*; 1727–30 in partnership with James Hoey, though a few items appear with his name alone)
172– B220, D190
1725 P208, T7, V123
1726 C48, N63, P1100, S210, Y22
1727 C46, D451, H130, M342, S214
1728 P107, P250, P770, S797, Y96
1729 B305, B390, D452, E312, F93, P782, R17, T178, W378
1730 B138, C483, D8, D480, D528, F159, G313–14, M389, N249, P516, T167, W356, Y118
1731 M252, P667
1732 B310, D9, D200, L336, P916, S873, S908, W363
1733 B67, B400–1, E388, G307, L74, P837, P842, P891–2, P930–1, S885, T390
1734 D522, D525, P847, P854, P922, W411
1735 A172, D529, H96, P804–5, P919, P971, T461–2
1736 B328, B395, B497, M260, P18
1737 A328, N347, P885, P902, P959, S759, Y15·2
1738 J80, M257, N338, P196, P880, P937, P940, S804–5
1739 G200–1, S926–30
1740 C57, D468, D520, E219, S403, S575–6, W338–9
1741 B352, B355, D521, F121, O96, P548, S931
1742 B357, P794, T351
1743 P1021
1744 A145, D519, M426, V53
1745 M10, M411, P870, T503
1747 D515, L340, M46–7, S400, S424, V54, V101, Y177
1748 A146, C142
1749 C214, E611, F153, M429, P874, P1157, V102
1750 A267

Fitz-Symons, James
1720 C330

Fleming, Thomas (at the Salmon in High Street)
1726 I38

Forrest, William (*printer*)
1727 A269

Fuller, Samuel (*printer?*)
1722 E301
1724 A338
1728 D176
1730 D177, G30

Garland, Halhed (*printer*)
1747 P655
1749 S137

Dublin (*cont.*)

Gill, P.
1702 W14

Golding, George (at the Blew Anchor in High Street)
173–? W146

Gowan, George
1735 W133–5

Gowan, John (*printer*)
1725/30 E609
1726 C68, F2, G60–1, P563, P596, P659, S221, S721
1727 B145, C45, M561, P578
1728 T300
1729 N239
1730 P59
1734 A357
1737 G3

Grierson, George (*printer* from 1721)
1711 D311, P809
1713 P990, W26
1714 G50, G72, T143
1715 P241·5, P976
1717 P75, P815, P1071
1721 B112
1722 B112·5
1724 L40
1725 B221–2, P221
1726 P219
1729 D196–7
1732 B115

Gunn, Matthew (or Gunne; T511 is a (mock?) elegy of 1724)
1701 E334
1702 D29·5, D135, U22
1702/14 P550
1704 D167
1706 D28, W34, W173
1707 E473
1708 K58, S640

Gunne, Richard
1709 S635
1735 S566

H., W. (*printer*)
1722 N153

Haite, John (at the back of Dick's-Coffee-house, in Skinner-row)
1710? D274

Hamilton, Edward
1728 P770

Hamilton, J.
1750 M113

Harbin, Thomas (*printer*; in partnership with Pressick Rider 1724–25)
1724 P51
1725 C277, G28, P217, P281–2, P542, T290, W138, Y113
1726 E536

Harding, John (*printer*)
1720 S414
1721 B60, D202, N174, P1169, V120
1722 E251, L63, R237, V82
1722/23 B227
1724 D21, E233, E541·5, E570, I66, L124, S846, S898, S902, T334

Dublin: Harding, J. (cont.)
 1725   N289, P660, S406, W447
Harding, Sarah (*printer*)
 1725   B78, O230, T373–4
 1727   S417
 1728   S95
 1729   S863
Heatly, William
 1733   D312
 1734   D11
 1735   H401, R139
Henly, John
 1710   M550
 1713   P236, S894
 1714   P945, S855
Hicks, C. (*printer*, at the Rein Deer in Montrath Street; succeeded by Christopher Goulding in 1736 according to *Plomer*. On the evidence of P501, which appears to follow an edition of Elizabeth Sadleir whose last work is 1726, Hicks's undated chapbooks are dated 1726/36)
 1726/36   C329, L10–11, P501–3, W448
 1726   H259
 1727   N27
 1730   I58
 173–   W147
Hoey, James (*printer*; in partnership with George Faulkner 1727–30)
 1727   D451
 1728   P107, P250, P770, Y96
 1729   B305, B390, D452, E312, F93, P782, R17, T178, W378
 1730   B138, G313–14, M389, Y118
 1730   (without Faulkner) D423, M393, Y119
 1731   D453, P688, T437, W263
 1732   R198, S831, T162
 1733   A364, C56·5, D179, N284, T390·5, W10, W573
 1734   P124
 1735   D454, W351
 1738   H400, S103
 1739   H181–2
 1741   C315
 1745   W270
 1749   B406, C538, U16
Hume, Thomas (or Humes, *printer*)
 1714   G56
 1715   T369
 1716   T287, W542
 1717   P75, P1071, S211
 1718   P634
 1719   S207
 1720   S711, W184
 1721   C395, P203
 1722   P1153, W376
 1723   C396, F156
 1724   S208
 1725   D36, E319, P591, S209
 1726   L252, P635, T215
 1728   R283
Hussey, Nicholas (*printer*)
 1729   I56, J102, N29, S864
Hyde, John (*printer* from 1726)
 1712   R334
 1713   T454

Dublin: Hyde, J. (cont.)
 1722   B506
 1726   T168
 1727   S358
Hyde, S. (*printer*)
 1732   S416
 1734   S890, T327
Jackson, Isaac (*printer*)
 1743   D180
 1749   D182
James, Richard (*printer*)
 1747   C345, P35, T42
 1748   M403, T185
 1749   B14, B362
 1750   M82, S200
Jones, E. (*printer*)
 1739   M170, O12
Jones, J. (*printer*)
 1738   P967
Jones, Theophilus (*printer*)
 1735   H163·2
K., J. (*printer*)
 1729   E174
Kelburn, James
 1739   L285, O12
 1743   S97
Kelly, Den.
 1728   I2
'Kilcock, Dorothy' (near Lucas's Coffee-house on Cork-hill; fictitious)
 1734   K33·5
Kinneir, J. & Long, A. (*printers*)
 1745   E469, F179
 1746   O232, P572
Knowles, T. (*printer*)
 1749   C149, C269
Lawrence, Thomas
 1727   C548
Leathley, Joseph
 1719   R294
 1728   P770
 1735   T190, T193
Leslie, Charles
 1745   A170
'Little, John' (fictitious)
 1727   L197
Lloyd, Edward (in Essex-street)
 1711   R323
Long, Augustus (*printer*; in partnership with J. Kinneir 1745–46)
 1745   E469, F179
 1746   O232, P572
 1748   H305
 1749   F145
Mason, J. (*printer*)
 1726/27   L195
Meres, A. (*printer*)
 1714   G56
Milner, M. (? widow of J. Milner, died 1701)
 1702   W14
Moore, T.
 1735   T193
Musgrove, Theophilis (*printer*)
 1729   N31

Dublin (cont.)

Neal, P. (in Georges Lane)
1725   B293

Needham, E. (*printer*; 1725 with R. Dickson)
1725   M560, N20, P223
1726   E383

Needham, Gwyn (*printer*; 1726 with R. Dickson)
1717   P76
172/-   S798, W132
1724   N165, T362
1725   O263
1726   A71
1727   D247, E568

Nelson, Oliver (*printer*)
1738   D379
1741   O250
1745   F72
1746   L103
1747   M102
1748   O32

Nicholson, James
1728   L196

Norris, Richard
1719   Y104
1727   B423, T206, T221
1728   N68

Owen, Robert
1731   P264
1735   S566

P., W. (*printer*, in Skinner-row)
1725   L59

Pattin, Ja. (in Coles-alley in Castle-street)
1726   E556

Pepyat, Jeremiah
1709   H241, H284, T166
1717   D32

Pepyat, Jeremiah & Sylvanus
1723   F156-7

Pepyat, Mary (*printer?*)
1743   F160, G288

Pepyat, Sylvanus (*printer*; 1723 in partnership with Jeremiah)
1723   F156-7
1731   D80
1733   P928, W11
1736   O81
1737   G286, P960
1738   D379

Powell, Stephen/Samuel (*printers*, father and son. According to *Plomer*, Stephen died in 1728 and was succeeded by Samuel; the imprint is always 'S. Powell', but I would guess Samuel took over between 1722 and 1725)
1706   M105
1707   I63
1710   P623
1713   P236, P990, T454
1714   G72
1716   A46, C71, G84, P954, R299, T282
1717   T280
1722   P520
1725   Y78, Y149-50, Y152-3, Y156-7, Y160
1726   H167, O11, O97, Y88, Y106, Y154, Y158, Y163
1727   B247, B423, C548, C548·5, G85, M100, O3,

Dublin: Powell, S./S. (cont.)
T206, T221, Y151, Y161, Y165
1728   B77, B543, H157·6, P289, R19, S96, T228, Y79, Y155, Y159, Y162, Y164, Y166-8, Y170
1729   B389, G77, P117, S108
1730   D6, G31, O62, O273, O285, T218, T224, T235, T241, Y84, Y97, Y114, Y120
1731   M295, P173-4, Y172
1732   Y107
1733   C102, O61, P632, P830, P843, P849, P929, S82, V49, W430
1734   D11, D524, P831, P838, P848
1735   A151, H401, M488, R139, T193, V89, W352, Y80
1736   S401
1737   W204
1738   M565
1739   B428-9
1740   T226, T232
1741   L17
1742   D194, S570
1743   B589, Y98
1745   B590
1746   D37, J94, T43
1747   B591, P695, S791, W416
1750   M113, P1158-9

Powell, William
1744   A298
1747   M102

R., J.
1725   N296

Ray, Joseph
1702   W14

Reilly, A. (*printer*; successor to Richard)
1742   P795

Reilly, Richard (*printer*)
1735   L139, N330, S566
1736   H26, H28
1737   A286, G192-3, O102
1738   P940
1739   W206
1740   C59

Rhames, Aaron (*printer*)
1709   H241, H284, T166
1711   P809
1716   A47
1722   B506, C118
1723   D209
1726   P220
1727   G51
1728   L173, P583
1729   S753
1730   T440

Rhames, Joseph (*printer*)
1744   S765

Rider, Ebenezer (*printer*)
1736   D517, D533, G103

Rider, Pressick (*printer*; in partnership with Thomas Harbin, 1724-25)
1724   P51
1725   C277, G28, P217, P281-2, P542, T290, W138, Y113

Risk, George
1716   A46, C71, C191, G84, R299, T282

Dublin: Risk, G. (cont.)
1717 T280
1726 O97
1727 B247, G85
1728 B543, T228
1729 G77, S108
1730 G31, O273, O285, T218, T224, T235, T241, Y84–5, Y97, Y114, Y120
1732 Y107
1733 P830, P843, P849, P929, S82
1734 P831, P838, P848
1737 O102
1738 P940
1740 T226, T232
1743 Y98
1748 Y121
Sadleir, Elizabeth (*printer*)
1715/26 P500
1723 E275, P1092
1726 B76, E80, F28, P675
Sandys, Edwin (*printer*)
1706 O51
1710 S215
1711 U15
1713 I4, W26
1714 G50, T143
1715 P241·5, P976
Shepheard, Thomas
1706 M105
Smith, John (in partnership with William Bruce, 1737)
1737 G192–3
1744 A298
Smith, William
1724 H163, P51, W145, W335
1725 W348
1726 T215
1727 B247
1728 B543, T228
1729 G77, S108
1730 G31, O273, O285, T218, T224, T235, T241, Y84–5, Y97, Y114, Y120
1732 Y107
1733 P830, P843, P849, P929, S82
1734 P831, P838, P848
1735 H163·2
1737 W204
1738 P940
1740 T226, T232
1748 Y121
'Stone, James, in High-street' (fictitious; probably a London publication)
1742 H159
'Telltruth, Timothy' (fictitious)
1736 F265
Thompson, James
1725 C501
1726 H167, O11, P417
1728 G76
1729 P950
1730 G320
Thornton, Thomas
1733 C102, V49
1735 N330

Dublin (cont.)
Tompson, Daniel (*printer*)
1714 B608, G57
1715 F206
Tompson, J. (*printer*, in High-street)
1726 P209
'Toybow, John, in Sheep-street, opposite the Bulls-head' (fictitious)
1728 S463
University Press
1746 L45
W., J. (*printer*)
1721 S838
Walsh, Thomas (*printer*)
1727 A342
1729 P522, T436
1733 C165
Ware, John (*printer* in 1726)
1707 D93
1726 S70
Waters, Edward
1708 O249, S640
1709 W515
1710 C178, M550
1710/14 H294
1711 R323, T446
1712 G38, S729
1713 C364, D439, E111, O123, P1132, W237
1713/14 L154
1714 E493, P721, T321
1716 P1033, S213, S642
1720 S502
1723 C278
1727 A358–9, G305, S643
1728 A356, B236, C482, C531, D527, L60, O190
1729 A355, G306, H357
173– S644
1731 E265
1733 S886, V108
1736 D251, J15, P1141, R187
1738 A135
1739 L242, R165
1740 W340
Watson, John
1731 P173–4
Watts, J. (*printer*)
1725 C501, W348–9
1726 P417
1728 G76
1730 G320
Whalley, John
1714 G291, W375
1722 P545
Whitehouse, Thomas
1725 Y78, Y113
1726 Y88, Y106
1728 Y79
Wilmot, William (*printer*)
1725 E92
1726 M573
1727 P621
Wilson, Peter
1743 C134, D14, D314, Y56

Dublin: Wilson, P. (cont.)
1745　W272
1746　L45, M190
1747　Y63
1748　C142
Wynne, Cornelius
1742　R278

IRISH PROVINCIAL

By towns

Armagh
　1745　F267
　Dickie, William (*printer*)
　1740　C58, C60
　1746　F214

Belfast
　Blow, James (*printer*)
　1707　E461
　Joy, Francis (*printer*)
　1738　D380
　Magee, James (*printer*; 1740–41 in partnership with
　Samuel Wilson)
　1740　S645
　1741　C309
　1748　L110
　Wilson, Samuel (*printer*)
　1740　S645
　1741　C309

Cork
　1729　T111
　Terry, Samuel (*printer*, in Cock-Pit-lane)
　1721　S901
　Welsh, Andrew (*printer*; 1733, next door but one to the
　Corke-Arms, near the Corn-market; whether this is
　the son has not been determined. *See also* Limerick)
　1723　S738
　1733　S874–5, V50

Drogheda
　Connor, James
　1728　W232

Limerick
　Brangan, Thomas (*printer*)
　1716　B560
　Welsh, Andrew (*printer*, at the sign of the Globe in
　Key-lane; the relationship of this printer with the
　Andrew Welshes of Cork has not been determined)
　1721　S840

Rathfarnam
　'printed at the Cherry-tree' (possibly the work of
　James Hoey & George Faulkner in Dublin)
　1730　P516

Temple-Oge
　'printed at' (possibly printed at Dublin for sale there)
　1730　M475·5

FOREIGN

No imprint
　1701　N348
　1704/05　D564
　1724　I55
　1740　L93·5
　1745/46　A1, C131, C383, I67, N302·5, O22, O58,
　　　　　O172

By towns

Amsterdam
　False imprint
　1710　V92–3
　1712　F258–9
　1741　C287

　'*For the author*' (*false imprint*)
　1741　C287

　Printers and booksellers
　Boussière, Henri
　1741　F167
　Joubert, Jean
　1746　M139
　L'Honoré & Chatelain
　1717　R229
　Petri, Johann
　1713　P1101·5
　'Swart, Weybran' (in false imprint)
　1721　P165

Annapolis, Maryland
　Parks, William (*printer*)
　1728　L165 (for the author)

Boston, Massachusetts
　1714　O242
　Hancock, T.
　1730　W256
　Phillips, J.
　1730　W256

'Brobdignagg, printed by Lamuel Hnhmyontrams,
printer to his majesty of Laputa' (fictitious imprint for
Dublin publication)
　1734　L321–2

Danzig
　False imprint
　1705　D97–9

Douai
　1710/16　B199

'Elguze, printed for Pedaneous, and sold by Circum-
foraneous, below the zenith' (fictitious imprint)
　1741　M162

Ghent
　1731　P259

Foreign (*cont.*)
the Hague
   Johnson, T.
     1716 A48, P814, P947
     1720 R295

Hamburg
    1710 W207

Holland
   False imprint
    1712 S769

Jamaica
   Baldwin, R. (*printer*, in Church-street in Kingston)
     1718 P288
     1719 P483
   Baldwin, Peter & Robert
     1740 L126, L128
   Letts, John (*printer*)
     1740 L126, L128

'Pandaemonium, printed for Venerable Merlin, at the Memento Mori' (fictitious imprint)
    1748 A163

Paris
   False imprint
    1749 S46
   No imprint
    1701 E160
   Gandouin
    1741 V115

Foreign: Paris (*cont.*)
   Piget
    1741 L219
   Prault, *père*
    1741 L219

Rome
   False imprint
    1715 C529

Rotterdam
    1746 S134

St Germains
    1701 E160

Switzerland
   False imprint
    1713 R123

Utrecht
    1712 D296
    1713 D298

Venice
   False imprint
    1727 E376

'Williamsburgh, printed for Fr. Maggot, at the sign of the Hickery-tree in Queen-street' (fictitious imprint)
    1702 L296

INDEX OF BIBLIOGRAPHICAL NOTABILIA

This index is inevitably subjective in its choice of subjects, and its completeness dependent on the notes made when books were examined. It makes no reference to details obtained from printers' ledgers, for which see Ackers, Bowyer, Ruddiman, Strahan, and Woodfall in the Index of Imprints; nor does it include sales of copyright by authors or by booksellers.

addenda

key to poem, M459, M460

leaf, P773, P775 (offered in advertisement to purchasers of early copies)

see also reissue – additional material added

advertisements: *see* fine-paper copies – advertisements removed

author's annotations and corrections, B352, B355, B356, B357, C298, G21, G173, V46

see also manuscript corrections

authorship statement

added to title of reissue, B265, B339, H270, M74, M80, T302, T551, T565, W81, W575; removed from title of reissue, C548·5, H269

changed by cancel dedication, W226

changed by cutting out previous author's name, H69, S252·2

changed in variant title, B412, B537·1, B581·5, E8·1, E46, F38, H11, H77·5, H80·2, H83·2, P556, W566·2

see also fine-paper copies – author's name

ballad: *see* imitations of popular ballads

begging poems

I have given this name to poor relations of the presentation poems listed under dedication; *they are clearly intended for soliciting gifts. The annual new year verses of bellmen, beadles and lamplighters are excluded from this catalogue.* B183 (marshal to trained bands), B526–7 (marshal), C238 (clergyman's daughter), C301–4, G156–68 (blind man), H5 (marshal), H110 (hawkers), H363 (marshal), M111 (blank form for wedding poem,) N245, P1008, S180–8 (blind clergyman)

binding

gilt edges to pamphlets (normally associated with presentation copies in marbled wrappers), A201, D199, K22, L70, L169, M566, N349, O250, P1066, T289, W353, Y76, Y105

'illuminated copies' of poems by Elkanah Settle (the text is mounted on heavy paper with a decorative border of gold-tooling and colour), S276, S286, S301–2, S304–8, S310–19, S322

label on spine gives author of anonymous work, B195, B301, B308, P786; *see also* the collected poems of Joseph Browne, Macnamara Morgan

pamphlets in original wrappers: black mourning wrapper, H278, W345; blue-grey paper, A14, D232, E93, P462, P771, P779, P893, P966, P974, S258, S571; blue-grey paper, printed with advertisements, Y25; marbled (usually for fine-paper or presentation copies, with gilt edges), C295, C426, L165, L169, P174, P808, P1066, S255, V71, W140, W353; printed white wrappers for part issue (title on upper cover, advertisements on lower), W105, W106, W111 ('with covers to keep it clean in order to be bound up')

binding *(cont.)*

pamphlets without wrappers, stitched, uncut, B121, B531, B612, C11, C189, C274, C324, G276, L236, O288, P765–8, P780, P789, P806, P888, P908, P909, S573, T216, T227, T233, T268, W40, W71, W116, Y125, Y128, Y130, Y132, Y136

presentation copies in morocco, B249, D12, F227, H146, K21, M8, M9, M10, M25, N247, N298, P237 (stipulated in author's agreement), R270, R293, T56, T73, T75, V112, V115, W530, Y95, Y101; in uniform calf, D232, P74, P238; *see also* presentation copies *and* Settle, Elkanah *passim*

text ruled in red, A22 (a half-sheet), M8 (in contemporary morocco)

blanks left in printing, E160 (in imprint), F149 (blank poem, published 1 April), H435 (charity hymn for use on successive occasions), K38 (in imprint), M111 (blank form for manuscript epithalamium)

blue paper: *see* paper

borders

mourning borders. *Normally found on half-sheet elegies and the titles of pamphlet elegies; these are not listed here, but may be traced under* Elegy *in the Subject Index. The following are exceptional:* B321 (black borders sewn on poem printed on satin), M544 (printed with mourning borders throughout), O227 (imprint cut on mourning border)

ornamental borders, B183, B525–7, C258–63, C518, C519, E119, E174, H5, H164–6, H363, N131; of texts, E277; of type-flowers, P521, R53, R99

cancel slip, B252, H183 (catchword), L100 (price), O249, S253, S260, S288, S327, S345 (catchword), S768 (one letter), T371, T451 (some copies with revised text); *see also* reissue – cancel slip over imprint

cancels

Cancels in the text have not been indexed; cancel titles, dedications, prefaces, etc. are normally entered under reissue. *The following are a few cases of general interest:* B426 (cancelland title), C477 (substantial changes), H97 (cancelland leaf with ms. correction), H98 (cancelland title), H144 (cancelland bears press-figure), K83 (two editions of cancels), N297 (cancel leaf substitutes politicians in power), O88 (cancel title), O249 (cancelland mispaginated), P74 (cancels to substitute engravings for fine-paper copies), P238 (cancel sheet), P776 (cancelland title slit), P781 (cancellanda slit), S563 (cancel bears press-figure), W47 (cancelland title), W56 (cancel marked with asterisk, cancelland found with ms. correction), Y61 (cancelland title)

collation

duodecimo signed 8/4 or 4/2 (usually Dublin), F75 (London), G31, G235 (Glasgow), H163, M426, M429, O254, P282, P783, P870 (smaller sections signed in lower-case), R119, R120 (London), W206

collation (*cont.*)

folio, 3 leaves. *This format appears to have been intro-
duced to avoid the stamp duties of 1712 by which any
pamphlet of one sheet or less had to be printed on stamped
paper; the same technique was used by newspaper pub-
lishers. The only earlier example seen is O72 (1708).
Most of the early examples of 1712, 1713 are printed on
one side of cheap paper in an attempt to equal the price of
the old half-sheets which were now taxed out of existence*
(B289, D497, D556, E307, F94, H244, L259, M174,
M175, O1, O269, R126, S445, T25, T492). *Their normal
collation is a half-sheet inserted in a folded sheet,* $A^2 < B^1$.
Other early examples of 1712–13 (G16, P526, P594,
P627, P1073, S647, T29, T33, T485, T544, T589) *are
printed normally on ordinary paper and this becomes a
standard format throughout the period, though the colla-
tion varies. The early form is* $A^2 B^1$, *but* $A^1 B^2$ *and* $A^2 < B^1$
*soon became common. There may be a number of unidenti-
fied cases where the signatures do not correspond with the
construction; see* H34, *printed as* $A^2 < B^1$ *but signed as*
$A^2 B^1$. *Some copies printed as* $A^2 < B^1$ *appear to be
signed as* A^3 (H244, J61, K10). *About half are completely
unsigned, and it is frequently impossible to determine
their construction.*
A235, A247, A277, A371, B26, B39, B41, B65, B91,
B289, B349, B424, B479, B568, B584, C6, C10, C106,
C264, C359, C430, C543, D353, D421, D497, D502,
D507, D556, E307, E348, E349, E362, E377, E378,
E394, E402, E431, E494, E495, E497, E498, E499, E512,
F4, F7, F23, F94, F139, F216, F257, G16, G299, H34,
H66, H83, H243, H244, H310, H406, J21, J34–6, J39,
J61, J83, K10, L150, L217, L228, L240·2, L259, L265,
M174, M175, M412, M471, M475, M500, M500·5,
M536, N15, N130, O1, O21, O38, O65, O72, O76,
O165, O224·2, O269, P2, P8, P44, P95, P141, P278,
P465, P470, P510, P526, P594, P599, P604, P627, P654,
P706, P711, P984, P1073, P1103, P1122, P1161, P1162,
Q3, R31, R126, R161, R199, R201, R232, R297, S12,
S16, S116, S129, S136, S178, S367, S397, S445, S454,
S498, S512, S592, S616, S647, S669, S715, S786,
S794, T25, T28, T29, T33, T34, T94, T293, T368,
T485, T492, T544, T589, V63, V77, W294

folio half-sheets signed 'A', B513, E353, P528,
P625, P1031, P1086, P1124, R291, S9, T518

printed on one side of the sheet only: folio, 3 leaves,
foliated 1–3, B289, D497, F94, L259, M174, R126,
S445, T25; folio, 3 leaves, paginated 1–6, D556, E307,
M175, O1 (irregular), O269, T492; folio, 2 leaves, inner
forme only (usually Edinburgh), H17, J5, K39–41,
K43–4, K46, M38, P366, P368, P381; others, A237,
B378–9 (engraved), H271 (engraved), P1113 (engraved),
T252 (with woodcuts)

quarto: gathering composed of two half-sheets
(Irish), C58, D524, O64, W274; in eights, O94, O105

signatures at variance with construction: A^4 signed
$A–B^2$, O233, W245, W523; A^6 signed $A–C^2$, C148; A^8
signed $A–B^4$, R94; $A^2 B^4$ signed A^6 (Henry Hills, 1709),
C79, H240, W71; miscellaneous, M170, P548, S150,
S235, Y61; *see also* folio, 3 leaves

signatures containing an odd number of leaves,
B198, D482, E309, G259, M212–13, N348, T145;
see also folio, 3 leaves; folio half-sheets signed A; wrapper
formed by first and last signatures

collation (*cont.*)

unusual collations, D128, P417, P906, U11, U35

variant collation for fine-paper copies, C373, D223,
P797, P826

watermark evidence contradicts expected collation
pattern (possibly the result of binder dividing sheets
before assembling copies), G81, P806, T181

wrapper formed by first and last signatures (the
common case of $A^1[=D1]$ $B–C^4$ $D^4(-D1)$ and the
alternative using D4 as A1 are not recorded), C85,
M212–13, M439, O104, P655, P806, S762, T145, T181,
W105–6; *see also* folio, 3 leaves

collection

new edition of part to complete sets, P832, P839,
P844, T219, T225–6, T231–2, T456, W92, Y28, Y35,
Y42, Y46, Y48, Y85, Y143, Y145

part issued separately, P961

preliminaries for collection of separately published
parts, G112, T217–18, T239, T241–2, Y167, Y170

printed so that parts may be separately issued, P815,
R32–109 *passim*, Y58, Y63, Y172

reprints designed for possible incorporation in collection, P835, P841, P846, P890, R32–109 *passim*,
S828, Y138–48, Y151, Y155, Y159, Y162, Y166

see also continuation; reissue – of single work in
collection

colour printing

red and blue paint over blind impression, C26–7

red paint over black ink, S460

red printing throughout, A345, D228, N110–12,
P586, S738

text in red and black, K87

white printing on black paper, M546

columns, editions printed in two (*used for cheap editions,
and hence usually a sign of piracy; half-sheets, where it is
common, are not indexed*), D26, D112, D118–19, D125–6,
D170, D448, D448·5, E20, F87, H406, H472, H472·5,
L143, M71, N132, P272, P423, P457, P490–1, P499,
R246–7, S3, S442·4, S442·6, S530, T76, T98, T491,
T575, W44, W73, W77–9, W124, W151, W202, W524,
Y7–11

conjugate printing of separate poems

*Though most slip songs and other small pieces must have
been printed two or more at a time, almost all that survive
undivided are Jacobite propaganda.*

eighth-sheets, B284, L117

half-sheets, N182, R2, R5, R48

quarter-sheets, B154, C13–14, C193, J111, P637,
P686, P1058

slip songs, B15, E288, E540, E560–1, E564, E566,
F44, F207–8, H303, K54, L301, N53, N55, N238,
P112, P194–5, P469, P1034, T396, T510

continuation (works published in separate books or sec-
tions), A294–5, B21–2, D278–84, D514, D523, E7,
E308, H302, O111, O130, P822–48, S157–8, T173–5,
T186–99, T211–35, T456–60, W70, W237, W464–7,
W470–3, Y24–54, Y122–37

periodical, O190 (Dublin), S685–6, T373–4 (Dublin)

see also collection; parts, publication in

copyright

actions against infringement, A307, P774, R83

author's request for it to be respected, E457

deposit copies: fine paper, P765, P882, T186, T191,

copyright (cont.)

T194, T196, T198, T208, Y95; later 'editions' (probably variant title), S703, S709; part 1 only of series entered, W193

entry in *Stationers' Register* claimed on title, not traced (a commonplace of nineteenth-century publishing; many examples not listed), D2, F192, W87

entry to author in *Stationers' Register*, A296, B10, B488–90, C23, C39, C47, C162, D226, F117, G171, G190, G197, H302, J57, M424, M500, P437, P453, P787, P932, P938, P965, Q17, R214, S109, S562, S571, S702, T208, T449, T548

ineffectiveness of protection commented on, copies signed, F117, R214

corrections to text

made by overprinting or stamping-in by hand, E604, H83·2, O249, P267 (price), P761 (page no.), P819 S260

see also cancel slip; cancels; manuscript corrections; variants

date

altered in ms. (sometimes clearly as a form of reissue), D64, E604, F88, G318, H69, H81·5, J29, L26, N232, P577, P994, S19, S245, S251, S253, S260·5, S565, S646, W185

misprinted, A5, A178, A360, B163, B410, B420, B439, B592–3, D387, E465, G73, G172, J45, K63, L174, L219, M87, P791, P798, S532, S814, S859, W351

For other changes of date, *see* imprint; reissue

dedication

A poet normally hoped for a financial acknowledgment from the person to whom he dedicated his poem (cf. B364, S112, S285 for such payment); he might also hope for reward from others to whom he presented copies (cf. B359). Since a dedication copy was more likely to produce results than a presentation copy, certain authors produced variant issues of their poems with different dedicatees. Such poems are listed below; they may exclude some later issues with new dedications. See Elkanah Settle passim for fuller exploitation of dedicatees, including variant texts of the same poem (S301–322).

dedicatee in title changed by press-variant, H67–8; changed by variant or cancel title, B132, D341–2, F39, F302, H82, H337–44, L263–4, N11–12, N40–9, O213–5, O244, S648–50

dedicatee's name stamped in by hand, N245, S241, S387, W222–36 (W227–31 written in ms.)

dedication cancelled for alternative dedicatee, S330, S525

dedication signed in type, apparently for presentation copies, B562, H71, H77·5, J74, P464; *see also* fine-paper copies – dedication signed

dedication copies, B241, D74, K25, M325, P10, P413, S226–349 *passim*, T130, W406, W412; *see also* binding – presentation copies; fine-paper copies; presentation copies

deposit copies: *see* copyright

duplicate setting, C535 (quarter-sheet poem), W259 (advertisement slip), Y44 (preliminaries)

edition

in part from standing type, A138, A140, A148, B234, B397–8, B544, C525, D96, D103, D124, D157, D187, D447, D521, E516, H57, H280, J41, J77, L213, L338, M47, M235–7, M449, M463, M465, M512,

edition (cont.)

P245, P248, P428, P766–7, P878, P883, P887, P910, P957, P969, R217, S428, S433, S820, S822, S906, S923, T90, T549, V40–1, W156, W248, W304, W479, W490, W540, Y26, Y41, Y124, Y127

so-called, but printed from the same type (press-variant or cancel title, or reimpressed), A43, A45, A66, A205–6, A332, B35, B57–8, B70, B73, B95·5, B136–7, B147–8, B190–1, B197, B250, B253, B255, B258, B264, B309, B317, B324, B327, B359, B419, B421, B431, B521, B523, B545–7, B565, C40, C74, C86, C112, C155, C389, C445, C524, D23, D29·2, D101, D133, D136–8, D141–2, D156, D201, D290, D314, D329–30, D406, D447, D475, D478, D484, D489, D491, E349, E409, E430, E489, E506, E511, E523, E526–7, E600, F245–6, F273, G49, G53–5, G71, G106, G144, G152, G201, G223, G296, H56, H58–9, H129, H145, H187, H223, H232, H270, H329, H369, I42, J2, J34–6, J52, J60, L109, L112, L131, L210, L248, L339, M4, M19, M47–8, M53, M79, M101, M123, M213, M237, M248, M256, M259, M262, M266, M311, M323, M334–8, M353–4, M381, M444, M448–9, M451, M458, M460, M463–6, M486, M505, O45, O234, O288, P30, P141, P266, P419, P483, P763, P766–8, P790, P812, P825, P911–12, P979, P989, P1005, P1014, P1091, P1173–4, R25, R107, R114, R120, R180, R261, R275, R277, R315, S76, S91–4, S101, S104, S160, S199, S494, S517, S539, S542, S697, S699, S701, S703, S708–10, S713, S726, S744, S805, S807, S820–4, S872, S882, S892–3, S905, S907, S923, S927–30, T5, T34, T54, T141–2, T164, T202–5, T213–14, T222, T229, T274–5, T278, T284, T293, T306, T423, T549, T551, T565, V4, V9, W41, W60, W93–4, W119, W249, W290, W299, W300, W304, W365, W381, W436, W504–5, W540–1, W566·5, Y6, Y30, Y38, Y40, Y76, Y77, Y92, Y110

miscellaneous, A141–2 (edition statement on half-title), M63–5 (three very similar editions, undifferentiated), S922 (edition number repeated), S924 (edition number repeated, possibly later reprint), T160 (edition number repeated, possibly later unauthorised reprint), V44 (Harley's note 'This which is called the fifth edition is not true but a sham of the booksellers'), W157 (called 'second impression', but new edition), W464 ('The first edition')

engraving

at head of broadside or half-sheet, A17, A270, A312, A349, B48, B611, C143, C272, C320, C497–8, D334, F29, F102, F177, F198, F295–6, G184, G265, G302, H193, H409, K31, M15–17, M231, M355, M525, N158, N296·5, N307, O188, P586, P1145, P1152, R137–8, S151, S718, S767, S857, T253, T537, V92–3, W557·5

emblems, P1113, T405

headpieces and ornaments, B88, B195–6, C88, D196, D368, G82, M275–6, M487, O93, O103, P74, P137, P787, P852, P893, P895, P941, P1158, S189, T134, T136, T281, T404·5, T444–5, V112, W169; omitted from copy, B88; substituted for woodcuts in fine-paper copies, G82, P74 (by cancellation); variant, T134

on title, A199, A207, A317, B385, B502, E379, E449, F151, G296, H12 (statement of authorship), H264, K35, M503, R195–6, R206, R315, S88, S179, S198,

engraving (*cont.*)

S549, S728, T129, T132, T165, T288, T473; omitted from copy, M413

title-page engraved, P771–4, P783, P860–1, T405, W325–30

work engraved throughout, books, B378–9, H271, P1113; single sheets, B48, B175, B211, B402, C225, D33, G187, H194, I38, I40, K49, O116, O211, P7, T295, T376, W557·5

see also frontispiece; plates

erasure of 'the end of part one' for separate issue, W121

errata

added to reissue, B190, H239

in ms., A108 (note of apology), C215, D232 (addition), M188, N303, P1142, S490

not present in fine-paper copies, P16, P228

note that pen corrections have been made throughout, E315

recorded in newspaper advertisement, B358, B569, F12, M228, P439, Y36

variant, K80, M98, P1061, T220, T516, Y47

errata leaf, A144, K82, N256, P365, P781, U32, W207

errata slip, B506, C534, D220, D414, D522, E459, G144, G283, G475, K77, L333, M84, M282, P120, P1016, P1144, S198, S816, T46, T155, T243, W29·5

error by printer

in imposition, C352, P922, S533, S665, Y74

in perfection, D138, D146, D252, E430, K95

see also sheets from different impressions mixed

extra-illustrated copies, P22

fine-paper copies (including cases of uncertainty), A28, A42, A81, A122, A180, A187, A189–90, A193, A195, A201, A203, A208, A297, A300, A304, A318, B6, B107, B128·1, B148, B215, B241, B243, B250, B353, B381, B384, B410, B500, B562, B570, B573, B606, B615, C24, C56, C56·5, C63, C65, C67, C173, C234, C255, C295, C358, C360, C371, C373, C376, C380, C423, C426, C512, C516, C523, C552, D12, D49, D91, D123, D129, D164, D221, D223, D225, D230, D295, D313, D345, D529, E93, E300, E310, E393, E422, E463, E491, E498, E501, E505, E508, E515, E518, E612, F63, F106, F111, F114, F154, F166, F170, F189, F229, G2, G12, G13·5, G19, G22, G26, G34, G46, G48, G67, G70, G82, G117, G154, G174, G191, G310, H27, H29, H52, H68, H72, H80, H91, H118, H185, H215, H224, H235, H378, H381, H383, H423, I64, I76, J75, K21, K23, K60, K86, K91, L70, L97, L100, L108, L150, L212, L227, L294, M9, M55, M57, M94, M129, M143, M145, M148, M194, M247, M274, M288, M310–11, M314–15, M322, M325, M345, M425, M544, M566, N247, N255, N257·2, N260, N265, N267, N273, N281, N292, N316, O98, O176, O250, P6, P10, P14, P16, P71, P74, P174, P205, P207, P227–8, P231, P238, P276, P413, P438, P440, P444, P452, P461·6, P582, P691, P764, P772, P787, P797, P808, P820, P824, P826, P845, P851, P853, P866, P882, P893, P909, P924, P942, P988, P1013, P1020, P1066, P1069, P1075, P1080, R16, R102, R112, R215, R258, R267, R270, R272, R281, R290, R293, R300, R302, S4·1, S84, S87, S120, S240·2, S244, S247, S254, S256, S259, S276, S277·2, S283–4, S286, S289, S292–3, S295, S370, S378, S396, S465, S492, S496, S501, S512, S519, S521, S526, S561, S707, S742, S772,

fine-paper copies (*cont.*)

S774, S909, T49·6, T51, T53, T56, T63, T65, T73, T75, T79, T83, T85, T87, T130, T135–6, T147, T169, T187, T192, T195, T197, T199, T201, T209, T273, T276, T289, T292, T294, T297–8, T304, T311, T405, T419, T441, T452, U32–3, V19, V36, V71, W54, W171, W176, W217, W219, W307, W359, W361, W519, W530, W577, Y51, Y53, Y70, Y73, Y75–6, Y83, Y87, Y91, Y95, Y101, Y103, Y109, Y123, Y126, Y129, Y131, Y133, Y135, Y137, Y175

see also format variant; leading of type; paper – blue paper; satin; vellum

fine-paper copies: (peculiar features)

advertisements removed, A28, A195, A318, C371, D230, M57, T289, Y87

author's name added to title, C423, N260, P228, P452, S283, S286, W519; removed from title, P16

corrected state of variants, P882, P956, Y131

dedication added, P174, R293; changed, S289; signed, C234, D164, P444

engraved headpieces substituted for woodcuts, G82, P74

errata not present, P16, P228

format changed, C516, N257, P765, R102, R215, R260, S284, S289, S293, T49·6

frontispiece added, T73

gilt edges, A201, L70, O250, P1066, T289, Y76

imprint changed: none, C63; 'printed for the author', S4·1, S286; 'printed in the year', no publisher, B128·1, M314, M322, N247, N260, P14, P16, T49·6; printer substituted for publisher, N273

inner margins enlarged (a frequent occurrence, but rarely noted), A28, B165, E393, F106, G14, G82, P276, P1080, S707, T201, T289

of later editions, G22 (sixth), G26 (seventh), T276 (third), T285 (third), Y103 (second)

price changed, H91, L294, W176, W217, W219; removed, A195, A201, A203, A297, A304, A318, C65, C423, C516, E393, F229, G2, H118, M57, M247, M322, P16, P582, P909, R281, S120, S465, S519, S521, S561, S707, T188, T192, T195, T197, T199, T209, Y75, Y95

printed to order only, P942

reimposition with leading, substitute for fine paper, W54, W171

signed by author, R102

superfine paper, S284, S293, T298

title changed, P882

variant collation, C373, D223, P797, P826

watermark the same as ordinary paper (Strasburg bend), T129, T136

format

eighth-sheets, A240, B284, C17, C41, I54, L117, O182, O187, P1131, P1136, S110

format obscure, A159, B156, H299, P19

format variant, P850, P893; instead of fine paper, P765, R260, T49·6; *see also* fine-paper copies – format changed

indeterminate pieces of paper printed on one side only, P294–409 *passim*

oblong quarter-sheets, B223, C535 (set in duplicate), P294–409 *passim*, P977

see also collation; slips

frontispiece, A14, A36–8, A134, A200, A204–6, B11–13, B48, B68–70, B162, B174, B193, B195–6, B383–9, B391, B396–9, B409, B418, B533–4, C5, C72–3, C76, C137, C151·5, C164, C250–1, C285, C468, C496, D68, D195, D407, E290, E360, E460, E530, F21, F43, F101, F199, G21–7, G29, G31–2, G69–71, G73–5, G78, H6, H48, H54–9, H230, H268–9, H271, H285, H328–9, H398–9, I14, I42, I74, J23–6, K34, K59, K60, K82–3, L107, L215, L284, L317, M6, M93, M147, M153, M199, M226, M251, M253–4, M309–12, M319, M347–8, M424–5, M427–8, M443, M501, M551, M557, N254, N297, N299, N323–4, O142–4, O255, O282–8, P29–30, P128, P137, P188, P237–8, P242–3, P719, P764–9, P776–81, P785–6, P800–1, P816–17, P860, P862, P867–74, P905–6, P941–4, P946, P948–9, P1106, P1159, Q2, R7, R11–13, R118–20, R136, R183, R254–9, R269, R274–7, R279–81, R292, R296, R320, S27, S35, S392, S525, S562, S716, T31–2, T37, T73, T134, T217, T223, T230, T233, T269–70, T444, T494, V9, V10, V112, W13, W15–18, W20, W36, W57–60, W93, W103, W109, W116–17, W128–9, W196–9, W212, W258–9, W325–30, W343, Y47, Y58–60, Y74–7, Y111–12, Y114–15

    added from another source, B140, F71, G130, T420
    in form of a fan, N319
    not ready for early copies, A133, H285, O142, P975, V8
    optional addition, C151, D128, P22, T217, T223, T230, T233
    woodcut: *see* woodcut frontispiece

funeral tickets, F297, F307, P177

half-sheets, folio
    intended for pasting up in houses, J15
    versos (*It was a normal practice in Dublin, particularly c. 1710–12, to reprint two London half-sheets back to back; it was not common in London, though some examples can be found* (G8). *Only unusual cases are noted here*): different versos in different copies, I39, W386; later work printed on verso, S140, W549; verso printed in some copies only, S414, S839, V83
    see also collation – folio half-sheets signed 'A'

hawkers, newspaper, 'new-year's gift', H110

imitations of popular ballads and slip songs, B32, D505–6, E546, H45–6, M60–1, N118, W38, Y20

imposition: *see* conjugate printing of separate poems; error by printer – in imposition; reimposition

imprint changed
    addition made in ms., H218, L223, V110
    addition of provincial publisher made in type, C503
    alteration in ms., B110, D34, R185
    deleted in ms., B607, S133, S386
    supplied in ms., C240
    see also fine-paper copies – imprint changed

imprint false
    Dublin imprint for original London publication, H159, K79–80
    'Dublin printed, London reprinted' for original London publication, D407, D409, E437, K82, P81, P692, P764–9, P1023, S809, S841, T532
    London imprint for original Dublin publication, C344, F53, H161·5, M67
    'London printed, Dublin reprinted' for original Dublin publication, A64, A170, A185–6, E386, G313,

imprint false (cont.)
    G320, N154, R157, S128, S382, S399, S913, T156
    original imprint copied for Dublin reprints, A94, C183, C246, D99, D104, D134, D167, D493, F77, J47, K99, M250, M367, M403, M455, N8, N67, N179, P181, P233, P529, S476, S885, T16, T32, T349, T578, V11, W396, W430, W508
    original imprint copied for Scottish (usually Edinburgh) piracies, A143, A307, B121, B155·5, B388, B399, C213, C526, D127, D288, D327, D370, D377–8, D386, D479, E158, E417, E427, E481, E606, F79, G149, G199, G271, G274, G284, H23, H160, J32–3, J78, L66, L127·5, L329, M5, M45, M52, M66, M169, M238, M294, M341, M350, M571, N337, N344, O86, P12, P232, P769, P793, P803, P828–9, P835, P841, P846, P879, P884, P890, P897, P918, P921, P927, P936, P939, P962, P966, P970, P983, R171, S423, S431, S438, S565, S574, S727, S758, S808, S811, S827 (Edinburgh bookseller named), S889, S925, S932, S940, T41, T184, T210, T234 (? suppressed), T326, T345, V42, W46·5, W415, W423–4, W429, W432–3, W437, W507, W513, Y15, Y27, Y33, Y39, Y45, Y116, Y138–9, Y176
    original imprint copied – other piracies, A93, B177, B527·6, C8, C465, D492, N66, N302, P214–15, P869, S670
    original imprint deliberately mis-spelt (piracies), B461, P774, P1077, S732, U13–14, W382; other mis-spellings, P17, P855–9
    place and publisher false, for original publication, C36–7, L67, L93·5, L122, L187, W278, W517
    place of publication correct, publisher false, D505, O165
    place of publication false, publisher correct (T. Johnson, the Hague), P814, P947, R295
    place of publication false, no publisher (*a number of entries under* piracy – no name in imprint *are of provincial origin though claiming to be London*), A238, C113, C287, C383, C529, D89, D97, E324, E376, F258–9, G110, H126–7, H175–9, H192, N150, N307, O22, R113–14, R123, S46, S667, S769, T13–14, V92–3

imprint fictitious or pseudonymous, A74, A78, A163, A250, A315, A329, B156, B228, B285, B514·5, C154–5, C243, C281, C286, C381, D40, D259, D271, D320, D353, D466, E24, E304, E313, E362, F15, F46, F168, F265, G248, G272, G299, H120, H159, H274, H354, H425, J56, J103, K33·5, K48, K51, L34–5, L197, L235, L265, L296, L300, L321–2, M77, M81, M159, M162, M412, M538, N70, N84, N141, N215, N326, O270–2, P46, P120, P143, P145, P165, P702, P1036, P1050, P1116, P1119, S130, S393, S463, S883, T317, T558, T586, W382, W386, W404–5, W558, Y20; *see also* A. Moore and W. Webb in the Index of Imprints

imprint of a descriptive nature (e.g. 'printed by a true blue'), B124, B542, B617, C313, C439, D255–7, E320, H411, L8, M239–40, M508, M514, N303, P480–1, P504, T153

imprint variant
Changes to imprint by cancellation are entered under reissue – cancel title. *Some entries here may be the result of reimpression.*
A280, A378, B350, B508, C186, D111, D135, D517, E472, F14, F63, F109, F193, F232–3, G157, H73

imprint variant (*cont.*)

H286, K5, M177, M366, M478, N324, N340, P807, P1097, Q13, R177–9, R233, S63, S246, S532, S731, S848, S854, T117, T138, U24, W58, W147, W271, W386, W482; *see also* fine-paper copies – imprint changed

imprint (miscellaneous), F62 (for the benefit of the author's widow and children), F191 (date of original copied in reprint), H108 (sold by all her majesty's running-stationers), J83–4 (for the benefit of Mrs Elizabeth Foster), R132–3 (imprint lists previous editions), U31 (to be had only of the author)

ink: *see* colour printing

large-paper copies

In this period, fine-paper copies are almost always printed on a larger paper; both are entered without distinction under fine-paper copies.

leading of type, used as substitute for fine-paper copies, W54, W171

legal

civil proceedings against piracy, A307, P774, P792

government action against publication, B528, B548, E83–4, F135, F144, M174, N18, O230 (Dublin), P2, P436, P1050, S841, S844, S890 (Dublin), W90, W278, W417

see also copyright; stamp act

Luttrell, Narcissus

Luttrell's manuscript dates in his copies are a valuable source for the dating of pamphlets until the year 1716, when his buying was much curtailed and his efforts at precise dating relaxed. A few anomalous entries by him are recorded here.

dated early, A173, C247, P717, T94; dated in a different hand, W96; dated late, C514, D95, G172 (1718 as '1721'; the frequent late dates of this period are otherwise ignored), P806, S740; dated twice, P1061; later edition than first dated, S680, W83; undated, P31, W333, W443

manuscript corrections (probably by printer) **in all or many copies**

date: *see* date altered in ms.

errata, A108, C215, D232, N303, P1142, S490

imprint, B100, R185; for other ms. changes *see* imprint changed

note by printer that pen corrections have been made, E315

price, C98, D433, F212, H85, M2, M253, M294, M311, N16–17, T33, W86, W475

text, A86, D110, D123, D151, D473, D522, E315, E397, F115, F238, G150, G282, H71, H73, H81·5, H97, J83, K83, P67, P1000, P1135, R113–14, R185, R250, S126, S155, S355, S444, S601, S647, S686, S736, T470, V88, W246, W255, W389, W426, W460, Y54, Y136

title, F64, H131, M540

manuscript corrections in individual copies (status uncertain), C108, C287, C425, E432, E480, F111, F166, J66, M316, M410, M504, N279, P370, P1012, R191, T47, T564, W86, W332

manuscript corrections in presentation copies, F80, F275, K22, M284, M285, S254, S264, S562, T124, W460

see also author's annotations and corrections; proof-sheets

music (usually on folio half-sheets)

added in manuscript, C175

engraved, B54, C240, C497, H17, I38

noted by letters, W458

printed from type, A235, B204, C258–63, C518–19, D502, D507, D541, D543, E478, E578, G44, H126, H164–6, H451, L151, M60, O205, O239, P64

woodcut, A236, D503–4, N197, R127, W180

newspaper

poems issued as supplement to, W44, W79

see also hawkers, newspaper; offprints

numbered copies, F117, P74, R214

offprints from larger works, D368, D552, H202 (from newspaper), L223, P211, T70

one side, printed on: *see* collation – printed on one side

ornaments

copied in piracy, W158

engraved: *see* engraving – headpieces and ornaments variant, B460, D434, P811, S878

paper

black paper for funeral elegy (printed in white), M546

blue paper (? for presentation copy), R256

mixed stock used, A198, B55–6, D326, J51, L226, L320, P810, S288, S560, U31

turned chain-lines (mark of manufacture in a double mould), no watermarks, A51, A55, A121, A123, A147, A151, B8, B155, B168, B273, B356, B458, B478, B517, B597, B616, C44, C119, C224, C254, C357, C417, C425, C457, C464–5, C469, D67, D70, D86, D163, D287, D305, D326, E217, E333, E385, E465, E475, F9, F73, F95, F103, F178, F203, F237, G87, G98, G116, G160, G247, G273, H24, H30, H143·5, H147·5, H201, H203, H208, H234, H256, H314, H328–9, H345, H350, H354, H396, H457, K4, K47–8, L79, L175, L206, L337–9, M36, M110, M118, M196, M239, M255, M261, M284–5, M372, M382–3, M431, M514, M567, N6, N19, N310, N322, O48, O88, O231, P2, P19, P46, P101, P267, P504, P510, P710, P821, P873, P1041, P1054, P1109, Q14, R234, S16, S19, S86, S100, S201, S525, S531, S569, S599, S601, S720, S785, T23, T49·5, T49·6, T70, T153, T257, T463, T492, T533, T542, T567–9, T591, W31, W212, W412, W461–3, W469, W496, W524, W531

turned chain-lines, with watermarks in various positions, A6, C522, D335, E226, E309, G323, H40, P669, P1110

variant (possibly indicating a reimpression or fine-paper copies), A226, C7, C141, D425–6, E93, E333, G310, L222, P190, S641, S735, T495, W487; *see also* fine-paper copies

parts, publication in

The following works appear to have many of the characteristics of 'number books'; see also continuation.

B192, B491–6, D131, G111, H217, O286, P727, P731–2, P737 (Edinburgh), R139, R139·2, T136, T238, W90–1, W103–8, W111, W114 (Edinburgh), W193–7; *see also* collection

perfection: *see* error by printer – in perfection

periodical

The daily slip, 1714 (some numbers contain verse only), J56, M159, M538

piracy

The term is not used here in its strictest sense of legal

piracy (cont.)

infringement of copyright, but in accordance with the custom of the trade. Unauthorized reprints are included here whether or not they were protected by entry in the Stationers' Register. Some early Scottish reprints of uncertain status have been given the benefit of the doubt, but the systematic reprints after the Act of Union are included. Dublin reprints are excluded.

Many piracies have false imprints; for these see imprint false.

different printer or publisher from original edition (the publications of Henry Hills, which were almost exclusively piratical, are omitted here; see the Index of Imprints), A351, B229, C44, D448·5, E3–4, G24, G87, G98, G304, H46, H120, J86, M526, N322, P19, P490, P498, P609, P791–2, P901, Q4, R234, S17, S677, S691, S732, S866, T76, T317, T324, W85, W151, W159, W421, W454, W496, W520, W524, Y17

no name in imprint (some probably of provincial origin, though claiming to be London), A117, A144, A174, B36, B370 (Edinburgh), B464, B527·7, B530·52, B530·55, B530·82, B542, C19–21, C177, D98, D103·5, D118–19, D125–6, D130–1, D152, D158–9, D161–2, D166, D169–70, D172, D183–4, D436, D448, D474, D476 (Northampton), D546, E522–3, F41 (Edinburgh), F87, G246, H240, H282–3, H287, H312, H460, H472, H472·2, K56, M43, M71, M220, M244, P220 (Dublin), P420, P423, P430, P433, P457, P491, P493, P499, P860–4, P1085, R38 (Edinburgh), R48 (Edinburgh), R65 (Edinburgh), R83 (Edinburgh), R109 (Edinburgh), R196, R246–7, S3, S430, S442·4, S442·6, S682, S851, S933–4, S939, T97–8, T491, T542, T575, W73, W77, W113·5, W124, W158, W191, W202, W402, W422, Y66–8

Scottish reprints of London editions (the majority are entered under 'imprint false – original imprint copied for Scottish piracies'), C404, O26, P216, P863, P915, P958, R38, R48, R65, R83, R109, S480, T429, W78, W250, W477, W483, W485, W500, W502, Y140–8

miscellaneous, B369 (author's report on), S429 (denounced in imprint), W158 (ornaments of original copied), W469 (pirated by shorthand when sung), Y50 (author reports piracy 'which, as to letter, and ornaments, mimics your's'; not identified)

plates, works containing, B71–4, B195–6, B426–7, C145, D233–4, D441, D460, F21, G11–14, G25–7, G29, G32, G69–71, G73–5, G78, H56–9, H267, M309–12, M424–5, M427–8, O142–4, O284, P119, P941–4, P946, P948–9, P1105, R11–13, R257–9, R269, R282, R284, R331–2, S655, S655·5, T134, T236, T243–6, V13, V112, W80, W130–1, W199, W212, W325–30, W559, Y74–7, Y111

Hayman's original drawings for, and early states, M425

wood-engravings, by Francis Hoffman, H268

presentation copies, A139, A190, A300, A376, A378, B250, B321, B491–5, B570, B606, C73, C76, C155, C162, C247, C411, C548, D12, D223, D232, D298, D347, D521, E33, E290, E518, F14, F166, F275, G13, G21–2, G67, G82, G135, H93, H332, H348, H377, K20, K22, K91, L211, L218–19, M144, M325, M408, M470, N260, N267, O236, P10, P16, P74, P174, P202, P227, P400, P440, P461·6, P463, P665, P765, P772, P797, P820, P866, P942, P1080, P1097, R89, R112,

presentation copies (cont.)

R179, R194, R256, S215, S226–349 *passim*, S396, S562, S653, S848, T124, T187, T237, T243, T289, T371, T456, T516, T548, W28, W219 (from publisher), W460, W517, W559, Y2, Y70, Y73, Y75, Y83, Y101, Y105, Y109, Y124, Y134, Y169

with ms. material added, M470, S254, S258, S262, S653, W559

see also binding – presentation copies; dedication copies; fine-paper copies

press figures, variant, D132–3, F106, H144 (sign of cancel?), H210, K74, P871, P881, P955

price

changed, by cancel slip, L100; by overprinting, P267; in ms., C98, D433, H20·5, H85, M2, M253, M294, M311, N16–17, T33, W86, W475

fluctuations of, W94

given away, *gratis*, B465, C41 ('at the theatre'), D353, H218 (a specimen), H443 (hymn sheet), S486, T46 ('to the subscribers'), T404·5, T464 (by bequest)

quoted by the dozen, T561; by the hundred, D67, D569, G162·6

variant, A350, A378, F16, J85, M88, M177, M307, T227, U24, W358

see also fine-paper copies – price

printing (miscellaneous), N256 (shared between two shops), P585 (printed on a wagon in Dublin procession), P873 (shared between two shops), P984 (printed 'at one pull')

private circulation, K83, P771, R194; see also presentation copies; title in half-title form

proof-sheets, N119, P434, S497, S509, S587

proposals for forthcoming edition, B374, H102, H183, N254, R81, T46, T136, T236, Y105; see also specimen; subscription editions

provenance

No general attempt has been made to establish the provenance of copies, but some copies belonging to the following have been noted; many have ms. notes.

Harley, Edward, *earl of Oxford*, A86, B326, H93, H157, M51, P802, P822, P827, P833, P840, P845, P894, P908, P917, P968, S884, V44, W360

Pope, Alexander, B396, D52, G21–2, H230, L335, M57, P10, P16, P74, P1026, R21, T187, T281, Y75, Y95

Walpole, Horace, A83, B39, D369, F174, G254, H331, J17, J63, J83, L265, O251, P45, P1103, P1166, P1170, R31, R199, R212, Y19, Y169

see also Luttrell, Narcissus

publishing history documented

Information from printers' ledgers and sales of copyright is not included.

B369 (piracy and London reprint of Edinburgh poem by Boyse), K12 (an indecent publication of White Kennet by Curll, with changed title, 'about 200 were sold...and the rest made waste paper'), M413 (booksellers' treatment of an indecent poem), P226 (royal bounty for John Philips's *Bleinheim*; copies with his name possibly circulated as propaganda), P237 (John Philips's agreement for *Cyder*; two dedication copies in Turkey leather and 100 on large paper)

red printing: see colour printing

reimposition

in different format, C516, N257, P765, P850, P893, R102, R215, R260, S284, S289, S293, T49·6

with leading of type, a substitute for fine paper, W54, W171

reimpression

concealed, B34, B164, B385–6, C64, C403, D155, D390, D426, F110, M123, M249, P888, P985–6, R217, S479, S813, S888, S917, W512

part reset: *see* edition – in part from standing type

with changed imprint, B56, D23, E582, J35–7, M130, P763; for changes made to fine-paper impressions, *see* fine-paper copies – imprint changed

with changed title, C63, C155, E42, E104, E173, E229 (these four apply one elegy to two different persons), G61, H329, P187, S122, S374; for reimpressions calling themselves 'second edition' etc., *see* edition – so-called; title – variant

with corrected text, B58, B521, C63, D23, D149, D406, L65, P187, P823, S122, S374, S429, S479, S726, S744, S779, S839, S872, S927–30, T202, T275, T284, W300, W418, W493; *see also* variants in the text

reissue

additional material added, B73, B172, B191, B218, B317, B565, B593, C112, D406, F63, F118, F202, F224, G140, H58–9, H77·5, H239, J33, L106, M25, M371, M405–6, O168·2, P82, P424, P773, P775, R86, R105, R184, R257, S260, S263, S332, S357, S442·2, S881, T5, T54, T164, T188, T229, T237–8, T464, V115, W94, W115, W128, W192, W211, W259, W366, Y58

cancel slip over imprint, L231, N298, S484, W46

cancel title changes title of poem, A324, A376, B95·5, B172, B190–1, B218, B427, B429, B431, B530·15, C548·5, D35, D389, F90, G152, G241, G306, H13·2, H82, H98, H145, H476, I42, M25, M53, M74, M80, M134, M368–9, M378, O168·2, O288, P262, P424, P786, P790, P973, P999, R180, R184, S191, S260·5, S263, S277, S442·2, S475, S542, S698, S881, T5, T302, T421, T576, V3, W55, W67, W115, W121, W140, W186, W192, W259, W366, W575, Y61, Y77, Y82

cancel title changes imprint (including changes to date alone), A301, A324, A376, B73–4, B95·5, B190–1, B218, B248, B265, B267, B339, B431, B563, C112, C413, C548·5, D14, D50, D201, D342, D411, E604, F90, F118, G152, G175, G241, G306, H13·2, H58–9, H82, H129, H145, H152, H232, H270, H338–9, H341, H344, H369, H476, I42, J60, K5, K61, L271, M25, M37, M48, M74, M79, M80, M101, M134, M262, M266, M368–9, M371, M378, M381, M442, M505, N47, N298, O168·2, O283, O287–8, P262, P419, P424, P476, P483, P485, P777, P786, P973, P999, R180–1, R184, R257, R259, R276–7, R315, S76, S104, S191, S260, S260·5, S261, S475, S542, S698, T5, T164, T229, T302, T421, T464, T551, T565, T576, T592, V115, W17, W48, W55, W62, W67, W81, W93–5, W115, W121, W128, W137, W140, W192, W211, W259, W326, W329, W366, W566·5, W575, Y61, Y76;

cancel title for new 'edition': *see* edition – so-called

date changed in manuscript: *see* date – altered in ms.

reissue (*cont.*)

of single work in collection or with other work, A34, A40, A75, A188, A190, A193, A200, A202, A315, A317, B19, B20, B68, B70–1, B129, B184, B256, B262, B330–1, B334, B399, B418, B524, B527·9, B530·86, B532, B552, C19, C71, C84, C174, C188, C190, C248, C252, C254, C319, C394, C476, C482, D60, D105, D113, D121, D168–9, D211, D213, D216, D259, D308, D450, D455, D458, D460–1, E6, E378, E402, E416, E483, F204–5, F222, F249, F274, G30, G72, G92, G115, G118, G125–7, G231, G309, H107, H307, H336, H365, H413, J23–4, J56, K60–1, K83, L34–6, L245, L288, L332, M2, M4, M104, M141, M159, M251, M267, M282–3, M538, O252, P188, P213, P234–7, P240–3, P249, P410, P431, P481, P497, P536, P612, P644, P690, P730, P795, P814–15, P819, P836, P850–1, P853, P906, P947, P992, P1036, R15, R20, R22–3, R32–109 *passim*, R176, R227, R264, R280, R282, R284, R288, S223, S389, S391, S436, S441, S537, S540, S614, S803, T10, T27, T37, T57, T61, T179–80, T188, T192, T195, T197, T199, T209, T217, T223, T230, T246, T282, T427, T497, T551, T558, U25, W53, W56, W58, W60, W70–1, W96, W102, W112, W120, W122, W127, W136, W141, W150, W153, W157, W162, W170, W175, W190, W201, W526, Y79, Y80, Y84–5, Y88–9, Y97–8, Y106–7, Y114, Y117, Y120–1, Y151, Y155, Y159, Y161–2, Y164–7, Y170, Y172

peripheral material cancelled, B190 (postscript), D201 (dedication), H82 (dedication), H232 (advertisement), O168·2 (preface), S257 (preface), S262 (dedication), S277 (dedication)

text of poem changed, A324, N298, O168·2, S104, S277, W55, W339

remainder issue or republication, B130, B257, R280, S252·2, S748, W94

satin, presentation copy on, B321

sheets from different impressions (or editions) **mixed,** B386, B396, C524, D390, G21, G49, P248, P871, R217, S927, T200, W155

slips

Slips are here taken to mean a quarter-sheet, cut from edge to edge across the shorter dimension of the sheet; towards the end of the century they were occasionally printed five to a sheet. For the propriety of the term, compare The daily slip (1714), J56, M159, M538. *The earliest example known to me dates from 1689. Popular slip songs of this period normally have a rough woodcut at the head; they are successors to the broadside ballad, usually undatable, and excluded from this catalogue except when they have a clear topical or political reference. A better printed style without woodcuts was popular between 1714 and 1718, particularly for Jacobite propaganda. Both styles seem to have evaded the provisions of the Stamp act, and this may explain their rise to popularity.*

A54, A61, A70, A74–5, A78, A102–3, A153, A271, A276, A353–4, B15–16, B23–4, B96–7, B105, B293, B453, B468, C35, C51, C53, C101, C132, C170, C204, C210, C275, C439, C458, C494, C546, D40, D53·5, D57, D208, D259, D319, D350, D360, D496, D506, D554, E126, E288, E318, E323, E325, E331, E335, E340, E342, E413, E537–40, E545, E548, E552–3, E558–62, E564–6, E573–4, F1, F37, F44, F207–8,

slips (cont.)

F220, F263, G41, G62–3, G170, G183, G189, G311, H35–6, H123, H152·5, H204, H250, H255, H257, H297, H303, H390, I2, I12, J56, J58, K54, K102, L34, L43, L50, L57, L61, L167–8, L195–7, L297, L301, L310, M1, M21, M132, M159, M183, M203, M208, M232, M281, M296, M359, M538, M572, N36, N53, N55, N57, N59–61, N77, N89, N106, N115–16, N118, N121–2, N139, N143, N157, N183–5, N192, N195, N199, N200, N207, N210, N216, N220–1, N223–6, N228–9, N235, N238, N304, N328, O108, O202, O204, O218, O247, O264, P97, P112, P179, P182, P194–5, P208, P469, P506, P571, P614, P714, P760, P952, P980, P1034, P1036–7, P1063, P1095, P1137, R5–6, R115, R122, R130, R172, R225, R286, S10, S15, S53, S67, S70, S79, S171, S174, S361, S458, S463, S477, S510, S536, S548, S579, S582–3, S591, S593–4, S597–8, S621–3, S626–8, S688, S777, S792, T263–4, T341, T358–9, T377–8, T396, T426, T498, T510, T514–15, T558–9, T571, V31–2, V84–7, W29, W183, W265, W371, W373, W398–9, W442, W452, Y108, Y178; *see also* conjugate printing – slip songs; imitations of popular ballads and slip songs

specimen (of forthcoming edition), B319, B374, H218, P592, R43, Y105; *see also* proposals

stamp act

early examples of halfpenny stamp (2 Sept 1712), S425, W255

half of double-sized sheet of stamped paper used for folio of two leaves, F73

penny stamp found on octavo pamphlet of one sheet, W343; on folio, C62

'register'd in the Stamp-office' in imprint, F192, L259, O1

stamp as evidence of date, M60

stamp omitted from some copies of half-sheet (imprint and price variant), M177, U24

stamp-office receipt for pamphlet duty, B6, W48

see also collation – folio, 3 leaves; slips

Stationers' Register: *see* copyright

subscription editions, B45, B153, B438, C185, C327, C415, C425, D194, E50, H6, H13, H20, H48, H102, H132, H332, L165, M78, M151, N254, O236, P196, R294, S754, T115, T236, T247–8, T405, T444–5, V112

see also proposals; specimen

title

endorsement, R110

in half-title form (often intended for private circulation), A20, B187, B221, B232, C157, C297, C374, D196, D296, D298, E438, E479, F185, L21, L221, M116, M122, M263, M401, O59, P221, P819–20, P866, R44, R85, R89, S117, S482, T353, T381, V26, V72, Y18

in the form of a dedication, no imprint, H65–8, P462, R80, S387, S648–50

variant (*Changes to titles by cancellation are entered under* reissue – cancel title. *Some entries here may be the result of reimpression*), B72, B412, B581·5, D46, E46, E472, E520, F38, G97, H11, H80·2, H83·2, H329, M56, M478, M530, N214, N324, P450, P556, T47, W65, W271, W566·2; *see also* authorship statement; fine-paper copies; imprint variant

type

black-letter, for traditional broadside or chapbook, J5, N240, P993; for sophisticated imitation, E546, M60, Y20

Grover's scriptorial, A349, F36, O114, R34, R127

typography

minimal use of capitals, M158

printing in the shape of a pyramid, P1180

unopened copies, A39, B121, R104, W24

variants

in the text (*not normally recorded, but the following may serve as examples; in some cases there may be a concealed reimpression*) B350, C39, C50 ('Finis'), C52, C186, D115, D177 (footnote added), D186, E2, E24, E517 (footnote added), E520 (first line), F64, F110 (three states of advertisement date), G47 (sheet B reset), L83–5 (obscenity removed), M221 (forme reset), M251 (three states), M449, O37, P294–409 (Pitcairne's poems appear to have been written in the printing-house and revised in type: cf. K41, R330), R427 (noted in new edition, R428), P1135 (early state has ms. corrections), R10 (obscenity removed), S509, S799, S800, T129, T246 (sheet reset), V37 (substantial changes)

see also errata – variant; imprint – variant; title – variant

vellum, copy on, E33 (a folio half-sheet)

woodcut

borders: *see* borders

frontispiece, A35, A64, B401, G23–4, G111, H269, K5–7, L187, L287, N18–19, N237, S387, S639, T248, W364–6

initials, used for first word of title, B25

'This indenture' used in first line, N52

title-page, O254

woodcuts

mourning (*The mourning borders and woodcuts normally used for elegies are not separately indexed: see the Subject Index under* Elegy), M409 (Norwich, cut for this occasion), P177 (with space for title – possibly originally intended for a funeral ticket), V12

pictorial: at head of half-sheets, slips, and on title-pages, A293, A351, A353, B32, B85, B96–7, B237, B294, B447, B449, B459, B463, B465, B553, C34, C123–5, C237, C242, C314, C337, C368, C392, C431, C440, C456, C484, C491, D131, D260, D271, D392, D496, D498, D501, D503, D505–6, D545–6, E293–5, E297, E304, E313, E325, E329, E331–2, E487, E535, E586, F140, F146–7, F220, F261, F263, G104, G114, G188, G263, G272, H46, H149–50, H204, H247, H259, H261, H266, H297, H428, H433, H435, H438–9, H444, H455, I1, I35, I39, J4–5, J53, J58, K50, L49, L71, L266 L281, L297, L299, L314, M20–2, M41, M61, M192, M203, M205, M359, M526, M568, N115–16, N118–19, N121–2, N157, N172, N183–4, N192, N194–5, N199, N202, N205, N207–9, N211, N213, N220, N225, N230–1, O4, P90, P271, P273, P284, P501–2, P757, P980, P993, P995–6, P1095, P1099, P1148–50, R26, R29, R54, R65, R115, R197, R307, R310, R316, S10, S140, S458, S472, S585, S589, S591, S603–4, S606, S777, S849–52, T30, T99, T104, T266, T315, T411, T477, T514–15, T526, U8, V7, V33–5, V86–7, W38, W177, W183, W239–40, W264, W275, W371, W398–9, W441–2, W444, W496,

woodcuts (cont.)

W498–9, W549; copied from engraving, A160, F29 ('beware of wretched halfpenny wooden cuts'); in text, E22, S58, S154, T252, V2–5

variant, in slip songs (possibly a sign of reimpression), L226·5, N116, T515

wood-engraving

John Cluer described as 'engraver on wood', H435
by Francis Hoffman, H266, H268, H269, H272
by F. Nixon, M539
by W. Pennock, G111

wrappers: *see* binding – pamphlets; collation – wrapper

INDEX OF DESCRIPTIVE EPITHETS

This index lists alphabetically the phrases describing the authors of anonymous books. It excludes those which are added to initials ('By M.N., late of Balliol College, Oxford') and those qualifying what may reasonably be called a pseudonym ('By Roger, the Observator's country-man').

an acquaintance of Dr. Eems, W555
an admirer, S70
an admirer of grace and truth, O115
an admirer of the fair sex, F28
an arch anti-whigg, F261
l'auteur de la tragédie de Didon, L82
the author of Age in distress, P612
the author of Albina, A155
the author of All men mad, W76
the author of the Apparition, E530
the author of Are these things so?, M249
the author of the Art of dress, B420, B425
the author of the Art of politicks, B396
the author the Battle of the sexes, B441
the author of the Benefit of farting explain'd, S218
the author of the Blackbird's song, S687, S698, S700
the author of the Blackbird's tale, S674, S685, S686, S696, S702
the author of Bleinheim, P246
the author of the British Apollo, C540
the author of the Cavalcade, W57, W117, W122, W128
the author of the Choice, P731, P732, P735, P736
the author of. . . Coffee, M287
the author of the Composition, M498
the author of the Country maid, W484
the author of the Country-man's companion, D417
the author of the Curious maid, J45, J46, J51
the author of the Deluge, and Bottomless tub, L251
the author of a Divine paraphrase, H13
the author of the Duel, P653
the author of the Dutch-catechism, B588, F124
the author of an elegy from the Dutch, S549
the author of the Epistle to Mrs. Nevil, S201
the author of the Essay on man, P982
the author of the Essay on the soul of man, P699
the author of Faction display'd, S437, S442
the author of the Female rake, and Rake of taste, D408
the author of the Fifteen comforts of matrimony, F131
the author of the Fifteen plagues of a maidenhead, F136
the author of the first [advertisement], L60
the author of the Foreigners, T574
the author of Friendship in death, R274
the author of the Generous muse, L305
the author of Geneva: a poem, B299
the author of the Golden age, L89
the author of the Great noise about nothing, R188
the author of Happiness, W204
the author of the Harlot's progress, P1106
the author of the Hebrew Campaign, and Review, T115
the author of Harlequin-Horace, M255
the author of Hudibras redivivus, W150
the author of the Humours of the Black-dog, W470
the author of the Hymn to the pillory, D102
the author of the Hymn to the victory in Scotland, T533

the author of Kick him Jenny, K35
the author of Kirkham Hunt, O217
the author of the Latin Mercury, H201
the author of Laugh and lye down, B539
the author of Leheup's ballad, L1, M117, N64
the author of the Letter to the patron of the Trip to Barleduc, E404
the author of the Letters from a nun to a cavalier, I14, L284
the author of the Lintoun-address, P147
the author of the London-spy, W50, W69, W70, W113, W129, W201, W241
the author of the Merchants advocate, G262
the author of Mr. W—— S——'s ballad, E544
the author of the Muse's treat, P1059
the author of My time O ye muses, &c, B620
the author of Namby Pamby, C47, H355
the author of One thousand seven hundred and forty-five, P100, P101
the author of a Pastoral elegy on the death of Mr. Creech, F275
the author of the Pleasures of a single life, C207, G245
the author of the Poet's ramble after riches, W200
the author of a Proper reply to a lady, C230
the author of the Proposal, &c, K73
the author of Protestant popery, A188
the author of the Prude, L30
the author of the Rapsody on the army, E464
the author of the Review, D106, E264
the author of the Roman relique, E15
the author of the satyr upon hoop'd petticoats, F94
the author of the sermon in praise of cuckoldom, P1116
the author of the Servitor, G122
the author of the Seven extinguishers, P437
the author of Seventeen hundred and thirty-nine: and the Hibernian politicians, B470
the author of the Silver piss-pot, W257
the author of the Sine-cure and Equivalent, M321
the author of the Summum bonun, A7
the author of the Tale of a nettle, L241
the author of a Tale of a tub, G218, K55, K62, K63, T495
the author of the Temple of war and Review, B153
the author of They are not, C311
the author of the Totness-address versify'd, M330
the author of the Totness and Sailor's address, E389
the author of the Trip to Jamaica, W141, W163
the author of the Trip to Nottingham, T487
the author of Tripatriarchicon, S945
the author of the True-born English-man, D110, D128, D132, D144, D151, G219, L162, L238, N132, N241, N331, T513
the author of the Two lurchers, &c, C326
the author of the Universal passion, Y94
the author of the Verses to the imitator of Horace, H21

the author of the Verses upon his grace's retiring into Germany, S371, S379

the author of...the Woful treaty: or, unhappy peace, E408

the author of the World unmask'd, G142

the author of Yes, they are, M507

the author of the Yorkshire horse-racers, P479

the authors of Britannia's loss, A156, P622

a bachelor in the college [Dublin], F265

a barber, A57

a blyth son of Bacchus, P40

a boy in the university [Edinburgh], M346

the bricklayer, J92, J94

a British author, N154

a British muse, F115

a British subject, O241

a brother volunteer, S466

a cabal of young ladies, U30

a candidate, E31

a Cantab, T3

a certain English nobleman, H161·5

a church of England minister, D45

a citizen, F45

a city lady, L8

a clergyman, C267

a clergyman of the church of England, P137, T337

a clergyman of Warwickshire, P103

the clerk of the parish, D251

a commoner, K16

the company of grey-headed gentlemen, C353

a country curate, M120

a country gentleman, R161

a country hind, E597

a country parson, E20

a craftsman of the city of Dublin, S752

a disobliged admirer of the fair sex, P163

a divine of the church of England, E246

an eminent hand, P898

an eminent soldier at home, E543

an English gentleman lately broke upon the wheel in France, A9

an English lord, G240

an experienced admirer of sanctified afflictions, T256

a famous master of the game [hare-hunting], A87

a fellow of a certain college in Oxford, C530

a fellow of All-Souls, H230

a fellow sufferer, L148

a fellow-sufferer in the hardships of the times, P559

a female, F304

the fool, R222

a footman, D388

a foreign bishop, now residing and preaching in his diocese in Terra incognita, L94

a free mason, F244, P595

a freeholder of Great-Britain, E394

a friend [i.e. quaker], B298

a friend, E217, P600

a friend of the light, G42

a friend to Dr. Sacheverell's club, F305

a friend to the German Doctor, A102

a gentleman, A123, B2, H47, K105, M13, P541, P1135, W295

a gentleman and a Christian, N248

a gentleman at Bath, M539, T371

a gentleman at Cambridge, B380

a gentleman at St. James's, V103

a gentleman at the university of Cambridge, E410

a gentleman at the wells [Bristol], B451

a gentleman commoner, M280

a gentleman-commoner of Oxford, C520, P666

a gentleman formerly of Trinity-College in Cambridge, O238

a gentleman from England, P542

a gentleman in a fever, occasion'd by hard drinking, W172

a gentleman in confinement, W464

a gentleman in England, under a fit of the gout, T300

a gentleman in New-England, P597

a gentleman in the army, E395

a gentleman in the navy, B160

a gentleman, late of Baliol College, Oxford, A14, M36, M118

a gentleman lately deceased, G280

a gentleman near the town of Lawder, E221

a gentleman of Cambridge, B193, P720, V68, V70

a gentleman of Christ-Church, Oxford, T271

a gentleman of Exeter, P651

a gentleman of Gray's Inn, S652

a gentleman of Lincoln's-Inn, L104

a gentleman of Magdalen College in Oxford, R265

a gentleman of New Inn Hall, A171

a gentleman of North-Britain, T502

a gentleman of one of the Inns of Court, D363

a gentleman of Oriel-College, Oxford, F242

a gentleman of Oxford, B176, C299, C385, C520, H107, H112, P628, S31, T91, V25

a gentleman of Scotland, E474

a gentleman of the Inner Temple, B100, H40, H109, M443

a gentleman of the navy, B131

a gentleman of the Temple, H188

a gentleman of the university of Cambridge, A157, B134, L319

a gentleman of the university of Oxford, A218

a gentleman of Trinity College, Cambridge, D189

a gentleman on board that fleet [at Porto Bello], H119

a gentleman who is much a lover of the reformation and the revolution, C430

a gentleman who saw the race perform'd, P1042

a gentleman who was unlawfully detained in custody by those merciless soul-hawlers [the press gang], S9

a gentlewoman, A86, E44, M23

a Gideonite, A327

a great poet lately deceased [Pope], D326

a Hanoverian, M254·5

a hearty lover of his country, A80

a hearty well-wisher to the welfare of Great Britain, U10

an honest sailor, D494

an honest whig curate, S794

Ille ego qui quondam, A265

an impartial hand, P1110, S486

an inhabitant near the Royal-Exchange, A121

an Irish laureat, P719

an Irish officer at Ostend, A1

a k——e [kite], S72

a lady, B198, B408, B409, C172, E23, F141, F143, G10·5, M224, N38, O20, O194, O221, P521, P616,

a lady (*cont.*)
P662, P676, P998, R144, R273, S71, S600, T380, T506, V39
a lady of Great-Britain, C93
a lady of honour, E447
a lady of quality, C351, D509, P650
a lady of real quality, M382
a land-waiter in the port of Poole, P1039, P1041, P1045
a late fellow of New-College, in Oxford, E43
— —, late of Westminster School, a king's scholar, P196
a late officer in the army, T123
a late prisoner confin'd in that place [the Poultry counter], H134
a layman of the church of England, S469
a lodger, R199
a lover of his country, E588
a lover of his country, and of the protestant succession, E472
a lover of his king and country, I19
a lover of liberty, N334
a lover of musick, S85
a lover of poetry, C228
a lover of the clergy, T154
a lover of truth, B218
Maggie Riddel's son, E220
the man in the moon, R152, T543
a Master of Arts, K67
a member of a society of gardeners, N8
a member of his [Benjamin Keach's] congregation, E165
a member of the catholic church, R139
a member of the club, held at Mr. Taplin's in Truck-street [Dublin], C350
a member of the company of players of which Mr. xxxxxxxx was manager, I40
a member of the Constitution Club at Oxford, A202
a member of the Easy Club in Edinburgh, R78
a milliner, A245
a modern hand, E595
a money'd man, F54
a native of Grub-street, H462
a native of New-York, C442
a nephew of the late Mr. John Milton, P254
no body, P427
no friend to William Woods, T519
no puff, P470
a Norfolk gentleman, P752
a northern bard, E61
a noted cuckold in the New-Exchange in the Strand, F127
the Observator, E203
an officer in his majesty's fleet, A250
an officer in the army, P577
an officer in the Duke of Argyle's army, L286
an officer of Major General How's regiment, C187
un officier irlandais étant à Ostende, A1
an old citizen, but a young poet, alias poetaster, C348
an old fox hunter, K53
an old gentleman, of Gray's Inn, lately retired to a country-life, H388
the old three, A191
the old wash-woman [at Dunleary], P193
one of her [Molly Smalley's] admirers, L147
one of his [Henry Barry's] schoolfellows, T372

one of the ministers of the gospel in Glasgow, C226, C229
one of the people called quakers, F234, H114
one who seeks the prayers of the godly reader, E451
one who thinks it an honour to be called a high-flyer, W397
an Oxford scholar, R312
a page of honor, N310
a parishioner of St. Mary Savoy, M155
a patient [in Bedlam], C225
a person altogether independent of ministerial influence, E471
a person of honour, E475, E550, F112, O178, P52, P1166, S41
a person of learning, F268
a person of quality, B477, N14, P426, P467, P722, R321, S634, T13, V107, W376, W572
a person who had some share in his [Lord Mountcashel's] education, S417
a person who has no mony to pay taxes in case of a war, D267
Philomathematicus's army of arguments, B95
a pious clergyman in Virginia, D61
a pious young divine, at Aberdeen, D277
a plain, right down lover of truth and honesty, N303
the poet laureat, S592
a poor brother in durance, B514
a principal actor, N208
a private gentleman, C495
a real barber, T481
the right honourable the Lady * * * *, A16
a Romish priest, lately converted to the protestant religion, R320
a sailor, Y81
a sailor on board the Shrewsbury, V33
a sailor on board the S---ness fleet, W523
a Salopian gentleman, W545
a serious person of quality, B186
a servitour of the university of Oxford, S222
a shoe-boy, D530
a Shrewsbury scholar, D565
a sincere lover of his prince and country, M542
Sir Francis Walsingham's ghost, N160
a soldier who was in the engagement [at Culloden], N194
some man of the law, B485
a star, B479
a state-boatswain, A160
a state lunatick, D243
a student at Oxford, A190, A193
a student in philosophy, E386
a student of Christ-Church College, Oxford, B205, P134
a student of Oxford, L293, W546
a student of philosophy in the university [Glasgow], B368
the suppos'd author of the Fifteen plagues of a maiden-head, F136
a tailor in Hamilton, P1008
a Templer, S203
a true-born English man, P456, V48
a true Briton, G223, S22
a true son of the church of England, W389
a true son of the church of Scotland, C144
an undergraduate of Jesus-College, Oxon, J96
an unknown author, M566

an unknown hand, A54, F3
a venerable person, P658
a very good acquaintance of esq; Toby, D76
a water-drinker, D534
a water poet, W364
a wel-wisher of 'em both, H170
a well-wisher of her's [Mother Blackham] in Trinity [Dublin], E59
a well wisher of the ministry, Z1
a well-wisher of the society [of Grubstreet poets], G305
a well-wisher to his king and country, T424
a well-wisher to this country [Ireland], I63
a young English maid, S559
a young gentleman, E38, F67, G226, H305, I45, P54, P573
a young gentleman at Rome, L331

a young gentleman going abroad, E435
a young gentleman of Hampsted, N315
a young gentleman of Oxford, H304, P706
a young gentleman of Trinity College [Dublin], F145
a young gentleman of Winchester School, L292
a young gentleman, who heard the doctor's [John Taylor's] lectures to the ladies in woman's habit, P566
a young lady, A220, J102, P576, R205, S55, W268
a young lady, now upon her departure for the New Atlantis, I3
a young lady of fifteen, P1108
a young lady of quality, G96
a young nobleman, B354
a young nobleman of the university of Oxford, F221
a young student at the university [Glasgow], V66

SUBJECT INDEX

This index attempts to list all proper names, key words of titles and sub-titles, verse forms (e.g. epistle, elegy, ode) as given in the titles, and certain broad subject headings (e.g. battles, medical, theatrical).

It was not originally intended to provide an index of this nature, and so no consistent attempt was made to study the poems themselves from this point of view. It will generally be found that notes on subject-matter vary inversely with the availability of individual works; half-sheets have usually been well described, anonymous verse frequently annotated, while poems by the better-known authors have been little studied. The following gaps should be noted:

  1 *no consistent attempt has been made to record dedicatees when they are not named in the title;*

  2 *headings are usually based on the wording of the title;*

  3 *political satires frequently attack so many subjects that it is impossible to deal with them fully; students should refer to the Chronological Index for the period that concerns them.*

It should be noted that this index does not duplicate references in the main catalogue; translations should be sought there under the author translated, and answers to individual poems under those poems. Reference is only made to the first edition of each work.

A.B.C., Christian's, R243

Abelard: to Eloisa, B81, C85, D6; Eloisa to, P801

Abel, John (musician), S587, W21

Aberdeen, K22, M207: execution at, A12; Marischal College, A159

Abergavenny, Katharine, baroness, B135, E363: elegies on, C10, P654

Abergavenny, William Nevill, 16th baron, B135, E363

Abernethy, John (addressee), W468

Abigail, *see* Masham, Abigail

Abingdon, execution at, B200

abjuration, oath of, B46

Abney, Sarah, elegy on, R328

Abney, Sir Thomas (lord mayor of London, *d.* 1722), elegy on, S239

Abney, Sir Thomas (justice of the common pleas), satire on, E569

Aboyne, George Gordon, earl of, birthday poem to, D54

Abra, Solomon and, S553

Abraham, the patriarch, A321, C475, L315, S944

Absalom, and Achitophel, C476, D448

academia, D34

academic, beau and, B337, H104

access, to virtue, W322

accident, the, A5

accomplished: hero, A6; leader, A7

Achates, to Varus, A15

Acheson, Lady, S868

Acheson, Sir Arthur, S868, S908

Achilles: Chiron to, J31; to Chiron, A16; dissected, J116

Achitophel, Absalom and, C476, D448

acquittal, the, A17

acrostics, A18, A19, C313, E328, M417, M419, P689, S195, T390·5

act: (university ceremony) at Cambridge, O275; for naturalizing foreign protestants (1709), C18; of indemnity (1703), S947

acting, art of, E469, H210, W274

active and retired life, M164

actors, discussed, R268

actress (Melissa), P700

Adam (de Cardonnel), fall of, C537

Adam (or Adams), Mordecai, A271, A272, D273, E556, M1

Adamia, epistle from Verax to, V27

Adams, Elizabeth (printer, of Chester), B617

Adams's weekly courant, B617

Addison, Joseph: *Cato*, E406, M208; his journalism, satire on, B476

  poems and epistles to: (1713) P61, R176; (1714) E492, I68, Y99; (1715) S365; (1716) T588; (1717) A190, E420·5, H348

  poems on death of, A279, C266, P201, R82, R273, S326, Y90

address: of Bolingbroke, H157·2; Bung's, B567: Cameronian, C9; Cheshire grand jury, A52; Church of England's, C179; clergy of Virginia, L296; country gentleman's, H121; country vicar's, C460; Dublin, I48; Dunfermline's, E454; Edinburgh's, R44; England's, E323; foreign, Y81; from Grubstreet, M356; of house of commons, A55; knights of the horn, K102; Lintoun, P148; London, L233, L235; muse's, M564; muses', S274, S285, T82; muses', R15, T61; poet's, P693, P694; poets', M332, P708; presbyterians, T388; quakers in Scotland, H389; sailors', S12; saints', S23; singing-bird's, B530·9; society of rakes, R32; Swaddling John's, S790; tories', T424; Totnes, A50, M333, S625, T427; Tower of London, T377; whigs', W392; widow's, B80; Windsor muse's, T88; wives of the bow, H391

  to the crown, C9, C460, E280, E454, H389, H391, P147, P148, P693, R15, S12, T61, T88, T377, T388; parodies and satires on, A50, A55, C193, D110, I48, L233, L235, L296, M332, M333, N96, S625, T424, T427, T587, W392

  to other recipients, A49, A52, A54, A56, A57, B80, E323, H157·2, H220, H390, H392, K9, K102, L48, L93, M142, M356, M421, M471, M564, P694, P1023, R32, R44, S23, S219, S240, S249, S250, S274, S285, S790, W204

'Addlebury, bishop of' (= Gilbert Burnet), W112

admonitions, seasonable, S164

Adonis: Pastora's lament for, P102; rape of, C394; Sappho to, S34

Adrastus, W435

Adrian (Dutch type-setter), W252

adulterous wife, W70: examples of, B135, E363, K101, L255, W456

217

adultery: à la mode, A63; rebuk'd, R320; sermon against, P973

adventures of three hundred years, D191

advertisements, poems occasioned by, D526, E389, E401, L60, S453

advice, S531: alderman's, A158·5; Beelzebub's, B159; church's, U19; country parson's, B528; Dr. Radcliffe's, D356; father's, F75; footman's, D389; freeman's, N69; French king's, F253; friendly, F268, S733; good, G217–19; Honest Clodd's, H295; Horace's, H317; humble, H393; Lucky Spence's, R60; moderate man's, M360; Oliver Cromwell's ghost's, O170; seasonable, S165, S555; serious, L139; Sir Tubal Cain's, O262; Tom the toper's, O126

from Caleb Smalley, A70; from fairyland, A71; from the stars, A72

to authors, A88, O258; barbers, D413; beaus and bachelors, G218; brethren of the livery, D389; child unborn, F268; children, F75; clergy, A89; John Dalgleish, S789; a daughter, A158·5; a certain dean, A73; Dr. Delany, L138, S555; England, A79; the fair, A90; fair sex, F235, R252; friend, B291, L137; Harry Gambol, A78; Great Britain, A80; Mr. Handel, A82; high church, A91, high-flying members, F253; Kentish long-tails, B507; ladies, A96, D356, G219, P752; ladies of Great Britain, A92; ladies of St. Michael's parish, A95; a lady, L328; lord keeper, B528; loyal Scots & English, H393; malcontents, W562; muse, A97; Oxford & Cambridge, U19; modern poet, O183; new-married husbands, P479; painter, see 'Advice to a painter'; the people, H418; would-be pirates, S165; a poet, A74, L139, O183; poets, B238, F170, H209, H291; the queen, A98; sailors, A101; Sappho, A86; Scribbog hare, A87; a son, H26, O126, W45; tories, A102; true representatives of old England, A104; whigs, A105; widow, A76; young fellows, C91; young gentleman, B439; young gentleman of fortune, A77; young gentlemen about town, P968; young lady, S59; young men, A106; young poet, L139; youth, G156

'Advice to a painter' poems, A83, A84, B254, D319, G184, I45, I46, N166, S78, W31

advocate: female, E23; merchant's, M184

advocates: complaint of, A107; faculty of at Edinburgh, M422; see also attorneys, lawyers

Aegon, in pastoral, A164

Aeolus, B347

Aesculapius, A108

Aesop: at Barcelona, A109; at the bear-garden, P1026; at the Bell-tavern, P425; Bickerstaff's, P424; at court, M385, Y1; dressed, M74; in Europe, A113; fables from (spurious?), E2, F60, N236, R173; Hibernian, A256; on this juncture, P1062; London, P433; in masquerade, P426; in mourning, A114; at Oxford, P422; at Portugal, A110; at St. James's, F243; in Scotland, A115; in Spain, A116; at Utrecht, A111; the wanderer, A118; at Westminster, A112

Aethiops, A119, A120

African prince, D361, D365

afterthought, the, A121

age: ass, A349; brazen, B403; in distress, A123; golden, G211; iron, L111; leaden, L89; of mad folks, A124; of wonders, A126; wooden, W558

aged father, A130

agent turn'd inside out, A131

Agility, Madam, M42

Ainslie, William, sergeant, L32

Aitkin, Heu, of Stirstrachen (dedicatee), K29

Aix-la-Chapelle, congress and peace of (1748–9), B505, C369, C431, C538, F145, G277, H328, L311, M412, O25, O50, O217, P134, P568, R309

Ajax, speech of, B430, F184, T49

alarm, A147: against popery, H273; Britannia's, G135; national, N6; to Scotland, A149; to the seceders, A150; to the wits, A151

'Albania' (= Scotland), A152, S145

Albanian animal, S449

Albemarle, William Anne Keppel, earl of (addressee), B153

Alberoni, Charles, cardinal, H80, L67

'Albertus the second', A153

Albina, A154, A155

Albion, T129: sighs of, S460

Albion's: glory, A156; naval glory, B527·1; triumph, A157, B358

Alblaster, Edmund (dedicatee), W222

alcaics, B185, B325

Alcander, A158

Alchemist, epilogue to, P7

Alcoforado, Marianna, the Portuguese nun, L287

alderman's: advice, A158·5; guide, S752

aldermen, Dublin, E111, R249

Aldrich, Henry, elegy on, P177

ale: cakes and, N238; price of, N296; see also beer

ale-wife, grunting, G308

ale-wives, O126

Alexander's: feast, B45, H50; overthrow, S1

Alexis (in pastorals), A39, A159, D406, E44, H167, L279

Alfred, the great, B240

Alkibla, by William Asplin, C459

Allan, 'the turncoat', B54, F186, N244

allegorical poem, B441, D234, T181

allegory, B467, H317

Allen, John, alderman of Dublin, L2

Allen, Joshua, viscount, S914, S916

Allen, Ralph (addressee), O88, S551

alliance, triple, T498

All-n, blacksmith, B269

alma mater, A171

Alma's complaint, A172

almanac-maker, S832

Almanza, battle of, B96

Almeria, T563

almonds for parrots, A173

aloe tree, A175

Alonzo, in The revenge, E346

alphabet, political, K49

alphabets, verse, W532

Alpheus, G251

Alphus, B207

Alrick and Isabel, D467

Alsatia amour, M117

Altamira's ghost, B340

Altamont (= Lord Abergavenny), B135, E363

Altham, Lord, elegy on, E42

Amarillis (in pastorals), C379, D20
Amazon, the, W269
Amazons, F32
ambition: address to, H157·2; ode to, W487; reward of, R173
ambitious father, W45
Amelia, A178
Amelia, princess (addressee), C108, H116
America: military successes in, P546; voyage to, K89
Amhurst, Nicholas: epistle to, E368; satire on, D323
'Aminadab' (dedicatee), G42
Aminadab's courtship, B298
Amintor, see Amyntor
amorous: groom, H401; jilt, A216; nun, A217; priest, N324; soldiers, P645; war, A218
amour: Alsatia, M117; new, N50; of Cytherea, M472; of Venus, M473
amours, B530·8
Amy, courtship of, C11
Amy, John (dedicatee), S241
Amyntas, B208, C379
Amyntor (or Amintor), A219, M44, T433, W296
anabaptists, L152, N78
anarchy, defeat of, T500
anatomy: art of, D303; of atheism, D67
ancient British music, T249
Ancient Briton, W286
Ancient Britons (= Welsh): poem dedicated to, E20; society of, G295, H379, S183; song to, S593
ancient philosophers, A220
Anderson, Rev. James, A265
Anderson, Rev. John, B368
Andrew, saint: dialogue with St. George, T585; Latin poem to, P360
Andrew, Merry, M198
Andrewes, Lancelot, Greek hymn by, E27
Andrews, Mordecai, elegies on, C283, G325, P605
angler, contemplative, W203; see also fisher
Anglesey, Arthur Annesley, earl of (addressee), D210
Anglesey, Richard Annesley, earl of, satire on, R192
angling, B531, I41, S464; see also fishing
animal economy, S942
Anjou, Philip, duke of, see Philip V, king of Spain
Anna, see Anne, queen
Anna Ivanovna, empress of Russia (addressee), M35
Annamboe, D365
Annandale, marchioness of (addressee), C420
Anne, queen:
  1698, dedicatee, W224
  1702, succession & coronation, A155, A156, A226, B80·5, B585, C180, C335, C356, D568, E280, E328, E329, E338, G263, H276, I30, M417, P255, P263, P689, P1148, T99, T388, W221; miscellaneous, H149, H256, I43, R168, R317, T107, T267
  1702/- (addressee), S387
  1703, F276, S947, T74; birthday poems, A228, M534, W21; dedicatee, W222, W328
  1703/04, A55
  1704, P184, Q14, R306, R322, V90; birthday poem, P1083; dedicatee, C488, W529
  1705, C14, D84, J72, P1101; birthday poems, C378, D268, E355, L5; dedicatee, B249, S7
  1705/07, V7
  1706, C376, D110, P1081, R310, T48, W33-4; birthday poem, E317
  1707, C460, C517, E357, F216, L132, S140, T513; birthday poem, O51; dedicatee, A367, D46·5
  1708, A366, C333, D339, H221, N88, O72, P270, T88, W525; birthday poem, M531
  1709, C247, E296, W515; dedicatee, E8
  1710, A98, B279, F36, H192, P352, S386; birthday poems, C550, P639·5, S215
  1710/14, H294
  1711, P1056, Q9, T400, W390; birthday poems, T77, U15; dedicatee, S288
  1711/14, O175
  1712, F8, F13, K85, N13·5, Q12, T507, W281; birthday poems, F113, I31, S212, T331
  1712/13, P294, P338
  1713, A24, A227, N269, S217, S468·5, S468·7; birthday poem, W26; dedicatee, P526
  1714, T50; birthday poems, H75, S216; funeral poems, B472, D226, E43-5, E467, H67, I5, I23, L130, M543, M549, O218, S329, S522, T140, T570, W125, W275, Y99
  1715-37, later memorial poems, N209, O204, O211, P130, P137, P650, S489, S585, T71
  1715-49, other poems, A346, L299, P98, S632
Anne, princess royal, subsequently princess of Orange: recovery from smallpox (1720), E512; marriage (1733/34), B86, B283, B393, C56·5, C115, D320, D473, D522, G326, O79, P252, P527, P579, P620, P632, S105, S183, U11, V30; dedicatee, S134
anniversary: birthday, O7, S7·5; ode, A228
annual book, C238
anointment, the, A229
anonymous authors, poem to, S910
'Anselmus', C127
Anstruther, Lady Margaret, elegy on, R73
Anstruther, Sir William, elegy on, E47
answers (these answers and replies are referred to under the poem which they answer in the main catalogue), A16, A54, A57, A86, A88, A96, A158·5, A165, A166, A173, A183, A191, A220, A230-54, A331, A370, A375, A377, B5, B34, B203, B300, B303, B307, B347, B507, B571, C91, C148, C209, C288, C311, C399, C462, C479, C536, D6, D26, D78, D87, D88, D89, D148, D163, D202, D356, D473, D562, D563, E23, E322, E333, E336, E342, E359, E371, E375, E396, E408, E414, E431, E485, F6, F10, F24, F53, F83, F90, F143, F162, F175, F186, F191, F194, F269, F271, G123, G203, G218, G231·5, G249, G253, H8, H9, H21, H125, H157, H194, H275, H298, H357, H395, I17, J67, J102, K36, K39, K51, K72, L8, L21, L25, L26, L77, L125, L128, L153, L154, L198, L202, L273, L308, L322, M23, M183, M185, M189, M191, M249, M299, M373, M389, M507, M509, M511, M572, N1, N144, N154, N166, N271, N282, N309, N329, O77, O258, O259-61, O263, O267, P31, P32, P36, P175, P435, P520, P535, P647, P658, P696, P1045, P1053, P1129, P1135, R56, R116, R144, R154, R165, R169, R204, R205, R219, R220, R238, R242, S44, S45, S54, S59, S68, S71, S85, S137, S167, S368, S384, S439, S446, S449, S455, S555, S584, S632, S654, S788, S795-7, S842, S858, S899, T1, T7, T9, T100, T126, T128, T150, T154, T321, T322, T361,

answers (*cont.*)
　　T380, T413, T481, T532, T547, T553, T565·5, T572,
　　U17, V76, V83, V98, W1, W64, W241, W247, W267,
　　W268, W270, W375, W380, W384, W390, W397,
　　W445, W486, W543, W557·5
antediluvian novel, P1044
Anthony, Dr, A255–64, I38
anthypochondriac satire, M80
antidote, the, C508
antigallican, the, F237
anti-Georgians, S486
Antigua, F209
anti-heroic poem, W189
anti-heroics, P10
anti-patriot, C464
antiquarians, British, R89
antisatirist, A267
Antoeus, A268
'Antoniettus, dux Corsorum', K66
Antrim, Elizabeth MacDonnell, countess of, elegy on, F294
Antrim, Randal MacDonnell, earl of, elegy on, I57
Anvers, Caleb d', *see* D'Anvers
ape and fox, M522
Apollo, C28: Marsyas and, C396; outwitted, S798; mock-
　　Apollo, B478
Apollo's: advice, A269; edict, B75; golden days, Y177;
　　maggot, W47; stratagem, J27
Apollo Society, L213
apologist, female, F85
apologue, E2
apology: the *Craftsman's*, A60; for a darling passion, B50;
　　friendly, B270; to Lady Carteret, S799; to the town,
　　A270
apostacy, female, F86
apostates, the, T574
apostles' creed, S186
apothecary: Mordecai Adam, A271, A272, D273; gentle-
　　man turn'd, E290
apotheosis, funeral, F286
apparel, original of, O244
apparition, the, A274–7, E517, S172: of Donald Mac-
　　donald, M2; of the Drapier, D429; of our Saviour,
　　G165; in Trinity College, Dublin, D514; *see also* ghost
appeal, to the people of Great Britain, G17
apple-pie, B418: buttered, B609
April 1st, F149, S856
April 23rd (Anne's coronation day), S468·5
Arabian: handsome, H33
　　tale, M357
Arabic, pretended translation from, M357
arbor vitae (*sens. obsc.*), N7
Arbuckle, James, C276: satires on, F286, G305, W537
Arbuthnot, John: epistle to, P802; possible reference to,
　　H155; *Three hours after marriage*, D444, W303
archers, young, of Edinburgh, P684; *see also* Royal
　　Company of Scottish Archers
Archimedes, P344
architecture, art of, M503
arch-types, or most accurate drawings with the pen,
　　H101
Ardelia, Venus and, V25
Argenson, R. L. Voyer de Paulmy, marquis d', L275
Argyll, Archibald Campbell, 1st duke of, elegy on, E48

Argyll, Archibald Campbell, 3rd duke of:
　　1716, C432
　　1739, E24
　　1741/42, B402
　　1748, dedicatee, D94
Argyll, John Campbell, 2nd duke of:
　　1705, C343
　　1709, R121
　　1715/16, C339, C359, C432, D260, F52, J90, T335
　　1719, H248,
　　1738, H246, K103
　　1740, H318, O68, T514
　　1741, G124
　　1742, E308, G247, O112
　　1743, elegies, E49, E50
Ariadne, C496
Arians, modern, P628
Ariel and Mirza, A291
ark, the, B569
Arlington, millers of, R231
Armagh, Hugh Boulter, archbishop of (1724–42), *see*
　　Boulter
armour: (= condom), K12; of God, W324
arms and the man, A292, S202
army: proceedings, A312; rhapsody on, R187
Arnall, William, P81, T474
Arniston, Robert Dundas, baron (1685–1753), E358
Arran, Charles Butler, earl of (dedicatee), T313
arrival, the, A315
Arroyo del Puerco, battle of, E57
Arscott, Mrs, presentation copy to, G67
art: of acting, E469, H210; of anatomy, D303; of angling,
　　I41; of architecture, M503; of baking, A359; of
　　beauing, G320; of beauty, A317; of breeding bees,
　　D316; of breeding pigeons, D315; of brewing, A356;
　　of charming, D381; of contentment, P697; of cookery,
　　K55; of courtship, A319; of cultivating peace, T544;
　　of dancing, J59; of dress, B418; encouragement of,
　　M269; of gardening, Z2; of getting preferment, B68;
　　of intriguing, A320; of life, A321, M246; of love,
　　A322, A323, H307, K60; of malting and brewing,
　　D402; of modern poetry, M251; of painting, C324;
　　of playing, W274; of poetry, A179, A325, B310,
　　D309, H313, H314, P416; of politics, B383; of preach-
　　ing, D376; of preserving health, A296; of printing,
　　P585; of punning, H155; of scribbling, A326; of spin-
　　ning, A360; of stock-jobbing, A327; of shooting-
　　flying, M98; of sinking in poetry, S542; of visiting,
　　L16; of walking the streets of London, G81; of weav-
　　ing, D400; of wenching, A328; of wrightcraft, D401
artful priest, A329
Arthur, prince, B266
articles: of peace, A330; of war, E564
arts, ingenious, O216
Arwaker, Edmund, imitation of, W566
A——s, M——t, Mrs, P573
ascent of the soul, A337
Asgill, John, satires on, S735, W260
Asplin, William, satire on, C459
Ashton, Tony, *see* Aston, Antony
Ashurst, Sir William, elegy on, S238
Asiniad, G312
Askew, Dr, of Newcastle (addressee), T165

Aspasia, Philander and, V102
aspiration, the, T590
ass: age, A349; fable of the lion and, T374
assassination displayed, S674
assemblies, town, T432
assembly, the, B82: of brewers, G100; of Church of
    Scotland, see Church of Scotland; fair assembly, R50
asses, congress of, C281
associate synods' procedure, P588
association, the, C201
Astley, Sir James (addressee), M407
Aston, Anthony, actor, A353: in Edinburgh, 1728, M200,
    P283
Aston, Walter, M200
Aston, Sir Willoughby, Y2
Astrea, K85, M474, M475, W222, W224: triumphans, A362
Astrea's: commission, A363; congratulation, A364
astrologers: Dr Anthony, A255; James Cathcart, R162;
    John Gadbury, M297; John Partridge, M297, S832;
    John Whalley, A72, W375
astronomers, M166
astronomy, D234, E19, H267, L150: bawdy tales on,
    L251, L253, S720
atheism, D67, E315
atheist, D71: practical, C228
atheists, modern, A26
Athenian philosophers, P876
Athens, plague of, S663
Athol, duchess of, elegy on (1707), E51
Atkins, Sir Henry, elegy on, S334
Atkinson, John, of Barnard Castle, B85
Atterbury, Francis (bishop of Rochester): made dean of
    Christ Church 1711, N123; dispute with Lord Con-
    ingsby 1718, R244; patron 1722, D51; plot 1722/23,
    A192, B227, C421, E366, P515, V68, W344; death
    of his daughter, Mary Morice, W355
Atticus, H161·6: British, M87
attorney (Hartley Hutchinson), satire on, D530
attorneys, Irish, A245, B53, D237, H139, M559, V94;
    see also advocates; lawyers
Atys, and Adrastus, W435
auctioneer (Edward Millington), B512
Audenarde, see Oudenarde
August 1st (George I's accession day), N40, N42, O204,
    O218
August 2nd, 1738, A370
Augusta (= London), A371, S226–42; Augusta's glory, D553
Augusta, princess of Saxe-Gotha: marriage to Frederick
    prince of Wales 1736, E399, F234, M308, O80; birth
    of daughter to, 1737, W306
Augustine, saint, A373
Augustus (= George I), T569
Auld-Reeky (= Edinburgh), G292
Aumont, Louis d', duke (ambassador to Great Britain,
    1713), T81: addressee, C95, S275; satires relating to,
    D497, M174, M183, N326, P139
auricula, the, A372
Austin (= St. Augustine), A373
Austin, Sir John, M229
author: sham, S382; letter to, L153, L154
authors, B530·9: anonymous, S910; of the age, Y117; of
    the town, S89; see also poets
autumn, T233, W570

Avignon, gentleman at, T272
Ayerst, William, D296
Ayr, execution at, L58

B——, major, P121
Babb, Mrs, actress, P1130
Babel, A150, B1: tower of, W189
Babel, William, composer, O54
Baber, Thomas, H104
baboon à la mode, B2
Bacchanalia, D44
Bacchanalians, B48
bachelor's: choice, B3; dream, B4; hall, W263; litany,
    A182
bachelors, F128; bachelors' answer, B5
backgammon, B174
backsliders, balsam for, B46
Badminton, Gloucs., T443
baffled hero, B8
bagpipes no music, C463
Bagwell, H. (dedicatee), V95
bailiffs, T438
baker: in Spittle-fields, W262; of Westminster, W38
Baker, Thomas, N228
baking, art of, A359
Balaam, R244
balancing captain, L64
Bald, Willy, elegy on, E52
ball, masquerade, B19, B20: ballad sung at, W563
Ball, Elizabeth, S195, S196
ballad: A102, A163, B21–42, B154, B424, B468, C407,
    C458, D496, D545, D557, G44, G59, G178, G181,
    G217, H108, H251, L12, L198, L260, L277, M114,
    M117, M132, M228, M412, N233, N328, O133,
    P465, P470, P710, P761, P903, P1147, R155, R232,
    S132, S752, T39, T512, T528, W29, W411, W561
    Captain Tom's, C34; city, F285; Coventry, H127;
    Drapier's, S406; Donore, D403, Dublin, D462;
    Flanders, E579; Geneva, G109; Grinsted, G299;
    Kentish, G110; Maldon, M38; Nottinghamshire,
    N329; prisoner's, W469; raree show, O1, R127;
    South Sea, A353, S611, W177; Spitalfields, W128;
    Temple Oge, P516, T115·5; university, U19; whig,
    W388
    excellent, E535; excellent new, B105, B582, C106,
    C203, C275, C402, C479, D328, E536–71, F239,
    L115, L255, L262, L288, M291, M395, N14, N18,
    O165, P755, P1007, S470, S510, S669, S843, T493,
    T584, Y16; excellent new play-house, D502; excellent
    old, E595; happy memorable, H45; most excellent,
    H7; new, A50, A263, A292, B65, B293, B340, B458,
    B459, B462, B479, B556, B618, C7, C39, C206, C212,
    C325, C367, C368, C392, C536, D41, D69, D420,
    D421, D440, D530, E311, E314, E599, F73, F257,
    F258, G207, G225, G265, G303, G308, H121, H158,
    H202, H406, I61, I71, J67, J89, J103, K47, K96, K97,
    K101, L13, L33, L91, L184, L211, L239, L240·5,
    M156, M205, M352, M358, M567, N53–107, N288,
    P2, P27, P46, P144, P145, P183, P510, P711, P1032,
    P1117, P1161, Q2, R31, R231, S16, S550, S624, T19,
    T404, T428, T587, U2, W239, W262·5, W344, W376,
    W425, W480, W481, W494, W497, W501, W503,

ballad (*cont.*)

W511, W563: new bloody, N110; new Kilmainham, N145; new Lilliputian, N149; new Norfolk, N159, N160; new masquerade, T541; new protestant, T119; new raree show, O1; new South Sea, A353; new test, S141; old, M59; proper new, E31, M379; tragi-comi-canonical-farcical, W453

see also congratulatory ballad; court ballad; historical ballad; humorous ballad; mock ballad; political ballad; satiric ballad

Ballantine, George, murderer, E231

Ballymore Loghsunderland, S446

Ballyspellin, S405

Balmerino, Lord (dedicatee), N245

Balmerino, Arthur Elphistone, 6th baron, elegy on, L18

balsam for backsliders, B46

Bambridge, Thomas, warden of the Fleet, B47

Banbury grumblers, B62

band, worn by lawyers, A245, B53

bandbox plot (1712), C514, T589

'Bang the broker' (= Allan the turncoat), B54

Bangor, Benjamin Hoadly, bishop of (1715–21): *see* Hoadly

Bangor, monks of, A373

Bangorian controversy, *see* Hoadly, Benjamin

banished beauty, B55

Bank of Ireland, B60, E175

bankers, of Dublin, E144, E554, H362, S900

bankrupt (Robert Cowan), G15

banks, abuses of, M269

Banks, John, prologue and epilogue to *The Albion queens*, P1121

Bar-le-Duc, trip to, S736

Barak, B325, D84, P95, T46

Barbados: governor of, P111; ode on, O55

Barbary, captives from, B79

barber, T481: and fireworks, B64; turned packer, B65

Barber, Dr, A233

Barber, John, alderman of London, B65

Barber, Rupert, of Dublin, A246

barbers, A57, B64, T481: advice to, D413

Barbier, Mme, singer, E381, M157

Barcelona, F62: Aesop at, A109

Barclay, Robert, quaker, *Apology* of, G280

bard: country, M440; wonderful, W553

bards, battle of, B104

bargains, new way of selling, K92

Barker, Samuel, marriage of (1706), S299

Barleycorn, Sir John, E294, P160, P168

Barlow, John (dedicatee), C513

Barnabas, dialogue of, C226

Barnaby, Protestant, O165

Barnard, Sir John: financial proposals of (1737), C210, W452; addressee (1738), F45, M18

Barnard Castle tragedy, B85

barometer, human, P200

Barret, Mr, composer, C258–63, C518, C519

Barrow, Miss, married Thomas Hilman, W453

Barry, Elizabeth, actress, C377, R287

Barry, Henry, the hon. (addressee), T372

Barry, Spranger, actor, P572

Barrymore, Margaret, lady, D73

Bartholomew fair, B90, B91, C41, F29, M134, P277, S350

'Basin, the', reservoir at Dublin, C276, T489

bastard, the, S90: Englishmen no bastards, E336

bastinado for a whig, F193

Batavia in tears, B92

Bateman, Sir James, elegy on, S236

Bath, Somerset, A339, B93, B94, C107, J19, O246: beauties, R190; charity children, H436, P633; company at D437; diseases of, D331; pleasures of, A354; royal visitors to, A352, F276, I43, M539, P184, R317, T371; toasts, B94

Bath, Wife of, N240

Bath, knights of the, E500

bath, the, a tale, C406

Bath, William Pulteney, earl of, *see* Pulteney

bathers: at Dunleary, P193; at Tynemouth, B180

Bathgate, news from, N293

Bathgate, James, elegy on, E55

bathos, S542

Bathsheba, R320

Bathurst, Allen Bathurst, earl: addressee, P923; distributes Pope's *Dunciad*, 1729, P771; park and woods of, S750

Battie, William, M172, M173

battle: or morning interview, R34; of the bards, B104; without bloodshed, W49; with boasters, B95; of Cambrians and mice, L165; of the colliers, B105; curatical, C543; of the friars, B174; of frogs and mice, P73, P1039, W342; of the giants, B87; between Jew and Turk, T554; of loggerheads, M228; of pamphlets, S98; of the poets, C408; between priest and porter, P1042; of the sexes, W333; of virtues and vices, P1155

battles, the, B106: *see* Almanza; Arroyo del Puerco; Belgrade; Bergen op Zoom; Blenheim; Bouchain; Bruges; Brussels; Cadiz; Cartagena; Culloden; Dettingen; Falkirk; Fontenoy; Ghent; Gibraltar; Glenshiel; Killiecrankie; Landau; Lille; Luzara; Malaga; Malplaquet; Mons; Oudenarde; Passaro; Peterwaradein; Preston; Prestonpans; Ramillies; Saragossa; Scheldt; Schellenberg; Sheriffmuir; Stavuchani; Toulon; Tournai; Turin; Vigo; Wynendael; *see also* victories

bauble, the, a tale, B108

Baucis and Philemon, S800

Bavius, Mr, D423

Bavius, Mother, B299

bawds, L316, W98, W445

bawdy house, the, B109

Bayn, Donald, execution of, H206

Baynton, Charles, elegy on, S230

'Bays' (= Cibber), N158

bays, candidates for, C409

bear and fox, fable of, T316

bear-garden: Aesop at, P1026; in mourning, B124

bears (stock-jobbers), S767

Beard, John, singer, P1095, W563

beast, blatant, C55.5

beasts: confession of, S804; congress of, C367, C369; in fables, B219, F3; in power, B125

beatific vision, C273

beau: and academic, B337, H104; college, M281; country, C448; Dublin, J102, M224, O110; in a wood, B127; *see also* beaux

beau-criticism, T72; beau monde, C39; beau philosopher, B193; beau-thief, B128

Beauchamp, George Seymour, viscount (addressee), D15

Beauclerk, Aubrey, lord and lady, T393

Beaufort, Charles Noel Somerset, duke of (dedicatee), C168

Beaufort, Frances, duchess of (addressee), P44

Beaufort, Henry Somerset, 1st duke of (elegy on), P186

Beaufort, Henry Somerset, 2nd duke of: dedicatee, S7·5, T443; elegy on, S270

Beaufort, Mary, duchess of (dedicatee), P188, T443

beauing, art of, G320

Beaumont, Charles (editor), B130

beauties, the, W31: Bath, R190; Canterbury, P43; celebrated, B527·4, B530·5, C89, M388; Cheltenham, R189; court, J17; Dublin, F28, T489; English, E330, W22; of Great Britain, E348; London, B530·5; Oxford, D446; reigning, M42; Richmond, B532, H114·5; St. James's, S19; see also fair; ladies; toasts

beauties of the universe, B131, N170

beautiful young nymph, S809

beauty, D381: advocate of, B134; art of, A317; no bribe like, G207; Cupid in quest of, C540; design and, B519, L108; line of, L188; love and, R263; ode on, C417, H20·5; power of, P1011; prize of, J30; progress of, D9; and proportion, B133; and simplicity, P1175; taste and, T45; triumph of, T499; universal, B491; victory and, R30; and virtue, C188; wit triumphant over, C438

beauty: the banished, B55; the cloistered, A217; the imperious, I13; the Spanish, W126

beaux: Dr. Garth's opinion to, D356; epilogue to, F177; good advice to, G218; prologue upon, P1134; rod for Tunbridge, R245; satire on, O110, W257

Beavan, Squire, N227

Beavis Marks, A216

bed: lady's, P563; of honour, B153

bed-tester-plot, B154

Bedford, Diana, duchess of: addressee, L328, L330; marriage, B348

Bedford, Elizabeth, duchess of (addressee), H84

Bedford, John Russell, 4th duke of: addressee, C239; assaulted at Lichfield races, L265; marriage, B348

Bedford, Wriothesley Russell, 2nd duke of (elegy on), L312

Bedford, Wriothesley Russell, 3rd duke of, B477: dedicatee, S30

Bedlam, B155, T28: England a great, W43; news from, F172; see also Bethlehem hospital

Bedlam, Tom o', H145·5, T409, T411

bee: adventure of, A65; beehive, old woman and, O131; bee-keeping, V14

beech-nut oil, H213, P506

beef, B157: roast, F198

beefeaters, S772·5

Beelzebub's advice, B159

beer: poems in praise of, B157, F104, H303, W172; see also ale; brewers; mum

Beeriad, B160

bees, art of breeding, D316, V14

beggar on horseback, B161; beggar's match, F156, T166

Beggar's opera, E550, L206, N64, P716, S80; see also Macheath, Captain; Peachum, Polly

beggars: poetic, F54; sturdy, L239, S777

begging, laws against, C323

Behn, Alderman, N307

Behn, Aphra, versification of, L284

Be——l, Miss F——y, D359

Belcher, Jonathan, governor of New England, W256

Belcher, Matthew, captain, B183

Beldam, William, elegy on, G137·2

Belgic fables, T252

Belgrade, B164

Belhaven, John Hamilton, 2nd baron: speech of, B165; imitation of his speech, E221; satires on it, D185, S384; elegies on, E53, E54

Belhaven, John Hamilton, 3rd baron, elegies on, P156, U8

believer, joyful death of, G210; believer's dowry, E451

believers, sad changes incident to, L39

Belinda, Strephon to, P60

'Belisarius' (= Duke of Marlborough), B171

bell, whip and, W400

Bell Tavern, T425: Aesop at, P425

Bell, Bessy, R36

Bell, John, epitaph on, P382

Bellamy, Miss, P570

belles, London, B530·5

Bellisle, Marshal, E487

bellman: and the captain, B611; of St. James's, B181; state bellman, S722

bells, B292, N295, W561

belly duel, C282

Belphegor, B184, D244

Belsize House, B186

Belvedere, B187, B188

Belvoir, in tears, H78

'Ben, Brother', (= Hoadly), L159

Benbow, John, admiral, elegy on, S162

bench, the, B189

Benedicite, F226

Benedict XIV, pope, F272

benefactress, the, S647

Benet, St, religious order of, at Ghent, P259

benevolence: rewards of, H337; royal, D477

Bengal, voyage from, M502

Bennet, Sir William, of Grubbet, R72: addressee, K18, P306

Ben-oni, dialogue with, C226

Benson, Samuel (dedicatee), S241

Benson, William, surveyor-general, satire on, N304

Bentham, Edward, satires on, C99, K73, W517

Bentley, Richard, B392, M51, P968

Bently, Madam: dialogue, C312; elegy on, E56

Benwell village, E298, T154

Bergen-op-Zoom, taking of, B33, C506

Berkeley, George, bishop of Cloyne, H394, M390, O259

Berkeley, Lady Henrietta, L284

Berkeley, James Berkeley, earl (dedicatee), N261

Berkeley, Louisa, countess, elegy on, N261

Berkley, Mrs, B26

Berkshire tragedy, B200, B201

Bermudas, projected college in, H394, O259

Bernard, Francis, judge, elegy on, S383

Berry, John, elegy on, W345

Bertie, Mr, election candidate at Brentford, M229

Berwick, James Fitzjames, duke of, mistaken elegy upon, E57

Bess, doctor and, D349

Bethlehem Hospital, C225, R335, S657

Betterton, Thomas: benefit for 1709, C377, R287; prologues spoken by, P486, P1022, P1125, T455; song from *The prophetess*, B204, E564

Bettesworth, Richard, N58, S72

Betty, John and, J68

Betty, Joseph, sermon satirized, D285, O270

Bevan, Arthur, M.P., N227

B—g—m, A—l, 'passau countess of Kerry', elegy on, E167

Bible: concordance, C162; extracts from, F103, S392; protestant king and, P1047; and stick, C313; versifications, B213, H61, H259, M135, W328; *see also* Old Testament; New Testament

bibliotheca, N246

'Bickerstaffe, Isaac' (pseudonym of Richard Steele, also used by others), D392, E209, M396, P424, P1118, S671, T253

'Bickerstaffe the younger', A370

'Bickerstaffe, Jacob', L130

Biddle, Edward, satire on, A191

bigotry, triumphs of, T506

bill: of complaint, T116; to prevent occasional conformity (1704), E58, E479, M32; *see also* occasional conformity

Billingsgate: charity boys, P94; fray (and language), B215

Billingsley, Grace, elegy on, B216

'Billy' in a peck of troubles, G8

Bindon, Francis, portraits by, D520, P661

Bingley, John, elegy on, F298

Bird, Dr (dedicatee), W224

birds: and beasts, B219; parliament of, S690, S695

Birnie, Patie, elegy on, R49

birth: of a son, congratulatory address on, S249; of manly virtue, B221

birthday poems: Aboyne, earl of, D54; Anne, queen, A228, A346, C378, C550, D268, E317, E355, F113, H75, I31, L5, M531, M534, O51, P639·5, P1083, S212, S215, S216, T77, T331, U15, W21, W26; Barry, Henry, T372; Bluck, Matthew, S294; Boyle, lady Elizabeth, B67; Caroline, queen, A278, B179, B233, C284, C499, D472, D524, F279, G1, H88, H377, H455, N48, O61, P638, S112–17, S401, S411, S649; Carteret, John, lord, C277; Charles Edward, the young pretender, B225; Colston, Edward, O7, S7·5; Cowper, William, earl, B343; Exeter, Brownloe, earl, S250; Frederick, prince of Wales, N341, O35, P592, S106, S512; George I, king, C395, C396, E494–6, F206, G95, H130, I46, N39, N43–6, N49, P225, P577, P591, P649, P1123, S207–11, S213, S582, V79; George II, king, B224, B349, B589–91, C194, F119, H65, O32, O62–4, P79, P251, P280, P569, P646, S214, S706, T115, T363, V89, W296; James Francis Edward, the old pretender, B26, B223, J111, N167, O222, P378, P634; Pelham, Thomas, lord, S248; Sheppard, Mrs Kitty, S402; Sunbury, George, lord, J88; Swift, Jonathan, D64, P596, P610; Vernon, Edward, admiral, T525; William III, king, E343, G37, H366, S590, W32; William Augustus, duke of Cumberland, D481, O41, O42; *see also* genethliacon

birth-night, the, A333

bishop, or no bishop, B228

Bishop, Cecil (dedicatee), N253

bishopric, way to, V82–3

bishops: and occasional conformity bill, 1704, E479; and Sacheverell, 1710, P453; Irish, S794

Bishopsgate ward, election, S473

Bishopsthorpe, B68

Biss, Edward, I1

biter bitten, R216, W537

bitter nut, W68

Blachford, John (dedicatee), W273

black upon blue, B236

Black Dog (Dublin prison), E162, W464

black knight, from Chaucer, D48

Blackall, Offspring, controversy with Hoadly, L159

blackamore, state, D340

blackbird, the, C287; in fables, F4, S675, S697, S685, S686, S700, T24; as the Old Pretender, B237

Blackburne, Lancelot, archbishop of York, B68, F146, M347, P1054

Blackerby, Nathaniel, freemason, O224

Blackett, Walter, election candidate at Newcastle, C148, I69, N309

Blackham, Mother, Dublin tart-woman, elegy on, E59

Blackmore, Sir Richard, epistle to, P31; satires on, E411, F107, F170, M140

blacksmith's recreation, B269

Blackwall, charity children, H438

Blackwood, Sir Robert, elegy on, E60

Bladen, Martin (dedicatee), H141

Blair, David, elegies on, S169, S719

Blair, James, of Virginia, L296

Blake, alias Blueskin, highwayman, N288

Blake, Mary, of Newport, W557

Blanche, Henry and, H146

Blandford, fire at, D318; royal bounty to, P421

Blandford, John Churchill, marquis of, elegies on, C379, E32

Blandford, William Godolphin, marquis of (dedicatee), W332

blank poem, F149

blank verse, poems in (only those stating this in the title are listed), A68, A123, B140, B280, B316, B374, B506, B554, C73, C76, M267, M438, P627, R22, R185, S571, S630, S771, T444, W39; *see also* Milton, poems in imitation of

blanket, the, L204

Blare, Brice, quartermaster, elegy on, E61

Blaregnies (= Malplaquet), victory at, T366; *see also* Malplaquet

Blas, Don, *see* Lezo, Don Blas de

blasphemers, society of, H136; warning to, T266

blasphemous clubs, C228

blasphemy, N248

blasted laurel, B281

Blasters, Dublin club, O75

blatant beast, C55·5

blazing star, B283

B—le, Madam, bawd, F135

Blenheim, battle of (also referred to as Höchstädt), A84, A157, B453, C217, C361, D123, D222, D555, E356, F115, F152, J71, N295, O168, O249, P226, P662,

Blenheim (*cont.*)
    P1079, Q14, R240, R306, R322, S488, V90, W529;
    see also Marlborough, John Churchill, duke of
Blenheim Palace, D275, L330
blessing, aged father's, A130
blind: Elymas, F20; harpers, H108, I47; poet (Thomas
    Gill), G156–68
blockheads, new crop of, N127
bloody ballad, N110
blot, B288
Blount, Sir John, epistle to, A196
Bluck, Matthew, birthday poem on, S294
blue: hero in, H152·5; true, T512
Blue, Sir (= Walpole), S471
blue bonnet, C314; Blue-coat School, T330; blue garter,
    see Garter, order of; blue-stone at Edinburgh, E62
'Blueskin' (Mr Blake), highwayman, N288
blunder of all blunders, B290
Blunderella, C39
'Blunt, Alexander' (= E. Bockett), B301
B—ns, Madam, assault on, S51
boarding-school, the, B293; encouragers of, H70; dedica-
    tion to boarding schools, C90
Bob: and Harry, M159, S717; for the court, B295;
    Bob's soliloquy, L260
'Bob' (= Robert Harley), A335, B295, M159
'Bob of Lynn' (= Walpole), C325
'Bob, Sir' (= Walpole), C367
Bobart, Jacob, epistle to, E530
bobtails (= whigs), history of, H255
Boccaccio, tales from, A374, F228, H401, N301, O95,
    P463, T93
Bockett, Elias, L153
bodkin, lady's, T28
Boeotia, D515
Boeoticorum liber, B310
Boerus, Thomas (addressee), P405
Boileau-Despréaux, Nicolas: discourse on satire, H98;
    letter to, P1079; satire on Paris, F183. (For verse
    translations of Boileau, *see* the catalogue.)
bold truths, S554
Boleyn, Anne, W434
Bolingbroke, Henry St. John, viscount: political poems
    upon
    170–, T350
    1708, N217
    171–, G311
    1712, B527·2
    1713, N218
    1714, A78, D259, E126, M159, N59, N83·5, O264
    1715, H299, H358, L257, L258, M201, N235, S129
    1716, P1035
    1727/–, P713
    1727/28, L261
    1728, L255
    1730, E380
    1732, A60
    1734, D69
    1736, D323
    1737, H157·2
    1739, L80
    poems addressed to, E217, P244, P850, P984, T451,
    W308, Y71

Bolton, Charles Paulet, duke of (dedicatee), P123
Bolton, Anne, duchess of (dedicatee), J17
'Bona-fide' (= Louis XIV), epitaph on, E439
Bond, William, T360
bonfire: bishop of St. Asaph's, E84; city, P436
bonnets, tale of three, R96
'Bonniface', F211
Bononcini, musical setting by, P876
booby, complete, B564
Book of common prayer, verses in, C433
book thief, A10
bookseller, T586
booksellers, complaint to, H48
'Booth, John' (? = Mr King), lecturer in Dublin, J94
boots and saddles, H324
'Booty, Bob' (= Walpole), B294
Borr, Christian, elegy on, E63
Borrowstounness, news from, N294
Boston, Mass., C135
bottle, delights of, W57
bottle hoax, A270, C80, C320, M15
bottle-screw, A185
bottomless tub, T10
Bouchain, taking of, T364
Boufflers, duc de, D541, G268
Boulogne fray, P1147
Boulter, Hugh, archbishop of Armagh, M8, N113, P661
Boulter, John (dedicatee), L263
Bounce: Duchess of Newcastle's dog, N326; Pope's dog,
    B326
bounty: fortune's, W72; royal, E296
Bourne, Charles, G113
Bower, Thomas, P405
Bowes, hon. Mrs E., elegy on, M569
Bowes, John, solicitor-general of Ireland, A245, B53
Bowhill, John Murray, lord, elegy on, E64
Bowman, William, sermon of, B299, D285, M292
Bowmont, Robert Ker, marquis of (subsequently duke
    of Roxburghe), K19
Bowyer, Anthony, funeral satire on, F305
boxing match, W409, W412
boy, and wolf, fable of, P178
Boyce, Joseph, *see* Boyse
Boyce, William, musical settings by, H99, L213, L216
Boyeck, Joseph (dedicatee), W230
Boyle, David, lord Boyle of Kelburn (subsequently earl
    of Glasgow) (dedicatee), C496
Boyle, Lady Elizabeth (addressee), B67
Boyle, Lady Harriet, elegy on, P655
Boyle, Henry (subsequently baron Carleton), satire on,
    C150
Boyle, Henry (subsequently earl of Shannon) (addressee),
    P124, V49
Boyle, John, lord (subsequently 3rd earl of Glasgow)
    (addressee), V66
Boyle, Michael, archbishop of Armagh (dedicatee), W223
Boyse, Joseph, elegies on, C161, E65
Brabant: Marlborough's forcing of the lines, 1705,
    O168·2, P1101; victory in, 1706, E411, J110, L149;
    see also Ramillies
Brace, Mrs, dedicate, L264
Bracegirdle, Anne, and earl of Scarsdale, R291; prologues
    spoken by, C377, G39

Bradbury, Thomas, travesty of his *The primitive tories*, S23; addressee, T506
Bradshaw, John, the regicide, fall of his head, D242
bragg, card game, N80
Bragge, Robert, elegy on, H90
Bramber, borough of, election, L326
bramble, vine and, fable of, G135
Bramhall, John, his *Consecration and succession*, W209
Bramston, James, satire on, M380
Brand, Mr, student at Edinburgh, elegy on, O196
'Brass, Sir Robert' (= Walpole), S474
brave Englishman, A25
bravery: British, B475; English, M349, O90, R263
brawny priest, C255
Bray, vicar of, V84
Brazen, Captain, E371
brazen age, B403
breach of promise, C530
bread, brown, and honour, B501
Bread-street: adventurers, U6; tatlers, T517; ward, P96
breasts, history of, J95
breathings, of a pious soul, H114
breeches, the, a tale, B407
Brent, D291
Brentford election, M229
Brett, Anne (addressee), N10, S90
brewer, hudibrastic, W96
brewers, G100, G292, H360, P154, P160, P168, T100
brewing, art of, A356, D402
Brewster, S., page to John Robinson, D298
bribery, M284, W50
bricklayer, poems by, J92, J94
bride: happy, H39; at her wits' end, O114; rape of, R119
bridegroom: condemned, C332; at his wits' end, B440
bridge: dialogue between old and new, W364; of life, B441
Bridgwater, Elizabeth, countess of, elegy on, H67·5
Bridgwater, Scroop Egerton, earl of (subsequently duke), addressee, A369, S649
bridle, for the French king, B447
Briggs (or Brigs), John, A239, B21-2, D397
brimstone, S155
Brisbain, James, elegy on, M541
Bristol, V22: compared with London, S100; fair quakers of, L188; journey to, J19; Loyal Society at, O7, S7·5; merchants, L240·2; Newgate, S100; opening of theatre at, F277; poetical description of, G216; progress of Methodism in, P1110
Bristol-wells, B451
Bristol, Elizabeth, countess of, and John, lord Hervey, A234, C444
Bristol, Elizabeth Chudleigh, countess of, *see* Chudleigh
Britain, T196: ancient and modern state of, C412; made free, B452
Britain's: apology, B466; consolation, D398; hero, J16; joy, B453, B454; jubilee, E478; lamentation, D399; ode of victory, B455; palladium, B527·2; recovery, C114; rejoicing, B456; triumph, B457; wrongs, B458
Britannia, B467, C517, M308, T101, T177, W51: excisa, B459, B462; invicta, B466; liberata, O164; rediviva, C114; triumphans, B80·5, D222, J97, P150
Britannia's: alarm, G135; glory, R312; gold-mine, L211; lamentation, B468; loss, B469; memorial, S687;

prayer, T48; precaution, B470; summons, B471; tears, B472, H60; triumph, B473; triumphs, B527·1
'Britannicus': signature, A133, L126; translator, L128
British: admiral, B474; antiquarians, R89; Atticus, M87; bravery, B475; censor, B476; court, B477, B527·4, S360; distillery, B301; empire, J29; fleet, Y81; frenzy, B478; general, A187; hero, B479, M84; heroes, G303; Homer, M497; Hudibras, W193; isle, F216; lion, T329; merchant, D544; Michael, B605; Mississippi, R127; muse, S275, T577; navy, O74; ode, B480; olympics, B527·8; phillipic, A133; piety, G111; plan, O241; prophecy, N114; shitters, M166, S206; swain, D72; valour, C491, M7; warrior, D27; whale, P357; wonders, W53; worthies, S518; *see also* Welsh
British magazine, M158
Briton: joyful, B568; loyal, L297; true-born, T513; Briton's thought, T514
Briton, Edward, ghost of, R151
Britons: loyal, R310; present corruption of, M490; true, C101, T516; thanksgiving of, B481; *see also* Ancient Britons
Brittain, Thomas, of Chatton, D476
Britton, Thomas, 'musical small-coal man', B482, S85
broad-bottomry, M461-2
broad brimmed hat, *see* hat
Broad-street ward, B404
Brobdingnagian verse, M332
Brodrick, Alan (subsequently viscount Midleton): lord chancellor, G291; departure from Ireland, I65; speaker of Irish house of commons, S620
Broggin, Mary, signs dedication, P196
brogue makers, D266
broken: mug, H303, W447; pipkin, B484
broker, court, C464
Bromley, trip to from Moorfields, W117
Bromley, William, satire on, D85
Brompton, lady of (= Katherine Field), L20
Brooke & Hellier, wine merchants, B487, B498·5, W149
Brooke, Ann, lady, elegy on, G202
Brooke, Henry, author, assisted Edward Moore, M424
Brooke, Henry, master of Manchester Grammar School, Q1
Brooke, Thomas, wine merchant, B487, B498·5, W149
Broschi, Carlo (called Farinelli), *see* Farinell
brothel, U6; *see also* bawdy house
brother in the country, letter to, I72
brotherhood-in-law, L1
brown bread and honour, B501
Brown, Adam, lord provost of Edinburgh, elegy on, E66
Brown, John, merchant in Holland, wedding song, W265
Brown, Margaret Cecil, lady, O251
Browne, Peter, bishop of Cork: book by, L254; elegy on, A151
Bruce, Robert, king of Scots, H102
Brudenell, George, lord (subsequently earl of Cardigan), marriage of, L95, S25
Bruges, taking of, S133
Brunswick, congress of, C281
Brunswick & Lunenburg, George Lewis, duke of, *see* George I
Brunswick mum, R209
brush, to the curry-comb of truth, B550

Brussels, siege of, P608, S133

'Brute, Sir John', C172

Brutus: the Trojan, founder of the British empire, J29; Et tu Brute?', E479

Bryan, a dog, E254

Bubb, George, subsequently Bubb Dodington, baron Melcombe, *see* Dodington

bubbies, secret history of, J95

bubble, the, S810: Westminster, W364; *see also* South Sea

bubbler's medley, B553

Bubo and Turturella, F2

Buccleugh, Anna, duchess of, P39

Buccleugh, Francis Scott, duke of (dedicatee), B369, H341

Buchanan, George: epistle to, P364; ode on, M318; works imitated, P753, P1056, T581

Buchans, imitation in broad, F184

Buckeridge's best intelligence, newspaper, H110

Buckinger, Matthew, elegies on, E67, S218

Buckingham, Edmund Sheffield, duke of: elegies on, B354, L220; ode to, L217

Buckingham, John Sheffield, duke of: addressee, H371; his *Brutus*, P876; imitation of, L80

Buckingham, Katherine, duchess of: addressee, L223, L226; verses upon, P984

Buckingham, Sir Owen, lord mayor, M533

Buckingham House, M104

Buckworth, Elizabeth, elegy on, T261

Buckworth, Hester, elegy on, T262

Buckworth, Sir John, S344

Budgell, Eustace, A232, C399, D323, E397, L240, M291, M397

budget, Sandys's, W480

Bugg, Francis, A8

Buissiere, John, poem on his marriage, S321

Bulger, Anthony, suspected Jacobite, N196

Bulkeley, Sir Richard, epistle to, P1140

'Bull' (= Bolingbroke), O264

bull baiting, T95

bulls (stockjobbers), S767

bully, high-church, H191

bum-bailiffs, T438; dedication to 'Bumbalio', T5

bum-bees assembly, B566

bumography, D534

Bumpstead, Edward (dedicatee), H344

'Bunch, Mother', M524

'Bung' (= Sir Gilbert Heathcote), B567

'Bungey, Dr' (= Sacheverell), D350

Bunhill burial ground, G327

Bunyan, John, versification of his *Pilgrim's progress*, H268

Burchett, Josiah: addressee, E1, R76; poems by, and answers, B571, R77, R86

Burgersdijk, Franco, E69

Burgess, Daniel, D333, D343, J7, L62, T26: elegy on, N136

burgess oaths, P588

burgesses, caution to, C80

Burgh, Thomas, mathematician, satire on, B288

Burgundy, Louis, duke of, B577, N251

burlesque, burlesque poem, burlesque verse (chiefly comprising those works that so describe themselves), A323, 8B, B184, B308, B430, B607, C286, C315, C405, C435, D34, D245, D285, D335, D360, D485, D494, D509, F100, F153, F272, H89, H180, H476, K52, L42, L60, M76, M217, M226, N236, N291, N294, O77, O114, O246, P1053, P1118, R8, R245, S37, S571, S655, T47, T156, T420, T529, V107, W11, W40, W90, W170, W257, W260; *see also Hudibras*, imitations of

Burley House, W567

Burlington, Charles Boyle, earl of, elegies on, P461, S264

Burlington, Richard Boyle, earl of: addressee, G88, L96, P908, S285; recovery of, 1707, T67

Burnbank, James Campbell of, *see* Campbell

Burnet, Alexander, *Achilles dissected*, 1733, J116

Burnet, Gilbert, bishop of Salisbury, L132: elegies on, E70, M167; satires on, P301, R128, W393; satiric elegies on, H262, W112

Burnet, Thomas, N259: Addison's ode to, M287, N275

burning of condemned books, E83, E84, P436

Burrowes, Henry, lord mayor of Dublin, H357, L119

Burton, Benjamin, alderman of Dublin, L2

Burton, John, fellow of Eton, satire on, K67

Burton, Samuel, banker of Dublin: addressee, C276; failure of his bank, H362

Bury, W531; Bury-fair, D60

business: idleness of, W575; and retirement, M87

butchers, Dublin, B602, B603; butchers' wives in Musselburgh, L37

butler, fifteen plagues of a, F132

Butler, James, duke of Ormonde, *see* Ormonde

Butler, Samuel, imitations of his *Hudibras*, *see* Hudibras

Butler, Theophilus, baron Newtown-Butler, *see* Newtown-Butler

Butler, Sir Toby, barrister, elegy on, E72

butterfly, fable of miss and, H19

button, and button-hole, B610

Button's coffee house, J27, T435: lion's mouth at, C507

Buxsted advocate, D212

B—y, Mr, elegy on, E200

Byng, George, viscount Torrington, admiral, E21: presentation copy to, T371

Byrom, John, imitation of, D406

bystander, B621

C., A. (addressee), C432, D53

cabal: mitred, E479; moderate, M230

Cadenus (= Swift), and Vanessa, S814

Cadière, Miss, M280, P38, S655, S720

Cadiz, attack on, P643, S458

Cadogan, William, earl Cadogan: entry at the Hague, 1718, S507; duel with Nicholas baron Lechmere, 1723, B42, D507, F140; elegy on, E73; addressee, A187, A192, B15, N279, O77, S505, W293

Caelia: Alexis to, H167; Palaemon to, W303

Caelia's: complaint, C90; marriage, L282; revenge, R242

Caesario (= Frederick, prince of Wales), D322, F271

'Cain, Sir Tubal', O262

cakes, and ale, H170, N238

Calder, Robert: elegy on, P164; used as *persona* by Pitcairne, P345, P353

'Caleb' (= 'Caleb D'Anvers'), H411, N130, P1161

Caledonia, D90; rediviva, C2

Caledonian songsters, A6

Cales (= Cadiz), S458

calicos: ballad on, W128; downfall of, S840; exposed, P1051

Calista: (= Lady Abergavenny), B135; (= Anne Oldfield), P104; (= Anne Vane), F199

Calista, opera, C104

Callistia, J30

Calmady, Shilston, H300

Calophilus, C388

Calpe, or Gibraltar, B420

calumny, essay on, S86

Calvert, Sir William, lord mayor, satire on, S470

Calves Head club, B608·5, K104, L298, L314, S911, T573

Calvin, John, D261, P298, P323, S705

Cam, and Isis, C6

Cambrai, François Salignac de la Mothe Fénelon, archbishop of, *see* Fénelon

Cambria, R260: sighs of, R194; triumphant, P717; Cambria's complaint, D234; *see also* Wales

Cambrians, battle of, L165; *see also* Welsh

cambric, bill concerning, L224

Cambridge: coach, B614; elections, C7, U19; George II visits, B557; ladies, P535; paintings, E513; poetasters, S38

  University: addressee, B505, M142; commencement, E515, L247, M129, P907, T103; disputes (1750), E387; fellow commoner (addressee), E387; friends, treatment of by Oxford, O275; George I's bounty to, S578; statutes, S734; theses, B169; tripos speech, C255; vote, S632; young student at (addressee), E390

  authors identifying themselves as from Cambridge, A157, B134, B193, B380, E410, L319, P720, T3, V68, V70

  St John's College, P1096; author (RS) from, T442

  Trinity College: authors from, D189, O238; servant at, B332

Cambridge, George, duke of, *see* George II, king

Cambro-British: gambols, S22; invention, T3

Cambro-Briton (= Sir William Morgan), S717

camera obscura, V57

Cameronian address, C9

Camilla, opera, prologue to, C200

Camillus, H211

Camisard prophets, E443; *see also* Cevennes, prophets of; Emes, Thomas

camp, humours of, R24

camp song, new, N115

campaign, the, A27: glorious, G180; Hebrew, H132; merry, M199; mock, M349; Wandsworth, S466; winter, C117

Campbell, curer of smoky chimneys, L313

Campbell, redcoat, H260

Campbell, A.: addressee, C432; recipient, P364

Campbell, Archibald, duke of Argyll, *see* Argyll

Campbell, Charles, elegy on, E74

Campbell, George, professor of theology, elegies on, E75, I28

Campbell, James, of Burnbank, criminal, B578, W550: banishment of, E76, P151, S606

Campbell, John, 2nd duke of Argyll, *see* Argyll

canary bird: elegy on, P281; robin redbreast turned, S586

'canary birds' (= foreign protestants) naturalized, C18

candidates: election, C22, C535, E31, W122; for the bays, C409

candle, reflections on, W28

candour, C23

Canons, house at, G151, H402

cantata, F198, M157, P1181

Canterbury: beauties, P43; ladies, G203; tale, C29; tales, P427

Canterbury, see of, contention for, F146, M347, M450, R7

Canterbury: John Potter, archbishop of (1737–47), *see* Potter; Thomas Tenison, archbishop of (1694–1715), *see* Tenison; William Wake, archbishop of (1716–37), *see* Wake

Canterbury, ship, S10

Canticles, essay upon, A7

captives from Barbary, B79

Cardigan, George Brudenell, earl of, *see* Brudenell

cardinal, A23; (= Cardinal Fleury), C498, K96, S669; cardinal's coach, C36; cardinals at Rome, C529

Cardonnel, Adam, C537, P277

cards, allegorical games of, B294, N199, P713, P1048–50, R308, R318, S724

Carestini, Signor, singer, E381

Carey, surgeon to Prince of Wales, M355

Carey, Henry: satire on, S71; *The honest Yorkshireman*, C41, C51–2

Carleton, Henry Boyle, baron, C150

Carlisle, siege of, S459

Carlisle, Charles Howard, earl of: addressee, C61; elegy on, G116

Carmarthen, Elizabeth, marchioness of: marriage, C508, C510, T66; elegy on, C509

Carmarthen, Peregrine Hyde Osborne, marquis of (subsequently duke of Leeds): marriage of, C508, C510, T66; dedicatee, C509

carmen seculare, C55, D295, M261, N250, P78, S362

Carnarvon, James Brydges, earl of (subsequently duke of Chandos), *see* Chandos

Carnarvon, John Brydges, marquis of: addressee, A281, R45; elegy on, Y69

Carnegie, lady Christian: marriage of, T397; elegy on, E194

carol, Christmas, *see* Christmas

Caroline, queen of George II:

  arrival in England (1714), G52

  at the Hague (1715), C92

  ode for happy delivery of (1716), H322

  birth of George William (1717), E507

  death of George William (1718), S375

  accession and coronation (1727), C45, E510, M141, N149, N266, R221, W253

  regency of (1729), M536; (1732), B52

  at Bath (1732), T371

  rebuilding of Queen's College Oxford (1733), T296

  death (1737), D433, D483, H116, M89, P651, R194, S118, S460, T415, V62, V65

  birthday poems, A278, B179, B233, C284, C499, D472, D524, F279, G1, H88, H377, H455, N48, O61, P638, S112–17, S401, S411, S649; poems addressed or dedicated to, A41, B77, B409, C472, D31, D477, H65, H82, L325, M147, M326, M332, M539, N306, P771, S32, S704, W296; satire on, P1063

carpenter of Oxford, C245

Carstairs, John, elegy on, P102

Cartagena, expedition to, A312, D56, D57, E332, E605, L126, L128, S617, V33

Carter, Cornelius, printer at Dublin, A72, W375

Carter, George, elegy on, S335

Carteret, Frances, baroness, poems addressed to while in Ireland 1725–30, B80, D205, D206, E383, R204, S799, T7

Carteret, Georgina (youngest daughter of preceding), P208

Carteret, Grace (eldest daughter), A372, B80, L195, N216, P27, P208, P221, Y108

Carteret, John, baron (subsequently earl Granville), secretary of state 1721–24, E502, S377, V68; lord-lieutenant of Ireland 1724–30, poems addressed to as, A358, A361, B78, B221, B403, D65, D196, D228, G7, I58, N35, P219, P542, P1123, S44, S497, T332, T440, V123; other poems occasioned by his stay in Ireland, C277, L196, L197, N113, P1, P533, P544, P683, S877; satires on his later career 1742–46, B517, D369, H158, K49, M462, W494; other poems addressed to, H220, N259, P474, R266

Carteret, Sophia, countess of Granville, elegy on, R266

Carthage revenged, C56

Carthy, Charles, satires concerning, B104, D514, D523, K1, L166, S127

Cartwright, Thomas, MP for Northampton, H125

Cary, Walter, marriage of, S309

Carvell, Hans, O114

case: Miss Cadiere's, M280; state of the, S450; a woman's, C97

Casimir, Isidora to, 170

Cass, Sir John, MP for London, T25

Cassandra, S24

'Cassaw, Comus', P269

Cassinus and Peter, S809

castle of indolence, T181

Castle Howard, C61

Castlemaine, Dorothy, viscountess (subsequently duchess) (dedicatee), T563

castrati, see Carestini; Farinelli; Nicolini; Senesino

Caswell, John, in Leominster election, T343

cat: death of favourite, S602; loss of ears of, B163; fables of, F13, W384; 'my grandmother's cat' (= Duchess of Kendal), L71; old cat's prophecy, B125; cat may look upon a king, B163; downfall of cats, C317

Catalonia, military success in (1706), O167

catches, C68, N320

catechism in metre, S527, W443

Cathcart, Charles, 8th baron: expedition of, R251; elegy on, H408

Cathcart, James, astrologer, mock elegy on, E79; reply to, R162

catholic poet, O165

Catiline, English (= Harley?), P41

Cato, the censor, L181

Cato, by Addison, A41, E406, M208

Cato major, by Cicero, C72, D213

caution: to the cits, S482; timely caution, to the ladies, G222

cavalcade: Grubstreet, G305; Kerry, K30; tumultuous, W155

cave: of Pope, D390; of poverty, T137

Cavendish, lord Charles (dedicatee), L98

Cayley, John, elegy on, E166

C——d, Dr, P565

Cebes's table, P998

Cecil, lady Elizabeth (subsequently countess of Orrery), marriage, S650

Cecilia, Saint, see St Cecilia's day

Celadon, C88

Celia, see Caelia

celibacy, C91

Cennick, John, G208, S219

censor (= Hugh Graffan), G313, G319; British censor (= Addison), B476

Cerealia, F104

Cesario, see Caesario

'Cethegus' (= Thomas marquis of Wharton), E375

Cevennes, prophets of, D278–84, P1140; see also Camisard prophets; Emes, Thomas

chain, of providence, O168·2

chair, hymn to, H456

chairman, at Bath, T371

Chamber, lady Mary, elegy on, S339

Chamberlen, Dr (Hugh the younger?), epistle to, W294

chambermaid, fifteen plagues of, F133; chambermaid's policy, C105

chamber-pot, P293, P627, T437

Chambrelan, Caesar, elegy on, S234

Chamillard, Mons. (French minister of war), vision of, P254

Champion, Sir George, candidate for lord mayor, C106

champions, three, T253

Chamyam, with her leg upon a table, C151

Chancery, court of, L229–30

Chancler, John (dedicatee), W230

Chandler, Edward, bishop of Lichfield and Coventry, subsequently of Durham, M150, P549

Chandos, Cassandra, duchess of, elegy on, S24

Chandos, James Brydges, duke of (dedicatee), G151, H402, I7, O82, S24, W289

'Change Alley, B308, S767, W177

changes, the, H10

chaplains, miserable conditions of, E607

Chapman, Richard, vicar of Cheshunt, satire on, E145

character (of William Gibson), B302, B303, B307, L153; (of Swift), C118: of Anselmus, C127; of Sir Willoughby Aston, Y2; of Mr Boyce, C161; of the Bread-street tatlers, T517; of a certain dean, W553·5; of a covetous citizen, W55; of the drabs, B610; of English poets, P31; of a fellow of Trinity College (Lambert Hughes?), W522; of a freeman, C121; of French officers, T487; of Frenchmen, N180; Gracchus, G233; of the Intelligencer, S887, T319; of the lord keeper (William lord Cowper), H109; of Louis XIV, F262; of a loyal statesman, D391; of a master of a vessel, C122; of a modern patriot, P705; of the nuns, M496; of Caius Asinius Pollio (= John duke of Argyll), H318; of a presbyterian, D216·5; of the Prince of Wales's poet (Sir John Vanbrugh), T518; of Strip-corps, F287; of Jonathan Swift, A237, H181, S884; of Marshall Tallard, T488; of Lord Timon, M40, W298; of Sir George Treby,

character (*cont.*)

T64; of a true-born Dutch skipper, S50; of a true churchman, S42; of a true country man, M68; of a turn-coat, C123; of the wooden monster, T519; of a Welshman, C126; of a certain whig (=Thomas marquis of Wharton), C119

characters, C129: of the British court, B477, B527·4, S360; of clergymen, D538–9; of the company at Bath, D437; of the fair at Stamford, P992; of the general officers, B98; of men, O88, P920; of quacks, E390; of sectaries, L152; of thirteen pilots (politicians), R211; miscellaneous, A96, B477, C130, C207, C407, G327, M166, M397, P180, P704, S486; of women, P917; *see also* beauties; fair; toasts

characteristics, C128

Charing Cross: dialogue with horse at, D270, N129; pillory scuffle at, P284

Charistes, poem to the memory of, T506

charity: beauty and excellence of, B132; description of C144; hue and cry after, W233; late, S403; planter's, P477; progress of, P1107

charity-boys, charity-children; *see* charity schools

charity schools, G162·5, H423, H429–30, H432–50, H473, P91–4, P96, P472, P633, T258, T330

Charlemont, James Caulfield, viscount (subsequently earl), epistle to, D519

Charlemont, William Caulfield, viscount, elegies on, E80–1

Charles I, martyrdom of, B608, C178, C304, E602, L4, R313, R314, R316, S5, S718

Charles II: restoration of, E595, F307, M408, N209, P686; song sung before, S592

Charles V of Austria, P407

Charles VI of Austria, F250, P348

Charles VII of Austria, death of, D75, E487

Charles III of Spain, *see* Charles VI of Austria

Charles XII of Sweden, A231, B530·2, C93, H152·5, P346: elegies on, C132, H85, M210

Charles Edward Stuart, the Young Pretender:
  1720, ode composed on his birth, O23
  1744, expedition from Dunkirk, B604, I72, L297
  1745–46, rebellion in Scotland: poems addressed to, A1, I67, O22, O66, P1058, T342; poems in praise of, A22, B225, B616, C131, C166, C383, O58, O187, O221, P575, P636; satires on, B230, C12, 7C43, H202, J58, L275, M411, N158, O243, P624, I₁d60, S599, T439; *see also* Jacobite rebellions
  1749, expulsion from France, S46; poems in praise of, M77, M81

Charleton, Capt. Edward, elegy on, E82

Charlett, Arthur, A177, D296

'Charley' (=Charles Lucas) in the chair, C133

charmers, the, C134

charming, art of, D381

charms: of indolence, M303; of liberty, C82; of music, P720, T399

Charnock, Robert, his remains, B413

Charteris, Colonel Francis, satires on, D396, E370, R117, R160, T584

Charteris, Janet, marriage of, R70

chase (=hunting), C136, S562: stag, P1012; *see also* hunting

chastity, C536, E39: female, F88

Chaucer, Geoffrey: poem on, D51; whims of, P431; wife of Bath reformed, N240; for modernizations and imitations, *see* the main catalogue

cheese, excise of, D557

Chelsea: trip to, C495; college, W559; monarch (= Walpole), C141

Cheltenham beauties, R189

Cherry and slae, imitation of, F22

Cheshire grand jury, A52

chess, Vida's poem on, translated, E460, J57, P1158

Chester, ladies, K51, L182, L200

Chester journal, B616

Chester, Francis Gastrell, bishop of (1714–25), *see* Gastrell

Chester, Robert (dedicatee), T357

Chesterfield, Petronilla, countess of (dedicatee), J92, W269

Chesterfield, Philip Dormer Stanhope, earl of: preface by, H22; lord-lieutenant of Ireland 1745–46, A170, D515, F72, J91, M190, T478, T503, V101, W270, W272, W274, Y177; other poems addressed to, B83, B351, C52, E421, F148, H419, J61, L320, N336, P67, P1160, S354, S714, S785, T39, T45

Chetham, Samuel, of Castleton, satire on, C287

Chevalier, the, *see* Charles Edward Stuart

Chevalier de St. George, *see* James Francis Edward Stuart

'Chevalier de St. Patrick' (=W. Dunkin), D7, I53

Chevy Chase, imitations of, H45, R223, W376, W539; *see also* tunes

Cheyne, George, epistle to, E398

Chichele, Henry, praise of, R111

Chichester, Francis Hare, bishop of (1731–40), B540

Chiesly, Captain, death of, P629

child, unborn, advice to, F268

Child, Emma, T563

Child, Sir Francis, the elder, M.P. (1702), R163

Child, Sir Francis, the younger, lord mayor (1731), C348

Child, Sir Richard, bart. (dedicatee), F173

children: art of getting pretty, C4, O142, R280; religious poems for, C218, D366, F75, G160, M135, N327, P1176, S467, S527, W443

chimerical patriot, C149

chimneys, patent for curing smoky, L313

chimney-sweeper: devil turned, L260; in disgrace, C150

china, passion for old, G79

china cups, metamorphosis into, T109

Chinese tale, C151

Chippenham election petition 1742, E544

Chiron, and Achilles, A16, J31

chivalry, no trifle, C152

Chloe: convinced, C156; Daphnis and, G44; monita, C157; Strephon and, S809; surpriz'd, S399; Thyrsis and, B333; triumphant, V26; fall of Chloe's piss pot, P627

choice, the, P722: bachelor's, B3; ladies', L9; libertine's, W101; maiden's, C449; for new members of parliament, L12; of life, W2; wise or foolish, C229

Cholmondeley, George Malpas, 3rd earl of (dedicatee), S88

Cholmondeley, Thomas, of Vale Royal, elegy on, P607

Choppin, Richard, B236, C161, C314, C531, L60, M203

choruses, for John duke of Buckingham's *Brutus*, P876

Christ, *see* Jesus Christ

Christ's Hospital: dedication to, C169; psalms sung by the children of, C258–63, C518–9, H164–6, H376

christening, the, C164

Christian, whole duty of, W443

Christian's: A.B.C., R243; epinikion, M438; exercise, C169; jubilee, T520

Christian: counsel to youth, B202; discourse, H385; duties, C146; hero, C166; life, R332·5; love, D301; priest, C167; religion, D366, P472; sabbath, L263; tales, G209; test, C168

Christianity: light of the moral world, H264; without persecution, W4

Christians: cure for dim-sighted, A114; fight with quakers, A8

Christie, James, P719

Christmas: hymn for, H422; carol, E20, H292; day, poems on, B411, M115, O191, P358, P1046, S26, W316; see also Jesus Christ, nativity

invitation, S497; trick, W535

Christmas box: for Dr. Delany, S842; answered, A246; maid's, M22; for Namby Pamby, C170

chronicle, scandalous, C407

Chudleigh, Elizabeth (subsequently countess of Bristol), epistle to, P702

church: declension of, L31; in danger, G273; in no danger, C175; in glory, J6; history of, R264·5; militant, C176, S696; monarchy and, M396; secured, T446; too hard for the state, C182; triumphant, D354, R333

ills, W555; memorial, burning of, E83; scuffle, B424

Church of England: best of all protestant churches, P265; defence of, D88; feasts of, S485; nature and proceedings of, S69; state of, S698; miscellaneous, C450, E13, L199; see also clergy; convocation

martyr, C178

Church of England's: address, C179; ghost, M362; joy, C180; lamentation, C176; new hymn, H466; new toast, T403

Church of Rome, protestants' charge against, F43

Church of Scotland: address of, T388; associate synods of, P588; and the covenanters, K84, M547, T385; lamentation of, K29; and oath of abjuration, B46; concerning plays, C181; Rome's legacy to, P170; shorter catechism of, S527; satires on the general assembly, A239, A244, A265; B21–2, B566, H205, H392, N201, S584

Churchill, family of, L330

Churchill, Brigadier Charles (addressee), L201, P104, P666

Churchill, John, duke of Marlborough, see Marlborough

Churchill, John, marquis of Blandford, see Blandford

Churchill, Sarah, duchess of Marlborough, see Marlborough

churchman: loyal, L299, W391; true, S42

churchmen: characters of, D538–9; weeping, W275

churchwarden, dialogue with lawyer, F81

churchyard, C184

Cibber, Colley, prologue spoken by (1713) T310; Nonjuror (1717) L48; poet laureate (1730) H462, U23; ode imitated, C195; controversy with Pope, C468, H156, O100, P761, S126, S153; Apology (1740) T128; at Drury Lane (1745) N158

Cibber, Mrs (Susannah Maria?), P702: poem to, T351

Cicely, Dermot and, D233

cider, P237

cindercola scrub, P539

Cipolla, Fra, F228

Circassian, fair, C520

Circe, F172

circumvention, the, C202

circular letter, D343

circus, in Hyde Park, B527·8

citizen, covetous, W55

citizen's: daughter, C208; honest citizen's wish, H294; procession, C203

citizens, poem to, T362

city: in glory, C204; in a hubbub, G225; triumphant, C212

ballad, F285; bonfire, P436; intrigue, C205; lady's choice, C206; madam, C207; mumpers, L134; ramble, C210; struggle, C211

civil wars of the Old Bailey, P594

Clanricarde, Michael Bourke, earl of, marriage of, S301

clans' lamentation, C216

Clara, Donna, J40

Clare, Thomas Pelham Holles, earl of (subsequently duke of Newcastle), see Newcastle

Claremont, G18

Clarendon, Edward Hyde, earl of, History versified, W80

claret, safe resolutions over a glass of, A330; claret-prone godson, S447

Claridge, Richard, elegy on, E292

Clarinda, fair libertine, R14

Clarissa, C221, R217, R219

Clark, Elymas, satire on, F20

Clark, Thomas, oculist, T352

Clarke, Alured, dean of Exeter, elegy on, O192

Clarke, Captain Edward, F46

Clarke, Henry, professor of divinity, E386

Clarke, Jeremiah, composer, N162

Clarke, John, G95

Clarke, Samuel, metaphysician, elegies on, C167, V61

classic quarrel, C230

Clause, King, L134

Clavering, Mary, marriage of, O208

Clavering, Robert, bishop of Peterborough (addressee), P1040

Clayton, John, dean of Kildare, elegy on, E85

Clayton, Robert, Irish bishop, his prize for poetry, G267, M356, T363

Clayton, Sir Robert, elegy on, S343

Clayton, Thomas, composer, H50

'Clean-cogue, Thomas', N182

Clelia, to Sappho, N282, N285; Princess Clelia, D191

Clement XI, pope, F284

clergy: advice to, A89, P1055; litany for, L193; petition of, P89; usefulness of, E533; London clergy, L233, L236; nonjuring, D289; Romish, F230

clergyman: and goldsmith, C237; of Virginia, D61; see also parson

clergyman's: daughter, C238; choice of a wife, L94

clerk, merchant's, E360

clerk of Oxford's tale, O95

Clerk, John, son of the following, elegy on, R101

Clerk, Sir John, of Pennecuik (addressee), R101

Cleveland, Barbara, duchess of: elegy on, F82; marriage to General Feilding, D464, F83

client's complaint, P753

Clifford, Jack, news-crier, elegy on, E86

Clio, C239, T552: and Strephon, T360

cloak: of dissenters, M203, T543; presbyterian, C240; woman's, F94

Clodd, honest, H295

Cloe, see Chloe

Clonmel, election at, M560

Closterman, John, portrait of Queen Anne by, T74

clouds, compared to woman, S410, S795

'Cloudy, Miss', M42

Clout, Colin, C284

clowns, S57: Irish, H400

Cloyne, George Berkeley, bishop of, see Berkeley

club: at Mr. Taplin's, C350, D251, D428, S381; blasphemous, C228; the Blasters, O75; drunken, D44; Hell-fire, H136; Kit-Cat, B257, K94, V16; see also Calves Head Club; Easy Club; October Club

Clubson, Andrew, G206

Clyde, river, A281, R271

clyster-pipe, satire on, A264

coach, overturning of, V58

coachman, D441: old, W494; fifteen plagues of, F132, F134; coachman's wish, C244

coalition, happy (1742), H40

coals, price of, P559

coat of arms, Jacobite, J53

Cobb, Samuel, notes by, Q16

cobbler: court candidate and, C535; of Gloucester, C264; in Patrick's Street, L118; a tale, W341; cobbler's poem, W270

Cobden, Edward, sermon on chastity, C536

Cobham, Richard Temple, viscount: his gardens at Stowe, W360; marriage, S302; poems addressed to, B315·5, C375, P920; poem in praise of, E426

Cochran, lady Anne (subsequently duchess of Hamilton), see Hamilton

'Cochrania' (=preceding), P152

cock, fable of, F8; cock-fighting, C269; cock-match, T26; cocks and ganders, F5

Cockburn's meeting-house, Glasgow, D419

cocker, the, H6

'Cock-lorrel, King', D40

'Codex, Dr' (=Edmund Gibson), D352, D352·5, P81

cod's-heads, fable of, P435

coffee, C274

coffee-house speculations, D75

coffee women turned courtiers, C275

Coffey, Charles, satires on, A256, E87, G305

Coghill, Marmaduke, satire on, W554

Coke, Edward, of Norfolk, elegy on, P109

Coke, Sir Edward, Reports of, R159

Coke, Thomas, MP for Derbyshire, portrait of, T350

Colcannen match, C282

Cole, William, inscription by, P259

Coleraine, Henry Hare, baron, elegy on, S340

Colin, Lucy and, T290

Colin's: complaint, R286; mistakes, P1065

college: eclogue, S31; examination, P173, V54; exercise, P264; life, P258; wit, C286

College of Physicians, M172-3

'Colley', see Cibber, Colley

collier's wedding, C147

colliers: battle of the, B105; thanksgiving for the, W323

Collins, Anthony: A discourse of freethinking (1713) V16; The scheme of literal prophecy (1726) P549

Collins, Nathaniel (dedicatee), N41

Colston, Edward, birthday of, O7, S7·5

Colt, Sir Henry Dutton, election candidate, D255

comedians, play-house, F169

comfort, crumbs of, C530, C531

comforts, see fifteen comforts

comical: dialogue, C312, F132, F133, N296; history, C313; revenge, K11; sonnet, C314

Comins, John (dedicatee), G229

commendatory poem, C316

commerce, progress of, G197

committee: of rats, C317; of secrecy (1715), T368, T377

common hunt, C318

common law, B394

commoner, C319: gentleman commoner, G122

commons, house of, see house of commons

commonwealth-man, L298, O4

companion to the bottle, C320

Company of Mine-adventurers, N263

complaint, the, D423, Y24: advocate's, A107; Alma's, A172; of beaux and bads, G294; of the black knight, D48; Caelia's, C90; Colin's, R286; doleful, D393; elegiac, P752; of a family, C321; fortunate, P731; freeholder's, P755; grove's, G302·5; hard-used poet's, H48; of Job, C322; penitent's, W233; Robert Penman's, R1; of the poor, C323; poor client's, P753; Robin's, R235; Voluminia's, N50; Jonathan Wild's, E319; young lady's, Y22

compliment, the, C326

composition, M472, M474-5

compositor, wedding of, W252

compromise, the, D243

Compter, see Counter

Compton, Henry, bishop of London, elegy on, A222

Compton, Sir Spencer (subsequently earl of Wilmington), see Wilmington

Comus, prologue to, J83

Con, Pro and, P1102

conclave dissected, C331

concordance to Bible, C162

condemned prisoners, hymn for, W317

condolatory poem, C333

condoms, A173, K12, M6

conduct, essay on, F280

confederate forces (under Marlborough), C336, C337

conference (=dialogue), C339, C464

Conference on the meaning of transubstantiation, C338

confession, H361: beast's, S804; false patriot's, H157·2; of M——D—— (Marcus Dowley), N314; Margaret Dickson's, M95; moderate man's, M361; of Peter Hough, C341; Observator's, O5; see also criminals

confessor, the, C342

confinement: hymn to, P442; satire against, H308

conflagration, general (=last judgement), C76, N259

conformity bill, see bill to prevent occasional conformity

congratulation: for arrival of Duke of Argyle, C343; to Duke of Ormonde, C344

congratulatory works (so describing themselves in the title): congratulatory address, S23, S250, S274; congratulatory ballad, E478; congratulatory epistle,

congratulatory works (*cont.*)

A188, A190; congratulatory hymn, P1138; congratulatory letter, C345, H348; line, S648; congratulatory ode, C346, C347, D302, H65; congratulatory poem, A227, A341, A358, A362, B393, B530·6, B585, C292, C348–64, D298, E338, E454, E471, F52, F276, G95, G252, H66, H403, I63, N10, N39, N162, P5, P255, R221, S241–2, S248, S275, S287, S299–322, S488, S649, T49·5, T50, T52, T55, T67, T267, W4, W25, W188, W280, W529; congratulatory verses, A191, B348, C365, J71, M307, M308

congress, the, C366: of asses, C281; of beasts, C367, C369; of excise asses, C368; Hampstead, H30; mournful, M542; *see also* Aix-la-Chapelle; Brunswick; Utrecht

Congreve, William: and the duchess of Marlborough, P261; elegies on, B315·5, M56; epilogues to *The way of the world*, N139, P611; poem 'corrected by', S43; poem inscribed to, B551; prologue and epilogue to *Love for love*, C377

Coningsby, Thomas, earl, dispute with Atterbury, R244

conjuror: bottle, C80, M15; Duke of Marlborough turned, D2

Connaught: attorneys, M559; squire, D254

connoisseur, the, C382

Conolly, William, speaker of Irish house of commons: addressee, O29; elegies on, E88, S753

Conolly, William (unidentified addressee), H417, S400

conquest, happy, H41

conscience: crutch for lame, C532; dialogue with, A106

Conscious lovers, by Steele, prologues and epilogues, N140, N176, P1133

consecration fee, E450

consolation, Y54: Britain's, D398; to Mira, C384

consolatory: epistle, C385; letter, W343; ode, C386; poem, C387, C388, T59; verses, S673

conspiracy, the, C390: report of a new (1716), G17; (=Atterbury plot, 1722/23), A192, C421, E366, V68

constable (Mr Dent), death of, P552; constable's trip, C391

constancy, trial of, P279

Constantine, Alderman, elegy on, E89

Constantinople, poem 'found' at, F120

constitution, the, G311: of Great Britain, H340; restored (1711), W278

consultation, the, C393

consummation, C394

contemplation, H14

contemplations heroical-divine, M39

contending candidates, W122

content, R41

contentment, art of, P697

contest: (theatrical) decided, C397; female, F34; stage, D427

contrast, the, C398: (=answer), C399

contretemps, the, C400

convent, the, C401: provisions for, P1152

conventicles, N142

convention (of Pardo, 1739), C349, C402, H306, L80, N18, P997, S478, S481, S725, T560

conversation, the, P1068: essay on, S757; midnight modern, B48; satire on female, L16; Sunday evening's, T154

converse, advice on, A90

conversion, heathen's, T567

convert, the, C424: and a half, C434; court convert, W224

convocation, A200, S98, S192: poem inscribed to, T534

cook-maid, fifteen plagues of, F133

Cook, Thomas, MP for Derbyshire, *see* Coke

Cook (or Cooke), Thomas, butcher of Gloucester, hanged 11 Aug 1703, E572, H458

Cooke, Edward, *Voyage to the South Sea*, V20

Cooke, Sir Samuel, elegies on, E90, F293

Cooke, Thomas, preface by, W333

Cooke, William, mayor of Norwich (dedicatee), C517

cookery, art of, K55

Coope, Richard (dedicatee), H340

cooper, more work for, F65

Cooper, John, of Fife, D557

Cope, Mrs E. (addressee), S856

Cope, Sir John, defeat of, at Prestonpans, B8, N14

Copernican system, E19

copper, on dome of St. Paul's, C541

copper coin, scarcity of, L116

coquet: dialogue with prude, B20; universal, U16; coquets, C434

cordwainers, Edinburgh, T398

Cordwainers Ward, London, P96

Cork, county of, M565

Cork and Ross, Peter Browne, bishop of (1710–35), *see* Browne

corkscrew, A185

Cornbury, Henry Hyde, viscount (addressee), N346

Cornhill, London, fire in (1748), A121

coronation, the, M141, W221; *see also* individual kings and queens for poems occasioned by their coronation

corruption, of Britons, M490

Corsicans, epistle to, K66

Corydon: and Cochrania, P152; querens, B329; and Thyrsis, T154

costume, *see* dress

Cotes, Miss, of Oxford, W251

Cotton Library: given to the public, S282; manuscript in, B392

Cotton, Charles, imitation of, F153

Cottrell, Sir Clement (dedicatee), N49

Cottrell, Lady (dedicatee), N48

council of hell, C439

counsel to Friends' children, P1176

counsellors, *see* lawyers

countenance, unembarrassed, U2

Counter (=Wood-street compter), F125, S639; *see also* Poultry compter

counterpart, *see* answers

countess's: epistle to her lover, C443; speech to her son, C444

country, E9: farewell hymn to, P1004; *see also* retirement bard, M440; beau, C448; courtship, C449; curate, C489; dialogue, O117; election, H398; gentleman, H121, L119, R161; girl, W475; gauger, D321; hind, E597; hob, C450; house, M476; Jack, M400; lamentation, C451; life, W566; maid, C207; man, *see* countryman; parson, B528, C454, E20, L242; people's recreation, C456; priest, C457; seat, H300; squire, C458; vicar, C459, C460

countryman: character of a true, M68; in Tutchin's *Observator*, B513, C461, H274

countryman's answer, C462; companion, D416; wish, H416

counts, downfall of, D420

courage: female, W269; Roman, R263

Courayer, Peter Francis, H104

court: Aesop at, M385, Y1; British, B477, B527·4, S360; change at, C113; fair, F28; honest man at, M415; of love, C69; mourning, M548, M549; new, N125; news from, P903; overthrow at, G275; panegyric on, G142; royal, in mourning, R307; unmasked, C1; view of, D551; visit to, P898; court's new toast, D499 ballad, A92, C141, G124, M199, N124, N127, O112, P762, S730; beauties, J17; broker, C464; convert, W224; dance, I15; fables, B179; lady's tale, C467; lord, T473; monkies, C468; penitent, W222; spy, C469; tale, L268; visit, C470

court-martial, A160

Court, Mr, musician, B373

Courtenay, hon. Elizabeth, K13

Courtenay, Kellond (addressee), K14

courtezan, C221: happy, H42; fate of courtezans, F73; see also harlot; whores

courtier, the, R174: crafty, C493; disbanded, P460; fickle, F116; Hob turned, H263; miser turned, C548·5; modern, M440, W46·2; old and new, O108

courtship, C471, C548: art of, A319; country, C449; love and, L280; platonic, K8

Cousser, John Sigismond, serenades composed by, C395–6, F206, H130, I4, S207–16, U15

covenanters, K84, M547, T385

Covent Garden: heiress, W257; humours of, B71; in mourning, C473; walk to, W12

Coventry ballad, H127

Coventry, Thomas, earl of, elegy on, S269

covetous citizen, character of, W55

cow: cure for, C545; Diggon Davy's resolution on death of his last, D362; (Mully of Mountown), K63

Cowan, Robert, bankrupt, G15

Cowper, lady Georgina Caroline, marriage of, D20

Cowper, John, kirk-treasurer's man, R46, R56

Cowper, Mary, countess: dedicatee, D341, N11; marriage of, O208

Cowper, Spencer, judge, and Sarah Stout, B146, L273

Cowper, William, 1st earl: character of, H109; elegies on, P210, P606, S327; marriage of, O208; poems addressed to, B528, D302, E309, P528, V36

Cowper, William, 2nd earl, B343

Cox, Mrs, marriage to Mr Gardiner, H242

coxcomb, curb for, A165

crab tree, the, C484

Crabtree, Sir Anthony, V77

cracked pitcher, W448

Craftsman, satires on, A60, B65, C478, C492, D41, D323, E380, E428, H33, J103, N130, P271, P1161; see also D'Anvers, Caleb

'Crafty, Lord', C202

crafty: courtier, C493; farmer, N232

Craggs, James (addressee), P204, S367

Craighall, Lady, P102

Craighead, Robert, elegy on, W468

Crambo's elopement, C495

cranes, battle with pygmies, P1179

Cratander, the perfidious, L282

Craven, William, lord (addressee), S320, W460

'Crawford', joint author, A239

Crawfurd, David, of Drumsuy, epitaph on, E444

Crawley, Miss, Irish poet, G305

creation: poems on the, B242, C28, C425, D341, G182, H212, P54, P707, S184; of women, C500

creator: hymns to, B575, C425, F226, H461, W295; ode to, H382; see also deity; God

credit: fall and rise of, S791; of Great Britain considered, C502; restored, M26

Creech, Thomas, elegy on, F273

creed: apostles', S186; deist's, D189; of Francis Hoffman, H266

Cremona fiddle, B41

Crewe, Nathaniel, baron, bishop of Durham, elegy on, C75

Crichton, William, elegy on, I26

cricket, D22, D233

cries of the oppressed, C506

criminals: Ainslie, William, L32; Aston, Tony, M200; Ballantine, George, E231; Bayn, Donald, H206; Blake, Mr, N288; Campbell, James, of Burnbank, B578, E76, P151, S606, W550; Christie, James, P719; Cooke, Thomas, E572; Cowan, Robert, G15; Curry, John, F197, M200, S629; Damere, Daniel, S603; Dickson, Margaret, M95; Fachney, George, B578, D258, P161, S788, W550; Forister, Elizabeth, P1099; Fuller, William, S130; Gibson, John, M302; Goodere, Sir Samuel, P291; Grant, Mr, woollen draper, W549; Gray, Arthur, V103; Green, Thomas, C31, C33, H323; Hamilton, Patrick, E142; Hamilton, William, E231; Huggett, turnip-man, W444; Johnson, Richard, F289, N204, P59; Kimberly, Daniel, E169; Kincaid, Thomas, P167; Layer, Christopher, C440; L——g——y, Mrs, L140; MacAlaster, Alaster, A12; MacDonald, Donald, M2, M3; Mackie, Musgrave, E231; McLeod, Margaret, A11, A275, E183, L49, L125, M302; Madder, Captain, C31, C340; Matthews, George, I71; Mauge, John, B201; Mooney, Captain, I61; Moore, Robert & Thomas, L58; Muschet, Nicol, E136, P155, S607; Paul, William, P86; Poe, Jo, E216; Porter, John, F289, N204; Price, John, S604; Riddle, Janet, L55; Sawbridge, Thomas, S843; Shepheard, James, S397; Sparrow, Sarah (Jane? Anna?), O274; Stevenson, William, S589; Swanson, Hogan, C332; Tubb, John, B200; Vert, Thomas, L56; Wilson, Andrew, P554; unidentified, B614, C237, L179, T493

Crisis, by Steele, C507, J69

Crisp, Sir Thomas, elegy on, S226

Crispin, kicked into good manners, S446

Crites, dialogue with Eugenius, O275

critical: essay, P699; minute, T437; poem, P476

criticism: beau-, T72; essay on, P806; verbal, M51

critics: modern, M477; Oxford, O268; session of, S225

Croft, William, musician, T448

Cromarty, George Mackenzie, earl of: addressee, I6; elegies on, E91, P106

Cromwell, Oliver, E273, O265, P57: his ghost, O170, S631

Crook, Japhet, R155

crooked sixpence, B392

Crosley, David, editor, O115

cross and crown, C226
Cross, Mrs, actress, P611
Crossly, Aaron, elegy on, E92
crow: dialogue with kite, N58; crow's nest, S127; crows and rooks, R265
Crowle, Mr, of the Temple, duel (1732), M199
Croxall, Rev. Mr (Samuel?), marriage of, S312
Croxall, Samuel, sermon satirized, D353
crucifixion, ode on, E27; *see also* Jesus Christ
Cruikshanks, James, of Monktonhall, elegies on, G294, H3
crumbs of comfort, C530, C531
crutch for lame conscience, C532
cryptography, D66
cuckold: greatest in the kingdom, W72; hasty, T479; northern, W127; in purgatory, C537
cuckolding, receipt for, D208
cuckoldom: cure for, L290; fifteen comforts of, F127; all manner of, F2
cuckolds: Edinburgh, E15; friendly, K11; London, F126; warning to, W239; (miscellaneous), R31, R131, W164
cuckoo: fable of, F6; pseudonym of W. Davidson, D57–8; three cuckoos, S220
cudgel, W67: cudgel-match, F308
Culloden, battle of, B100, C539, F236, G185, H142, H204, M136, N76, N194, N260, P268, P624, S548, S600
Culquhalzie, laird of, E267
Cumberland, William Augustus, duke of, *see* William Augustus
Cunningham, John, professor of law, elegy on, I18
Cupid, C436: in quest of beauty, C540; proclamation of, S372
cupola, of St. Paul's, C541
cur, and lap-dog, C542
curate: country, C489; mourning, P66
curatical battle, C543
curb for a coxcomb, A165
cure: for the cow, C545; for cuckoldom, L290; for the gout, I37; for love, U34; for the presbyterian itch, M12; for a scold, C544; for scolding ladies, A158·5; for shame, L27; sick lady's, C205
Curio (=William Pulteney), epistle to, A136
curious: females, C546; maid, C547, J34 (and replies); wife, M104
Curll, Edmund, H151, M423, N261, P978, W343
Curll, 'Ethert', R56
Curll, Henry, H151
Curry, James, elegy on, D82
Curry, John, forger, F197, M200, S629
curry-comb of truth, B550, C549, D516
curses against the stars, C550
Curtis, George, banker of Dublin, elegies on, E94, F181
customs, commissioners of, C511, C515, L104
'Cut, Mr, tobacco-merchant', F283
'Cut-Arse, Madam', S51
Cuthbert, James, elegy on, E456
Cutts, John, baron: addressee, D27; elegies on, E473, G289, N138
Cutts, John, lord (unidentified), poem on his wife's death (1708), T59
Cuzzoni, Francesca, singer, satire on, C400
Cyclops, Latin poem to, P299

Cydippe, Philander and, C420
Cymbeline, song from, C300
Cymena's epistle to Cratander, L282
Cynegetica, M147, M443
cynic laughing, C555
Cynthio, Y69
Cyprian, St, epistle to Donatus, T548
Cytherea, amour of, M472

D—, Charles (addressee), C6
da Costa, Mendez, F26
Daily Journal, E401
Dalacourt, James, satires on, B104, D514, L166
Dalgleish, John, hangman, of Edinburgh, L125, P161, P162, S789
Dalkeith: palace of, B369; prison house of, K29
Dalkeith, Henrietta, countess (dedicatee), W235
Dalrymple, Sir David, elegies on, M305, S142
Dalrymple, Sir Hew, lord North Berwick (addressee), M421, P310
Dalton, Father Nicholas, elegy on, E95
Daly, Denis, Irish judge, elegy on, E96
Damere, Daniel, queen's waterman, S603
damned, place of, S897; damned's doom, G138
Damocles, D19
Damon: and Amaryllis, D20; and Thyrsis, P114; steals maids of honour's shifts, B128; Damon's case, D21
dancing: art of, J59; characters in, C130; satire against, S41; *see also* Terpsichore
devils, W56; dogs, F29; master, C497, D24
Dandridge, Bartholomew, painter (addressee), M331
danger: over, D25; of writing verse, W438
'Daniel the prophet' (=Defoe), D26
Daniel, Richard, skit on, P60
Danniston, Walter, name used by A. Pitcairne, P341, P354, P364, P366, P369
'D'Anvers, Caleb', editor of *The Craftsman*, D69, F283, H411, N130, P271, P1161
Daphne, story of, D515
Daphnis, B498, F273: and Chloe, G44
'Dapper, Beau', L14
Darius's feast, D47
dark penitent, W233
darling passion, B50
Darlington, Countess of, E413
Darnley, Edward, earl of, L33
Dartington, D53
Dartmouth, William Legge, earl of, K94, T303
'Dash, Mr, a rich vintner', F283
daughter: parson's, W578; alderman's advice to, A158·5; old man's legacy to his daughters, O115
Davenant, General, E543
David: and Bathsheba, R320; and Goliath, O253; life of, E299; and Venus, P355
David's: lamentation, L212, T46; troubles, W27
David, saint, poems in praise of, C126, T4; *see also* St David's day
Davideis, E299
Davids, Miss, breach of promise to, C530
Davidson, tailor and poet, M185
Davis, Mrs, actress, P1134
Dawes, Sir William, archbishop of York, elegy on, A224

Dawley, D69

dawn of honour, D70

Dawson, Thomas (addressee), C151

day of doom, W457

dead: complaints of, P159; express from, N141; raising and selling of, A13

Deal in an uproar, D76

dean: advice to a certain, A73; character of a certain, W533; and country parson, L242; curry comb of truth for, D516; epistle to, E386; dean's answer, D78; dean's provocation, M416·5

Dean, Christian Riddel, lady, elegy on, P105

Deane, Mrs, oculist, P541

Deane, Joseph, alderman of Dublin, L2

death, D80: cogitations upon, C279; fear of, W379; happiness of, W458; night thoughts on, Y24; pomp of, H86; prospect of, P733, S525; serious thoughts on, P63; temple of, S390; terrors of, R22; triumphant, B185; death's vision, R177; see also elegy; four last things; grave

death-bed, G210: displayed, U31

Death, Miss, O179

Deborah, D83: and Barak, B325, D84, P95, T46

decade, doctor's, B110, D358

de Cardonnel, Adam, see Cardonnel

deception, general, G102

deciphering, art of, D66

declaration: by cardinals of Rome, C529; of Old Pretender, F282, M140, N71, P1035, P1036; without doors, D85

declarations, of corporations of Dublin, E593

decoy, lady's, L26

decree of the stars, W375

Deer, 'rabbling of', M214

defeat: of anarchy, T500; grand, G242; patriot's, T271; wisdom's, L59, O230

defection, the, D86

defence: of the Church of England, D88; of Mr Graffan, M389; for the ladies, D87; of the Scottish vision, S167; of women, S372

Defoe, Daniel: preface by, D388; satires on, A233, A252, B511, C18, D26, F6, F186, G42, H8, H9, H352, L62, N57, N331, P456, R154, S449, T253, W282

dehortatory poem, S447

deist's creed, D189; lesson for deists, A26

deity, B359: hymn to, H457; see also creator; God

Delany, Patrick, A73, B75, G205, S887, S913: Christmas-box for, S842; defence of, A246; letter of advice to, L138; libel on, S877; seasonable advice to, S555

Delape, William, preacher, elegy on, E97

Deleau, Madam, F84

Delemar, Richard, counsel at law, elegy on, E98

Delia, Strephon and, P736

delights of the bottle, W57

deluge, the, D211; (last judgement), N275

delusive gold, F223

Demar, Mr, famous rich man, elegy on, S836

Demas chastised, D212

Demophoon, Phyllis to, E436

Denbigh, Isabella, countess of, B26

Denham, Sir John, imitation of, D319

Dennis, John: dedicatee, M479; invitation to Richard Steele, J69

Dent, John, constable, P552

dependant, the, D229

depravity of human nature, T564

Derby: gentlewoman at, B616; silk-mill, B382

Dermot, and Cicely, D233

deserted mistress, epistles from, A178, B541, D305, D322, F33, F181, F199, F271, H157·5, L27, N50, S463, Y20; see also Vane, Anne

design and beauty: epistle on, B519; essay on, L108

Desmarets, Mrs, French prophecy by, V105

desolation, B556

despairing lover, A39

Despauterius, Joannes, V100

Dettingen, battle of, B38, B101, B341, B358, B457, B475, D39, D471, E471, H208, J108, J109, L228, M119, M254·5, N110, N211, N276, P590, S588, V48, Y16

de Veil, Sir Thomas: elegy on, E99; satires on, D244, D252

devil, S619: disappointed, D532; and the doctor, M14, M80; downfall of, Q8; feast for, D40; Hodge and, N296·5; in a fish kettle, J106; in a frying-pan, H140; in a whirlwind, D242; in mourning, B513; knows what, D243; marriage of, B184, P68; mess for, M204; net for, N37; outwitted, W552; reprieved, D244; take the hindmost, N14; tired with matrimony, H135; to do about Dunkirk, D245; to do on the death of Old Nick, D247; to do at Westminster, T149; to pay, R210; turned chimney sweeper, L260; upon Dick, D300; upon dun, S442·2; upon two sticks, D251, W76; visit paid to, W100; war with, K2; weaver turned, W262

devil's: exchange, S747; summer house, T490; tavern, B159, J53·5

Deviliad, D252

devils, dancing, W56

Devon, grand jury, M289

Devonshire, William Cavendish, 1st duke of, elegies on, E101, S265

Devonshire, William Cavendish, 2nd duke of, B477, L313: elegies on, L98, P604

Devonshire, William Cavendish, 3rd duke of (addressee), W204

Diack, Paul, P129

dialect, poem in Cheshire, A52; see also Scotch dialect

dialogue, poems describing themselves as in, A96, A106, A267, B20, B203, B337, B411, B511, B513, B577, B616, C10, C128, C150, C172, C226, C244, C339, C388, C464, D239, D243, D254–87, D340, D396, D514, D549, E13, E289, E322, E601, F81, F125, F247, F270, F283, G42, G162·5, G240, G272, H33, H122, H161·5, H400, I17, J53·5, J116, L19, L38, L62, L283, M14, M121, M200, M249, M285, N58, N128, N129, N181, N326, O54, O100, O101, O115, O117, O275, P20, P64, P154, P756, P886, P932, R134, R212, S2, S8, S140, S168, S178, S225, S419·5, S619, S662, S914, S916, T126, T257, T479·5, T543, T585, W113, W129, W148, W364, W442, W478; see also comical dialogue; discourse; pastoral dialogue; poetical dialogue

diamond cut diamond, D289

Dibben, Thomas: Latin translation by, T371; page to John Robinson, D298

Dick: and Amy, C11; devil upon, D300; Kitty and, K95; and Tom, O117

Dickinson, Richard, of Scarborough spa (dedicatee), W47

'Dicko-ba-nes', F211

Dickson, David (addressee), W521

Dickson, Margaret, M95

'Dicky and Dolly', S831

'Dicky, Jubilee', P1129

dictator, modern whig, M387

'Diego, Don' (=Sir Thomas Fitzgerald), N18

diet of Poland, D97

difference: between keeping and marriage, D305; between verbal and practical virtue, H156

Digby, Edward, distributor of Pope's *Dunciad*, P771

Digges-Latouche, James (addressee), M82

Diggon Davy, D362

dildo, B108, B607, M413

Dildoides, B607

Dillon, Arthur, I55

'Dingle, Miss', E28

'Dingle, Tom' (=Thomas Sheridan), N143

directions: how to gain by losses, D318; to a painter, D319

directors, the, A331

dirge: on the death of Dorinda, E485; satirical, B472

disappointed doctor, B228

disbanded: courtier, P460; officer, T11

discarded fair-one, D322; *see also* deserted mistress

disconsolate shepherd, E485, E609

discontent, C291, D323, D324

discontented virgin, D325

discord, D326

discourse: familiar, G241; visionary, E26

discovery, the, D328, E374: best, T510

disease, R250: diseases of Bath, D331

'Dismal' (=Earl of Nottingham), D235

dispensary, the, G21: transversed, D332

dissenter, the, W63

dissenters: in England, V109; protestant dissenters, M524; dissenters' triumph, D333; miscellaneous satires on, E13, F207, L199, L300, M203, M359, M370, N142, P445, S23, T431

dissenting: clergymen, D538-9; hypocrite, W97; minister, B608·5; piety, D334

dissertator in burlesque, D335

dissolution (of parliament, 1710), B574, D336

distemper, pastoral on, D362

distillers, E132

distracted lady, Y20

distress, A313

distressed: maid, D337; shepherd, D406

ditty, R223: country squire's, C458; sorrowful, S602

diverting dialogue, D340

divine, progress of a, S109

divine: attributes, M188; essay, M194; lessons, A130; love, P1108, S6, S392; majesty, P1030; ode, B540; poem, B268, C1·5, D341, E292, H234, H417, M97, P1144, S181, S184, S186-8, S251, T46; right, D128; right of kings, E475, M538, O269, W237; soliloquy, W566·7; union, W236; vengeance, T266; wisdom, B443

divinity: dispute with law and physic, M559; united with love, L281

divorce, C345, P488

Dixie, Sir Wolstan (dedicatee), H301

Dobbs, Arthur (dedicatee), F266

Dobbs, Richard, L232

doctor: and Bess, D349; and the devil, M14, M80; disappointed, B228; of divinity, T328; German, G132; militant, D354; old woman and, F1; quack-, F134, Q1; strolling, N73; doctor's decade, B110, D358; duel between two doctors, S640; *see also* medical subjects

doctrine, fanatical, F57

Dod, Benjamin, linen-draper, elegy on, E102

Dodington, Ann (lady Brooke), elegy on, G202

Dodington, George Bubb (subsequently baron Melcombe): addressee, F123, S107, S773, Y128; satires on, B39, S168, W478

dog: in the wheel, D391; miller and his, D269; fable of shepherd and, F10; poems concerning, B326, H6, N326; P678, S666; *see also* cur; lap dog

dog-kennel to be let, D392

dogs: dancing, F29; of Egypt, Y5; fable of F7; without doors, C43

Dolben, John, elegies on, E103, S556, S671

doleful: complaint, D393; swains, M304

doll worship, A62

'Dolly' (=Dorothea Gorges), elegy on, S831

Dolly, Dr, L50

dolphin, P357: (=Godolphin), tale of, T12

Domitian, state of Rome under, S725

Don, river, D394

Donaides, K22, M54

Donaldson, Capt. James, marriage of, E447

Donatus, St Cyprian's discourse to, T548

Donegal, Arthur Chichester, earl of, marriage of, S306

Doneraile, Arthur Mohun St. Leger, viscount, W425

Donore ballad, D403

doom: damned's, G138; day of, W457; forger's, F197; universal, H343

door (to eternal life), H272

Dorchester, G43

Dorinda: Frontello and, L323; (=countess of Euston), D404, E485

Doron, and Alexis, E44

Dorset, Charles Sackville, earl of: epitaph on, P931·5; parody of, N125

Dorset, Lionel Cranfield Sackville, duke of, lord lieutenant of Ireland, D529, N169, R157, T9: dedicatee, W288, W302, Y122

Dorset Garden, playhouse in, D236

dotage, D410, D412

Douai, English college at, B199

'Double, Tom', D274

double-shaver, D413

Douglas, Archibald, earl of Forfar, *see* Forfar

Douglas, James, man-midwife, L26, M69, S453

Douglas, John, controversy with William Lauder, P28

dove, the, P1070; doves, V15

dove-cote, D315

Dover, John, quaker, N78

Dowdwel, Sir Daniel, elegy on, E104

Dowley, Marcus, E200, N314

Down Hall, P1072

downfall: of the counts, D420; of Cockburn's meeting house, D419; of the devil, Q8; of Westminster Bridge, D421

Downing Street: in the dumps, C204; speech in, G270

dowry: believer's, E451; Mary queen of Scots', M122

dozen, new, at Westminster, N130

drabs, character of, B610; *see also* harlot; whores

dragon: (of excise) demolished, E599; roaring, W56

Drake, Sir Francis, ghost of, S7

Drake, Sir Francis Henry, marriage of, S315

Drake, James, *Memorial of the Church of England*, E83

Drake, Montague Gerard, marriage of, S314

dramatic: composition, H407; performance, C520; poem, D194; poetaster, D425; sessions, D427

dramatizations of *Song of Solomon*, B280, C520

'Drapier' (=Swift): his attacks on Wood's halfpence, D403, D428, L124, M436, S406; later references, B550, D251, D429, P610, P675; *see also* Swift, Jonathan

Drapier's head, sign of (Mr Taplin's), D251, D428, S381

drawing room, poem on, P611

dream, D29, D430, D433, D437, D438, E611, M472, M474, P258: bachelor's, B4; dreamer's, D439; maiden's, B4, M21; poet's, P695; of Solan goose, D434; sylvan, S943

dress, A90, O244, V58: art of, B418; *see also* band; cloak; fashion; hats; hoop-petticoat

dressing room: lady's, G123, M416·5, R242, S399, S869; London lady's, L238

drink, progress of, B160

drinking: by authority, D440; extravagant, M360; immoderate, S447

match, W376; song, B157

Drive on, coachman, D441

Drogheda, Henry Moore, earl of, elegy on, E105

'Drogheda, Paddy' (William Tisdall), S887

Drummond, Captain, H323

Drummond, David, K17, P356: elegy on, D443

Drummond, George, E476: elegy on, E106

Drummond, James, lord Stobhall, P312

Drummond, May, quaker, F101

Drummond, Thomas, L144

Drummossie moor, battle of (=Culloden), N76

drunkard's looking glass, E293

drunken: club, D44; ramble, T96; wives, T100

drunkenness: advice against, O126; praise of, E483

Drury Lane: humours of, H54, R10

cats, L71; monster, D444; lamentation from play-house, L33

Drury Lane theatre: quarrel between Rich and the actors (1710), P487; opening of (1714), S739; performance for freemasons (1730), O224; dispute with patentees (1733), T126, T127; rejection of Carey's *Honest Yorkshireman* (1735), C52; riot, 23 Jan 1740, S166; opposition to Pretender at (1745), N158; opening of (1747), J85

Dryades, D292

Dryden, John: *Fables*, H371, W435; imitations of, D412, R173, S8, W435; his judgement of Tassoni, O287; *MacFlecknoe* parodied, B413; translation of Virgil's *Georgics*, B195–6

Dublin: address, I48

aldermen, E111, L2, L135, R249, S752

ballad, D462

bankers, E94, E175, E554, H362, S900

Basin, C276, T489

beauties, C89, T489

beaux, J102, M224, O110

castle, N239, P557, P614

citizens, T362

corporations, A342, A344, A345, A347, B602, B603, C68, D266, E593, G104, H355, M11, N26–32, N154, N168, N171, N206, O3, P540, P593, P621, P639, S66, S79, S838, T7, T314, T504, V123

day spent in, D73

dunces, L166; *see also* poets and poetasters *below*

elections, (1713/14), D439, D462, T321; (172–), N69; (1727), B25, C316, E31, E389, E557, L28, V124; (1728), B236, C531, E125, L60; (1729), O262; (1733), A364; (1749), C269, C549, H326, L115·5, R249, S137

executions, E169, E175 (mock), E216, F289, N204, P59

franchises, riding of, M11, N20–1; *see also* corporations *above*

freemen, L115·5, O19; *see also* elections *above*

guilds, *see* corporations *above*

hospital, V52

intelligence, D463

jubilee, N20

ladies, F28, L196, M291, P193, T380

lady, L27, S863

lord mayors, dispute over (1713), D462, E111; Henry Burrowes (1729), H357, L119, P559; Humphry French (1732), C56·7, S752

magistrate, H351

Mall on George's Hill, A64

parliament house, N33

playhouse, *see* theatre *below*

poets and poetasters, A71, B63, B104, D509, G305, I44, L166, S62, S67

poor house, N79

prisons, E162, W464–7, W469–73

protestant nunnery, proposals for, P1141

St Andrew's parish, H440, P534; St Mary's, P534, V106; St Michael's, A95; St P——, P117, St Warborough's, A56

scuffle, G306

statues, P550, P623, U20, V22

Society, A286

Swan tripe club, T496

theatre: opening of new playhouse in Ransford-street (1732), P1128; riot at Theatre Royal (1747), D420

Trinity College: speech of the provost (1716), S633; dedication to (1719), O9; character of the fellows (1724/26), C331; satires on and answers (1725–6), A71, O261, O263, P1; character of a fellow of (1725/30), W522; furniture of a certain gentleman of (1726), L155; Dr Clayton's prizes for poetry (1727), G267, M356, T363; college beau (1728), M281; Patrick Murphy, porter, (1728), C482, D527; elegy on Mother Blackham, college-tart-woman (1730), E59; elegy on Burgersdijk's Logic (1730), E69; college-examination (1731), P173; mock elegy on John Taylor, suffocated in the college (1732), E257; teacher of Hebrew at (1733), T554; apparition at, (1734), D514; library of (1735), N330; satire on (1736), F265; dedication to young gentlemen of (1739), H181; petition to (1740), O13;

Dublin: Trinity College (*cont.*)
riot of members at Theatre Royal (1747), D420; college examinations (1747), V54; picture of Frederick prince of Wales (1749), J93; poem by member of (1749), F145
Dublin, William King, archbishop of (1703–29), *see* King
Dubourg, Matthew, odes set to music by, B589–91, D524, O61–4, P280, S401, S411, V89
duchess, conquered, W486
duchess's epistle to her son, D465
Duck Island, M329
Duck, Stephen, B554, C288, C543, D383, D422, D423, D466, G282, Y14
Dudley, (Elizabeth?) Lady, B26
duel, C230: between two doctors, S640; belly, C282; mock, N74
duelling, folly of, F46
duels: Lord Mohun and James duke of Hamilton (1712), D496, E440, E535, H353, L259, N313; Nicholas Lechmere and Sir John Guise (1720), D502; Nicholas Lechmere and Earl Cadogan (1723), B42, F140; John lord Hervey and William Pulteney (1731), C444, D488, E371; Viscount Micklethwaite and Mr Crowle (1732), M199; Sir Chaloner Ogle and Edward Trelawney (1743), D494; Captain Clarke and Captain Innes (1750), F46
Duick, John, B180
duke upon duke, D502
Dulcinead, D508
Dullardiad, W1
dullness, W298: cherished, D509; island of, M299; *see also* dunces
dumb: bells, of Worcester, W561; farce, W56
dun, devil upon, S442·2
Dun, Sir Patrick, S640
Dunblane, *see* Sheriffmuir
Dunbo, Mrs, J43
Dunbreck, Charles, elegy on, E107
dunces: Dublin, L166; epistle to, S153; female, F91; of Norfolk, B95·5; state, W426; out of state, V28; *see also* scribblers
Dunciad: Pope's, P764 (for works in answer, *see* Pope); new book of, D363; sequel to, S206; Tom o' Bedlam's, H145·5
Duncomb, Sir Charles, elegy on, N137
Duncomb, John (dedicatee), N47
Dundonald, John Cochrane, earl of, elegy on, S349
Dunfermline's address, E454
dunghill, and oak, B203, B499, D513
Dunkellin, Michael Bourke, lord (subsequently earl of Clanticarde), marriage of, S301
Dunkin, William, satires on, B104, D7, I53, L166, S127
Dunkirk: Pretender's expedition from (1708), D245, I51, T484; surrender of (1712), D235, D532, F261, N311, S769, S895; restored (1730), S16; fortified by French (1740), C59; Young Pretender's expedition from (1744), L297
Dunleary, petition from, P193
Dunlop, William, professor of divinity, elegy on, T383
dunoscope, D533
duns, D533
Dunstable, downright, P475
Dunton, John, T435, U4, W343

Dupplin, George Hay, viscount (subsequently 8th earl of Kinnoull), P307
Dupplin, Thomas Hay, viscount (subsequently 9th earl of Kinnoull), prologue spoken by, P1084
Durgen, D554, W66
Durham, executions at, L56, S589
Durham, Edward Chandler, bishop of (1730–50), *see* Chandler; Nathaniel Crewe, bishop of (1674–1721), *see* Crewe
Dutch: B92, D532, D556, F266
bribe, D557; catechism, B588; deputies, D1; embassy, D558; memorial, P131; riddle, W164; skipper, S50; tale, P165
Dutchman, fifteen comforts of, F124; Dutchmen's answer, P435
duties of servants, D559, S787
dutiful son's lamentation, C98
Dutry, Lady (dedicatee), B132
duty: family, M104; of children, G162·5; of a Christian, W443; of a husband, D562, D563; of magistrates, O245; of a wife, J12
duumvirate, D564, H252
dyers, of Dublin, P621
dying: groans of John Dunton, D537; heathen, S749
Dysart, 'battle' of, E532

Eagland, Daniel, B95
eagle: address to, B530·9; fable of, E1; falconer and hawk, E7; and robin, E2; vulture and, V124
Eames, Mr, A263
'Earl Harold' (=Earl of Thanet?), W376
Earl Robert's mice, P1073
Earle, Giles, dialogue with Bubb Dodington, S168, W478
earthquake (1750), A79, A123, C434, M231, P612, S761, V64
East Grinstead, election, G299
East India companies, D544, S243
East Indies, voyage from, M501, V121
Easter Sunday, P289
Easy Club, at Edinburgh, R75, R78
Ebenezer and Ralph (Erskine), V105
Eboracum, M152
Eccles, John, composer, C370, M534, T69, T77, T78, T80
Eccles, Sir John, elegy on, E108
ecclesiastical history, R264·5
Eccleston, John (dedicatee), M502
Echlin, Sir Henry, elegy on, E109
Eckhardt, John Giles, painter (addressee), W31
eclipse (1715), E14, R75: hue and cry after, H356
eclogue: Newgate, N286; Persian eclogues, C298; other eclogues, A291, A352, B189, B207, B208, B550, G1, H44, J66, K74, L333, M145, T474; *see also* college eclogue; pastoral eclogue; piscatory eclogues; sacred eclogue; sea eclogues; town eclogues; tragi-comical eclogue
economy of love, A303
ecstasy, the, A366, H374
Eden Hall, W376
Edinburgh: address to the country, R44
advocates, M422
blue stone on Castle Hill, E62
brewers, *see* brewers

Edinburgh (*cont.*)

castle, blockade of (1745), B287

cuckolds, E15, K102

election (1713), H427; (1744), P613

executions, E142, E183, F299, H206, L32, L49, L55, L125, P554, S607

fires, N245, O201, P1001

fruit maids, K102

fruit wives, L38

guilds, M185, M445, T398

hangmen, John Dalgleish, L125, P162; Harry Ormistoun, S605; Sutherland, S789

High School, archers of, P684

instructions to their MP, E24

Katy, R108

knights of the horn, K102

ladies, E16, J70

lockman, *see* hangmen *above*

low life, E130, E177, K102, L38, L316, P157, T100, W446

magistrates, P165

observator, E16

playhouse, *see* theatres *below*

Porteous riots, *see* Porteous riots

prerogatives, K103

resurrection men, A13, G300, P159

Revolution Club (addressee), H251

Royal Company of Scottish Archers; *see* Royal Company

salutation, R45

taverners, T100

theatres, C181, F169, P283, R100

town council, L145

university, lament of, L6; poem by boy at, M346

West-kirk parish, P1027

whores, W446

see also Auld-Reeky

Edinburgh, Alexander Ross, bishop of (1688–89), *see* Ross

Edinburgh, Thomas Rattray, bishop of (1739–43), *see* Rattray

Edmonds, Joseph, L326

'**Edoarda**' (= Miss Edwards), D305

'**Edrisa**' (= Miss Edwards), elegy on, E17

education: essay on, F280; method of, C99

Edward III, king: and the cobbler, C494, S171; his ghost, C494

Edwards, Miss, D305; elegies on, E17, E110

Edwards, John, actor, elegy on, P290

Edwards, Oswald, anabaptist, N78

Eems, Thomas, *see* Emes

Edwin, Charles, election candidate at Westminster, (1741), I33, W373

effigies: of the legion, E22; of love, C436; to be burnt by the whigs, 17 Nov 1711, K94, Q8, T119

Egmont, John Perceval, earl of (addressee), S484

Egypt: dogs of, Y5; plagues of, P468

elect lady, T124

election of peers, D58

elections: (1702), S784; (1705), H126, U17, U19; (1710), B471, H295, N155–6, T403; (1715), H250; (1722), O127, W122; (1734), H398, M379, P1055; (1741), B470, C325, F239, G232; Ireland (1727),

A269, E31; unidentified, C22, C206, C535, E30, L12, N227; *see also* Bramber; Brentford; Cambridge; Chippenham; Clonmel; Dublin; East Grinstead; Edinburgh; Hereford; Leicestershire freeholder; Leominster; Lichfield; London; Middlesex; Newcastle; Northamptonshire health; Norwich cavalcade; Oxford; Southwark; Staffordshire; Sussex; Westminster; York; Yorkshire

elegiac: complaint, P752; essay, O207, R326; ode, E35; pastoral, E36, R328; pastoral dialogue, G116; poem, B175, B332, C54, C301, D29, E17, E38, E456, F209, G136, H174, I27, O193, T36; song, W220; verse, C32

elegies: love, H22; mournful, E39, O254

elegy (so described in title), A2, A15, A162, A343, A355, B92, B124, B127, B170, B218, B276, B440, B512, B574, B579, B581, C222, C461, C509, D17, D82, D102, D132, D415, D534, E32–288, E456, E461, F82, F144, G137, G137·2, G139, G169, G253, G319, G321–5, G327, H21, H60, H171, H172, H296, I57, L63, L260, L312, M123, M186, M210, M400, M409, M420, M523, M538, M544, N52, N131–8, N148, N287, O53, O177·5, O256, P44, P155–7, P164, P167, P177, P186, P189, P201, P290, P434, R46, R48, R49, R162, S136, S142, S162, S169, S170, S218, S383, S420, S529, S545, S671, S689, S831–4, S836, T511, T542·5, T583, V12, V24, W112, W313, W449, W450; *see also* excise elegy; false elegy; funeral elegy; habbiac elegy; love elegies; panegyrical elegy; pastoral elegy; satirical dirge

other poems occasioned by the death of individuals, A132, A151, A154, A159, A187, A221, A223, A224, A273, A291, B151, B152, B216, B235, B275, B306, B315·5, B320, B322, B324, B354, B367, B368, B372, B442, B468, B469, B472, B502, C17, C75, C88, C98, C132, C161, C167, C188, C266, C283, C294, C330, C333, C379, C388, C416, C473, D36, D44·5, D55, D81, D224, D226, D332, D339, D405, D418, D442, D443, D483, E289, E326, E397, E405, E467, E473, E485, E510, F80, F181, G163, G202, G294, G301, H20·5, H77, H78, H85, H90, H103, H116, H137, H168, H206, H233, H254, H278, H404, H408, I5, I18, I23–6, I28–30, J16, J53·5, K18, L6, L18, L39, L98, L144, L164, L189, L201, L220, L318, L319, L337, M56, M89, M90, M124, M158, M167, M171, M221, M282, M304, M305, M316, M317, M468, M470, M518, M542, M543, M545, M546, M548, M549, M570, M573, N193, N202, N222, N258, N261, O8, O43, O44, O68, O72, O192, O194, O196, O197, O199, O200, O210–12, O227, P66, P102, P109, P111, P116–18, P130, P166, P172, P190, P210, P217, P285, P286, P374, P415, P518, P538, P551, P553, P555, P562, P597–607, P629, P647, P650–7, P665–70, P672, P682, P691, P1028, P1040, Q17, R68, R69, R73, R78, R82, R88, R101, R110, R194, R239, R262, R266, R273, R307, R310·5, R327, R329, S24, S30, S107, S118, S224, S264, S365, S375, S460, S516, S522, S524, S549, S556, S557, S559, S601, S608, S715, S719, S735, S741, S745, T38, T59, T64, T71, T140, T144, T200, T208, T260, T261, T265, T333, T381–4, T393, T415, T434, T477, T506, T527, T561, T570, V61, V62, V65, V66, V69, V70, V72–4, W5, W24, W37, W275, W295,

elegy (cont.)
W308, W343, W354, W355, W407, W468, W516, W521, W560; see also elegiac complaint etc.; epitaph; funeral poem etc.; habbiac; habby

elements, wars of, W201

Elford, Richard, singer, D549

Elias and Enoch, E289

Eliza, B249

Elizabeth I, queen of England, N88, Q8, P270

Elizabeth, queen of Spain, W442

Elizabeth Christina, empress consort of Charles VI of Germany (dedicatee), R253

Ellis, Lieut.-col., H5

Ellis, John, painter (addressee), N265

Ellis, Sir Richard (addressee), W30

Eloisa, and Abelard, B81, C85, D6, P801

eloquence, force of, B431

Elrington, Thomas: prologues and epilogues spoken by, C277, L102, N174, P1120, S413; epistle to, E406

Elton, Sir Abraham, speech of, O184

Ely, William Fleetwood, bishop of (1714–23), see Fleetwood

Ely, John Moore, bishop of (1707–14), see Moore

Elymas (= Elymas Clark), F20

embarrassed knight, J61

embassy from heaven, A334

emblems, E304, M41, T405

emblematical essay, A7

Emes, Thomas, 'the prophet', E443, F260, W555

Emma, E305

emperor, the dead (Charles VII), D75

emperor of the moon (dedicatee), C103

empty purse, E306

enchanted garden, B560

encomium, A14, E309, H38, H70, O90

end to our sorrows, E576

enemies, unequal, M499

England: advice to, A79, H317; bobbed, P754; a great bedlam, W43; in miniature, E311; miseries of, M278; prosperity to, A238; in tears, T263; triumphant, E313; see also Old England

England's: alarum bell, E314; danger and duty, S146; doom, B210, E315; exhortation, E316; glory, B279, E317, E318, P255, R225, W373; happiness, P256; ingratitude, E319; late jury, E320–2; most humble address, E323; passing-bell, E324; reformation, W207; resolution, E325; sorrow, E326; surprise, E327; triumph, E328, E329

English: beauties, E330, W22; bravery, M349, R263; Catiline, P41; courage, E331, E332; excise-man, P154; gentleman, E333; grenadiers, B38; Haddock, E335; hero, C217; Jesuit, E364; monster, C123; muse, E338; padlock, E339, P1076; psalm, B416; rap, S382; sailor, C315; sailors, E340, E341

Englishman, M234, M511, S140: brave, A25; impartial, B568; modern, M365; true, A233; true-born, D153; trusty and true, E584

Englishman's: answer, E342; grace, F191; thought, E343

Englishmen no bastards, E336

Englishwoman, true-born, F86, L8

enigma, D66

Enoch, E289

enquiry: after virtue, M504; grand, G243; modest, M390

entertainment, Irish, S642

enthusiasm, H181, S469

enthusiast, the, W243

envy: epistle on, G229, T254; fame and, G101; goddess, G205

epic: poem, B240, B249, B488, I7, K79, L215, O3, P1016, T437, W412; poesy, M499; satire, B89

epicedium, A132, I25, I28

epicure, innocent, I41

epidemical madness, E345

epigram, C257, D514, D523, N330, P1056, P1082, T60, W578: panegyrical epigram, P42

epilogue, A82, C377, C410, E346–55, F102, F177, F277, J85, L54, L102, M187, M346, N139, N140, N163, N164, N173, N176, O224, P7, P203, P446, P486, P611, P1022, P1120–2, P1124, P1129, P1132, P1133, R287, S415, S838, W32, W310

epinikion, D555, E21, E356, E357, M35, M438, S217

epistles (translations, as of Horace's epistles, are excluded), A15, A101, A136, A168, A178, A188, A190, A193, A194, A196, A256, A279, B50, B83, B135, B315·5, B415, B439, B483, B519, B583, B584, B612, B613, C52, C75, C92, C93, C97, C129, C233, C288, C410, C415, C443, C463, D15, D16, D196, D324, D371, D383–5, D397, D407, D465, D469, D509, D519, D520, D567, E358–436, E465, E466, E488, F33, F72, F95, F101, F106, F123, F162, F200, F204, G45, G88, G125, G130, G147, G148, G229, G276, G283, H38, H42, H43, H157, H175, I44, I70, J40, J42, J43, J55, J107, K1, K66, K68, K88·5, L14, L94·8, L224, L279, L282, L304, L331, M51, M85, M86, M88, M91, M142, M144, M164, M246, M255, M305, M382, M434, M479, M480, M487, M497, M535, N251, N282, N285, N336, O82, O83, O85, O87–9, P10, P128, P204, P206, P364, P802, P908, P917, P923, P1006, P1027, P1054, P1119, P1160, R32, R56, R71, R87, R106, R140, R160, R331, S99, S102, S153, S179, S203, S363–5, S498, S536, S615, S617, S667, S706, S714, S751, S841, S842, T44, T45, T139, T254, T272, T532, T564, T565·5, T591, V27, W31, W289, W291–3, W301, W302·5, W312, W434, W438, W440, W538, Y23, Y71, Y72, Y117; see also burlesque epistle; congratulatory epistle; consolatory epistle; ethic epistle; expostulatory epistle; familiar epistle; friendly epistle; heroic epistle; heroi-comical epistle; love epistles; panegyrical epistle; poetical epistle; satirical epistle; see also letter

epistolary: canto, L258; essay, A90; letter, E437; poem, B163, B605, D217, R117, R251; satire, W244

epitaph, A222, C135, D59, E438–46, I22, N339, P382, P931·5, R186, S149, T573

epithalamium, C508, C510, E447, E448, G3, H47, H242, I2, M111, M351, S25, S183, S650, T66; see also marriage

epitome, of the Bible, H259, M135

epode, M408

Epping forest, B614

equal distribution of happiness, P704

equivalent, the, M344: for Defoe, H8; for fasting, E450

Erichtho, Sextus and, H368

Erskine, Ebenezer, A150, H258, V105

Erskine, Mary, elegy on, E112

Erskine, Ralph, H258, V105

essay (so described in title), B443, B502, C76, C115, C411, D102, D106, D192, D307, D323, E461–76, F163, F185, F280, G138·5, H93, H98, H317, L108, M85, M146, M149, M188, M469, M481, M484, M499, M518, N336, O169, P11, P63, P70, P265, P410, P699, P709, P806, P822, S27, S30, S86, S282, S388, S757, W439, Y2; *see also* divine essay; elegiac essay; emblematical essay, epistolary essay; heroic essay; metaphysical essay; occasional essay, odaic essay; pastoral essay; philosophical essay; pindaric essay; poetical essay; satiric essay

Essex, miller of, M232

Essex, Robert Devereux, earl of (analogue to Marlborough), N88, P270

Essex, William Capell, earl of, instalment as K.G., T370

estate, poetical, P69

Estcourt, Richard, prologues and epilogues spoken by, E347, L246, S737

Este, Mr, singer, C41

Esther, T472: queen of Persia, H144

eternity, E482: theoretic view of, A314; time and, T313

ethic: epistles, B51, P850, T254; poem, M36

ethi-comico-satirical poem, B539

ethnic tales, T405

Eton: college, G254; Jack of (=John Burton), K67; schoolmaster of (=Andrew Snape), S510

'Eubulus' (=Eubule Thelwall), E483

eucharist, the, E484, S251; *see also* Lord's supper; sacrament

Eugene, prince of Savoy:
    1702, E466, H70, H71, H153, L162, P257, P1059
    1705, O168·2
    1706, F278
    1707, B315
    1708, G93, G268, P608
    1709, S133, S137·5
    1712, B295, C256, D235, G101, P1060
    1716, T250
    1717, B164

Eugenio, B122, E485, H161·6

Eugenius, and Crites, O275

eunuchs, *see* Carestini; Farinelli; Nicolini; Senesino

Europe, G214: Aesop in, A113; affairs of, A117·2, B83, G240; commotions in, B89; fate of, W332; in a flurry C498; peace of, S159; state of, K31, S161, V118; tranquillity of, N262; transactions of, A118

European mourners, E487

Euston, Dorothy, countess of, death, D404–5, E485, G96

Euston, George Fitzroy, earl of, G96

Evans, Major-general, N317

Evans, Abel (dedicatee), M14

Evelyn, Lady (dedicatee), H342

evening, ode to, O65

evening thought, E531

every man in his own way, D469

Evesham, vale of, B415

Ewelme, Oxfordshire, maypole at, H256

examinations, college, P173, V54

Examiner, The, O264

example, the great, M557

exception, the, W270

exchange, the devil's, S747

Exchange-alley bubbles, W177; *see also* 'Change alley

excise: bill of 1733, B459, B462, C203, C212, C368, C462, E598–9, E600·5, F283, G225, H121, L239, L240·5, O203, P1117, R135, R231, S204, S482, S777, T404·5; 1734, P126; 1744, W29; of cheese, D557; of glass, G178; *see also* gin act; malt tax

excise: asses, C368; elegy, E599; monster, C212; sermon, E600·5

exciseman: English, P154; Scots, S144; *see also* gaugers

excursion, the, M50

excursory view, E601

executioners, *see* hangmen

executions, *see* Aberdeen; Abingdon; Ayr; Dublin; Durham; Edinburgh; Leith; London; Southwark

Exeter: grand jury (1710), M289; gaol, B438; journey to, G88

Exeter, Brownlow Cecil, earl of (addressee), D47, S250

exhortation: England's, E316; to undertakers, G104; to youth, A340

expedition, the, E605, F201

experienced student, E607

explanation, of a tale, E608

expostulation, E609

expostulatory epistle, R273

express: from the dead, N141; from Parnassus, E610

extempore prayer, N142

extravagant wish, E611

exultation, the, M387

Eyre, Mr, Dublin poetaster, B63, G305

F., M. (=Martin Folkes), letter to, B614

Fabené & Campbell, curers of smoky chimneys, L313

fables (including those describing themselves as 'tales'), A65, A282, B77, B125, B179, B203, B219, B484, B499, B501, B530·1, B530·3, B530·9, C29, C321, C369, C467, C469, C493, D60, D203, D434, D482, D513, E1, E2, E7, E308, F1–20, F60, F243, G135, G137·5, G243, H19, H325, H326, L72, L190, L191, L241, M70, M82, M218, M330, M398, M522, O111, O131, O132, P47, P77, P80, P178, P435, P437, P447, P449, P454, P455, P458, P460, P756, R134, R173, R216, R237, R239, S127, S220, S417, S578, S674, S675, S679, S685–6, S690, S695, S700, S702, S791, S847, T8, T10–13, T18, T19, T24, T26, T27, T29, T30, T33, T316, T374, T534, T535, T540, U16, W384, W400: collections of fables, A109–18, F21, M73, M385, M424, N236, O190, P422, P425–7, P431, P1062, T252, W287, Y1

facetious poem, F22

Fachney, George, Scottish criminal, B578, D258, P161, S788, W550

faction, the, C478, F23: displayed, F24–5, S427; essay on, D323, E462; funeral of, F295; revived, W125; vanquished, H10

faction's secretary (=John Tutchin), T104

Fagge, Sir Robert, F26

fair: advice to the, A90, F235; forsaken, F199; of Great Britain, B407; irresistible, D359; *see also* beauties; ladies

fair (*cont.*)

assembly, R50; court, F28; impostor, P25; libertine, R14; quakers, B217, S173; question, F30; sex, F32, F235, R34, R252; shell, W68; suicide, F33; thinker, F35; warning, F36, W390

fair-one, matchless, D238; characters of the fair-ones of Stamford, P992

fairy: feast, K62; king, F37; tale, H290

Fairy Queen, Spenser's, new cantos of, C522, C527, N117, W357

fairyland, advice from, A71

faith: act of, V95; free thoughts upon, H216; life of, W318; and practice, F39; and reason, C168; triumphs of, T505; true, A26

faithful: few, F40; shepherd, P158

Falconer, Sir James, elegy on, W450

Falkiner, Daniel, banker of Dublin, H362

Falkirk, battle of, A22, E93, F102

fall: of Chloe's piss-pot, P627; (of Florella), T268; of man B572, B613, F42; of virtue, L111

falling out, the, F44

false: brethren, P178; elegy, R162; fame, W301; happiness, F45; honour, F46; patriot, F47–50, H157·2; taste, P908

falsehood, truth and, D482

fame: description of, M498; false, W301; love of, Y169; prologue between fame and envy, G101; rebellious, R142; temple of, B551, P974

fame's mausoleum, F163

familiar: answer, F53; discourse, G241; epistle, A198, B301, C244, F54, M307, S500, S503; epistles, B610, R51

family: complaint of, C321; duty, M104; unfortunate, U3

fan, the, F55, G47

fan painter (Thomas Loggan), A83, K36

fanatical doctrine, F57

fanatics, modern, M370

Fanciad, H214

fancy, force of, D437

Fanny (= John lord Hervey), F162, T474

farce: dumb, W56; is over, F58

farewell: Mr Budgell's, M291; to passive obedience, F59; Alexander Robertson of Struan's, R226; Tom Punsibi's, T412; to the world, W565

last: of William Ainslie, L32; to Dolly, L50; of Christopher Layer, C440; of Mrs M'Leod, L49

hymn, to the country, P1004

Farinelli (= Carlo Broschi) castrato singer, C315, E400, F73, H42, S179

farmer: crafty, N232; and fisherman, B69; and friar, C140; golden, W460

farmer's: daughter, B68; yard, F60

Farquhar, George, epilogue to his *Recruiting officer*, E347

Farquharson, John, elegy on, F292

Farringdon within, charity children of, H433, H437

fart: Miss Vane's, O180; Spanish, S618

farting, praise of, P49

farthingale, N172: revived, F65, L272; *see also* hoop petticoats

fashion, F67, W244; modern fashions, M372; present fashions, T158; *see also* dress

'Fashoner, Mr', N172

fast day, B17

fasting, equivalent for, E450

fat vicar's race, P1042

fatal: love, F68; union of France and Spain, F69

fatality of forced marriage, F71

fate: of courtesans, F73; of an Hibernian muse, F72; of traitors, F74

father, ambitious, W45

father's: advice to children, F75, M572; blessing, A130; instructions to his son, S147

Faulkner, George, Dublin publisher: edition of Swift, D429; letter to, G317; offer of knighthood to, C152

Faustina (Faustina B. Hasse) singer, A230, C42, C400, E376, E379, F175

Faustus, eclogue of Mantuan, B208

favourite, the, S366: female, P270; royal, P445

Fawden, Mary, murdered near Hartlepool, S589

Fazakerly, Nicholas, P1166

F——ce, W——m, P269

F——d, Ashy, L200

Fealding, Handsome, *see* Feilding, Robert

fear: of death, W379; and interest, F81

feasts of the church, S485

felicity: real, D192; rural, M487

Feilding, Robert: bigamous marriage with the Duchess of Cleveland (1706), D464, F83, F84; her death, F82; elegy on him, E113

fellow of a college, letter from, C530

female: advocate, E23; apologist, F85; apostacy, F86; chastity, F88; combatants, C345; contest, K34; courage, W269; dunces, F91; empire, H111; faction, F92; favourite, P270; folly, F94; honour, F95; monster, F97; moralist, F98; muse, D568; nightwalker, L29; Phaeton, P1094; philosophy, T532; piety and virtue, F99; proselyte, F100; rake, D407; reign, C247; sex, fables for, M424; skirmish, B68; speaker, F101; volunteer, F102; worthies, F103

females, curious, C546

Fénelon, François Salignac de la Mothe, allusion to, C81

Fenton, Lavinia, actress, A242, E550, N64

Fergusia (= Scotland), complaint of, M162

Fermanagh, Viscount (dedicatee), L263·5

Fermor, Arabella (dedicatee), P951

Ferns and Leighlin, Josiah Hort, bishop of (1721–27), *see* Hort

Ferris, Paul, lieutenant colonel, H363

Fetherston, Heneage, elegy on, S228

feu de joie, F115

fickle courtier, F116

fiddle, Cremona, B41

fiddler's fling at roguery, F117

field: sports, S569; spy, W69

Field, Katherine, heiress, L20

Fielding, Henry, epistle to, Y23

fifteen comforts: of cuckoldom, F127; of a Dutchman, F124; of a lawyer, F125; of matrimony, F128; of a Scotchman, D107; of a single life, M23; of a wanton wife, F126; of whoring, F131

fifteen plagues: of a coachman, *etc.*, F132; of a cook-maid, *etc.*, F133; of a Frenchman, A9; of a lawyer, *etc.*, F134; of a maidenhead, F135

fifteen pleasures of a virgin, F136

fifth monarchy men, L152

fifth of November, F182

fight: and no fight, F140; between Christians and quakers, A8

Finall, Peter, elegy on, P107

finance, A163, C103, C210, C348, C464, E552, I62, L116, M26, M269, P506, P522, S791, V111, W394, W452; *see also* bank; bankers; South Sea; stock-jobbers; stocks

Finch, Daniel, baron (subsequently earl of Nottingham) (addressee), F231

finches, tale of, T27

fine gentleman, modern, J63

fine lady, modern, D407, M373

'fir-bush' (Forbes?), elegy on, E125

fire, B506: at Blandford, D318; in Cornhill, A121; in Edinburgh, N245, O201, P1001; and faggot, E84, F144, P436; in the Pope's breeches, F284

'Firebrass, Aminadab', L124

fireside, the, B517

fireworks, celebrating peace of Aix-la-Chapelle, B64, C431, F145, G277, M412

first of April, F149, S856

fisher, successful, M495; *see also* angler

Fisher, Thomas, Edinburgh merchant, elegy on, M420

fisherman, farmer and, B69

fishery, F151: advantages of, S558; herring, L211; Irish whale, F266; North-Sea, R81

fishes, O236

fishing, O236; *see also* angling

FitzGerald, —, Irish blood, D420

FitzGerald, Mr Prime Serjeant, elegy on, E114

Fitzgerald, Eleanor, marriage to Viscount Mountjoy, P626

Fitzgerald, Sir Thomas, Spanish envoy, L126, L128, N18

Fitzharding, Viscountess, elegy on, S278

Fitzsimons, Father James, elegy on, D17

Flanders: Marlborough's victories in (1706), B228, T338; *see also* Ramillies; (1709), C187, S133; Duke of Ormond's departure for (1712), E354; war in (1747), E318, F201, P574

Flanders ballad, E579

'Flavia' (=Lady Mary Wortley Montagu), F162

Flavius, opera by Handel, E402

fleet: British, O90, Y81; pacific, P2; stay-at-home, G257; *see also* naval affairs

Fleet prison, A67, B47, B514, D537, F231, P21

Fleet, Sir John, MP for London, R163

Fleetwood, Charles, epistle to, O89

Fleetwood, William, bishop of St Asaph: *Four sermons*, 1712, E84; thanksgiving sermon, 1716, B226

Fleming, Christopher, baron of Slain, elegy on, E240

Fletcher, Lady (dedicatee), O214

Fletcher, Andrew, of Saltoun (addressee), P336

Fleury, André Hercule de, cardinal: addressee, L219; satires on his diplomacy, C497, C498, K96, S669

flies, horse and, H325

flight: for fame, S37; muse's, M565; from Westminster, F168

flogging, I14

flood in Ireland (1 Jan 1726), W240

Flora triumphans, F173

Florinda singing, H412

Florio, epistle to, T591

Florio, Prince, D191

florist's lamentation, P103; *see also* gardener

flowers: loss of, P103; state, C285

flute, silent, J46

Flutter, Sir Fopling, P1133

fly, getting into widow's eye, P659

flying: general (Ormonde), B582; man, R224

F——ne, R., C312

foetus, description of, H183

Fog's journal, versified, M286; Fog's delirium, H33; Fog's triumph, D69

Foley, Paul, P1166

Folkes, Martin, letter to, B614

folly: D408, F176; female, F94; Green-park, G277; and knavery, T579; of industry, W574; love and, S198; of love, A182; triumphant, F177; of vice, W532

Fontenelle, imitation of, B415

Fontenoy, battle of, F178

fool: pulpit, D538; well fitted, F126

fools have fortune, F180

Foord, Joseph, elegy on, M316

football, match at, C327

footguards, speech of Marlborough to, S627

footman: epistle from, D383; poem by, D388; fifteen plagues of, F132, F134

Fop, dog at court, B326

Forbes, election candidate in Dublin (1728), E125, L60

Forbes, Duncan, of Culloden, epistles to, R71, R100

Forbes, Robert, kirk treasurer's man, elegy on, H1

Forbes, William, of Disblair, satires on, A165, A166, N244

force: of fancy, D437; of religion, Y74; of truth, D47

Ford, alderman of Dublin, elegy on, E116

Ford, Joseph, minister of Edinburgh, E115

foreign address, Y81

foreigners, the, T574

Forfar, Archibald Douglas, earl of, elegy on, E117

forger's doom, F197

forgiving husband, W70

Forister, Elizabeth, murderer, P1099

fornication: essay on, R32; spiritual, S655

Forquar, earl of; *see* Forfar

forsaken: fair, F199; lover, G113; *see also* deserted mistress

Forrester, Captain, travelling in the Highlands, P564

Forrester, Miss, playing with her shadow, C265

Forster (or Foster), John, recorder of Dublin, L2, R323

Forth, river, P589

fortunate complaint, P731

Fortunatus, eclogue of Mantuan, B208

fortune: not blind, F206; fools have, F180

fortune's bounty, W72

fortune-book (fortune-telling), N51

Fortune, Robert, elegies on, E118, E119

forty-one: (1641), F207; (1741), M261; in miniature, F209

Foster, Elizabeth, actress, J83

Foster, James, on heresy, D43, F101

Foster, John, recorder of Dublin, *see* Forster

Fountaine, Sir Andrew (dedicatee), A316

Fountainhall, Lady, elegy on, I29

Fountainhall, Sir John Lauder, lord, I29, M357

Four-courts Marshalsea, prison in Dublin, W466

four last things, B316, P1144, S525, T37, T456; *see also* last judgement

Fowke, Martha, poem occasioned by her *Epistles*, T360
Fowns, Sir William, MP for Dublin, O262
fox: ape and, M522; bear and, T316; caught in his own trap, F26; death of, Y19; a friar, H80; and geese, B530·1; lion and, F9, L190; lion, wolf and, R216; and monkey, G137·5; in mourning, F220; unkennelled, F221, P437; catching of foxes, H392
fox, old (= Walpole?), O111–13
fox-hunters, poem inscribed to, C185
fox-hunting, C185, K53, Y19; *see also* hunting
Fox, Henry, ode to, W488
Fox, John, signs verses to an author, P122
Fox, Sir Stephen: dedicatee, S387; elegy on, S348
frailty, human, W27
frame-work knitters, C272, O3
Frampton, Matthew, M.D., ode to, H34
France: glory of, G184; royal family of, E120; union with Spain, 1701, F69
Frances Harris's petition, imitated, D77, D337, R169
franchises, Dublin, M11, N20, N21
Francis, Father, J57
'Francisco, Colonel, or Don' (= Francis Charteris), D396, T584
Francklin, Richard; *see* Franklin
Frankfurt, University of, jubilee, O17
Frankland, Elizabeth, elegy on, V72
Franklin (or Francklin), Richard, bookseller: E368; his acquittal (1729), B65, N130, P1161
Fraser, James, of Aberdeen, K22
Fraser, Simon, baron Lovat, S178: ghost of, L277
Frederick II, king of Prussia, letter to, V116
Frederick, prince of Orange, *see* William IV, prince of Orange
Frederick, prince of Wales:
  1723, dedicatee, B240
  1727, with Le Heup, L94·8
  1728, birthday, S512
  1728/29, arrival in Britain, E503, H403, P581
  1729, dedication to, L67; epistle to, S751
  1732, child by Miss Vane, C164, L279, V8, Y20
  1736, birthday, S106; marriage, E399, F199, F234, M308, O80
  1737, disgrace, H231; dedicatee, S102
  1738, addressee, S756
  1739, birthday, N341, O35; dedicatee, M440
  1741, addressee, N343, O241; birthday, P592
  1742, addressee, S569; reconciliation, H40
  1744, addressee, S86
  1745, dismissal of Lady Hamilton, D322, F271
  1747, dedicatee, P574
  1749, picture of, J93
free thoughts on faith, H216; *see also* freethinking
Freebairn, Robert, P354, P401
freedom, B438: ode to, S582; of will, T254
freeholds, splitter of, B530·95, S659
freeholder, the, F239; freeholder's complaint, P755
freeholders: advice to, on elections, G232, L28, P24; Irish, A269; Kentish, P57
freeman, character of, C121
freeman's: advice, N69; litany, F241
Freeman, Sir George, elegy on, B322
Freeman, R., Irish judge, elegy on, E122
freemason: a poet, H474; poem by, P595

freemasons, L113: prologue and epilogue for, O224; songs, B220, D190; satires on, F61, F244, M355, O69
freethinker's: confession, T533; creed, D189; Iliad, W40
freethinkers, F247
freethinking, F35, H216: vanity of, V16
French: poems in, A1, C131, C383, D278–84, E40, E41, F183, G184, H385, H386, I67, L4, L5, L158, M139, N302·5, O22, O58, O172, P48, P146, S46, T107, T118·5, V79–81, V112, V116, Y21; translations into, A48, A278, C95, L93·5, L219, R228; works claiming to be translated from, but probably original, G240, L258, O44
  the, satyr against, B2; scourge for, W401
  generals, B577, T488; Huguenot, G241; invasion, F251; king, *see* Louis XIV; marshal, F257; officers, T487; pedlar, P140; policy, B89; preliminaries, F258; pride, D543; privateers, C30; prophet (Thomas Emes), F260; sincerity, F261; standards in Westminster Hall, D268; strollers, P143–4; tyrant, F262
French, Henry, alderman of Dublin, A364
French, Humphry, lord mayor of Dublin, C56·7, S752, T332
French, Matthew, fellow of Trinity College Dublin: elegy on, E121; speech of, A251, L156
Frenchman: fifteen plagues of, A9; lamentation of, F264; letter of, F263; Jack Frenchman's lamentation, J1; young Frenchman's lampoon, Y21
Frenchmen, character of, N180
frenzy, British, B478
freshman, university, F265
friar, fox a, H80
friars, battle of, B174
friend: advice to, B291; epistle to, E358, E365, E388 (poems where 'epistle to a friend' is the sub-title are only entered under epistle); letter to, C107, F185, L42, L142, L144, M300, W12; letter from, L120; ode to, S552; in the country, letter to, B76, G158, L122, L141, M504; in England, letter to, F263; at London, letter to, B620, L137; in Wolverhampton, letter to, L187
friendly: advice, F268, S733; cuckolds, K11; epistle, F269
friendship, B440: of Christ, C144; essay on, E474, P50; Horatian canons of, S493; and love, F270; power of, D552
Friends' children, counsel to, P1176; *see also* quakers
frigate, S785
'fringes' in Dublin, U20
frogs and mice, battle of, P73, P1039, W342
frolic, ladies', L13
Frontello, and Dorinda, L323
fruit wives of Edinburgh, L38
fruits of solitude, T176
fuddle-caps, rambling, W150
Fulham, organ at, M566
full moon, F285
Fuller, Joseph, minister at Reading, elegy on, E124
Fuller, William, the impostor, S130
funeral, the, D36: of Councillor Howard, B235; of faction, F295; of the low church, F297

funeral (*cont.*)
apotheosis, F286; discipline, F287; elegy, F289–
94, H171, H172, I56; idyll, O166; oblation, S331;
pindaric ode, H67; poem, C98, F298–304, G105,
G289, H67·5, L231, L305, M541, P158, P439,
P448, S226–39, S265–73, S278–81, S296–8, S323–9,
S334–41, S343–9, S753, T259; satire, F305; sermon,
hymn to, H458; tear, F306, J11, S264, S333; ticket,
F307; *see also* elegies
'fur-bush' (Forbes?), elegy on, E125
Furnesse, Sir Henry, elegy on, S231
furniture, of a woman's mind, S857
Fustiad, the, F308

G., G., the honourable, epistle to, E466
Gadbury, John, astrologer, elegy on, M297
Gaffeny, Miss, B440, H170, S53
Gage, Lady, W42
Gainsborough, Baptist Noel, 3rd earl of, elegy on, S298
Galatea, love letter to, P191
Gale, Oliver, speech of, G7
Gall, Monakey, E549, M281
gallant, unfortunate, N300
gallant: exploits, L64; tale, L20
gallantry, plain truth on, P476
gallery, upper, L74
galloper, the, W74
Galway, Henri de Massue de Ruvigny, earl of: in Spain
(1706), E57; lord justice in Ireland (1716), I8; loss of
(1717), F264
Gamball, Miss B—ll, N77
'Gambol, Harry' (=Bolingbroke), A78, D259, E126, S129
game: at cards, N199, P1048 (*see also* cards); backgammon, B174; bragg, N80; picquet, R318; put, B49
games, D8: rural, S571; *see also* sports
gamester: Norfolk (=Walpole), N319; prosecuted, G8
gamesters: royal, R308; state, S724
gaming, folly of, B174
ganders, cocks and, F5
garden: enchanted, B560; Wanstead, F173; plot, G10
gardener: Boileau's epistle to his, S615; Hanover, H35;
gardener's congratulatory poem, B393
gardenhouse intrigue, W127
gardening: art of, Z2; *see also* flowers
gardens, G11
Gardiner, Mr, marriage to Mrs. Cox, H242
Gardiner, James, colonel, death of, E127, O200, P268
Gardiner, Robert, elegy on, I24
Gardiner, William (addressee), I24
garland: for a bankrupt's brow, G15; Lancashire, L41;
Newgate's, N288; Norfolk, Y19; younger brother's,
Y178
garlands, origin of, M153
Garrard, Sir Samuel, lord mayor of London, D239, L81
garret, gentleman in, C555
Garrick, David: quarrel with Macklin (1742), C236;
amour with Peg Woffington, L33; *Miss in her teens,*
(1747), N208; marriage (1749), M431; prologue
spoken by (1750), J83; presentation copy to, C155
Garter, order of, W358: installation of 1712, B289, C494,
G16, S171; of 1741, K48; congratulatory poems to
individual knights, B143, H66, L96, N277, T370, Y86

garters, Whitehaven, W411
Garth, Sir Samuel: *Dispensary* transversed, D332;
epistles to, E412, W292; opinion, to the beaux,
D356; *Poem to the Earl of Godolphin* answered, E28,
V76; satire on, S657
Gastrell, Francis, bishop of Chester: presentation copy to,
T124; elegies on, T260, W354
gates of hell, G42
gaugers, of Great Britain, D321; *see also* exciseman
Gaulstown house, S861
Gay, John: *Beggar's Opera*, E550, L206, N64, P716, S80
(*see also* Macheath, Captain; Peachum, Polly);
Fables, imitated, B77, H19; *Journey to Exeter*, imitated, W12; *Polly*, subscribers to, F92; *Three hours
after marriage*, D444, W303; dedicatee, B331; imitation of, C471
Gazette, dialogue between English and Paris, P64
G——e, Mr, the usurer, A10
Geddes, Janny, H258
geese, and fox, B530·1
genealogy, the, G99: of Christ, L292
general: (=Marlborough) cashiered, G101; wronged,
S131; (=Ormonde), T426; flying, B582
general assembly: of the brewers, G100; of the Church of
Scotland, *see* Church of Scotland
general: conflagration, C76, N259; deception, G102;
mistake, R55
General remark, periodical, P1118
generous: exhortation, G104; muse, G105
genethliacon, K19, P150, T545
geneva; *see* gin
Geneva ballad, G109
genius, the, W294
Gent, Thomas, ms. translation by, D232
gentleman, the, G120: country, L119, R161; in the country, epistle from, S667; of fortune, A77; in a garret,
C555; in Holland, letter to, L130; in Lincolnshire,
letter from, L187; modern, M358; modern fine, J63;
of the Temple, B613; in town, letter from, I72;
see also young gentleman
gentleman-commoner, the, G122
gentleman's study, G123, S399
gentlemen, young, epistle to, E435
genuine epistle, G125
George I, king of England:
1708, dedicatee, G153
1713, E545; addressee, T386, T589
1714, accession, arrival, and coronation, A168, A316,
B456, C114, C227, C437, C456, C521, D226, E297,
E454, E492, E537, E573, G132, G176, G183, H37,
H67, H68, H123, H243, H376, H389, H391, H449,
M419, M538, N15, O28, O164, P147, P185, P275,
P284·5, P580, P584, P671, P679, P680, S371, S489,
S781, T341, T358, T379, T569, W280, W291,
W387, W392, Y99; Jacobite satires, C275, D558,
H35, L117, N89, O218, T479
1715, A41, B417, C9, C96, C310, C450, E343, H372,
H451, O223, R209, S262; birthday poems, F206,
P225, S582; Jacobite satires, B284, E413, E558,
H250, M519, N36, N124, P98, S579, T377
1716, B408, K10, M532, P673, P1033, S560, T424;
anniversary poems, H76, N40, P1126; birthday
poems, N44, S213; Jacobite satire, D319

George I (*cont.*)

1717, C487, K25, T430, W451; return from Hanover, B454, D31, D304, R241, S544, W9; birthday poems, N49, P577, S211; Jacobite satires on his quarrel with the Prince of Wales, E288, E541, E560, F44, N53, S597

1718, K27; anniversary poems, C355, N42, T92; birthday poems, G95, N45, P150; Jacobite satires, B154, B468, C193, D270, E565, K54

1719, R312; return from Hanover, C363, C486, G266, O39, P618; birthday poems, N46, S207; Jacobite satires, D5, H249, N95, N304

1720, E497, H266, I68, J21, N250, S712; return from Hanover, F138, R271, S362, S367, V63; birthday poems, E494, N43, V79; Jacobite satire, M218

1721, E499, N174; birthday poems, C395, E495, I46

1722, U20; Jacobite satires, O127, R212

1723, K26, O30, W538; birthday poems, C396, E496, N39, W6

1724, O257; return from Hanover, C353, G290; birthday poem, S208

1725, A285, S578; birthday poems, P591, P1123, S209

1726, M149, M500, P533; birthday poem, S210

1727, N96; birthday poems, H130, P649; death of, A223, B175, B324, B442, B537, E128, E510, H171, H172, N202, P116, R239, S107, W560

1749, S632

George II, king of England:

1714, arrival in England, as Duke of Cambridge, A315, C430; birthday poem, as Prince of Wales, H65

1716, E412, S633; birthday poems, P1127, W296

1717, addressee, W7; quarrel with George I, satires on, E288, E541, E560, F44, N53, S597

1718, C499

1719, S352; addressee, P618

1720, reconciliation, J21; birthday poem, S706

1722, O127; birthday poem, P569

1723, birth of Princess Mary, M103

1726, birthday poem, P646

1727, accession and coronation, A257, B144, B179, B324, B537, C45, D537, E510, F119, I48, L170, M144, M332, N149, N266, P5, P128, P578, P595, R221, S12, V80, W253; birthday poems, S214, T363

1728, B557, M324, R15, T587, Y94

1729, L99, P771

1730, C469, M467, Y82; birthday poems, B349, O62

1731, C198, P133, P421, T115; birthday poems, C194, T115

1732, A60, B52, C199, C292, C354; birthday poem, P251; dedicatee, W374

1733, M539, O184, S32

1734, B79, T118; birthday poem, P280

1735, C77, S624; birthday poem, V89

1736, P78

1737, B364, H419

1738, G272; addressee, S118

1739, T560; birthday poem, P79

1740, H311, N271, S653; birthday poem, O63

1741, B155

1742, P524, R254

1743, H354; battle of Dettingen, D39, D471, J108, J109, M119, N211, N276, P590, V48; birthday poem, B589

1744, L297, N276, T133

1745, K47; birthday poems, B224, B590

1746, L218, P664, P760, P1109; birthday poem, O64

1747, birthday poem, B591

1748, birthday poem, O32

1749, P702

1750, H425, N75

undated, F191, M145

George III, king of England (dedicatee, as Prince George), R260

George, prince of Denmark (consort of Queen Anne): recovery from illness, 1702, S515; dedicatee, T55; elegies on, B581, C88, C333, D339, E40, E129, G251, M548, O72

George, saint: and the dragon, H273; ballad in honour of, G303; dialogue with St Andrew, T585; *see also* St George's day

George William, prince (1717–18): birth of, A181, A191, B212, B314, E507, O40; dispute at christening of, E288, E541, E560, F44, N53, S597; death of, S375

Georgia (colony), G128

Georgic (satire against Hanoverians), T571

'Geraldino, Don Thomas' (=Thomas Fitzgerald), L126, L128

Germain, Lady Elizabeth (dedicatee), Y136

German, poem in, W276

German Caesar, P257

'German doctor' (=George I), A102, G132 (*see also* High-German doctor); German knight, A64

Germanicus, conference with malcontent party, H231

Germany: trip to, T485; war in, W245.5

ghastly wound, G133

Ghent: taking of (1709), S133; English convent at, P259

ghost: Altamira's, B340; of Edward Briton, R151; Cato's, M208; Church of England's, M362; of John Cowper, R56; Oliver Cromwell's, O170, S631; of Dorothy, countess of Euston, G96; Drake's, S7; of Sir Fopling Flutter, P1133; grandsire's, G250; of Mr G——e, A10; of William Gregg, A276; Guido's, G310; Guiscard's, A274, G311; Duke of Hamilton's, D497; Grandsire Hampden's, G249; Henry VIII's, K48; Admiral Hosier's, G186; Ignatius's, L162; of James II, O172; of Sir Joseph Jekyll, W503; Lord Lovat's, L277; Donald Macdonald's, M2; of Margaret M'Leod, A275; of Queen Mary, A334; Mazarin's, F262; Lord Mohun's, L259; Alexander Pope's, P761; Captain Porteous's, C32; Raleigh's, S7; reformer's, R151; Bishop Ridley's, B230; Scelus's, S132; of Andrew Snape, A277; Spenser's, D459; Waller's, W22; Sir Francis Walsingham's, N160; Dr Woodward's, D357; other ghosts, A363, D514, E189, G250, N286, P198, T1; ghost and the miller, G134; *see also* apparition

giants: battle of, B87; contest with Jupiter, H130; wars with gods, M76

Gibbie: Marjorie and, W264; and Wattie, B276

Gibbons, Thomas, epistle to, E418

giber (=jiber), T318

Gibeonites discovered, A169

Gibraltar, B420, E314: battle at (1705), S472; siege of, M146

Gibson, Edmund, bishop of London (1724), C358: Heydegger's letter to, H169; contention for see of

Gibson, Edmund (*cont.*)
  Canterbury (1731), F146, M347; opposition to Thomas Rundle's appointment to Gloucester (1734), D352, P81; alliance with Walpole (1734), K97; pastoral letter (1739), D352·5; contention for see of Canterbury (1747), R7
Gibson, John, accomplice of Mrs M'Leod, M302
Gibson, Lucky, E130, L316
Gibson, William, controversy with Elias Bockett, B300, B302, B303, B307, L153
Gideon, H217
Gideonite, A327
Giffard, Andrew, elegy on, E131
Gillespie, John, elegy on, L39
Gillmertoun caves, G169
Gilmour, Sir Charles, P613
gin: presentment against (1729), B304; epistle on behalf of (1730), B301; act permitting (1733), B554; 'death' of (1736), B556, E132, M521, N225; Sandys's gin act (1743), W480, W503
'Gin, Mother', M521
'Gineva, Madam', mock elegy on, E132
Girard, Jean Baptiste, P38, S655, S720
girdle of chastity, E339
Girolamo and Sylvestra, U5
Gissippus, Titus and, D552
Gladsmuir, battle of, *see* Prestonpans
Glasgow: Cockburn's meeting-house, D419; university, poems by students at, B368, V66
Glasgow malt-man, P154
glass, excise of, G178
Glenshiel, battle of, H467
glimpse of hell, G179
Gloriosa, man of war, M7
glorious: campaign, G180; warrior, G181; year, G183
glory: progress of, P1109; of France, G184; of Spain, M7; Vernon's, T525, V31, V33
Glotta (= the Clyde), A281
Glottiades, R271
Gloucester: butcher of, E572; cobbler of, C264; *see also* Rundle, Thomas, for his cancelled bishopric
Gloucester, duke of (= Richard III?), and Jane Shore, J55
Gloucester, William, duke of, elegies on, D332, P597
Glover, Richard, preface by, G283
G—mb—ll, Miss B—ll, N77
God, L205: the creator, D30; eternity of, S495; goodness of, S392; hymns to, B446, H452; judgments of, G114, G204, P1001; perfections of, C145; poems to, P1030, P1178; whole armour of, W324; *see also* creator; deity
Godfrey, Edward, elegy on, S297
godly: lessons, H405; Sarah, G206
Godolphin, Lady Henrietta (subsequently duchess of Marlborough), *see* Marlborough
Godolphin, Lady Henrietta (subsequently duchess of Newcastle), marriage of, E504
Godolphin, Sidney, earl of: character of, S360; death of, P363; dedicatee, R301; fall of (1710), D336, E28, G36, P437, P447, P458, S935, T8, T12, V76, W394; praise of, M24; satires against, C393, D564, V111
Godolphin, William (subsequently marquis of Blandford) (addressee), W332

gods: chat of, P129; in debate; G207; revels of, W163; wars with giants, M76
Godschall, Sir Robert: election in Bishopsgate ward (1739), S473; defeated as candidate for lord mayor (1740), C204, C211
Godwin, Edward, G208
Gogmagog's confession, F180
gold, delusive, F223
golden: age, G211; apple, D2; farmer, W460
Golden Eagle, meeting place, L314
goldfinch, linnet and, M82
goldsmith, and clergyman, in the pillory, C237
golf, M137: described, A281
Goliath, David and, O253
Gooch, Thomas, C7
good: advice, G217–9; manners, D569; nature, G226, O82; old cause, O2; shepherd, B486; stewards, H337; Good Friday ramble, W75
Goodere, Sir Samuel, P291
Goodman's Fields theatre, L235: epithalamium performed at, H47
Goodwin, Peter, elegy on, G137
Goodwood, Italian paintings at, N264
goose: good, don't bite, G225; old woman and, O132; pie, G227
'Goose, Philip' (satirizing Stephen Duck), D466
Gordan, Mary, elegy on, E133
Gordon, Alexander, 2nd duke of, M107
Gordon, Elizabeth, duchess of, P362
Gordon, John, incumbent of Deer, M214
Gordon, Thomas, author, N1
Gordon, Thomas, captain in Scots navy, C30
Gore, Lady (dedicatee), C134
Gorges, Dorothea, countess of Meath, elegies on, S666, S831
Gorges, Richard, elegies on, S666, S831
gospel, propagation of, S288
gossip, state, P713
gossips' wager, H401
Gostling, William, S451
Gostwick, Ann (dedicatee), W227
Gotham, wise men of, B507, M526
Gothenburg frolic, D246
Gothic hero, B530·2
Goupy, Joseph, as copyist of Guido Reni, G310
gout: first fit of, F112; remedies for, B538, I37
government: happy, H340; order in, O241; original of, O245; of the human body, G232
governor, the, S712
Gracchus, character of, G233
grace, G234: means of, W319; wonders of, D560
Graffan, Hugh, of Trinity College Dublin: satires on, G312, G313, G316, G318, G319, P32; defence of, M389
Grafton, Augustus Henry Fitzroy, 3rd duke of: addressee, E399; dedicatee, W531
Grafton, Charles Fitzroy, 2nd duke of, lord lieutenant of Ireland (1721–24), I60, N174, O27, P203, S498
Grafton, Henrietta, duchess of, N174, P203: addressee, D209; elegy on, B320
Graham, William, dean of Wells, elegy on, P189
grammar, B95, B592, B597, E69, W458
Granby, John Manners, marquis of (subsequently 2nd Duke of Rutland) (addressee), V38

grand: defeat, G242; Khaibar, O69; mistake, G245; question, S908; rebellion, W80; removal, G247; sale at Westminster, G248; Schemifl (=Walpole), P1117
grand-jury, Dublin, E571, E594, N165
'Grandevus', barrister at law, M227
grandsire's ghost, G250
Grant, Mr, woollen-draper and homosexual, W549
Grant, Sir Francis, elegy on, P166
Grant, Roger, oculist (addressee), O238
Grantham, society of sportsmen at (addressees), H6
Granville, George, baron Lansdowne, A54, R291, T350: addressee, P987, Y72
Granville, John Carteret, earl, see Carteret
Granville, Sophia, countess, elegy on, R266
gratitude, M191
gratulatory poem, see congratulatory poem
grave, the, B271: groans from, G300, P159
grave makers in Edinburgh, A13
Gray, —, shoemaker of Montrose, elegy on, G253
Gray, Arthur, footman, V103
Gray, Mary, and Bessy Bell, R36
Gray, Dr Robert, P364, P402
Gray's Inn, poems by members of, H388, S652
Great Britain, D302, G215: advice to, A80; in danger, G255; constitution of, H340; credit and interest of, C502; fair of, B407; gaugers of, D321; inhabitants of, O70; ladies of, A92, I32, W269; patriots of, B530·6; people of, G17; poets of, M332
Great Britain's: glory, G257; happiness, G261; hope, G262; joy, G263; joyful triumph, G264; triumph, N203; union, G265; welcome, G266
great man (=Walpole): address to, P1023; fatigues of, F76; soliloquy of, S550; great man's answer, M249; true great man (=Charles, lord Talbot), T527
great men newly made, ode to, W484
great: noise about nothing, G273; overthrow at court, G275
greatness, true, F123
Grecian knabbs, Ajax's speech to, F184
Greece, T191
Greek: poems in, D390, E27, H408; pretended to be translated from, A178, F120
Greek: hymn, E27; measures, I49; play, S415
green-cloth, the, G276
Green Park folly, G277
Green, John, marriage of, S316
Green, Captain Thomas, executed as pirate, C31, C33, C340, E134, H323, M192, S165, T483
Greene, Maurice, poems set to music by, P95, P907
Greenwich hunting-match, N59
Greenwich Park, H332
greeting to youth, A340
Gregg, William, ghost of, A276
Gresham, Sir Thomas, statue of, C464
Gresham College, T94
Grey, Forde, baron (subsequently earl of Tankerville), L284
grey-headed gentlemen, company of, C353
Griffin, Edward, lord, elegy on, N135
Griffith, Thomas, Irish actor, prologues and epilogues spoken by, A285, P203, P1132, S839
Grimaldi, Nicolino, castrato singer, S461
'Grimaria', P700

Grinstead ballad, G299
Grizel, and Thomas, C244
Grizelda, and Gualtherus, O95
groans: from the grave, G300, P159; of the people, G301; prison, P1099; Smithfield, S530
Grobianus, B564
groom, amorous, H401
groom-porter's house in the castle of Dublin, P614
grotto, the, G282: in Richmond garden, N276; at Twickenham, D390
grove, the, F275, P258: in tears, D404; the grove's complaint, G302·5
Grove (Lord Doneraile's house), W425
Grove, Joseph (dedicatee), B188
grounds, the, G302
Grub-street, R56: address from, M356; cavalcade, G305; debate, G316; poetical senate, P1064; politicians of, P711; society, B299; tribunal, D516
grumblers, Banbury, B62
Grumbletonians, the, C43
grumbling: hive, M70; traders, H121
grunters' request, G307
grunting ale-wife, G308
Gualtherus and Griselda, O95
guard, call to the, C3
guardian, the (Duke of Cumberland), F236
Guelphs, history of, H257
guide: alderman's, S752; for malt-worms, V5; from cradle to grave, G309
Guido (=Guido Reni), G310
Guildford, jury at, L140
Guildhall, lottery at, L274
guinea, last, L51; fall of guineas (devaluation, 1717), E552
Guinea, naval action on the coast of, S342
Guiscard, Antoine de: attack on Harley (1711), A9, F255, P1089, S64, S674, T391, T394, T466; elegy on, E135; ghost of, A274, G311
Guise, Sir John, quarrel with Nicholas Lechmere, D502
Gulliver's travels, poems occasioned by, B290, S356, T586
'Gulliver, Martin', satires on, S45, W1
'Gundi, Sir Solomon', T247
Gunne, Matthew, elegy on, T511
guns on Tower-Wharf, dialogue of, D268
Guy, Alice, G113
Gymnasiad, W412

habbiac, H2
habbiac elegy, H1
habby, H3
Hackabout, Moll, H54
hackney scribblers, R33
Haddington, Thomas Hamilton, earl of (addressee), A279
Haddock, Nicholas, admiral, B338, E335
Hague, the: peace negotiations at (1709), R318; Earl of Cadogan's entry (1718), S507
Hair, James, druggist in Edinburgh, E112
hairy monster (sens. obsc.), S51, W164
Hales, Ann, nun, epitaph on, E446
Half Moon tavern, H76

half-pay officer, epistles from, E365, E366

halfpence, Wood's, *see* Wood, William

Halifax, Charles Montagu, baron, subsequently earl of: addressee, A39, A168, E420, P206, S157, S158, T569; honours conferred in 1714, R297; elegies, P217, S325, S365

Halifax, George Montagu, 1st earl of (addressee), S578

Halifax, George Montagu, 2nd earl of, birthday poem (as Lord Sunbury), J88

Hall, Justice, jacobite, executed 1716, O174

Hall, Margaret, elegy on, E136

Hallam, Thomas, killed by Charles Macklin, I40

Halsey, Anne, marriage to Lord Cobham, S302

halter for rebels, H7

'Haman' (=Walpole), fall of, O107

'Hamilla' (=Lady Archibald Hamilton), D322

'Hamillio' (=Lord Anne Hamilton), D305

Hamilton, tailor in, P1008

Hamilton, Lady (wife of Sir Francis) (addressee), M470

Hamilton, Alexander, of Stirling, elegy on, E456

Hamilton, Anne, duchess of (suo jure, and wife of the 3rd duke), elegy on, E137

Hamilton, Anne Douglas (formerly Cochran), duchess of: marriage (1723), P152, R66; elegies on, G301, R68

Hamilton, Anne Douglas (formerly Spencer), duchess of, marriage (1737), B342

Hamilton, Lord Anne, marriage of, D305

Hamilton, Lord Archibald, governor of Jamaica, P715

Hamilton, Lady Archibald, D322, F271

Hamilton, Lord Basil, elegies on, E138–9, M545, O227, P118

Hamilton, Sir Francis, elegy on, M470

Hamilton, James, lord Pencaitland, elegy on, E210

Hamilton, James Douglas, 4th duke of, P33, P681, U1: addressee, A21, L307; fatal duel with Lord Mohun, D496, E535, H353, L259, N313; elegies on, E440, G163, I27, P374; ghost of, D497

Hamilton, James Douglas, 5th duke of: marriage (1723), P152, R66; captain of Royal Company of Archers, P48, R74; marriage (1737), B342; elegy on, E140

Hamilton, Jane (Lady Archibald), D322, F271

Hamilton, John, baron Belhaven, *see* Belhaven

Hamilton, John, minister of Edinburgh, elegy on, E141

Hamilton, P., Scots lawyer, M357

Hamilton, Patrick, of Green, elegy on, E142

Hamilton, Sir Robert, elegy on, B170

Hamilton, William, of Gilbertfield, verse epistles, R51

Hamilton, William, murderer, E231

Hamilton's Bawn, A237, S908

hammer-men, in Edinburgh, M185

Hammond, Anthony: character of Lord Orford, S30; epistle to, R106

Hammond, Francis (dedicatee), H89

Hampshire: description of, H275, L68, R195; gentry of (dedicatees), S634

Hampstead: congress, H30; epistle from, S363; young gentleman of, N315

Hampstead Wells, H31–2

Hampden, John, ghost of, G249

Hampton Court, Raphael's cartoons at, B252

Ha——n, Mr P., satire on, M357

Handel: advice to, A82; epistle to, E402; odes to, O67, P1017; oratorio of, P720; satire on, C400

hangmen: *see* Dalgleish, John; Ketch, Jack; Murray, Richard; Ormiston, Harry; Price, John; Sutherland

Hanmer, Elizabeth, lady, elopement with Thomas Hervey, W456

Hanmer, Sir Thomas, W456; edition of Shakespeare, C299

Hannes, Dr, ode to, N275

Hannes, Sir Edward, T352

Hanover: gardener, H35; heroes, M254·5; succession, C489, S253

Hanover Square: statue of George I, D270; consecration of St George's, E450

Hanoverian: leeches, H36; tory, H37

Hanoverians, satires on, H257, M254·5, W22

happiness, W205: England's, P256; epistles on, G229, T254; essays on, N336, P704; false, F45; Great Britain's, G261; human, C551, J18; Ireland's, I60; man's chief, P199; of death, W458; of retirement, H38

happy, way to be, P658

happy: bride, H39; coalition, H40; conquest, H41; courtezan, H42; deliverance, F231; government, H340; island, D191; isle, G215; life, H43; marriage, H44; North Briton, B342; nuptials, H47; pair, H30, S193; reign, M145; rival, N253

Harcourt, Simon, viscount: attack on, N217; lord chancellor (1713), C513

Hardecanute, W213

Harding, John, Dublin printer, elegy on, E143

Harding, Sarah, Dublin printer, imprisoned, L59, O230

Hardinge, Nicholas, law reader, T356

Hardwicke, Philip Yorke, baron (subsequently earl) (dedicatee), C534, J62, S653, V110

Hardyknute, W213

hare hunting, A87, S768: at Houghton, H331

Hare, Francis, bishop of Chichester (addressee), B540

Harlequin, C320: Horace, M251; Doctor Faustus, M197

harlequinade, B478

Harley, Edward, 2nd earl of Oxford, *see* Oxford

Harley, Lady Elizabeth (subsequently marchioness of Carmarthen), *see* Carmarthen

Harley, Lady Henrietta Cavendish Holles (subsequently countess of Oxford): recovery from sickness (1708), S287; verses spoken to, P1096; dedicatee, B152

Harley, Lady Margaret (subsequently duchess of Portland), *see* Portland

Harley, Robert (subsequently earl of Oxford):
　1701, speaker of the commons, dedicatee, H277
　1702, dedicatee, P451
　1705, dedicatee, P226
　1706, C454
　1708, intrigues with Abigail Masham, A3, F251, N90, N217; resignation, W282; dedicatee, W305
　1709, B125, D434
　1710, M268
　1711, attacked by Guiscard, A9, P1089, S64, S674, T391, T394, T466; created earl of Oxford, C66, J99, M437; praise of, O267, Q9, T400, T446, W385; satires on, A274, C158, E576, M26, N332, P41; addressee, C64, M410, O175, P1078, P1089, T391, T394, T466
　1712, praise of, particularly his peace moves, A335, B295, D235, F9, P508, P754, T68; attack on, H298; addressee, C514, M273, N311, S369, V20

Harley, Robert (*cont.*)
1713, praise of, B336, Y5; attacks on, P42, R175, T33; addressee, C509, (occasioned by the peace) C62, H184, H244, S520, T502
1714, satires on fall of, C113, C522, D259, J56, L34, L61, M159, N83·5, N186, O264, P506, T358, W311; defence of, I45; dedicatee, H213, T358
1715, satires on, A276, H299, R238, S586, W539; addressee, T368
1727, praise of, T392
harlot: progress of, B426, H54, P1105; repenting, W98; wanton, C160; *see also* courtezan; drabs; whores
Harmonia sacra, P720
harmony: hymn to, C370, J100; power of, C427; temple of, P1016
harp, Irish, S738
Harper, Mr, singer, S581
harpers, blind, H108, I47
Harrington, William Stanhope, earl of: addressee, B344, B345, M255; lord lieutenant of Ireland (1749), C214, F153
Harris, Benjamin, publisher of the *London Post*, P434
Harris, Frances, petition of, S801: imitations of, D77, D337, R169
Harrison, Mr, banker of Dublin, elegy on, E144
Harrison, Sir Edmund, elegy on, S345
'Harry', S717: (=Bolingbroke), M159
Harry the eighth, K48
'Harry the IXth' (=Henry Pelham), K49
Hart, Josiah, writer on quadrille, N58
Hart, Philip, composer, H380
Hartford, Frances Seymour, countess of, *see* Hertford
Hartup, Sir John (dedicatee), N49
Harvey, Miss, a day old, Y108
Harvey, John, baron, *see* Hervey
Harvy, Mrs (dedicatee), S525
Hasse, Faustina B., singer, A230, C42, C400, E376, E379, F175
Hastings, Lady Elizabeth, elegies on, P602, V74
Hastings, G., page to John Robinson, D298
hasty: cuckold, T479; wedding, H105
hat: broad brimmed, D87; old (*sens. obsc.*), B610
hats, ladies', F32, O206
hate, vulgar, P705
Have at you all, M507
Haversham, John Thompson, baron: impeached (1701), S291; attack on, D391
hawk, dialogue with robin, P756
Hawke, Sir Edward, ode to, N268
hawkers, in mourning, M186; hawkers' new year's gift, H110
Hayes, William, professor of music, ode set by, C295
Haymarket, Queen's (subsequently King's) Theatre: design of, N173; first opening of (1705), G39; opening (1706), F64; ridotto at, B19; Heidegger's company at (1727), C400
health, B110, R57: art of preserving, A296; essay of, E398; invocation of, B10
health (= toast), H123: high church, H192; to honesty, H124; loyal, B279, N155, T99; loyal churchman's, W391; loyalist's, G263; new, C101, C550; Northamptonshire, N320; to the Northamptonshire sneakers, H125; royal, R310; Suffolk, S783; tory, N235; valiant soldiers and sailors', V7; to the tackers, H126

Hearne, Thomas, letter to Sir Hans Sloane, E437
Heathcote, Sir Gilbert: election as MP (1702), R163; deputation to queen (1710), M160; lord mayor of London (1710), D239; address of, satirized (1727), B567
Heathcote, William, marriage of, S317
heathen, the dying, S749; the heathen's conversion, T567
heaven, T459: embassy from, A334; glory and happiness of, S456; orbs of, H267; *see also* four last things
heaven-drivers, the, H131
Hebrew: campaign, H132; poetry, H212; *see also* Jews
Hecate, Orpheus and, O251
Hector, P371
Hedges, Sir Charles, elegy on, S347
Heidegger, John James: masquerades and ridottos of, F122, H169, M131, R207, R208; epistle to, E400; satire on his opera company, C400; tale attributed to, after his death in 1749, A329
Helen, of Troy, rape of, R118
Heliocrene, M195
hell, T460; council of, C439; dream of, F262; upon earth, H134, H135; in epitome, H133; gates of, G42; glimpse of, G179; journey to, W100; news from, C103; parliament of, P68; in an uproar, B586; *see also* four last things
Hell-fire Club, H136
Hellier, John, wine merchant, B487, B498·5, W149
help, to patience, H137
Helsham, Richard, S408
helter skelter, H139, H140, W76
hemp, H141
Henley, rural poet from, C291
Henley, John: ms. note by, C104; satires on, D42, E367, F61, H474
Henriade, L215
Henry: and Blanche, H146; and Minerva, B424·5
Henry IV, answered by Robert III of Scotland, F191
Henry VIII: and Ann Boleyn, W434; ghost of, at the garter installation, K48
Heosphoros, H147·5
Hepburn, Margaret, wedding of, W265
Hepburn, Robert, P400
Heptarchus, M162
Heraldiad, G316
Hercules, judgment of, L79, L293, M313, S394
Hereford, election of 1741, A240, I54, P1007
heresy, D43, F101
heretics, God's judgment on, G204
Heriot (George?), poem written under his name, P353
Heriot's walks, R26
hermaphrodite, poem on advertised, K72
hermit, M44, P72
hermitage, M510, R226; Queen Caroline's at Richmond, B409, L325, M326, S778
'Hermodactyl' (=Bolingbroke), D259
Herne, Clement, elegy on, M409
hero: accomplished, A6; baffled, B8; Britain's, J16; British, B479, M84; famed, F52; Gothic, B530·2; great, and little, G268; royal, R310·5; tory, T426; in blue, H152·5; in miniature, H153; revived, F152
Hero, and Leander, B44, C70, E490, S754
heroes, the, W481: British, G303; Hanover, M254·5

heroic: epistle, B326, D305, D322, L275, M509
  essay, H154
  poem (frequently mock-heroic), A14, A356, A357, B8,
    B160, B192, B266, B530·7, C12, C89, C114,
    C221, C408, C475, C476, D22, D218, D252, E145,
    F173, G120, H74, H214, L315, M118, O248, O249,
    P764, P1156, R21, R239, S7, S35, S137·5, S243,
    S245, S253, S290, S768, T4, T35, T312, V118, Y5
  satire, M166
  tale, D244
  verse, C70, C78, C136, D552, H13·2, S154
heroi-comic oration, T21
heroi-comical: epistle, H155; poem, B6, B82, B90, B426,
    C189, C548, F55, H105, H107, H112, H304, J23,
    L200, M137, M443, P941, P1139, P1171, R34, W406;
    see also heroic poem
heroi-comic-historic poem, J19
heroi-satirical mythological poem, Q7
herring fishery, L211
Hertford, Frances Seymour, countess of: addressee, D16;
    dedicatee, S4·5, T227
Hervey, John, baron: duel with Pulteney (1731), A234,
    C444, D488, E371; satires on (1734), E359, F162,
    T473, T474; dedicatee, S460
Hervey, Miss Lepel, marriage of, L222
Hervey, Thomas, elopement with Mrs Hanmer, W456
Hester, P136; see also Esther
he-strumpets, the, D536
Hibernia: in mourning, H171, H172; out of mourning,
    A358; resurgens, H173; Hibernia's lamentation, H174
Hibernian: muse, F72; politicians, H175, H177, H179
Hick's Hall, trip to, C391
Hickford's dancing-room, P1084
hieroglyphic, high-church, H193
Hiffernan, Paul, satire on, M114
Higden, John, of Hampstead, N62
Higgins, Francis: trial for seditious preaching (1707),
    H191; second trial (1712), N145, S580; elegy on,
    E146
high: mass, H201; sheriff's feast, K30; treason, P153;
    wind, M97
high-boys (=high church), H188
high church, H189, H194, H199, L300: advice to, A91;
    and low church, C450, C490, N4, S2, T29, W76
high-church: bully, H191; champion, E295; health, H192;
    hieroglyphic, H193; hornets, B530·3; lovers, H195;
    loyalty, A238; miracles, H196; passive obedience,
    E147; spectacles, H198
high-flyer, W397
high-flying: members, F253; party, I3; squadron, H189
'High German', translation from, M254·5
High-German: doctor, H200; (=Harley), L61; ('Mez-
    ereon'), H293; (=John Thomson), T247; speaking-
    dog, S621
highland (of Scotland): fair, C143; invasion, H202;
    laddie, R58; man, H204–6; reformation, H207
Highland-man, John, J70
highlands (of Scotland), F22, P564, W297: farewell to,
    B448
'Hilaretta, Lady' (=Lady Abergavenny), elegy on, C10
Hill, Aaron, beech nut project, P506
Hill, Abigail (subsequently Lady Masham), see Masham
Hill, Janet, elegy on, E148

Hill, John, congratulatory poem by, D192; his British
    magazine, M158
Hill, Sir Scipio, epistle to E413
Hilman, Thomas, marriage of, W453
Hilpa, Shalum and, P1043
Hinde, Mr (dedicatee), N41
hints to a schoolmaster, D470
Hippocrates, discourse with, E26
Hist, H251
historic poem, H153
historical: ballad, H252, S202; poem, A342, A359, A360,
    D289, H144, H254
historico-satirical poem, H328
history: of the bob tails, H255; of bubbies, J95; of the
    Guelphs, H257; of the honest whigs, W64; of the
    mitre and purse, N57; of the New Testament,
    H259, W325; of an old shoe, S177; of the Old Testa-
    ment, H259, W328; of the secret expedition, H260;
    of 29 years rebellion, H261; true, D199; of the white
    staff, N57; see also comical history; ecclesiastical
    history
hive, grumbling, M70
H—lt, Miss (addressee), T112
Hoadly, Benjamin, bishop of Bangor etc.: controversy
    with Blackall and Sacheverell (1710), L159, S2,
    V92, W64, W148; Bangorian controversy (1717–20),
    A200, A277, A373, P120, S503, S510, W189; con-
    tention for see of Canterbury (1731), F146, M347;
    (1747), R7; character, B477
Hoadly, John, archbishop of Dublin (dedicatee), M888
hob: country, C450; turned courtier, H263
Hobbinol, S571
Hoby, Ann, lady Brooke, elegy on, G202
Höchstädt, battle of, see Blenheim
Hockley in the hole, bear garden at, B124
Hodge and the devil, N296·5
Hodges, Sir William, elegy on, S232
Hoey, Abraham van, letter to, L275
hog ('Robin Hog'=Robert Stephens) tossed in a blanket,
    H274
Hogarth, William: Harlot's progress, B426, H54, P1105;
    Marriage à-la-mode, M110; Midnight modern con-
    versation, B48; Rake's progress, P1106, R10; Roast
    beef of Old England, F198; epistle to, M331; instruc-
    tions to, S78
Hogg, Thomas, elegy on, E149
Hogland, description of, H275, L68, R195
Holbeach, John (dedicatee), W225
Holdecombe, Mr, ballad set to music by, D502
holiday ramble, H289
Holland, gentleman in, letter to, L130
Holles, Lady Henrietta (afterwards Harley, countess of
    Oxford), see Harley
Hollings, daughter of John (Margaret?), B541
Hollis, John (addressee), R327
Hollis, Thomas, elegy on, R327
Holmes, John, his Greek grammar attacked, B95
holy: life, E534; Parnassus, H291; poem, H292; spirit,
    D560
Holy Roman Empire, succession to, E487, N75
Holywell, N. Wales, brawl at, L200
Homer: address to, M471; essay on, P699; poem to,
    P309; poems occasioned by English translations of,

Homer (*cont.*)
M479, M480, M489, M496, M497, M500·5; for translations and imitations of, *see* the main catalogue; *see also* Iliad

homosexuals, C286, D536, P81, W549: female, E376, S35

homunculus, H293

honest: jury, P1161; man, H297, M415; whigs, W64; citizen's wish, H294; Clodd's advice, H295; Tom's resentment, H298

honesty: the best policy, H300; in distress, W82; yet to be found, H301; health to, H124; progress of, D551; search after, S163

honour, B43, B504, W414: brown bread and, B501; dawn of, D70; false, F46; female, F95; love and, D194; man of, M63, M68, M415; retrieved, C249

Hood, Robin, L198, R232

hoop, for the broken mug, H303

hoop-petticoats, B206, D87, F65, H304, H305, L25, L272, N172, O206, O242, P196, W10

hoops, *see* hoop-petticoats

hope, M439

Hopkins, Edward, master of the revels, P1167

Hopkins, John, imitations of Sternhold and Hopkins's style, K67, L34, O171

Horace: critical thoughts on, P475; dissertations on, S157, S158; to Fannius, T474; Harlequin-, M251; to Lucifer, P372; metres of, imitated, M24, P526; poem to, P399; satire on Allan Ramsay translating, S73; sober advice from, P968; turned whig, H315; for imitations of, *see* imitation

horn-book, poem in praise of, T300

Horncastle, Lincs., Justice Howgrave of, M227

Horneck, Anthony, *Fire of the altar* versified, M558

Horner, Laury, barber in Oxford, B64

hornets, high-church, B530·3

horse: and away, H324; and the flies, H325; and the monkey, H326; and the olive, P77; stumbling, S776; white (= George II), G272, H354; dialogues between horses, D270, M121, N129

racing, G265, H150, J75, L265, P480, P640

Hort, Josiah, bishop, epigram on, H327

Horwood, Mr, music composed by, H164–6

Hosier, Francis, admiral, ghost of, G186, P1045

hospital: Bethlehem, C225, R335, S657; at Dublin, V52; at Northampton, P1107; madman's, M12

hostages, the, H328

Hotchkis, Leonard (dedicatee), W242

Hottentot knight (= Josiah Owen), B618

Houblon, Sir Richard (dedicatee), N44

Hough, Peter, proprietor of Sadler's Wells, C341

Houghton: Sir Robert Walpole at, H406, N160, N318, Q3, S786, Y19; hare-hunting, H331; prosperity to, F174

hounds, monkey and, M398

Hounslow Heath, W461: troops encamped on (1740), N115

house, country, the, M476

house of commons, A104: address of (23 Dec 1703), A55; muse's address to, M564; proceedings of, B34; *see also* parliament

house of lords, sentence on Sacheverell, O219

housewife and her cock, F8

How, Dr John, elegy on, E150

Howard, Lady Elizabeth (subsequently duchess of Gordon) (addressee), P362

Howard, Sir Ralph, S640

Howard, William: in Dublin election (1727), B25, C316, E557, V124; death of, B235, C531, E151, H296

Howe, Mr (dedicatee), H339

Howe, John, MP (addressee), P1111

Howe, Scrope, viscount, governor of Barbados, elegy on, P111

Howe, Sophia, H157·5

Howell, William, proprietor of Belsize House, B186

Howgrave, Justice, satire on, M227

Howland, Madam, elegy on, H84

'Howlet, Don Juan', F211

Howson, Miss, of Barnard Castle, B85

Howth, Thomas St. Lawrence, baron, elegy on, E152

Howth, William St. Lawrence, baron, hare hunting of, A87

Hoyle, Dr Richard, elegy on, E153

Hubbard, Mother, M522

Hubbard, John, elegies on, E38, G323

hubble bubbles, D545

Hudibras, F211: British, W193; redivivus, W90

Hudibras, imitations of, B404, D233, H299, M225, P1036, S474, W97, W277; *see also* the following entries

hudibrastic: brewer, W96

cantos, F211

poem, B604, D300, F244, H293, I72, R119

verse (poems describing themselves as in), C450 D397, D508, F100, H54, K104, M110, M347, P197, P261, P479, P1042, P1106, P1110, P1112, R10, S23, S37, S451, S942, T529, W103, W466; *see also* burlesque

hudibrastics, E290, F46, P20

hue and cry, D498, H361, H362: tradesman's, T438

after Lord Bolingbroke, H358; brewers, H360; bum bailiffs, T438; charity, W233; city magistrate, H351; Daniel Defoe, H352; the Drapier's club, D251; Dublin poor-house, N79; eclipse, H356; E——s, A263; George Fachney, P161; flying man, R224; *Letter to the lord mayor*, H357; George Macartney, H353; M——k, H355; money, E304; *Observator*, H359; outlandish monster, D320; Madam Yarmouth's white horse, H354

Huet, William (dedicatee), S768

Huggett, turnip-man, W444

Huggins, John, warden of the Fleet prison, B47

Hughes, Mr, singer, O57

Hughes, John, sends poem by Welsted, W294

Hughes, John Roydon, captain of foot, elegy on, V69

Hughes, Lambert, of Trinity College Dublin, satire on, W522

Huguenot: French, G241; true-born, P456; act for naturalizing (1709), C18

human: barometer, P200; body, G232; frailty, W27; happiness, C551, J18; life, P11, P1144, R250; nature, C28, T564; passions, H387; wisdom, H388; wishes, vanity of, J87

humble address: of the muses, T61; of the quakers of Scotland, H389; of the wine-merchants, etc. of York, H390; of the wives of the bow, H391; to the general assembly, H392; *see also* address

humble advice, to loyal Scots and English, H393

humble petition: of a beautiful young lady, H394; of Philip duke of Wharton, H396

Hume, Sir David, of Crossrig, elegy on, E154

Hume-Campbell, Alexander, his dedication satirized, L67

humility, admonition to lowly, D543

humorous: ballad, C345, W523; tale, A329, D441

humours: of the Black-dog, W464; of the camp, R24; of the Fleet, P21; of the university of Oxford, D34; of the Wells, S747

'Humpus', town-poet, O229

hundred godly lessons, H405

hunter: hunted, H406; parson-hunter, P85

hunting, C136, M147, M443, O118, S562; fox-hunting, C185, Y19; hare-hunting, A87, H331, S768; after money, H409; of the Pope, C318; of the senator, K53; of the stag, H410, P1012

Huntingdon, Francis Hastings, earl of (addressee), A137

Huntly, Alexander Gordon, marquis (subsequently duke of Gordon), M107

huntsman, tale of lady and her, T540

Hurd, Tom, bookseller, A10

Hurlothrumbo, by S. Johnson, M187: dialogue of Hurlothrumbo with death, P782

hurricane, C488

husband, H413: duty of a, D562, D563; forgiving, W70; loving, L283; letters from lady to her, B541, L121

husbands, advice to new-married, P479

husbandmen's petition, H414

husbandry, Virgil's, B195–6

Husbands, Mr, prologue spoken by, N176

Hussey, Edward, H346: marriage to the Duchess of Manchester, W486, W488

Hutcheson, Archibald, epistle to, E394

Hutchinson, Francis, bishop of Down & Connor, satire on, E536

Hutchinson, Hartley, satires on, B270, D530, P47

Hyde Park: military camp in, N115, R24; ramble through, R24; review in, H132; ring in, B527·8

Hyde, Lady Katherine (subsequently duchess of Queensberry), P1093

Hyde, Lady Theodosia (addressee), O156

hydra, modern, L42

Hymen, quarrel with Venus, Q7

Hymenaeus, H420

hymn, C488, D301, H421, H424, H427, P751, S361: Church of England's, H466; congratulatory, P1138; farewell, P1004; sacred, B325, B341; thanksgiving, Q14

    for Christmas, H422, W316; for the condemned prisoners, W317; among the dead, D103·5; on the death of the bishop of Cork, A151; for the use of high-church, E573; on the nativity, H319; on peace, W331; at the sacrament, P738–50, W315; for St Cecilia's day, *see* St Cecilia's day; on the sufferings of Christ, H426; of thanksgiving, H425; for the thanksgiving day, B416, D109, H451

    sung by the charity children, H376, H423, H429–50, H473

    to the birthday, H455; to the chair, H456; to confinement, P442; to the country, P1004; to the creator, B575, C425, F226, H461, W295; to the deity, H457; to the funeral sermon, H458; to God, H452; to the

goddess of silence, J44; to harmony, C370, J100; to the incarnation, W569; to James III, P1138; to liberty, C414; to the light of the world, B252; to May, T171; to the mob, D114; to money, H453; to the moon, S190; to Neptune, P443; to the new laureate, H462; to Alderman Parsons, H428; to peace, D110, N141; to the pillory, D115; to the pope, H463; to the redeemer, H81, P472; to St Tack, H454; to the scaffold, H465; to the supreme being, B446; to the tories, R158; to the Tower, B227; to the trinity, S397; to Tyburn, H471; to victory, D123, H467, S240

hymns, D560, N299: annual, L231; of consolation, C531; sung by the charity children, H473

Hyp-doctor, H474

hyperbole, poem on the, H89

hypochondria, H475

hypocrite, dissenting, W97

hypocrites: portrayed, F90; satires on, H477, P253, S42

iambic: match, I2; ode, I2; poem, C176

Iberia liberata, O167

idleness of business, W575

idol: the new, N144; of Paris, I3

idyll: funeral, O166; on the peace, I4

Ierne's (= Ireland's) answer to Albion, T380

if, the monosyllable, M402

Ignatius's ghost, L162

ignorance, poem in praise of, H180

Iliad: freethinker's, W40; in a nutshell, W342; sequel of, M193

Illia's plain, I5

Ilton, Baron, Hanoverian general, satires on, B38, M254·5, Y16

imagination, pleasures of, A139

imitation:

'Imitation' is used in titles to cover everything from direct translation to imitation of style or metre. The works listed here are those which describe themselves as imitations or as being 'in the manner of' earlier poems. All translations that have been identified as such are entered under the original author in the main catalogue, whereas works in the manner of other authors are only to be found in this index. For a complete list of 'imitations' of all kinds, the author entry in the main catalogue and in this index should be consulted.

    of Arwaker's *Pia Desideria*, W566; Lord Belhaven's speech, E221; Boileau, D217; Buchanan, T581; Byrom, D406; Calpurnius Siculus, M145; Chaucer, C245, P202, P1073; *Cherry and slae*, F22; *Chevy Chace*, H45, R223, W376, W539 (*see also* tune); Cicero, C72; *Donaides*, M54; Dryden, D412, R173, S8, W435; Du Bartas, B569; *Epistle to William Pitt*, S452; Fontenelle, B415; *Frances Harris's petition*, D77, D337, R169; Gallus, Cornelius, I14; Gay, John, B77, C471, E549, H19, W12; Holdsworth's *Muscipula*, L276; Homer, Virgil, Dryden, and Pope, M6; Horace, A170, A327, B15, B351, B356, B383, B408, C56·7, C59, C138, D243, D254, D272, D293, D376, E345, E384, E469, F137, F150, F214, F215, F236, G147, G320, H15, H49, H157·2, H311, H322, H419, I21, I50, J62, J65, J69, J109, K55, K72, M91, M165, M168, M246, M258, M328, M503, N15, N304, O21, O36, O70, O91–4, O100, O101, O103–6, P124, P877,

imitation (*cont.*)

P881, P886, P896, P897, P932, P955, P961, P965, P1078, P1157, P1166, P1181, R53, R291, S81, S88, S407, S483, S484, S493, S577, S737, S854, S859, S860, S891, S911, T255, T283, T332, T357, T440, T562, T566, W30, W33, W274, W297, W311; *Hudibras*, B404, D233, H299, M225, P1036, S474, W97, W277 (*see also* hudibrastic); Irish poetry, A71; Juvenal, G141, J76, J87, M184, S355, T155; Ker, John, M54; La Fontaine, M73, T158; long verses, S452; Lucan, M146; Lucretius, H183, I20; Machiavelli, D244; Mallet's *William and Margaret*, G96, L277, P761, S132, T290, W503; Milton, A167, B91, B176, E528, F104, J101, K12, L174, L204, M124, M551, N254, P65, P67, P137, P246, P264, T168 (*see also* Miltonic verse); *Molly Mog*, E549; *Mousetrap*, L276; Ovid, C496, E218, H157·5, I8, K60, O97, S34, S800, U33, V27; Persius, A77, D42, H161·5, L291; Phaedrus, B530·9; Philips, Ambrose, S53, Y108; Philips, John, B392, B554, D533; Pindar, Y82; Pitcairne, P366; Pope, B160, G5, J116, O231, P63, P1026, W242; Prior, E339, S151, S487; Psalm 77, R336; Psalm 137, H16; *Qui mihi*, E483; Ramsay, M2, M3; Rapin, B378; Richards, Thomas, L68; Rochester, C495; Scarron, M76; *Session of poets*, S223; Shakespeare, T137; Sheridan, Thomas, L155; six several authors, B520; *Spectator*, 159, B441; Spenser, A365·5, J100, P1004, P1065, P1081, P1113, S395, T181; Sternhold & Hopkins, B299, K67, L34, O171; Swift, D77, D337, R169, S126, W270; Theocritus, P1172; Virgil, A352, B550, H6, H44, L242, M521, N13, O9, P110, T434, T435, T474; Waller, A74, C75, E69, O220

immortality: night thoughts on, Y24; revealed, C415

impartial, the, H220: Englishman, B568; judge, B404; narrative, I9; satirist, I10

impeachment (of Sacheverell), F30, I11, R333

imperious beauty, the, I13

impertinent, the, C39, P898

impiety exposed, B515

important triflers, B405

imports, *see* trade

impossible thing, C372

impostor, fair, P25; impostor's doom, S130

impotent lover, I14

imprisonment, comforts of, B514

impudence: ode to, H387; satire against, T517

incarnation, of Christ, H364, M271, O48, W569; *see also* Jesus Christ, nativity

incendiaries, modern, O209

incendiary (=Charles Lucas?), scourge for, S150

independent sectaries, L152

index, metrical, to the Bible, C162

Indian: calicos and silks, P1051; kings, E353, H108, R321; pastoral eclogue, H69

indolence: castle of, T181; charms of, M303

industry: folly of, W574; virtue and, A360; *see also* business

infatuation, the, M556

infernal spirits, junto of, E315

infidelity, check to, H457

infidels, lesson for, A26

Ingoldsby, Richard, lieutenant-general (addressee), P543

ingratitude, satire against, A122

inhabitants of Great Britain, ode to, O70

iniquity displayed, F231

injured: ghost, G96; merit, M86; patriot, N278

Inkle and Yarico, M434, S380

Inner Temple, poems by gentlemen of, B100, H40, H109

Innes, Alexander, elegy on, A159

Innes, Thomas, killed in duel, F46

innocent lampoon, I43

Inns of Court: members of (addressees), M228; poem by gentleman of one, D363

inscription: on John Bell, P382; modern, A365·5

insect war, B530·3

insects: emulation of, E308; seditious, S192

inspired poet, I44

installation (as K.G.), K48

instalment (of Walpole as K.G.), Y86

institution of order of the Garter, W358

instructions: for children, G160; to freeholders, P24; to a painter, I45, I46; for young men and maids, G156; a father's instructions to his son, S147

instructors instructed, I47

intelligence, Dublin, D463

Intelligencer, character of, S887, T319

interest, fear and, F81

interlude, D396

intrigue, the, S31: city, C205; garden-house, W127; governor's, C384

intrigues, of Miss Cloudy, M42

intriguing, art of, A320

invasion: (1708), F251, H221, I51; (1717), I50; (1719), N203; (1746), D37; French, F251; Highland, H202; of the Spaniards, N203; *see also* Jacobite rebellions

inventory, G248, I52, L155, S419

invitation, S407, S512, W252: Christmas, S497; John Dennis's, J69; royal, R312

invocation of health, B10

Iphigenia, Miss Chudleigh's appearance as, P702

Ipswich, voyage to, P23

Iredal, Francis (addressee), W468

Ireland: poems to, P675, S859; in mourning, I56; in universal mourning, I57

attorneys, A245, B53, D237, V94

Bank of Ireland, B60, E175

description of, H162

elections, A269

house of commons, speaker of, S620, V49

ladies, H305, S840

linen manufacture, C56·5, D522

lord chancellor, I65, P631

lord lieutenants, *see* Carteret, John, baron; Chesterfield, Philip Dormer Stanhope, earl; Devonshire, William Cavendish, 3rd duke; Dorset, Lionel Cranfield Sackville, duke; Grafton, Charles Fitzroy, 2nd duke; Harrington, William Stanhope, earl; Ormonde, James Butler, duke; Pembroke, Thomas Herbert, earl; Rochester, Laurence Hyde, earl; Shrewsbury, Charles Talbot, duke; Wharton, Thomas, 1st marquis

mint proposed, P522

music, P282

parliament, G227

poets, *see* Irish poets

Ireland (*cont.*)
  potatoes, E219, R165
  Roman catholics, F267, R139
  squires, I59
  woollen manufactory, S840
Ireland's: answer to Albion, T380; black day, I58; blessing, I59; eye, P721; happiness completed, I60; lamentation, I61; mourning flag, I62; prospect of happiness, I63; universal loss, I65; warning, I66
Irene triumphans, S275
Irish: translation from, D199
  the, I67; poem to, G307
  bar, V94; bishops, S794; clowns, H400; cry, H13; entertainment, S642; fortune-hunter, B425; gimlet (*sens. obsc.*), D233; harp, S738; historical library, H173; howl, H13·2; legs, W491; manufactures, A286; nobleman, death of, S557; poetry, A71; poets, A229, E383, G267, G305; Polly Peachum, E550; Pretender (=William Dunkin), D7; shilling, J8; whale fishery, F266
Irishman, L300; Irishman's joy, E583·5, P757; *see also* Teague
iron age, L111
ironical poem, B564
Ironmonger, Joshua, marriage of, S307
'Ironside, Nestor', description of Bath by, B94
irregular ode, I68, P252, P1109, S552, S785, W28
irresistible fair, D359
Isaac, the patriarch, C475, S944
Isabel, Alrick and, D467
Isabella's sparrow, K95
Isaiah, poem upon, E451
Isham, Sir Justinian, MP, H125
Isidora to Casimir, I70
Isis, M123: Cam and, C6; triumph of, W247
island, happy, D191
Islay, Archibald Campbell, earl of (subsequently 3rd duke of Argyll), *see* Argyll
isle: happy, G215; of love, B162; of moderation, R128
Isleworth, private school at, P1122
Islington, New Tunbridge Wells at, S59, W200
Israel: restoration of, H217; triumphs over Jabin, B530·7
Israel in Egypt, by Handel, A82
Italian: poems in, M93, R186, R253–5; works claiming to be translated from the Italian, but probably original, C286, E386, P712
  canzone, R53; opera, O251; paintings, N264; policy, I72
Italy: ancient and modern compared, T186; letter from, A39; Prince Eugene's successes in (1702), E466, H71, L162, P257; (1706), B315
itch, poem in praise of, S155
Ithuriel's spear, A15

J., C. (addressee), G283
Jabin, king of Hazor, B530·7
Jack: Country, M400; of Eton (=John Burton), K67
jackdaws: tale of, A112; magpies and, T29
Jacks (=Jacobites), J8: Perkinite, P183; of Great Britain, C385
Jackson, chaplain to William King, S426
Jackson, musician, G63

Jacob, the patriarch, C475, S944: and Rachel, I49
Jacobite: discourse with French Huguenot, G241; and Swedish conspiracy, F23
Jacobite propaganda:
No attempt has been made to include the many high tory poems which have Jacobite implications
  1704/05, D564
  1714/15, accession of George I, B284, C275, C321, C439, D558, G41, H250, L43, L117, L191, L310, M208, M519, M522, N36, N89, N124, N125, N185, N209, N235, N325, O131, O218, O223, P98, P1063, P1136, R172, S110, S579, T377
  1716, aftermath of the rebellion, B448, O174, O210, P571, P576
  1715/20, propaganda campaign, largely of slip songs, B15, B23, B154, B237, B468, C193, D5, D319, E288, E323, E413, E540, E541, E552, E558, E560, E563, E564, F1, F44, H35, H249, H255, H257, H261, I21, L301, M132, N53, N55, N223, N224, N304, O204, O220, P194, P469, P1034, P1137, P1138, S593, S597, S621, T263, T396, T571
  172–, M218, N93
  1722, R212
  1742, B157
  1745/46, rebellion, B103, B225, C383, C398, E567, H17, N302·5, O172, O221, P575, P686, P1058
  1746/50, aftermath of the rebellion, H16, L18, M3, M77, M81, P525, R103, S595
  see also Charles Edward Stuart; James Francis Edward Stuart
Jacobite rebellions:
  1708, D245, F170, F251, H221, I51, I73, M140, T315, T484
  1715/16, A97, C216, C339, C359, D260, E412, E586, F52, F74, H7, H372, M107, P1033, R2, R142, S290, S376, T335; *see also* Argyll, John Campbell, 2nd duke; Mar, John Erskine, earl; Sherrifmuir
  1719, H467, N203, N213
  1744, B604, L297, N207
  1745/46, A147, A292, B87, B230, B455, C201, C267, D37, D398–9, D417, E575, E597, G135, G235, G255, H202, H310, H393, L218, M139, N6, N34, N200, N212, N321, O169, O182, P624, P710, P1109, P1131, R141, R143, R311, S134, S146, S459, T439, T556, V56, W32, W272, W481; *see also* Charles Edward Stuart; Culloden; Falkirk; Prestonpans; William Augustus, duke of Cumberland
  1747, F182
Jacobites: protestant, O169; challenge to, A105; insurrection of, T556; *see also* Jacks
Jacobites': coat of arms, J53; downfall, H7; lament for King James, J53·5; purgatory and prayer, T430
Jacobites, satires against:
No attempt has been made to include the many attacks on the high tories, or on the Pretender himself
  1701, A116
  1713, E545
  1714, E573, P182
  1715, C9, S700
  1716, G17
  1717, L200
  1718, E364, P634
  1722, N196, P515

Jacobites (*cont.*)
  1747, P470, P510
  see also Charles Edward Stuart; James Francis Edward
    Stuart
Jaconitism, S35
Jamaica: politics and patriots of, P715; governors, *see*
    Lawes, Sir Nicholas; Trelawny, Edward
James II: consolatory poem to (1688), C387; elegies on,
    A273, E155–7, E160, E161, G105, H254, J53·5, O44,
    O53, O194, O212, T577; fable concerning, C321;
    ghost of, O172; Latin poems on, P376, P383; reign
    of, C489
James Francis Edward Stuart, the Old Pretender:
  1701, birthday, O222; proclamation as king, K52,
    P693, P1061, P1062
  1708, lamentation for the small pox, P1031; attempted
    invasion, D245, F170, I51, I73, M140, T315, T484
  1710/–, addressee, B199
  1711, T581; effigy of seized, K94, Q8, T119; medal of,
    L308, W278; 'expedition to Switzerland', T425
  1711–13, Pitcairne's Latin poems to, P309, P313,
    P315, P361, P378, P386, P388, P391
  1712, B46, D556
  1713, P507; ode to, R175; renounced by Louis XIV,
    B514·5
  1714, H37, P182, P1057; declaration, P1036
  1714/–, E323, S110
  1715, H358, L43, P179, P1032, R172, S585; birthday,
    B223, N233
  1716, declaration, F282, P1035; landing, A97, E412;
    letter to the tories, P1037; routed, P1033
  1716/–, picture, O220
  1717, P1034; birthday, E540; epistle to, A193
  1718, P1171; birthday, P634; epistle from Princess
    Sobieski, A194
  1719, marriage to Princess Sobieski, E448, M351,
    N213; Spanish attempt at invasion, N199, N203,
    N213, P1138
  1722, declaration, N71
  1726, birthday, N167
  1727, birthday, B26
  1745, M411; birthday, J111
  1749, N307
  1750, birthday, E362
James, George (addressee), S558
January, poem to, P316
January 30 (martyrdom of Charles I), B608, C304, S5
Jandrau, Mrs, S525
Janssen, Sir Stephen Theodore (addressee), L224
Janus, P318, S514: (=Harley), J56; Secretary (= Sir
    John Murray), S178
Jaquo', the monkey, E162
Jefferies, Mother, of Tunbridge Wells, elegy on, D534
Jehosaphat, life of, T567
Jekyll, Sir Joseph: ghost of, W503; manager of Sachev-
    erell's trial, A52; wife of, J67
Jemmy's pedigree, J58
Jenney, Henry, correspondent of Swift, A237
Jenny: the fish, E163; maid, at Derby, B616; and Meggy,
    R59; Kick him, Jenny, K32
Jeremiah, Lamentations of, B516, E459
Jericho, taking of, W322
Jerningham, Sir Francis (dedicatee), W225

Jersey, Edward Villiers, earl of (dedicatee), W225
Jerusalem, of Tasso, B319, B488, H302
Jesina, F223
jest and earnest, P432
Jesuit, epistle from an English, E364
Jesus Christ, D341, G298, H272, R185; God's glorious
    perfections shining in, C145; intercourse with the soul,
    B130; poems addressed to, B252, K9, P320, W331;
    star that leads to, D217; wisdom of choosing, C229
  acts and miracles of, W325; apparition and ascension
    of, G165; circumcision of, G164; coming of, C1·5;
    crucifixion of, E27, T91; divinity of, B169;
    friendship of, C144; genealogy of, L292; life and
    death of, W236; life and miracles of, G115; love
    of, C222, S6; nativity of, A333, B318, B486, C171,
    C302, C303, C553, G168, H81·5, H292, H319, H364,
    M271, N120, O48, O191, O213, P630, T520, W29·5,
    W514, W569 (*see also* Christmas); nuptials of, N348;
    passion of, B140, P706, S4·5, S27; resurrection
    of, L315, P289; second appearance of, P730;
    sufferings and death of, H426; temptations and
    sufferings of, M557; transfiguration of, R198; *see
    also* Messiah; Redeemer
'Jet Black' (=Jonathan Smedley), H356, L118, O258
Jew, battle of, with Turk, T554; Jew lady, marriage of,
    A216
jewel, in the Tower (= Sir Robert Walpole), O205
Jews, H132, T587
J——h, Ben, T554
jiber jibed, T318
jilt, the amorous, A216
jilts: wheedling, W383; and hypocrites portrayed, F90
jingle, a new, N143
J——o, jolly old, E555
Joan, Pope, M520
Job: complaint of, C322; history of, B9; lamentation for
    his children, A123; life and death of, G118
jobbers, fate of, P642; *see also* stock-jobbers
jockeys, P480
'Jocky, Sir', B404
John: and Betty, J68; (=Marlborough), N332
John, king, K51
John, Sir, epistle from Lady Traffick to, A63
Johnson, Richard, elegies on, F289, N204
Johnson, Samuel, his *Hurlothrumbo*, M187, P782
Johnston, Maggy, elegy on, R46
Johnston, Richard, criminal, P59
joke, merry new, M203
jolly: patriots, J89; soldier, J90
Jonah, M309
Jonathan, P324: David's lamentation for, L212
Jones, Mr, 'the soldier's advocate', elegy on, V24
Jones, Edward, printer, elegy on, M186
Jones, George (addressee), H400
Jones, John (dedicatee), W230
Jones, Robert, of Fonmon Castle, elegy on, W313
Jones, William (dedicatee), W233
Jonson, Ben, epilogue to his *Alchemist*, P7
Joseph, archduke of Austria, N75
Joseph, emperor of 'Germany' (=Holy Roman Empire),
    elegy on, E164
Joseph, the patriarch, C475: history of, N327, R269,
    R274, S154; Joseph's old cloak, M203

Joshua, J101: poem on text from book of, A169

Jotham, Uzziah and, U35

journal, the, S861; of a Dublin beau, J102; of a Dublin lady, S863; of pastime à-la-mode, B405

journalists, G42, M72, P1025, T253: displayed, J103

journey: to Bath and Bristol, J19; to the county of Cork, M565; from Evesham to Oxford, B415; to hell, W100; to Mayfair, T490; to Somerset House, T492; *see also* trip

journeymen-weavers, *see* weavers

Jove, liberty of, R206; Jove's ramble, J105

joy: Irishman's, E583·5; upon joy, J106

Joye, Charles (addressee), C97

joyful ode, J108

Jubilade, the, J109

jubilee, Britain's, E478

judge: impartial, B404; politic, P710

judgement, M469, T458: of Hercules, L79, L293, M313, S394; of Paris, B205, C115, D2; upon heretics, G204; of the muse, H418

judgement-day, G138, H222, S525; *see also* four last things; last judgement

judgements, God's, G114, G204, P1001

Judoign, battle of, J110; *see also* Ramillies

jugglers, political, W398

Juggy, Munster, M561

Julius Caesar, prologue to, by Thomas Sheridan, S416; opera by Handel, E402

July 25, 1713, poem on, P409

'Jumpedo, Don', C320

June, 1712, Latin poem to, P327

June 10 (Old Pretender's birthday), B223, J111, N167, O222

junto, the, B30, J112, M204, R334·5: little (1732), L199

Jupiter: and the giants, H130; Mars and, C395; Jupiter Ammon, P370

jury: England's late, E320; honest, P1161; Dublin grand-jury, E571, E594, N165

justice: picture of, M227; political, N346; throne of, B536; triumphant, B340

justice, of peace: apology for, B270; curious, A153; Westminster, W372

Juvenal, poem occasioned by, E9

Katy, Edinburgh, R108

Kavana, Mrs, singer, S581

Kaven-bail poem, K1

Keach, Benjamin, elegy on, E165

Keck, Robert, elegy on, P600

keeping, and marriage, difference between, D305

Keith, George, missionary, A8

Keith, William, earl Marischall (dedicatee), P384

Kello, Commissioner, elegy on, E166

Kelly, E., originator of riots at Thomas Sheridan's playhouse, D420

Kempster, Bartholomew, S634

Kendal, Ehrengard Melusina von der Schulenburg, duchess of, satires on, B154, L71, N95

Kenmure, William Gordon, viscount, elegy on, O210

Kenn, Thomas, bishop of Bath and Wells, elegies on, P190, S689

Kennett, White (dedicatee), N49

Kensington, trip to, T486

Kensington Garden, T288

Kent: trip into, S451; poem to loyal gentlemen of, C355

Kent, Henry Grey, 11th earl (subsequently duke) (addressee), N44, P462

Kentish: ballad, G110; freeholders, P57; long-tails, B507; men, K16, S56; petitioner, K104; petitioners, T409; spy, K104; worthies, T62

Kentish, Mrs Frances, epitaph on, E445

Ker, Joan, marriage to Walter Aston, M200

Kerry: county of, O11; cavalcade, K30

Kerry, Countess of (A---l B---g---m), elegy on, E167

'Ketch, Jack' (London hangman), N286, R160, S604

Kick him: Jenny, K32; Nan, K35

Kidd, Captain William, pirate, elegy on, E168

Kielmansegge, Baroness, E413

Kilkenny, C142

Killiecrankie, battle of, K39

Kilmainham ballad, N145

Kilmallock, Limerick to, L183

Kilmarnock, Countess of, her lamentation, L18

Kilmarnock, William Boyd, earl of, execution of, L18

Kilmorey, Thomas Needham, viscount (addressee), M569

Kimberly, Daniel, elegy on, E169

Kincaid, Thomas, of Gogar-Mains, murderer, P167

king: beasts and their, F3; and the cobbler, C494; fairyking, F37

King, Mr (alias Mr Booth), J94

King, Charles, composer, O34

King, Sir John, elegy on, E170

King, Moll, memoirs of, C473

King, Sir Peter (subsequently baron King of Ockham) (addressee), H337, R145, T116

King, Tom, B71

King, William, the gazetteer (1663–1712), elegy on, O156

King, William, archbishop of Dublin (1650–1729): opposition to Wood's halfpence (1724), S846, T334; addressee, S426, T334; elegies on, E171–4, I56, N193

King, William, principal of St Mary Hall (1685–1763): attacks on Edward Bentham, C99, W517; editor of Swift, S920

King's Bench prison, poems from, B86, L148

Kingston, Evelyn Pierrepont, duke of, K48

Kingston, James King, 4th baron, satire on, I9

Kingston, William Pierrepont, earl of, elegy on, S338

Kinnoull, George Hay, 8th earl of, P307

Kinnoull, Thomas Hay, 7th earl of (addressee), P307

Kinnoull, Thomas Hay, 9th earl of, prologue spoken by, P1084

Kinsale, Gerald de Courcy, lord (dedicatee), T129

Kintore, John Keith, earl of (addressee), H103

Kintore, William Keith, earl of, elegy on, H103

kirk: and covenant, K84; *see also* Church of Scotland

Kirton, George (addressee), P305

kiss, struggle for, C448, W150

Kiss my arse, K92

Kit-Cat club, B257, K94, V16

kitchen, Yarhell's, Y5

kite: (=lawyer), B6, S72; blackbird and, F4; and crow, N58; paper kite, P47

Kitty: or the female Phaeton, P1095; and Dick, K95

Knap, Mrs, epilogue spoken by, N140, N176
knave: of trumps, H411; at the bottom, P713, P1050
knavery, poem in praise of, T579
knaves turned honest, M70
Kneller, Lady (addressee), S224
Kneller, Sir Godfrey: addressee, A41, P977, T311; death of, S224
knight, the: M211; and the cardinal, K96; and his lady, C152; and his man John, D287; and the prelate, K97; and the purse, K100; embarrassed, J61; outrid, K101; overthrown, C182; unfortunate, P1116; upon squire, L261
of the Garter, see Garter; of the kirk, M212; of Malta, L20; of the sable shield, F107
Knight, Robert, cashier of the South Sea Company, V119
knighthood: no trifle, C155; new order of, C326
knights of the horn, K102
knitters, stocking-frame, C272, O3
Knole, epitaph at, P931·5
Knolls Hill, Essex, B84
know yourself, A290
knowledge of men, P920
Korath, K105
Kountze, Mr, kettle-drummer, G63
Kræuter, Philip David, marriage of, O47
Kremberg, James, composer, E317

L., C., letter to, F151
labour: in vain, W494; lost, L2
labyrinth, the, L3
Lacey's bagnio, S453
La Chetardie, J. J. Trotti, marquis de (addressee), C386
Lacy, J., tobacco merchant, T404·5
Lacy, John, Camisard prophet, E443, F260
laddie, highland, R58
ladies: poems addressed to, H307, J94, M372, N8, P566; metamorphosed into china cups, T109; of pleasure, L14, W257; poetical, P709
advice to, A92–6, D356, P752; defence for, D87; epilogue to, P1124; good advice to, G219; lecture to, P163; new simile for, S409; Punch's petition to, P1167; treason against, T469
at Bristol-Wells, B451; Cambridge, P535; Canterbury, G203; of Dublin, T380; of Edinburgh, E16, J70; of Great Britain, A92, I32, W269; in the Earl of Meath's liberty, F28; of Ireland, S840; London, L238; of Michael's parish (Dublin), A95; of Munster, E542; of St Warborough's parish (Dublin), A56; of the three kingdoms, P709
see also beauties; fair; female sex; toasts; women
(titles where 'ladies' may represent either a singular or plural possessive): answer, L8; choice, L9, L12; defence, C172; dressing room, L238; frolic, L13; hoops and hats, O206; libraries, A95, F28, P520, S55; opera, L15; screen, N108; tails, D534; tutor, L16
lady: and her huntsman, T540; and the linnet, L17; in the country, letter from, S201; in the lobster, V108; in town, letter from, B76; surprized, L317
advice to; L328, ballad set by, S611; consolatory verses to, S673; epistle from, T272; epistle to, P917, S841; journal of, S863; letter from, B541, L121; letter to, G52

Dublin, S863; in England, T272; in St Mary's parish (Dublin), V106; in St P— parish (Dublin), P117
see also young lady
lady's: answer, D562, L21–5; bed, P563; bodkin, T28; decoy, L26; dressing room, M416·5, R242, S399, S869; lamentation, S602; last shift, L27; letter, L28; ramble, L29; transformation, P218; watch, L30
Lady Jane Grey, tragedy, N163
'Laelius' (addressee), C130
La Fontaine, imitations of, M73, T158
Laguerre, Louis, painter, A215
laird, the young, R108
Lake, Sir John, congratulation to, B323
lamb, nuptials of the, N348
Lambert, George, painter, epistle to, M331
Lambeth: first oars to, F146; bishops rowing to, M347
lament: highland man's, H206; Jacobites', J53·5; Pastora's, P102; town officer's, R1; true Scotsmen's, T530; white regiment's, W407; zealous countrymen's Z1
lamentation: for Miss P——p, N82; for the departure of Mr No-body, N2; on the death of Duke Hamilton, G163; over the sad changes, L39; over Sion, L31
Mordecai Adam's, M1; of William Ainslie, L32; Doctor Anthony's, A258; Lady Balmerino's, L18; Britain's, D399; of Anthony Bulger (and others), N196; of the butchers' wives in Musselburgh, L37; of James Campbell, S606; a certain dutiful son's, C98; Church of England's, C176; Church of Scotland's, C181, K29; clans', C216; of Mrs Cooke, E572; country, C451; of Daniel Damere, S603; David's, L212; from Drury-lane playhouse, L33; florist's, P103; of Elizabeth Forister, P1099; Frenchman's, F264; Jack Frenchman's, J1; of the fruit-wives, L38; William Fuller's, S130; Hibernia's, H174; Ireland's, I61; lady's, S602; Lady Kilmarnock' s, L18; Kit-Cat club's, K94; Little Beau's, L195; lord's, L265; of Mrs M'Leod, L49; of Nicol Muschet, S607; of Harry Ormistoun, S605; Oxenard's, O266; pretended Prince of Wales's, P1031; of John Price, S604; Protestant Barnaby's, O165; sailor's, S10; of a sinner, L34; soldiers', S546–7; Spuddy's, S666; Sutherland's, S789; of Hogan Swanson, C332; Swedish, S792; women-hater's, W549
lamentations: of Jeremiah, B516, E459; of Mary Magdalene, L40; of the non-juring clergy, D289
La Motte, French general, H154
Lampe, John Frederick, composer, G63, O32, S4·5
lampoon, C540, D534, N315, P535, T361: innocent, I43; young Frenchman's, Y21
Lancashire, epistle from, H38
Lancashire garland, L41
'Lancaster, Duke of' (=Nicholas Lechmere), R232
Lancaster, William, vice-chancellor of Oxford, O279
Lancelot (Blackburne) to his ladies, P1054
land, of love, B162
land-leviathan, L42
Landau, taking of, C337
landing, the, L43
landlord's tale, L44
landscape, the, L45: gardening, B402
Lane, Mary, marriage to Lord Parker, E509

Lane, William, C160
Langdon, near Plymouth, H300
Langton, Ludovic, H104
language, progress of, M149
Lansdowne, George Granville, baron, *see* Granville
Laodamia to Protesilaus, P1041
lap dog: rival, R214; and cur, C542
La Pillonière, F. de, S23
La Rochefoucauld, François de, duke, verses occasioned by, S926
lark, pheasant and, D203
Larwood, Francis, recorder of Norwich, P192
lash: for the laureate, L48; for Levi, T406
last: day, B561, Y109; epiphany, P730; farewell, C440, L32, L49, L50; guinea, L51; judgement, N254, O173, W457 (*see also* C76, G138, H222, H259, N275, P730, S525, T458); shift, L27; speech, L55–60, P162, R64; will and testament, A259, B127, F297, L61, L316, P151, W284
Latin: poems in, A14, A20–4, A176, A177, A221–4, B45, B88, B185, B202, B231, B232, B312, B314, B324, B325, B329, B331–4, B394, B442, B592, B597, C13–17, C54, C78, C135, C157, C215, C227, C255, C257, C301, C428, C476, C486, C538, D54, D55, D59, D74, D219, D227, D231, D232, D295, D296, D302–4, D344, D346–8, D368, D390, D520, D527, D555, E9, E21, E32, E34, E39, E305, E483, E496, E603, F80, F165, G1, G4, G6, G290, H34, H74, H142, H143, H143·5, H148, H226, H229, H237, H276–9, H327, H408, I6, I7, I18, I22–31, I74, J75, J107, K17–22, K25–7, K40–3, K66–8, K73–8, K88, L6, L205, L315, L318, M24, M35, M167, M195, M207, M223, M271, M328, M404, M407–10, M417, M419, N34, N270, N293, N297, N299, N311, N312, N330, O17, O18, O65, O235, O249, P177, P184–6, P190, P191, P244, P294–409 *passim*, P526, P537, P688, P1016, P1101, P1142, P1156, R113, R194, R195, R271, R304, R329, S38, S39, S137·5, S149, S217, S245, S253, S275, S387, S485, S489, S490, S544, S608, S613, S749, S763, S768, T95, T118, T129, T132, T166, T172, T312, T448, T449, T470, U26, V14, V15, V18, V21, V82, V95, V100, V117, W517, W518, W571
  works claiming to be translated from, K79, R103
  measures, I49
Latin Mercury, H201
latitude, for longitude, S720
Lauder, town-piper of, E220
Lauder, Alexander (addressee), I29
Lauder, George, elegy on, E176
Lauder, Sir John, lord Fountainhall, I29, M357
Lauder, William, satire on, P28
Lauderdale, John Maitland, 1st duke of, H207
laugh: and be fat, L71; and lie down, B538; upon laugh, B539
laughing, satire upon immoderate, M272
Laughlin, H400
laureate: (Cibber), S153; hymn to, H462; (Rowe), lash for, L48; volunteer (Savage), S112–18
laurel: blasted, B281; and the olive, S773; and the ox, L72
Laurie: Thomas, minister at Bathgate, N293
law, B394, B485, N3, R159: corrupted, L73; poem upon, H109; students of, dispute with sheriffs, P594
law-suit, B69

Law, Lucky, elegy on, E177
Law, John, P616: addressee, R99
Law, William, *Spirit of prayer*, B613
Law, William, professor at Edinburgh, poem to the memory of, B275
Lawes, Sir Nicholas, governor of Jamaica, P288
Lawles, Sir Patrick, letter to, G125
laws of England tried, L229–30
lawyer: dialogue with church-warden, F81; fifteen comforts of, F125; fifteen plagues of, F134; mock duel with physician, N74; turned butcher, L76; whimsical, F180
lawyer's: answer, L77; escape, M205; warning piece, S132
lawyers, D242, L229–30, M228, P197, P710, T116: disbanded, H310; satire on, S57; scuffle with physicians, B586; *see also* advocates; attorneys; kite
Layer, Christopher, C440
Layfield, Mr, singer, N197
layman, resolution of, R161
leaden age, L89
leader, accomplished, A7
Leake, Sir John, S472
leaky vessel, L90: Beware of leaky vessels, B206
Leander, Hero and, B44, C70, E490, S754
leap year, intercalary day in, D234
Leason, John, of Bath, H436
lechers: satire on modern, I14; Westminster, V1
Lechmere, Nicholas, baron: escape (1705), M205; quarrel with Sir John Guise (1720), A235, D502; duel with William, earl Cadogan (1723), B42, D507, F140; satire on (1727), R232
lecture: by John Taylor, P566; to the ladies, P163; in verse, L91
lecturers' combat, L92
Lee, William, inventor of the stocking-frame, C272, O3
Leech, Mr, answer to, A240
leeches, Hanoverian, H36
Leeds, Peregrine Osborne, duke of: addressee, C509; marriage, C508, C510, T66
leek, the, G295, T4
legacy, old man's, O115
legacy-hunting, O101
Leghorn, celebration of George I's coronation at, T92
legion, effigies of, E22
Leguerre (=Laguerre), Louis, painter, A215
Le Heup, Isaac: at Hanover, L94·3; embassy to Hanover, L1; epistle to Prince Frederick, L94·8; satires on, I17, K92, L1, L94·3, L94·8, M117, N107
Leicester, Thomas Coke, earl of, P1160
Leicestershire: poem in praise of, H301; freeholder, L101
Leigh, Francis, prologue spoken by, P1129
Leigh, John, epilogue spoken by, P1132
Leigh, William, inventor of the stocking frame, *see* Lee
Leith: executions at, C31, C33, C340, E134, T483; late misfortune at, P1002; packet from, D434; race at, P640
Leixlip, L103, P570, S400
Lempster, George Fermor, lord (subsequently earl of Pomfret), N305
lent: litany for, L193, L194; poem for, D341
Leominster election, T343
Leonidas, G190
lesbians, E376, S35

Leslie, Charles, A8, F151, R175

lessons: divine, A130; for the use of children, D366; state, P426

Lestock, Richard, admiral, at Cartagena (1741), V33; at Toulon (1744), N195; court martial (1746), A160

L'Estrange, Sir Roger: burlesque of, V107; fables from, P425; elegies on, E178–9, L319

letter, A39, A72, A251, B76, B299, B514·5, B541, B614, B620, C107, C375, C530, D27, D343, D541, E492, F84, F107, F185, F263, G52, G113, G158, G317, H157·5, H169, I13, I72, L28, L42, L118–58, L187, M300, M504, M553, N317, N346, O15, P534, P736, P1037, P1079, S67, S137, S201, S418, S463, S546, S863, S876, T328, T433, V98, V116, W12, W343, Y90: of advice, L137–9; of thanks, L140; *see also* congratulatory epistle; epistolary letter; love letter; merry letter; pastoral letter

letters, W456: between a nobleman and his sister, L284; to the king, A60; from a Portuguese nun, L287

levee-haunter, the, L161

levellers, S192

Leven, Anne, countess of, elegy on, E180

Leveridge, Richard: singer, D549, O57; song composed by, S590

Levet, Sir Richard, elegy on, S280

Levi: lash for, T406; tribe of, T476

leviathan, L159

levity and steadiness, M88

Lewis upon Lewis, L163; *see also* Louis

Lewis, Sarah, maidservant, E546

Lewis, Thomas (dedicatee), P422

Leytonstone, H70

Lezo, Don Blas de: epistle from, S617; letter from, L126; letter to, L128

L—g—y, Mrs, L140

Lhuyd, Edward, R195

libel, B617, D530, L59: on Dr Delany, S877; on the Dublin dunces, L166

libertas triumphans, G153

Libertina, and Sylvia, D407, T532

libertine: fair, R14; libertine's choice, W101

liberty, B160, B505, G229, L169–72, S704, T186: asserted, M146; cause of, C77, E348; charms of, C82; fountain of, D70; hymn to, D70; loss of, L270; love of, R23; lover of, L167; and loyalty, C201; offering to, R206; and property, B530·4; regained, L174; temple of, K77

liberty-beggars, L134

library: Cottonian, S282; ladies', A95, F28, P520, S55; modern, N246; of Archibald Pitcairne, K42; of Trinity College Dublin, N330

Lichfield: trip to, T487; elections, H150, L175; races, G265, H150, L265; squabble, L175

Lichfield, George Henry Lee, earl of (dedicatee), R170, Y47

Lichfield and Coventry, Edward Chandler, bishop of (1717–30), *see* Chandler

'Lick-ladle, William', N182

life: art of, A321; bridge of, B441; choice of, W2; Christian, R332·5; conduct of, J15; country, W566; of faith, W318; happy, H43; night-thoughts on, Y24; view of, F205; virtuous, B122; *see also* human life

Liffy, river, L103, O97

light: extinguished, W235
of the world, hymn to, B252

Lightfoot, William (dedicatee), S241

lightning, A149

Lille, capture of (1708), G268, S133, T88

Lilliput, fop's observation on, B290

Lilliputian: ballad, N149; Kate, K51; ode, C45, T586; queen, K51; verse, W10; widow, L182

Lillo, George, prologue and epilogue to his *George Barnwell*, P1120

Limerick to Kilmallock, L183

Lincoln, Edmund Gibson, bishop of (1716–20), *see* Gibson

Lincoln, Henry Clinton, earl of: elegy on, F301; marriage of, S310

Lincolnshire, letter from gentleman in, L186

Lincoln's Inn, poem by a gentleman of, L104

Lincoln's Inn Fields, theatre in, P486

Lincoln's Inn squire, L184

Lindsay, Robert, poem to, P335

line of beauty, L188

lineage and succession, essay upon, E475

linen, Irish, C56·5, D522

linnet: and goldfinch, M82; lady and, L17

Lintot, Bernard, publisher, O165, T435

Lintoun: address, P148; Lintoun's lamentation, L189

lion: and fox, F9, L190; wolf and fox, R216; British, T329; sick, and ass, T374; lion's proclamation, L191

Lister, Martin: elegy on, S324; letters to, K57

Lister, Matthew (dedicatee), W231

litany, L167: freeman's, F241; for lent, L193, L194; new, C264, N150–3; for the present year, H250

'Little Beau' (=Patrick Walsh), I2, L195–7, S53, S463

Little John's answer, L198

little junto, the, L199

Little Merlin's cave, W168

Little Preston, L200

'Little Whig', I71

Littleton, Sir Edmund, marriage of, S313

Liverpool, L179: trip to, L104

liveryman's answer, L202

Livingstone, George, epitaph on, D59

Lloyd, Henry (dedicatee), W226

Lloyd, William, bishop of Worcester, satire on, W561

L——n, J., letter to, L129

lobby, step to, S748

lobster, lady in the, V108

lock, the: rape of, P941; princess's, P1063

Lock, John, of Athyoe, elegy on, O256

Locke, John, poem 'writ at the request of', R180

lockman, *see* hangmen

locusts (=lawyers), L229–30

Lodge, Mother, J43

Loggan, Thomas, painter, A83, K36

loggerheads, battle of, M228

logico-astrologico-physico-mathematician, L232

Lombe, Sir Thomas, B382

London, G197, J76: art of walking the streets of, G81; blind man's case at, G158; and Bristol compared, S100; in a hubbub, G225; in mourning, N133; new year's gift for, C55; and Paris, dialogue between, D267; poems addressed to, D553, S240; Terpsichore at, T118·5

London (*cont.*)
address, L233, L235, N96
Aesop, P433
belles, B530·5
clergy, L233, L236
coal merchants, B105
common council, T428: election for (1739), S473
cuckolds, F126
elections: (1701), E29; (1702), R163; (1705), C554;
 (1722), N62; (1734), L262; (1741), H36
executions, C440, E168, E572, L18, N286, O174,
 P571, S604
fires, A121, N36
guilds, C272, E280
ladies, L238
lieutenancy (dedicatee), S241–2
liveryman's answer, L202
lord mayor, M154; *see* Calvert, Sir William; Child,
 Sir Francis; Garrard, Sir Samuel; Heathcote, Sir
 Gilbert; Parsons, Sir Humphrey; Williams, Sir John
magistrates, C55, L235
merchants, L239
mob, T491
prisons, *see* Fleet; Marshalsea; Mint; Newgate;
 Poultry compter; Queen's bench; Tower of London;
 Wood Street compter
sheriffs' feast, O57
Spa, M153
tale, L241
theatres, *see* Dorset Garden; Drury Lane; Goodman's
 Fields; Haymarket; Lincoln's Inn Fields
trained bands, B183, B525–7, H363, W49
London, John Robinson, bishop of (1714–23), *see* Robin-
son
London, Edmund Gibson, bishop of (1723–48), *see*
Gibson
London Journal, M524
London Post, P434
Londonderry, city of, N63
long vacation, L243: prologue, L246
Long, Andrew, recovery of, J98
Longford, Christopher Fleming, viscount, *see* Slain
Longford's Glyn, D199
longitude: discovered, L251; found out, L253; latitude
 for, S720
Longleat, B41
Lonsdale, Henry Lowther, 3rd viscount (addressee),
 B504, N345
Lonsdale, Richard Lowther, viscount (addressee), T299
looking glass, the, L254: drunkard's, E293; love's, C90;
 projector's, P1119; for smokers, S661; tories', G95;
 see also mirror
lord: epistle to a noble, A168; upon knight, L261; letter
 to a noble, T328; and no lord, L255; new, N154·5;
 lord's lamentation, L265
Lord's: day, L263; prayer, S181; supper, F39
lord chancellor, complaint to, T116
'Lord Crafty', C202
lord mayor, *see* Dublin; London
lords, house of, sentence on Sacheverell, O219
Lorenzo, Altamont to, E363
Lorrain, Paul, H458
loss of liberty, L270

losses, how to gain by, D318
Lothario: (=Spencer Cowper) and Sarah the quaker,
 B146, L273; (=Frederick prince of Wales) and
 Calista, F199
lottery, the, L274
Loudoun, Hugh Campbell, earl (dedicatee), N44
Louis, 'a French marquis', G240
Louis XIV (usually as 'the French king'), satires on:
 1701, N180
 1702, F262, L162
 1704, F25, T105
 1705, F253
 1706, B447, C233, F256
 1708, E313, I51
 1709, D498, D541, E123 (false elegy), N251, R318
 1710, C550
 1711, F255
 1712, E327
 1713, B514·5, B548, E307
 1715, epitaph, E439
Louis XV: and Pope Benedict (1744), F272; and the
 Young Pretender (1745/46), L275, S599; satire
 against (1747), G184
Louisa Maria, princess, P329, P385, P388
louse-trap, the, L276
Lovat, Simon Fraser, baron, S178: ghost of, L277; *see
 also* Scotch plot
love, A218, A320, D410, P1088: after enjoyment, L279;
 alone, D217; and courtship, L280; and divinity,
 L281; and folly, S198; and honour, D194; and resentment, M485; atones for little crimes, B51;
 drowned in the South Sea, L282; fatal, F68; for
 love, L283; friendship and, F270; given over, G230;
 in a quandary, F116; of fame, Y169; of liberty, R23;
 patriotic, J48; triumphant over reason, P732; unlicensed, M473; vanquished, Y74; without affectation, L287; *see also* amorous
 art of, A322, A323, H307, K60; court of, C69; cure for,
 U34; economy of, A303; effigies of, C436; elegy
 on, O177·5; essay on, P50; folly of, A182; land of,
 B162; odes on, F200; picture of, H229; power of,
 H167, W309; praise of, R263; progress of, L333;
 remedy of, U33; satire against, M109, S43; temple of
 C215, L209; test of, A212; triumph of, H14
 affairs, C11; elegies, H22; epistles, C496, S553;
 letter, E407, L93, P191; letters, L284; poems, P736;
 tale, C420; verses, L286
love's: invention, L288; looking-glass, C90; mystery,
 B130; preservative, M6
Love for love, prologue and epilogue to, C377
'Loveall, Sir William', C172
Lovel, Sir Salathiel, charge to Devon grand jury, M289
Lovel, Thomas Coke, baron (subsequently earl of
 Leicester), P1160
'Love-merit, Richard', D423
lover, D424: letter from, I13; letter to lover in town, S201
 despairing, A39; forsaken, G113; impotent, I14; of
 liberty, L167; of nature, W243; reverend, aged, and
 greatly mortified, C530; vanquished, A218
lover's web, D522
lovers: high church, H195; of their country, B568, F40;
 platonic, T360; sanguine, H13; unfortunate, U5;
 warning to, W241

loving husband, L283

low church: funeral of, F297, F307; and high church, C450, C490, H188, N4, S2, T29, W76 man, D265; ode, H315

Low, Mary, suicide of, F68

Lowrie, the traitor, R3

Lowther, Anthony, H157·5

Lowther, Sir Thomas, marriage of, S322

loyal: address, L296; Briton, L297; Britons, R310; churchman, L299, W391; health, B279, N155, T99; Irishman, L300; Margaret, E184; member of parliament, N156; poem, K85; resolution, L301; trimmer, L302; wish, L303; worthies, L304

Loyal Society in Bristol, O7, S7·5

loyalist, the, L305, L307

loyalists, the, S7·5; society of, N215

loyalty, S7: high church, A238; liberty and, C201; soldier's, S544; displayed, L308; honoured, L309; restored, E577; revived, L310; triumphant, C539, L311

Lucan, essay in the spirit of, M146

Lucas, Charles, election campaign of 1748/49, C133, C149, C269, C549, H326, N56, N72, R249, S137, S150, T528

Lucas's coffee house, Dublin, L136

Lucifer: Horace to, P372; Lucifer's defeat, L313; grand emissaries found out, L314

lucky mistake, L317

Lucretius: essay on, P699; his description of the plague of Athens, S663

Lucy: a pastoral, L320; and Colin, T290

Lueders, Herr, marriage of, W276

lullaby, for the dean of St Patrick's, L321

lunacy, the, L326

lunatic, the, F172, L327

lunatic paraphrase, F172

lust, priestcraft and, P1054

lustful priest, P719

Luther, Martin, dialogue with Jack Calvin, D261

Luxborough, Lady (dedicatee), P103

luxury of the age, satires on, C42, G250

Luzara, H71

Lyddal's, Mr, theatre in Dame Street Dublin, S1

Lyddel, Richard, C10, E363

Lympany, Robert, gift of organ by, M566

'Lyn, Frank', R136

lyre, the, B139

lyric, naval, Y82

lyric: ode, W47; poem, L212; rhapsody, D423

Lyttelton, George (subsequently baron Lyttelton), M433, S602: addressee, S394

Lyttelton, Lucy, lady, elegy on, L337

Lytton, Lytton, elegy on, S296

M., J., (addressee), C338

Maben, Alexander, elegy on, B276

Macareus, and Aeolus, B347

Macario (= George MacCartney), N313

M'Aulay, Watty, elegy on, T583

MacCartney, George, E440: death of, N313; hue and cry after, H353

McCarthy, Dennis, priest of Cork, elegy on, E181

Macclesfield, Anne, countess of (subsequently Mrs Brett) (addressee), N10, S90

Macclesfield, Thomas Parker, baron (subsequently earl): addressee, E509, H136; conviction of, E369, T30

MacDermot, Irish fortune-hunter, B425

McDermot, Murtagh, satire to, S45

McDermot, Thaddeus, priest, elegy on, E182

Macdonald, Donald, ghost of, M2

MacDrummond, banker, epistle to, E401

Macheath, Captain (in Beggar's Opera), P716

Machiavelli, imitation of his Belphegor, D244

Machiavellian, the, L190

machine, the, M6

Mackalaster, Alastair, account of, A12

Mackenzie, George, Latin poem to, H148

Mackie, Musgrave, murderer, E231

Mackintosh, William, his farewell to the highlands, B448

Macklin, Charles, C236, I40

Mackworth, Sir Humphry: dedicatee, Y3; candidate at Oxford election (1705), D393, U17

MacLauchlan, David, address to, R32

Maclean, James, highwayman, B198

M'Leod, Margaret, forger, A11, E183, L49, L125, M302: ghost of, A275

Maculla, James (addressee), P522

mad: dialogue, O54; dog, G58; folks, age of, A124; poem, B155, M13, T409, T510; all men mad, W43

madam, city, C207

Madden, Samuel, V54

Madder, John, executed for piracy, C31, C340

Maddox, Isaac, bishop of St Asaph's (dedicatee), R194

madman's hospital, M12

madness, M13: epidemical, E345; political, P711

Madrid, news from, W126

madrigal, Colin Clout's, C284

Maecenas, R297

Magdalen-grove, M14

magician, the, M15: Sid Hamet, S935

Magician, The, by John Rich, song in, A353

magistracy, burlesque upon, T156

magistrate, the, M18

magistrates: duty of, O245; mock, P165

magnanimity, M397

magpies, and jackdaws, fable of, T29

Mahanaim, or striving with a saviour, T256

maid: country, C207; curious, C547, J34; distressed, D337; wishing, W535

maid's: answer, B5; Christmas box, M22; vindication, M23

maiden's: choice, C449; dream, M21

maidenhead: elegy on, B440; fifteen plagues of, F135; loss of, P534; restored, L272; Richmond, R201

maidens, address to, L93

maids of honour, theft of their shifts, B128

Main, James, P315

Maine, victory on, see Dettingen,

Mainwaring, Arthur (father and son), M34

Maitland, Sir Charles, of Pittrichie, elegy on, H233

Maitland, John (addressee), P684

Malaga, battle of, B527·1, P443, W529

Malcolm, Alexander, writer on music (dedicatee), M319

malcontents, word of advice to, W562

Maldon ballad, M38

malice defeated, M40

malice's masterpiece, M41

Mall, the, M42: satire on, S58

Mallamour, Amelia to, A178

Mallet, David, imitations of his *William and Margaret*, G96, L277, P761, S132, T290, W503

Malpas, George Cholmondeley, viscount (subsequently 3rd earl Cholmondeley) (dedicatee), S88

Malpas, Mary, viscountess, elegy on, H404

Malplaquet, victory at, D541, S529, T366

malt tax, dispute over in Scotland (1725), G292, L38, P154, P160, P168

malt-worms, vade mecum for, V2, V5

malting, art of, D402

man: complete, H413; essay on, P822; fall and restoration of, F42; nature of, B263; passions of, R331; satire against, A183, O178; tale of a man and his mare, M218; woman's, W547; wonderful, W554; What is man?, V91

    of honour, C399, D391, M63, M68, M415; of taste, B396, C382

man's: chief happiness, P199; uncertainty of man's life, U3

man-midwife (James Douglas), L26, M69

Man, Jenny, E365

'Man, Thomas', editor, J95

manager, wicked, of a theatre, I40

managers, theatric, H48

Manchester, St Anne's church, sermon at, B612

Manchester Grammar Schoool, Q1

Manchester, Isabella, duchess of: addressee, C542; remarriage of, W486, W488

mandragora, M78

mankind: ode to, N343; redemption of, C1·5; satire on, S52; vain pursuits of, J42

Manley, Mr, libelled, L104

Manlius: Patricius to, P122; (=Young Pretender), M81

Manlius Capitolinus, M., F108

manly virtue, birth of, B221

Manly, Captain, commander of the Southwell frigate, S785

manners, W417: of the age, N256; deciphered, M189; good manners for schools, D569

Mansfield, William Murray, earl of, *see* Murray

mantua-makers, M92

manuscripts, inventory of stolen, I53

Mar, John Erskine, earl of: dedicatee, E474; in Jacobite rebellion, C216, C339, D260

Marcellus, dialogue with Louis, G240

Marchmont, Alexander Campbell, 2nd earl of, death of, O68

Marchmont, Hugh Hume-Campbell, 3rd earl of (addressee), O68

Marchmont, Patrick Hume, 1st earl of (addressee), M421

mare, tale of a man and his, M218

Margaret, William and, M59

Margaret, loyal, elegy on, E184

Margaret, saint, queen of Scotland (d. 1093), P386

Margaretta, S54, S385

Margarita, Mrs, singer, M157

Maria, M475·5: Rupert to, M509

Marischall, William Keith, earl (dedicatee), P384

Marjorie, and Gibbie, wedding of, W264

market, the chevalier's, C143

Market Hill (Sir Arthur Acheson's house), S868, S869

Marlborough, Charles Spencer, duke of: addressee, C412, H208, H214, S83; installation as K.G., K48

Marlborough, Henrietta, 2nd duchess of (formerly Godolphin), S425: dedicatee, G45, M56, R240; love for William Congreve, M56, P261

Marlborough, John Churchill, duke of:

In general, only those poems which specifically refer to Marlborough are included here; others relating to him will be found under his battles

    1702, dedicatee, D568

    1703, campaign of 1702, B551, H64; departure for Holland, S457; death of Marquis of Blandford, E32

    1704, battle of Schellenberg, F115, O168; battle of Blenheim, A27, A84, C217, C361, D218, D555, D565, E356, F115, F252, J71, O168, R306, S488, S737, V90, W529 (*see also* Blenheim); grant of Woodstock park, B555, H271; return to England, S488; addressee, A27, C361, D555, S488, V90

    1704/–, addressee, B480

    1705, success of 1704, F152, G131, H386, W332; return to England, A157, T509; welcome in London (6 Jan 1705), D95, H247, M533; success in Brabant, C336, O168·2, P1101, T123; praise of, D84; Jacobite satire against, D564; addressee, A157, D95, G131; dedication copy to, B250

    1706, victory at Ramillies, B238, B530·7, C15, J110, L149, P65, T338, W3; other eulogies, A365·5, C139, C334, F256, J101, L146, L158, M105, O46, P287, T508; odes to music performed in honour of (Dec) D549, N162; addressee, C334, J101, P65, T338, W3

    1707, return to England, S587; departure for Holland, H49; character of, S360; praise of, E420, E478, H74, W576; addressee, B498, T336

    1708, victory at Oudenarde, G93, G153, H45, O109, W518; welcome to, A368; poems on Elizabeth and Essex, implying Anne should dismiss him, N88, P270; referred to, A176, D275; addressee, A368, W518

    1709, previous successes, A158, B254, C187, L142, S133; arrival, W288; Malplaquet, T366; Tournai, G180; welcome to England, D501; praise of, B605, P1115, S137·5; attack on, B125; addressee, C187, P1115, T366

    1710, successes of 1709, E309; satires against, B30, B171, W38

    1711, capture of Bouchain, T364; welcome home, H122; praise of, W527; satires against, N332, S770, T22; addressee, T364

    1712, dismissal, E327, F8, G101, I12, M106, S131, S546, T11, T337, T540, W400; defence of, D338, D500, E578, F10, P42, S425, V97; satires and fables against, A335, C56, C393, D2, D269, E354, F5, F9, F13, F108, G243, L42, N243, P1003, Q12, R173, S847, T316, T521, U7; departure for Germany, S373, T485, V77; addressee, S373, T337

    1714, return to England, A74, D499, N154·5, O202, W280; defence of, V122; satires against, N228, P1057, W155; addressee, S371, W280

    1715, defence of, M191; satires against, F221, N192, S627; addressee, S376

    1716, addressee, C188

Marlborough, John (*cont.*)

1717, character of, B477; view of his battles, A215

1722, elegies and funeral poems on, A187, C54(1723), C416, D36(1725), E36, E185, E405, F302, G45, H86, I22, J16, L318, M84(1733), N279, P555, S331, S379, S545, S547, W292, W294

Marlborough, Sarah, duchess of:

1704, dedicatee, C217, J71, P662

1706, dedicatee, N13

1710, dismissal from court; C470, S36, satires on, B30, B171

1711, satires against, T22, T148; defence of, H122

1713, attack on, E375

1742, memoirs, O129, S37

1744, addressee, C357, V52

1746, possible verses upon, P984

Marlborough bowling-green, Dublin, G63

'Marral, Sir Robert' (= Walpole), P1119

'Marrall, Sir Martin', M441

marriage, M109, S422: à-la-mode, M110; comforts of, A253; of the devil, P68; disappointed, D320; essay on, F185, P50; fatality of forced, F71; happy, H44; mock, M352; remarks upon, W551; revengeful, H146 unhappy, D467; of Venus, M112

poems concerning, A76, A90, B3, B5, B291, B609, C91, C172, D410, D562, D563, G219, H420, J12, L9, L94, O237, P479, R119, T148, T166, W267, W268; *see also* bride; bridegroom; husband; matrimony; nuptials; wedding; wife

poems occasioned by specific marriages, A216, B342, B348, C392, D20, D305, D320, D473, D567, E399, E504, E509, E555, G326, L95, L222, M111, M122, M200, M308, M352, O47, O49, O73, O79, O80, O208, P152, P252, P579, P620, P626, P632, R66, R70, S299–322, T397, U11, V30, W252, W264–6, W276, W453; *see also* epithalamium

bed, R285; dialogues, W113; mouse trap, R9

married man, U4

Mars: and Jupiter, C395; and Plutus, D549

Marseilles, plague of, G114, P414·5

marshal's humble offering, H5

Marshall, Mr, victorious in Munster election, M560

Marshall, J., author of poem, C134

Marshall, Sir John (dedicatee), W231

Marshalsea prison, B514: description of, H133

Marsyas, and Apollo, C396

martial: discipline, W49; law, N84; virtue, C418

martin, and the oyster, M117

Martin, Irish blood, D420

Martinique ships, victory over, N119

martyr, royal (Charles I), R313–6, S718

martyrdom, of Charles I, E602, S5

martyrs, Edinburgh, F299

marvellous, rhapsody upon, R187·5

Mary, the blessed virgin, T312

Mary, the cook-maid, D77

Mary, Lady, L19, T390·5; *see also* Montagu, Lady Mary Wortley

Mary, princess, birth of (1723), E366, M103

Mary, queen, ghost of, A334

Mary, queen of Scots, M122

Mary of Modena, queen of James II (dedicatee), N348

Mary Louisa, queen of Spain, C315

Mary Magdalene, lamentations of, L40

Maryland, voyage to, C405

Masham, Abigail, intrigues with Harley, A3, F251, N90, N217

masks all, W563

masonry, L113; *see also* freemasons

masque, R66

masquerade, the, C95, F122, M131: Ovid in, B430; trip to the, T492; town mistress in, M133

masquerade: ball, B19, B20, W563; ballad, T541; plot (1716), G17, M132

masquerades, H169: ballad on, L288; downfall of, R208; *see also* ridotto

Massalina, M133

master of a vessel, character of, C122

masterpiece: the cardinal's, C498; Taffy's, T3

Masterton, Francis, apothecary, elegy on, E186

mastiff, the, W347

Mat's peace, M30

match, the, D8: beggar's, F156; drinking, W376; at football, C327; unequal, J51

matchless fair-one, D238

mathematician, L232

matrimonial scenes, J9

matrimony, G224, M138, S193: devil tired with, H135; fifteen comforts of, F128; miseries of, L290, P488; modern, M376; pleasures of, C392; *see also* marriage

Matt, of the Mint, E372

Matthews, George, printer, I71

Matthews, Thomas, admiral, A61, A160

Mauge, John, murderer, B201

Maurice, Peter, I1

mausoleum, the, T140

Mawson, Matthias, bishop of Ely, R7

Max Emanuel, elector of Bavaria, epistle from, C233

maxims: for the conduct of life, J15; of Louis XIV, F262

May, hymn to, T171

May 28, birthday of George I, P150, W6; *see also* George I

May 29: restoration of Charles II, F307, P686; birthday of Old Pretender, B26, E362, N233, P361, P378; *see also* James Francis Edward Stuart

May day, M153, S592.

May-fair, journey to, T490

mayor, and the mob, M154

maypole: at Ewelme, H256; new year's gift of, M155

Mazarin's ghost, F262

Mead, Richard, D357, S487, T94: dedicatee, R264

'Meagre, Paul', F287

means of grace, W319

Meath, Chaworth Brabazon, earl of, P1128

Meath, Dorothea, countess of, elegy on, S831

Meath, Edward Brabazon, earl of, elegy on, E187

medal: old, O116; (of the Old Pretender) welcome to, W278

medallist, the, M156

meddlers, the, M160

medical subjects, poems on, A13, A108, A158·5, A258–64, A296, A303, B110, B335, B538, B586, C4, C480, D303, D328, D331, D332, D356–8, D387, E26, E385, E390, E398, E568, F112, F134, F165, F213, G21, G300, H183, H475, I37, I39, L26, M69, M78, M172, M559, N188, O14, O142, O238, P159, P267,

medical subjects (*cont.*)
    P541, P566, P703, P1139, P1157, Q1, Q2, R152, R280, S18, S453, S487, T39, T72, T94, T352, W42; *see also* doctor
medicine, for scolding ladies, A158·5
meditation, the, M157: in the fields, M158; on a turd, O180
meditations: on the day of judgement, G138; on the fall of Bob and Harry, M159; on the four last things, T37; upon the love of Christ, C222; morning and evening, C220; pleasant, L178; seven, P758; on the soul, D416
medley: new, N157; on the times, M161; Tom of Bedlam's, T411
Medlicott, Sir Thomas, colonel of trained bands, H5
meeting house, elegy on, L260; *see also* conventicles
Meggy, Jenny and, R59
melancholy, pleasures of, W246
melancholy sonnets, M162
Melazzo, H83
Melcombe, George Bubb Dodington, baron, *see* Dodington
Meldrum, George, elegies on, E188, S149, T384
Melfield, spa well near, N323
Melibiæ, Aegon and, A164
Meliora's tears for Thyrsis, C330
Melissa, C172: (actress), P700
Melpomene, M316
member, city lady's choice of standing, C206
member of parliament: Edinburgh's instructions to her, E24; letter from a, L122
members to their sovereign, J45
members of parliament: ladies choice, L12; loyal, N156
Memmius, Caius, speech of to people of Rome, S630
memorial: Britannia's, S687; Church of England's, C176, P436; Duchess of Cleveland's, D464; Dutch, P131; muse's, T67-8
men: characters of, O88; knowledge and characters of, P920; poetic essays on, T165; modern men of taste, C382
Menalcas, M171: and Palaemon, B411
Mercer's Hall, treat at, K16
merchant: à-la-mode, M174, M183; British merchant's glory, D544
merchant's: advocate, M184; clerk, E360; wife, M104
merchants: Bristol, L240·5; London, L239
merchants' complaint, against the tailors, M185
mercury hawkers, M186
merit, M190: and gratitude, M191; injured, M86
merits of piracy, M192
Merlin, B409, N305: dialogue with Sir Walter Raleigh, O101; prophecies of, P1137, S849, Y14
Merlin's Cave, Y14; little Merlin's Cave, W168
Merrideth, Mathias, elegy on, E189
merry: campaign, M199; dialogue, M200; letter, M201; poem, W155; tale, G134, L71, L317, N323, P1063, W364
Merry Andrew, M198
Merry, John, elegy on, E190
Merton walks, D446
mess for the devil, M204
Messalina, M133
messenger, defeated, M205

Messiah, B540, M194, O235
metamorphosis, A164, M224, P1019, S504, T109, T499: of the town, T158; *see also* transformation
metaphysical essay, S184
meteor, Whiston's account of, L150
Methodism, progress of in Bristol, P1110
Methodist reproved, S469
Methodist poem, A169
Methodists, satires on, M225-6
metres: Greek and Latin in British poetry, I49; Horace's imitated, M24, P526
metrical index to the Bible, C162
'Mezentius' (= Charles Carthy) on the rack, D523
'Mezereon', the High German doctor, character of, H293
mice, W384: Earl Robert's, P1073; Welshmen and, H279 (and translations)
Michael, the British (= Marlborough), B605
Michaelmas term, M228
Micklethwaite, Joseph, viscount, duel of, M199
microscope, poems on, B232, D60
Midas: fable of, S847; tale of, T414
midden-fight, E476
Middle Temple, author from, F85
Middlesex: election (1705), N320; grand jury, B304; patriots, M229; trained bands, H5
Middlesex, Charles Sackville, earl of (subsequently duke of Dorset), ode to, L225
Middlesex, Grace, countess of, ode to, L225
Middleton, Sir Hugh, G9
Midleton, Alan Brodrick, viscount, *see* Brodrick
midnight modern conversation, B48
midwife, *see* man-midwife
military affairs, poems on (excluding campaigns), B153, E318, E564, H310, H474, M349, N84, N115, N310, P1131, R24, R311, S627, T396, W481
military prophet, the, M231
milkmaid, K95, S592
miller: and his dog, D269; of Essex, M232; ghost and, G134; of Trumpington, M233
Miller, James, satires on, B407, N271
millers, of Arlington, R231
milliner, poem by, A245
Millington, Mrs (dedicatee), D342
Millington, Edward, auctioneer, elegy on, B512
Mills, John, C391
Mills, John, actor, prologues spoken by, O224, P1022
Milton, John: Bentley's edition of, M51; controversy between Douglas and Lauder concerning, P28; poems falsely attributed to, K68, P253; prologue to his *Comus*, J83; hij sublimity asserted, M267
    poems in imitation of, A167, B91, B176, B392, E528, F104, J101, K12, L174, L204, L313, M124, M551, N254, P65, P67, P137, P237, P246, P264, T168, V122
Miltonic: style, rhapsody in, C130; verse, poems in, A133, B305, B382, D405, F145, F237, M394, O197; *see also* blank verse
Miltonics, poem in, E306
Mincing Lane, trip to, A216
mind: woman's, furniture of, S857; well fortified against disappointment, H41
Mindana, history of, T93
Mine-adventurers, Company of, N263, Y3

Minerva: Henry and, B424·5; to Phoebus, M268; Minerva's remonstrance, M269
mines, late of Sir Carbery Price, Y3
ministers' address to King George, H391
ministry, ballad on (1743), B458
mint, proposals for Irish, P522
Mint prison, J69; Matt of the, E372
Mira: consolation to, C384; ode to, K71
miracle, Northumberland, N323
miracles, high-church, H196
miraculous sheep's eye, W408
mirror: of man's misery, C279; schemer's, G178; statesman's, S733; *see also* looking glass
mirth in ridicule, M272
Mirza, Ariel and, A291
miscellaneous poem, M273
miscreants, club of, O75
miser, the, M270: last speech of, R64; turned courtier, C548·5
miser's feast, O100
miseries: of England, M278; mountain of, M540
mishap, the, M279
miss: and the butterfly, H19; in her teens, N208
Mississippi Company, R127
mist (= Mist's *Weekly Journal*?), M286
Mist, Nathaniel, in the pillory (1721), D122, P284
mistake: general, R55; grand, G245; lucky, L317
mistress: in the country, letter to, E407; favourite, letter to, M201; town, M133; *see also* deserted mistress
Mitchel, David, marriage of, S303
Mitchel, William, 'Tinklarian doctor', wives of, E148, W266
Mitchell, Joseph: ode to Alan Ramsay, R107; satire on, F54
mite, widow's, P758
mitre, the, M347: in dispute, K100
mitre'd cabal, E479
M——k, late master to a Dublin corporation, H355
M——k——n, Mr, panegyric on, E367
mob: contra mob, M214; hymn to, D114; mayor and, M154; London, T491; town, C450
mock: ballad, G204; campaign, M349; epithalamium, M351; magistrates, P165; marriage, M352; masonry, M355; ministry, P180; moralist, F186; mourners, D132; patron, M356; poem, C306, S517, T3; senator, M357
mock-heroic poem, B71, C306, C473, H275, N300, O282, O286, S517, T268; *see also* burlesque; heroic poem; heroi-comic poem
mocking, C47
model, the, M358
moderate: cabal, M230; man, C449, M359
man's: advice, M360; confession, M361
moderation: displayed, M362, S437, S442; elegy on, E191; flaming isle of, R128; truth and, T537
modern: courtier, W46·2; courtiers, M440; critics, M477; Englishman, M365; fanatics, M370; fashions, M372; fine gentleman, J63; fine lady, D407, M373; gentleman, M358; incendiaries, O209; inconsistencies, H196; inscription, A365·5; languages, M149; lechers, I14; matrimony, M376; patriot, P705; patriotism, M377; patriots, M379; poet, M380, O183; poetry, M251; poets, M494; quality, M382; reasoners,

D385; turn-coats, M385; virtue, M386; whig dictator, M387; wit, M388, O83, P709
modest: defence, M389; enquiry, M390; petition, M392; praise, M393
modesty, satire against, H115
Mogg, Molly, G59, M561
Mohocks, the, M394; Mohocks' revel, M395
Mohun, Charles, baron: duel with James duke of Hamilton, D496, E440, E535, N313; ghost of, L259
Molesworth, Miss, J30
Molesworth, hon. Mrs Mary, marriage of, G3
Molesworth, Robert, viscount: dedicatee, B536; elegy on, E192
Molineux, Peter, writing master, elegy on, P598
Molly Mogg: imitation of, E549; *see also* Mogg, Molly
Momus mistaken, A282
monarchy: and church, M396, T446; rightful, R211, R212; triumph of, T500
Moncrief, John, editor of Wardlaw's *Hardyknute*, W215
money, P67: corrupt use of, W50; hue and cry after, E304; hunting after, H409; hymn to, H453; Old Mother Money, O117
Monimia to Philocles, H157·5
monk, and the merchant's wife, M104
monkey: (Jaquo), E162; bitter nut for, W68; fox and, G137·5; horse and, H326; and the hounds, M398
monkies, court, C468
Monmouth Street, M400
monody, C283, L337, M124, M401
monosyllable 'if', M402
Mons, battle near (1709), *see* Malplaquet
monster, the, M414: all-devouring, A163; female, F97; hairy, S51, W164; northern, N321
Montagu, Charles, earl of Halifax, *see* Halifax
Montagu, Christopher (dedicatee), N44
Montagu, John, 2nd duke of: addressee, A215, C406, H332; character of, B477; elegy on, M158
Montagu, Mary, duchess of (dedicatee), H67·5
Montagu, Lady Mary, marriage to Lord Brudenell, L95, S25
Montagu, Lady Mary Wortley: addressee, M489, N38; ms. note by, E392; satires on, A86, F91, F162, P1135, S34, S177
Monteego, Count, A64
Montgomery, Colonel Alexander, elegy on, E193
months, emblematical representation of, P1113
Montrose, Christian, marchioness of: elegy on, E194; marriage, T397
Montrose, James Graham, 4th marquis of, marriage, T397
monument, the (= elegy), D224, M317
monumental poem, T64
Moody, Lieutenant, elegy on, P629
moon: emperor of, C103; hymn to, S190; *see also* full moon
Mooney, Captain, kidnapper, I61
Moore, family of, in Clonmel election (1725?), M560
Moore, Rev. Mr (dedicatee), W223
Moore, Arthur, economist, satire on, T414
Moore, John, bishop of Ely, satire on, C150
Moore, John, vendor of worm powder, D369, M423, P978
Moore, Robert, last speech of, L58
Moore, Samuel, penman (addressee), H101

Moore, Thomas, last speech of, L58
Moorfields, trip from, W117
Moors, invasion of, M560
moral: emblems, T405; poem, O84; precepts, D317; satires, N256; story, D552; writing, F205
moralist, female, F98
morality in vice, B426
morals, essays on, T165
Mordecai triumphant, O107
More, John, see Moore
'Morecrave, Priscilla', B485
Morell, Thomas, satire on, C543
Morforio, Pasquin and, D262
Morgan, Macnamara, commendatory verses by, P1000
Morgan, Richard, marriage of, S308
Morgan, Thomas, *Philosophical principles* of, B335
Morgan, Sir William: addressee, G297; satire on, S717
Morice, Mary, elegy on, W355
Morley, William, epistle to, E433
morning, the, M469: interview, R34; meditations, C220; star, H147·5
morning's salutation, B608
Morphy, Mr, performer on the Irish harp, S738
Morris, Edmund, marriage of, S319
mortality, state of, H343, T531
Mortimer, Earl (=Robert Harley), J99
Mortimer, Cromwell, E385
mother: godly lessons of, H405; unveiled, N10
Mother Hubbard's tale, M522
Mother Red-cap's prophecy, P1057
motion, the (for Walpole's dismissal), M525: patriot's, M526
Motly, Mrs, Dublin whore, elegy on, E195
motto, the, M538
mottoes, M539
Mount Alexander, M404, R226
Mount Caburn, H117
Mount Parnassus, applause of, U15
mountain of miseries, M540
Mountcashel, Edward Davys, viscount (dedicatee), S417
mountebank, infallible, I39
Mountfort, Susanna, epilogue spoken by, E351
Mountjoy, William Stewart, 3rd viscount, marriage of, P626
Mountney, Richard, revises poem, J94
Mountown, Mully of, K63
mourner, the, M541, R336
mourners, mock, D132
mournful: congress, M542; copy of verses, M543; muse, M544, M545; poem, B216, M546, W516; shepherds, P166; song, M547
mourning: court, M548, M549; curate, P66; muse, A39, W468; muses, S943; poet, B514; prophet, W125
mousetrap, the, H279 (and translations): marriage, R9; More, Welsh, W283
Mowdiwart, Mouldy, R64
Moyer, Sir Samuel, elegy on, S235
M——pp, quack, E390
muff, the, L268
mug, broken, H303, W447
mug-house, Mr Smith's, P1126, P1127
mug-house song, V6
Mullan, David, letter of, D78

Mullen, John, doctor, elegy on, A355
Mully, of Mountown (a cow), K63
mum, L114; see also beer
mumpers, city, L134
Mumpsimus III, king of the Gipsies, K47
mundus delirans, M556
Munster, ladies of, E542
Munster: attorneys, M559; combat, M560; Juggy, M561; wedding, M562
'murder', barbarous and bloody, of Mr Eyre, B63
Murphy, Paddy, porter of Trinity College Dublin, C482, D527
Murray, Elizabeth, murdered, P167
Murray, Lady Emilia (dedicatee), T256
Murray, Griselda, attempted rape on, V103
Murray, John, lord Bowhill, elegy on, E64
Murray, Sir John, secretary to Young Pretender, S178, T345
Murray, Richard, hangman, elegy on, N287
Murray, Samuel, of Glasgow, elegy on, E196
Murray, Thomas, painter (addressee), T350
Murray, William (subsequently 1st earl of Mansfield), M446, M457
Murray-Kynnynmound, Hugh, elegy on, P665
Murtagh and Laughlin, dialogue between, H400
Musaeus, M124
Muschet, Nicol, of Boghall, E136, P155, S607
muse: advice to, A97; an advocate, M86; in distress, M563; judgement of, H418; poet and, P692
British, T577; English, E338; female, D568; generous, G105; Hibernian, F72; mounful, M544, M545; mourning, A39, W468; sylvan, P119; weeping, L164; Windsor, T88
muse's: address, M564, T82; bower, T66; flight, M565; friend, T38; memorial, T67–8; paradise, P258
muses, P478: mourning, S943; rival, F275
farewell to, T412; magistrates against, L235; seat of, H128; solemnity of, S549; tears of, B367, H231
muses': address, R15, S285; congratulatory address, S274; essay, S282; humble address, T61
Musgrave, Sir Christopher, W376
music, M566, W10: charms of, P720, T399; in good time, M567; ode for, P904; power of, H12, M319, S613; praise of, H380, O34; progress of, in Ireland, P282; prologue for, P1124; taste of the town in, N335; see also harmony; opera; St Cecilia's day
meeting: Britton's, B482, S85; Nicolini's, S461
speech, at Cambridge, L247, T103
musicians, session of, S223
Musidora, M569
Musidorus, M570
Musselburgh: panegyric on, D219; butchers' wives of, L37
Mustapha, page to George I, mock elegy on, B468
musty snuff, S74
mutineers, T126
Myddleton, Sir Hugh, G9
Myrtillo, M573

N——, R——, esq, F72
Naas, vicar of, S450
naked truth, M38
Nales, Mrs (dedicatee), W227

SUBJECT INDEX

'Namby Pamby' (Ambrose Philips), C49: answer of, N1; Christmas box for, C170; his lamentation, N2

Namby Pambaick strain, poem in, P38; *see also* D554, O180, P209, P523, P678, S53, S385, S452, T344, Y108

Nan, Kick him, K35

Narcissa, Y36

narration, of the wonders of grace, D560

narrative, the, N3: of high and low, N4; impartial, I9; poetical, M7

poem, P23

Nassau, house of, H375

nastiness, poem in praise of, P539

nation run mad, N5

national: alarm, N6; covenant, T385 (*see also* covenanters); vices, F213

nativity (of Christ), B318, C302–3, C553, G168, H81·5, H292, H319, P630, W514, W569; *see also* Christmas; Jesus Christ

natural: history, N7; philosophers, N9

nature, F202, F203, H183, T165: displayed, C293; lover of, W243; of man, B263; in perfection, N10; nature will prevail, B50; *see also* human nature

naval affairs: poems on, A61, A101, A160, B40, B338,, B474, B527·1, C30, C122, C257, C491, E21, E331, E335, E340, E341, F263, G257, H119, K89, M7, M118, M120, M272, M349, M501, N81, N84, N119, N195, N196, N224, O36, O74, O90, P2, P443, P531, P546, P712, P1112, P1156, R225, S4, S8–16, S50, S78, S342, S472, S785, T55, T422, T507·5, U8, V33, V121, W523, W529, Y81, Y82, Y94; *see also* Cartagena; Vigo

panegyric, H350

navy, poem inscribed to officers of, P562

Neapolitan woman of quality, F71

neck or nothing, N14

Needham, Elizabeth: mock elegy on, M523; dialogue with Francis Charteris, D396

negotiators, the, N18

'Negro, Tom', chimney sweeper, C150

Nelson, Henry, mock elegy on, A343

Nelson, Robert, elegy on, P538

Neoptolemus, N34

Neptune: to Lord Carteret, N35; hymn to P443; court of V122; Neptune's triumph, K54

Nereides, D294

Nereo, P448

Nereus, prophecy of, T283

Nero: state of Rome under, S725; the second, N36

'Nessuno, Viscount' (addressee), D425

net for the devil, N37

Netterville, John, viscount, elegy on, E197

nettle: contention for, S225; tale of a, T13

neuropathia, F165

neuter, the, N38

Nevil, Mrs, epistle to, E407

New England, governor of, W256

New light, sect, C532, S790

New River, G9

New Testament, history of, W325

New Tunbridge Wells, S59, W200

new year: odes for, C195, C198, C199, E497, E499, F110, R298, S514, T69, T84, T118; songs for, T78–80

new year's gift, C55, C116, D556, G164, H417, N242–5, S145, S387, T510: Dr Anthony's, A260; hawkers', H110; maypole's, M155

Newburgh, Frances, countess of, K71, K79: elegy on, E198

Newbury, Shuff of, B32

Newcastle: election (1741), C148, I69, N309; ladies of, B180

salmon, T18

Newcastle, Henrietta, duchess of (addressee), H117

Newcastle, John Holles, duke of (addressee), S287

Newcastle, Margaret, duchess of, benefactress, S647

Newcastle, Thomas Pelham-Holles, duke of:
1714, birthday, B29; addressee, H68, O164, S248, T395
1715, addressee, G18
1716, created duke of Newcastle, W296
1717, marriage, E504; addressee, R241
1718, S621; dedicatee, N42
1732, addressee, N262
1738, addressee, M89
1739, dedicatee, C24
1745, satire on, F137
1746, dedicatee, Y54
1749, satire on, T31
1750, N75

Newgate (London), H458: collegians of, N287; description of, G179; ordinary of, J116; trip to, I71; Newgate's garland, N288
(Bristol), satire written in, S100
(Dublin), humours of, W470
divine, N248; eclogue, N286

Newman, John, elegy on, G322

Newmarket, K53, N290: George II's journey to, B557; welcome from, B530·1

news, N291: from Bathgate, N293; from Borrowstounness, N294; from court, P903; from hell, C103; from Madrid, W126; from Oporto, B498·5; from Parnassus, D202; from St James's, G272, S772·5; from Worcester, N295

news-cryer, elegy on, E86

newspaper, unrecorded, H110

Newton, Sir Isaac, P398: elegies on, F80, R69, T200

Newtonian system, D234

Newtown-Butler, Theophilus Butler, baron, elegy on, E71

N——g, Countess of, S508

Nicander, Michael, notes of, R118

Nichols, Benjamin, sermon by, B612

Nicholson, Sir Francis, panegyric on, F222

Nicolini's music-meeting, S461

Nicolson, Sir James, satire on, U30

Nicolson, William, bishop of Derry: *Irish historical library* of, H173; and Swift, O230

night, R18: night's ramble, N300

night-piece, F225; night-thoughts, Y24

night-walker, female, L29

nightingale, the, N301

Nisbet, William, elegies on, E199, P172

Noailles, Marshal, D39

Noailles, Louis Antoine de, cardinal, archbishop of Paris, L132

nobility, C411, W440

noble duellists, N313

Noble, John, elegy on, R326
nobleman: love-letters of, L284; Irish, death of, S557; *see also* young nobleman
'No Body', dedication to, F149
'Nobody, Mr': departure of, N2; (=Marcus Dowley), E200, N314
nocturnal, the, N315
Nod, plagues of, P469
noise: about nothing, G273, N317; about something, A248
nonconformists, essay to, P265
nonjuring clergy, lamentations of, D289
non-resistance: death of, E147; farewell to, F59
nooning, the, P8
Nore, mist cleared up at the, M286
Norfolk: dunces of, B95·5; Suffolk and, S782; in tears, F168
    ballad, N159, N160; congress, N318, Q3, S786; gamester, N319; garland, Y19
Norfolk, Henry Howard, duke of, elegy on, E201
Norris, Isaac, L121
Norris, Sir John, admiral (addressee), F224, P531
north, voyage to, I73
North Briton, happy, B342
North-country wedding, B506
North Sea fishery, R81
North, William, baron North: addressee, S274, S648, satire on, P515
Northampton, hospital at, P1107
Northampton mercury, D476
Northamptonshire: health, N320; sneakers, H125
northern: cuckold, W127; monster, N321; star, H225
Northesk, Anne, countess of (addressee), O73
Northumberland: miracle, N323; prophecy, D486
Northumberland, Catherine Fitzroy, duchess of, satire on, N326
Norwich, A119–20, I10, P192
    cavalcade, N334, Q2
nose, captivity of, C255
Nostradamus, prophecy of, N325
nothing: noise about, G273, N317; but truth, N328
Nottingham: politics, E431, I47; printing, W458; races, J75; trip to, T488
Nottingham, Daniel Finch, 2nd earl of: dedicatee, H68, W567; satires on, D235, N329, S844, S911
Nottingham, Daniel Finch, 3rd earl of (addressee), F231
Nottinghamshire ballad, N329
novel, P201: antediluvian, P1044
novels, poetical, M81, M275–6
November 4th (birthday of William III), G37, H366
November 5th, F182
nun: amorous, A217; Portuguese, L287
nunnery, protestant, in Dublin, P1141
nuns, P643: battle with, P645; character of, M496
nuptial dialogues, W129
nuptials, O80, R66: happy, H47; of the lamb, N348; *see also* marriage
nurse, wife and, W511
nursery maid, fifteen plagues of, F133
nut, bitter, W68
nutshell, *Iliad* in, W342
Nuttley, Richard, judge, elegy on, E202
N—v—l, Mistress, epistle to, E407
nymphs' prophecy, D292

oak, and the dunghill, B203, B499, D513
Oates, Titus, elegies on, E203, E204
oath of abjuration, B46
Oberon, King, declaration of, A71
observator, L137: Edinburgh's, E16; of the times, N195; trimming, W154; walking, W69
Observator, John Tutchin's paper, B513, C461, C554, E203, E262–4, E355, G42, H274, H359, O4, O5, P273, P446, T253
occasional: conformist, P272, S619, W97
    conformity, H124, K105, P112, S138; bill to prevent (1704), E58, E479, M32
    essay, C23; ode, M77; poem, E329, O6, O7, W5; satire, H106
ocean, Y94
Octavius, prince of Syra, T406
October, poem to fox-hunters, C185
October 30 (birthday of George II), P646; *see also* George II
October club, P425, T425
oculists, poems to, O14, O238, P541, P566, T352
odaic essay, B318
oddity, the, O15
ode (*so described in title; translations, as of Horace's odes, are not normally included*) A20, A137, A167, A172, A364, B86, B101, B143, B179, B185, B194, B224, B225, B231, B283, B358, B363, B364, B380, B455, B480, B589–91, C57, C62, C131, C139, C195, C198–9, C247, C294, C295, C341, C417, C418, C521, C534, C538, D302–3, D524, D549, E27, E494–9, E605, F40, F110, F119, F200, F234, G128, G254, G279, G290, G297, H12, H17, H19, H20·5, H34, H75, H243, H315, H320, H364, H374, H377, H380, H382, H386, H387, J48, J108, J109, K27, K71, L171, L216–20, L225, L315, M103, M129, M318, M319, M343, M375, M431, N13, N34, N162, N258–68, N275, N280, N306, N339–45, O17–76, O79, O80, O177·5, O251, P79, P124, P210, P244, P251, P280, P720, P904, P1017, P1044, P1081, R15, R68–70, R89, R107, R175, R298, S26, S32, S134, S362, S367, S368, S401, S411, S460, S491, S505, S514, S515, S551, S610, S616, S653, S756, S801, T84, T89, T103, T115, T172, T249, T291, T293, T415, T586, V22, V89, V91, V99, V101, W6, W21, W35, W245, W253, W294, W296, W297, W379, W451, W475, W484, W486–8, W492, W539, Y94
    see also anniversary ode; congratulatory ode; consolatory ode; divine ode; elegiac ode; funeral-pindaric ode; iambic ode; irregular ode; Lilliputian ode; lyric ode; occasional ode; odaic essay; philosophic ode; pindaric ode; religious ode; sacred ode; triumphant ode; votive ode
ode-maker, O77
Odell, Thomas, L235
Oedipus, prologue to, S412
offering to liberty, R206
officer: disbanded, T11; half-pay, E365; peace, A131; town, R1
Ogle, Sir Chaloner, D494, V33: addressee, S342
Ogle, George (dedicatee), S754, T131
Oglethorpe, James Edward, G128
O'Hara, Kean (dedicatee), P173
oikographia, W302

old: age, C301, D213, D321, D410, D412, I14, M109; cheese, K65; coachman, W494; fox (= Walpole), O111–13; hat (*sens. obsc.*), B610; maid's fortune, O114; maids, S75; man's legacy, O115; man's wish, C142, P993; medal, O116; pack, O118; shoe, S177; tack, O124; wife's tale, O129; wives' tales, O130; woman, D211, F1, O131–3; woman's tale, O134

Old Bailey, civil-wars of, P594

Old England: roast beef of, F198; triumph of, O109

Old Mother Money's farewell, O117

Old Nick, death of, D247

Old Pretender, *see* James Francis Edward Stuart

'Old Shepherd' (dedicatee), R88

Old Testament: history of, W328; questions on, G166

Old Tom the toper's advice, O126

old-fashioned song, O110

Oldfield, Anne: epilogue spoken by, E348; elegies on, L201, M34, P104, P666

olive, the, B364: horse and, P77; laurel and, S773

'Oliverus secundus' (= Marlborough), P1003

olympics, British, B527·8

omega, O173

one thousand seven hundred: and thirty eight, D286, N272, P932

    and thirty nine, D286, O233, S354

    and forty four, D326

    and forty five, O231, W497

Onslow, Arthur (addressee), R250, Y25

Onslow, Thomas, baron, M352

opera, O182: Handel's, E402; Italian, N335, O251; ladies', L15; *see also* castrati

opera-epilogue, N163–4

opera theatre, B19; *see also* Haymarket

Ophelia (= Anne Oldfield), M34

Oporto, great news from, B498·5

optics, the, O238

oracle, the, N268

oracles for war, O239

Orange, Anne, princess of, *see* Anne, princess royal

Orange, William IV, prince of, *see* William IV

oration, heroi-comic, T21

orators, satire on, D42

order, O240: in government, O241

Orford, ship, S12

Orford, Edward Russell, earl of, S291: dedicatee, P1156; elegy on, S30

Orford, Maria, countess of, *see* Skerret, Maria

Orford, Robert Walpole, earl of, *see* Walpole

organ: benefaction of, M566; Handel playing, P1017

original: and conduct of the Young Pretender, O243; of apparel, O244; of government, O245

Orkney, George Hamilton, earl of, elegy on, E205

Orleans, Duke of, F278: death of, P518

Ormiston, Harry, hangman in Edinburgh, S605: elegy on, E206

Ormonde, James Butler, duke of
    victory at Vigo (1702), A362, B551, O248, P622, S458, V96
    lord lieutenant of Ireland (1703), A362, C352
    return to England (1704), O248
    lord lieutenant of Ireland (1711), L309, R323, T339, T446

    appointed commander in chief (1712), C344, C351, E354, Q12
    impeachment and flight of (1715), B582, F221, N192, N234, N235, O247, P567, P757, S458, S591, T426
    Jacobite expedition (1719), N213
    elegy (false alarm, 1730), E207
    satiric reference to (as Jemmy Butler, 1744), B604

Orpheus: fragments of, H382; and Hecate, O251; redivivus, S738

Orrery, Charles Boyle, 4th earl of, P515: marriage, S650

Orrery, Henrietta, countess of, elegies on, P691

Orrery, John Boyle, 5th earl of (addressee), C428, D11, D77, D520, P691, P1181, T139

'Orthodox, Parson', letter from, B299

'Osborne, Francis' (= James Pitt), M524, T474

osiers, the, B173

Oswald, James, music by, S535

Otway, Thomas, *The orphan*, prologues and epilogues to, M346, P1084, P1122

Oudenarde, battle of, A369, B98, B577, C82, E8, G93, G153, H45, O109, P608, S133, T125, W305, W518

overthrow at court, G275

overture, called negative, H205

Ovid: answer to an epistle of, B347; burlesques of, B430, R8; imitations of, C496, H157·5, O97, S34, V27

Ovidian style, poems in, D322, S35

Ovington, John, his *Essay on tea* burlesqued, W11

Owen, Josiah, satire on, B618

owl: tale of, T24; parrot and, P80; raven and, R134

ox: laurel and, L72; roasted, O264

Oxenard, an Irish priest-catcher, H361, O265, O266

Oxenden, Lady, elegy on, R110

Oxenden, Sir George (addressee), D229

Oxford, T299: the seat of the muses, H128; miscellaneous, A217, I7

    Aesop at, P422; barbers, A57, B64; beauties, D446; carpenter of, C245; critics, O268; election (1705) D393, U17, U19; epistles to, A198, T591; journey to, B415; letter from, H348; oyster women, S191; poetasters, S38; reformation, W175; riddle, O269; sermon, H199, O270; toasts, A207, A317; tragedy, O274; trip to, T482; visit of Queen Anne (1702), R317; visit of William prince of Orange (1734), M58

    University: epistle to, C75; heroi-panegyrical poem on, A199; humours of, D34; prologues to, N173, P486, P1022, S740, T310, T455

    act at, A168, B337, H104, N173, O275; botany professor, E530; George I's bounty to, S578; reformations at, C99; statutes, S734; theatre, odes and exercises performed at, C295, D355, O34, S515, T448; vice-chancellor, (dedicatee) M194, (election of) H454

    authors identifying themselves as from Oxford, A190, A193, A218, B176, C299, C385, C520, C530, E298, E324, E483, F221, H107, H112, H192, H304, L293, P628, P666, R312, S31, S222, T91, V25, W546

All Souls, R111; author from, H230

Balliol College, authors from, A14, M36, M118

Christ Church, new dean and canon (1711), N123; authors from, B205, P134, T271

Constitution Club, poems by members of, A202, R303

Oxford (cont.)
Jesus College, author from, J96
Magdalen College, author from, R265
Magdalen Grove, M14
Magdalen Hall, author from, D533
Merton Walks, D446
New College, author from, E43
New Inn Hall, author from, A171
Oriel College, author from, F242
Queen's College, rebuilding of, T296
St John's College, author from, A171
St Mary Hall, song performed at, B373
Tennis Court, players at, P486
Trinity College, patroness of J.C.R., W251
Wadham College, author from, P486; homosexual scandal at, C286
Oxford, Edward Harley, 2nd earl: addressee, C66, H186, M142, T392, V70; distributes Pope's *Dunciad*, P771
Oxford, Henrietta Cavendish Holles Harley, countess, *see* Harley
Oxford, Robert Harley, 1st earl, *see* Harley
Oxfordshire, O276: election (1710), O279
Oxfordshire Society, P532
Oxonian, ramble of modern, R10
oyster: guinea gave for, F180; martin and, M117; two clowns and, S57
oyster woman, S190: Oxford oyster women, S191
oysters, O281

pacific fleet, P2
pack, old, O118
Pack, Richardson, epistles to, M304, S364
padlock: English, P1076, (unlocked) E339; political, P712; Dr Sacheverell's, O269
Page, Alderman, of Dublin, H362
Page, Samuel, of Jamaica, P715
pain and patience, D387
painter, *see* 'Advice to a painter' poems
painters, session of, S224
painting: art of, C324, M331; poems on, A215, B252, B555, E513, G310, L103, N264, N265, T350; *see also* picture
pair, happy, S193
Palaemon, G5: to Caelia, W303; dialogue with Menalcas, B411
Palatines, Queen Anne's bounty to, E296
Palladio, P908
palladium, Britain's, B527·2
Pallas: gift of, C56·5; and Venus, P1082, S402
Pamby, Namby, *see* Namby Pamby
Pamela, or the fair impostor, P25
Pamela versified, B192
pamphleteers, the, M72
pamphlets, battle of, S98
Pancharilla, P27
Pancridge (= St Pancras), walk to, H289
pandemonium, P28
Pandora's box, P29
panegyric, A267, C49, D219, D400–2, E367, F65, G142, G203, H350, K103, L272, M24, N269, P32–41, P146, P150, P169, P256, P257, P717, T484

panegyrical: address, S240; characters, P992; elegy, H86; epigram, P42; epistle, G64, P31; poem, M8, M141, P43, T144
Panthea's confinement, P735
pantheon, the, P45
pantin, the, P46
paper kite, P47
Paphian grove, B71
papists, F81, N151; *see also* Roman catholic
parable, B530·3
'Parabocka, Don', T156
parade: Glasgow's, G176; of Scottish archers, P48
paradise: lost, *see* Milton in the main catalogue; regained, Z2; reviewed, E374; muse's, P258; poet's, P697; Turkish, T555
paradox, P49, S29: state, B530·1
parallel, the, E502, P50
paraphrase, *poems so describing themselves (most commonly used for verse based on the Bible)* A323, A365, D569, E457, E459, F226, H99, H143·5, H342, K20, L105, M438, M490, M519, P51–62, P95, P753, P961, P1053, S181, S186–8, S854, W318, W321, Y100; *see also* lunatic paraphrase; poetical paraphrase; versification
parasites, satire on, L161
Pardo, convention of (1739), C349, C402, H306, L80, N18, P997, S478, S481, S725, T560
Paris: archbishop of, L132; dialogue with London, D267; idol of (= Sacheverell), I3; satire on, F183; St Victor's in, W408
gazetteer, P64
Paris, judgement of, B205, C115, D2
Paris, John, satire on, T6
parish: gutt'lers, W136; priest, W345
Parke, Daniel, governor of the Leeward islands, elegy on, F209
Parker, Lady (dedicatee), W235
Parker, Sir Thomas (afterwards earl of Macclesfield), *see* Macclesfield
Parkinson, Christopher, captain of trained bands, B526
Parkyns, Sir Thomas (dedicatee), B194, T545
parliament:
1701, poems to the new, I19, T52; Kentish petition to, B507
1702, assembling of, T69; panegyric on present, P256; address to ensuing, P694
1705, satire on, D97
1706, address to queen, D110
1710, dissolution, B574, D336, J6
1711, husbandmen's petition to, H414
1713, account of expiring, S445
1718, poem on, W8
1722, elegy on, L63
1728, meeting of, L172
1732, meeting of, W374
1735, address to, C77; *see also* house of commons
of birds, S690, S695; of hell, P68
Parnassus: duck drowned in, D466; equity of, E449; express from, E610; holy, H291; news from, D202; plea of, M320; proclamation from, D526; to be sold, P69; view of, C127
Parnell, John, Irish judge, elegy on, E208
parody, poems so describing themselves, B413, S602
parrot, and the owl, P80

parrots, almonds for, A173

parson: bewitched, P84; and his clerk, P81; and his maid, P82; married, O237; preferred, P87; receipt to roast, R145; roasting of, R223; ship's mate and, S426; squire and, J66; *see also* clergyman

parson, country: advice of, B528, C454; dean and, L242; poem by, E20

parson, Scots, roast for, R222

parson's: compassion, P89; daughter, W578

parson-hunter, P85

Parsoniad, P88

Parsons, Sir Humphrey, lord mayor of London: (1730), N205, P90; addressee, A371, H428, V51, W188; (1740), C204, C211, F220, W441

parties: all agreed, D25; satire on all, G143

Partridge, John, astrologer: elegy on John Gadbury attributed to, M297; mock elegies on (1708), E209, S832

party against party, P1146

party scuffle, C450

Pasquin: and Morforio, D262; at Paul's, P97; to the queen's statue at St Paul's, P98

Passaro, naval victory at, E21

passing-bell, England's, E324

passion: of Jesus Christ, B140, P706, S4·5, S27; fits of, H267; universal, Y122

passions, the: C295; duel with, A218; human, H387; of man, R331

passive obedience, I3: elegy on, E147; farewell to, F59

past and present, P100–1

Pastora's lament for Adonis, P102

pastoral (poems describing themselves as), A159, A164, A223, A333, B173, B276, B329, B531, C53, C88, C330, C379, C471, D21, D362, F223, G5, G202, H400, I49, L320, L323, L324, M171, M485, O9, P110, P111, P114, P150, P152, P166, P172, R59, R76, R82, R88, R266, S522, S721, T38, T154; *see also* elegiac pastoral

dialogue, B467, E44, G116, G206; eclogue, D20, H69, S24; eclogues, E460, W245·5; elegy, A219, C10, D404, F273, G251, M569, P103–8, P281, P461; epithalamium, H47; essay, A5, M40, P109; lamentation, C47; letter, D352, D352·5, P112; poem, B498, M573, O168, P115–18; recitative, R70; soliloquy, B517; stanzas, L222; welcome, S513

pastorals, D72, G69, P211, P1172, P1175, W570

Pastorella, P119

patch, the, H107

patchwork, P120

patentees, of Drury Lane, T127

paternity case, F26

Paterson, George, smith, elegy on, G169

Paterson, Thomas, elegy on, P158

Patie, and Roger, R76

patience, P121: help to, H137; pain and, D387; trials of, G118

patriarchs, lives of, C475, S944; *see also* Abraham; Jacob; Joseph

Patricius, P122

Patrick, Saint, *see* St Patrick's day

patriot, the, D445, P123, P124, S369, S714: chimerical, C149; false, F47–50, H157·2; injured, N278; modern, P705; real, N280, V99; true, T528; unbiassed, U1; the patriot prostituted, D86

patriot's: defeat, T271; motion, M526; triumph, P126

patriotic love, J48

patriotism, P125: modern, M377; power and, P1010; progress of, P1111

patriots, the, F187, H158, P451: assembled, W374; Broad-street, B404; jolly, J89; Middlesex, M229; modern, M379; true, U10

Patroclus, B95

patron, mock, M356

pattern: of piety, G118; royal, R252

Paul, saint, poems occasioned by his words, F42, T505

Paul, William, the Jacobite, M296, O174, P86, P571

peace, V117: and plenty, A359; art of cultivating, T544; articles of, A330; best argument for, Y81; hymn to, D110; poem sacred to, C551; praise of, B365; prophecy of, N114, V21; prospect of, G252, N306; reviving, D75; no peace for the wicked, N307

(=peace of Utrecht, 1711–13), A24, C513, D74, H184, L259, P131, P633, S520, T451, T502, W385: bowl of punch upon, B336; congratulatory poem on, A227, S275; declaration of, P526; and Dunkirk, S895; happy conclusion of, S468·7; hymn on, W331; hymns on occasion of, H473; idyll on, I4; Mat's, M30; on earth, W25; or no peace, G249; prospect of, P61; ratification of, T544; safe peace or none, W388; shortest way to, S455; speech against, S631, S844; triumph of, T81; triumphant, P1132; war and, P77; *see also* Utrecht, peace of

(=peace of Seville, 1729), E428, M535, N141, Y82

(=peace of Vienna, 1731), P133; of Europe, S159; hymn to, N141; *see also* Vienna

(=convention of Pardo, 1739), speech upon, S478; *see also* Pardo

(=peace of Aix-la-Chapelle, 1749), B505, O217, P134; ode on, C538, O50; poetical essay on, L311; *see also* Aix-la-Chapelle

peace-haters, P135

peace-keeper, M320·5

peace officer, A131

Peachum, Polly, A242, L151, N64, N139: on fire, P716; Irish, E550

Peadie, James, lord provost of Glasgow, elegy on, V73

Peddie, John, captain, M118

pedlar, the (=Louis d'Aumont), P139: French, P140

Pedro, Don, D465

peeper, the, P141

peers, S518: congratulatory poem to, B530·6; election of Scottish, D58; modern, S354

'Peg Trim Tram' (= Lord Trentham), P143–5

Pelham, Henry: addressee, B198, P1010, P1170, S651, V81, Y49; satires on, K49, T31, W29

Pelham, Thomas, baron, (subsequently duke of Newcastle), *see* Newcastle

Pellet, Thomas, F.R.S. (addressee), P703

Pemberton, Ebenezer, elegy on, C135

Pembroke, Thomas Herbert, earl of: lord-lieutenant of Ireland, I63; dedicatee, G262, H68, H77·1, N297, S522, W301

pen, drawings with, H101

Pencaitland, James Hamilton, lord, elegy on, E210

Pendergrass, Lady, fight with Mrs Phips, C345

Penelope to Ulysses, epistle of, E436

penitent: court, W222; dark, W233

penitential confession, M95

Penkethman, William, *see* Pinkethman

Penman, Robert, town officer in Edinburgh, R1

Penman's magazine, T70

Penn, William, *Fruits of solitude* versified, T176

Pennecuik, Alexander (1652–1722), elegy on, L189

Pennecuik, Alexander (*d.* 1730), satire on, D258

pennyworth of wit, C160

Penshurst, C474

pentecost, wonderful, W556

Peploe, Samuel, bishop of Chester, libel on, B617

Peppard, Jacob, MP, elegy on, F291

Pepusch, J. C., music by, D355, H377, M157

Perceval, John, viscount (subsequently earl of Egmont), (addressee), S484

Percival, William, archdeacon, A177

perfume, the best, P49

perils of false brethren, P178

Perkin (= James Francis Edward, the Old Pretender), P1062: priest of the order of, E573; redivivus, P179; *see also* James Francis Edward Stuart

Perkin's: cabal, P180; farewell, P182

Perkinade, the (on the Young Pretender), C12

Perkinite jacks (= Jacobite tackers), P183

'Perpendicular, David', A18

Perrault, Charles, French translation by, F21

Perry, Elizabeth (addressee), C474

Perry, William (addressee), C474

Persian eclogues, C298

Persius: satire in the manner of, H161·5; Sheridan's translation of, T355; Persius Scaramouch, D42

person of quality: epistle to, J42; letter to, S863

perspective, the, C104

Perth, James Drummond, earl and titular duke of (dedicatee), T333

Peter, P192: Cassinus and, S809

Peter, the great, czar of Russia, H225–6: death of, B151

Peter, saint: dialogue with low-churchman, D265; never in Rome, H463; poem occasioned by his words, O173; supposed author, P395

Peterborough, Anastasia, countess of, E377

Peterborough, Carey, countess of (dedicatee), O167

Peterborough, Charles Mordaunt, earl of: addressee, B144, H211, P1009; campaigns in Spain, F62, H211, O167, P1009; elegy on, B372

Peterwaradein, victory at, T250

petition, B198, O257, P194: Dr Anthony's, A261; apothecary's, A272; Bambridge and Huggins's, B47; of beautiful young lady, H394; distressed maid's, D337; Mrs Harris's, S801; hungry poets', G305; husbandmen's, H414; Kentish, B507, K104, T409; John Ker's, K25; little beau's, L196; London clergy's, L236; Lord Mountcashel's, D65; David Mullan's, M554; of Murroughoh O'Connor, O13; of old washwoman of Dunleary, P193; pigs', P277; poetical, M321, M329, M344; printers', P1064; prisoner's, P1100; Punch's, P1167; quaker's, Q5; of water-drinking poets, M332; of Duke of Wharton, H396; of the whigs, M392

petitions, poets', P709

Petrarch, tale from, O95

Petronius Arbiter, feigned fragment of, R192

petticoat, the, C189: whale-bone, O242; *see also* hoop petticoats

Petticoat Lane, tabernacle in, charity children of, T258

pettifoggers, the, P197

Pettit, Clement, elegy on, S272

Pettus, Lydia, lady, F55

Petworth, C419

Phaedra and Hyppolitus, prologue to, S408

Phaedrus, feigned fable of, B530·9

Phaeton, M217, P557: female, P1094

phallic poems, C206, J45, N7, T586, W533

phantom, the, P198; *see also* ghost

Phaon's answer to Sappho, C496

pheasant, and the lark, D203

Philadelphia, elegy on death at, B306

Philadelphian Society, C441, E211

Philander: and Aspasia, V102; and Cydippe, C420; and Sacharissa, P201; and Silvia, L284

Philanglus, and Astraea, K85

Philemon, Baucis and, S800

Philenis, Sappho's epistle to, E374

Philip V, king of Spain, C315, C402, D498, H245, P169, W442

philippic, British, A133

Philips, Ambrose: defence of, S71; parodies in 'namby pamby' verse, L21, O180, P38, P209, P523, P678, S53, S385, Y108; satires on, C49, C170, N1, N2, O229, S62, T344

Philips, John: elegies on, S516, W308; imitations of, B392, B554, D533

Philips, Katherine (the matchless Orinda), B392

Phillips, Elizabeth (addressee), P259

Phillips, Teresia Constantia, F73, H42, S179: memoirs of, F85

Philocles, Monimia to, H157·5

Philopolites, K103

'Philosarchus' (= David MacLauchlan), address to, R32

philosopher, the beau, B193

philosophers: ancient, A220; Athenian, chorus of, P876; characters of, M166; tippling, W183; *see also* natural philosophers

philosophic: ode, P260; poem, P200

philosophical: essay, P1019; poem, B242, D71, L110, R177

philosophy, H41, J94: female, T532; religion and, P9; stoic, H236; wisest, W312

Phino-Godol, P261

Phipps, Mrs, fight with Lady Pendergrass, C345

Phipps, C., marriage to Miss Lepel Hervey, L222

Phipps, Sir Constantine, elegy on, E212

Phocylides, proposed edition by R. Monteith, M421

Phoebus: Minerva to, M268; poems to, M268, P332, P334

phoenix, P263

phonetic alphabet, W458

Phosphorus, P265

Phyllis to Demophoon, epistle of, E436

physic, M559, P267: new method of treating, B335; poetical essay on, P703; praise of, N275; progress of, C480; *see also* medical subjects, poems on

physician: duel with lawyer, N74; prophetic, P1139; regular, R152; turned cook, L76; young, epistle to, P1157

physicians: addressees, P1139; consult of, D332; scuffle with lawyers, B586

picquet, R318

picture: of Hugh Boulter, P661; of a church militant, S696; of an English monster, C123; of a female favourite, P270; of the first occasional conformist, P272; of W—m F—ce, P269; of his majesty (the Old Pretender), O220; of love, H229; of Maria, M475·5; by Thomas Murray, T350; of the Observator, P273; of Mr Pope, M298; of pictures, P271; prince's (Young Pretender), O187; of a sot, E293; state, N230

Pierce, alias Allan, the turncoat, B54, F186, N244

Piercy, Henry, colonel, elegy on, P668

Pierpoint, Lady Grace, elegy on, E213

piety: British, G111; dissenting, D334; female, F99; pattern of, G118; pleasures of, P505

pig, the, W347

pigs' petition, P277

pigeons: art of breeding, D315; fable of, O190; Robin's, T33

Pigott, Nathaniel, lawyer, S203

pike, the, P278

Pilgrim's progress versified, H268

Pilkington, Matthew: arrest of, S841; letter to, C345

pill: for pork-eaters, F188; for *The craftsman*, H33

pillory, the: dialogue with Defoe, B511; hymn to, D115; new hymn to, C237; Mr Stephens's triumph over, C454; trip to, T493

pillory scuffle, P284

Pimlot, Mr, murdered attorney, P1099

Pindar: poems in the manner of, C247, P210, Y82; Mr West's translation of, W245

pindaric, C363, D418, O228, P57, P1059, W514
essay, A315, P284·5, P733; illustration, H212; ode, A156, A273, A366, A367, B378, B536, C335, C376, F141, G318, H64, H70, H71, H84, H168, H375, J72, M468, O55, O156, P130, P225, P285–9, P730, R110, S457, T146, T384, T478, T570; ode, discourse on, C376; poem, F163, L254, N348, P717, S288, S392, S524, W24, W474, W569; verse, V91

pindarics, English, B380

Pinkethman, William: his company in mourning, P290; new opera in Bartholomew fair, F29; prologues and epilogues spoken by, E352, L54; prologue answered, P1129

pious: soul, breathings of, H114; youth, P292

pipe of tobacco, B520

pirate: sailor turned, S9; *see also* Green, Thomas; Kidd, William; Madder, John

piracy, merits of, M192

piscatio, S464

piscatory eclogues, B531

piss-pot, P293, T437: Chloe's, P627

Pitcairne, Anne, Latin poem to, P295

Pitcairne, Archibald: dissertations and poems of, K40; library of, K42; ode to, O18; death of, D55, E214–15, K24, R78, R329, W521

Pitcairne, Elizabeth, Latin poem to, P325

Pitcairne, James Andrew, Latin poem to, P311

Pitcairne, Joaneta, Latin poem to, P321

Pitcairne, Margaret, Latin poem to, P330

pitcher, cracked, W448

Pitt, James, M524, T474

Pitt, Samuel, of Keir (dedicatee), W225

Pitt, William (subsequently earl of Chatham): addressee, E434, S452; satire on, U2

place of the damned, S897

place bill, E24, P465

place book, W497

plague: fears of, B481; of Athens, S663; of Marseilles, G114, P414·5

plagues: of Egypt, P468; of Nod, P469; *see also* fifteen plagues

plaid, the, R97: hunting, P470

plain: thoughts, W501; truth, P473–5

plantation, sugar, S784·5

planter's charity, P477

platonic, the, P478

platonic: courtship, K8; lovers, T360

play, the, L206

player and poet, dialogue of, S225

players: the, P484; turned academics, P486

playhouse: Alan Ramsay's, F169, R100; in Dorset garden, D236; *see also* theatre

playhouse: ballad, D502; rioters, S166; scuffle, P487

playing, art of, W274; *see also* acting

pleasure: sailor's, S15; virtue and, C422, T117

pleasures: of Bath, A354; of imagination, A139; of melancholy, W246; of piety, P505; of a single life, P488; of Tunbridge, C78

plenty, prospect of, R81

plot: detected, W42; discovered, F58, P506–7, R131; or no plot, P508, P510; upon plot, T589
band-box, C514, T589; bed-tester, B154; garden, G10; masquerade, G17, M132; Scotch, A55, S350; screw, S152; *see also* Atterbury plot

plotters, the, P515

Plume, Captain, E371

Plumptre, John, MP for Nottingham, I47

Plumstead, C., satire on, L121

Plutarch, tale from, M320·5

Plutus, dialogue with Mars, D549

P——n, Miss, V25

Poe, Jo., elegy on, E216

poem, *see* allegorial poem; blank poem; burlesque poem; commendatory poem; condolatory poem; congratulatory poem; consolatory poem; critical poem; dehoratory poem; divine poem; dramatic poem; elegiac poem; epic poem; epistolary poem; ethic poem; ethi-comico-satirical poem, facetious poem; funeral poem; heroic poem; heroi-comical poem; heroi-satirical mythological poem; historic poem; historical poem; historico-satirical poem; holy poem; hudibrastic poem; iambic poem; ironical poem; loyal poem; mad poem; merry poem; mock-heroic poem; monumental poem; moral poem; mournful poem; narrative poem; occasional poem; panegyrical poem; pastoral poem; philosophical poem; pindaric poem; sacred poem; serio-comic poem; spiritual poem

poet, H182: advice to, A74, L139, O183; dialogue with player, S225; dialogue with his grandmother's ghost, D514; letter from one to another, C345; and the muse, P692; Dr Anthony turned, A255; tailor turned, T6
catholic, O165; hard-used, H48; inspired, I44; modern, M380, O183; mourning, B514; town, O229, S67; young, L139, M479

poet's: address, P693, P694; complaint, H48; dream, P695; fancy, P191; free thoughts, P696; paradise, P697; prayer, D525; ramble after riches, W141; reply, P696; *see also* poets'

poet laureate: dialogue with, O100; (Cibber) expelled the house of lords, U23; mock title, C347

poetaster: austere, C495; dramatic, D425

poetasters: Oxford and Cambridge, S38; Dublin, *see* Dublin, poets and poetasters

Poetastro, Don, D397

poetess, the, G231·5

poetic: beggars, F54; epistle, P698; essays, T165; sermon, R79

poetical: abridgement, K73; character, G233; description, G216, K35, P700; dialogue, S126; epistle, D361, M116, M331, P702, P1010; essay, A26, A303, A313, A319, B515, B527·1, L311, M283, M439, P199, P699, P703–5, S422, S495, T128; estate, P69; harvest home, N127; ladies (addressees), P709; meditations, T37; narration, K89; narrative, M7; novel, M81; novels, M275–6; paraphrase, F226, H143·5, L235, M312, T168, W13; petition, M321, M329, M344; recreations, S662; senate, P1064; tales, M275–6; thought, P707

poetry: art of, A179, A325, B310, D309, H313, H314, P416; art of modern, M251; art of sinking in, S542; critical poem on, P476; essay on, S388; essay on different styles of, P70; imitation of present Irish, A71; in praise of, N275; present state of, C418, M491, M563, T67; prospect of, D11; rhapsody on, S888; satire concerning, D459; state of in England, C417; taste of the town in, N335; true test of, C477

poets, B281, C128, C184, C365, C407, C477, E401, M307, N127, P764, S206, T433: advice to, B238, F170, H209, H291; battle of, B104, C408; essay on, M481, M483; legacies to, A259; modest satire on, N38; satire on, R153; satiric essay on, M477, M494; session of, C429, T475; short critical poem on, P476; *see also* authors; dunces

English, P31; hungry, G305; Irish, *see* Irish poets; tory, M351; of the town, D509, S62, S67 (*see also* Dublin, poets); of Trinity College Dublin, G267, T363; water-drinking, M332

poets': address, P708; petitions, G305, P709

Pointis, French admiral, at Gibraltar, S472

Poland, diet of, D97

'Pole, Lord', translated, L260

Polemo-middinia, E476

Polhill, D. (dedicatee), P57

politic judge, P710

political: alphabet, K49; ballad, L114, P84, S204; jugglers, W398; justice, N346; madness, P711; padlock, P712; pair, P713; touch of the times, P714; writers, M378 (*see also* journalists)

politician, amorous successful, C202

politician's advice to his son, W45

politicians: Hibernian, H175; rival, R216; three, T257

politics: art of, B383; of Jamaica, P715; rural, N232

policy, Italian, I72

politeness, M255: island of, M299

Pollio, Milton's epistle to, K68

Pollio, Caius Asinius, character of, H318

Polly, letter to, L151; *see also* Peachum, Polly

Poltis, king of Thrace, M320·5

Polyarchus, epistle to, C443

polygamist, the, P719

Polyphemus: evaporated, T248; his farewell, P721

Pomfret, George Fermor, earl of, N305

Pomfret, Samuel, elegy on, L231

pomp of death, H86

Ponty (= Pointis), French admiral at Gibraltar, S472

Pooley, John, bishop of Raphoe, eulogy to, T353

poor, the, complaint of, C323

poor client's complaint, P753

poor-house, Dublin, N79

pope, T529: effigy of, K94, Q8, T119; congratulatory epistle from, to Dr Snape, A188; epistle from English Jesuit to, E364; fire in his breeches, F284; French king's lamentation to, C550; hymn to, H463; and Pretender in a quandary, P760; pursuit of, C318

Pope Joan, *see* Joan, Pope

Pope, Alexander:

Answers to individual published works (with the exception of the Dunciad) *are entered under each work in the main catalogue*

1713, addressee, G66, R175

1715, addressee, B94

1716, epistle to, E404; satire on, O165

1720, preface to, H212

1722, epistle to, E405

1725, poem on Mr Pope's works, P282

1728, satire on, S504

1730, epistles to, L331, W302·5, Y117; preface to, C231

1732, addressee, W360; epistle to, T565·5; satire on, O183

1733, addressee, F91, F215, P88, V28, V39, W426, W572; dedicatee, E470; epistle to, E415, M51, S203; publication of Swift's *Life and genuine character*, S884; quarrel with Lady Mary Wortley Montagu, A86, F91, P1135, S34, V39

1734, addressee, C468, T473; epistles to, D384, F50, G130; quarrel with Lord Hervey, E359, F162, H157, T322, T473

1735, dedicatee, D409; epistle to, E392

1736, poem corrected by, W29·5

1737, addressee, B122; epistle to, K88·5

1738, addressee, M18; epistle to, P10

1739, epistle to, C129; satire on, S83; editor of Swift, S920

1740, ode on, D520; satirical epistle to, L269; and Walpole, M234, M249, M511

1742, epistles to, H156, M497; satire on, C55·5; defence of, against Cibber, S153

1743, grotto and gardens of, D390; picture of, M298; verses on, S201

1744, death, B502, E217, E218; ghost of, P761; satire on, D326

1745, elegy on, P752; satire on Pope's patrons, R170

1747, monody in memory of, M124

Dunciad, D363, D554, H98, H145·5, R21, S206, S542, W47, W66; imitations of, B160, D508

Eloisa to Abelard, answer to, D6

First satire of the second book of Horace, imitation of J116

Homer, H181, M479, M496, M500·5

Pope, Alexander (*cont.*)
    One thousand seven hundred and thirty eight, attack on,
      D286; imitations of, A370, O231
    Pastoral, imitation of, G5
    Temple of fame, imitation of, P1026
    Three hours after marriage, D444, W303
    Universal prayer, imitation of, P63
    Windsor Forest, imitation of, W242
popery: alarm against, H273; antidote against, F43; blind-
    ness in, A225; resolution to down with, E325
    protestant, A200; true popery no foppery, T529
popes, fate of, F182
popish impostor, F230
Poplar, charity children of, H438, H439, H450
popular convention (of Pardo), P997
porch and academy opened, P998
Porcupinade, P1000
pork-eaters, pill for, F188
portents, A149
Porteous riots, B483, C32, H246, H258, H260, K103,
    L145, P554, V105
porter, battle of priest and, P1042
Porter, John, murderer, elegies on, F289, N204
Portland, Margaret, duchess of: dedicatee, Y36; marriage,
    O49
Portland, William Bentinck, duke of: dedicatee, H340;
    marriage, O49; K.G., K48
Portland, William Bentinck, earl of, S291
portrait of a just and honourable man, H388
portrait-royal, T74
portraiture of Oliverus secundus, P1003
Portsmouth, theatre at, S581
Portugal: Aesop at, A110; expedition to, C257
Portuguese nun, L287
post office feast, M531
postillion in his master's saddle, K101
potatoes: elegy on (1739/40), E219; resurrection of, R165
Potter, John, archbishop of Canterbury, M450, R7
Poultney, Lady (dedicatee), W224
Poultry compter, character of, H134
pound, for Hereford freemen, P1007
Poussin, French chargé d'affaires, E322
poverty: cave of, T137; epistle concerning, M307; praise
    of, H236
poverty's coat turned, P1008
Povey, Charles, satire on, P1118
Powell, George, prologue spoken by, F277
Powell, Jacobella, epilogue spoken by, F277
power, O84: of beauty, P1011; of harmony, C427; of
    love, H167, W309; of music, H12, M319, S613;
    and patriotism, P1010; of union, D220
Powers-court House, P548
pox, poem in praise of, A262
Poyntz, Stephen, ode to, B231, W492
P——p, Miss, N82
praise: of God, P1178; of peace, B365; of poverty, H236;
    of the pox, A262; of Miss Smalley, M393; of tea, I32,
    M527
Pratt, Benjamin, speech of, S633
prayer: nature of, N11; Britannia's, T48; poet's, D525;
    universal, P63, P982; *see also* Lord's prayer
preaching, art of, D376
preceptor, epistle from, D15

prediction, A370, P1018: of Merlin, S849; *see also* pro-
    phecy
pre-existence, E528, P1019
preferment, F146: art of getting, B68; despised, E7;
    essay on, E464; *see also* promotion
prelate, knight and, K97
prerogative, woman's, C472
presbyter unmasked, P1024
Presbyter, Jack: triumphant, H59; downfall of, J6; trium-
    phant rejoicing of, J7
Presbyter, Sir John, M212
presbyterian, without disguise, D216·5
presbyterian itch, M12
presbyterians, B46, D274, T388: satires on, A150, A265,
    C36, C240, C433, G109, K105, L152, N151, P395;
    of Scotland, V109
present, past and, P100, P101
present: fashions, T158; state of men and things, E601;
    times, S77
press restrained, P1025
press-gang, scourge for, S9
press-yard, present to, P121
Preston: battle of (1745), B103, N302·5; dissenting
    preacher at, M370; encomium on, H38; quaker
    anniversary (1738), H4
Preston prisoners, W543
Preston, Christopher, master of the bears, elegy on, B124
    (*see also* P1026)
Preston Baggot, labourer poet from, C291
Prestonpans, battle of, A22, B8, H17, N14, O66, O200,
    O221, P575
'Pretendant, Monsieur', M411
Pretender, *see* Charles Edward Stuart; James Francis
    Edward Stuart
Pretender's godson, I9
'Pretenderillo, Signior', M411
pretext, sad, S6
Priapeia presbyteriana, A265
Price, Sir Carbery, mines of, Y3
Price, John, hangman, elegy on, S604
Price, Richard, marriage of, S311
Prichard, Lady (dedicatee), F39
'Pricklove, Roger', B485
Priddon (alias Salisbury), Sarah, G133, R263
pride, R71: French, D543; will have a fall, A263
pride's exchange broken up, P1051
priest: amorous, N324; artful, A329; beast's confession
    to, S804; brawny, C255; country, C457; lustful,
    P719; outwitted, C105; parish, W345; and porter,
    P1042; turned poet, P1053; and widow, P1052
priest-catchers, advice to, H361
priestcraft, P1055: and lust, P1054; more, W123; war
    with, W40
prince, the, P1056: and no prince, P1057
prince of peace, hymn to, W331
prince of Wales, *see* Frederick; George II; James Francis
    Edward Stuart
Prince Frederick, ship, R225
princess royal, *see* Anne, subsequently princess of Orange
Princess Scocia, E235
princess's lock, P1063
princesses, the young (dedicatees), B532
principles of Christian religion, D366

Pringle, John, town-piper of Lauder, elegy on, E220

Pringle, Rorie, drawer in the Tolbooth, P157

printers' petition, P1064

printing, art of, P585

Prior, Matthew:
    1701, satire on, B281
    1706, attack on, A365·5; letter to, L149
    1711, satire on his peace mission, M30; addressee, F209
    1712, addressee, C515, P340
    1714, epistle from, G125
    1715, letter to, L148
    1721, dedication to, J18; death of, B152, C365, R88, T434, V70
    imitations of, E339, O114, S151, S487

Prior, Thomas, on tar water, T39

prison, poems from, B86, B438, B514, L148, P1100, S397, T546, W469, W543

prison groans, P1099

prisons opened, W353

prisoner's: ballad, W469; petition, P1100

prisoners: condemned, hymn for, W317; for debt, M564; Preston, W543

Pritchard, Hannah, epilogue spoken by, W32

Pritchard, Sir William, MP, R163

prize of beauty, J30

Pro and Con, P1102

Proby, Charles, elegy on, E222

procession, B235: republican, W155; see also Dublin, corporations

proclamation, P1103: of Cupid, S372; concerning farthing-ales, N172; from Parnassus, D526

proctor's banquet, G318

prodigal son, P1104

prodigy, B76: Tunbridge, F142

prodigies, W53

progress, the, P1116: harlot's, H54; rake's, R10; royal, R317; Vanella's, V13
    of beauty, D9; of charity, D1107; of commerce, G197; of a divine, S109; of divine love, P1108; of glory, P1109; of a harlot, P1105; of her majesty's arms, C376; of her majesty's forces, R168; of honesty, D551; of language, M149; of love, L333; of methodism in Bristol, P1110; of music in Ireland, P282; of patriotism, P1111; of physic, C480; of a rake, P1106; of religion, J49; of sacerdotal sanctity, R213; of Spain, B338; of time, P1113; of valour, P1115; of the war, P1112; of wit, H230

projector, the: (= Charles Povey), P1118; (= Walpole) at his last shift, S716; defeated, W452; in the dumps, P1117; his looking-glass, P1119

prologue, A285, C200, C277, C377, C378, C410, F64, F277, G37, G39, G101, H138, J83, J85, L48, L54, L246, M187, N173–6, O224, P23, P446, P486, P1022, P1083, P1084, P1120–34, S166, S408, S412, S413, S415, S416, S737, S739, S740, T310, T455, W310

Prometheus, S898

promotion, the, M321: way to, P1055; see also preferment

property, liberty and, B530·4

prophecy, A162, B540, C270, D390, D565, G41, G293, P407, P1136, V20, W311, W555: ancient, N243, P149; Bickerstaff's, B210, D392; British, N114; Latin, Y14; by Merlin, P1137; negative, N16; of Nereus, T283;

Northumberland, D486; Nostradamus's, N325; nymph's, D292; old cat's, B125; Mother Red-cap's, P1057; of peace, V21; of David Rowland, R305; Scotch, T287; Whitehall, N16, W410; Windsor, P459, S938, W527; see also prediction

prophet: French (Thomas Emes), E443, F260; military, M231; mourning, W125

prophetess, royal, B530·7

prophetic: hymn, P1138; physician, P1139; postscript, D286

prophets, the, of the Cevennes, D278–84, P1140

proportion, beauty and, B133

proposal of a certain little tutor, C99

proposals: for erecting a protestant nunnery, P1141; proposals for publishing books will be found in the index of bibliographical notabilia

proselyte, female, F100

Proserpina: ode to, C534; rape of, H368

prosody, I49, M24, P526, P1142, V18

prospect, the, P1144, R191, T198: of death, P733; of peace, G252, N306, P61, T303; of poetry, D11

prosperity to Houghton, F174

prosphoneticon, H276, H277

protector, the modern (= Marlborough), P1003

Protesilaus, Laodamia to, P1041

protest, the, P1145

protestant turned papist, L184

protestant: ambulators, W170; ballad, T119; Barnaby, O165; director, H273; divisions, P1146; Jacobites, O169; king, P1047; knock, P1147; nunnery, P1141; popery, A200; queen, P1148; religion, W4; scourge, W123; session, A202; toasts, P1151

protestants' charge, F43

proverb made true, B161

providence, B443, D477: chain of, O168·2; vindication of, F203; works of, G182, W557

provisions for the convent, P1152

prude, the, P1153: demolished, H42; dialogue with a coquet, B20; epistle from, E416; metamorphosed, T499; purgatory of, J50

Prue, Miss, C208

Pryce, Lady, elegy on, O8

Pryer, John, elegy on, P553

psalm: English, B416; of thanksgiving (Christ's Hospital), C258–63, C518–19, H164–6

Psyche, B130

psychomachia, P1155

pteryplegia, M98

pubic hair, B26, C372, C546, J34, S51, W164, W552

public: affairs, H220; credit, S767; good, O85; houses, V2; spirit, F222, S102; virtue, S651; works, S102

publicans, dialogue with their customers, N296

publishing, P475

'Puddle-dock, Duchess of' (dedicatee), G99

Puerto de Santa Maria, taking of, P643

Pullen, Tom, letter to, P480

pulpit, tub and, T543

pulpit: fool, D538; war, W148

Pulteney, Anna Maria (wife of William), L255

Pulteney, Charlotte, poem to, P217

Pulteney, Peggy, poem to, P217

Pulteney, William, earl of Bath
    1727–28, satires against, L255, L261, P713

Pulteney (*cont.*)

1731, duel with Lord Hervey, C444, D488, E371; dialogue with Walpole, D243, D272; mock elegy on, P653; eulogy of, D445; addressee, P519; dedicatee, H229

1733, R231; satire on, P705; addressee, N291, W558

1739, ode on, N339

1741, epistle to, E361; contrast with Walpole, B467

1742, epistle to, E429; eulogy of, H418; satires on, A268, F48, J65, W475, W494

1744, epistle to, A136; satire on, E449

1745, addressee (?), R148

1746, ode to ambition, W487

'pun broker', N148

punch: bowl of, B336; curse upon, M328

Punch (the puppet): out of humour, T156; his petition to the ladies, P1167

punning, art of, H155

'Punsibi, Tom' (= Thomas Sheridan), L157, O258, S418, T318, T412, T413

puppet show, P1167, P1169, P1170, T156: state, C1

puppies, Lord Wharton's, L262

Purcell, Henry, song by, B373

purgatory, prude's, J50

purging potion, B236

puritan preacher, B608

Purney, Thomas, editor, B562

purse: knight and, K100; empty, E306, M328

pursuit of the pope, C318

put, game of, B49

Putland, Thomas, banker in Dublin, elegy on, E223

Putland, Thomas, boy at Sheridan's school, S408

pygmies and cranes, battle of, P1179

pyramid to memory of William III, P1180

Pyrrha, B356, P1181

Pythagoras, P397

quack: triumphant, Q2

doctor, A158·5, F134, I39, Q1; vintners, W149

quacks, E390, F213, M78

quadrille, N58, P1141: as played at Soissons, Q3

quadruple alliance, G266

quaker's: affirmation, L236, P89; letter, V98; petition, Q5; sermon, T491; song, Q6; wedding, B298

quakers: dispute with anabaptists, N78; fight with Christians, A8; 'Change-alley, B308; fair, B217, S173, (of Bristol) L188; at Preston, H4; in Scotland, H389; (miscellaneous references), A339, E113, F101, F234, H114, L152, P1176, W238

qualities of the British court, S360

quality, modern, M382

quarrel: classic, C230; between Venus and Hymen, Q7

Queen's Bench prison, B514

Queen's chapel, battle for, C543

Queen's Theatre, Haymarket, *see* Haymarket Theatre

Queensberry, James Douglas, duke of, poem on his receiving the Garter, H66

Queensberry, Katherine, duchess of, B55, P1093

Queensberry, Mary, duchess of, elegy on, D415

question: fair, F30; grand, S908

questions and answers, G166

Qui mihi: imitation of, E483; paraphrase of, D569

Quidnuncs at St James's coffee-house: letter from, L136; poem to, P518

Quin, James, C236

Quixote de la Mancha, Don, W103

R., J. (addressee), A321

'rabbit-woman' (Mary Toft), S18

rabble of writers, L226

'rabbling o' Deer', M214

race at Sheriffmuir, R2

racers, Yorkshire, P480

races: Leith, P640; Lichfield, G265, H150, L265; Nottingham, J75

Rachel, Jacob and, I49

Radcliffe, John, his advice to the ladies, D356

Radnor, John Robartes, 4th earl of (dedicatee), A313

Ragoo, Monsieur, M412

rake: female, D407; in fetters, R9; progress of, P1106, R10; reformed, G171; of taste, D409

rakes: letter to, G171; poem inscribed to, N300; Society of, R32

Raleigh, Sir Walter: dialogue with Merlin, O101; ghost of, S7

Ralph (Erskine), V105

Ralph, James, satires on, B39, N271

ram feast, description of, B160

ramble: austere poetaster's, C495; city, C210; disguised statesman's, C469; drunken, T96; Good Friday, W75; through the heavens, W163; holiday, H289; through Hyde Park, R24; lady's, L29; night's, N300; poet's, W141; royal strangers', R321; to Smithfield, B91; Teague's, G119; unfortunate, U6; vacation, V1; *see also* trip

rambling fuddle-caps, W150

Ramillies, battle of, C15, C139, C233, D27, D106, D220, D553, E411, J73, J110, L149, N13, O37, O228, P52, P56, P64, P65, P254, P1081, S240, T338, W3

rams all, R31

Ramsay, Allan: elegies (premature) on, H2, P108; epistle to, H15; pastoral in praise of, S721; satires on, A164, B286, C463, S73; his theatre, F169, R100; poems in imitation of, M2, M3

Ramsay, Elizabeth, Latin poem to, P300

Ramsay, Lord George, epistle to, R87

Ramsay, Lady Jean, elegy on, E224

Randolph, Sir John, C368; *see also* excise, bill of 1733

Randolph, Thomas, epigram to, P1056

Ranelagh House, balls at, P702, W563

rap: English, S382; at the rhapsody, R116

rape, E169, P643, R117, S843, T472, V103: of Adonis, C394; of the bride, R119; of Helen, R118; of the lock, P941; of Proserpine, H368; of the smock, J23

Raphael, cartoons of, B252

Raphoe, John Pooley, bishop of (1702–13), *see* Pooley

Raphoe, Edward Synge, bishop of (1714–16), *see* Synge

raree-show, H324, O1, R122, R126, R128, S174: ballad, O1, R127; man, R130

rat catcher, at Chelsea College, W559

Ratho, M324

rats, committee of, C317

rattlesnake, F192

Rattray, Thomas, of Craighall, bishop, elegies on, D442, L144

raven: and blackbird, S700; and owl, R134

Rawdon, Sir John, elegy on, E225

Rawlings, Pleasant, abducted heiress, C332

Rawlinson, Sir Thomas, elegy on, E226

Raymond, Anna, elegy on, S336

R——by, Miss, B269

Read, Sir William, poems to, O14, T352

Reading, free school at, M194

Reading, Miss, abducted heiress, E169

real: felicity, D192; patriot (Walpole), N280, V99

reason, R137: asserted, F35; essay on, H93, P63; love triumphant over, P732; religion of, H216, M493; rhyme and, R188

reason's tribunal, F267, R139

reasoners, modern, D385

reasons for writing verse, R140

rebel: army in Scotland, F236; Scot, R141

rebellion: history of the grand, W80; history of 29 years of, H261; (Jacobite, 1715–16), F74, R142, S290, S376, T335; (Jacobite, 1745–46), A147, B230, B455, C201, C267, D417, F236, G135, G235, L218, M139, O182, P624, P1109, R141, R143, S134, S146, V56, W32, W272; see also Jacobite rebellions

rebellious fame, R142

rebels, Jacobite: (1715–16), F52, H7, P1033; (1745–46), E575, N34, N321, R143; see also Jacobite rebellions

rebuke, seasonable, S166

rebus, R144

recantation, the, B588: Dr Bungey's, D350

receipt: for cuckolding, D208; to dress a parson, R145; to make a junto, M204; to make a soup, P952; to tame a shrew, N177; see also recipe

recipe to make a wicked manager of a theatre, I40; see also receipt

reconciliation, joyful, H40

recorder's (John Foster's) speech, R323

recreation in vogue, L288

recreations, poetical, S662

recruiters, letter from, S546

recruiting captain, fifteen plagues of, F134

Red-cap, Mother, prophecy of, P1057

Redeemer, hymn to, H81, P472; see also Jesus Christ

redemption, B268, C1·5: man's, H81·5; sinner's, C171

reflection, the, M151: rural, H346

reflections: on a candle, W28; on the victory over the French, R149

reformation, R150, S148: more, D144; England's, W207; Highland, H207; of manners, D145; Oxford, W175

reformer's ghost, R151

regency, B23, B52, M536, N95, R148: and return, W9

regeneration, poem on, D417

Reid, Archibald, Latin poem to, P296

Reid, Jean, marriage of, E447

Reid, John, Edinburgh printer, P296

Reid, William, freemason, O224

reign: female, C247; happy, M145

reigning beauties, M42

religion: and philosophy, P9; poet's, R153; protestant, W4; of reason, H216, M493; soldier's, M39

force of, Y74; principles of Christian, D366; progress of, J49; search after, B530·95, K9; wisdom of, W532

religious: disputes, F213; ode, C267; piety, F169; poems, F75; toleration, S450; turncoat, W154

verse (the following religious poems do not fall under any of the obvious headings, such as are listed below), A7, B11, B481, B533, B535, D192, D277, D417, E10, E315, F75, G309, H407, J15, L40, L93, M469, M558, O115, P414·5, R132, T256, T590; see also believer; catechism; Christian; Christmas; convert; creator; death; deity; divine; eternity; eucharist; faith; four last things; God; grace; heaven; holy; hymn; Jesus Christ; last judgement; Lord's day; meditation; nativity; penitent; prayer; providence; psalm; repentance; resurrection; sabbath; sacrament; sacred poem; sin; sinners; soul; trinity

remark, upon the baths, A339

remarker, remarked, P1118

remarks (=answer), O259, O260, P658, R154, R155: upon remarks, R156

remedy of love, U33

remonstrance, the, R157

removal, grand, G247

Renaut, Lawrence (dedicatee), W225

renegado, the (=Allan), F194, N244

Reni, Guido, copyist of, G310

Renwick, James, elegy on, S420

repentance: call to, C116, W238; stool of, P170

repenting harlot, W98

reply, see answer

report, the, R158

representatives of Old England, A104

reprieve, the, R160

reproof, S534: seasonable, M258

republican procession, W155

resentment, love and, M485

resignation, poem on, P576

resolution, A79: of a layman, R161; loyal, L301; sailors', E340; valiant soldiers', T315

resolve, the, M138

restoration, the, F210, R163

resurrection, the, A204, D414, S525, W273, W564: of Christ, L315, P289; of the potatoes, R165; Tom Punsibi's, T413

resurrection men, in Edinburgh, A13, G300, P159

retired life, M164

retirement, A54, B366, C387, C470, H38, M36, M87, M487, N267, O71, P722, P1006, R167, W566, W566·7

retreat, the, T590: sight's, W234

retrievement, the, R168

return, see answer

revels of the gods, W163

revenge: Caelia's, R242; comical, K11; Strephon's, A207; Sylvia's, A183

Revenge, by Edward Young, epilogue to, E346

review, the, R170, T324: in Hyde Park, H132

Review, Defoe's, G42, T253

revolution: new, N178; upon revolution, R172; tyranny, R211, R212

Revolution club, Edinburgh, H251

reward of ambition, R173

rewards of virtue, P463

Reynard the fox: death of, Y19; fable of, C493

Reynolds, James (dedicatee), C422

Reynolds, Thomas (dedicatee), N40

R——f, preacher of Preston, M370

rhapsody, C130, C422, M327, M380, O233, R186, R187, R187·5, S888, W274: lyric, D423; rap at, R116

rhetoric, system of, S763

rhyme: 250 lines in one continued, O15; and reason, R188

rhythmical composition, C305

rich vintner, W551

Rich, John, B478, P487, S737: his *Harlequin Doctor Faustus*, M197; his *Magician*, A353

Richard the third, opera-epilogue to, N164

Richardiad, R192

Richards, Katherine, elegy on, S346

Richardson, Samuel, his *Pamela*, B192, P25

riches: poet's ramble after, W141; use of, P923

Richmond, Surrey: addressee at, B188; royal hermitage at, B409, L325, M326, S778

 beauties, B532, H114·5; Garden, N276; maidenhead, R201; Park, R203

Richmond, Yorkshire, R202

Richmond, Charles Lennox, 1st duke of (addressee), L259, N263, R202

Richmond, Charles Lennox, 2nd duke of (addressee), N264, N277

Richmond, Sarah, duchess of (dedicatee), C438

Richy, and Sandy, R82, R88

Riddel, Christian, lady Dean, elegy on, P105

Riddel, Maggie, E220

riddle: Oxford, O269; upon riddle, H87; other riddles, D205–8, M388, R204, R205, S508, S899, W164

Riddle, Janet, last speech and confession of, L55

ridicule, essay on, W439

riding hood, plague of, F94

Ridley, Matthew, of Newcastle, C148

Ridley, Nicholas, bishop of London, ghost of, B230

Ridley, Richard, of Newcastle, C148

ridotto, R208: al fresco, R207; *see also* masquerade

ridotto-ladies, B19

Ridpath, George, (?) editor of *Observator*, T253

Rigat, Jo, E546

right triumphant, R210

righteous, happy end of, E534

rightful monarchy, R211–12

ring in Hyde Park, B527·8

Rings-end, whipping club at, W239

rioters: at Drury Lane, S166; at Theatre Royal, Dublin, D420

rival: happy, N253

 lap dog, R214; muses, F275; politicians, R216; queans, C400; sisters, P565; wives, R217

rivals, the, R220

Rivers, Richard Savage, earl, poem to, T49·5

roast, for a Scots parson, R222

roast beef, F198

roasting, of a parson, R223

Rob Roy, S788

robbery, in Epping Forest, B614

Robert, Richy, and Sandy, R88

Robert: the raven (=Walpole), L180; the rhymer, R224

Robert, Earl, P1073

Robert III, king of Scotland, F191

Roberts, 'Squire, elegy on, E228

Roberts, Lady Olympia (dedicatee), S525

Robertson, Lucky, L38

Robertson, Alexander, of Struan: addressee, M404, O59; elegies on E438, T381

robin: eagle and, E2; and hawk, P756; and tom tit, T30; and Will, R231; (=Harley), A335, B125, N332, T33; (=Walpole), F168, P755, R135, R136, R230, R231, R239, T30; *see also* robin red-breast

Robin's: pathetic tale, R239; song, B125, P756; tame pigeons, T33

'Robin Hog' (=Robert Stephens), H352

Robin Hood, L198, R232

robin red-breast, R235–8: and vulture, S674; and wren, R235; turned canary-bird, S586; (=Harley), D434, R238, S586, S674, S702

Robinocracy, C158

Robinson, Anastasia (subsequently countess of Peterborough), E377

Robinson, John, bishop of Bristol and of London, P754: addressee, C366, D296, O31

Robinson, Samuel, captain of trained-bands, B527

Robinson, Sir Thomas (subsequently baron Grantham), ode inscribed to, O50

Rochester pad, R244

Rochester, Francis Atterbury, bishop of (1713–23), *see* Atterbury

Rochester, John Wilmot, earl of, imitation of, C495

Rochester, Laurence Hyde, earl of: elegy on, S323; lord lieutenant of Ireland, S513, W474

Rochester's prophetic answer, F256

Rochford, Anne, C275

Rochford, Robert, Irish judge, elegy on, E229

Rochfort, Robert, marriage of, G3

Rock, Dr, epistle from, E367

rod: for the author of the *Election*, S137; for somebody, C479; for Tunbridge beaus, R245; in piss for the aldermen, R249; Sid Hamet the magician's, S935

'Roderigo' (=Lord Hervey), A234, C444

Roger: Patie and, R76; trial of, T472

Roger, 'the Observator's country-man', E355; *see also Observator*

Roger, Sir, his speech, S477

roguery, fiddler's fling at, F117

Rollance, George, king's boatman, elegy on, T583

Roman: bravery, A157; courage, R263; senate, H318; songstress, C42

Roman catholic church, satires on, C529, F43, F230, H201, W408

Roman catholic: clergyman, elegy on, M171; satires, P120, S69; version of the first psalm, P953; *see also* Ireland, Roman catholics; papists; popery

romance of the rose, P202

Rome, T194: advice to the people of, H317; declaration of cardinals at, C529; fall of, L270; ruins of, D566; speech to people of, S630; state of under Nero and Domitian, S725; statues in, D262

Romish clergy, frauds of, F230

'Romulus of Athens', 'translation' by, P149

Rooke, Sir George: dedicatee, P443; elegy on, P448; victory at Vigo, B551, S11, T418

rooks, and crows, R265

Rosalind, R266

Rosciad, the, R268

Roscommon, Wentworth Dillon, earl of, imitated, T440

rose, romance of, P202
Rose Tavern cabal, S580
Rose, Aquila, elegy on, B306
Roseingrave, Daniel, music by, O24
Ross, Alexander, bishop of Edinburgh, elegies on, A291, E230, E289, P672
Rouse, college servant at Trinity College, Cambridge, B332
Rowe, Nicholas: his prologue to Cibber's *Non-juror* attacked, L48; *Fair penitent*, prologue for, P1125; *Lady Jane Grey*, cantata in, M157; *Tamerlane*, (epilogue to) W32, (prologue for) G37
Roxburgh, Robert Ker, duke (addressee), K19
Roy, Rob, S788
royal: benevolence, D477; boroughs of Scotland, R80; conqueress, R306; conquest, B204; court in mourning, R307; family, B477, P150, T588; royal family of France, E120; favourite, P445; gamesters, R308, R309; guardian, B52; health, R310; hermitage, B409, L325, M326; hero, R310·5; invitation, R312; martyr (=Charles I), R313–6; martyrdom, S5; pattern, R252; progress, R317; prophetess, B530·7; shuffler, R318; sin, R320; strangers, R321; triumph, R322
Royal: Anne, galley, shipwreck of, U8
College of Physicians, A108
Company of Scottish Archers, B363, K17, K43, P48, P401, P641, R72, R74
Exchange, paper stuck up at, M154; statue of Sir Thomas Gresham, C464
Hunters, Yorkshire regiment, R311
Oak lottery, P446
Society of London, R69
royalist, epistle from, E362
Royston, W571
Rue, William, elegy on, E231
ruffs, ladies wearing, B26
Rufinus, C231, S775
Rufus Hall, M228
ruin, poor land's, P755
ruins of Rome, D566
Rule, Gilbert, elegy on, E232
rules for a Christian life, R332·5
rump, the, D535
runaway general, T426
Rundle, Thomas, cancellation of his appointment as bishop of Gloucester, B228, D352, P81
Rupert to Maria, M509
rural: felicity, M487; games, S571; politics, N232; sports, G66
Russel, man of war, M7
Russel, William, baptist minister, elegy on, J11
Russell, Lord John (subsequently duke of Bedford), *see* Bedford
Russian: court, C386; victory at Stavuchani, M35
Rutland, John Manners, 1st duke of, elegy on, S268
Rutland, John Manners, 2nd duke of: commissioner for union with Scotland, V38; elegy on, H78
Ruvigny, Henri de Massue de, earl of Galway, *see* Galway
Rye, George I's landing at, C456

S., A., esq. (addressee), P569
S., Sir E., congratulatory poem to, C362
S., W., life and actions of, L179

sabbath: act for keeping, P153; Christian, L263
sacerdotal sanctity, R213
Sacharissa, Philander and, P201
Sacheverell, Henry:
1709, sermon of, H199, P1053; dedication to, R195; poem by a friend to, F305
1710, acrostic on, A19; healths to, B279, H192, T401; poem on, E295; satire addressed to, W545; sentence passed on, O219; sermons, elegy on, F144; and Hoadly, S2, W148; poems occasioned by his trial and ensuing controversy, A52, A112, A124, A254, B62, B413, C34, C178, C433, C467, D25, D239, D274, D336, D343, D350, D354, E103, E147, E191, E324, F30, F36, F59, G217, H108, H189, H195, H196, H315, H465, I3, I11, J53, L62, L81, L241, L281, M12, M41, M396, N4–5, N73, N98, N103, N178, N295, O2, O118, P178, P453, R145, R223, R333, S121, S671, S718, T2, T19, T26, T401, T482, T534, T543, W51, W154, W287, W367, W553
1712/–, his padlock, O269
1713, poem on, P361
1714, dialogue with the devil, M14; satire on, M538
1715, Lord Bolingbroke's epistolary canto to, L258; song of, R265
1719, dispute with William Whiston, B424
1720, dispute at St Andrew's, Holborn, H200, L92
1724, elegy on, E233
Sackville, Lady Caroline (dedicatee), D522
Sackville, Lord George (subsequently viscount Sackville), poem inscribed to, P264
sacrament, the, F39; hymns at, P738–50, W315; poem of Grotius on, L69; *see also* eucharist; Lord's supper
sacred: eclogue, B486; ode, D83, S4·5; poem, B9, C168, E299, F39, L263, R177, R336, S456, U31, W27
sad pretext, S6
saddle, put on right horse, M3
Sadler, Richard, of Dublin, P688
Sadler's Music house, Islington, W200
Sadler's Wells, Islington, C341
sailor, S8: lamentation of, S10; letter from, O15; turned pirate, S9
sailors, advice to, A101
sailors': account of Vigo, S11; address to George II, S12; health to Queen Anne, V7; pleasure before the mast, S15; song S16
English, resolution to fight Spaniards, E340; triumph over French, E341
saint, the, A374
St Albans, trip to, S36
St Albans, Charles Beauclerk, duke of, installation as K.G., K48
St André, Nathanael, anatomist, S18
St Andrew's, Holborn (Sacheverell's church), B424, H200, L92, R265
St Andrew's parish, Dublin: charity children of, H440; letter to young lady of, P534
St Ann's, Aldergate, charity children of, H435
St Asaph, William Fleetwood, bishop of (1708–14), *see* Fleetwood; Isaac Maddox, bishop of (1736–43), *see* Maddox
St Botolph's, London, vestry of, W136
St Bride's, London, charity children of, H432, H441, H442, H447, H448

St Cecilia's day, odes and songs for, B373, C87, C370, H12, L216, O24, P904, S491, T249

St Clement Danes, vestry of, V78

St David's day, A278, G295, H377, H455, P91, S22, S393, S593

St Dunstan's in the west, charity children of, H443, P93

St George, chevalier de, *see* James Francis Edward Stuart, the Old Pretender

St George the martyr, charity children of, H444, P92

St George's, Hanover square, consecration of, E450

St George's chapel, Ormond Street, charity children of, H434

St George's day, L299, N209

St Germains: James II's arrival at, C387; king of (= Old Pretender), K52; poem written at, A273

St Giles Cripplegate without, charity children of, H445

St Giles's: fortune, H105; workhouse, E189

St James Clerkenwell, charity children of, H446

St James's: Aesop at, F243; beauties, S19; bellman of, B181; news from, G272, S772·5; nobleman at, E359; pleasures of, C39; tale from, T8; trip from, S36; walk from, W12; young lady living near, N118

St James's coffee-house, London, L136, P518

St James's park, B530·8: adventures in, C495; Duck Island, M329; fireworks in, C431; Walpole's new house in, M307

St John, Henry, viscount Bolingbroke, *see* Bolingbroke

St John, Sir Walter, elegy on, A2

St Leonard's hill, M510

St Margaret's parish, Westminster, C150

St Mary Savoy, poem by parishioner of, M155

St Mary's (= Puerto de Santa Maria, Cadiz), P643

St Mary's parish, Dublin: poem addressed to lady of, V106; letter from young lady of, P534

St Michael's parish, Dublin, advice to ladies of, A95

St Pancras, walk to, H289

St Patrick's church, Dublin, E13

St Patrick's day, pastoral on, P114

St Patrick's Well, S20

St Paul's cathedral: S21, W170; building of, C541, N241, S152, W568; Pasquin at, P97, P98; Queen Anne's welcome to (1702), H149; Queen Anne's statue at, N13·5, P98, W281

St Perkin (= Pretender), priests of, E573

St Stephen's chapel, picture for the use of, S696

St Tack, hymn to, H454

St Taffy's day, S22, S393, S593; *see also* St David's day

St Victor's, Paris, miraculous sheep's eye at, W408

St Warborough's parish, Dublin, address to ladies of, A56

Saintloe, Arabella (dedicatee), M434

saints': congratulatory address, S23; rich treasure, P1029

'Salamander', song on death of, N222

Salisbury: journey by way of, J20; song sung at, S581

Salisbury, Jacobite ship captured (1708), M140

Salisbury, Brownlow Cecil, earl of (addressee), D47

Salisbury, Gilbert Burnet, bishop of (1689–1715), *see* Burnet

Salisbury, James Cecil, earl of, poem on marriage of, S300

Salisbury, Sally, poems inscribed to, G133, R263

Sally: Fagg him, F26; whore from Shrewsbury, R156

salmon, Newcastle, T18

Salters' Hall, discourse at, S705

salutation, W474: Edinburgh's, R45; morning's, B608

Samber, Robert, ms. verse referred to, L284

Sambrooke, Sir Jeremy (dedicatee), E410

Samford, John, letters from, W559

Samson's foxes, N152

sanctity, sacerdotal, R213

Sandwich, Burchett's farewell to, B571

Sandwich, John Montagu, earl of (dedicatee), D22, H350, P134

Sandy: Richy and, R82; Robert, Richy and, R88

Sandys, Samuel, baron: (1741) motion to dismiss Walpole, F295, G242; (1743) gin act, W480, W503; (1743) created baron, C346

sanguine lovers, H13

Sannazaro, Jacopo: account of, B173; Latin poem to, P369

Saphirah, British ship, C491

Sapho, *see* Sappho

Sapphic: muse, P150; verses, H148, K20

Sappho, Clelia's epistles to, N282, N285

Sappho (the poetess), P309: to Adonis, S34; epistle to Philenis, E374; passion of, H50; Phaon's answer to, C496

Sappho (= Lady Mary Wortley Montagu), A86, S34

Sappho-an, S35

Sara, Colonel (or Sarah, Captain), elegy on, E234, W407

Saragossa, battle of, T376

Sarah: godly, G206; the quaker (= Sarah Stout), B146, L273

Sarah (= Duchess of Marlborough): farewell to court (1710), S36; dialogue with John, H122; Sarah-ad, S37

Satan: dialogue with young man, D277; defeat of, H59; King Satan, K53

satire: dissertation on, A267; essay on, B502, H98

satiric: ballad, F178; epistle, O231; essay, M477

satirical: ballad, L163; dirge, B472; epistle, F48, L269; essay, M494

satiriser satirised, S85

satirist, the, S81: impartial, I10

satirists, satire on, S83

Saul, David's lament for, L212

Saunders, Mr, musician, B373

Saunders, John, painter, E513

Savage, Richard, royal pardon to, N10

save-alls, six, A254, S121

saviour, the, G298; *see also* Jesus Christ

Savoy, Victor Amadeus, duke of, campaign in Italy (1706), B315

Sawbridge, Thomas, dean of Ferns, S843

Sawney (= Alexander Pope), R21

Scaeva, Horace to, S88

scaffold, the: hymn to, H465; in Westminster Hall, S291

scale, the, T102

Scaliger, Joseph, Latin poem to, P325

scamnum, K74

scamperer, the (= Bolingbroke), S129

scandal, W298

scandal club, Defoe's, D26

scandalous chronicle, C407

Scaramouch, Persius, D42

Scarborough, belles of, B180

Scarborough, Richard Lumley, earl of (addressee), B537, L325, P5

Scarron, Paul, imitation of, M76

Scarronides, S517

Scarsdale, Robert Leke, earl of: love for Mrs Bracegirdle, R291; funeral poem on, S266

Scelus's ghost, S132

scenes, matrimonial, J9

Scheldt, defeat of French at (1708), P608, S133

Schellenberg, victory at (1704), F115, O168

schemer's mirror, G178

schism: causes of, S469; danger of, K105

schism act, P112

scholar, soldier and, S904

Schomberg, Isaac, dispute with College of Physicians, M172–3

schoolboy's elegy, S136

schoolboys, play acted by, P1122; see also Sheridan, Thomas

schoolmaster: of Eton, S510; hints to a, D470; schoolmaster's letter, S137

schoolmistress, the, S395

schools: good manners for, D569; system of rhetoric for the use of, S763; see also boarding schools

Schulenburg, Ehrengard Melusina von der, duchess of Kendal, see Kendal

science, epistle on its decline and revival, F204

Scipio Britannicus, S137·5

Sclater, Alexander, life of, S448

Scocia, princess (= Scotland), decease of, E235

scold, cure for, C544

scolding: ladies, A158·5; wife, F196, T580

Scot, rebel, R141

Scot, Mrs Jean, marriage of, E447

Scot, William, of Thirlestane, elegy on, K18

Scotch: cloth, S138; countryside, C451; dialect, poems in, F184, G307, M304; mist, S141; peers, N102; plot, A55, S350; prophecy, T287; riddle, C2; song, N181; taste, B402

Scotchman: complaint of against Sacheverell, D274; dialogue with Englishman, S140; fifteen comforts of, D107

Scotchmen's lament, T530

Scotland: Aesop in, A115; alarm to, A149; flight of religious piety from, F169; genius of, poem to, A152; highlands of, B448, F22, P564, W297; nobility and representatives of, K28; parliament of, F195; poem in honour of, D90; rebellion in, see Jacobite rebellion; royal boroughs of, R80; tears of, S535; trip to, T483; union with England, see union; victory in (1719), A250, H467; welcome to, H248

Scotland's: grievances, E454; nurseling, N321; tears, S142, S143

Scots: answer, H9; excise man, S144; genius reviving, F195; lancet for an English swelling, F188; nation, D90; ode, R89; parson, roast for, R222; poem, S145; poetry, satire on, C463; songs, R90, R92

Scott, Lady Jane (dedicatee), H342

Scott, Marjory, epitaph on, E442

Scott, Lady Mary (dedicatee), H342

Scottish vision, S167

scourge: for the author, O261; for the French, W401; for ill wives, A158·5; for the incendiary, S150; for the town, L91

screen: (Walpole's), N308, S151; detected, H87; ladies', N108; state, S716

screw plot, S152

'Scribble, Innuendo', W282

scribblers, B559: advice to, C454; hackney, R33; lashed, R93; satire on, D42; (= spinners), A358, N206

scribbling: art of, A326; (= spinning), A360

Scribleriad, S153

Scriblerus: changed into Snarlerus, S504; prolegomena of, P771

Scriblerus Maximus, critical observations of, D22

Scriblerus Tertius, prolegomena of, W412

Scriblerus, Erasmus, editor, T35

Scribogg Hill, near Dublin, A87

scrub, scrub, S155

'Scrub, Timothy' (= Eustace Budgell), death of, C399

scrutiny, the, S157–8

Scudamore, Frances, viscountess, elegy on, P44

scuffle: party, C450; playhouse, P487

scuffle-royal, A64

sea: eclogues, D294; fight, B527·1; officer, M272; piece, K89; storm, W201; see also naval affairs

Seafield, James Ogilvy, earl (dedicatee), N312

Seale, John, elegy on, S233

seamen's sorrow, S162

search: after honesty, S163; for religion, B530·95, K9

seasonable: admonitions, S164; advice, S165, S555; rebuke, S166; reproof, M258; satire, F54

seasons, the, B153, P1113, T236

seceders, led by Ebenezer Erskine, A150

second thoughts, S176

secrecy, committee of, T368

secret: committee, C103; expedition, H260; history, J95, S177

secretary of state, dialogue with Connaught squire, D254

secrets of a woman's heart, S179

sectaries, characters of, L152

sedition, S189, S190

seditious insects, S192

self-denial, P576

Selim, the Persian, trial of, M433

Sempronia, epistle to Cethegus, E375

senate, poetical, P1064

senator: hunting of, K53; mock, M357; young, Y23

Senesino, castrato singer, C47, C400, E416: letters from and answers, A230, E377, E379, F175

Sephalissa, to Sylvius, S201

sequel, M461, S202–6, S442: better, B203

serenades, for birthday of George I, C395, F206, S207–10

serenata: da camera, S211, U15; for royal birthday, S215, S216; theatrale, S212–14

Sergison, Thomas, S610

serio-comic poem, B538

serious address, S219

sermon: against adultery, P973; court, C536; funeral, H458; Oxford, O270; quaker's, T491

sermon hunters, W75

sermons, poems occasioned by: (Joseph Betty) D285, O270; (William Bowman) D285, M292; (Henry Clarke?) E386; (Edward Cobden) C536; (Samuel Croxall) D353; (William Fleetwood) B226; (Paul Lorrain) H458; (Benjamin Nichols) B612; (Henry Sacheverell) F144, H199; (Edward Synge) E589; ('Robert Vyner') E600·5; (unidentified), E419, F57, M520

servants: duties of, D559, S787; poem in behalf of good, D388

services and sufferings, S220

servitor, the, S222

servitude, D388

session: of the critics, S225; of musicians, S223; of painters, S224; of the poets, C429, T475; protestant, A202

sessions, dramatic, D427

seven: extinguishers, P453; wise men, S350, S352

seventeen hundred and thirty-nine, S354; see also one thousand . . .

seventeen hundred, forty-five, place book for, W497; see also one thousand . . .

Seville, peace of (1729), E428, G257, M535, N262, Y82

Sewel, William, letter from, L135

Sewell, George, prefaces by, R77, R106

sex, poems on, A303, C4, I14, O142, R280; see also castrati; condoms; dildo; homosexuals; phallic poems; pubic hair; rape

sexes, battle of, W333

Sextus and Erichtho, story of, H368

'Shaccoo, Monsieur', E322

shades, letter from the, B514·5

Shadwell, Charles, elegy on, M573

Shaftesbury, Anthony Ashley, 3rd earl of, poem occasioned by reading his Characteristics, P549

Shaftesbury, Susanna, countess of, epistle to, C410

Shakespeare, William: actors of, R268; imitation of, T137; prologue and epilogue on, C410
Sir Thomas Hanmer's edition of, C299; Lewis Theobald's edition of, M51
Cymbeline, song from, C300; Henry IV, prologue and epilogue to, O224; Measure for Measure, prologue and epilogue for, W310; Richard III, opera-epilogue to, N164

Shakespeare Club, dedication to, S166

Shales, Richard, of Hatfield Broadoak, elegy on, P599

Shalum and Hilpa, P1043

sham author, S382

shame, cure for, L27

Sharp, John, archbishop of York, L262: dedicatee, A19

Sharp, Thomas, archdeacon of Northumberland (dedicatee), W28

Sharp, Sir William, of Stonnie-hill, elegy on, O199

sharpers, downfall of, D392

Shaw, Sir John, collector of the port of London, elegy on, S273

Shaw, Sir John, of Greenock, elegy on, E236

Shaw, Peter (dedicatee), D387

She-land, C158

Shea, Nicholas, conversion of, P537

sheep, and wolves, fable of, T535

sheep's eye, miraculous, W408

sheermen, of Dublin, P621

Sheffield, poem with local associations, S943

shell, fair, W68

shepherd: and his dog, F10; disconsolate, E485, E609; distressed, D406; faithful, P158; wolf and, C210, W545

'Shepherd, Old' (dedicatee), R88

shepherd's: day, P119; dog, N128; tale, R237; tears, P172; week, G69

shepherds: dialogue between two, N181; mournful, P166; oppressed by the war in Germany, W245·5

shepherds' jubilee, S513

Sheppard, Sir Fleetwood, L148

Sheppard, John, criminal, epistle from, E369

Sherburn, Mrs, epilogue spoken by, O224

Sheridan, Thomas, actor, D420, P572

Sheridan, Thomas, schoolmaster: Alexander's overthrow, L157, S1; defence of, O258, R220; imitation of poem by, L155; Julius Caesar, S416; mock elegy on, E237, (answers to it) P647, T413; translation of Persius, T355; plays performed by his school, E346, H138, S408, S412, S415–16; poems inscribed to, A89, L157, T355, T437; poems written at his school, D65, T372; puppet show of, P1169; satires on, N143, T318, T412

Sheriffmuir, battle of, C432, J90, M107, M221, N181, R2

sheriffs, dispute with students, P594

Sherlock, Thomas, bishop of London: in Bangorian controversy (1718), A277; contention for see of Canterbury (1747), R7; Appendix on the fall of man (1749), B613

Sherwin, William, Latin letter of, T328: answer to, H157

Shields, Alexander, elegy on, T542·5

shifts, maids of honour's, stolen, B128

shilling, splendid, P246

shining sisters, S425

ship's mate, and the parson, S426

Shippen, William, quoted, V92

ships, description of, S8

shitters, British, M166, S206

shoe, history of an old, S177

shoe-boy (=Hartley Hutchinson), D530

shoe-heel, the, M327

shoemakers, society of, at Dublin, A342, A344–5, P593: dialogue with brogue-makers, D266

shooting-flying, M98, S444

Shore, Jane, epistle to the Duke of Gloucester, J55

short verses, S452

Shorter, Catherine, see Walpole, Catherine, lady

Shorter, John, satires on, L184, L327

Shovel, Sir Cloudesly, elegies on, D44·5, F300, N134, P439, P562, T144

Shower, Sir Bartholomew, elegy on, E238

shrew, receipt to tame, N177

Shrewsbury: scholar, poem by, D565; whore from, R156; 'Salopian gentleman', W545

Shrewsbury, ship, sailor on board, V33

Shrewsbury Quarry, W242

Shrewsbury, Adelaide, duchess of, B548, E307: epilogue to, L102

Shrewsbury, Charles Talbot, duke of: lord chamberlain (1710), D438; and peace of Utrecht (1713), D497, T81; lord lieutenant of Ireland (1713–14), C364, P721; dedicatee (1714), H67

shrine, the, M90

Shuff, of Newbury, B32

shuffler, royal, R318

shuttlecock, the, W406

Sican, Irish poetaster, B104

sick-bed soliloquy, M328

sickness, T173–5: thoughts in, T251

sighs of Albion, S460

sight's retreat, W234

signal, the, H115

signor in fashion, S461

silence, hymn to goddess of, J44

silent: flute, J46; woman, B76

Silenus, imitation of Virgil's, B550

silk, manufacture of, W459

silk-mill, Derby, B382

silks: imports of French, E547; Indian, P1051

silkworm, the, P1159

silkworms, P264, S462

Silva, to Strephon, S463

Silvester, Tipping, *Critical dissertation* versified, D43

Silvia, and Philander, L284

simile, P1087, S151, S366: for the ladies, S409

simnel cake, V23

simony, bribery and, W50

simple style, poem in, C47

Simpson, Thomas, grammarian, B95

Simson, John, suspended by general assembly of Church of Scotland, A239, A244, B21-2, B566

sin, sincere sorrow for, W224

sincerity, French, F261

Sinclare, Alexander, elegy on, E239

sinecure, the, M329, M344

singing-bird's address, B530·9

single life: fifteen comforts of, M23; pleasures of, P488

Singleton, Henry, P480

S——ini, Father M——r, P712

sinking, in poetry, art of, S542

sinking fund, Walpole's, P506

sinner: lamentation of, L34; redemption of, C171

sinners, warning to, E316, G138·5

Sion: comforted, S469; lamentation over, L31

sister, poem addressed to, A90

sisters, shining, S425

sixpence, the crooked, B392

skating, B232, N270

Skelton, French 'spy', L163

Skerret, Maria: Walpole's mistress, S177; marriage to Walpole (1738), C392, G272, L324, R217, R219

sketch, of some characters, S486

Skipwith, Sir George, marriage of, S304

Skira (or Skirra, = Maria Skerret), R217, R219

Slain, Christopher Fleming, baron, elegy on, E240

slaves from Barbary, B79

sleep, D368, H20·5: power of, A167

Sloane, Elizabeth, lady (dedicatee), O213

Sloane, Sir Hans: dedicatee, A108, B359, B538, F302, H338, H340, N43-6, N49, W234; letter from Thomas Hearne to, E437

Sloper, William (addressee), O76

Smalley, Caleb, advice to his daughter Molly, A70, M572

Smalley, Molly, A70, E555, I13, L120, L147, M393, M572

small-pox, D357, S487: lamentation for, P1031

Smallridge, George, bishop of Bristol: made canon of Christ Church (1711), N123; elegy on, P1040

Smart, John, of Chelsea Hospital (dedicatee), N44

Smedley, Jonathan: answers to his poems, F53, O261, S858, S876; burlesque of poem by, O77; misidentification of, L120; satires on him as 'Jet Black', H356, L118, O258

Smedley, Mary, misidentification of, L120

Smith, Aaron, solicitor to the treasury, elegy on, E241

Smith, Edmund, student of Christ Church, elegy on, O197

Smith, James, principal of Edinburgh University, elegies on, L6, P657

Smith, John Christopher, composer, L214

Smith, Samuel, minister of Newgate, epitaph on, E441

Smith, William, marriage of, S301·5

Smith's mug-house, prologues spoken at, P1126, P1127

Smithfield, ramble to, B91

Smithfield groans, S530

Smithing, Samuel (dedicatee), N39

smiths, of Dublin, N31, T7, V123

smock, rape of, J23

Smoke the doctor, S510

smokers, looking-glass for, S661

smoking spiritualized, E456

smuggler's success, C203

smuggling, L224

'Smut' (= Swift), epistle to the Whigs, S536

snake in the grass, L163

Snape, Andrew, satires on, A188, A277, S510

sneakers, Northamptonshire, H125

Snow, Thomas, epistle to, G64

snuff, A287: musty, S74; satire against, P29

sober advice, P968

Sobieski, Maria Clementina, princess: epistle to Old Pretender, A194; marriage to him, E448, M351, N213

societies for the Reformation of Manners, D145, H131, P552, T409

society: of loyalists, N215; of rakes, R32

Society for the Propagation of the Gospel, S288

Society of Antiquaries, ode to, R89

Socinian controversy, H108

Socrates, portrait of, C73

Sodom's catastrophe, S543

sodomite club, satire on, D536

Soissons, congress of, Q3

solan goose, D434

soldier: and a scholar, S904; jolly, J90

soldier's: loyalty, S544; religion, M39; resolution, T315

soldiers: amorous, P645; of Great Britain, T396; in tears, E326

soldiers': elegy, S545; lamentation, S546; loyal health, V7; praise, S548

solemnity of the muses, S549

soliloquies, early, E10

soliloquy, H18: Bob's, L260; divine, W566·7; of a great man, S550; sick-bed, M328

solitary, the, S551

solitude, S552: fruits of, T176; ode upon, S801

Solomon, B45, D346-8: and Abra, S553; prayer of, T46; *see also* Bible, Song of Solomon, in the main catalogue

solstice, winter, O177·5

Somers, John, baron: impeachment and acquittal (1701), S291, T501; addressee, P254

Somerset House, journey to, T492

Somerset, Lord Charles Noel (subsequently duke of Beaufort) (dedicatee), C168

Somerset, Charles Seymour, duke of (dedicatee), C411, C419, H71

Somerset, Elizabeth, duchess, satire on, S938
Somervell, James, Dublin alderman, N69
something, noise about, A248
son: advice to, H26; father's instructions to, S147; lamentation of, C98; statesman's advice to, W46·2
son of God, *see* Jesus Christ
song (poems so describing themselves), C300, D355, D428, F270, J90, L310, M531, N113, O109, P1095, S481, S580–600, T77–80, T290: of a bird in the park, R265; blackbird's, S675; choice new, C158; drinking, B157; elegiac, W220; entered prentices', B220; excellent, E597; excellent new, D260, E575–94, I66, J1, M26, M30, M32, P139, S780, S844, S846, S895, T113, W278; fellow craft's, D190; Leicestershire freeholder's, L101; mournful, M547; mug-house, V6; new, A12, B54, B206, B463, C51, C175, C549, D428, F255, H126, H152·5, L64, L94·3, M232, N183–228, O267, P135, R26–30, R65, R115, R222, R225, S660, T425, T480; new camp, N115; new occasional, S717; new Scotch, N181; new weather-cock's, N239; old, R172; old fashion, O110; pleasant new, C34; quaker's, Q6; rare new, R121; right, H273; sailors', S16; second, S381; South Sea, W57; swan's, L178; thanksgiving, T125; of triumph, M254·5; true English-boys', T525; turnip, T571
songs, F61, L15, L113: Scots R90, R92
sonnet, comical, C314
sonnets, melancholy, M162
Sophia Dorothea, divorced wife of George I, T479
Sophron, S601
sorrow for sin, W224
sorrowful ditty, S602
sorrows, end to, E576
sot, picture of a, E293
sot-weed factor, C405
Sou Ma Quang, C151
soul: ascent of the separate, A337; breathings of a pious, H114; essay on, E468; intercourse betwixt Christ and, B130; meditations on the valuableness of a precious, D416; war of, P1155; soul's departure from the world, R182
soup, receipt to make, P952
South Britain, S609
South Carolina, epistle from, K88·5
South Saxon ode, S610
South Sea: poem on (1723), P642; decline of, S364; love drowned in, L282; weaver's new ballad on, W262·5
    ballad, A353, S611, W177; bill, T407; couple (1724), D60; song, W57; stock, F223, P561; whim (1711), M33; other poems concerning the bubble, B553, D545, H297, P506, R87, R104, R113, R127, S810, T539
South Sea Company, directors of, A331, C103, G64, P149, P676; poems addressed to directors, A196, E433, F19; epistle to Charles Joye, deputy governor, C97; Robert Knight, cashier, V119
Southampton, F242: song sung at, S581
Southerne, Thomas, epistle to, F106
Southwark, borough of: election, L326; execution at, C332
Southwell, collegiate church at, S647
Southwell, frigate, voyage in, S785
Southwell, Thomas, 1st baron, elegies on, C330, H174

Southwell, Thomas, 2nd baron (addressee), C330
Spain:
    1701, Aesop in, A116; union with France, A116, F69, W401
    1706, victories in, O167
    1719, attempted invasion, N199, N203, N213, P1138
    1729, peace of Seville, E428, M535, Y82
    1738–39, agitation for war with, A133, B568, E340, N122, N183, P714, S483, T329 (*see also* Pardo, convention of)
    1740–41, war with, B189, B338, C57, C315, F191, M120, M349, N219, N280, P546, P560, P615, R130
    glory of, subdued, M7; progress of, B338
Spalding, gentlemen's society at (dedicatee), W29·5
Spaniard, song sung by, N213
Spaniards: armaments against, T329; defeat of, V33; English sailors' resolution to fight, E340; insults of, A133; intended invasion of, N203; whip for, W401
spaniel, poem upon, P678
Spanish: works claiming to be translated from, A116, C385
    armada, S616; beauty, W126; courage, S617; descent, D151; expedition, F62; 'farst', S618; net, E335
    West-Indies, Vernon's achievements in, P615
sparrow: death of a lady's, T36; Isabella's, K95; turtle and, P1090
Sparrow, Sarah (?), murderer, O274
spas, N175, S747, T491: *see* Bath; Bristol; Hampstead Wells; Islington; London Spa; Melfield; Sunning Hill; Temple Oge; Tunbridge; Whitby
speaker, the, S620: female, F101
specimen, of a larger work, D72; *see also* the index of bibliographical notabilia
spectacles, high church, H198
Spectator: epigram on, T60; poem addressed to, M394; poems based on, B441, J57, M540, P1043, S380
spectre, the, P1045; *see also* ghost
speech: of John Curry, S629; of the first stone laid in the parliament-house Dublin, N33; of John Foster, R323; Oliver Gale's, G7; of George I, M519, S632; of George II, O184, S624, T560; by the High-German speaking dog, S621; 'Little Beau's', L197; of Marius, S630; of the Duke of Marlborough, S627; Earl Mortimer's, J99; of the Earl of Nottingham, N329, S844; of Oliver's ghost, S631; of Benjamin Pratt, S633; Sir Roger's, S477; by Tom Tattle, T558; of Sir Robert Walpole, G270, S478
    last: to the election, L60; of Thomas and Robert Moore, L58; of James, duke of Ormond, E354; of William Paul, M296; of Janet Riddle, L55; of the statue at Stock's-market, L57; of Thomas Vert, L56; of *Wisdom's defeat*, L59
    see also music speech
speeches of Ajax and Ulysses, B430, T49
Spellerberg, Elizabeth, marriage of, O47
Spence, Lucky, R60, W446
Spencer, Anne, marriage to Duke of Hamilton, B342
Spencer, Anne, countess of Sunderland, *see* Sunderland
Spencer, Charles, earl of Sunderland, *see* Sunderland
Spencer, Lady Diana (subsequently duchess of Bedford): addressee, L328, L330; marriage to Lord John Russell, B348
Spencer, John: addressee, T128; elegy on, O207

Spenser, Edmund: poems in imitation of, A365·5, J100, P1065, P1081, S395, T181; in stanza of, B358, B364, C521; tale from, M522

    Epithalamion, imitation of, P1004; *Fairy Queen*, new cantos of, C522, C527, N117, W357; imitation of, P1113

Spenser's ghost, D459

spent time, glance upon, G170

Sphinx, S910

spider, bee and, A65

spinning, art of, A360

spinsters, A358, N206

spirit, work of the, D560

spiritual: fornication, S655; poem, B202

Spitalfields ballad, W128

spite and spleen, S657

Spithead, fleet at: (1729), G257, P2; (1740), P1112

spleen, the, F141, G283, S658: spite and, S657

splendid shilling, P246: imitation of, D533

splitter of freeholds, B530·95, S659

sponge, the, S660

sports, rural, G66; *see also* games

sportsmen, society of, at Grantham, H6

spring, T227, W570

Spring Gardens, Vauxhall, R207; *see also* Vauxhall

Spuddy's lamentation, S666

spy: in armour, L13; court, C469; field, W69; French, L163

squabble, theatric, T126, T127

'Squash', D235

'Squat, Squire', L255

squib, M412, S667

squire: and the cardinal, S669; and the parson, J66; turned ferret, D328; country squire's ditty, C458

squirelin, the, S672

squires, Ireland's blessing on her hopeful, I59

squirrel, the, P1086

Staffordshire election, L175

stag: chase, P1012; hunting of, H410

stage, the, R176: clear, C236; rhapsody on, W274; use and improvement of, O89

stage: contest, D427; tyrants, C52

Stair, John Dalrymple, 1st earl of, elegies on, E244–5

Stair, John Dalrymple, 2nd earl of: addressee, B475, H208, L304, M305, O85; recovery from illness (1744), C357

Stamford toasts, P992

Stanhope, George, translator of Epictetus, P999

Stanhope, Hugh, poems to, A331, C463

Stanhope, James, 1st earl: (1710) victory at Saragossa, A25, T376; Westminster election, E543, G181; addressee, T347; (1714) dedicatee, H68; (1715) dedicatee, S577; (1718) voyage to France, T293; dedicatee, T92; (1719) addressee, A202; (1721) elegies on, D418, E35, P415, S715

Stanhope, Lucy, countess (addressee), P415

Stanhope, William, earl of Harrington, *see* Harrington

Stanley, Sir William, travels of, L41

Staples, Mrs Elizabeth, elegy on, E246

star: blazing, B283; northern, H225; that leads to Christ, D217

star-gazer, the, S720

starling: imprisoned, P153; song of, C469

stars: advice from, A72; curses against, C550; decree of, W375

state: of man, A314; of the nation, S706; of Rome, S725 affairs, O190; bell-man, S722; blackamore, D340; boatswain, A160; dunces, W426; fables, Y1; flowers, C285; gamesters, S724; gossip, P713; lessons, P426; paradox, B530·1; picture, N230; puppet-show, C1; screen, S716; weather-cocks, S728, S729

statesman, the: (=Walpole), S652, S730; on his travels, C347

statesman's: advice to his son, W46·2; lecture, O111; mirror, S733

statue: of Queen Anne at St Paul's, P98, W281; of George I, in Hanover Square, D270, in Dublin, U20; of Sir Thomas Gresham in the Royal Exchange, C464; of William III, in London, V22, in Dublin, P550, P623, at Charing Cross, D270, N129, at Stock's Market, L57, N129

statues, P279: dialogue between two, D262

statutarian, the, S734

Stavuchani, battle of, M35

steadiness, levity and, M88

Stebbing, Henry, epistle to, F101

Steele, Elizabeth, marriage to John Trevor, D567

Steele, Sir Richard:

    1709, *Tatler* satirised, T253

    1710, *Tatler* pirated, P1118

    1711/13, letter from Robert Hepburn to, P400

    1714, *The Crisis*, C507, J69; attack on, I45, L7; addressee, L181, S854, W291, W311

    1716, dedicatee, L286

    1717, addressee, J97

    1718, dedicatee, S23

    1720, epistle to, R273

    1722, *Conscious lovers*, prologues and epilogues to, N140, N176, P1133

    1729, elegy on, M317

    see also 'Bickerstaffe, Isaac'

Steeleids, the, L7

Stennett, Joseph, elegies on, P669, Q17

step to the lobby, S748

Stephens, Robert, messenger to the press, C454, H274, H352

Stephens, William, *Letter* of answered, J101

Sterling, Mrs, actress, prologues and epilogues spoken by, N139, N163, N164, P1120

Sterling, James, satire on, G305

Sterne, John, bishop of Clogher (addressee), A172

Sternhold, Thomas, imitations of, B299, K67, L34, O171

Stevenson, Sir Archibald, Latin poems to, P300, P343, P381

Stevenson, William, murderer, S589

steward (=Stuart), good, C321

stewards, good, H337

Stewart, —, A239

Stewart, Ann, marriage to William Mitchel, W266

Stewart, Lady Barbara, Latin poem to, P373

Stewart, Sir James, of Good-trees, elegies on, E250, I25, S170, T382

Stewart, Lady Margaret, Latin poem to, P373

Stigand, F237

Stilton hero, S762

Stinchcomb Hill, R191

stinking fish, D540

Stock's Market, statue at, L57, N129
Stockell, Samuel, elegy on, E247
stocking-frame, invented by William Lee, C272, O3
stockjobber, bankrupt, R87
stockjobbers: fate of, P642; yea and nay, B308
stockjobbing: art of, A327; prophecy concerning, P149
stocks, S767: abuses arising from, M269; rise and fall of, R87
stoic philosophy, H236
Stoke by Nayland, inn-sign at, H193
stool of repentance, P170
Stopha, Signor, boxer, W409
stoppage no payment, S769
storm: (of 26 Nov 1703), C488, D102, P625; sea storm, description of, W201; see also high wind; tempest; thunder and lightning
Stormont, Anne, viscountess, elegy on, B367
Stormont, Marjory, viscountess (dedicatee), T256
story: moral, D552; to the purpose, P454
Stote, Sir Bertram, Latin poem to, P297
Stourbridge, H237
Stout, Sarah, B146, L273
Stowe, gardens at, W360
Stoyte, John, alderman of Dublin, L60, O262: elegy on, E248
'Stranger, Sir Peter', R155
strangers, royal, R321
stratagem, Apollo's, J27
Stratford (London), Venus at, C540
Strathmore, John Lyon, earl of, elegy on, M221
Strathnaver, William Gordon, baron, elegy on, E249
Strephon: to Belinda, P60; and Chloe, S809; Clio and, T360; to Delia, P736; Silva to, S463; and Sylvia, C205
Strephon's revenge, A207
Stretch, puppet-show man, P1167
strife and envy, B572
'Strip-corps', F287
strollers, French, P143, P144
strolling hero, B604
Stuart, Alexander, master of Gairlies, elegy on, V66
Stuart, Archibald, Jacobite, P525
Stuart, Sir James, of Goodtrees, see Stewart
Stuarts, the, A367
student, experienced, E607
study, gentleman's, G123, S399
Stukeley, William (dedicatee), W229
stumbling: block, S775; horse, S776
sturdy beggars, L239, L240·5, S777
styles of poetry, P70
subscribers: (to a religious test), S780; Gay, F92
subsidy treaties, ballad on, N75
success, of her (his) majesty's arms, C139, C334, C376, D27, J109, O167, P1081, R168, T267, W21
successes, of her majesty's arms, B106, C334, E420, G173, P52, P56, P543, R301, T84, T107; see also battles; victories
succession, the, S781: essay upon, E475
sufferings, services and, S220
Suffolk, S782
Suffolk health, S783
Suffolk, Henrietta Howard, countess of: epistle from, F95; letter of Swift to, S830

sugar plantation, S784·5
suicide, the fair, F33
Sullivan, Mr, singer in Dublin, N80
summer, T220, W570
summer-house, T490
summum bonum, the, W312
sun: ode on, P260; ode to, F110
Sunbury, George Montague, viscount (afterwards earl of Halifax) (addressee), J88
Sunday: evening's conversation, T154; thoughts, B533–5
Sunderland, Anne, countess of, S425, W255: elegies on, C188, M468, P601, W5
Sunderland, Charles Spencer, earl of: (1710) dismissal, M160, P455; (1716) death of his wife, W5; (1720) addressee, S500, T291; (1722) elegies on, E251, S136
Sunning Hill, in Windsor Forest, M195
superstition, O87: exposed, B515
supper, beef-eaters' last, S772·5
supplication, whigs', C306
supreme being, B446, S495; see also God
surprise, the, E290
Susan, Sweet William's farewell to, B331
Susanna, story of, F238
Sussex, election, S610
Sutherland, executioner of Edinburgh, S789
Sutherland, George Gordon, earl of, elegies on, E242–3
Sutherland, William, elegy on, M223
'Sutorioso, Don Francisco' (= Francis Taylor), D395
'Swaddling John', S790
swain: bashful, P1175; British, D72
Swan tripe-club, in Dublin, T496
swan's song, L178
swans, the, S791
Swanson, Hogan, criminal, C332
swearer, thundering poem to, T266
Sweden, king of, see Charles XII
Swedes, naval expedition against, N224
Swedish: conspiracy, A193, F23; invasion, D246; lamentation, S792
sweet William, the, S793
Swift, Jonathan:
    1712, fable inscribed to, W384
    1713, band-box plot, T589
    1714, addressee, C507, D293; satires on, G125, O264, S536, T435
    1719, satire on, O77
    172–, imitations of, D337, R169
    1720, invitation from Sheridan to, S407
    1722, character of, C118
    1724, satire on, T318, (answer) R220; poems occasioned by his campaign against Wood's halfpence, E571, E594, E610, L123, L124, M436, N165
    1725, congratulatory poems on his campaign, A341, B75, C350, D403, D428, P660, S175, S381, S406; birthday poems, D64, P610; satire by Smedley, S509, (answered) O261, O263, S68
    1725/–, letter to, S67
    1726, birthday poem, P596; as Drapier, P675; inventory of his goods, S419; young lady's complaint for his stay in England, Y22; Gulliver's travels, B290
    1726/–, recipe sent to, P952
    1727, dedicatee, A346, O3; letter to, S418; poem revised by, E389; Gulliver's travels, S356, T586

Swift, Jonathan (*cont.*)
  1728, satire on, S504
  1730, addressee, G5, I44; advice to, A73; epistle to, E386, E396; panegyric on, P36
  1731, addressee, T437; attack on, E608
  1732, addressee, S658; character of, A237
  1733, addressee, L74, T390; life and genuine character of, S884
  1734, addressee, A357; lullaby for, L321; satire on, M416·5
  1735, addressee, F100; letter to, M553; publication of his works, A282
  1736, addressee, O132, P786; as Drapier, B550, D251; praise of, D516, E464; satires on, B550, W553
  1739, addressee, B43; character of, H181; and country parson, L242; epistle to, E395; satire on, S83; verses on death of, S920
  1740, Francis Bindon's portrait of, D520
  1742, poem in manner of, S126
  1744, essay inscribed to, E465
  1745, elegy on, F290; apparition of, concerning Faulkner's edition of his works, D429; imitation of, W270
  1745/–, thoughts from a ms. of, D77
Swinton, John, of Wadham College, Oxford, C286
S——wll, J., usurer, elegy on, N52
Sword, —, parish schoolmaster, E252
syllabus of animal economy, S942
sylvan: dream, S943; muse, P119
Sylvestra, Girolamo and, U5
Sylvia: poem to, T360; and Libertina, D407, T532; Strephon and, C205
Sylvia's revenge, A183
Sylvius, Sephalissa to, S201
Synge, Edward, bishop of Raphoe, sermon on toleration, E589
synods, associate, P588
syphilis, poem in praise of, A262
system of rhetoric, S763

T——, John, minister of the gospel at M——, elegy on, E252
tabernacle in Petticoat-lane, charity children of, T258
table-talk, K37
tack, the old, and the new, O124
Tack, Saint, hymn to, H454
tacker's: character, H124; ghost, T1
tackers, the, D45, O276, S783: health to, H126; new ballad on, P183
tacking club, T2
Taffy's: masterpiece, T3; triumph, B176
Taffydeis, the, T4
tailor: in Hamilton, P1008; turned poet, T6; tailor's vindication, D53·5
tailor craft, poem on, M445
tailors: Dublin society of, poems in honour of, N26, N29, N30, N168, P540; satires on, A347, B602, P639, S79, T504; annual procession of, N27, N32, N154, S66; dispute with the smiths about precedence, T7, V123
  Edinburgh, M445; merchants' and hammer-men's complaint against, M185
Talbot, Charles, baron, elegies on, P551, T208, T527
tale (*Many political fables were published as 'a tale' but have been entered under* fable. *Those remaining here have been roughly divided between simple tales (often erotic, in the manner of La Fontaine's* Contes) *and those with a political purpose which are not clearly fables.*)
  A65, A175, A185, A216, A247, A374, B49, B64, B108, B139, B407, C39, C43, C102, C156, C202, C230, C274, C342, C372, C401, C406, C484, C547, D211, D233, E290, F228, F284, G58, G133, G310, H135, H146, J34, J51, J68, J105, K11, K32, K65, K95, L3, L13, L17, L27, L44, L90, L251, L253, M117, N9, N177, N296·5, N301, O95, O114, O134, O237, P9, P82, P278, P279, P478, P1024, P1052, P1068, P1088, P1153, R201, R214, S20, S380, S672, S720, T28, T93, T158, T320, V23, V25, W309, W341, W372, W435, W559, W578
  (political), C490, F182, G232, H188, J8, J56, M160, M218, M320·5, M347, M522, O129, P192, R96, S654, S769, T9, T21–3, T25, T31, T414, T436, W400
  see also Arabian tale; Chinese tale; court tale; Dutch tale; fairy tale; gallant tale; London tale; love tale; merry tale; Tartarean tale; tragical tale; tragi-comic tale; true tale
Talent, hon. —, elegy on, E253
tales, W347: ethnic, T405; old wives', O130; poetical, M275–6
talk of the town, M431
Tallard, Marshal: character of, T488; letter to, L146, L158; to the Duke of Vendôme, A176
Tamerlane, by Rowe: epilogue to, W32; prologue for, G37
Tamiad, the, T35
Tamworth, Robert Shirley, viscount, elegy on, S271
Tankerville, Forde Grey, earl, L284
tapestries, in Dublin castle, P557
Taplin, Mr, club at his house, at the sign of the Drapier's Head in Truck Street, Dublin, C350, D251, D428, S381
tar, tale of a, T19
tar water, T39
tarantula turning, T247
'Tariff, Arthur' (=Arthur Moore), T414
tartan, R97
Tartarean tale, T43
Tash, —, vintner, W149
taste, H20·5, T44: observations on, C417, C418; à-la-mode, H89; and beauty, T45; false, P908; Scotch, B402; of the times, M85; of the town, N335; true, T532; *see also* man of taste; rake of taste; woman of taste
'Taste, Mr', tour of, M299
Tate, Nahum: poem of, adapted, E171; satire on, S56
Tatler, Steele's: attack on, T253; imitation of, P400; piracy of, P1118
Tatler, at the sign of, Calves-head club, L298
'Tattle, Tom', new speech by, T558
tattoo, the, T91
Tauris, entertainment for the ladies of, C298
Tauronomachia, T94
tavern: hunter, T96; query, T99
taverners' answer, T100
Taylor, Captain, in Edinburgh, B287
Taylor, Francis, Yorkshire lawyer, D395, U25
Taylor, John, of Cambridge, J100

Taylor, John, oculist: character of, E390; defence of, N188; his lecture to the ladies, P566; mock elegy on, E257

Taylor, Nathanael, minister of the gospel, elegy on, S745

Taylor, William, Dublin attorney, elegy on, E258

Te deum, B80·5, T105, T107

tea, T108, T109: poem upon, C11, T72; in praise of, I32, M527; satires against, P163, W11

tea-bill, to the promoter of, L224

tea-kettle, T112: metamorphosis of Dublin beau's head into, M224

tea-pot, or the lady's transformation, P218

tea table: chat of gods at, P129; conversation, L16; satire on, N238, P163; war with cakes and ale, N238

teachers, miserable condition of, E607

Teague: poor, P757; Teague's ramble, G119

Teague-root, botanically considered, W534

tears: of Amaryllis, C379; of the muses, B367, H231; of Scotland, S142, S143, S535; tribute of, T477

Telemachus, adventures of, A68, A69, M83

tell tale, the, T271

temperance, commended, C502

tempest, the, R22, S4

temple: of death, S390; of fame, B551, P974; of harmony, P1016; of liberty, K77; of love, L209; of Venus, C215, S197; of war, T115; temples of virtue and pleasure, T117

Temple, the, in an uproar, H310; flying horse in, F125; epistle to gentleman of, B613; poem by a gentleman of, H188

Temple Oge, C278: ballad, P516, T115·5; trip to, T489

Templer, poem by, S203

Templer's: bill of complaint, T116; exit, P1106

ten commandments, S187–8

Tenison, Thomas, archbishop of Canterbury (addressee), O28

tennis-court, song sung in, S587; see also Oxford, Tennis Court

Teresa, Donna Clara to, J40

Terpsichore, T118·5

terrors of death, R22

test: of love, A212; of poetry, C477
  act, G307, T13; ballad, S141

'Testo, Sir', L20

Thame, T35

Thames, royal appearance on (1727), N149

Thames Street, fire in, N36

Thanet, Thomas Tufton, earl of, W376

thanksgiving, T119, T123, T124: for the colliers, W323; hymn for the, D109; poem occasioned by the, G10·5

  day, (1704) R322; (1706) D109, G10·5, W35; (1713) H436, P633, P1132, T81; (1715) H451, O223; (1716) B416; (1749) B64, O25

  hymn, (1704) Q14; night, (1746) S583; poem, (1743) B341; sermon, (1716) B226; song, (1708) T125

theatre: turned upside down, T126; recipe to make a wicked manager of, I40

Theatre Royal, see Drury Lane theatre

theatres, essay on, E469; see also Bristol; Dorset Garden playhouse; Drury Lane theatre; Dublin, theatre; Edinburgh, theatres; Goodman's Fields theatre;

Haymarket, Queen's Theatre; Lincoln's Inn Fields theatre; Oxford University, theatre

theatric: managers, complaint to, H48; squabble, T126, T127

theatrical, see acting; actors; actress; Aston, Anthony; Carestini; Cibber, Colley; comedians; dramatic; Elrington, Thomas; epilogue; Farinelli; Garrick, David; Hallam, Thomas; Harlequin; Hasse, Faustina B.; Heidegger, John James; Macklin, Charles; Nicolini; opera; Penkethman, William; play; players; playhouse; playing; prologue; Quin, James; Rich, John; Senesino; Sheridan, Thomas; stage; tragedy; Woffington, Margaret

theatrical volunteer, T128

Thelwall, Eubule, satire on, E483

Theobald, Lewis: author of *Martiniad*(?), P782; edition of Shakespeare, M51

Theocritus, pastorals after the manner of, P1172

Theodora, Amyntor and, M44

'Theodore, King', K54

Theophilus, dialogue with Calophilus, C388

Theseus, answer to Ariadne, C496

they are not, T150

thief slain, J26; see also beau-thief

thimble, the, H112

thing, an impossible, C372

'Thing, Monsieur', M413

thinker, the fair, F35

thirty marks of a fine woman, A65

thirty seven articles, satire on, E337

Thistlethwaite, Robert, of Wadham College, Oxford, C286

Thomas: dialogue with Grizel, C244; redivivus, T157

Thomson, James: elegies on, C294, M570; poem on his *Seasons*, D11

Thorn, tragedy of, P685

Thornhill, Mr, ride of from Stilton to London, S762

Thornhill, Sir James, epistle to, S363

Thorold, Sir Charles, elegy on, S227

Thorold, George (dedicatee), W228

thought: Englishman's, E343; evening, E531

thoughts: in sickness, T251; upon the four last things, T456; plain, W501; second, S176

three: bonnets, tale of, R96; politicians, T257

Three hours after marriage, D444, W303

threnody, G319, H278, H408, I21, S323–41, T259–65

throne of justice, B536

Thucydides, description of plague of Athens, S663

Thumb, Tom, history of, T157

thunder and lightning, W556

thundering poem, T266

Thurmond, Mrs, epilogue spoken by, P611

thyme, old woman spinning of, O133

Thynne, Henry, elegy on, S267

Thynne, Thomas, elegy on, S333

Thyrsis: and Chloe, B333; Corydon and, T154; Damon and, P114; Meliora's tears for, C330

Tickell, Thomas: epistles to, B583, B584; letter to, Y90; ode to, S368; poem to, P533; verses to, M500·5

tickler, the: (= Thomas Tickell), B584; (= Paul Hiffernan), M114

Tiger, elegy on, E254

Tighe, Richard, satires on, T373–4

Tilden, Sister Petronilla Maria, N348

tilt-yard, epistle from an half-pay officer at, E365

time: glance upon spent, G170; progress of, P1113; and eternity, T313

time-servers, attacks on, B219, T353

timely caution, G223

times, the: essay on the vicious bent and taste of, M85; medley on, M161; new song on, S660; odes on, O76, S756; poem on, H33; political touch of, P714; satire on, O2, T494; touch of, T21, T428, T430; true touch of, N122, T533; verses on the present, N121

Timon, Lord, Pope's character of, M40, W298

tin-plate workers of Dublin, complaint of, T314

Tindal, Matthew: *The rights of the Christian church asserted*, E517; *The defection considered*, E408; *Christianity as old as the creation*, C127; dedicatee, W40; elegy on, E397

'Tinsel, Sir Billy' (= Sir William Calvert), S470

tippling, ancient philosophers vindicated against, A220

tippling philosophers, W183

Tisdall, William: poem thought to be his, A237; *The true character of the Intelligencer*, S887

Tissey, John, elegy on, N148

tit for tat, T321, T322, T328

tit-bit, the, T320

Titchfield (Hants), M283

tithe hops, advocate for, D212

tithes, quaker's petition for exemption from, Q5

Titus, and Gissippus, D552

toast, the, K79: for all true hearts, T401; for Anne and Robin, T400; independent Westminster electors', I34; real, S19

new: N233; Church of England's, T403; Duke of Marlborough and the court's, D499; to Duke of Ormond, N234; queen's and the Duke of Ormond's, Q12; queen's and my lord of Oxford's, Q9; whigs', W393

toasts, the, T404: Bath, B94; Oxford, A207, A317; protestant, P1151; Stamford, P992; *see also* beauties; fair; ladies

tobacco, B209, C405, E456, P479, P482, S661, T404·5: pipe of, B520; *see also* snuff

tobacco merchant, dialogue with, F283

Toby: (= Swift), T435; Esquire, D76

Toft, Mary, 'the rabbit-breeder', D328, S18, S453

Tofts, Catherine, satire on, F284

toilette, the, T269

Toland, John: elegy on, E256; invitation to Dismal, S911; poems occasioned by his pamphlets, I45, J101

Tom: Dick and, O117; in the suds, W470

Tom of Bedlam, T409: Tom o' Bedlam's Dunciad, H145·5; Tom of Bedlam's new medley, T411

Tom, Captain: dialogue with Sir Henry Dutton Colt, D255; Captain Tom's ballad, C34

Tom, Honest, H298

Tom, the toper, O126

Tom King's, Covent Garden, B71

'Tom-tit' (= Sir Thomas Parker), and the robin, T30

Tomo Chachi, G128

Tonson, Jacob: F107; and the Kit-Cat club, B257, K94

topographical poems, A281, B84, B93, B366, B369, B451, B620, C2, C61, C107, C276, C278, C419, C474, C541, D52, D53, D232, D236, D291, D394, D566, E298, F242, G9, G18, G43, G128, G216, G254, H31, H32, H51, H117, H162, H271, H275, H300, H332, H402, J98, L103, L330, M152, M195, M283, M510, N241, O11, P548, P589, P987, P1038, R191, R195, R202, R203, R260, R335, S21, S400, S750, T288, T299, T443, T486, V2, W242, W360, W461, W525, W531, W567, W568; *see also* trip

Torbay expedition, P1112, T422

tories: advice to, A102; hymn to, R158; Pretender's letter to, P1037; vagabond, V6

tories': address to King George, T424; looking-glass, G95; triumph, T425

tory: whig and, W387

health, N235; hero, T426; wits, epithalamium inscribed to, M351

tory's downfall, R303

Torrington, George Byng, viscount, *see* Byng

Totnes address, A50, B567, M333, P708, S625, T427

touch of the times, T21, T428, T430: political, P714; true, N122, T533

Toulon, naval action off (1744), A61, A160, N195

tour, Mr Taste's, M299

Tournai, victory at (1709), G180

tower, the, F227, M343; of Babel, W189

Tower of London: humble adddress of, T377; hymn to B227; in mourning, F168; jewel in, O205

Tower-wharf, guns on, D268

town, the, K15: displayed, N37, T433; metamorphosis of, T158; scourge for, L91; taste of, N335; vices of, V88; view of, G148; way of, W257

town: assemblies, T432; eclogues, B415, T434, T435; life, pleasures of, F131; mob, C450; officer, R1; poets, D509, O229, S62, S67; talk of, M431

Towne, (Richard?), Dr (addressee), B139

Townsend, Isaac, victory of (1745), N119

Townshend, Charles, viscount: addressee, B151, E8, O6, O71, S249; recovery of (1728), H333; retirement from court (1730), O71; sponsor of Stephen Duck (1730), D466

Towzer, T436

trade: downfall of, M30; elegy on death of, E259, N132; encouragement of, M269; plot against, P506; (miscellaneous poems concerning) A286, A356–60, B382, C56·5, C272, D400–2, D522, D544, D545, F151, F266, H306, L211, L224, L313, O3, P559, P1051, R81, S143, S243, S558, S840, W459, Y178; *see also* commerce; Dublin, corporations; excise; merchant; South Sea

traders: satire addressed to disconsolate, L243; grumbling, H121

trades, song on, S581

tradesman's hue and cry, T438

'Traffick, Lady', A63

tragedy, W82: Berkshire, B200, B201; youth's, S419·5

tragedy speeches burlesqued, D360

tragical tale, U5

tragi-comi-canonical-farcical ballad, W453

tragi-comic tale, B174

tragi-comical eclogue, M521

traitors, fate of, F74

tranquillity of mind, H388

transfiguration, the, R198

transformation, lady's, P218; *see also* metamorphosis

translated verse, essay on, D307
transmigration, P1019
transportation, M343
transubstantiation, B169, C338
Trapp, Joseph, poem occasioned by his sermon *The royal sin*, R320
Trapp, Joseph (son of the preceding), P1122
Traquair, porter in, E52
Traulus, S914, S916
traveller, wanderer and, H407
travellers: merry, W117; three, C102
travelling, abuse of, W357
Travers, Dr, elegies on, E260, N131
travesty: of Ovid, R8; of Virgil, S517
treason against the ladies, T469
treasure, the saints' rich, P1029
treaties, subsidy, N75
treaty: woeful, W539; of Worms, D369
Treby, Sir George, elegies on, P286, T64
tree of life (*sens. obsc.*), N7, W533
Trelawny, Edward, governor of Jamaica, D494
Trentham, Granville Leveson-Gower, lord (subsequently marquis of Stafford), in Westminster election of 1749–50, C313, M285, N198, N210, P143–5
Trevers, Dr, elegies on, E260, N131
Trevor, Mrs Elizabeth (addressee), D567
Trevor, John, marriage of, D567
trial: of constancy, P279; mock, W550; of Roger, T472; of Selim the Persian, M433; of skill, T473–5; of wit, L7
trials of patience, G118
tribe of Levi, T476
tribunal, reason's, F267, R139
Tribune, The, by James Arbuckle, F286
tribute: of the muses, T478; of tears, T477
trick: for trick, T479; upon trick, T479·5
trifle, the, T480
triflers, important, B405
trimmer, T481: loyal, L302
trimmers, satire against, T353
trimming observator, W154
trinitarian combat, S705
trinity, the, T416: doctrine of, B169, S780; hymn to, S397
Trinity College, Dublin, *see* Dublin
trip: from Beavis Marks to Mincing Lane, A216; from Moorfields to Bromley, W117; from St James's to St Albans, S36; from Turnstile to Hick's Hall, C391; from Westminster Hall to Oxford, T482
to Ballymore Loghsunderland, S446; to Bar-le-Duc, S736; to the board, the court, and the temple, H33; to Chelsea, C495; to the devil's summer-house (Mayfair), T490; to Dunkirk, T484; to the fleet, A67; to Germany, T485; to Kensington, T486; into Kent, S451; to Lichfield, T487; to Liverpool, L104; to the masquerade (Somerset House), T492; to Newgate, I71; to Nottingham, T488; to the pillory, T493; to St Paul's, N241; to Scotland, T483; to Temple Oge, Stephen's Green and the Bason, T489; to Vauxhall, T494; to Westminster, S748; *see also* journey; ramble; voyage; walk
tripe club, T495; Swan tripe-club, T496
triple alliance, the, T498

triumph, the, T84: of beauty, T499; Britain's, B457; Britannia's, B473; Great Britain's, G264; of Isis, W247; of love, H14; of monarchy, T500; Old England's, O109; Parson's, P90; patriots', P126; of peace, T81; royal, R322; of the great Lord Somers, T501; Taffy's, B176; of union, T82; of virtue, T502; widows and orphans', W452; of wisdom, T503
triumphant ode, D553
triumphs: of bigotry, T506; of faith, T505; of the lady of the ocean, T507
Triumvirade, the, M462
triumvirate, the, W303
trivia, G81
trooper's elegy, V24
trophies, the, D553
trophy bucket, the, O286
Trosse, George, of Exeter, elegy on, M518
Troy, destruction of, M193
Truby, —, vintner, W149
true: blue, T512; Briton, C101, T514; Britons, T516; churchman, S42; countryman, M68; English boys, T525; greatness, F123; hearts, T401; history, D199; patriot, T528; popery, T529; Scotsmen, T530; tale, C535, F72, G96, N232; taste, T532
true-born: Briton, T513; Englishman, D153, P456; Englishwoman, F86, L8; Huguenot, P456; Welshman, S393
True intelligence, P658
Trumbal, Lady (dedicatee), N12, O215
trumpeter, the, T534
Trumpington, miller of, M233
trusty and true Englishman, E584
truth, A375, A377, B345, T536: curry-comb of, B550, C549, D516; discovered, L81; in disguise, T540; and falsehood, D482; force of, D47; found out at last, T539; and honesty, P434; and moderation, T537; at last, T538; naked, M38; nothing but, N328; plain, P473–5; on all sides, T541; to some tune, E311; speak truth, and shame the devil, S619; Is this the truth?, I69; No, this is the truth, C148
truth's champion, T542·5
truths, some bold, S554
tub: tale of a, T21; new tale of a, H188; tale and no tale of a, C490; tale of a bottomless, T10; and pulpit, T543
Tubb, John, murderer, B200
tubs: tale of two, T31
Tullamore, Charles Moore, baron (addressee), S403
Tullamore, John Moore, baron, elegy on, E261
Tullibardine, John Murray, marquis of, elegy on, S529
Tunbridge (and Tunbridge Wells): description of, B94, B620; familiar epistle from, A198; pleasures of, C78; poems written at, A83, D534, H412, S425, W255
Tunbridge: beaus, rod for, R245; prodigy, F142
tunes:
   A beggar of all trades is the best, N328
   A begging we will go, B424, E558, G308, H331, T571, W480, Y19
   A cobbler there was, F257, H251, L80, N58, P710, U2; (? = The cobbler)
   A hundred and thirty four, T1
   A soldier and a sailor, H108, L298
   A trifling song you shall hear, N159

tunes (*cont.*)

A whim-wham's lately come over, N14
Ah how happy is he, that's from business free, W459
Aim not too high, G114, R307
All in the land of Essex, W561
An ape, a lion, a fox and an ass, F174
An old courtier of the queen, N151
An orange, G263
And a begging we will go, *see* A begging . . .
And as I was going to Derby, E583
As down in a meadow, C210
Auld lang syne, H393, S595
Avast! honest mess-mate, R225
Balhaven's voyage, T556
Bartholomew fair, C41
Belinda, N213
Bob in Joan, I15
Bonny Dundee, C325, Q8
Bonny Katharine Ogie, C216, R30
Brave boys, W239
Brave Vernon's triumph, V33
Bumpers 'squire Jones, F178, S583
But we'll be as merry with our comrades, H121
By Jove I'll be free, R249
Captain Johnston's lament, A12, C340 (? = Johnson's farewell)
Catharine Ogie, *see* Bonny Katharine Ogie
Catholic brother, *see* Dear catholic brother
Charles of Sweden, *see* Glorious Charles of Sweden
Chevy Chase, A126, B32, B39, B293, B468, B567, C150, D328, E546, E560, G242, I71, M1, N59, N84, N85, N88, R223, R311, S586, S780, S792, V103, W376, W539, W557·5
Clack, clack, W38
Come and listen to my ditty, E314, G186, N121
Come lay thee down my Phillis, D419, H37
Come let us prepare, D428, I34, T525 (cf. The free masons)
Come prithee, Horace, hold up thy head, O267
Come sit thee down my Phillis, *see* Come lay thee . . .
Commons and peers, *see* Ye commons and peers
Constant Anthony, B85
Daniel Cooper and his man, P1034
Dear catholic brother, M228, N89, P757, S597
Derry down, D420, H158, M114, N212, O25, S550
Did you not hear of a gallant sailor, P1148, V96
Diogenes surly and proud, H200, W371
Down, down, down, derry down, *see* Derry down
Down with 'em, S130
D'Urfey's fart, E563
Fair Rosamund, G181, N90
Farewell joy and farewell pleasure, S36
Forgive me if your looks I thought, E572, S603
Forty-eight, G109
Forty-one, N154·5
Fye soldiers, fye, why so melancholy, boys, H123
Glorious Charles of Sweden, C431, E331-2, N211, S588, W441
God prosper long our noble king, H406, T113
God save our noble king, N210
Golden hair, H195
Gossip Joan, H202, P713
Green sleeves, L163, M30

Hark, hark, the thundering cannons roar, N235
Hey boys up go we, D328, D343, F44, M205, N73, N93, P713
Highland laddie, bonnie laddie, *see* The highland laddie
Horse, foot and dragoons, I61
Hosier's ghost, H36
How happy are we, T426
How pleasant a sailor's life passes, J89
Huzza! Bomb, B279
I am a silly old man, R27
I am the Duke of Norfolk, T99
I laugh at the pope's devices, E576
I'll tell thee Dick, J1
I'll tell thee, Estcourt, a pleasant tale, C368 (? = preceding)
Ireland's lamentation, N202
Joan stooped down, G225
John Anderson my jo, E551, P406, T557
John bobbed in, and John bobbed out, I15
Johnson's farewell, C332, C440, F68 (? = Captain Johnston's lament)
Jolly Bacchus, T99
Killiecranky, B103, E597
King Charles's martyrdom, N204
King George's march, R115
King John and the abbot of Canterbury, B41, B105, B618, C7, C212, D270, D421, E450, E554, E569, F239, K97, L13, L184, L198, N95, N102, N318, P139, P1147, R232, S171, S470, S471, S478, S599, S669
Lang unkenn'd, E220
Last parliament sat as snug as a cat, M392
Let Caesar live long, R310
Let the soldiers rejoyce, E564
Lillibullero, B30, C339, C369, E541·5, E591, F253, J103, N189, N217, P179, Y16
Lochaber no more, R65
London is a fine town, *see* Oh! London is a fine town
Marlborough push 'em again, N218
Moggy's lamentation, P760
Mortimer's-hole, L308, W278
My bleeding heart, T477
My nanny O, B456
My virgin's treasure, M192
Near Thame a town in Oxfordshire, O274
Now now comes on the glorious year, E327, G183, N203, N209
Now ponder well, H362
Of noble race was Shinkin, E565, S593
Oh! London is a fine town, B29, E593, H257, **L288, N96,** N225, O202, S660, T428
Oh rare popery, S472
Old long syne, *see* Auld lang syne
Old Noll, H427
Old Sir Simon the king, D541, N110, T480, W391
On the fourteenth of August, B40
Over the hills and far away, D545, N233, S140
Packington's pound, B65, B462, C34, C242, D354, E599, F258, G257, G270, I66, L91, N18, N75, N98, N160, N289, P471, P1161, S510, Y178
Peggie I must love thee, R29
Poultrane poverty, P1008
Preston fight, E318 (cf. The battle of Preston)

tunes (*cont.*)

Pretty parrot say, E550, F251, N64
Pretty Polly say, *see* preceding
Randel a Barnaby, E583·5
Remember ye whigs what was formerly done, E577
Saint George for England, K47
Sally in our alley, W481
Sarsefield's lamentation, N196
Sawny's to be married to Moggy, M562
Set the glass round, L299
Since Celia's my foe, N193, S589
Sing tantararara fools all, R31, T541, W563
Sound the trumpet, C337
Such a parcel of rogues in a nation, U30
Such charms has Phillis, G113
Tantararara, masks all, *see* Sing tantararara fools all
The abbot of Canterbury, *see* King John and the abbot...
The apprentices song in masonry, *see* Come let us prepare
The battle of Preston, N76 (cf. Preston fight)
The black joke, N69
The blacksmith, H255, N103 (? = Twangdillo)
The bleeding heart, E326
The bonny black laddie, E567
The bonny boat man, R1
The bonny broom, E586
The broom of Cowden knows, O243
The Cameronians' march, N182
The Campbells are coming, J90
The caping trade, R121
The catholic ballad, P135
The children in the wood, E288, O247
The cobbler (of Canterbury), E30, M379, N201, S584 (? = A cobbler there was; The honest cobbler)
The cobbler's end, N318 (? = preceding)
The cuckoo, B38
The cut-purse, G260, N288 (cf. You cut-purses all)
The dame of honour, D464, F83
The drums and the trumpets command me from Shear, H248
The Earl of Essex, N194
The fine lady's airs, L33
The first of August, G265, N206
The fisherman, H192
The free masons, I33 (cf. Come let us prepare)
The frolicsome lord Duke of Buckingham, E549
The gallant Grahams, G235
The glorious twenty-ninth of May, W452
The good old cause revived, L159
The grand elixir, W177
The hare merchant's rant, D260
The high church health, D88
The highland laddie, N94, P640
The highland rant, H204
The honest cobbler, S481 (cf. The cobbler)
The horseman's sport, R2
The Irish dear-joy, S597
The Irish trot, L300, P84
The jovial beggars, M395
The king and the abbot of Canterbury, *see* King John and the abbot...
The king and the miller of Mansfield, E335, I15, L64, M232, M254·5, N115, N212, T514

The king of France's lamentation, E313
The king shall enjoy his own again, E545, H150, K96, N83, R303, R316, S895
The lad's a dunce, T115·5
The ladies fall, M32
The leather bottle, G178
The London 'prentice, S406
The married man's item, N227
The merchant's daughter of Bristol town, P681
The miller of Mansfield, see The king and the miller...
The nurse's ballad, L321
The old wife she sent to the miller her daughter, H7
The old woman poor and blind, W264
The Oxfordshire lady, R317
The philosopher's stone discovered, W177
The pious Christian's exhortations, T520
The protestant flail, W409
The raree show, F263
The royal forester, W262
The sailor's delight, E341
The Scotch wedding, J7
The tackers, N155
The tippling philosophers, P1007
The winter is cold, my cleeding is thin, G176
There was a jovial beggarman, C549
There's no hopes of peace, T500
This great world is a bubble, C68
To all ye ladies now at land, *see* To you fair ladies...
To the weaver if ye go, S165
To you, dear Ormond, cross the seas, P1037 (= following)
To you fair ladies now at land, A241, B582, C458, E547, F285, L183, M33, M291, N106, N107, N125, N219, N222, P112, P762, P903, S16, S352, S473, S546, S600, T404, T546, T552, W262·5
Troy town, M548–9, W275
Twangdillo, B269 (? = The blacksmith)
'Twas when the seas were roaring, N223
Under the greenwood tree, N307
Valiant Jockey's marched away, T315
We have catcht you in the nick, E588
What is greater joy and pleasure, L281
When she was brought before my lord mayor, P145
When Troy town for ten years wars, *see* Troy town
Which nobody can deny, A78, E570, L81, M174, M352, N130, N224, N228, O165, P194, P465, T538, W239
Why, this is the devil, L61
Wigmore's galliard, H405
William and Margaret, L277, P761, S132
Winchester wedding, T480
Women's work is never done, U8
Would you have a young virgin of fifteen year, N57
Ye bold presbyterians, N156
Ye commons and peers, A50, B25, C275, D41, E31, E556, G180, L92, L101, N62, N71, N79, N145, P1032, P1151, S204, S752, T358, T528
Ye gallants, come, N72
Ye lads and ye lasses, L57
Ye pretty sailors all, W549
Ye rebels of England, D88
You commons and peers, *see* Ye commons...
You cut-purses all, E568 (cf. The cut-purse)

turd, meditation upon a, O180

Turd-man, Tom, his epistle, K1

Turin, victory at, F278, S240

Turk, battle between Jew and, T554

Turkish paradise, T555

Turks: victories over, B164, T250
the two (George I's pages of the back stairs), B468

Turnbull, Dr (addressee), D470

turncoat, T557: character of, C123; new way of, E551;
religious, W154

turncoats, the, T558: modern, M385

turnip-man: trial of, W444; old (= George I), D5, O127

turnip song, T571

Turnstile, trip from, C391

turtle: and the sparrow, P1090; wandering, C29

Turturella, Bubo and, F2

Tutchin, John, B513, E203, H274, H359, N331, O4, O5,
P273, T104, T572, W282: elegies on, C461, E262–4,
T573; *see also Observator*

tutor: celebrated (= Sheridan), poem inscribed to, A89;
certain little (= E. Bentham), proposal of, C99;
ladies', L16

twelve blessings, of a scolding wife, T580

Twickenham: dog at, B326; gentleman at, E359; grotto at,
D390; little satyrist of, E415; squire, T473 (all refer
to Pope)

Twiford, Esquire, adventures of, A67

twitcher, the, N197

two kingdoms, union of, *see* union

two tubs, tale of, T31

T—y, Lady Mary, T390·5

Tyburn: courteous invitation of, S443; hymn to, H471;
petition from, P194; stanza upon, G311

Tynemouth bathers, B180

Typhon, M76: story of, S770

tyranny exposed, T577

tyrant, French (= Louis XIV), F262

tyrants: fate of, F182; stage, C52

Tyrconnell, Eleanor Brownlow, viscountess, recovery of,
S111

Tyrconnell, Frances Talbot, countess of, elegy on, E255

Tyson, Edward: addressee, S657; elegy on, S341

Ulrica, queen of Sweden, P388

Ulysses: Ajax and, speeches of, B430, T49; epistle of
Penelope to, E436; his men transformed to beasts,
F172

unbeliever, awful death of, G210

unbiassed patriot, U1

undertaker, character of, F287

undertakers, exhortation to, G104

unembarrassed countenance, U2

unequal match, J51

unfortunate: family, U3; knight, P1116; lady, H157·5;
lovers, U5; married man, U4; ramble, U6

ungrateful world, U7

unhappy: marriage, D467; voyage, U8

union, U10, U11: divine, W236; fatal, of France and
Spain, F69; of whig and tory, O169
with Scotland (1707), poems celebrating, B530·6, C16,
C517, D46·5, D107, D220, F216, G93, G261, G264,
O226, P461·5, P619, R304, S140, S245, T82, T146,

T513, T585, V38; Scottish controversy concerning,
B165, D148, E235, H9, M68, M162, P681, P687
S143, S167, S384, S945, T530, V109
commissioners for, B530·6, F216, P461·5, V38
dialogue, S140; parliament, B165; top-knot, U12

universal: beauty, B491; coquet, U16; doom, H343;
elegy, G327; misery, D324; passion, Y122; prayer,
P63, P982

universe, the, B11: beauties of, B131, N170; essay on,
E470, M484; philosophic ode on, P260

universities: news from both, C255; poem addressed to
three, D533

university: fresh-man's entry into, F265
answer, U17; ballad, U19

unlicensed love, disasters of, M473

upper gallery, the, L74

upstart, the, U25

upstarts, vanity of, W190

Upton, Arthur, elegy on, E461

Upton, John, notes by, B518

usurer, the, U30

usurers, Irish, A10, L129, N52

Utopia, Y177: canary-birds naturalized in, C18

Utrecht: Aesop at, A111
congress of, C366
peace of (and negotiations before), A24, A91, A111,
A227, B159, B295, B323, B336, B514·5, B548,
C29, C62, C366, C513, D74, D235, D296, D298,
D497, D532, E111, E307, E547, E591, F258, F261,
G249, H184, H244, H436, H473, I4, L259, M30,
M174, N13·5, N85, N189, N269, N311, N328, O1,
P61, P77, P97, P131, P135, P340, P526, P633,
P1132, R122, R126, S217, S275, S455, S468·7, S520,
S631, S769, S844, S895, T81, T303, T400, T451,
T502, T535, T544, W25, W331, W385, W388, Y72

Uxbridge duplicate, T584

Uzziah, and Jotham, U35

vacation: long, L243; ramble, V1

vade mecum for malt-worms, V2

vagabond tories, V6

vain pursuits of mankind, J42

valour, progress of, P1115

Vanbrugh, Sir John: character of, T518; epilogue to his
Pilgrim, P611; epilogue to his *Provok'd wife*, P611

Vandeput, Sir George, and the Westminster election of
1749–50, M285, N210, P698

Vanderbank, John, instructions to, B254

Vane, Anne: her child by Frederick prince of Wales,
C164, L27, L279, O180, V8, Y20; illness and death,
F199, V12, V13

Vanella (= Anne Vane), V12: epistle to Alexis, L279; in
the straw, V8; Vanella's progress, V13

Vanessa, Cadenus and, S814

vanity: of free-thinking, V16; of human life, R250; of
human wishes, J87; of upstarts, W190; and worth,
D60

variety, B347

Vario, the painter, *see* Verrio

Varus, Achates to, A15

vaticinium, V20

Vaughan, Parson, P1042

Vauxhall: trip to, T494; gardens, R207, T555

veillée, V23

Vendôme, duc de, A176, B577, H45, L162

Venice, voyage to, S785

Venus: amour of, M473; and Ardelia, V25; and David, P355; enraged, P82; and Hymen, Q7; marriage of, M112; mistaken, N253; ode to, P896; Pallas and, P1082, S402; poem to, T399; revenged, V26; at Stratford, C540; temple of, C215, S197

Verax, to Adamia, V27

verbal criticism, M51

Verdoen, Sir Peter, elegy on, E265

Vereilles, John, Dublin juror, E594

verge, of the court, G276

Vernon, Mrs (addressee), P1041

Vernon, Edward, admiral: answer of, P1045; glory of, T525, V31, V33; letters from Don Blass to, L127, S617; resolution of, G124; in the West Indies (1739–42), A312, B474, E331, E332, E342, E605, F120, J96, M120, N81, P615, P1045, S78, T257, U26; election campaign of 1741, B470, I33, P23, T525, W371, W373

Vernon, honble Edward (? = preceding) (dedicatee), C225

Vernum, Mr, tailor (dedicatee), O244

Verres (= Walpole) and his scribblers, B559

Verrio, Antonio, painter: advice to, A84; letter to, B555

verse: danger of writing, W438; reasons for writing, R140

versification (mainly limited to those works which so describe themselves), A50, A68, A69, B192, B213, B226, D43, D352·5, E290, E598, E600·5, G115, H61, H245, H259, H268, H474, I74, J57, K73, K103, L67, L127, L284, M83, M135, M140, M286, M292, M296, M333, M519, M520, M524, M540, M558, N7, N318, O270, P1, P81, P86, P463, P1043, R332·5, S527, S944, T176, T427, T505, W80, W325, W328; see also paraphrase

Vert, Thomas, last speech of, L56

Vertumnus, E530

vessel, leaky, L90

vestry: (of St Clement Dane's), V78; select (of St Botolph's), W136

veteran scheme, P1131

vicar: of Bray, V84; of Cheshunt (R. Chapman), E145; country, C459, C460; fat, P1042

vice: folly of, W532; morality in, B426; triumphant, C271

viceroy, the, D529

vices of the town, V88

Victor Amadeus, duke of Savoy, campaign in Italy (1706), B315

victories: over the French and Bavarians (1704), C249; over the French king, F216; see also battles; successes

victory, V90: and beauty, R30; Britain's ode of, B455; essay on, D123; over the French, R149; hymn to, D123, H467, S240; in Scotland, A250, H467; welcome to, C336, W529; see also battles; success

Vida, M. G., account of life and writings of, S462

Vienna, peace treaty of (1731), N141, N159, N262, P133, S159

view: of the court and city, D551; of the creation, C425; of eternity, A314; of the Irish bar, V94; of life in its several passions, F205; of the present fashions, T158; on the present state of men and things, E601; of the town, G148; of Westminster, P1146, V1

Vigo, victory at, A362, C385, P622, S11, S458, T418, V96

Villars, duc de, marshal of France, letter to General Evans, N317

vindication: of the Duke of Wharton's answer, V98; of the libel, D530; the tailor's, D53·5

vine, and bramble, fable of, G135

vintner: complete, W57; rich, F283, W551

vintners, B487, B498·5, W149: panegyric on, P40

Vintners' Hall, entertainment at (1706), D549

Violante, Madam, play acted at her booth, S416

Violenta, P463

Violetti, E. M., marriage to Garrick, M431

Virgil: character of, M479; critical thoughts on, P475; ode to, P897; description from, M498; dramatic poem taken from, D194; imitations of, A352, B550, H6, H44, L242, M521, N13, O9, P110, T434, T435, T474; travesty of, S517

virgin, S831: discontented, D325; fifteen pleasures of, F136

virgin sacrifice, A329

Virginia: address of the clergy of, L296; poem by a pious clergyman in, D61

virtue, F200, S19: beauty and, C188; and industry, A360; in danger, V103, V106; in distress, T93; enquiry after, M504; fall of, L111; female, F99; manly, B221; modern, M386; and pleasure, C422, T117; rewarded, B192; rewards of, P463; triumph of, T502; verbal and practical, difference between, H156

virtuous: wife, dialogue with loving husband, L283; women, catalogue of, F103

vision, the, A25, C528, D185, D193, D483, N13, R103, S525, V104, V106: beatific, C273; Belhaven's, B165; British, H9; of Mons. Chamillard, P254; death's, R177; Ormond's, O247; Scottish, S167; of two brothers, V105; (other visions), B560, D425, L209, P45, P974, R199

visions, V107

visit, the, V108: court, C470

visiting, art of, L16

Voguells, Jungfer, marriage of, W276

voice from the north, V109

Volkra, Cristoforo (dedicatee), R253

Volminia's complaint, N50

Volpone, B530·1: (= Godolphin), P458, V111; (= Lord Hardwicke), V110

Voltaire, poem attributed to, R213

volunteer: female, F102; theatrical, T128 company, P674; laureate, S112–8

'Volusenus, Joannes', professor, poem to, D55

votive ode, H322

vox: britannica, V118; populi, V119

voyage: to the court of Neptune, V122; from the East Indies, M501, V121; from Europe to America, K89; to the gulf of Venice, S785; to Ipswich, P23; to Maryland, C405; to the north, I73; unhappy, U8; see also trip

Vulcan's speech, V123

vulgar praise, poetical essay on, P705

vulgus britannicus, W193

vulture: and eagle, V124; robin red-breast and, S674

'Vyner, Robert' (= Walpole), excise sermon of, E600·5

W——, Mrs (addressee), H290

W——, Sir, W261

W., S. R. S. (dedicatee), D40

Wade, George, general: dedicatee, A152, N45; epistle to, H43; ode to, on disarming the highlands, W297

Wade, John, usurer, L129

Wadhamite prologue, P486; *see also* Oxford, Wadham College

'Wadie', satire on, N94

Wadsworth, Mary, marriage to Robert Feilding, F84

wager, the gossips', H401

Wager, Sir Charles (addressee), P1044, T507·5

'Wagstaff, Dr', T157

'Wagstaffe, A.,' his *True account of the late pyracies of Jamaica*, P715

Wagstaffe, John, quaker, elegy on, O193

Wake, Ethelreda, elegy on, A221

Wake, William, archbishop of Canterbury: contention for see on his illness (1731), F146, M347; dedicatee, A221, N46

Wakefield, sermon of W. Bowman at, B299, D285, M292

Waldo, Sir E., elegy on, S279

Wales, P1038, R260: complaint of, D234; panegyric on, P717; sighs of, R194
Company of mine-adventurers in, N263

walk: to Islington, W200; from St James's to Covent Garden, W12; to St Pancras, H289; *see also* trip

Walker, Mr, scandalous reflections on, L104

walking the streets of London, art of, G81

walking observator, the, W69

Wall, Mary, elegy on, W220

Wallace, Sir William: life of, H20; poem to the memory of, T333

Waller, Edmund: imitations of, A74, C75, E69, O220; ghost of, W22

Wallmoden, Amalie Sophie Marianne, countess of Yarmouth, *see* Yarmouth

Wallup, Mrs, epistle to, C92

Walpole, Mrs (dedicatee), S525

Walpole, Catherine, lady, R217, R219: elegy on, E266

Walpole, Sir Edward, B541

Walpole, George (subsequently 3rd earl of Orford), painting of, N265

Walpole, Horace (subsequently 4th earl of Orford) (dedicatee), M270

Walpole, Horatio (subsequently baron Walpole): dedicatee, O21; at Norwich, N334, Q2; satires on his foreign policy, H252, L64, N18, N107, S669

Walpole, Maria, patent of precedence for, M382

Walpole, Sir Robert (subsequently 1st earl of Orford):
1712, 'the patriot', S369; imprisonment in the Tower, F168, O205, R173, S366, T316
1716, recovery from illness, O181; addressee, S560
1718, epistle to, E408
1721, satire on, H87
1723, epistle to, W538
1725, impeachment of Sir Thomas Parker, T30; epistle to, D371; poetical petitions to, M329, M344
1726, installation as K.G., B143, N277, T512, Y86; epistle to, E488; poetical petitions to, M321; dedicatee, Y132
1727, Lechmere's complaint against, R232; recovery from illness, M537; and death of George I, R239;

and Isaac Le Heup, I17; quarrel with Bolingbroke and Pulteney, L261; praise of, O6; dedicatee, T200
1728, house party at Houghton, F174, Y19; satirized as Norfolk congress, C367, H406, N318, Q3, S786; epistle to, E424; addressee, H333
1729, house party at Houghton, H331; and peace of Seville, E428, M535; presents Pope's *Dunciad* to the king and queen, P771; satire on, C492; petition to, B47; addressee, B304, L161, M317, M536
1730, house party at Houghton, N160; praise of, R230; satires on, C231, C469, F76, F117, H252, T584; epistles to, B301, D353, E425, E428; petition to, H396
1731, and *The craftsman*, D41; negotiations with Fleury, K96; and Pulteney, D243, D272; and Vienna treaty, N159, S159; satires against, C141, H410, N230, S471, S474, S730
1732, satire on, B559; epistles to, M326, S99; ode to, M343; addressee, S159
1733, and excise bill, C368, E600·5, P1117, R135, R231 (*see also* excise, bill of 1733); at Norwich, July, Q2; praise of, M38; satires on, O184, P1119, R136; verses to, N278
1734, and Edmund Gibson, K97; satires on, N319, P755, S177, S716; epistle to, M86; addressee, S40
1735, praise of, C77; satire on, S782; epistle to, M307; addressee, M87
1736, addressee, S189
1737, dedication to, B364; epistle to, M85
1738, marriage to Maria Skerret, C392, L324, R217, R219; negotiations with Spain, N18
1739, peace with Spain, C349, P714, S478, S725 (*see also* Pardo, convention of); satires on, D287, M168; epistle to, E426; ode to, P79
1740, and Pope, M234, M249, M511; satires on, B292, F220, L114, L174, N219, R130, S550, Y178; addressee, N280, S652
1741, motion of Sandys for his removal, A17, F295, G242, G302, M525, P1145, R137, T271, T537; contrast with Pulteney, B467; satires on, C325, F263, G124, G248, M156, P1023; defence of, P125, V99; friendly advice to, S733; addressee, G124, P546, P1023, V99
1742, defeat and resignation, A268, B294, G247, L180, N308, O107, O112, S151; satire on, C497; created earl of Orford, O39·5; poems to, as earl of Orford, F58, N267, P547
1743, enquiry into his administration, G270; 'the old fox', O111, O113
1744, and Pulteney, E449; redivivus (as Henry Pelham), W29
1745, poem to, W536
(undated poems concerning), D19, E360, F191, L152, M398, N258, P271, T498

Walsh, Patrick, 'the Little Beau': deserted mistress of, S70; satires on, C35, I2, L195–7, P209, S53, S463

Walsh, William, 'translation from Homer' of, A3

'Walsingham, Francis' (= William Arnall), T474

Walsingham, Sir Francis, ghost of, N160

Walters, Peter, *see* Waters

wanderer, the, H407, S119

Wandesford, Susannah (dedicatee), P196

Wandsworth campaign, S466

Wanstead garden, F173

wanton: baker, W38; wife, F126

war, B89, O90, W39: amorous, A218; with the devil, K2; insect, B530·3; oracles for, O239; and peace, P77; preparations for, A133; with priestcraft, W40; progress of the, P1112; pulpit, W148; of the soul, P1155; temple of, T115; *see also* Spain, war with

'Warbeck, Perkin', *see* James Francis Edward

Warburton (?), Molly, C35, L195, S70

Warburton, William: dialogue with Pope, D326; dedicatee, B503, S493; editor of Pope, P800, P819, P865; satires on, D363, P1103

Ward, brewer's son in Dublin, B440, H170

Ward, Edward: satires on, U4, W96; poem in manner of, H289

Ward, John, of Hackney, V55

Ward, Joshua, quack doctor, E390, W42

Ware, Henry, death of, W220

warming-pan, the, N200, P454

warning, W237: to cuckolds, W239; fair, F36, W390; to Ireland, I66, W240; to lovers, W241; ominous, W523; to the queen, W390; to sinners, G138·5

warning-piece, W238: to Englishmen, N84; to sinners, E316

Warren, Benjamin (dedicatee), W227

Warren, Borlace, MP for Nottingham, I47

Warren, Sir Peter, ode to, O74

Warrington, George Booth, earl of (dedicatee), B417

warrior, the glorious, G181

wars: between gods and giants, M76; broke out in the city, N307; of the elements, W201; new song of, N207

Warton, Thomas, professor of poetry (addressee), C365

washer-woman, poem by, C288

Wat, John, grieve to the laird of Culquhalzie, elegy on, E267

watch, the lady's, L30

Waters (or Walters), Peter, moneylender, I52

Watson, James, Edinburgh printer, W252

Wattie, Gibbie and, B276

Watts, Isaac: elegies on, G136, M282, P656; ms. notes by, Y102; satires on, A15, D334

Watts, John, marriage of, S318

Watts, May, presentation copy to, P463

way: to a bishopric, V82; to heaven, W260; to peace, S455; of the town, W257; of the turncoat, E551

W—d, J—n, letter from, L129

W—e, A—r—n, elegy on, E268

wealth, R104

weather-cock, N239: state weather-cocks, S728–9

weather-glass, living, P200

weather-menders, S654

weaver: turned devil, W262; poems by, C287, W262·5, W459

weavers: Dublin corporation of, B603, C68, G104, N171; prologue and epilogue in behalf of, S413, S838; Sisyphian society of, C287; humble thanks of, W459

weaving: art of, D400; neglect of, P1051; trade, A357

Webb, John Richmond, general, victory at Wynendael, H154

Webster, James, elegy on, T259

wedding: collier's, C147; hasty, H105; Munster, M562; north-country, B506; quaker's, B298; Welsh, H107; *see also* marriage
    night, K35; song, W264–6

wedlock: a paradise, W267; vindicated, W268

Weedon, Cavendish (addressee), T375

Weekly journal, D122

Weemys, earls of, *see* Wemyss

weeping: church-men, W275; muse, L164

Weighley, *alias* Wild, Jonathan, *see* Wild

Weims, Thomas, advocate (dedicatee), W236

welcome: to Queen Anne, H149; Duke of Argyll's, F52, H248; Prince Charles's, P1058; Prince Eugene's, B295, P1060; to King George I, W280; to Duke of Marlborough, A368, D95, D501, H247, W280; to the medal, W278; to Duke of Ormonde, L309; to Earl of Rochester, S513; to victory, C336, W529

Weldon, John, poems set to music by, D549, M533

Wel-he, Captain, *see* Walsh, Patrick

wells, the, N175, S747, T491; *see also* spas

Welsh: poems in, A278, B480, E287; metrical form, E20 the, poems addressed to, H455, N55; satire on, H279; *see also* Ancient Britons; leek; St David's day; Taffy ambassador, B186; charity children, P91; engagement with the mice, Q15; health, N320; monster, W282; mouse-trap, W283; poet, H346; wedding, H107

Welshman, C381, E565: character of, C126; true-born, S393

Welshman's: last will and testament, W284; prophecy, R305; scuffle with the mice, M552; tales, W287

Welsted, Leonard: controversy with Pope (1732), M40, O183, T565·5; dedicatee, M492; epistle to, M480

Wemyss, David Wemyss, earl of, elegy on, E269

Wemyss, James Wemyss, earl of, marriage, R70

wenching, art of, A328

Wentworth, Thomas, general, at Cartagena, A312

Wesley, Samuel, poem revised by, L107

West India heroes, D494

West Indies: banishment to, E76; war in, M120, P615

West Kirk, Edinburgh, P1027

West, Gilbert, translation of Pindar, W245

West, Richard, lord chancellor of Ireland, P631: elegy on, E270

Westerham, Kent, K104

Westfield, William, marriage of, S305

Westminster: Aesop at, A112; devil to do at, T149; flight from, F168; grand sale at, G248; step to, S748; triumphant, W373; view of, V1; wanton baker of, W38; whigs' farewell to, A161
    elections, (1708) C150; (1710) E543, G181; (1715) P24; (1741) I33, I34, T525, W371, W373; (1749–50) C313, M285, N70, N198, N210, P143–5, P698
    bubble, W364; choice, I33; combat, W367; electors, I34; justice, W372; scuffle, M199

Westminster Abbey, A14

Westminster Bridge, D421, W364

Westminster Hall, P1146: devil in a whirlwind at, D242; French standards in, D268; scaffold in, H465, S291; trip from, T482

Westminster Journal, poem from, H202

Westminster School: Edmund and Henry Curll at, H151, W343; metrical grammars for, B592, B597; new dormitory at, S285; play acted by scholars of, P1084; poems written by scholars of, L318, P196, V21

Weymouth, Frances, viscountess, elegy on, S337

Weymouth (? Grace), Lady, B41

whale: British, P357; Irish whale-fishery, F266

whalebone petticoat, O242; *see also* hoop petticoat

Whalley, John: letter to, A72; mock elegy on, S834

Wharton, Philip, duke of: and Bolingbroke, E380; dedicatee, H87; drinking match with 'Earl Harold', W376; turns Roman catholic, V98; and Walpole, H396

Wharton, Thomas, 1st marquis of, lord lieutenant of Ireland, H320, H361, O266, T23: elegies on, P670, W112; satires on, C119, E375; tale of his puppies, L262

Wharton, Thomas, professor of poetry, *see* Warton

Wheatstone, Dr, his explanation of a prophecy, R305

wheedlers, touch to, T431

wheedling jilts, W383

wheel, dog in, D391

Whetty, James, of Edinburgh, elegy on, E271

whig: bastinado for, F192; character of a certain, C119; conjuring, C381; dialogue between whig and tory, T539, W387

whig: ballad, W388; dictator, M387

whiggery displayed, W389

whiggish fair warning, W390

whiggism laid open, W391

'Whiglove, Lord' (Thomas, marquis of Wharton), elegy on, W112

whigs: advice to, A105; epistle to, S536; history of the honest, W64; no plunderers, W394; petition of, M392; triumphant, C176; turned Jacobites, N178; whip for, W404; at their wits' end, O116

whigs': address, W392, W397; farewell to Westminster, A161; idol, F221; last will and testament, F297; mortification, N156; new toast, W393

whim, South Sea, M33

'Whim, Sir Valetude', H476

whimsical age, W398

whip: and a bell, W400; for the Spaniards, W401; for the whigs, W404

whipping, D534; *see also* rod

whipping club, at Rings-end, W239

'Whipstaff, Ned', A101

Whiston, James, elegy on, E272

Whiston, William: his account of late meteor, L150; his principles exposed, M300; Sacheverell's proceedings against, B424

Whitby, J98

White Cross Street, wheedling jilts of, W383

white-haired gentlemen, R209

white horse (= George II), G272, H354

white regiment's lament, W407

White, Jeremiah, elegy on, E273

White, Thomas, prebendary of Lichfield, elegy on, A132

Whiteacre, boxer, W409

Whitefield, George: lament for absence of, Z1; addressee, M226, P292

Whitehall: newly erected folly at, T518; prophecies found under ruins of, N16, W410

Whitehaven garters, W411

Whitehead, George, elegy on, E274

Whitehead, Paul: addressee, C129; *Manners* answered, M189; mock procession organized by, M355

Whitie, Nanny, of Edinburgh, L38

Whitshed, William, lord chief justice, Dublin: addressee, P55; elegy on, E278

Whittam (= Wytham) miller, B201

Whittington: defeat, L265; revived, W441

whores, J43, R156: of Edinburgh's lament, W446; *see also* courtezan; drabs; harlot

whores' and bawds' answer, W445

whoring, fifteen comforts of, F131

W—h—t, Dr, N141

Widdrington, Lady, inscription to, N348

widow: advice to, A76; and her cat, F13; poem on, S385; poem to, P659; priest and, P1052

widow's: address, B80; answer, W241; mite, P758

widowers, poem dedicated to, F128

widows bewitched, N323

widows' and orphans' triumph, W452

wife: the, O252; clergyman's choice of, L94; duty of, J12; and the nurse, W511; and no wife, W453, W456

adulterous, W70; of Bath, N240; curious, M104; Jekyll's, J67; scolding, F196, T580; virtuous, C160, L283

Wilcox, Daniel, elegies on, F306, G321

Wild, Jonathan, N288, W277: complaint of, E319; epistle to Colonel Charteris, E370

Wilhelmina Charlotta, princess of Wales, *see* Caroline, queen

Wilkie, Thomas, minister of Edinburgh, elegy on, E279

Wilkinson, A., libel of John Gaynam on, G95

Wilks, Robert, prologues spoken by, F64, S739, S740

will, of: Dr Anthony, A259; beau, B127; Burnbank, P151; Lucky Gibson, L316; High German doctor (Harley), L61; Welshman, W284; whig, F297

Will, Robin and, R231

William and Margaret (by Mallet), M59: translation of, B333; imitations of, G96, L277, P761, S132, T290, W503

William, sweet, farewell to black-eyed Susan, B331

William, duke of Gloucester, death of, D332, P597

William III, king of England:

1701, birthday poem, S590; poems addressed to, D295, I19, T61

1702, poems addressed to, L296, P693; proclamation of the Old Pretender, P693, P1061; poems on death and funeral of, A154, B92, B469, B579, D29, D132, D224, E41, E280-2, F163, H60, H77, H168, H278, I30, L164, L305, M90, M542, M544, M546, O43, O166, P66, P285, P682, P1180, R307, R310·5, S524, S549, S559, S608, S741, T265, T477, U21, W24, W37, W516

anniversary poems on his birthday, B204, E343, G37, H366, W32

poems to the memory of, H333, L208, P545, R212

statues of, P550, P623, V22

William IV, prince of Orange, marriage to Anne, princess royal (1733–34), B86, B283, B393, C115, D320, D473, G207, G326, M58, O79, P252, P527, P579, P620, P632, S32, S105, S183, U11, V30

William Augustus, duke of Cumberland:

1725, addressee, E500

1732, birthday, D481

1743, wounded at Dettingen, L228

1745, praise of, B224

1746, victory at Culloden, F236, H142, N76, N194, P268, S548; successful campaign and return, B452, B455, B479, F214, H143, L171, L218, O52, O56,

William Augustus (*cont.*)
O200, P146, R115, S793; reported death at battle of Falkirk, E93; Jacobite attack on, C398; addressee, B87, C326, D37, H147·5, N252, N260, O20, P704; birthday, O42

1747, victory at Culloden, D398, G185, M136; expected at Bath, A352; going to Flanders, F201; addressee, B473, M136; birthday, O41

1748, P568; addressee, A20, C347

1749, addressee, G279

1750, addressee, T101

Williams, reverend Mr (dedicatee), W226

Williams, Sir Charles Hanbury: Edward Hussey to, H346; satire on, J61

Williams, Francis (dedicatee), W222

Williams, Griffith, *Antichrist revealed* of, G249

Williams, Henry (dedicatee), M400

Williams, Sir John, lord mayor of London (addressee), M320

Williams, Thomas, of Oxford, E483

Williamson, David, minister of Edinburgh, elegy on, E283

Willis, Captain, U8

Willis, Mrs, song sung by, Q6

Wills', poem to worthy gentlemen at, A173

Willson, Samuel, *see* Wilson

Wilmington, Spencer Compton, earl of (dedicatee), Y32, Y130

Wilmot, Miss, of Oxford, W251

Wilson, Andrew, execution of, P554

Wilson, John, minister at North Leith, elegy on, G139

Wilson, John, professor of mathematics, poem to, D55

Wilson, Maggie, poultry-wife in Edinburgh, elegy on, P157

Wilson, Nathaniel, prebendary of Worcester, guilty of breach of promise, C530

Wilson, Samuel, elegies on, E284, T561

Winchester: journey by way of, J20; song sung at, S581; window of college chapel at, L292

wind: in the east, W523; late high, M97

Windsor: muse, T88; prophecy, P459, S938, W527

Windsor Castle, W525: dialogue with Blenheim House, D275

Windsor Forest, P987: chalybeate well in, M195; stag chase in, P1012; poem by a forester of, R115

Windsor Great Park, lodge in, C326

wine, G89: satire against, W172; poems in praise of, P400, P479, W57; *see also* vintners

Winefride, saint, G111

Winfield, Edward, elegy on, E285

winter, T89, T211, W570: celebrated at London, H111 campaign, C117; evening, W571; night, A225; ode, T172; solstice, O177·5

wisdom: human, H388; of religion, W532; revealed, W533; triumph of, T503

wisdom's defeat, L59, O230

wise, word to, P84

wise men: four, M160; seven, S350, S352

wish: country-man's, H416; extravagant, E611; happy, B3; honest citizen's, H294; loyal, L303; old man's, C142, P993

Wishart, William, moderator of Church of Scotland, P345

wishing maid, the, W535

wit, W536: abuse of, C23; choice pennyworth of, C160; progress of, H230; trial of, L7; triumphant over beauty, C438; upon crutches, W537

modern, M388, O83: essay on, P709

Witham, —, vintner, W149

Witless, Miss, L14

wits, P1103: alarm to, A151; tory, M351

wives: of the bow, H391; drunken, T100; ill, A158·5; rival, R217, R219; scolding, J106

woeful treaty, W539

Woffington, Margaret: addressee, C397; amours of, L33; epilogue spoken by, F102

wolf: stripped of his shepherd's clothing, W545; turned shepherd, C210; dialogue with shepherd's dog, N128; fable of boy and wolf, P178; fable of lion, wolf, and fox, R216

Wolfe, Sir Joseph, elegy on, S229

Wolverhampton, letter to a friend in, L187

wolves, and sheep, fable of, T535

woman: a cloud, S410, S795; in miniature, W546; of taste, N282, N285; unmasked and dissected, F89; weighed with man, T102; satires on, A182, A183, E23, F90, G230

fine, thirty marks of, A65; silent, B76; *see also* old woman

woman's: case, C97; labour, C288; man, W547; mind, S857; prerogative, C472

women: characters of, P917; creation of, C500; defence of, S372; virtuous, F103; satires on, B207, E401, F88, F97, F99, M109, P479, P917, T10, T433, U12, Y134, Y136

women-hater's lamentation, W549

wonder, the, W552: new, N241; of wonders, W551

wonderful: bard, W553; man, W554

wonders: age of, A126; British, W53; of grace, D560; upon wonders, W557·5; year of, Y14

Wood Street: compter, S639; meeting-house, dialogue with, E13

Wood, Lieutenant-general, elegy on (1712), F304

Wood, James, elegy on, G324

Wood, Lucky, elegy on, R46

Wood, William, poems occasioned by the introduction of his halfpence to Ireland, D81, E541·5, E570, E583·5, E588, E593, E610, I66, L123, L124, M301, M436, O29, O257, O260, P660, S175, S443, S846, S898, S902, T334, T519

woodcock, remarks on, S444

Woodcock, Robert, composer, H12

wooden: age, W558; man, G312, T248; monster, T519

Woodford, Anna Maria (dedicatee), H112

Woodstock Park, B555, H51, H271

Woodward, John, M80, T94: epistle to, E416; ghost of, D357

woody, the, R104

Woolfe, Margaret, lady, elegy on, S281

woollen manufacture, S840, W459

Woolrich, Thomas, G206

Woolstain, Mr, carried away by the devil, G204

Woolston, Thomas, freethinker, G204, M300, N248

Worcester, bells of, N295, W561

word: of advice, W562; of tender caution, A339; in season, R188; to the wise, P84

workhouse: St Giles, E189; hymn for children of, H376

'Workit, Dolly', S463
works of creation, G182
world: affairs of, C305; farewell to, W565; in disguise, W563; in hieroglyphic, A349; origin of, C28; run mad, C271; turned topsy-turvy, F97, M414; ungrateful, U7; unmasked, G150
worm-powder, John Moore's, M423, P978
Worms, 'treatise' of, D369
Worth, —, of Rathfarnham, elegy on, E286
worthies: British, S518; female, F103; Kentish, T62; loyal, L304
Wotherspoon, Patrick, death of, P1027, P1028
'Wou'd-be, Lady', C155
wound, ghastly, G133
Wray, Sir Daniel, elegy on, S237
wren, robin red-breast and, R235
Wren, Sir Christopher, elegy on, S328
Wright, Robert, elegy on, S601
wrightcraft, art of, D401
wrinkle, the, O246
writers: lady insulted by, L226; political, M378; satire on, F213
writing masters, B211, H101, P598, T70
wrongheads, the, W572
W—t—n (? = Warburton), Molly, S70
Wyndham, Sir William (dedicatee), W231
Wynendael, battle of, H154
Wynn, Sir Watkin Williams: addressee, O111; elegies on, E287, R262
Wynne, James (addressee), H175
Wytham (Berks), miller of, B201

Xantippe, F196
Ximenes, Charles, composer, O51

Yarde, Robert (dedicatee), R79
Yarhell's (= Harley's) kitchen, Y5
Yarico and Inkle, M434, S380
Yarmouth, Amalie Sophie Marianne Wallmoden, countess of, D387·2, F95, G272, H354, L268
year: glorious, G183; of wonders, Y14
yellow sash, Y16
Yester, palace and park of, B366
Yonge, Sir William: addressee, M563, O83; excise scheme, C368; see also excise, bill of 1733
York, D232, M152: elections, H390
York, John Sharp, archbishop of (1691–1714), see Sharp
York, Sir William Dawes, archbishop of (1714–24), A224
York Buildings, concert at, N162

Yorke, Joseph (subsequently baron Dover), election of, G299
Yorke, Philip, 1st earl of Hardwicke, see Hardwicke
Yorke, Philip (subsequently 2nd earl of Hardwicke): dedicatee, Y43; ode to, J65
Yorkshire: elections, P480; Royal Hunters, R311
Yorkshire-racers, P480
young: archers, of the High School, Edinburgh, P684
Chevalier, see Charles Edward Stuart
club, the, D298
distracted lady, Y20
fellows, advice to, C91
Frenchman's lampoon, Y21
gentleman, advice to, B439; love-letter from, E407; poems to, P1088, T36
gentleman of fortune, advice to, A77
gentlemen, epistle to, E435
ladies, instructive poem for, R285
lady, complaint of, Y22; dialogue with, D340; epistle from, F33; humble petition of, H394; letters from, L123, P534; picture of, M475·5; poems addressed to, E362, F270, N242, O97, S402, U16; psalm for use of, P953; verses on, L281, N118, V58, W309
laird, and Edinburgh Katy, R108
maiden's tragedy, F68
man, dialogue with Satan, D277
men, advice to, A106
nobleman, epistle to, D15; letter to, H157·5; satire to, M376
physician, epistle to, P1157
poet, epistle to, M479; letter of serious advice to, L139
Pretender, see Charles Edward Stuart
senator, the, Y23
student, epistle to, E390
Young, Edward: addressee, M490, S89, T564; letter of, N261; *The revenge*, epilogue to, E346; *The universal passion*, poem occasioned by, S841
Young, Sir William, see Yonge
younger brother's garland, Y178
youth: advice to, G156; Christian counsel to, B202, C218; dialogue with conscience, A106; pious, P292; tender greeting and exhortation to, A340
youth's tragedy, S419·5

Zara, D361, D365, R328
Zariana, Belisarius and, B171
zealous countrymen's lament, Z1
Zeuma, R23
Zoilus, life and remarks of, P73

AN	National Library of Wales, Aberystwyth
AdU	Aberdeen University Library
BP	Birmingham Reference Library
BU	Birmingham University Library
BaP	Reference Library, Bath
BlL	Linenhall Library, Belfast
BlU	Queen's University Library, Belfast
BrP	Central Library, Bristol
C	Cambridge University Library
CJ	St John's College, Cambridge
CK	King's College, Cambridge
CM-P	Magdalene College, Cambridge, Pepys Library
CQ	Queens' College, Cambridge
CT	Trinity College, Cambridge
CdP	Central Library, Cardiff
DA	Royal Irish Academy, Dublin
DG	Gilbert Collection, Municipal Library, Dublin
DK	King's Inns, Dublin
DM	Marsh's Library, Dublin
DN	National Library of Ireland, Dublin
DT	Trinity College Library, Dublin
DrU	Durham University Library
DrU-U	Durham University, Ushaw College
E	National Library of Scotland, Edinburgh
EN	New College Library, Edinburgh
EP	Central Public Library, Edinburgh
ES	Signet Library, Edinburgh
EU	Edinburgh University Library
EtC	Eton College Library
ExI	Devon and Exeter Institution, Exeter
ExP	Exeter City Library
ExU	Exeter University Library
GM	Mitchell Library, Glasgow
GT	Trinity College, Glasgow
GU	Glasgow University Library
GlP	Gloucester Central Library
HU	Hull University Library
HrP	Hereford City Library
IP	Ipswich Public Library
L	British Library, London
LDW	Dr Williams's Library, London
LF	Society of Friends Library, London
LG	Guildhall Library, London
LL	London Library
LLP	Lambeth Palace Library, London
LMA	Methodist Archives, London
LPR	Public Record Office, London
LSA	Society of Antiquaries, London
LSC	Sion College, London
LU	London University Library
LUC	University College Library, London
LVA	Victoria and Albert Museum Library, London
LVA-D	— Dyce Collection
LVA-F	— Forster Collection
LWS	Westminster School, London
LdP	Reference Library, Leeds
LdU	Leeds University Library
LdU-B	— Brotherton Collection
LpU	Liverpool University Library
MC	Chetham's Library, Manchester
MP	Central Library, Manchester
MR	John Rylands Library, Manchester
MR-C	— Crawford Deposit
NeA	Society of Antiquaries, Newcastle
NeL	Literary and Philosophical Society, Newcastle
NeP	Central Library, Newcastle
NeU	Newcastle University Library
NtP	Nottingham Public Library
NwP	Central Library, Norwich
O	Bodleian Library, Oxford
O-JJ	— John Johnson Collection
OA	All Souls College, Oxford
OC	Christ Church, Oxford
OM	Magdalen College, Oxford
OQ	Queen's College, Oxford
OW	Worcester College, Oxford
PrP	Harris Public Library, Preston
RP	Reading Public Libraries
SaU	St Andrews University Library
ShU	Sheffield University Library
SrS	Shrewsbury School Library
WaP	Warrington Public Library
WcC	Winchester College Library
WgP	Wigan Public Library
WrP	Worcester Public Library
YM	York Minster Library
YP	York City Library
YU	York University Library

Broxbourne   Broxbourne Library (on deposit at the Bodleian Library)

Chatsworth   Chatsworth House Library, Bakewell, Derbyshire

Forster   H. B. Forster, Woodstock, Oxon.

Longleat   The Marquis of Bath, Longleat

Madan   The late F. F. Madan (on deposit at the British Library)

Rosebery   The Earl of Rosebery, South Queensferry, West Lothian

Rothschild   Lord Rothschild (at Trinity College, Cambridge)